The Essential Guide to Pricing Businesses and Franchises

2017
BUSINESS
REFERENCE GUIDE

Important Note to the Reader

This publication is designed to provide accurate and authoritative information with regard to the subject matter covered. It is sold with the understanding that the authors, editors and publisher are not engaged in rendering legal, accounting or other professional advice. If legal advice or other expert assistance is required, the services of a competent professional should be sought.

Notes to the *2017 Business Reference Guide* and the *Business Reference Guide Online*

Just a few explanations concerning the information in this year's *Guide*:

- Some quotes in the sections may be grammatically incorrect or some words improperly capitalized. We attempt to remain true to the original source and make changes only to improve readability.

- Due to space requirements, some information such as General Information and Advantages and Disadvantages are not included in the hard copy *Guide*, but are available in the online edition.

Pricing Methods

Pricing methods such as multiples of SDE (Sellers Discretionary Earnings), EBIT (Earnings Before Interest and Taxes) and EBITDA (Earnings before Interest, Taxes, Depreciation, Amortization), all have two things in common: each requires that the actual earnings be calculated and then a multiple based on many factors relating to the business must also be calculated. Multiplying the two should then produce the price for that business. Unfortunately, these methods are based on the figures being calculated and by the person doing the pricing.

The other method used is the rule of thumb that calls for a multiple of sales. The big advantage to this method is that it doesn't call for calculating the figures as other methods require. One simply takes the total annual sales (less sales taxes) and multiplies it by a percentage that people in the know are comfortable with, based on their knowledge and experience. In many cases there is a universal rule of thumb for the multiple based on many transactions. And, the annual sales of a business are usually a provable figure.

An argument could be made, especially in very small businesses, that the owner could be taking money off the top, thus reducing sales. However, unless the owner is really stealing from the business, small amounts shouldn't influence the price dramatically.

The purpose of the above information is to show that, although multipliers may stay about the same, the final result is based on figures that do reflect the impact of the economy. Sales are down and costs go up, especially in relation to sales. Therefore, we are comfortable with the final pricing results. As we keep saying, rules of thumb are just that. The purpose in supplying other information and data is so the user can adjust the rule of thumb up or down based on such information.

Introduction

The pricing of a business is based on the sales and earnings, for the most part. However, another major factor in pricing a business is whether the seller will finance a portion of the selling price. If the seller won't finance a portion of the selling price, the price will generally be lower than if the seller will finance a portion of the selling price. The rule is usually the lower the down payment, the higher the full price; and the seller who demands an all-cash transaction will receive, in most cases, a lower full price.

The price of a business is ultimately what someone will pay for it—it is market driven. Or, as the old saying goes, the price is what a buyer will pay and that the seller will accept.

Using the Rules of Thumb

Despite all the caveats about using rules of thumb in pricing businesses, they are commonly used to do just that. The answer is quite simple—the rules are very easy to use and almost seem too simplistic. But how accurate are they? A lot more accurate than many people think. They may supply a quick fix, but if used properly, rules of thumb can come pretty close to what the business will ultimately sell for.

Rules of thumb usually come in two formats. The most commonly used rule of thumb is simply a percentage of the annual sales, or, better yet, the last 12 months of sales/revenues. For example, if the total sales were $100,000 for last year, and the multiple for the particular business is 40 percent of annual sales, then the price based on the rule of thumb would be $40,000.

Quite a few experts have said that revenue multiples are likely to be more reliable than earnings multiples. The reason is that most multiples of earnings are based on add-backs to the earnings, which can be a judgment call, as can the multiple. Sales or revenues are essentially a fixed figure. One might want to subtract sales taxes if they have not been deducted, but the sales are the sales. The only judgment then is the percentage. When it is supplied by an expert, the percentage multiplier becomes much more reliable.

The second rule of thumb used is a multiple of earnings. In small businesses, the multiple is used against what is termed Seller's Discretionary Earnings (SDE). SDE is also called Seller's or Owner's Cash Flow and similar names. It is usually based on a multiple (generally between 1 and 5), and this number is then used as a multiple against the earnings of the business. Many of the entries also contain a multiple of EBIT and/or EBITDA.

The terms used to express earnings are as follows:

EBDIT (EBITDA)—Earnings before depreciation (and other noncash charges), interest, and taxes

EBDT—Earnings before depreciation (and other noncash charges), and taxes

EBIT—Earnings before interest and taxes

SDE —Seller's Discretionary Earnings

Source: Pratt et al., *Valuing a Business*

Seller's Discretionary Earnings (SDE): "The earnings of a business enterprise prior to the following items:

- income taxes
- non-recurring income and expenses
- non-operating income and expenses
- depreciation and amortization
- interest expense or income
- owner's total compensation for one owner/operator, after adjusting the total compensation of all owners to market value."

Source: The International Business Brokers Association (IBBA)

The above definition of Seller's Discretionary Earnings, although accurate, is a bit confusing. If you change the words prior to the and substitute the word plus it may be easier to understand. We would also suggest that the highest salary be used in the calculation of SDE. The reason is that we must assume that the buyer will replace the highest compensated employee or owner—at least for the SDE calculation. We should also add that this is our definition and not necessarily that of the IBBA.

Keep in mind that the multiples for the different earnings acronyms mentioned above will be different than the multiple of SDE, which, as mentioned, generally is a number between 0 and 5. The rules contained in the *Guide* are specific about what is being used. It will say 2.5 times SDE or 4 times EBIT, etc.

The Basics

The businesses are arranged alphabetically. In some cases, the business may go by two name descriptions, for example, gas stations and service stations. We use the one that we feel is the most common, and we try to cross-reference them. If you can't find what you are looking for, see if it is listed under another name. If there is a particular franchise you are working on and it's not in the rules, check the type of business for more information. For example, if the franchise is an ice cream shop, check the name of the franchise; and if it's not there, go to ice cream shops and other ice cream franchises. If the business is not listed, find a similar business and start there.

Name/Type of Business

The information just below the type of business is the approximate number of businesses of that type in the U.S. Where there was an IBISWorld report, we generally use that number. In the top section where the type of business is located, in some cases we have rounded the number of businesses for ease of use.

IBISWorld provides excellent reports on many, many different businesses: www.ibisworld.com. Most of these reports are well over 20 pages and are not only extensive, but most informative. They are well worth the price.

We have also provided the Standard Industrial (SIC) Classification code and the North American Industry Classification System (NAICS). For NAICS and SIC codes, go to www.naics.com.

The Rules of Thumb

The price, based on the rule of thumb, does not include inventory (unless it specifically states that it does), or real estate, and other balance-sheet items such as cash and accounts receivable. We have noticed an increase in Industry Experts telling us that inventory is included in the multiples. The price derived from the rule of thumb is for the operating assets of the business plus goodwill. It also assumes that the business will be delivered free and clear of any debt. If any debt is to be assumed by a purchaser, it is subtracted from the price based on the rule of thumb method.

In other words, the rules, unless mentioned otherwise, create a price that includes goodwill, FF&E (furniture, fixtures & equipment), and leasehold improvements, less outstanding debt, including, accounts payable, loans on FF&E, bank loans, etc. The business, unless otherwise mentioned, is assumed delivered to a purchaser free and clear of any debt or encumbrances.

Accounts receivable are not included as they are generally handled outside of any transaction and also almost always belong to the seller. Work in progress, prepaid memberships, etc. also normally belong to the seller. Items such as these may be divided between buyer and seller. For example, in a dry cleaning business, the seller may have taken in a customer's clothing for dry cleaning, but the buyer may take over the business before the work has been completed and delivered back to the customer. This is generally handled outside the transaction and does not usually figure in a pricing or valuation.

Pricing Tips

After the rules of thumb are the Pricing Tips. These provide information from industry experts and other sources. They areintended to amplify the rules themselves. We include lots of new information every year, while maintaining important information from prior years.

Industry Experts' Comments

This section allows our Industry Experts to add their own personal comments about this type of business. These comments may amplify a particular area or provide additional pricing information. Many times these Industry Experts provide information or data that can't be found anywhere else. We should add that some Industry Experts, who own or manage an office with associates, list themselves under more than one business. It may just mean that one or more agents in that office are experts in that industry.

Benchmark Data

This is a valuable section. We feel it is very important, in analyzing and pricing a business, that you compare it to similar businesses, or benchmarks, that are unique to this type of business. One common benchmark unique to each business is the expenses. We have included as many of these as we could find. Many have been contributed by Industry Experts. If no source is mentioned, then you can assume that an Industry Expert(s) has supplied them. In many cases we have used a breakdown of expenses from IBISWorld.

The figures in Expenses as a Percentage of Annual Sales may not always add up to 100 percent. We provide only the major categories, and there may be other expense items not included which would make up any difference. Also, in many cases, we have had to meld the figures from several different Industry Experts or sources. This may also cause some totals to slightly exceed 100 percent.

We recommend *Nation's Restaurant News*, an invaluable resource, and *Franchise Times,* also an excellent resource, for information on pricing businesses and lots of other information. Still other information is from Industry Experts, local newspapers, magazines, newsletters, etc. Some of the benchmark data is from IBISWorld, a subscription research service, which we use. It is an excellent resource, as we have previously mentioned.

Introduction

We mentioned, at the beginning of this section, that if the rule of thumb was used properly, the price derived could be more accurate than simply multiplying the sales by the percentage rule or the SDE multiple. Reviewing market-driven data, one can reasonably assume that a 10 percent swing (that's our number; yours may be higher or lower) on either side of the percentage multiple would allow for the additions or subtractions to arrive at a more accurate multiple of annual sales. Using our example above, the 40 percent figure, and then using available benchmark data could lower or raise that percentage by 10 percent. The multiple then might be more accurate.

Critics of rules of thumb claim that a rule is simply an average and doesn't allow for the variables of each individual business. Comparing the business under review with industry standards—benchmarks—can allow one to raise or lower the percentage accordingly. A 40 percent figure then could be as low as 30 percent, or as high as 50 percent.

The Benchmark section can help you look at the vital signs of the business and compare them to similar businesses. Looking at the expenses as a percentage of annual sales can be a good start. For example, if the business under review has an occupancy percentage of 12 percent against an average 8 percent benchmark, perhaps the price then should be reduced to compensate for the higher rent. The rent is pretty much a fixed expense; but the higher the rent, the lower the profit. Certainly a new owner could lower some of the expenses, but a trained labor force, for example, is hard to replace. Obviously, reducing the percentage multiple is a judgment call; but let's face it, even business valuation is not a science, but an art—and judgment plays a large part in it.

Resources

Also included in Resources are trade associations related to the particular types of businesses. For most of the associations, we have included their website if available. Some are very informative; others are really only for members or consumers. However, many of the associations offer books or pamphlets or studies that can be informative. Every year, we find that more and more associations are offering research materials to members only and offer them to non-members at a much higher price. Don't forget that IBISWorld has great reports on many, many different businesses including franchises and many mom and pop type businesses.

Franchises

This edition contains more franchise data than any previous one. For a quick rule for many franchises, go to the Franchise entry. Additional information can be found under the entries for the specific franchise.

If you can't find the one you are looking for, see if there is a similar type of franchise that has one. If that fails, go to the particular type of business that the franchise represents. You may add to or subtract from that rule of thumb based on your assessment of the value of the franchise—is it a plus or a minus? Even if there is a rule of thumb, it is always wise to refer to the type of business for more information.

Some Final Notes

Some associations conduct their studies and surveys only every other year or even further apart. In some cases, we have done a particular section prior to the new data becoming available; however, we attempt to keep the information as current as possible.

We know that some of the information may be contradictory, but since we get it from those whom we believe to be experts, we still include it. The more information you have to sort through, the better your final conclusion. We think the information and data are reliable, but occasionally we find an error after the book has been printed.

Also, keep in mind that rules of thumb can vary by area and even by location. For example, businesses on the West Coast tend to sell for a higher price than the East Coast businesses which sell for a higher price than the Midwest ones.

Thanks to our Industry Experts

We want to thank all of those who contributed rules of thumb, industry data, and information. It is a tribute to them that they are willing to contribute not only a rule of thumb, but also their knowledge on pricing.

We are focusing on the Industry Experts and are offering to put them on our website, provide BBP industry logos and anything else we can do to set them apart, in gratitude for their contribution. And, we also give them a complimentary copy of the current copy of the *Business Reference Guide*. If you're interested and feel that you are qualified, go to www.bbpinc.com and click on Industry Experts

And When All Else Fails

Keep in mind that if it's not in the *Guide*, we really don't have a rule of thumb for that business. We get calls from people asking for a rule of thumb for some oddball type of business like Elephant Training Schools (not really). Honestly, if we knew of one, it would be in the *Guide*. We're always happy to help if we can, but unless there is sufficient sales data, there generally isn't a rule of thumb available. Here are some suggestions if you can't find what you need.

- Call a similar business in your area and see if they are aware of one.

- Check with a vendor, distributor, or equipment manufacturer and see if someone there can help.

- Call a trade association for that particular industry and see if they can direct you to someone who can help. Don't do it by email or fax, but call and speak to someone. Trade associations really don't want to get involved, but an individual might get you to the next step.

If none of the above helps, then we're afraid you just have to accept the fact that there just may not be one for the business you are checking on.

Thanks to our Sponsors

(For more information on any of the resources below, please see the blue pages in the center of the Guide.*)*

Capital Business Solutions

Bizcomps

Business Transition Academy

Business Valuation Resources

BusinessBroker.net

AICPA

Diamond Financial

GCF Valuation

International Business Brokers Association

International Franchise Professionals Group

Nation-List International

Nationwide Valuations

PeerComps

Deal Studio

Toons 'N Tips

Lawyers Escrow

Businesses in the 2017 Guide

Business Reference Guide **2017**

Introduction

Introduction

Introduction

Business Reference Guide **2017**

Business Reference Guide **2017**

Franchise

AAMCO Transmission (See also Auto Transmission Centers, Franchises)	
Approx. Total Investment	$227,400 to $333,000
Estimated Annual Sales/Unit	$645,000

SIC 7537-01	NAICS 811113	Number of Businesses/Units 671

Rules of Thumb

➢ 40 to 42 percent of annual sales plus inventory

➢ 2 to 3 times EBITDA

Pricing Tips

- "One observation is that franchised shops that are following the model with a good manager are successful. The typical shop has three technicians, a rebuilder and two mechanics, and a manager. Most of the franchised shops have an owner who oversees but might be considered absentee."
- "The better way to analyze a business is from a well-defined proforma as opposed to tax returns and financial statements. Looking at the top line on the tax return, I sell from a proforma using market values for parts, cost and labor."
- "Detailed weekly reports provided to the franchisor are more important documents for analyzing historical performance than financial statements and tax returns, as these reports will reveal the prices charged ratio of major/minor repairs and warranty repairs."

Expert Comments

"Typically a buyer assumes responsibility for warranty repairs. In my analysis I look at this very carefully and at the compensation to the rebuilder to see if it is too low."

"The Internet has changed the marketing and advertising model—lowering cost but making it more difficult for the small independent to compete with the franchises in the major market areas."

Benchmark Data

Expenses as a percentage of annual sales

Production labor costs	20%
Sales/Labor	08% to 10%
Occupancy	06% to 10%
Profit (estimated pretax)	10% to 20%

Cost of Sales

Parts & Fluids	22%
Production Labor (All Technical Employees)	20%
Towing	1%
Misc. Production Supplies	3%
Total Cost of Sales	46%

Sales & Administration Expenses

Salaries (Center Mgr. & Office)	10%
Rent	08%
Insurance	03%
Utilities	01%
Advertising-Yellow Pages	08%
Telephone	01%
Legal/Accounting	01%
Bank Fees/Bad Debt	01%
Training	01%
Total Sales & Administration Expenses	34%
Net Profit	20%

Seller Financing
- "50 percent down—five (5) years"

Questions
- "Following are some suggested questions:
  - ✓ Does the shop meet AAMCO standards?
  - ✓ Historic sales and change in demographics?
  - ✓ What is ratio of major to minor repairs?
  - ✓ Ratio of general auto to transmission repair?
  - ✓ Ratio of 'Fleet' (commercial) vs. Retail?
  - ✓ Percentage of 'Comebacks' warranty repairs?
  - ✓ Is the manager following the AAMCO 'Spiel'?"

Resources

Websites
- AAMCO Franchises: www.aamcofranchises.com

Accounting Firms/CPAs (See also Accounting Firms)		
SIC 8721-01	NAICS 541211	Number of Businesses/Units 97,680

Rules of Thumb
➤ 100 to 125 percent of annual revenues plus inventory

➤ 1.8 to 3 times SDE plus inventory

➤ 2 times EBIT

➤ 2.2 times EBITDA

Pricing Tips
- "Accounting and CPA firm selling prices are a function of Gross Revenue, Customer Profile, (business client versus individuals), mix of revenue by type. What is being sold is the customer list, goodwill and the revenue stream from the customers."
- "Most accounting and tax practices will sell based on a multiple of gross billings. This multiple will typically include a client retention clause. If no retention clause, the multiple will be reduced significantly."

- "Small accounting and tax practices and CPA firms tend to sell for a multiple of gross revenue equal to 100–130%. Deals are structured basically one of three ways. The first way deals are structured is the earnout. This is where a buyer pays a % of the revenue he/she collects post closing. If terms agreed were 100% of revenue, the buyer might pay the seller 20% of what they collect from the seller's client list each year for 5 years. Because this structure puts the majority, if not all, of the risk on the seller's shoulders, the multiples can be higher, sometimes as high as 200%. The second way deals are structured is a fixed price. This structure is fairly self explanatory. Buyer and seller agree to a price and there are no post closing adjustments. The buyer assumes the majority of the risk in this structure. The third way deals in this industry are put together is a combination of the two, call it a modified earnout structure. A buyer offers to pay a multiple of gross revenue for the seller's clients based on the first year following closing. This structure gives buyers the confidence to pay a little higher multiple while at the same time giving a seller the security that the buyer will not be able to cherry pick the clients. We see deals in this industry put together every day using all three deal structures."
- "Most practices will sell for a minimum of 1 x earnings. Anywhere from 1.0 to 1.5 x sales. Profitability and location are some of the most important variables when determining asking price."
- "In Florida I find the multiples of SDE to be slightly lower than 2. Important to understand that generally speaking CPA and accounting practice sales will require the seller to stay on for at least one tax season and that there typically will include an earnout structure. It is important that purchaser has a similar style to seller to maximize client retention."
- "Product mix and any special areas of practice can affect selling price to the right buyer. There is always the possibility to split up a practice among two or more buyers if specialty work is involved."
- "Revenue composition is important; retail tax, writeup, monthly accounting, review work, audit, consulting, types of revenue streams—all have an effect on sale's price."
- "Biggest factor is the terms and whether seller will guarantee part or all of the income."
- "Location is paramount. Same practice will sell for 1.3 times gross revenue in one location and 1 times gross revenue in another."
- "The composition of billings is important. The split between recurring/one time. The split among taxes/accounting/audit/consulting/other is important in determining staff composition. Labor costs are extremely important in bottom line. Accounts receivable levels may indicate problems with billings and/or clients."

Expert Comments

"Have a strategy. It is a long process from both the seller and buyer perspective. Be prepared as this will not happen overnight."

"We have encountered all of these scenarios over the years. When a seller meets two prospective qualified buyers, he or she will sell the practice to the one that feels right. The wise buyer will be sensitive to the feelings and emotions of the seller, and the wise seller will be sensitive to the feelings and emotions of the buyer."

"Buyers like consistency. Having a consistent 3-year revenue pattern without significant influxes shows the buyer stability in the practice and client base. Obviously with the shape of the economy over the last few years, a 5–10%

decrease would not be too alarming. On the contrary, if revenues have spiked greatly over the years, you as a seller should be ready to explain this pattern. Increasing to stable revenue patterns will show the buyer that your practice is on solid financial ground."

"Buyers that are looking to buy your CPA or accounting practice are looking long-term. They are not buying your client base with the expectations that clients will turnover or leave after a tax season or two. They want your client base to adapt and become clients over the long haul. Practices that have a good reputation in the area and have been well established in the area will yield a higher market demand."

"The higher the average fees per client, the more value the buyer will find in the practice. Below-average individual tax returns fees is not always a negative. If you are charging $100 per return, but this return only takes 15 minutes to complete, then your average billing rate would be $400, not bad. However, the problem is that some buyers will not dig deep enough to understand this point and dismiss the practice right off the bat because their firm's minimum 1040 is $200. They may be doing more complicated and difficult returns for $250 and it may take them 30 minutes to complete. The key is to explain to the buyer why your fee structure is what it is and how they too can make this a profitable business."

"Buyer will need to be a CPA or have an accounting background in order to buy the business. It is a specialized and niche field. Buyers will need this education and background in order to retain the existing client base. Not everyone who wants to buy a business will be able to buy an accounting or tax practice."

Benchmark Data

Statistics (Accounting Services)

Number of Establishments	97,680
Average Profit Margin	17.9%
Revenue per Employee	$186,500
Average Number of Employees	5.6
Average Wages per Employee	$72,865

Products and Services Segmentation

Financial auditing services	30.1%
Other services	21.9%
Corporate tax preparation and representative services	16.8%
Individual tax preparation and representative services	11.2%
Tax planning and consulting services	8.2%
General accounting services	5.7%
Financial statement review services	3.2%
Other financial assurance services	2.9%

Major Market Segmentation

Finance sector	22.2%
Individuals	15.6%
Manufacturing sector	13.8%
Retail sector	12.6%
Other businesses	12.5%
Utilities and mining sector	10.9%
Public sector	7.3%
Nonprofit organizations	5.1%

Industry Costs

Profit	17.9%
Wages	39.2%
Purchases	2.8%
Depreciation	1.5%
Marketing	0.8%
Rent & Utilities	6.2%
Other	31.5%

Market Share

PricewaterhouseCoopers	9.9%
Deloitte Touche Tohmatsu	9.6%
Ernst & Young	9.5%
KPMG International	5.9%

Source: IBISWorld, April 2016

- "Accounting and CPA firms with more than 60% of revenue from tax preparation are not as profitable as firms with less than 60%. As a rule of thumb, the more revenue coming from monthly accounting versus tax preparation the more profitable."
- "Employee should bill out $100k per year."
- "Small one-owner firms tend to show 40–60% SDE. Larger firms with more than one partner/owner show lower SDE but still typically remain in the 30–40% range."

Expenses as a percentage of annual sales

Cost of goods	0% to 05%
Payroll/labor Costs	25% to 35%
Occupancy	10% to 20%
Profit (estimated pretax)	35% to 45%

Industry Trend

- "Due to the Baby Boomer curve there will be an increase in the number of firms being offered for sale or merger."
- "Aging accountants will be selling off. New regulations have also moved more people towards the sell side."
- "More sellers with the baby boomers retiring. There are different opinions as to the liquidity of small accounting firms with more sellers entering the marketplace. I believe practices in major metro areas will continue to be in high demand while practices in more rural areas will struggle to find buyers at times."
- "Industry trend is upward due to increased tax and government regulations on businesses and individuals."
- "Still a seller's market"
- "Industry regulation makes entry difficult yet demand for services continually increase."
- "An increase in the number of small single-owner firms billing $100K or less as laid-off industry CPAs open their own firms."

Seller Financing

- "Majority of funding from buyer and outside funding. Average term 2 to 3 years. Past experience has shown the seller getting 100% of selling price at closing."

- "Buyer 10–25%, seller 10–25%, bank the balance."
- "The transactions I've participated in were based on notes based on client retention, or earnouts over a 1–3 year period. Most commonly through 2 tax seasons. Heaviest weight of earnout based on first tax season."

Questions

- "Access to 3 years of financials and tax returns for review. Non-compete agreement? Seller financing?"
- "How long will you help me with transitioning the clients?"
- "How is your staff? What are the terms of the lease? How close are the clients to the office?"
- "What type of services do you perform? Who is on staff that has primary contact with customers?"
- "What period of time will they guarantee the billings?"
- "Any client concentrations, risks of client losses."
- "Why are you selling? Is any individual client fee over 10% of the Gross Revenue? Is any single industry over 10% of Gross Revenue? How much of Revenue is earned from tax return preparation and how much from accounting or auditing? What percent are corporate returns or individual returns? What type of client audits? What type of work does your staff do? What tax and accounting software do you use? What is the billing rate per hour? Do you bill by hour or project? How long have your clients been with this firm? How long have the employees been with this firm?"
- "Info relating to clientele, fee structure, employee information, pending litigation, office lease, type of services performed, need for licenses/ certifications"
- "Do you do any audit work? Are your licenses current? How many hours do you personally bill per year?"
- "The quality of the fees should be investigated both by looking at the cash flow percentages and investigating the billing rates of the personnel and the owner. Post-sale competition is a major risk factor so this possibility should be investigated carefully."

Resources

Trade Publications
- accountingTODAY: www.accountingtoday.com

Associations
- American Institute of CPAs: www.aicpa.org

Accounting Firms/Practices
(See also Accounting Firms/CPAs/Tax Practices)

SIC 8721-01	NAICS 541219	Number of Businesses/Units 140,000

Rules of Thumb

➤ There are three Rules of Thumb generally cited: #1—.75 to 1.25 times annual revenues, depending on characteristics of practice; #2—9 to 15 times monthly net sales, depending on characteristics of practice; and #3—2 to 5 times the seller's SDE. Rules of Thumb normally include FF&E, Lease and Intangibles. Current assets, real estate, and all related liabilities must be considered separately.

➢ 2.5 to 3.5 times SDE plus inventory (if any)

➢ One to 1.25 times annual revenues (non-CPA) plus inventory

➢ Generally sold for a multiple of 1 to 1.5 times gross revenues depending upon net earnings. Rarely sell below one times gross.

➢ One times gross for low-level billings, up to 1.5 times gross for high-level billings

➢ 100 percent to 115 percent of one-year's revenue + FF&E with one-year guarantee of gross

➢ 90 to 110 percent of anticipated annual revenues under new ownership, subject to seller guarantee and earnout provisions

➢ 100 to 115 percent of annual revenues, plus fixtures & equipment; seller keeps accounts payable & accounts receivable

➢ Sales price generally 100 to 125 percent of annual revenue; higher in some metropolitan areas such as New York City, Dallas, Atlanta, etc.

➢ 45 percent times EBIT

Pricing Tips

▪ "Net profit margins for the average company in the accounting category rose to 22 percent in 2015, up from 18 percent in 2014. Over the past five years, the margin was 16.2 percent. Profit growth, however, dropped to 19.5 percent from 2014's 23.8 percent. But 2015's profit growth indicated improvement over the 17.6 percent overall average for the last five years."
   Source: http://www.accountingweb.com/practice/growth/accounting-firms-saw-solid-sales-growth-in-2015

▪ "Almost all of the deals will be subject to attrition and retention clauses. But it is equally important for the deal to also include a clause for the growth within the portfolio."

▪ "Fee structure, client complexity, location and overall staffing requirements affect practice desirability."

Expert Comments

"Locate well established practice with experienced staff, great fee structure, and growing location."

"As taxes get more complicated the need for good accountants keeps increasing. There is lots of consolidation in this industry as the older accountants start to retire and the newer ones know that to grow their practice faster, they need to acquire."

"There seem to be plenty of buyers for a good accounting practice."

"With technology today, accountants can process the client's work from anywhere. Office location is not as important unless it is an all-1040 tax practice."

A - Rules of Thumb

Benchmark Data

- "Labor at less than 33% is best."
- "Each employee should generate around $100k–$150k in annual billings. Owners/Partners—$200k–$250k."
- "Generally revenue based on employee costs."
- "Not moving the office will help retain the client base."
- "Number of repeat clients on the book; it usually takes at least 250–350 to break even and above that to be profitable."

Expenses as a percentage of annual sales

Cost of goods	n/a
Payroll/labor Costs	30% to 35%
Occupancy	08% to 12%
Profit (estimated pretax)	30% to 45%

Industry Trend

- "Continuing to grow at a rapid rate as the economy improves."
- "More people preparing own returns with 'off-the-shelf' software."
- "Steady to upward"
- "Generally an upward trend"
- "Consolidation and firms sending work offshore"

Seller Financing

- "We are continuing to see more practices sold with outside financing. Generally buyers are being required to pay 70 to 80% upfront at closing with minimal seller financing. Very strong seller's market."
- "5-year financing period"
- "Typical seller financed over 2 to 3 years and it is tied to the retention of the clients."
- "Earnouts are very typically between one and two years."
- "30 percent down payment, 70 percent seller carry back, five years, 8 to 10 percent"
- "20 to 40 percent down, financing three to five years for small practices; seven to 10 years for larger ones"
- "30 to 35 percent down, balance financed over three to five years with one-year client retention guaranteed by the seller to the buyer"

Questions

- "1) What do you plan to do after you sell the practice 2) How often do clients come in to the office to meet with you? 3) How many personal taxes do you do a year vs. corporate tax returns? 4) What percentage of your work includes 'specialty' consulting work? 5) Does your practice also provide bookkeeping services?"
- "Demographic of the client base. Number of years average client has been with the firm."
- "Gross revenue, revenue type, number of clients, fees generated from each client, employee compensation and experience, lease on facilities, type of software used, net income."
- "Will clients likely stay with new owner?"

- "Break down the composition of fees on an annual basis (percent from tax, bookkeeping, payroll, accounting, auditing, technology, consulting, etc.). Also ask if fee structure is based on hourly or fixed-fee arrangements. What is the effective percent of production hours (total firm hours billed/total firm hours spent)? What are the rate realizations (total fees billed/standard rates x hours billed)? Clients making up over 10% of annual fees? Any major clients coming to end of
- service agreements, and details? Answers indicating poor production and rate realizations have a negative impact on pricing, while positive statistics have positive impacts on pricing."

Resources

Websites
- Buying a Practice by Leon Faris and Vance Wingo: www.cpasales.com

Associations
- American Institute of Certified Public Accountants (AICPA): www.aicpa.org
- National Society of Accountants: www.nsacct.org

Accounting/Tax Practices (See also Accounting Firms/Practices/CPAs)

SIC 7291-01	NAICS 541213	Number of Businesses/Units 131,538

Rules of Thumb

➤ 1 to 1.35 times annual revenues plus inventory

➤ 2 to 3 times SDE plus inventory

➤ 5 to 7 times EBIT

➤ 4 to 6 times EBITDA

Pricing Tips

- "Many factors may add a premium or discount to the 'rule of thumb' multiple: years established, billing rates, net earnings, reputations, location, type of work performed, established clientele, trained staff, etc."
- "Diversification of client industry and no client over 20% of the practice gross revenue. Should have a good mix of accounting and tax."
- "Practices in urban areas are priced higher. Practice prices do not include equipment or inventory."
- "Most practices are sold on a multiple of the gross billings. This is typically anywhere from 1.0 to 1.30."
- "Even distribution of revenue from tax return preparation and accounting fees is better."
- "Buyers generally want earnouts, sellers want cash."
- "Repeat clients, accounting vs. tax preparation work."
- "Tax related revenues are priced at 1 to 1.25 times annual revenues. Monthly write-up revenues are priced at 1.25 to 1.5 times annual revenues. Other revenues priced at one times annual revenue."
- "National franchises can hurt sale price due to franchise, royalty, and advertising fees charged."

- "Higher average price per return results in higher asking price."
- "Higher end practices will net 40%"
- "Dependent on type of clients; 1040 clients result in lower pricing; monthly and retainer clients result in higher pricing. Audit only preferred by a minority of firms."
- "Typically practices sell for multiples of revenue from 1x to 1.75x based on location and demand in area and type of practice."

Expert Comments

"While there are lots of accountants and tax preparers, satisfied clients are very loyal. Small businesses need help and often look for help from their accountant."

"Accounting work growing due to outsourcing"

"The profit trend and industry trend is upward due to increased tax and government regulations on businesses and individuals. There is a greater need of business bookkeeping and records for proof of compliance with government regulations. Location and facilities are located in office or retail locations. A profitable, well balanced practice is highly marketable to those entering the profession from corporate and established firms to expand their client base. Replication or opening a practice is not difficult. Establishing a client base is the challenge for a new accounting practice."

"Historically profitable practices will sell for a higher price."

"Lots of competition. Marketing for new clients is difficult, so building a large client base takes time."

"The major concern for any buyer should be retaining the clients they are purchasing. An owner willing to stay on after the sale to help with transition should help the buyer feel more comfortable. Practices where owners do not stay on should be sold at a discount and less than market price."

"Tax preparation has become a commodity. Anyone with $5,000, a PC, and software can easily open a tax prep office. A number of recent national franchises have over-saturated the market."

"Fair amount of competition in the industry. Very profitable businesses when compared to many others. Accounting practices in major metro areas are highly marketable."

"Industry is in need of personnel and has no lack of new regulations which necessitate new audit or forensic work."

"Not a location-dependent business...service usually at the client's business address. Tough business to grow organically but many with financial wherewithal to purchase firms or accounts."

"High risk, as it is easy to duplicate this type of business. Customer loyalty is not as strong in this business as in a CPA practice."

"Easily transferable. High visibility of offices necessary to attract large number of walk-in clients. Majority of clients are seen only once a year for tax preparation and filing of tax returns. Office location is critical."

Benchmark Data

Statistics (Tax Preparation Services)

Number of Establishments	131,538
Average Profit Margin	14.0%
Revenue per Employee	$36,000
Average Number of Employees	2.3
Average Wages per Employee	$10,076

Products and Services Segmentation

Standard tax preparation services	57.0%
Basic tax preparation services	23.0%
Full-service tax preparation services	14.0%
Tax-related financial products	6.0%

Industry Costs

Profit	14.0%
Wages	28.6%
Purchases	5.8%
Depreciation	3.7%
Marketing	12.0%
Rent & Utilities	4.9%
Other	31.0%

Market Share

H&R Block Inc.	23.4%
Intuit Inc.	17.5%
Jackson Hewitt Inc.	2.2%

Source: IBISWorld, February 2016

- "$100,000 billings per staff person"
- "A successful accounting practice should have Seller's Discretionary Earnings of 45% to 60% of revenue. The larger firm will earn 40% to 50% of revenue and the smaller firm should be 50% to 60% of revenue."
- "Well-run practices have profits of 30% to 45% of revenues."
- "Write-up work and monthly payroll preparation should provide approximately 75% of total revenues. Taxes should provide the remaining 25%."
- "Taxpayers may also benefit by obtaining tax preparation estimates from more than one preparer from different size companies. For example, the survey found that tax preparation fees for an itemized Form 1040 with Schedule A and a state tax return averaged only $217 at one-person firms, and rose to an average of $245 for firms with three or more staff."

Expenses as a percentage of annual sales

Cost of goods	02%
Payroll/labor Costs	25% to 30%
Occupancy	05% to 10%
Profit (estimated pretax)	30% to 45%

Industry Trend

- "Up and possibly up sharply depending on the IRS Tax Code changes and effects of the Affordable Care Act"
- "Computers are making it easier and easier for businesses and individuals to

prepare their own taxes, but people will always need professionals to help with audits, the tax code, etc."
- "More industry regulation from IRS."
- "Any new tax laws would greatly affect the accounting and tax industry."
- "I see the trend to remain about the same as it has been the past 10 years."
- "Growth...consistent growth due to regulations"
- "Continued demand for acquisitions and continued exiting by aging population of CPAs"
- "IRS free e-file along with PC software continues to pull customers away from paid preparers. More tax preparation franchises opening will take business away from established firms."

Seller Financing

- "Generally seeing more outside financing, with a combination of owner and bank financing in place."
- "Usually, an accounting practice is sold for 1 to 1½ times annual gross revenue, with 25% to 50% down payment. The balance is paid to the seller as a percent of revenue received from a purchased client list over a negotiated period of time (may be 2 to 6 years). The payments may be paid monthly or quarterly or annually as a percent of revenue received from the previous period. EXAMPLE: Annual Revenue $100,000, Purchase Price $ 125,000, 30% down payment $37,500, Balance due $87,500, Annual Revenue $100,000 = 87.5 %/4 years = 21.875% per year. For each dollar of revenue received from a purchased client list, the buyer would pay 21.875% to the seller for four years. Balance check: Annual revenue received $100,000, 21.875% = $21,875 for 4 years = $ 87,500 Balance due"
- "Almost always has some seller financing which is usually 5 years for moderate or larger practices and 2 to 4 years for smaller practices."

Questions

- "Why are you selling? Is any individual client fee over 10% of the Gross Revenue? Is any single industry over 10% of Gross Revenue? How much of Revenue is earned from tax return preparation and how much from accounting or bookkeeping? What type of work does your staff do? What tax and accounting software do you use? What is the billing rate per hour? Do you bill by hour or project? How long have your clients been with this firm? How long have the employees been with this firm?"
- "Why do you want to sell your business? What will you do after closing. Are you willing to sign a broad Non-Competition Agreement?"
- "Repeat clients, accounting vs. tax preparation work"
- "Strengths and weaknesses of the firm. Information about the area."
- "What is the breakdown between tax, write-up, consulting and audit revenues? Also, who else in the firm can do the tax and write-up work? Who reviews the work?"
- "How long has the firm been in business? List of clients that have left within the past 3 years. List of new clients within the last 3 years. Does the owner plan on being available after the sale? Review sample returns and work papers to get a feel for the amount of work that is done for each client."
- "Why are you selling? Are the clients leaving because of location or other reason? What type of software is used now? If the clients are not walk-in,

how long have they been tax clients? What industry are most of the clients? What % of clients are personal returns or business returns? Are bookkeeping services included with any client?"

- "What are the seller's goals in the sale of the practice? They are not the same for all sellers."
- "Fee structure, number of clients, services performed, employee costs, franchise fees paid, licenses required."
- "Any clients not in the local service area?"

Resources

Associations
- American Institute of CPA's: www.aicpa.org
- National Association of Enrolled Agents: www.naea.org
- National Association of Tax Professionals: http://www.natptax.com/Pages/default.aspx

Ace Cash Express (See also Check Cashing Services, Franchises)		
SIC 6099-03	NAICS 522390	Number of Businesses/Units 1,750

Rules of Thumb
➤ 1.25 times annual sales plus inventory

Resources

Websites
- Ace Cash Express—this company is publicly held, and their annual report is available online and is an excellent resource.: www.acecashexpress.com

		Franchise
Ace Hardware (See also Hardware Stores, Franchises)		
Approx. Total Investment		$400,000 to $1,100,000
SIC 5251-04	NAICS 444130	Number of Businesses/Units 4,166

Rules of Thumb
➤ 45 percent of annual sales plus inventory

Pricing Tips
- Sales seem to indicate that smaller sales bring a higher multiple (50%+) than stores with sales over $1 million, which seem to bring lower multiples. Price is plus inventory, and that may be the reason for lower multiples for larger stores.

Resources

Websites
- www.myace.com

A - Rules of Thumb

		Franchise

Adam & Eve Stores (See also Franchises)

Approx. Total Investment	$100,000–$300,000

	NAICS 451120	Number of Businesses/Units 55

Rules of Thumb

> 35 percent of annual sales plus inventory

Resources

Websites

- Adam & Eve stores: www.adamevestores.com

Advertising Agencies

SIC 7311-01	NAICS 541810	Number of Businesses/Units 68,801

Rules of Thumb

> 50 percent of annual revenues (billings) plus inventory. May require an earnout.

Pricing Tips

- "What are agencies worth? This is a tough one, but typical agencies are valued at 2–5 times EBITDA (I mean realistic EBITDA that includes having the CEO actually paying himself and other agency mangers what they are worth). Digital firms have higher multiples at 8 plus. The digital sweet spot is a firm with technological prowess, owned IP, strategic vision and industry-leading expertise in a hot category like mobile, social, etc.

  "A good start is to take a look at what kinds of agencies or digital media companies have been purchased in the past couple of years." – Peter Levitan
  Source: https://www.linkedin.com/pulse/8-tips-how-sell-your-ad-agency-wpp-peter-levitan

Benchmark Data

Statistics (Advertising Agencies)

Number of Establishments	68,801
Average Profit Margin	7.7%
Revenue per Employee	$171,600
Average Number of Employees	3.8
Average Wages per Employee	$74,145

Products and Services Segmentation

Advertising services	64.1%
Creative services	19.5%
Other	8.0%
Media planning, buying & representation	6.3%
Public relations services	2.1%

Major Market Segmentation

Retail sector	22.0%
TMT	21.0%
Automotive sector	13.0%
Financial services	13.0%
Travel & entertainment	13.0%
Other	7.0%
Consumer packaged goods	6.0%
Pharmaceutical & Healthcare sector	5.0%

Industry Costs

Profit	7.7%
Wages	43.0%
Purchases	43.6%
Depreciation	0.7%
Marketing	2.0%
Rent & Utilities	2.3%
Other	0.7%

Market Share

Omnicom Group Inc.	10.7%
Interpublic Group of Companies Inc.	8.4%
WPP PLC	7.0%

Source: IBISWorld, April 2016

Industry Trend

- "The blockbuster $4.8 billion sale of Yahoo's core assets to Verizon communications, announced on Monday, could generate deep shifts on the global advertising industry's playing field. Verizon plans to merge the Yahoo assets with AOL, which the company bought in 2015. AOL head Tim Armstrong will spearhead the integration of the two companies along with Verizon EVP Marni Walden, a process that is sure to be tedious and lengthy. The newly bolstered telecom giant hopes to compete with Google and Facebook in an industry where 'scale is imperative.'"

  Source: "Verizon, Yahoo could Reshape the Advertising Industry," by Tobi Elkin and Philip Rosenstein, July 26, 2016 http://www.mediapost.com/publications/article/281071/verizon-yahoo-could-reshape-the-advertisingindus.html? adMPA_Daily_News_Roundup&MPA_Daily_News_Roundup_=

- "'Retail advertisers continue to represent the largest category of Internet ad spending, responsible for 22% percent last year, followed by automotive and financial services which each accounted for 13% of the year's revenues,' the report states.

  "Google, the leading Internet search provider, and Facebook, the biggest social network operator, claimed 64% of the $59.6 billion in online advertising revenue, according to Pivotal Research analyst Brian Wieser. Google scooped up $30 billion and Facebook gathered $8 billion, while other smaller companies lost market share, the analyst noted. 'Smaller companies will continue to operate in the shadows of the industry's two dominant players,' Wieser wrote in a note to investors."

  Source: "U.S. mobile advertising grows 66% in 2015," by Tracy Maple, April 22, 2016 https://www.internetretailer.com/2016/04/22/us-mobile-advertising-grows-66-2015

- "There are three trends in particular that marketers need to get ahead of: 1) Social media increasingly means paid media. The rules are changing. Facebook has now decreed that brands need to pay to get visibility, even when it comes to reaching people who opt in to follow those brands. With Twitter, Instagram, and other social platforms, the only way to ensure wide reach is to support strong creative with paid media.

2) Default social activity shifts from public to private. Social media usage keeps skyrocketing. Yet much of the growth is coming from private social activity, where people are sending messages and multimedia directly to select individuals or groups of friends, rather than sharing everything publicly.

3) People are buying from each other instead of from brands. What if it doesn't matter how big your brand is, how many locations you have, how great your products are or how good your service is? What if, instead, people would rather buy products and services from each other?"

Source: "Three Seismic Threats to Marketers Hitting in 2015" by David Berkowitz, http://adage.com/article/digitalnext/seismic-threats-marketers-hitting-2015/296406/ 12/31/14

Resources

Websites

- American Association of Advertising Agencies: www.aaaa.org

		Franchise
Aero Colours, Inc. (See also Franchises)		
Approx. Total Investment		$49,000 to $174,000
SIC 7532-02	NAICS 811121	Number of Businesses/Units 200+

Rules of Thumb

➢ 70 percent of annual sales

Resources

Websites

- www.aerocolours.com

Aircraft Cleaning (See also Airport Operations)		
SIC 4581-04	NAICS 561720	Number of Businesses/Units 3,807

Rules of Thumb

➢ 100 percent of annual sales plus inventory

➢ 3 times SDE plus inventory

Pricing Tips

- "Minimum 3 yrs. in business, 2.5 x net if owner operated, as much as 4x net if work is performed by a crew or crews."

Expert Comments

"Cleaning an airplane after the passengers leave is no easy job—it's messy, sometimes disgusting, and can even be downright dangerous, employees told ABC News. 'We encounter human feces, sometimes blood, most of

the time vomit from passengers that get motion sick'" said Joel Castillo, who works for Air Serv, a company that handles the cabin cleaning for commercial flights. Castillo's job is to empty the blue liquid that's in the toilets on airplanes. Cabin cleaners are also responsible for sweeping the plane to see what passengers left behind, and they say they often find dirty diapers and half-eaten food stuffed into the seat pockets."
Source: http://abcnews.go.com/Health/airplane-cabin-cleaners-demanding-protection/story?id=26075813

"Strong barrier to entry; quality equipment is a must; high profit; labor intense; and a current downturn in general aviation"

"Aviation is a very difficult industry as a startup business."

Benchmark Data
- "Labor should run approximately 25% of sales."
- "Corporate aircraft cleaning is a very specialized service; if it survived the first 18 months, chances are it will do well."
- "All services are mobile."

Expenses as a percentage of annual sales

Cost of goods	05% to 10%
Payroll/labor Costs	25% to 35%
Occupancy	10%
Profit (estimated pretax)	55% to 60%

Industry Trend
- "The industry will bounce back, as always."
- "Increase in demand"
- "Private aviation is a rapidly growing industry."

Questions
- "Number of accounts, how long servicing those accounts, percentage of sales from which accounts"
- "How many aircraft do you service per week, per month? Number of employees? The buyer is going to need to keep the employees."
- "Transition period is very important."

Resources

Associations
- National Business Aviation Association: www.nbaa.org

Aircraft Manufacturing—Parts, Supplies, Engines, etc. (Kit-built & Ultralight aircraft industry)		
SIC 3724	NAICS 336412	

Rules of Thumb
➢ 40 to 70 percent of annual sales includes value of equipment
➢ 4 times EBIT

Pricing Tips

- "Add for any FAA approvals and for high-value equipment."
- "FAA approvals and/or contracts with major OEM's very important."
- "Each business varies so greatly from the next. It takes someone who knows the industry to know the exact business being described before a price can be established."
- "When very specialized equipment is needed, add some if a good business. Add value of real estate."

Expert Comments

"Sales and profits declining due to technological factors such as increased time between overhauls"

"Low competition based on high barriers to entry."

Benchmark Data

- "Revenue per employee should be at least $100,000 per annum."

Expenses as a percentage of annual sales

Cost of goods	35%
Payroll/labor Costs	35%
Occupancy	20%
Profit (estimated pretax)	10%

Industry Trend

- "Another reason why the aircraft market has become less cyclical—and now less likely to crash—is the advent of no-frills airlines. Because they are prepared to vary prices to ride out the ups and downs of demand for flights, their demand for planes is smoother. The rise of budget carriers in emerging markets is also helping. Budget airlines account for around 60% of seat capacity in India and South-East Asia; in Europe, the figure is around 40%, according to CAPA, an aviation-consulting firm."
  Source: http://www.economist.com/blogs/economist-explains/2016/01/economist-explains-10?zid=293&ah=e50f636873b42369614615ba3c16df4a
- "Highly cyclical with the economy and military spending"

Seller Financing

- "3 years max, 1 year least"
- "We've never sold a 'seller-financed' ultralight aircraft business. It is always a cash deal."

Questions

- "Approvals and contracts"
- "What is the reputation of the aircraft or related product being sold? What is the reputation of the company? Is business up or down? What about accidents—any deaths? A company with a great reputation may be worth little because of their product—or, vice versa."
- "Where are sales today in comparison to one, two . . . years ago? Why are they up or down?" Have there been any structural failures or successful liability suits against them? Is it movable or must buyer move?"

Airport Operations (See also Aircraft Cleaning)

SIC 4581-06	NAICS 488119	Number of Businesses/Units 2,242

Rules of Thumb

➢ 90 to 100 percent of annual sales includes inventory

➢ 4 to 5 times SDE includes inventory

➢ 4 times EBIT

➢ 5 times EBITDA

Pricing Tips

- "Pricing would be highly dependent on the sector. In certain segments there is lot of personal goodwill. A prospective buyer should separate the personal goodwill from the business goodwill in calculating a purchase price. Many smaller businesses are highly dependent upon the owner's talent or specialty. These businesses should be valued with consideration to an earnout or employment contact to ensure ongoing stability."
- "FBOs and MROs are about real estate. Revenues per square foot can be a good metric, but most transactions above $3MM use a multiple of EBITDA plus inventory"
- "The FBO business is really a real-estate play. Take a careful look at the city leasehold agreements and the fuel farm, as EPA regulations can be costly to implement. Most fuel farms now must be built above ground. For air charter companies, take a close look at the age/condition of the aircraft used and existing contracts."
- "Multiples are dependent on market. Large market FBOs will generally be in the 4–5 x EBITDA range with second and third tier market FBOs valued at 3–4 x EBITDA. There are, however, several important factors affecting value including lease terms, services offered, and airport as well as area competition. The shorter the leasing terms and more restrictive the lease, the lower the multiple will be. If new facilities or improvements must be made, a 20-year lease is often needed for financial feasibility. FBOs with a monopoly on local operations will be valued higher than those facing competition. Buyers tend to value the diversity of income streams differently: Larger chains tend to shy away from maintenance and hangar rentals due to the added complexity while owner/operators tend to appreciate the more stable income these additional sources provide. Fueling rights are also an important factor in pricing. Airports often restrict who is able to install fuel tanks and for what purpose. An entity which has the exclusive right to sell fuel on the airfield carries significant value; however, if co-op fuel arrangements are common place on the field, this may drastically reduce local demand."
- "First, if a fixed base operator, perform due diligence on EPA regulation adherence (e.g., fuel farm) and hangar leases with city or county."

Expert Comments

"An operator's location is the primary determinant of volume and marketability."

"A major source of income is from fuel sales. Margins vary greatly depending on competition. Location is a key factor that affects the amount of traffic at an airport and thus the volume of business. Smaller FBOs are harder to market because most require owner operators with a passion for aviation. After a long down period the industry is tending up. FBOs are difficult to duplicate as the property is generally owned and controlled by some government entity. The number of operators allowed at any given airfield in limited."

Benchmark Data

Statistics (Airport Operations)

Number of Establishments	2,242
Average Profit Margin	4.3%
Revenue per Employee	$266,800
Average Number of Employees	43.5
Average Wages per Employee	$30,164

Products and Services Segmentation

Fixed base operations	63.6%
Airport administration and operation services	13.0%
Handling services for goods	11.4%
Other services	8.5%
Repair and maintenance services for aircraft	3.5%

Major Market Segmentation

Passenger airlines	47.6%
Households and business consumers	42.6%
Cargo	4.9%
Other	4.3%
Government	0.6%

Industry Costs

Profit	4.3%
Wages	11.4%
Purchases	3.2%
Depreciation	35.0%
Marketing	2.1%
Rent & Utilities	5.5%
Other	38.5%

Market Share

The Port Authority of New York and New Jersey	11.1%

Source: IBISWorld, June 2016

- "For FBO labor costs should be 20–35%. Occupancy could be variable depending on the airport and real estate costs. Rent+utilities, 14%"
- "Standard & Poor's benchmarks are a good starting place. Premiums placed on location, e.g., Van Nuys, CA or major cities."
- "High private-jet-traffic airports. Jet fuel sales a plus. General aviation service only and/or airports with less than 5,000-foot runways sell at a discount."

Expenses as a percentage of annual sales

Cost of goods	30% to 40%
Payroll/labor Costs	25% to 35%
Occupancy	05% to 10%
Profit (estimated pretax)	05% to 15%

Industry Trend

- "Industry consolidation expected as smaller operators are displaced from the market. Improving economic conditions expected to result in revenue growth."

- "The airport operations industry will continue to expand over the next five years as the U.S. economy continues to improve and travel rates grow. Several airports will invest in new infrastructure to expand capacity and ease congestion. The federal government, through its airports improvement program, has budgeted more than $3.0 billion annually over the five years to 2020 to assist airports with capital improvements to improve safety and capacity as well as to alleviate environmental concerns. Despite this projected investment, capacity constraints at airports are expected to suppress revenue growth to some degree. Industry revenue is expected to increase 1.9% per year on average over the next five years, totaling $26.6 billion in 2020.

  "The total number of domestic trips is forecast to increase 1.6% per year on average through 2020. Likewise, the number of inbound international trips by foreigners is anticipated to grow an annualized 4.2% over the same period. Lower ticket prices resulting from increased competition among airlines, especially those offering budget fares, will assist this growth."

  Source: http://clients1.ibisworld.com/reports/us/industry/industryoutlook.aspx?entid=1194

- "Although the slow growth of the U.S. economy and the European recession has dampened the near term prospects for general aviation, the long-term outlook remains favorable. We see growth in business aviation demand over the long term driven by a growing U.S. and world economy especially in the turbo jet, turboprop and turbine rotorcraft markets. As the fleet grows, the number of general aviation hours flown is projected to increase an average of 1.5 percent a year through 2033."

  Source: FAA Aerospace Forecast Fiscal Years 2013-2033

- "Private jet aviation is the main driver of many of these airport businesses; how the business jet industry goes is how these services will go."

- "Major research firms are showing a delivery of over 10,000 private jets in the next 10 years, implying a need for more airport service providers, including FBOs. City governments are now taking ownership of some FBOs, which is a threat to entrepreneurship. The inability of FBO owners to get more than a 25-year lease from a city is also a threat to profitability."

Seller Financing

- "Outside and partial seller financing. Depends on the particular sale"
- "3–5 years"

Questions

- "Why sell? How long is lease with city? Any renewable lease clauses? If so, at what rate?"
- "Insurance can be a major cost component. What is the company's safety record? Does the business operate under any FAA certificates (IE 135 charter or 141 flight school)? Is maintenance involved with the FBO? How

many IAs and A&Ps are employed? Are they contract workers? Is it an FAA certified repair station? Is it an authorized repair station for an OEM? What is the hangar occupancy rate? Is there a waiting list? How long? What are the average rates per square foot?"

- "Why sell now? Any trouble with city/local governments? Status of existing leases/agreements? Trouble with EPA? Labor issues?"

Resources

Websites
- Federal Aviation Administration: http://www.faa.gov/

Trade Publications
- Aviation International News: http://ainonline.com

Associations
- Aeronautical Repair Station Association (ARSA): www.arsa.org
- Professional Aviation Maintenance Association (PAMA): http://pama.wildapricot.org/
- Aircraft Electronics Association (AEA): www.aea.net
- Aviation Suppliers Association (ASA): www.aviationsuppliers.org
- National Air Transportation Association (NATA): www.nata.aero
- Aircraft Owner's and Pilot's Association (AOPA): www.aopa.org
- General Aviation Manufacturers Association: http://www.gama.aero/
- International Air Transport Association (IATA): www.iata.org

		Franchise
Allegra Marketing-Print-Mail (See also Franchises, Printing)		
Approx. Total Investment		$162,010 to $593.392
	NAICS 323114	Number of Businesses/Units 275

Rules of Thumb

➢ 60% to 65% of annual sales plus inventory

Resources

Websites
- www.allegranetwork.com

		Franchise
All Tune and Lube		
(See also Auto Lube, Franchises, Grease Monkey, Jiffy Lube)		
Approx. Total Investment		$150,000
SIC 7549-03	NAICS 81191	Number of Businesses/Units 358

Rules of Thumb

➢ 20 to 25 percent of annual sales

Resources

Websites

- www.alltuneandlube.com

AlphaGraphics (See also Franchises)		Franchise
Approx. Total Investment		$258,300 to $395,900
Estimated Annual Sales/Unit		$1,125,700
SIC 7336-02	NAICS 541430	Number of Businesses/Units 245

Rules of Thumb

➢ 60 to 65 percent of annual sales plus inventory

Resources

Websites

- http://alphagraphicsfranchise.com/

Aluminum Smelting Machinery		
	NAICS 331316	

Rules of Thumb

➢ 70 percent of annual sales plus inventory

➢ 5 times EBITDA

Pricing Tips

- "If balance sheet is sound, business is worth an average between twice net assets and 5 times EBITDA."

Expert Comments

"Highly specialized market. Vendor must establish himself on short list of major EPCMs through references. Spare parts market captive and profitable."

Benchmark Data

- "$250,000 per employee"

Expenses as a percentage of annual sales

Cost of goods	70%
Payroll/labor Costs	25%
Occupancy	05%
Profit (estimated pretax)	10%

Industry Trend
- "The aluminum market is growing fast. New smelters are being built. Older are being extended or revamped. Market for machinery will be excellent for next 5 years at least."

Questions
- "Indebtedness? Officers' loan or debt? Backlog and list of references"

Ambulance Services		
SIC 4119-02	NAICS 62191	Number of Businesses/Units 28,341

Rules of Thumb
➤ 40 percent of annual revenues plus inventory

➤ 2 to 4.0 times SDE includes inventory

➤ 2.75 to 5.2 times EBITDA

Pricing Tips
- "There is a very wide range of value for these businesses as there are 12–14 different characteristics that affect the pricing and multiples paid. EBITDA multiples range from 2.75 to 7.5 X EBITDA depending on company size, EBITDA, call mix and 10-12 other major factors, all of which affect value and risk, etc."
- "Owner's level of involvement is definitely a major contributor to a multiplier. Revenue per vehicle is a very top level gauge of company's performance. Revenue per vehicle varies with geography. For example, in No. California revenue per vehicle is 20% higher than in So. California. Two major expenses to watch after are payroll and cost of fuel."
- "Large pricing range due to a larger number of key variables that affect valuation. Transition period with seller is critical (should be at least 6 months to a year, even on smaller businesses)."
- "Payer mix & breakdowns very important; breakdowns on advanced life support (ALS) vs. basic life support (BLS) transports; reimbursements; rural vs. urban mix; wheelchair transports diminish profitability."

Expert Comments
"Most ambulance services have high recurring revenue business model; high fragmentation. Most owners are former medics and lack skill sets required to grow these businesses beyond $2–5 MM in sales and maintain margins and maximize utilization and effectively manage payroll costs."

"Very few companies consistently provide a high level of service and generate solid EBITDA margins in the 18–25% range. The industry is very fragmented, with companies over $10 MM in net cash sales and solid earnings securing premium pricing."

"Amount of competition varies by region. Some areas in California are very densely populated and the density is connected to a number of medical facilities in the area. Location of the office is irrelevant to the business, however parking availability for the fleet is definitely a benefit."

Government cut rates several times, therefore profits suffered and owners had to streamline their businesses and cut expenses in order to maintain profit margins. Threshold of entry in the industry is pretty high, especially if company wants to get paid by the government. The approval process is quite lengthy."

"Aging baby boomers will drive increased transport volume. Regional and statewide Medicaid brokerage contracts are becoming more common, but only account for a small percentage of transports and are low-profit runs. Implementing appropriate technologies is becoming a requirement for operators in order to maintain profit levels. It is very hard for startups to steal customers away from high-level providers."

"Growing number of transports, but tougher for the smaller provider (all under $5–$7 million in sales) to compete effectively against the mid-sized players; trend is to sell, merge or acquire; knowledge of ambulance billing is very important."

Benchmark Data

Statistics (Ambulance Services)

Number of Establishments	28,341
Average Profit Margin	13.9%
Revenue per Employee	$82,500
Average Number of Employees	7.3
Average Wages per Employee	$32,649

Products and Services Segmentation

Emergency surface ambulance	53.3%
Nonemergency surface ambulance	19.5%
Emergency air ambulance (rotary wing)	16.9%
Other	5.3%
Emergency air ambulance (fixed wing)	3.2%
Nonemergency air ambulance	0.7%
Standby ambulance and/or first-aid services	0.7%

Major Market Segmentation

Sprains or strains of neck and back	21.9%
Contusion with intact skin surface	21.5%
Open wounds	16.5%
Fractures	13.4%
Sprains or strains excluding neck and back	13.2%
Spinal disorders	8.8%
Other	4.7%

Industry Costs

Profit	13.9%
Wages	39.7%
Purchases	7.5%
Depreciation	3.6%
Marketing	1.0%
Rent & Utilities	2.8%
Other	31.5%

Market Share

Envision Healthcare	15.4%
Air Methods	8.2%

Source: IBISWorld, June 2016

- "EBITDA margins vary significantly from company to company. Most owners who lack proper skill sets to effectively manage these businesses typically generate 8–12% EBITDA; however owners with proper business skill sets who know what drives profits and have high levels of service, etc. typically generate 17–22% EBITDA consistently."
- "Industry average EBITDA is 7–8% of net cash sales per year; well-run operations generate 18–25% EBITDA margins and these companies sell for a premium compared to equally sized companies in the market. Keeping total payroll costs down and having a good billing process/dept. are keys to drive profitability."

Expenses as a percentage of annual sales

Cost of goods	02% to 12%
Payroll/labor Costs	45% to 58%
Occupancy	01.5% to 03.0%
Profit (estimated pretax)	07% to 22%

Industry Trend

- "Heavy competition, strong growth, consolidation expected to continue."
- "Smaller companies with sales under $3 MM per year will have a tougher time competing with larger operators. More technology and software modules are required today, than compared to 5 years ago and these advances help improve efficiencies, but they also are costly to purchase and implement."
- "During the next five years, ambulance providers will exhibit revenue growth as healthcare reform bolsters the number of insured individuals, thereby lowering the occurrence of bad debt. Nevertheless, to cut healthcare costs, the federal government will likely lower reimbursement rates, causing the industry to grapple with rates that may not cover the cost of care. However, the burgeoning elderly population requires more physician care, personnel and medical equipment than any other age demographic, which will provide need-based demand for both nonemergency and emergency ambulance services."

  Source: http://clients1.ibisworld.com/reports/us/industry/industryoutlook.aspx?entid=1581
- "GIA announces the release of a comprehensive global report on Ambulance Services. The global market for Ambulance Services is projected to exceed US$63 billion by 2020, driven by the growing demand for emergency and non-emergency medical care by the elderly."

  Source: http://www.strategyr.com/pressMCP-6103.asp
- "Increased technology & efficiencies improvements will become a requirement to survive"
- "I believe any industry related to servicing aging and ill population will grow over the next 20–30 years. People live longer and get sick and need transportation to get to medical offices. Therefore demand for medical transportation will only grow."
- "Increased volume, more technology being utilized to maximize profits"
- "Higher CAPEX cost due to need to implement technology for both logistics management and patient record management"

Seller Financing
- "Outside financing"
- "All across the board; typically 50–80% cash at close, with 5–10% held in escrow for reps & warranties. Working capital is true'd up within 60–90 days post close and is normally included in the purchase price, based on historical avg."
- "Although we use both (outside financing and seller financing), seller financing is more typical lately."
- "3–5 years"

Questions
- "Payor mix, market share, patient demographic data."
- "Knowledge of medical billing; logistics management; attention to details"
- "Except regular financial due diligence, buyers should be watching for lawsuits against the company and traffic tickets. High level of lawsuits and traffic tickets indicates that the business doesn't have good driver education and discipline in place."
- "Lots—There are a lot of fraudulent practices and brokers need to understand the industry and billing guidelines or they should avoid taking a listing/ representing the owner; need to know the quantity of dialysis patients; businesses with a high percentage of dialysis runs get discounted in valuation/ pricing"
- "Who does billing: in-house or sub out to 3rd party? What software is used? What systems do you have in place & utilize for billing and for logistics? Do you prescreen your transports/patients?"

Resources
Websites
- EMSWorld: http://www.emsworld.com/

Associations
- American Ambulance Association- primarily for members: www.the-aaa.org

	Franchise
American Poolplayers Association (APA)	
(See also Billiards, Franchises)	
Approx. Total Investment	$16,695 to $19,865
SIC 7999-12 | NAICS 713990	Number of Businesses/Units 297

Rules of Thumb
- ➤ 1.4 times annual sales
- ➤ $1,000 to $1,800 per team in sales: selling price—$2,000 to $2,500 per team

Pricing Tips
- "These franchises are purchased by areas. Pricing is normally based on the number of teams in the area. The general rule of thumb is $2,000 per team in a well-managed area."

Expenses as a percentage of annual sales

Cost of goods	n/a
Payroll/labor Costs	n/a
Occupancy	n/a
Profit (estimated pretax)	35%

Industry Trend

- "Increase in popularity and participation in recreational billiards"

Resources

Websites

- www.poolplayers.com

	Franchise

Andy OnCall (See also Franchises)	
Approx. Total Investment	$35,650 to $47,050

	NAICS 236118	Number of Businesses/Units 1,398

Rules of Thumb

➤ 25 percent of annual sales

➤ Andy OnCall connects unemployed craftsmen with homeowners who need home repairs.

Benchmark Data

Statistics (Handyman Service Franchises)

Number of Establishments	1,398
Average Profit Margin	5.4%
Revenue per Employee	$182,200
Average Number of Employees	10.2
Average Wages per Employee	$71,235

Products and Services Segmentation

Maintenance services	63.1%
Plumbing	8.6%
Electrical	7.5%
Others	7.3%
Decks and Fences	5.1%
Painting	5.1%
Flooring	3.3%

Major Market Segmentation

Households	68.2%
Property owners and managers	14.8%
Commercial clients	10.0%
Other	7.0%

Industry Costs

Profit	5.4%
Wages	39.2%
Purchases	41.2%
Depreciation	1.3%
Marketing	1.4%
Rent & Utilities	1.5%
Other	10.0%

Source: IBISWorld, May 2016

Resources

Websites
- www.andyoncall.com

Antique Shops/Dealers		
SIC 5932-02	NAICS 453310	Number of Businesses/Units 1,258

Rules of Thumb

➢ 20 percent of annual sales plus inventory

Resources

Websites
- Art and Antique Dealers League of America: www.artantiquedealersleague.com

		Franchise
Anytime Fitness (See also Fitness Centers, Franchises)		
Approx. Total Investment		$80,000 to $130,000
	NAICS 713940	Number of Businesses/Units 3,036

Rules of Thumb

➢ 2.5 times SDE plus inventory

Pricing Tips
- "Multiples of SDE vary based on size of the owner benefit. SDE less than $75k, typically we see multiples in the 1 range. $75–$150k, we see multiples in the 1.8 to 2.5 range. Greater than $150k multiples may be higher."

Expert Comments

"'We've never had any major incidents in our 12 years. I think people love getting their own key and going anytime they want. I should mention that we're not completely unstaffed; a franchise owner will likely work 30 to 50 hours a week, depending on the time of year. In January they're going to work longer, and in the summer months less.'

"'When we came up with the concept, it was a new category in the fitness industry. There was no such thing as a nonstaffed club. By using technology we dramatically minimized overhead—taxes, utilities, rent, payroll. So-called industry experts said it would never work. They felt there was no way people would join if they didn't get hands-on service with every single visit.'"

Source: "Anytime Fitness," quotes from Chuck Runyon and Dave Mortensen, edited by Cristina Lindblad & Dimitra Kessenides, *Businessweek*

Seller Financing
- 2 years

Questions
- "How much in prepaid memberships?"

Resources

Websites
- www.anytimefitness.com

Apartment Rental

SIC 6531-11	NAICS 531110	Number of Businesses/Units 518,186

Rules of Thumb
➢ 80 percent of annual revenues

Pricing Tips
- "This is generally a secondary revenue source to real estate sales."
- Note: A real estate license is required for the operation of this business in many states.

Benchmark Data

Statistics (Apartment Rental)

Number of Establishments	518,186
Average Profit Margin	33.1%
Revenue per Employee	$226,700
Average Number of Employees	1.5
Average Wages per Employee	$25,960

Products and Services Segmentation

Rental of one-unit structures	35.4%
Rental of two- to four-unit structures	19.2%
Rental of five- to nine-unit structures	12.5%
Rental of 10- to19-unit structures	11.9%
Rental of 50- or more unit structures	8.7%
Rental of 20- to 49-unit structures	8.4%
Rental of manufactured homes, mobile homes or trailers	3.9%

Major Market Segmentation

1 person	36.2%
2 persons	27.2%
4 or more persons	21.2%
3 persons	15.4%

Industry Costs

Profit	33.1%
Wages	11.5%
Purchases	9.4%
Depreciation	19.9%
Marketing	1.4%
Rent & Utilities	3.5%
Other	21.2%

Source: IBISWorld, April 2016

- "Fees are most often paid by the apartment owner, usually about 10% to 15% or one month's rent."

Questions

- "How long have they been in business? How do they locate apartments? Do they have an online database? How many apartment communities do they work with?"

Source: www.austinapartmentfinder.com,

Appliance Stores		
SIC 5064	NAICS 443111	Number of Businesses/Units 33,760

Rules of Thumb

➢ 2 times monthly sales plus inventory

Benchmark Data

- "Markup is about 27 percent with some discounters working on a 25 percent markup."

Resources

Associations

- Association of Home Appliance Manufacturers: www.aham.org
- North American Retail Dealers Association: www.narda.com

Appraisal (Valuation Services)		
SIC 7389	NAICS 541990	

Rules of Thumb

➢ "For a firm with less than 10 professionals—1.25 to 1.5 EBITDA. This would include all FF&E and related software and exclude accounts receivable and accounts payable."

Pricing Tips

- Most of the deals are where there is a merger of firms or a buyout by a CPA firm wanting to get into the appraisal business. They usually want the seller to manage the operation for several years."

A - Rules of Thumb

Benchmark Data

Statistics (Real Estate Appraisal)

Number of Establishments	50,166
Average Profit Margin	14.3%
Revenue per Employee	$111,700
Average Number of Employees	1.5
Average Wages per Employee	$37,531

Products and Services Segmentation

Real estate appraisal—commercial	50.2%
Real estate appraisal—residential	26.5%
Real estate consulting	10.9%
Appraisal management	6.6%
Real estate brokerage and other services	5.8%

Major Market Segmentation

Financial institutions & brokers	58.0%
Law offices	15.0%
Private owners	13.0%
Government and other	8.0%
Accountants	6.0%

Industry Costs

Profit	14.3%
Wages	33.9%
Purchases	9.3%
Depreciation	1.3%
Marketing	2.6%
Rent & Utilities	7.8%
Other	30.8%

Market Share

CBRE Group Inc.	6.9%

Source: IBISWorld, March 2016

Statistics (Business Valuation Firms)

Number of Establishments	81,835
Average Profit Margin	10.2%
Revenue per Employee	$81,835
Average Number of Employees	1.0
Average Wages per Employee	$19,775

Products and Services Segmentation

Capitalization of income valuation	34.8%
Asset valuation	31.4%
Owner benefit valuation	22.1%
Market valuation	11.7%

Major Market Segmentation

Private firms	58.6%
Government institutions	30.8%
Other	6.9%
Individuals and households	3.7%

Industry Costs

Profit	10.2%
Wages	38.4%
Purchases	10.9%
Depreciation	1.0%
Marketing	1.7%
Rent & Utilities	4.2%
Other	33.6%

Source: IBISWorld, July 2016

Resources

Associations

- National Association of Certified Valuators and Analysts (NACVA): www.nacva.com
- American Society of Appraisers: www.appraisers.org
- Institute of Business Appraisers (IBA): instbusapp.org

Arcade, Food & Entertainment Complexes		
SIC 7993-03	NAICS 713120	Number of Businesses/Units 6,594

Rules of Thumb

➤ 25 percent of annual sales includes inventory

➤ 3 times SDE includes inventory

➤ 3 to 3.5 EBITDA

Pricing Tips

- "The typical floor space for Family Entertainment Centers runs from 8,000 Sq Ft (2400 Sq M) to 50,000 Sq Ft (15,000 Sq M) or more, and the typical 'standalone' arcade game room ranges from 1,500 to 5,000 Sq Ft (475-1525 Sq M) in size, with a complete turnkey budget for FEC's starting about $1,000,000 and smaller traditional arcades starting about $250,000. A very good 'rule of thumb' for budgeting many facilities uses $125–$300 per Sq Ft or $410–$985/Sq M for total project costs, but it depends a great deal on where in the world the facility will be located.

  "Of course, if you already have built out, unused space, and are adding 'non-redemption' arcade and sports games into locations such as hotels, resorts, casinos and cruise ships, a better way to estimate startup costs would be to use 10 to15 games per 1,000 Sq Ft (300 Sq M) and using an average equipment cost of $6,000–$8,000 per game, for budgetary purposes."

  Source: http://www.bmigaming.com/commercialarcades.htm

- "Make sure the equipment is either owned and is in current, 'fashionable' condition, or make sure there is an attractive lease arrangement that enables simple trade-in for more current gaming. These games are only as valuable as the current trend. There are 'stability' games such as air hockey, certain pinball games and redemption games where you can win toy prizes straight from the machine. The store must have a mix of current trend equipment and the stability games. Stability games are the work horses but the trendy games are very expensive to stay on top of."

A - Rules of Thumb

- "This industry is not for everyone! Although, if you are an experienced retailer and have a stomach for high rent-to-gross sales percentages, this could be a great opportunity for you to enter into a fun and rewarding industry! It is a simple business model and can be improved significantly by introducing customer promotions combining game tokens with redemption prize incentives and local food retailers."

Expert Comments

"Games must also be attractive/specific to area demographics. Interestingly, my clients that owned a chain of stores in and around New York City found that the Asian neighborhoods demand more high-tech, challenging games and they will correspondingly pay a higher price per use. This is not a business that a client should jump into ill-informed or insufficiently researched. Only buy tried and true locations. Don't build new locations unless on a massive scale like Dave & Busters. They are a one-stop entertainment supercenter including food, bowling and usually booze. The smaller locations in malls and plazas are way too risky given the fact that kids don't need to leave the home anymore to get the most current and challenging gaming. So, if there is a location that has withstood the transition to home-based gaming through the 80s, 90s and up to now, it is likely a winner. These arcade formats only now work in certain neighborhoods, need high volume given the price of commercial real estate, etc. Get a long lease."

"Location is KEY. This is a capital-intensive industry but a proven location is a very valuable semi-absentee opportunity. If you are buying existing units, you can use the assets in the purchase to back part of the financing."

Benchmark Data

Statistics (Arcade, Food & Entertainment Complexes)

Number of Establishments	6,594
Average Profit Margin	13.4%
Revenue per Employee	$43,000
Average Number of Employees	6.6
Average Wages per Employee	$11,967

Products and Services Segmentation

Debit-card and coin-operated games and rides	45.1%
Food and beverages	35.9%
Admissions	14.2%
Corporate and party event services	4.2%
Other	0.6%

Industry Costs

Profit	13.4%
Wages	28.0%
Purchases	26.6%
Depreciation	7.4%
Marketing	2.7%
Rent & Utilities	9.4%
Other	12.5%

Market Share

Dave & Buster's Entertainment Inc.	32.4%
CEC Entertainment Inc.	29.5%

Source: IBISWorld, June 2016

Statistics (Golf Driving Ranges and Family Fun Centers)

Number of Establishments	53,817
Average Profit Margin	4.9%
Revenue per Employee	$87,300
Average Number of Employees	2.3
Average Wages per Employee	$21,129

Products and Services Segmentation

Other	31.6%
Amusement and recreation services	30.5%
Coin operated games and rides	14.0%
Amateur sports teams and club services	6.7%
Meals and beverages	5.5%
Fitness and recreational sport center services	5.1%
Registration for sports tournaments and matches	3.8%
Golf course and country club services and memberships	2.8%

Industry Costs

Profit	4.9%
Wages	24.7%
Purchases	26.0%
Depreciation	2.7%
Marketing	3.0%
Rent & Utilities	9.5%
Other	29.2%

Source: IBISWorld, February 2016

- "Game costs range from $2,500 to $15,000 per new machine. You do not have to buy new machinery! Sell older technology online and buy new circuitry for new games and put them in your existing game machines. It will save tremendous operating capital and the customer will not know the difference."

Expenses as a percentage of annual sales

Cost of goods	05% to 10%
Payroll/labor Costs	15%
Occupancy	40% to 50%
Profit (estimated pretax)	15% to 20%

Resources

Websites
- Coaster Grotto: http://www.coastergrotto.com/theme-park-attendance.jsp

Architectural Firms

SIC 8712-02	NAICS 541310	Number of Businesses/Units 85,114

Rules of Thumb

➢ 40 percent of annual sales plus inventory

Pricing Tips

- "Larger Firm: Value = Earnings X Multiple Earnings = $1,200,000 Market Multiple Range: Three (3) to Five (5)
  Smaller Firm: Value = Earnings X Multiple Earnings = $100,000 Market Multiple Range: One (1) to Three (3)"
  Source: http://www.aianewmexico.org/aianmprograms/d.arne3.23.07.pdf

- "Consulting firms that specialize in ownership transitions develop a fair-market value based on a handful of factors including adjusted net worth (book value), weighted net income, weighted net fees, projected fees, and backlog of unearned fees.
  "These factors produce a range of a firm's value. For example, some consultants value a firm at between 1 and 1.5 times adjusted net worth for an internal transition or between 2 and 3 times for an external sale. Other consultants value a firm at between 3 and 5 times weighted net income or apply a percentage of their average earnings to their backlog of unearned fees."
  Source: "How Much Is Your Firm Really Worth?" excerpted and adapted from an AIA Architect article by Michael Strogoff

- "Goodwill is at a minimum due to the non-repetitiveness of the clients. It is also a personal service business. The stature, reputation and contacts of the principal(s)are generally not transferable, especially in a smaller firm."

Expert Comments

"Tools for Small Firms: Simple Business Practices that Reduce Risk
  ✓ Not documenting advice given or decisions made during conversations with the client.
  ✓ Not using a written agreement.
  ✓ Beginning work before having a signed written agreement.
  ✓ Not following the written agreement once it is in place.
  ✓ Taking any job that walks through the door"
Source: Rena M. Klein, FAIA, principal of R.M. Klein Consulting, in Seattle, Washington, is a member of the Soloso Editorial Content Review Board and serves as the Subject Matter Expert for Practice.

Benchmark Data

Statistics (Architects)

Number of Establishments	85,114
Average Profit Margin	12.2%
Revenue per Employee	$180,200
Average Number of Employees	2.6
Average Wages per Employee	$67,749

Products and Services Segmentation

New project architectural services	58.0%
Renovation and rehabilitation architectural service	42.0%

Major Market Segmentation

Institutional construction	51.8%
Commercial and industrial construction	27.1%
Residential construction	17.1%
Other	4.0%

Industry Costs

Profit	12.2%
Wages	38.8%
Purchases	8.9%
Depreciation	0.7%
Marketing	1.3%
Rent & Utilities	4.7%
Other	33.4%

Source: IBISWorld, June 2016

Industry Trend

- "Profitability will also improve over the next five years, driven by an increase in demand for new construction projects. As a result, IBISWorld expects that average industry profit will marginally increase from 11.8% of revenue in 2015 to 11.9% in 2020. Growth in industry revenue and high profit margins will bring more operators to the industry, especially small companies and sole proprietors that left as a result of poor business conditions after the recession. Consequently, the number of industry operators is forecast to increase at an average rate of 1.6% per year to 77,150 companies during the five years to 2020."

Source: http://clients1.ibisworld.com/reports/us/industry/industryoutlook.aspx?entid=1401

- "There are currently over 102,000 firms in the architectural services field and on average, successful firms are seeing profits as high as 21%! Competition is fierce, but opportunity is plentiful due to a decaying infrastructure and positive construction activity."

Source: http://www.vikingmergers.com/blog/2016/how-to-prepare-an-architectural-services-firm-for-sale/

Resources

Websites

- www.aia.org: The American Institute of Architects, an excellent site

Art Galleries and Dealers		
SIC 5999-69	NAICS 453920	Number of Businesses/Units 23,221

Rules of Thumb

> ➢ 30 percent of annual revenues plus inventory

Pricing Tips

- "In some galleries, much of the art work may be on consignment."
- "A surprising number of people search for answers to these and similar questions in attempts to quantify the art market. The art market, however, is not quantifiable, and the answers to these questions don't exist. To begin with, art is not a commodity that can be regulated. Anyone can call him or

herself an artist, anyone can call anything that they create 'art,' and anyone can be an art dealer. Anyone can sell art wherever, whenever and under whatever circumstances they please, and price or sell whatever they call 'art' for whatever amounts of money they feel like selling it for, as long as that art is offered without fraud or misrepresentation."

Source: www.artbusiness.com

Expert Comments

"5 tips to building your own art business:
- ✓ Find your niche
- ✓ Know and understand basic business principles and essentials
- ✓ Build and maintain a network of professionals already running their own successful art business
- ✓ Learn to brand yourself, and start with social media and a functioning Website
- ✓ Don't get down on yourself and don't give up"

Source: http://theartcareerproject.com

Benchmark Data

Statistics (Art Dealers)

Number of Establishments	23,221
Average Profit Margin	7.7%
Revenue per Employee	$257,100
Average Number of Employees	1.5
Average Wages per Employee	$62,676

Products and Services Segmentation

Paintings	42.0%
Drawings	29.0%
Prints	18.0%
Sculptures	6.0%
Photography and other media	5.0%

Major Market Segmentation

Modern art	47.0%
Post-war art	25.0%
19th century art	12.0%
Contemporary art	11.0%
Old masters	5.0%

Industry Costs

Profit	7.7%
Wages	24.3%
Purchases	58.2%
Depreciation	0.6%
Marketing	4.0%
Rent & Utilities	1.9%
Other	3.3%

Market Share

Christie's International	5.4%
Sotheby's Holdings Inc.	4.5%

Source: IBISWorld, April 2016

Industry Trend

- "The Art Dealers industry is in the mature phase of its life cycle because of the industry's market acceptance and relatively low technological change. This indicates that the industry is outperforming the general economy."

Source: http://clients1.ibisworld.com/reports/us/industry/industryoutlook.aspx?entid=1104

Resources

Associations
- Art Dealers Association of America: www.artdealers.org

Arts & Crafts/Retail Stores (See also Hobby Shops)		
SIC 5085	NAICS 45113	

Rules of Thumb

➢ 35 percent of annual sales plus inventory

➢ 2 times SDE plus inventory

Pricing Tips

- "Inventory should be priced separately and should include any costs associated with shipping the inventory to the place of business. Also, any needed labor required to re-package product should be part of COGS and not part of labor. As with most other business valuations, look hard at attractors and detractors to the 36% rule of thumb."
- "You should be able to tell if a 'crafter' is operating the business as opposed to a 'business person,' by their financials."
- Note: The people who actually create the finished arts and crafts (craftspeople) are unique and their business might be difficult to sell because of the very nature of what they produce. Their skill is usually not transferable.

Benchmark Data

Statistics (Fabric, Craft & Sewing Supplies Stores)

Number of Establishments	24,003
Average Profit Margin	14.6%
Revenue per Employee	$78,500
Average Number of Employees	2.7
Average Wages per Employee	$10,715

Products and Services Segmentation

Fabrics	40.0%
Sewing and craft supplies	33.0%
Other	12.0%
Seasonal decorations	8.0%
Fabric home decor	7.0%

Industry Costs

Profit	14.6%
Wages	13.7%
Purchases	59.0%
Depreciation	0.9%
Marketing	2.2%
Rent & Utilities	6.0%
Other	3.6%

Market Share

Michaels Stores Inc.	47.0%
Jo-Ann Stores Inc.	25.0%
Hobby Lobby Stores Inc.	18.0%

Source: IBISWorld, July 2016

- "A benchmarking study on the business practices of private store front and home-based businesses that sell crafts directly to the public was recently released by Craft & Hobby Association (CHA). The purpose of the study was to explore best practices that make an independent craft retailer successful and to share the data with CHA members and industry suppliers.

  "Business practices that were common among the top 15% of the independent retailers were:
    - ✓ 86% were store front businesses
    - ✓ 46% were paper related businesses
    - ✓ 47% had a strong customer database and did outbound marketing
    - ✓ More than half use social media to market their business; with Facebook as the most active
    - ✓ More than half invested time in continuing education and professional development"

  Source: Craft and Hobby Association, May 2015

- "Rent at 10% of GAS (Gross Annual Sales). Sales per square foot at $150–$175. Sales per employee at $75,000–$125,000. Advertising at 3%–4% of GAS."

Expenses as a percentage of annual sales

Cost of goods	50%
Payroll/labor Costs	15%
Occupancy	15%
Profit (estimated pretax)	20%

Industry Trend

- "Locating wholesalers and distributors for products won't be difficult, and the profit potential is tremendous as product markups can be 100 percent or more."

  Source: http://www.entrepreneur.com/businessideas/craft-supply-store

Resources

Websites

- Craft and Hobby Association (CHA): www.craftandhobby.org

Trade Publications

- Handmade Business magazine: www.craftsreport.com

Art Supplies (See also Arts & Crafts/Retail Stores, Hobby Shops)		
SIC 5999-65	NAICS 453998	

Rules of Thumb

➤ 25 to 30 percent of annual sales plus inventory

Pricing Tips

▪ "Many hobby stores and related businesses may carry a line of art supplies. A store specializing in just art supplies requires an owner with the appropriate knowledge."

Benchmark Data

▪ For Benchmark Information see Retail Stores—Small Specialty

Assisted Living Facilities (See also Nursing Homes)		
SIC 8361-05	NAICS 623311	

Rules of Thumb

➤ 75 percent of annual sales

➤ $30,000–$60,000 per bed. Pricing above this range typically raises a red flag for individual buyers.

➤ This business is based on net operating income divided by a capitalization rate of 10 to 14 percent.

Pricing Tips

▪ "Real-estate-intensive business. SBA pays extra attention to this industry to ensure that the buyers are not acting as 'passive real-estate investors,' but rather as small-business owners."

▪ "Capitalization of income for going concern value including real estate"

▪ "Occupancy in market area. Going cap rates at that specific time. Whether Medicaid or private pay?"

Benchmark Data

Statistics (Nursing Care)

Number of Establishments	33,845
Average Profit Margin	7.2%
Revenue per Employee	$75,500
Average Number of Employees	54.6
Average Wages per Employee	$30,587

Products and Services Segmentation

For-profit skilled nursing facilities	43.6%
For-profit nursing homes	33.0%
Nonprofit skilled nursing facilities	10.3%
Nonprofit nursing homes	7.8%
Government nursing homes and skilled nursing facilities	4.7%
Hospice centers	0.6%

Industry Costs

Profit	7.2%
Wages	40.8%
Purchases	18.4%
Depreciation	2.2%
Marketing	0.3%
Rent & Utilities	7.4%
Other	23.7%

Source: IBISWorld, October 2015

Long-Term Care Spending by Payer:

Medicaid	42%
Medicare	25%
Out of Pocket	22%
Private Insurance and Other Sources	11%

Source: www.leadingage.org/facts

- "The average assisted living center resident is an 85-year-old female who pays close to $3,000 a month—though many needing greater care pay closer to $4,000 or $5,000. While the assisted living industry is currently strong, experts said a major shift in demographics and the looming threat of federal regulation could transform the industry over the next two decades."

  Source: "Assisted Living Centers Are Costing the Elderly a Pretty Penny" www.foxbusiness.com
- "Total expenses excluding debt service should average 68 percent."
- "Operating expense ratio—65 to 70 percent"

Industry Trend

- "Between 2007 and 2015, the number of Americans ages 85 and older is expected to increase by 40 percent. By 2020, 12 million older Americans will need long-term health care."

  Source: HIAA, "A Guide to Long-Term Care Insurance"

Seller Financing

- 5 to 10 years

Resources

Websites

- National Center for Assisted Living: www.ncal.org
- A Place for Mom: www.aplaceformom.com

Associations

- Leading Age: www.leadingage.org
- Argentum: www.alfa.org

Franchise
Atlanta Bread Company (See also Bakeries, Franchises)

Approx. Total Investment	$650,000 to $1,000,000
Estimated Annual Sales/Unit	$1 million

SIC 5812-08	NAICS 722211	Number of Businesses/Units 167

Rules of Thumb

> ➢ 25 to 30 percent of annual sales plus inventory

Audio and Film Companies

	NAICS 512120	Number of Businesses/Units 12,755

Rules of Thumb

> ➢ 4 to 6 times EBITDA

Pricing Tips

- "Ownership of the intellectual property is key to value. Companies that provide work-for-hire services are not as valuable as those that own the final production. Since this medium ages quickly, the economic life span of the films/videos is critical."

Benchmark Data

Statistics (Audio Production Studios)

Number of Establishments	5,106
Average Profit Margin	12.4%
Revenue per Employee	$121,300
Average Number of Employees	2.0
Average Wages per Employee	$41,737

Products and Services Segmentation

Postproduction sound editing & design (audio works)	24.7%
Music recording services	23.8%
Other sound editing & design	18.1%
Postproduction sound editing & design (video works)	13.2%
Radio recording services	12.8%
Spoken word recording services	7.4%

Major Market Segmentation

Music industry	50.0%
Film producers	17.0%
Advertising agencies	16.0%
TV and video producers	12.0%
Multimedia developers	5.0%

Industry Costs

Profit	12.4%
Wages	34.5%
Purchases	20.3%
Depreciation	3.6%
Marketing	2.1%
Rent & Utilities	10.0%
Other	17.1%

Source: IBISWorld, September 2015 (latest available)

A - Rules of Thumb

Statistics (Movie & Video Production)

Number of Establishments	7,649
Average Profit Margin	16.4%
Revenue per Employee	$512,400
Average Number of Employees	11.2
Average Wages per Employee	$98,607

Products and Services Segmentation

Action and adventure films	39.4%
Comedy films	27.1%
Thriller/suspense films	16.8%
Dramas	8.7%
Other films	8.0%

Major Market Segmentation

Domestic distributors of feature films, short films and other	56.2%
International distributors of feature films, short films and others	43.8%

Industry Costs

Profit	16.4%
Wages	19.3%
Purchases	28.4%
Depreciation	2.9%
Marketing	9.0%
Rent & Utilities	3.6%
Other	20.4%

Market Share

The Walt Disney Company	16.2%
21st Century Fox	13.7%
Comcast Corporation	12.5%
Viacom Inc.	6.1%

Source: IBISWorld, July 2016

Seller Financing
- 3 to 7 years

Audio/Video Conferencing

SIC 4822-06	NAICS 518210	

Rules of Thumb
➢ 3 to 4 times EBITDA

Expert Comments
"Cost of setting up public centers is substantial. Industry is upgrading services and equipment."

Industry Trend
- "New technology is outdating old. Tele-presence is the new upgrade name."

Questions

- "How long are the contracts? What services are being provided?"

Auto Body Repair		
SIC 7532-01	NAICS 811121	Number of Businesses/Units 124,155

Rules of Thumb

➢ 25 to 35 percent of annual sales plus inventory

➢ 1.5 to 2.3 times SDE plus inventory

➢ 3 times EBIT

➢ 2 to 4 times EBITDA

Pricing Tips

- "Initial Questions to Ask the Seller of an Auto Body Shop—By compiling the following information, a buyer should be able to get a full picture of the auto body shop they are looking at:
  - ✓ Size of the building
  - ✓ Size of the total lot
  - ✓ Monthly rent, including the CAM (Common Area Maintenance). If business is owned by seller: What rental amount does the seller want from a buyer? What rent does the seller currently charge himself on his company books?
  - ✓ Number of spray booths? How many are heated and what type of heated spray booths? (downdrafts and side drafts are the two main types of heated spray booths.)
  - ✓ Number of frame machines and the make and model number, if the seller knows.
  - ✓ Does the business have any DRP (Direct Repair Program) contracts? If yes, what are the names of each insurance company?
  - ✓ What % of the volume is DRP business?
  - ✓ What is the annual gross income of the business?
  - ✓ What is the real owner's take home earnings from the business, regardless of the form that it is received (salary, personal expenses written off by the business and cash income not reported)."

Source: http://www.businessbuyingservices.com/what-you-need-to-know-in-order-to-value-an-auto-body-shop/

- "Annual volume is critical. Low volume (below $600K) shops are difficult to sell. The higher the volume the higher the multiple. Franchises sell for lower multiples. Lease terms are very important."
- "Shops doing a volume of $500,000 are worth $125,000 or less."
- "Pricing usually 2.5 x owner benefit [SDE] plus fair market value of FF&E."
- "Shops doing less than $100,000 monthly sales are worth $125,000 or less, regardless of any other rule of thumb. Shops doing less than $40,000 in monthly sales are worth $75,000 or less."
- "Market value of FF&E is critical to accurate price development. Also—number of years in business, diversity of supplier base; with auto body shops the number & quality of DRP contracts, stability of labor pool, ease of replacing skilled employees & diversity/stability of supplier base."

A - Rules of Thumb

Expert Comments

"The industry is dominated by insurance companies. Contracts are not assumable by buyers. Without a contract, your volume is going to be very small. Regardless of how well the current owner is doing, when the business is transferred, the contracts are cancelled."

"Insurance referrals can go away very easily with ownership changes."

"Volume continues for a good quality shop even in a flat to declining economy."

"Body shops should only be purchased by experienced buyers in this industry. Shops doing less than $100,000 a month in sales all make around the same profit, which is $60,000 to $100,000 for a working owner. Working owner means one who physically works on cars some of the time. Only shops with a multiple of insurance contracts are easy to market. Shops without insurance contracts are very difficult to sell."

Benchmark Data

Statistics (Car Body Shops)

Number of Establishments	124,155
Average Profit Margin	6.2%
Revenue per Employee	$120,900
Average Number of Employees	2.6
Average Wages per Employee	$35,677

Products and Services Segmentation

Body repair services	59.7%
Painting services	20.7%
Glass replacement and repair	11.6%
Merchandise sales	3.0%
Detailing services and body conversions	1.7%
Upholstery and interior repair	1.7%
Other services	1.6%

Industry Costs

Profit	6.2%
Wages	29.6%
Purchases	47.2%
Depreciation	1.4%
Marketing	1.9%
Rent & Utilities	5.5%
Other	8.2%

Source: IBISWorld, July 2016

Expenses as a percentage of annual sales

Cost of goods	35% to 40%%
Payroll/labor Costs	20%
Occupancy	05% to 10%
Profit (estimated pretax)	15% to 20%

Industry Trend

- "Upward for established, quality-oriented operations with DRP relationships with clients, mainly insurance companies."

Seller Financing

- 3 to 5 years
- 5 years
- "Sellers carry for three to five years with SBA requiring the seller not to receive payments for the first two years."

Questions

- "How much of their time does the owner work on cars? When does your paint supplier contract expire? Lease terms. Employee census. Worker's comp mode rate. Reason for selling. Upside potential."
- "Percentage of volume that is DRP Contracts? (Insurance Contracts) Percentage of rent to gross sales? How much space is there indoors for car storage?"
- "Do you supply loan cars? If so, do you get rebates from rental companies for the loaners? When will a job be booked as a sale? Do you have steady referrals from dealerships? When are initial assessments made? Is any charge made for them? After the initial estimate is made, how are contacts made with the insurance company?"
- "What is your real sales volume? How many DRP contracts do you have? Which insurance companies are your DRP contracts with? What is the labor rate paid by the insurance companies? How many employees do you have? Are your employees paid a salary or a percentage of the production they produce? How many frame machines do you have? is your spray booth heated?"
- "Show me your profit & loss statements, tax returns, environmental compliance & OSHA documents."

Resources

Trade Publications

- AutoInc.org—great, great site: autoinc.org
- Body Shop Business is an excellent publication and Web site; it also offers back issues. : www.bodyshopbusiness.com

Associations

- Automotive Service Association, (ASA) - Great site with lots of information: www.asashop.org

Auto Brake Services (See also Auto Repair)		
SIC 7539-14	NAICS 811118	

Rules of Thumb

➢ 30 percent of annual sales plus inventory

➢ 4 times monthly sales plus inventory

Auto Dealers—New Cars

SIC 5511-02	NAICS 441110	Number of Businesses/Units 22,448

Rules of Thumb

➤ Depending on the franchise, it's three to six times EBITDA plus real estate and hard assets

➤ Blue Sky—two to four times EBIT Earnings

➤ Total transaction value in the industry currently ranges from two to four times pretax earnings

➤ Blue Sky—two to three times net profit or new unit sales (most recent year) times average front-end gross profit per unit

➤ Hard assets at cost—new parts, FF&E– Book + 50 percent depreciation,

➤ Blue Sky—3 times recast earnings

➤ The goodwill component of the sale price of an auto dealership (franchised only) normally falls within the range of two to six percent of gross revenues. Where added to the assets or book value of the business, this is a reliable method of determining price.

➤ Goodwill = 1 to 3 times pretax earnings (recast)

➤ Parts = current returnable parts

➤ FF&E = book value + one-half depreciation

➤ New Vehicles = net dealer cost

➤ Used Cars = as agreed

Pricing Tips

▪ "Be aware of rental cost paid to owners of dealerships. Be aware of compensation to owners, family members, and general managers."

▪ "Automobile dealerships should have net income of around 2% of total revenue if domestic and higher if import. Service department customer pay labor, gross profit should be between 65% and 70%, parts GP between 35% and 40%. A multiple of 4 to 6 times net income is typical. Imports bring a higher multiple than domestics. Larger stores in a mid-size or large market bring a higher multiple than smaller, rural stores."

▪ "The two most important characteristics are brands sold and location within a market. Competing outlets affect value. Market analysis, including measuring consumer demand in the area, is critical. Facility age is also a factor."

▪ "The brand is the key factor when buying or selling a dealership; Toyota and Honda are about the most difficult to buy and make the highest profits."

▪ "New auto dealerships usually have 4 profit centers, parts, used cars, F&I, and service. New car sales typically have very little margin. Ask the dealer about their absorption ratio (an industry term that indicates how much of their back-end is absorbing their overhead). Any new buyer would have to be approved by the manufacturer (Ford, GM, Toyota, etc.) Key people: used car manager, parts manager, service manager."

▪ "The current value is two to four times net profit of the most recent year. However, the new car franchises that are bringing up to five times net profit are Honda, Toyota and Mercedes Benz."

- "Other pricing methods include: (1) application of industry averages for gross profit as percentage of sales to the total revenues of the dealership being evaluated; (2) assessing financial data and applying appropriate multiples to recast net profit; (3) projection of potential based on industry average penetration statistics times appropriate multiples."
- "The goodwill of an auto dealership can generally be valued at one year's pretax profit plus the dealer's salary and benefits, plus any adjustments from normalizing the financial statement against standard industry operating data."

Expert Comments

"All dealerships are governed by state franchise laws and controlled by the various manufacturers and/or distributors. Transfer of ownership is very difficult and restricted. Capitalization demands are high."

"New-car profits are weak. In fact, the used cars they generate (trades) are the lifeblood of a new-car dealership."

Benchmark Data

Statistics (New Car Dealers)

Number of Establishments	22,448
Average Profit Margin	0.5%
Revenue per Employee	$781,200
Average Number of Employees	48.5
Average Wages per Employee	$53,482

Products and Services Segmentation

New vehicles	57.7%
Used vehicles	26.6%
Parts and repair services	12.9%
Finance and insurance	2.8%

Industry Costs

Profit	0.5%
Wages	7.0%
Purchases	86.0%
Depreciation	0.2%
Marketing	1.0%
Rent & Utilities	1.6%
Other	3.7%

Market Share

AutoNation Inc.	2.6%
Penske Automotive Group Inc.	1.4%

Source: IBISWorld, May 2016

Profile of dealerships' service and parts operations, 2014 (average dealership)

Total service and parts sales	$5,594,388
Total gross profit as percent of service and parts sales	46.14%
Total net profit as percent of service and parts sales	6.39%
Total number of repair orders written	17,070
Total service and parts sales per customer repair order	$255

Total service and parts sales per warranty repair order.. $230
Number of technicians (including body).. 17
Total parts inventory...$328,114
Average customer mechanical labor rate $135

Source: NADA Industry Analysis Division, 2014

Average Dealership Profile—2014

Total Dealership Sales.. $49,165,223
Total Dealership Gross $6,459,256
Total Dealership Expense $5,365,451
Net Profit before Taxes $1,093,805
Average Net worth $3,749,838
Net profit as % of net worth 29.2%

Source: 2014 National Auto Dealers Association (NADA) Data,
We can't say enough about how valuable this site is for anyone doing their homework
on the retail auto sales industry. It is one of the very best sites we have seen.

Share of total dealership sales dollars in 2014

New Vehicle... 57.6%
Used Vehicle... 31.0
Service and Parts 11.4%

Market Share, by segment:

Small Car... 17.0%
Midsized Car.. 15.8%
Large Car... 1.8%
Luxury Car 6.2%
Pickup 14.5%
Crossover 31.1%
SUV 7.4%
Van... 6.2%

Source: 2015 National Automobile Dealers Association (NADA)

- Highlights from 2015 report on America's franchised new-car dealerships:
  - ✓ Franchised new-car dealerships sold a record 17.3 million-plus new cars and light trucks.
  - ✓ Total dealership revenue, including new- and used-car sales, as well as parts and service sales, eclipsed sales from 2014 reaching a new high of $862 billion in 2015, an increase of 6.9% from 2014.
  - ✓ Dealerships wrote more than 200 million repair orders, with more than $9 billion in service and parts sales.
  - ✓ New-car dealership employment reached 1,110,700, up 4.3% from 1,064,000 employees in 2014.
  - ✓ Average number of employees per dealership was 67, up 3.1% from 65 employees in 2014.
  - ✓ Annual payroll at new-car dealerships was $62.8 billion in 2015, up nearly 8% from 2014.
  - ✓ Average dealership payroll was $3.8 million, up nearly 8%

Source: National Automobile Dealers Association (NADA)

Expenses as a percentage of annual sales

Cost of goods..75% to 80%
Payroll/labor Costs... 08% to 10% of gross profit
Occupancy .... 10% of gross profit
Profit (estimated pretax) ....01.5% to 03%

Industry Trend

- "NADA Forecasts a Record 17.7 Million New-Car Sales in 2016 DETROIT (Jan. 8, 2016)—U.S. sales of new cars and light trucks will set an all-time record in 2016, said Steven Szakaly, chief economist of the National Automobile Dealers Association. 'More than 17.7 million new light vehicles will be purchased or leased this year, about a 2-percent increase from 2015, and setting back-to-back records,' Szakaly said. 'It will be the seventh consecutive year of auto sales growth.'

   "In 2015, a record 17.4 million new light vehicles were retailed, up 5.8 percent from 2014, according to WardsAuto. The average transaction price of a new car and light truck was $33,269 in 2015, according to NADA.

   "Sustained sales momentum in 2016 is also dependent on expectations that auto financing rates will remain competitive, with interest rates rising modestly—by less than 1 percentage point—by the end of 2016; wages will grow about 2.5 percent this year; and the economy will add more than 2 million net new jobs in 2016, Szakaly added."

   Source: https://www.nada.org/CustomTemplates/DetailPressRelease.aspx?id=21474843413

Seller Financing

- "Can be a mixture of both seller and outside financing."
- "3 years—very small percentage of selling price is carried."
- "Seller financing occurs in less than 30 percent of our transactions and does not normally extend beyond a five-year term."
- "5 years—only goodwill is seller-financed."

Questions

- "How many cars per month do they sell? How is their CSI rating? Is the manufacturer requiring upgrades to the facility? If so when?"
- "What is your motivation for selling? Any family members part of your succession plan? Are you retiring or moving to a different location/life structure? What is your ideal 'deal'? Are you interested in holding the real property—or selling with a carry back note? What tax attributes are associated with your business (LIFO, Goodwill, etc.)?"
- "What is your parts obsolescence percentage? CSI Scores?"
- "Staff that will stay on? Building lease if not owned. Franchise ratings and CSI ratings."
- "Are you ready to sell for market value?"
- "Is financing in place for new and used sales? Do you have a floor plan? Does the factory have any future plans for your facility—new or larger?"
- "Employee retention is key at this time with the downturn in the economy and sales."
- "Age of key personnel? What is the absorption ratio? Can I see your claims history? Who finances the new and used inventory? If this is a multiple-franchise operation under one roof, discover if the manufacturers are pushing for the dealership to split the franchise out into separate facilities."
- "Sales trends; consumer satisfaction survey results; recent market studies commissioned by manufacturer; facility standards adopted by manufacturer"
- "How many family members on the payroll? What dollar amount of personal items is being deducted from the financial statement?"

A - Rules of Thumb

Resources

Websites
- Ward's Auto: www.wardsauto.com

Trade Publications
- Automotive News: www.autonews.com

Associations
- National Automobile Dealers Association: www.nada.org
- American International Automobile Dealers: www.aiada.org
- Business Valuation Resources: www.BVResources.com

Auto Dealers—Used Cars

SIC 5511-03	NAICS 441120	Number of Businesses/Units 133,320

Rules of Thumb

➤ Wholesale book value of cars; no goodwill; add parts, fixtures & equipment

Benchmark Data

Statistics (Used Car Dealers)

Number of Establishments	133,320
Average Profit Margin	2.6%
Revenue per Employee	$445,800
Average Number of Employees	1.8
Average Wages per Employee	$25,221

Products and Services Segmentation

Used vehicles	38.9%
Parts and services	29.9%
Financing and insurance	29.1%
Other	2.1%

Industry Costs

Profit	2.6%
Wages	5.7%
Purchases	83.1%
Depreciation	0.3%
Marketing	1.0%
Rent & Utilities	3.0%
Other	4.3%

Market Share

CarMax Business Services LLC	11.9%

Source: IBISWorld, May 2016

Dealer Operating Information

Average units sold per dealer (BHPH deals only)	610
Average cash in deal per vehicle sold	$4,926
Average ACV per vehicle sold (includes recon)	$5,487
Average reconditioning cost per vehicle sold	$1.026
Average gross profit per vehicle sold	$4.509
Average cash down payment	$1,134
Average amount financed	$9.664
Average term of loan (in weeks)	143

Source: http://usedcarnews.com 3/1/15

Industry Trend

- "Used-car sales expected to grow into 2016

  'We are looking for used-vehicle sales to continue to grow as we move into 2016,' Fleming (Kelley Blue Book analyst Tim Fleming) said. 'The new-car market is incredibly strong right now, but that growth is expected to level off in 2016 and 2017.'

  "According to Chris Hopson, IHS Automotive's manager of North American light vehicle sales forecasting, his organization is still holding to its predicted peak of 18.2 million units to be sold in 2017, before tapering off to around 17 million units by 2022. This continued influx of new vehicles bodes well for the next few years of used sales."

  Source: http://www.autoremarketing.com/trends/used-car-sales-expected-grow-2016

Questions

- "General Questions

  What types of sales transactions did you have for the year under examination?

  a. Any sales at auctions? If yes, which?

  b. Any sales to wholesalers? If yes, which?

  c. Any sales to other dealers? If yes, which?

  d. Any consignment sales? If yes, describe.

  e. Any scrap sales? If yes, describe.

  f. Any in-house dealer financing sales?

  g. Any third-party financing sales?

  h. Did you have any other types of sales transactions?

  i. Did you have any sales that resulted in a loss on the sale? If yes, describe the nature of these sales.

  j. What sales did you have to relatives or family friends during the year? Identify."

Resources

Trade Publications

- Used Car News: www.usedcarnews.com

Associations

- National Independent Automobile Dealers Association (ADA): www.niada.com

A - Rules of Thumb

Auto Detailing (See also Car Washes/Coin Operated, Full Service)

SIC 7542-03	NAICS 811192	Number of Businesses/Units 14,000

Rules of Thumb

➢ 40 to 45 percent of annual sales plus inventory

Benchmark Data

Detailer Type — % of Total

Detailer Type	% of Total
Freestanding Detail Shop	44%
Full-Service Conveyor Car Wash	28%
Mobile Detailing	12%
Self-Service Car Wash	07%
Exterior-only Car Wash	02%
Oil Change/Lube	05%
In-Bay Automatic	07%
Gas Station	09%
C-Store	05%

Operating Costs as Percentage of Revenue

Rent	13.4%
Equipment/Supplies/Maintenance	8.9%
Chemicals (incl. soap, wax, compound, etc.)	4.3%
Labor	36.7%
Utilities (incl. water/sewer)	5.4%
Advertising & Promotion	2.8%
Insurance	5.6%
Customer Claims	0.3%

Average Number of Cars Detailed Annually

Freestanding	1,310
Car Wash Combo	1,157
Mobile Service	1,560

Average Package Price Retail—Free-Standing

Complete Interior/Exterior Detail	$200.77
Interior Detail Only	$114.23
Exterior Detail Only	$135.83
Average Gross Revenue Per Car (Car Wash Sales Only)	$19.36
Average Number of Cars Washed Per Month	2,907

Average Monthly Gross Income (Detail Services Only)

Freestanding	$12,333
Car Wash Combo	$14,200

Source for the above 5 charts: "Detailing Survey 2016—Results from Auto Laundry News," www.carwashmag.com. This is a very informative site—and publication—for Car Washes and Auto Detail—all sites should be this good.

- "A skilled detailer, who is working hard but not rushing, can probably complete a car in about 4 to 4.5 hours and make it look great. The average car would be only a few years old, be a mid-size, and be in average cosmetic condition with no major scratches or blemishes, and no major stains or excessive dirt on the interior."

Source: www.dealermarkclicks.com

Resources

Websites
- Auto Detailing: www.autodetailingnetwork.com

Trade Publications
- AutoLaundry News: www.carwashmag.com

Auto Glass Repair/Replacement

SIC 5231-10	NAICS 811122	

Rules of Thumb

➢ 45 to 50 percent of annual sales plus inventory

➢ 1.8 times SDE plus inventory

Benchmark Data

Statistics (Auto Glass Repair & Replacement Franchises)

Number of Establishments	206
Average Profit Margin	5.4%
Revenue per Employee	$102,300
Average Number of Employees	6.0
Average Wages per Employee	$27,701

Products and Services Segmentation

Windshield repair	65.0%
Windshield replacement	24.0%
Window repair	7.0%
Window replacement	4.0%

Major Market Segmentation

Households	45.0%
Commercial clients	25.0%
Insurance companies	18.0%
Other	12.0%

Industry Costs

Profit	5.4%
Wages	27.6%
Purchases	39.4%
Depreciation	2.0%
Marketing	2.5%
Rent & Utilities	6.5%
Other	16.6%

Market Share

Glass Doctor 42.8%
Source: IBISWorld, March 2016

Industry Trend

- "Smart glass in the automotive industry is expected to become a $2.1 billion market by 2019, compared with $1 billion in 2014, according to Smart Glass Opportunities in the Automotive Industry–2014, a recent report from NanoMarkets. The report defines smart auto glass as any kind of glass used in the automotive sector that is made 'intelligent' with the addition of layers of smart materials or the embedding of sensors and other kinds of electronic and electrical functionality into the glass."
Source: "Market Trends: Smart Auto Glass Continues Growth"
http://www.ceramicindustry.com/articles/93976-market-trends-smart-auto-glass-continues-growth 6/2/14

- "A number of factors are impairing the ability of independent auto-glass-replacement shops to compete with large chains. Johnson Auto Glass and Trim Shop Vice President Dan Johnson said those factors include rising prices for replacement auto glass, lower reimbursements from insurance companies and efforts to steer insured parties away from independent auto-glass-replacement companies."
Source: "Business Tougher for Independent Auto-Glass-Replacement Companies" by Dan Heath, www.pressrepublican.com

Resources

Trade Publications

- Glass Magazine—an informative site with archived articles of past issues: www.glassmagazine.com

Associations

- National Windshield Repair Association: www.nwrassn.org/
- National Glass Association (NGA): www.glass.org

Auto Lube/Oil Change (See also All Tune & Lube, Grease Monkey, Jiffy Lube)		
SIC 7549-03	NAICS 811191	Number of Businesses/Units 35,821

Rules of Thumb

➢ 40 percent of annual sales (tune-up) plus inventory

➢ 3 times EBIT (tune-up)

➢ 45 percent of annual sales (only auto lube businesses) plus inventory

➢ 1.5 to 2.25 times SDE plus inventory

Pricing Tips

- "There are two different service and working environments applicable to this business. The first being an oil and lube facility only, no service work is performed. The second being a tune-up business, performs oil and lube, in addition to service work, brakes, tune-ups, smog inspection, etc.
"The first auto lube business generally shows a greater multiple, 2.5 SDE, while the auto tune-up business described above normally shows a 2.0 SDE.

"The reasoning for the difference in the multiples above is the first business described is generally in a low-tech environment, with non-specialized training and employee wages are lower in comparison to specialized standards in this industry. In addition, most owners have multiple locations. The owner is mostly absentee in this operation and a manager is trained to perform all facets of operation and office functions as required. Demand is also higher.

"The second business described above requires a higher skilled employee (usually certified) and in most states the employees need to be tested. In addition the owner needs to be involved in the everyday functions of the operation, if only as an administrator. Most have a manager in place as well.

"Critical factors affecting business value are as follows: franchise vs. independent, manager and staff, customer base and vehicle count per day, average ticket per day, lease terms, equipment leased, owner's participation and location."

Benchmark Data

Statistics (Oil Change Services)

Number of Establishments	35,821
Average Profit Margin	13.5%
Revenue per Employee	$74,300
Average Number of Employees	2.6
Average Wages per Employee	$21,387

Products and Services Segmentation

Oil changes	52.4%
Cabin air filters	21.0%
Tire rotations	14.9%
Transmission flush services	7.0%
Other	4.7%

Industry Costs

Profit	13.5%
Wages	28.8%
Purchases	38.9%
Depreciation	3.2%
Marketing	1.8%
Rent & Utilities	10.3%
Other	3.5%

Market Share

Royal Dutch/Shell Group	7.9%

Source: IBISWorld, June 2016

Seller Financing

- 4 years

Resources

Trade Publications

- AutoInc.: www.autoinc.org
- National Oil & Lube News: www.noln.net

Associations
- Automotive Service Association: www.asashop.org

Auto Mufflers (See also Meineke, Midas)		
SIC 7533-01	NAICS 811112	

Rules of Thumb
➢ 35 to 40 percent of annual sales plus inventory

➢ 1 to 1.5 times SDE plus inventory

Auto Parts and Accessories—Retail Stores		
SIC 5531-11	NAICS 441310	Number of Businesses/Units 36,427

Rules of Thumb
➢ 40 percent of annual sales plus inventory

Pricing Tips
- "New cost of fixtures and equipment plus inventory at wholesale cost, nothing for goodwill. The inventory should turn over 4–6 times per year."

Benchmark Data

Statistics (Auto Parts Stores)
Number of Establishments	36,427
Average Profit Margin	4.2%
Revenue per Employee	$162,400
Average Number of Employees	9.0
Average Wages per Employee	$25,629

Products and Services Segmentation
Critical parts (new)	69.6%
Critical parts (used)	10.8%
Maintenance parts	9.8%
Performance parts	7.0%
Accessories	2.8%

Major Market Segmentation
Household and individuals	56.3%
Repair shops	22.7%
Retailers and Wholesalers for resale	12.8%
Other	8.2%

Industry Costs
Profit	4.2%
Wages	15.8%
Purchases	70.0%
Depreciation	0.9%
Marketing	1.0%
Rent & Utilities	2.9%
Other	5.2%

Market Share

Advance Auto Parts Inc. 18.5%
AutoZone Inc. 18.0%
O'Reilly Automotive Inc. 16.2%
Genuine Parts Company 12.8%

Source: IBISWorld, March 2016

Miscellaneous Sales Information:

Average store size ....6,350 sq. ft.
Average per store sales $1,573,000
Inventory turnover 1.81
Average net sales per store sq. ft. $248

Expenses as a percentage of annual sales

Cost of goods 61.3%
Payroll/labor Costs 19.9%
Occupancy 03.4%
Profit (estimated pretax) 05.3%

Resources

Associations
- Automotive Aftermarket Industry Association: www.aftermarket.org

---

Auto Rental (See also U-Save Car and Truck Rental)		
SIC 7514-01	NAICS 532111	Number of Businesses/Units 10,434

Rules of Thumb

➢ 45 percent of annual sales plus inventory

➢ Number of cars times $1,000

Pricing Tips
- "Reservation system, and national sales efforts, are critical. Many airport locations receive 70% or more of their business from this source. Off-airport locations are different; they can survive on local advertising as well as national."

Benchmark Data

Statistics (Car Rental)

Number of Establishments 10,434
Average Profit Margin 11.5%
Revenue per Employee $338,500
Average Number of Employees 11.2
Average Wages per Employee $42,924

Products and Services Segmentation

Leisure car rental 50.5%
Business car rental 27.3%
Car leasing 20.2%
Car sharing 2.0%

Major Market Segmentation

Off-airport market 40.9%
Airport leisure customers 38.4%
Airport business customers 20.7%

Industry Costs

Profit 11.5%
Wages 12.6%
Purchases 31.7%
Depreciation 28.4%
Marketing 1.5%
Rent & Utilities 2.7%
Other 11.6%

Market Share

Enterprise Rent-A-Car Company 36.1%
Hertz Global Holdings Inc. 16.9%
Avis Budget Group Inc. 13.7%

Source: IBISWorld, June 2016

"2015 U.S. CAR RENTAL MARKET FLEET, LOCATIONS AND REVENUE"

Company	U.S. Cars In Service (Avg.) 2015	# U.S. Locations	2015 Revenue Est. (in millions)
Enterprise Holdings	1,166,828	6,250	$13,880
(Includes Alamo Rent A Car, Enterprise Rent-A-Car, National Car Rental)			
Hertz	499,000	5,410	$6,350
(includes Dollar Thrifty, Firefly)			
Avis Budget Group	365,000	3,250	$5,445
(includes Payless, not Zipcar)			
Fox Rent A Car	19,000	19	$225
Advantage Rent-A-Car	30,000	50	$325
ACE Rent A Car	11,000	65	$100
Advantage Rent-A-Car	18,000	43	$200
U-Save Auto Rental System	12,000	140	$123
(owned by FSNA)			
International Franchise Systems	5,000	143	$41
(Rent-A-Wreck of America, Priceless & Nextcar)			
Affordable/Sensible	3,620	190	$32
Independents	70,000	5,500	$585
Total:	2,181,548	21,067	$27,106

Source: "Fact Book 2016" Auto Rental News

- "Income comes from two sources: operating income from rental and add-on services (such as CDW); and resale of vehicles (if the risk has not been assumed by the OEM in the fleet agreement). Accounting treatment (depreciation schedules for vehicles) can distort these sources."

Expenses as a percentage of annual sales

Cost of goods	82%
Payroll/labor Costs	08% to 10%
Occupancy	04%
Profit (estimated pretax)	06%

Industry Trend

- "In North America, rental days are predicted to increase 2% to 4% in 2016. Per-unit fleet costs are expected to be approximately $305 to $313 per month in 2016, an increase of 3% to 5% from $297 in 2015, says the company. For total company fleet costs, Avis Budget expects $280 to $290 per month in 2016, compared to $277 in 2015."

  Source: http://www.autorentalnews.com/channel/rental-operations/news/story/2016/02/avis-budget-s-full-year-revenue-increases-5.aspx

- "Though aspects of carsharing have existed since 1948 in Switzerland, it was only in the last 15 years that the concept has evolved into a mobility solution in the United States. In that time, the carsharing market has grown from a largely subsidized, university research-driven experiment into a full-fledged for-profit enterprise, owned primarily by traditional car rental companies and auto manufacturers. Today, Zipcar (owned by Avis Budget Group), car2go (owned by Daimler), Enterprise CarShare and Hertz 24/7 control about 95% of the carsharing market in the U.S.

  "Compared to car rental, total fleet size and revenues for carsharing remain relatively small. The Fall 2014 Carsharing Outlook, produced by the Transportation Sustainability Research Center at the University of California, Berkeley, reports 19,115 carsharing cars in the U.S., shared by about 996,000 members. Total annual revenue for carsharing in the U.S. is about $400 million, compared to the $24 billion in revenue for the traditional car rental market."

  Source:"CarSharing: State of the Market and Growth Potential" by Chris Brown, http://www.autorentalnews.com/channel/rental-operations/article/story/2015/03/carsharing-state-of-the-market-and-growth-potential.aspx

- "Increasing transparency of pricing with Internet travel sites. Increasing use of 'yield management' in pricing. Regulatory scrutiny of merged entities."

Questions

- "Relationships with franchisor; license agreement and royalty rate"

Resources

Trade Publications

- Auto Rental News: www.autorentalnews.com

Auto Repair (Auto Service Centers)

SIC 7514-01	NAICS 811111	Number of Businesses/Units 259,023

Rules of Thumb

- 25% to 30% of annual sales plus inventory
- 1 to 2.5 times SDE plus inventory, ($75,000 to $100,000 SDE)
- 3 times SDE plus inventory ($150,000 + SDE)
- 3 to 3.5 times EBITDA
- 1.25 to 1.75 owner's provable net income includes inventory

A - Rules of Thumb

Pricing Tips

- "Most auto repair shops/service centers for pricing should be based on SDE and not on EBITDA. The multiple for an average shop is 2x and this would normally increase to 2.5x if the business is showing an SDE of $200k or higher. This business is not priced on revenues due to the fact there are too many variables between the sales, gross profit and expenses that overall affect the bottom line. Too many CPA's who try to value this business for their clients look at the revenues as a benchmark to determine value and this is wrong."
- "Most buyers of shops need to work in the front of the shop doing estimates and customer service. There is a lot of information for people coming from different industries to get schooled on how to run a profitable shop. Also feedback I am getting in 2016 is that the amount shop owners need to pay good technicians is going up by 20% or more."
- "3.0 to 3.5 SDE for SDE $150,000 and up to about $500,000; around 3.0 for $100,000-$150,000 and about 2.0-2.5 for under $100,000."
- "The reason it is important to understand whether the business sale is an asset sale or stock sale is that the categories for the purchase price allocation are a bit different. For stock sales, the entire purchase price may be allocated to the value of the stock. The seller pays the capital gains rate for stocks held more than one year, and the buyer does not get a write-off and must accept assets at the current book value. Occasionally, the parties may agree to allocate a portion of the purchase price to the non-compete agreement and/or the training/consulting agreement. For the portion allocated to the non-compete agreement, it is ordinary income to the seller and the buyer gets to amortize it over 15 years. For the portion allocated to the training/consulting agreement, it is ordinary income to the seller and the buyer gets to expense it out as paid."
  Source: http://www.acbrokersinc.com/blogs/purchase_price_allocation_business_sale.html
- "Size matters. Larger shops with enough volume to hire a full time manager command a higher multiple. Conversely small shops where SDE is equal or less than an average technician's wage are worth only equipment and leasehold value."
- "Inventory on hand is usually small. Most parts can be delivered in a few hours. Must be a great mechanic. Small shops make a small return. Need a busy shop to make any real money."
- "Lack of owner dependence is very important. Auto repair is a customer service oriented business with many owners working the front counter. Buyers often ask themselves what will happen to the customer base if the owner is not there to greet them. Advise sellers to distance themselves from the front desk and hire a service writer. One-man shows almost never sell. Tire stores grossing over $1 million are very desirable, despite low margins, and are fetching a 3–3.5 multiple. Employee costs should be around 25%; oftentimes an owner can trim some fat to boost SDE to justify a higher asking price."
- "A business with fleet and commercial customers is worth a higher multiple than a full retail business. Having more than one bay and one lift per technician is important, since many times a vehicle is waiting on parts after being torn down so it's important for the technicians to have more than one work space to move from job to job. Shops that do heavy line work, such as power train and transmission repairs, also are worth a higher multiple than shops that just do light duty work only."
- "Typically when pricing a shop location is a large part of the valuation and marketability of the business. If a shop has $1 million plus in revenues the multiplier can be higher vs. a shop that does a few hundred thousand in revenues. If a shop has too much equipment the owner may believe his business is worth more, but we let them know that is just 'stuff' that helps you

generate your revenues. For example if a shop's value is $200,000 based on SDE and they have $400,000 in assets I may have the client not include every tool they own in the deal. I let them know to sell that equipment another way because they will never get paid for it on the transaction."

- "Large volume shops tend to get a larger multiple percentage. If inventory is valued at less than 15% of selling price, it is often included. Shops with a high tire volume may have larger inventories and these inventories would not be included."

- "If the business is an independent service repair shop the % to SDE will normally be higher than if the business were a franchise. A franchise has a royalty fee as an added expense; this lowers the % of gross profit to SDE. That being said, a franchise center, such as Meineke, Honest 1, or Midas, etc. will also bring forth a higher value to the owner when it comes time to sell the business. The market continues to shift towards the preference of a well-known franchise brand name for buyers. The key for an auto repair center is to obtain revenues of $700k or higher on an annual basis. This brings a strong SDE to the bottom line."

- "1. Distinguish between Personal Goodwill that goes home with the owner at night and might not transfer versus Business Goodwill that will transfer to any Buyer. Personal Goodwill needs to be addressed through adjustment in Sales Price or with an Earnout. 2. Are any customers tied to a key employee? If so address with an employee contract or discount Sales Price. 3. Determine ratio of commercial accounts to retail. If the Seller has multiple shops the commercial accounts might leave."

- "Length of lease is very important. Percentage of tire sales if significant can reduce SDE and sales ratio and affect price. Condition of equipment, cleanliness of shop and brand or banner will affect local desirability and price. Reputation is also very important."

- "Rent can be added to the SDE if the seller also owns the building and is selling the building with the business. If the seller hires too many employees, it is sometimes possible to show the buyer why the business can be run with fewer employees, and add the soon-to-be-terminated employee's salary to the SDE."

Expert Comments

"This industry has shown a good steady growth over the last twenty years, however many smaller shops have closed their doors due to more competition from the dealerships and larger auto repair centers. The ratings reflect this going forward."

"It helps if the shop has been in the community for a few years and has developed a reputation of being honest and doing good work. Shops used to carry significant amounts of inventory 10 or more years ago. Now shops have virtually zero inventory because parts are delivered quickly."

"Make your employees a priority. In this sometimes fast paced and always super competitive industry, most owners put all of their emphasis on taking care of their customers and not their employees. Take care of your employees and they'll take care of your customers. Set realistic expectations and monitor where you are versus where you need to be; spend time to help your employees learn and earn; because the happier they are, the more you'll make."

"Profit trend is up as people keep vehicles longer. Location and facilities are very important. Auto repair has been primarily a recession- proof industry so the trend is favorable. Replication takes space, technicians and specialized equipment."

"It is becoming extremely difficult in many places to get permits to construct new automotive repair shops and the cost of entry is difficult. If you have a decent lease or own a building in a good traffic area that is reasonably solid with adequate parking, there is a lot of demand. However the returns are very sensitive to the cost of occupancy and if occupancy is above 15% of sales it is usually not viable."

"Any mechanic with a tool box can open a shop. Many closed gas stations available for rent. Auto repair shops on every corner in most towns."

"Although competition is extremely high, most customers will be loyal to an auto repair center that provides reliable service in a reasonable amount of time. People like knowing who they're trusting their vehicle to, and repair shops that can provide that personal touch should always be in demand."

"There are always going to be many shops and car dealers that work on vehicles as competition, but the good thing is there are millions of vehicles on the road and they always break or need regular service. Vehicles seem to last longer these days, but that just means people are waiting for service and repairs. The end results being higher ticket values per job.

"The risk in getting into this industry usually has to do with location. If the location is hidden away it may be harder to build the business. If the location is in a prime spot the rent may become too expensive. A good technician is hard to come by and that makes it difficult, but with a good shop and location the good techs are always available. Buyers are always intrigued by this industry and see the potential in a sound investment by purchasing a shop. An owner does not need to be a mechanic, which drives the demand."

"Multiple shops can be started or purchased, but it comes with a whole new set of challenges. It may be easier than some industries, but is still not simple. Personnel and location will be your main factor that makes it difficult."

"In this marketplace there is competition, however you will see a good number of auto centers come and go if they fail to provide honesty and quality service to their customers. Many smaller auto centers have gone out of business; those shops that are underachievers normally have sales under $300k annually and are not profitable. If you list a shop with sales over $500k annually you'll have a good chance of selling that business; the key is to have a good staff in place with mgt. that will stay."

Benchmark Data

Auto Repair (Auto Mechanics)

Number of Establishments	259,023
Average Profit Margin	7.2%
Revenue per Employee	$107,500
Average Number of Employees	2.1
Average Wages per Employee	$28,299

Rules of Thumb - **A**

Products and Services Segmentation

Powertrain repair services	24.4%
Scheduled and preventive repair and maintenance services	22.9%
Brake repair services	15.8%
Other repair and maintenance services	11.4%
Electrical system repair services	8.6%
Heating repair services	6.6%
Wheel alignment and repair services	5.5%
Muffler and exhaust repair services	4.8%

Industry Costs

Profit	7.2%
Wages	26.8%
Purchases	44.5%
Depreciation	1.5%
Marketing	1.1%
Rent & Utilities	6.8%
Other	12.1%

Source: IBISWorld, April 2016

- "The common denominator in this industry is that sales should average $20k per each tech per service bay. So if you have five bays with four techs, the shop should average $80k per month as a minimum. Other critical elements you should look for when listing this business are: at least one mgr., three techs—at least two techs being certified, a reasonable lease and terms going forward. However you will find franchise auto centers with higher rent factors for the most part. Lastly, go to yelp.com to see the rating the business has; it should be at least three stars or higher." "68% gross on labor sales and 35%-40% on parts. $100,000–$125,000 sales per employee. Need two bays per technician. Quick lube or quick service lane is a plus. Need plenty of lifts."
- "Rent per bay not to exceed $1500.00, sales per bay over $150,000 minimum, with $250,000 per bay reaching capacity."
- "Mechanics must generate revenue of at least $1500 to $2000 per week to cover their own salary. Many mechanics learn the business then leave and open their own shop. Customers are easy to find, but hard to keep."
- "Average ticket should be between $400 and $550 per car. A very busy and well-staffed shop can produce on a regular basis $35K per month per technician. Cost of parts and labor should not exceed 20% of total revenues."
- "$100,000 to $150,000 in annual sales per bay is typical. Any shop that is on the high side of this scale is likely to be significantly more profitable if costs are controlled. I like to see gross rent under $1500 per month per bay."
- "Estimated average annual sales is $475,000."

Expenses as a percentage of annual sales

Cost of goods	30% to 40%
Payroll/labor Costs	20% to 30%
Occupancy	08% to 14%
Profit (estimated pretax)	10% to 18%

Industry Trend

- "This industry is being segmented by large dealerships and therefore the Mom and Pop auto repair shops are slowly diminishing. Auto centers doing over $750k annually in revenues should survive however. Moving forward, shops that do not bring in state-of-the-art equipment and do not change from their

own ways will not survive in the next five years."
- "Wages for good technicians are going to continue going up as less and less people want to go into the industry. In more rural areas shops are pressured to allow customers to bring in their own parts thus reducing profits that the shop would enjoy if they sourced the parts. Labor rates are 20–30 percent lower then in large cities because of competition from 'back yard mechanics.'"
- "The industry will probably plateau for the next few years and then pick up again in two or three years as more and more used vehicles enter the market. 2016 will be a record year for new vehicle lease turn-ins, which will put more used vehicles on the road as dealers clear their inventory. As these vehicles come out of their factory warranty periods, they will need to be serviced."
- "Market forecasts are looking good for the American automotive repair industry. According to the Automotive Aftermarket Industry Association, forecasts show a compounding 3.4% growth through 2017—just 1.5% shy of the rest of the U.S. economy's forecast growth. Although that seems low, it's certainly growing for the long term. While new car and truck sales are rebounding faster than expected, people are holding onto their vehicles longer than ever before: 11.4 years on average in 2014. The market's growth is being driven by three trends. "Trend 1: Changing Cars—Today's vehicles are much more complicated. "Trend 2: Changing Customers—An auto repair shop's next customer may be a former do-it-yourselfer who's finally stumped by increasingly complicated engine designs. "Trend 3: Changing Shops—Auto shop customers and their cars aren't the only things changing. Since vehicles are getting more complex, the business cost involved in serving every single make and model is getting steeper every year."

Source: "3 Trends Sending Customers to Auto Repair Shops" by Youssef Sleiman, June 19, 2015, http://blogbattery.com/2015/06/3-trends-sending-customers-to-auto-repair-shops

- "Trend is more volume for shops with good employees. Population keeping cars longer and having them repaired instead of replaced."
- "The trend that we are seeing is that shops are having to invest in original equipment manufacturers' diagnostic equipment and tools. This leads to additional costs for an independent or franchised auto repair shop. The upside is that those shops that are willing to make that investment are taking customers and jobs from other shops. Technician wages and ongoing training requirements are on the rise."
- "Less cars entering a shop because of the quality of newer cars and the high cost of used cars. Newer cars on the road, but when they do come in, the average ticket seems to be increasing"

Seller Financing
- "Seller financing, average 3- to 5-year loan at 6% interest. If the value of the business is over $750k then bank financing is the norm."
- "Banks are big fans of transferable skills so a lot of these deal are done with seller financing to maximize value for the sellers. Terms are 30% down over 5–7 years at 6% interest."
- "Typically there is some seller financing involved in the sale of auto repair businesses. Outside financing is more typical but many lenders would require some sort of seller financing along with buyer cash. I would think you could expect about 10% to 20% down, and about 10% to 20% in seller financing with the rest outside financing."
- "A portion of seller financing tied to a longer transition period is important in a non franchised business where the seller's reputation is the basis of the client following. Bank financing is easier to get for most reputable franchised shops."
- "Mostly sold at a discounted level for heavy cash down. It is impossible to find

bank financing for business only shops without real estate as collateral."

- "Bank financing is very easy to obtain, if the books are clean and the numbers work, as with any business."
- "Seller financing is a must for an automotive repair business."
- "Banks will fund these deals with 25% down. The banks do like to see the seller carry minimum of 10% of the purchase price."
- "Financing for this business is usually easy to obtain with the seller showing good books and records for at least three years, seller carry note is normally for three to five years at 6% interest."

Questions

- "The norm of three years' books and records, tax returns. List of staff and their positions and tenure. Have they been fined by the state or county for overselling? What is their car count and average ticket per customer? What software are they utilizing and how many customers are active in their database? Does the owner work within the business as a tech or hopefully as the administrator and PR person?"
- "Ask the seller when his last shop labor rate increase was. Ask the seller how long his top techs have been with him. See if the techs are on commission or salary."
- "Average hours per repair order; average dollars per repair order; average repair orders per day; how may bays; how many lifts; how many techs; do you repair transmissions; do you sell tires or provide wheel and tire services? What do you not sell that you think should be added to the product or service line?"
- "Are customers in a computer base? Amount of advertising needed to keep customers. Promotions used to generate new business."
- "How many technicians, how many bays, how many lifts do you have? What are your hours per RO, dollars per RO? Do you do fleet or commercial repairs? How many repair orders per month do you average?"
- "Price your business according to these terms or it will just sit on the market and not sell. If you are buying a business in this market try and buy one that has at least $500,000 in revenues and has a location with drive by traffic. Ask how many cars per week do they work on (should be minimum 25). What is the average RO (should be minimum $450). What is your mark up on parts (should be 60% but if it's not, don't be too concerned; you will have room for better profits)."
- "Ask the seller if he is an active mechanic in the business. If not what are his daily functions? Are there any family members in the business? Is there a good mgr. in place who will stay on after the sale? Will the key mechanics stay after the sale? Does the owner have a good software program in place and does the owner have all his customers in the database? Any hazardous waste issues in the last five years? Does the owner pay all his employees on a W-2 ? Are any employees paid under the table?"
- "Profit margins on parts should be 55% to 60% average."

Resources

Websites
- AutoInc: www.autoinc.org

Associations
- Automotive Service Association—an excellent site for both auto services/ collision businesses: www.asashop.org

- The Automotive Maintenance & Repair Association (AMRA) : www.amra.org
- National Institute for Automotive Service Excellence: www.ase.com

Auto Transmission Centers (See also AAMCO Transmission)		
SIC 7537-01	NAICS 811113	

Rules of Thumb

➢ 35 to 45 percent of annual sales includes inventory

➢ 1.5 to 2 times SDE includes inventory (as the SDE increases so will the multiple, i.e., SDE $50,000 the multiple will be 1.5 times, SDE $200,000 the multiple will be 2 times—all include inventory)

➢ 3 times EBITDA

Pricing Tips

- "Parts cost for classic shop focused on rebuilding transmission ranging from 18%, increasing as added general repair increases to 25%-28% of sales. Lower parts cost indicates use of used parts, which should be cause to examine warranty repair issues. If the owner is the manager or the manager will be leaving, an examination of personal versus business goodwill should be looked at, as the one dealing with the customers is a good barometer to determine why the business can be improved or affected by an ownership change. Considering that the industry is changing where general auto repair becomes a major factor, an analysis of the ratio of retail versus business from referrals from auto repair shops should be analyzed. Ask if the shop has plans to incorporate 'remanufactured units' to avoid high priced labor."

- "Shop labor target is about 20% of sales and typically there are three employees. Parts cost lower than 18% is indicative of using used parts. If bottom line EBITDA is higher than 20% of sales."

- "Parts Cost
   ✓ 8–22% for classic shop without general auto repair.
   ✓ Lower than 18% it is a red flag indicating significant used parts which trigger high warranty (comeback) costs
   ✓ Higher than 30% indicates that there might be some green cash not reported

   Labor Cost
   ✓ A traditional shop has four employees three technical employees—a builder and two mechanics, paid weekly/hourly, representing about 20% of the booked sales, and a manager paid on commissions, typically 10% of sales with oversight by the owner.
   ✓ A progressive shop has labor related to general auto repair paid a flat rate percentage of shop rate, or 'flag rate.'

   General Information
   ✓ Ratio of commercial accounts to retail is a topic that can affect pricing if the account is tied to the owner or will not transfer to a buyer.
   ✓ Adding back the manager's compensation to inflate discretionary earnings is a red flag, as most buyers do not have industry experience."

Expert Comments

"Visiting with an owner of a shop that looks busy in a different market place will be much more helpful, as he will tend to be more open. Contact a good business broker who has sold these type businesses."

"This is a recession resistant segment that is changing. Technology is affecting the industry in a positive way, but also negatively, as the quality of new automobile transmissions, extended warranties and high cost encourage trading up rather than repairing, especially if the shop is in an affluent area."

"The industry has competition from general auto repair shops using after market transmissions and from dealerships, especially on high-end automobiles. Transmissions have become very reliable. High cost of advertising makes it hard to compete for small independent shops in major markets."

"People keeping cars longer is a positive. Parts distributors are consolidating and fixing prices. Technology and the economy are encouraging total car repair which destroys classic parts and labor models."

Benchmark Data

- "Keep the Gross Profit at or below 50%, which includes parts cost and shop labor. Maintain a ratio of 80% retail, not to exceed 20%. Fleet/commercial with low concentration of accounts. Address the issues concerning a changing market regarding labor pricing methods where historically transmission shops paid hourly rates and general auto repair by 'flag' hours as percent of shop rate."
- "Rules of Thumb for shop labor is 20% of sales, maintaining gross profit of 50%. Typical breakeven is $12,000 per week."

Expenses as a percentage of annual sales

Cost of goods	18% to 24%
Payroll/labor Costs	20% to 25%
Occupancy	08% to 15%
Profit (estimated pretax)	10% to 20%

Industry Trend

- "The industry does not seem to be consolidating as is the body shop arena. High cost of Internet advertising is affecting the small independents; in major market areas the ones doing much better are part of a franchised group with co-op advertising."
- "Manufacturers are providing longer warranties. Competition from general auto repair shops has forced migration into general auto repair. Smaller shops with less than $500,000 sales in a major market might not be in business. The costs of real estate and zoning are a problem. Many locations desired will be too expensive to justify any auto repair shop. Transmission services are considered by many cities to be heavy auto repair and often require special use permits. Attracting and keeping a highly skilled workforce."

Seller Financing

- "Typically all sellers want cash but end up having to address financing to sell with half down, balance paid over five years. Outside financing typically involves the buyer providing outside collateral to add to real estate loan at a conventional lender. SBA loans for a franchise without real estate is an option to get by the industry experience required."
- "Seller financing unless real estate is included"

Questions

- "None until he has signed a confidentially agreement. Ratio of retail to commercial sale. Ratio of major to minor repairs. Are there concentrations at any account? Seasonality of the business. How many and job description of employees. Discuss the manager."
- "Who is your competition?"
- "Why are you selling? What are the sales trends for last few years? How stable is the manager if ownership changes? What is the percentage of transmission service to general auto repair? How are your employees compensated? What is the ratio of retail/walk-in versus commercial? What is ratio of major to minor repairs? What is the average invoice for a major? What is percentage of warranty returns (comebacks)? Do your expenses include Workman's comp or alternative insurance?"

Resources

Trade Publications
- Gears Magazine: www.gearsmagazine.com
- Transmission Digest: www.transmissiondigest.com

Associations
- Automatic Transmission Rebuilders Association (ATRA): www.atra.com

Auto Wrecking/Recyclers/Dismantlers/Scrap/Salvage Yards (Auto parts—used & rebuilt)

SIC 5015-02	NAICS 441310	Number of Businesses/Units 4,792

Rules of Thumb

- "Auto wrecking yards sell for 2 to 2.5 times the owner's provable net income. Parts inventory is included, but cars for sale inventory is not included."
- "Values are based on the following: 3–5 times earnings, land and improvements, vehicle and parts inventory discounted based, anticipated time to liquidate. Goodwill such as customers, strategic location, and permitting can be fairly significant."
- 100% of Annual Gross Sales including inventory
- 25% times EBITDA

Expert Comments

"Sellers should expose their opportunity to several potential buyers."

"Self-service auto recycling is the trend, due to lower personnel costs."

Benchmark Data

Statistics (Used Car Parts Wholesaling)

Number of Establishments	4,792
Average Profit Margin	4.8%
Revenue per Employee	$225,600
Average Number of Employees	4.2
Average Wages per Employee	$32,281

Products and Services Segmentation

General auto recycling	55.0%
Specialized motor vehicle dismantling and parts sales	45.0%

Major Market Segmentation

Automotive mechanics and repair shops	42.0%
General auto parts wholesalers	19.2%
Auto parts rebuilders and remanufacturers	14.5%
Other	11.3%
Do-it-yourself customers	6.7%
Auto parts retailers	6.4%

Industry Costs

Profit	4.8%
Wages	14.5%
Purchases	52.3%
Depreciation	0.8%
Marketing	1.0%
Rent & Utilities	4.5%
Other	22.1%

Market Share

LKQ Corporation Inc.	13.8%
Schnitzer Steel Industries Inc.	5.0%

Source: IBISWorld, May 2016

Expenses as a percentage of annual sales

Cost of goods	40% to 50%
Payroll/labor Costs	10%
Occupancy	14%
Profit (estimated pretax)	25%

Industry Trend

- "Consolidation is a trend that will continue. Smart operators will have to manage their businesses better every year."
- "Wrecking yards do well in good and bad economies."

Seller Financing

- "Quality buyers pay in cash, or lease facilities long term. Some seller financing takes place, usually when involving a first time buyer."
- "6 years for self-service yards, and 12 years for full-service yards."

Questions

- "Are they able to pitch the sale of their yard to at least ten potential buyers?"

Resources

Associations

- Automotive Recyclers Association of New York: www.arany.com
- Automotive Recyclers Association : www.a-r-a.org
- Institute of Scrap Recycling Industries: www.isri.org

Aviation and Aerospace

Rules of Thumb

➢ 80 percent of annual sales

➢ 3.8 to 6.0 times SDE

➢ 4 times EBIT

➢ 5 times EBITDA

Pricing Tips

- "To provide a rule of thumb for the industry as a whole would be misleading. A regional airlines SDE multiple will vary greatly from an avionics supplier or repair shop."
- "Type of aircraft, market served, age of aircraft, revenue per flight hour and asset utilization."
- "Must use both inventory and sales."

Expert Comments

"Aviation is a closed community—relationships are easily verified and confirmed. New entrants—unless they have an unheard of capability—are generally short lived."

"Aviation has always been a 'darling' industry. Buyers aren't hard to find if you're making money."

Benchmark Data

- "Revenue per flight hour"

Expenses as a percentage of annual sales

Cost of goods	20%
Payroll/labor Costs	50%
Occupancy	10%
Profit (estimated pretax)	20%

Industry Trend

- "Very high growth"

Seller Financing

- "Outside financing"

Questions
- "Age of aircraft, maintenance costs, revenue flights per hour, % of utilization of assets, marketing and sales"

Resources

Associations
- www.rotor.com: Helicopter Association International

	Franchise
A&W Restaurants (A&W Root Beer) (See also Franchises)	
Estimated Annual Sales/Unit	$325,000

SIC 5812-06	NAICS 722513	Number of Businesses/Units 1,000 +

Rules of Thumb
➢ 45 percent of annual sales plus inventory

Benchmark Data
- "Recommended square footage is between 1,500 and 2,000 square feet."

Resources

Websites
- www.awrestaurants.com

Bagel Shops (See also Bagel Franchises, Bakeries)		
SIC 546101	NAICS 722513	

Rules of Thumb
➢ 30 to 35 percent of annual sales plus inventory

➢ 2.5 SDE plus inventory

Pricing Tips
- "Generally worth 1/3 of gross sales volume, with a decent rent. Higher rent or upcoming increase will lower price."
- "Rent a large factor; hand-rolled or frozen product?"

Expert Comments

"As the team from Always Bagels in Lebanon, PA, put it, a bagel is a bagel, which means carbs and calories. Even whole grain, fiber-packed attempts at added nutrition carry a calorie count that scares off consumers today. While items such as cake and cookies can enjoy their treat status, and loaf bread can benefit from whole grains, bagels still must contend with their rotund size and everyday breakfast positioning."

Source: "Walking the bagel line," by Charlotte Atchley, www.foodbusinessnews.net 6/25/2014

- "Easy to duplicate. Setup cost expensive. Most shopping centers already have a bagel shop."

Benchmark Data

- For additional Benchmark Information see also Restaurants—Limited Service
- "Rent and payroll the most important factors"

Expenses as a percentage of annual sales

Cost of goods	10%
Payroll/labor Costs	25%
Occupancy	20%
Profit (estimated pretax)	20%

Industry Trend

- "This precarious position has the bagel field staring down flat sales, and bagel bakers looking for new ways to jump-start sales momentum. According to data from IRI, a market research firm based in Chicago, for the 52-week period ending Jan. 26, the entire bagel category only grew 2% in dollar sales and 2.8% in unit sales, with private label seeing the biggest boost at 9.1% growth in dollar sales. Shrinking the bagel's size to reduce calorie and carb counts, cleaning up ingredient labels and reenergizing old channels with new promotions and creative uses for these rolls all provide opportunities to bring new life to the breakfast product."

    Source: "Walking the bagel line," by Charlotte Atchley, www.foodbusinessnews.net 6/25/2014

Resources

Websites
- New Yorker Bagels: www.newyorkerbagels.com

Associations
- Independent Bakers Association: www.bakingnetwork.com

Bait and Tackle Shops (See also Sporting Goods Stores)		
SIC 5941-0101	NAICS 451110	

Rules of Thumb

➤ 30 percent of annual sales plus inventory

Benchmark Data
- For Benchmark Information see Sporting Goods Stores

Bakeries (See also Bakeries—Commercial, Food Stores/Specialty)		
SIC 5461-02	NAICS 445291	

Rules of Thumb

➤ 40 to 45 percent of annual sales plus inventory

➤ 2 times SDE plus inventory

Pricing Tips

- "Receivables; years in business; scope of market; new 'state-of-art' equipment vs. old."

Benchmark Data

Expenses as a percentage of annual sales   :

Cost of goods sold (Food) .... 05% to 10%
Payroll/Labor Costs .... 30% to 35%
Occupancy Cost .... 06% to 08%
Other Overhead .... 10% to 15%
Profit (estimated) .... 20%+

- "Percentage of full-line retail bakery operators offering the following items:
  1. Sodas, juices, teas 61%
  2. Conventional coffee service 56%
  3. Sandwiches 45%
  4. On-site dining 31%
  5. Espresso, other gourmet coffee 30%
  6. Other deli (salads, cheeses, etc.) 30%"
  Note: Figures above are approximate.
- For additional Benchmark Information see Food Stores—Specialty

Industry Trend

- "According to the report, the global bakery market is anticipated to grow at a Compound Annual Growth Rate (CAGR) of 7.04% between 2014 and 2019. Key trends:
  ✓ Increase in demand for gluten-free products
  ✓ Increase in demand for organic products
  ✓ Constant product innovations increasing revenue
  ✓ Price fluctuations around commodities used to produce bakery products"
  Source: Global Bakery Market 2015–2019 report from Research and Markets

Resources

Trade Publications
- Modern Baking: http://supermarketnews.com/product-categories/bakery

Associations
- Independent Bakers Association: http://www.ibabaker.com/

Bakeries—Commercial (See also Bakeries)		
SIC 5149-02	NAICS 311812	

Rules of Thumb

➢ 65 to 70 percent of annual sales plus inventory

➢ 2 times SDE plus inventory

➢ 3 to 5 times EBITDA

B - Rules of Thumb

Pricing Tips

- "The following table illustrates the relationship between two price multiples and company revenues, using data from a study of thousands of sales of small and very small businesses across all industries:

Size of Company	Sale Price/ Revenue	Sale Price/ Discretionary Earnings*
Up to $1 million revenue	0.51	2.2
$1 to 5 million revenue	0.62	2.9

- "Gross sales in retail & wholesale; operating hours; location."
- "The above price/earnings Rules of Thumb assume a 'minimal asset sale,' meaning fixed assets, inventory and intangibles only. Assumes the buyer replaces all other elements of working capital, and that the assets are transferred free of liabilities. Typical light manufacturing value drivers and risk factors apply (customer concentration, brand, product differentiation, growth prospects, distribution channel, longevity in the market, condition and capacity of equipment, management depth, etc.)"
- "Age & sophistication of equipment; convenience of bakery to major transportation hubs allowing for plentiful pool of employees."
- "Gross sales . . . what portion is from retail sales & how much from wholesale; inquire as to the amount of 'bags of flour' purchased weekly; loaves of bread sold weekly."
- "The SDE multiplier is subject to increase or decrease based on the age and type of equipment. Further, large commercial bakeries require specialized human resources which may be the seller(s) whose expertise will need to be replaced. Oftentimes sellers minimize the difficulty in replacing their expertise, but this should be carefully evaluated and valuation adjustments made accordingly."
- "Be careful to check if one or two customers comprise a high percentage of the bakery's revenues."
- "Don't be fooled by the owner's overstatement of the value of the equipment. Most bakery equipment is valued at between 10% and 25% of replacement cost new. The larger equipment requires riggers to move it. The dismantling and re-installation of ovens requires specialized skill and knowledge."
- "Price will vary greatly depending on the volume and types of labor-saving equipment. This is an industry where payroll can be significantly reduced by machinery. Commercial contracts with restaurants, hotels, etc. are also a source of value."

Expert Comments

"Overall commercial bakeries are generally a high risk/high competition industry."

"Fastest growing market segments are functional foods, organic, low calorie, all natural, gluten free."

"This industry over the past several years has been under a tremendous squeeze on profitability. Price of flour & other needed ingredients has been most volatile, yet the market place has been most resistant to price increases...thus profit margins (& profit) have been reduced!!!"

"Industry is declining due to eating habits of population. Cost of entry is very high due to equipment cost, unless used equipment is purchased.

Marketability is limited by the size of the marketplace of professional bakers. In some parts of the U.S., facilities tend to be old. Competition is growing a bit due to the business education of young professional bakers."

"Receivables are very important since they determine the amount of start-up capital needed. It was the cause of the demise of many a big wholesaler in New York."

"Price will vary greatly depending on the volume and types of labor-saving equipment. This is an industry where payroll can be significantly reduced by machinery. Commercial contracts with restaurants, hotels, etc. are also a source of value."

Benchmark Data
- "Pounds of flour used; # of loaves of bread baked/sold."
- "Cost of goods should be no more than 20% tops . . . just as rent should be no more than 10% of sales."
- "22%–25% cost of goods"
- "Direct cost of goods varies significantly from product to product. There is no little commonality between a bread bakery and a cake and pastry bakery. A well-run facility with reasonable market share should result in an SDE of 15%–20% of Gross Revenues."
- "Difficult to measure since many of these businesses operate from facilities that are old and much larger than required with new highly automated equipment available."

Expenses as a percentage of annual sales

Cost of goods	25% to 30%
Payroll/labor Costs	30% to 40%
Occupancy	15% to 20%
Profit (estimated pretax)	15% to 18%

Industry Trend
- "There will be less and less small bakeries, with the larger ones of each regional area dictating market price."
- "Down, as the major bakers take over the industry."
- "As obesity becomes more of an issue, I anticipate a slight decline in the industry."
- "Fewer and fewer competitors . . . with a growing trend toward baking artisan products."

Seller Financing
- "If it is a high asset business with relatively new baking equipment, equipment loans may be available to finance the purchase. Otherwise seller financing must be in place."
- "Mostly seller financing...but if equipment is modern (which most are not) then outside financing can be arranged."
- "5 to 7 years or the length of the lease if building is not owned"

Questions

- "Determine the geographic scope and customer type of its customer base."
- "Ask for flour and water bills, cost/price list of major items carried, aging of receivables & payables; see gas/electric bills; determine age and condition of equipment."
- "Is location of any importance to sales . . . if so how long is lease?"
- "Review and interview key customers—evaluate equipment carefully—check for expansion opportunity."

Banks—Commercial		
SIC 6021-01	NAICS 522110	Number of Businesses/Units 78,575

Rules of Thumb

- ➤ 1 to 2 times Book Value
- ➤ 350% of Annual Gross Sales includes inventory
- ➤ 15 times SDE includes inventory
- ➤ 15 times EBIT

Expert Comments

"The post-recession regulatory environment has burdened smaller community banks with compliance issues that are forcing many of them to consolidate in order to achieve the necessary economies of scale required to enable compliance."

Benchmark Data

Statistics (Commercial Banking)

Number of Establishments	78,575
Average Profit Margin	25.2%
Revenue per Employee	$468,300
Average Number of Employees	19.9
Average Wages per Employee	$74,388

Products and Services Segmentation

Depository services and other noninterest-income generating products	34.8%
Real estate loans	31.3%
Commercial and industrial loans	14.2%
Other	8.8%
Loans to individuals excluding credit cards	5.6%
Credit card loans	5.3%

Major Market Segmentation

Corporate clients	49.0%
Retail customers	48.0%
Other clients	3.0%

Industry Costs

Profit	25.2%
Wages	16.7%
Deprecation	3.6%
Marketing	2.1%
Rent & Utilities	9.7%
Other	42.7%

Market Share

Wells Fargo & Company	10.4%
JPMorgan Chase & Co.	8.3%
Bank of America Corporation	6.5%

Source: IBISWorld, March 2016

Expenses as a percentage of annual sales

Cost of goods	25%
Payroll/labor Costs	35%
Occupancy	05% to 10%
Profit (estimated pretax)	25%

Industry Trend

- "U.S. News spoke to four financial and banking experts to find out what's on the horizon for the banking sector in 2016. Here are 10 trends they told us to watch.
  1. Fewer people will head to branches.
  2. The digital and branch experience will merge.
  3. Branches will start to go digital.
  4. Investment options at the bank aren't likely to expand.
  5. Savings account interest rates should go up, but you won't get rich.
  6. Banks could start charging for convenience.
  7. Online banking will remain popular but won't replace branches.
  8. Mobile payments will continue to make inroads.
  9. Regional banks will get in on mobile deposits.
  10. Chip cards may finally see some action.

Source: "10 Banking Trends for 2016" by Maryalene LaPonsie, January 7, 2016, http://money.usnews.com/money/personal-finance/articles/2016-01-07/10-banking-trends-for-2016

- "Consolidation of smaller banks, high scrutiny of risk in making loans, lower profit due to building up of capital and reserves."

Questions

- "Are you now or have you ever been involved in banking? How much liquid capital do you have to invest? Have you spoken with any bank regulatory authorities about your plans to acquire a bank?"

Barber Shops (See also Beauty Salons, Hair Care, Franchises)		
SIC 7241-01	NAICS 812111	

Rules of Thumb

➢ 10 to 25 percent of SDE plus inventory; add $1500 per chair

Benchmark Data
- For Benchmark Data see Hair Salons

Bars (See also Cocktail Lounges)		
SIC 5813-01	NAICS 722410	Number of Businesses/Units 70,736

Rules of Thumb

➢ 35% to 45% percent times annual sales—business only plus inventory

➢ 2 to 2.5 times SDE plus inventory

➢ 1.5 to 2.5 times EBIT

➢ 2 to 2.5 times EBITDA

➢ 4 times monthly sales + game revenue (net) plus inventory

➢ 4 times monthly sales + liquor license and inventory

Pricing Tips
- "You have to understand how the licenses and permits impact value."
- "A bar serving alcohol only should have a higher profit margin than one selling food. It is a cash business. A lot of due diligence is necessary to verify cash expenses and receipts."
- "High volume locations bring higher multiples. Value very location driven. Location often times more important than financials. Value of liquor license can also drive value dependent upon ease of obtaining liquor licenses in particular area where business is located. Prices have not recovered from 2009 economic woes. Good financial documentation also helps sale process and value."
- "Competition, number of available licenses in town, previous violations"
- "Top-line method is used due to the perception of a cash business. This is changing and it is much more difficult to sell bars without documented earnings."
- "Understand the value of liquor license and percentages of alcohol vs. food."
- "Main variable is the fair market value of the liquor permit, as some areas have a high number of available permits which results in the permit having no, or limited, additional value, while in other areas limited number of available permits may cause the permit to have a substantial value. One will need to research type of permit and its availability and if in fact a market exists for the permit itself. I have seen liquor permits being sold for as high as $150,000, which obviously impacts the value of the business."
- "The location, lease rate, and restrictions on the conditional use permit or liquor license will largely impact any given operation's value. As some licenses are valued at $75K plus, there is always some 'floor' value regardless of profitability."

- "Discretionary cash flow (DCF) can be very different from deal to deal. There is one very important DCF item that should be identified: Does the bar or taproom have any vending? (Examples of this are video poker, tobacco, juke box, pool tables, etc.) If the answer is 'Yes,' then the next question should be, is there a vendor arrangement, or does the seller own the machines? A vendor arrangement means that the vendor owns the machines and collects a portion of the proceeds. If the seller owns the machines, the seller collects all of the proceeds, and can use these funds to reduce their COGS and labor considerably. In each case, (with the seller as owner or the vendor as owner of machines) OFF BALANCE SHEET seller financing or vendor financing can be a very powerful source of funds. There are a few little things that can alter the valuation in a bar or taproom. Generally, these types of establishments derive a lot of revenue from draft beer. (COGS for draft beer 25%–30%, gross profit 70%–75%). If the establishment is operating on an antiquated draft system, glasses may not appear clean, spouts look discolored, this could warrant a discount. Most states require that draft system/draft lines are cleaned weekly. A potential buyer should ask for vendor beer invoices to determine the 'popular' products of the establishment. This is important if the buyer has a potential age group in mind as the primary patrons. This is a forward cash flow assumption that should be acknowledged. If vendor beer invoices are not made available, check the trash dumpster on a regular basis, it is an excellent source of information. If liquor is being served, the pouring routine should be observed. Measured shot or free pour can materially change COGS. 750ML bottle yields 26 ounces, which is 14 shots at a 1.75oz free pour, and 21 shots at a 1.25oz measured shot. This difference could be the cost of 1.5 bottles. (Generally these establishments sell mostly beer/draft beer, but this scenario should be included in forward cash flow assumptions.)"

- "Never trust the books. Check sales tax returns, bank statements, etc. Also, check the price points and compare to the actual COGS. Are the comps legitimate on the P&L? Are COGS high due to the owner skimming, or are they giving the house away? We never address a value to skimming and never represent it to buyers. Experienced buyers will recast the financials using their own labor percentage, etc."

Expert Comments

"For a buyer—work in a bar first and make sure you understand the business. Do your homework about cash receipts and where the money really goes."

"Location seems to be a driving factor here. Young people going out to a bar seem to prefer going to an area with a cluster of bars which allows for 'bar hopping.'"

"All of the reality shows glamorizing the industry have popularized the business."

"Having practical work experience in the industry is a definite plus. Avoid a 'bad' lease situation. Be comfortable with customers. Sellers should make the place look presentable and not have a bunch of broken equipment around. Police runs and bad health department Inspections drive down value. "

"True bars (without food) are becoming less profitable. Bars in good, dense, urban locations are still strong but suburban bars are struggling. Stronger drunk driving laws, smoking bans, etc. have contributed. Plus full-service restaurants with bars have cut into some of the business."

"These businesses are highly marketable due to the public demand (and dream) of owning their own bar. The difficulty of obtaining new permits adds significant value to existing operations."

"Neighborhood bars seem to be popular despite a good or bad economy. Sometimes the closer to home the better with tougher DUI laws."

Benchmark Data

Statistics (Bars & Nightclubs)

Number of Establishments	70,736
Average Profit Margin	5.4%
Revenue per Employee	$62,800
Average Number of Employees	5.7
Average Wages per Employee	$16,146

Products and Services Segmentation

Sale of beer and ale	33.6%
Sale of distilled spirit drinks	35.4%
Sale of meals and nonalcoholic beverages	14.1%
Sale of wine drinks	7.7%
Admissions to special events and nightclubs, including cover charges	2.6%
Other	6.6%

Industry Costs

Profit	5.4%
Wages	25.7%
Purchases	44.6%
Depreciation	2.4%
Marketing	3.0%
Rent & Utilities	6.6%
Other	12.3%

Source: IBISWorld, August 2016

- Liquor pouring costs should be at 25% or less. Beer and wine at 33%.
- "Food costs under 34% helpful."
- "High rents have been the cause of many failures."
- "There is no greater markup than that of liquor."
- "Small easily operated bars are the most desirable. Rent at 10%–12% (or less) of sales help."
- "Benchmarks vary widely with markets and types of establishments; food costs tend to be 25%–33%; however, productivity per square foot is a function of size and location (and subsequent lease rate)."

Expenses as a percentage of annual sales

Cost of goods	20% to 30%
Payroll/labor Costs	20% to 28%
Occupancy	06% to 10%
Profit (estimated pretax)	10% to 20%

Industry Trend

- "More alcohol-only bars with leased space for food trucks."
- "With the amount of new products emerging from the market with flavored wines, vodka, whisky...one has to stay up on what is in."
- "Increasing cost inflation and changing consumer tastes, e.g., craft beer, local foods, etc. Smoking blue collar 'sports' bars on the decline."
- "Most bars are improving on their food to drive more bar business."
- "Increasing costs and increasing competition from chains"
- "More bars, more craft beers, wines from different regions. I think we will see more pub-type concepts."
- "Increased governmental regulation, e.g., smoking bans"
- "More wine bars, tapas bars; drinking is always popular. More pricey drinks."
- "Liquor licenses in certain areas where there are high concentrations of establishments within major cities have become extremely difficult to obtain, thus driving the value of those licenses very high."

Seller Financing

- "Mostly cash or buyer supplied financing."
- "All cash or some element of owner financing is usually necessary to make a deal happen. Bank financing very difficult"
- 3 to 7 years

Questions

- "How much do you pay the help? Are you paying any of the help in cash? Are your ASCAP BMI fees paid and current?"
- "Length of time employees have been at work, number of employees, tax audits? Recent violations?"
- "Violations, invoices for purchases, customer count and sales"
- "Unpaid taxes? Liquor license violations? Police runs?"
- "Please provide me with a copy of the permit or conditional use permit, as provided by the city and the state Alcohol Control Board."
- "The variance between the internal books and records versus the tax returns. Purchase invoice availability."
- "What conditions have been placed on the license restricting the hours, use, or entertainment associated with the license?"
- "Scrutinize happy hour, comps, etc. Many buyers think they can increase sales by eliminating giveaways which usually does not work. Ask to see all liquor invoices and cash receipts from liquor purchases."
- "For the tax returns, why they are selling? Cooperation is key in this business. Bars are difficult to sell when there are unreported sales, weak returns. Many of the sellers in our market will not hold notes."
- "Discretionary Cash Flow should be evaluated very carefully. There can be a huge difference from deal to deal."

Resources

Websites
- BarProducts.com: www.barproducts.com

Bars—Adult Only (Adult Clubs/Nightclubs)		
SIC 5813-01	NAICS 722410	

Rules of Thumb

➢ 100 to 120 percent of annual sales includes inventory

➢ 3.5 times SDE includes inventory

Pricing Tips

- "Real estate typically will lease out at a 12%–20% premium to market. Alcohol licenses may have intrinsic value to be added to cost of purchase."
- "A recasted, SDC Flow is the best starting point. Be sure to examine either property or rental costs to make sure they are in line with area...Typically rental costs show a premium of 10%–20% above comparable market rates. FFE is a consideration related to its age."
- "Additional income is available from dancers and door."
- "The industry has experienced a shake-out of weaker performing clubs being swallowed by larger operators as they become available. Although we have experienced recessionary forces, as the entire industry has, the Adult Club industry by and large has been more resilient than mainstream bars and nightclubs to the effects of discretionary dollar competition and distribution. The more troubling aspects are more related to legal issues of Independent Contractor Status and the efforts of the Citizens for Community Values (CCV)."
- "Adult clubs are of course cash heavy operations. Verifying internal ratios of cost can lead to a back-ended method of providing gross cash flow."
- "A true EBITDA + owner's compensation recast is a necessity . . . "
- "The best thumbnail is SDE. It stands up well to real-world numbers on the sales prices. Real estate, inventory, FFE all should be considered separately as add backs to total sale price. Some states allow the sale of inventory alcohol to the buyer, some do not. MAI appraisals do well for real estate. FFE is a 'swag' and over 3 years old stuff ought to write down to 10%–20% of initial cost."

Expert Comments

"Industry is vital, and succeeding....the average club life can be measured almost in decades."

"Major risk is from legislative actions. Operator chooses location and level of sophistication and markets accordingly."

"The economy really hits discretionary earnings spending . . . "

"Conservative nibblings at the edges of law have served to limit growth of the industry. There has been a generalized effort on the part of the larger chains and owners to absorb reasonably priced clubs in targeted areas. Past the big and midsized players, the single and small operators struggle to maintain a stable cash flow with controlled labor costs, dancers, and stable legal environments."

Benchmark Data

Statistics (Strip Clubs)

Number of Establishments	4,074
Average Profit Margin	19.8%
Revenue per Employee	$105,900
Average Number of Employees	14.6
Average Wages per Employee	$22,360

Products and Services Segmentation

Alcohol	41.3%
Service revenue	39.7%
Food and merchandise	13.4%
Other services	5.6%

Industry Costs

Profit	19.8%
Wages	21.1%
Purchases	19.3%
Depreciation	3.2%
Marketing	3.9%
Rent & Utilities	5.6%
Other	27.1%

Source: IBISWorld, April 2016

- "Liquor cost should be in the range of 18%–22%; Rent: optimally in the 8%–10% range of gross sales."
- "SDE x 2.5–3.5 = possible sale price."
- "Should be reporting an SDE in neighborhood of 23%–26% or higher."
- "There are basically three revenue streams, in addition to the fees from dancers: cover charges, which can top $20; food and drinks; and services, which include the renting of private rooms. A customer may pay the club $400 to $500 for a spell in one of those rooms."
- "Rent: 10%; liquor cost: 15%"

Expenses as a percentage of annual sales

Cost of goods	20%
Payroll/labor Costs	n/a
Occupancy	<10%
Profit (estimated pretax)	25%

Industry Trend

- "Continue to maintain growth with more mainstream investments in the industry and more robust economy"
- "Markets have remained relatively stable throughout the U.S. with the exception of the Las Vegas market. Stable; but more concentration of clubs under a few chains."
- "Like so many other 'sin' categories, the business seems to be resistant to economic downturns, especially as the customer base keeps expanding."

Seller Financing
- "Usually 2–4 years"
- "Usually all cash"

Questions
- "What is the legal status of licenses and permits: alcohol, privilege, local?"
- "Detailed explanation of all income sources. Current political atmosphere. Security of license."
- "What violations have been charged? Is the owner aware of any pending litigation or legislation (either local or state) which will have a negative impact? There are others but the rest are more site specific."
- "How would he replace the Cash Flow of this business with something comparable?"
- "Why is he/she selling? What is wrong with this picture? I have yet to have an owner list a club with me because he woke up one morning, said, 'Gee, I think I'll let someone else make a bunch of money off my club, and I'll finance it to him on easy terms, too!' Inevitably, if someone wants to sell, there is usually a serious reason that is material! Caveat Emptor, and make sure that both buyer and seller have their own individual attorneys."

Resources
Trade Publications
- Several magazines devoted to the adult nightclub industry: www.edpublications.com

Associations
- Association of Club Executives: www.acenational.org

Bars—Nightclubs (See also Bars)		
	NAICS 722410	Number of Businesses/Units 70,736

Rules of Thumb
➤ 40 percent of annual sales
➤ 2.5 times SDE plus inventory
➤ 3 times EBIT
➤ 2 times EBITDA

Pricing Tips
- "The conditions or potential restrictions on the liquor license are paramount. Are there abbreviated hours, are happy hours or door fees allowed, what is the security-guard-to-patron ratio, does a significant percentage of sales need to be derived by food sales, etc."
- "Buyers of nightclubs are generally going to implement their own concept and theme. Sellers rarely seek to sell when they are at the peak of their game, but when revenues begin to slide. The lifespan of a 'hot' club rarely lasts beyond 3 to 4 years, so at that point an owner may need to give the business a 'face lift'

or sell it to a new owner who will implement a new theme. That in mind, value based on cash flow becomes less relevant since a new owner's investment will be the same regardless."

Expert Comments

"This industry is highly volatile as trends are constantly changing. Also, clubs on the Strip in Las Vegas, in Hollywood or in South Beach are significantly different from main street America."

Benchmark Data

- See charts under Bars
- "Of the Top 100 survey participants, 42.8% identified their venues as nightclubs; 70.6% of them described their hotspots as dance clubs. Of those identifying their venue as bars, 31.7% are sports bars and 29.3% are traditional bar/taverns. DJs and live entertainment are featured by 88.3% and 73.6% of total respondents, respectively. Nearly 80% offer a dance floor, 70.1% provide VIP areas, and 65% offer bottle service.

  "Drinks generate the lion's share of venue revenues—56% of sales from alcohol is the mean among Top 100 survey participants. While in the venues, partyers favored spirits, which generate 44% of alcohol sales. Beer contributes 25% and wine 9%. A full food menu is offered by 68% of survey respondents' venues. Gaming, such as pool tables, video games systems and jukeboxes, are available at 42% of respondents' venues. Nearly three quarters (73%) have outdoor patio, terrace or rooftop space, which is an increase from 63% a year ago.

  "Small companies can compete effectively by serving a local market, offering unique products or entertainment, or providing superior customer service. The industry is extremely labor-intensive: average annual revenue per worker is $60.000.

  "Size varies greatly, from small corner taverns to warehouse-sized dance clubs. The majority of nightclubs range from 3,500 to 7,000 square feet, according to nightclubbiz.com. Experienced owners tend to run the largest nightclubs, which range from 10,000 to 30,000 square feet. A 3,000 square foot club can gross between $24,000 and $64,000 per month. A 15,000-square-foot club can gross between $100,000 and $260,000 per month."

Source: National Club Industry Association of America www.nciaa.com

Expenses as a percentage of annual sales

Cost of goods...25%
Payroll/labor Costs..30%
Occupancy...15%
Profit (estimated pretax) 20%

Industry Trend

- "There will always be a market for such venues, and buyers willing to pay premiums to A+ locations for venues."

Questions

- "Original invoices for liquor sales, and, with your fingers crossed, door counts per night."

Resources

Websites
- Nightclub & Bar: http://www.nightclub.com/

Associations
- National Club Industry Association of America, NCIAA: www.nciaa.com

Bars with Slot Machines (See also Casinos/Casino Hotels)		
	NAICS 722410	

Rules of Thumb

➤ 3 times SDE plus inventory

Pricing Tips
- "Drinks are free to slot players. Pay close attention to only the net, providing other operating costs are in line."

Expenses as a percentage of annual sales

Cost of goods	32%
Payroll/labor Costs	30%
Occupancy	10%
Profit (estimated pretax)	17%

Seller Financing
- "Where the debt service does not exceed 35 percent of the SDE."

Franchise

Baskin-Robbins Ice Cream (See also Franchises, Ice Cream/Yogurt Shops)		
Approx. Total Investment		$90,350 to $396,100
Estimated Annual Sales/Unit		$225,000
SIC 2024-98	NAICS 722515	Number of Businesses/Units 7,300

Rules of Thumb

➤ 46 to 56 percent of annual sales plus inventory

Resources

Websites
- Baskin Robbins: www.baskinrobbins.com

Franchise

Batteries Plus Bulbs (See also Franchises)		
Approx. Total Investment		$208,450 to $385,750
	NAICS 441310	Number of Businesses/Units 626

Rules of Thumb

➤ 30 to 35 percent of annual sales plus inventory

Resources

Websites
- Batteries Plus: www.batteriesplus.com

Beauty Salons (See also Barber Shops, Hair Care, Nail Salons)		
SIC 7231-06	NAICS 812112	Number of Businesses/Units 1,364,091

Rules of Thumb
➤ 35 percent of annual revenues; add fixtures, equipment & inventory
➤ 2 times SDE plus inventory
➤ 4 times monthly sales plus inventory
➤ 2.5 times EBIT

Pricing Tips
- "In the larger full-service salons you may sometimes have more equipment value to consider such as skin care, facial. Some salons may still owe money, these leases can also sometimes be assumed by the buyer decreasing the sales price."
- "Take into consideration the working owner and how much of the sales belong to their work performed. Will they stay on and pay commission or rent, or will they slowly flow their customers to the buyer."
- "The larger the gross sales, the higher the multiples. For instance if I have a salon that is doing $1 million in sales annually, my high number will be $500,000, then I look at the true owner benefits."
- "25% to 35% of annual sales"
- "Whether the operators are W-2 or #1099—and also how the chemical product costs are debited."
- "What percentage of the gross sales is generated by a service generating owner and how may the change in ownership shift the owner's income? The most effective pricing point is utilizing the SDE."
- "Check reason(s) for empty stations—turnover? Are stations rented?"

Expert Comments
"Do not tell your staff or clientele that you are selling until you have closed on the transaction. Then seller will take buyer to the salon and have all employees or staff there for an introduction to the new owner. Take lots of food and drink (no alcohol) and buyer should speak to each of the staff individually and openly. Listen to the concerns of the people and tell them how you will not change anything for at least 3 to 6 months so you can learn more about the needs and desires of both the staff and the clientele. Suggestion box is great."

"It is very expensive to start a beauty salon from scratch with all of the build out, equipment, impact fees from the county government, not to mention the time it takes from signing the lease, construction. You will be out approximately $250,000 from the start. Purchasing a salon that has good equipment, location, technicians and clientele in place will be far more appealing at the end of the first 12 months. Buyers always change the looks

B - Rules of Thumb

in some way that appeals to them whether it is major cleanup or paint and new floors depending on the salon itself."

"The beauty industry is as old as mankind and essentially a replenishment industry; the resale possibilities are endless; rebranding is the next frontier."

"Location and marketing are big factors in the success of a salon."

"Highly competitive industry with a fair level of risk. Can be easily replicated. Location, location, location."

"Market saturation has occurred likely due to the creative nature of the salon professional wanting to expand yet not completing the necessary business market research. The risks are considered low because of the small monetary initial investment. The beauty industry trends will always grow due to vanity and fashion."

Benchmark Data

Statistics (Hair & Nail Salons)

Number of Establishments	1,364,091
Average Profit Margin	7.9%
Revenue per Employee	$31,300
Average Number of Employees	1.3
Average Wages per Employee	$13,173

Products and Services Segmentation

Haircutting services	45.5%
Hair coloring services	17.1%
Nail care services	15.9%
Merchandise sales	9.7%
Other hair care services	4.7%
Other beauty care services	3.6%
Skin care services	3.5%

Industry Costs

Profit	7.9%
Wages	42.0%
Purchases	21.7%
Depreciation	1.8%
Marketing	2.3%
Rent & Utilities	11.9%
Other	12.4%

Source: IBISWorld, March 2016

Economic Trends: Percent of Gross Revenue by Category

Hair Color Service Sales	34%
Hair Cutting Service Sales	31%
Retail Sales	17%
Skin Care, Body Care, Spa-type Service Sales	08%
Nail Service Sales	04%
Chemical Service Sales	03%
Other	03%

Source: "Salon Today"

- "If seller earns commission credits, do not include them in the owner's benefit—just what is earned as solely an owner."

Expenses as a percentage of annual sales

Cost of goods	06% to 12%
Payroll/labor Costs	50% to 60%
Occupancy	10% to 20%
Profit (estimated pretax)	07% to 15%

Industry Trend

- "Wellness products. Business Focus: Wellness + Technology + Science, the New Beauty Market."
- "The demand for organic and natural-based salon products is sky rocketing! Not only is the organic salon product market growing, but so are the salons that have chosen to be a part of the movement. Now, with the ingredient lists of salon products available at the push of button, it comes to no surprise clients are demanding safer products that still perform at the professional level."

  Source: "Salon Industry Trends 2015," January 6, 2016,
  http://hubpages.com/style/Salon-Industry-Trends-2014
- "More and more foreign buyers and growth in chain operations."
- "Growing trend with the Baby Boomers being more concerned with aging and graying."
- "Mainstream beauty services will continue. Natural processes for beauty treatments. Minor cosmetic surgery/treatments will interchange with spa and salon services. Male client services are increasing."

Seller Financing

- "Seller financing is suggested in this industry as most banks do not lend money on the majority of these businesses. Never take less than 50% down payment. I typically see 75% down payment or all-cash balance over 2 to 3 years."
- 3 to 5 years

Questions

- "How much of the sales belong to your performance, will you stay on? If the buyer is a stylist and so is the seller, will the clientele slowly flow to the buyer? You cannot make a client stay with you. They are yours to lose or gain. Honesty is the best policy.
- How long have the employees been with you? What is the turnover of technicians and why? Commission or rental? What type of products do you use and how old is the product on your shelf and why? How often and where do you advertise? Who does your website, Facebook page? Where do you find your employees? How often do you offer education classes and what company"?
- "What percentage of the gross sales is generated by the seller?"

Resources

Trade Publications

- Modern Salon: www.modernsalon.com

Bed & Breakfasts (See also Inns)

SIC 7011-07	NAICS 721191	Number of Businesses/Units 7,531

Rules of Thumb

> 550 percent of annual sales includes inventory and real estate

> 4.2 times gross room sales for small B&Bs (less than eight rooms); a little higher for dinner-service inns, 4.5; these are for businesses as opposed to real-estate-driven small properties

> 8 to 9 times SDE includes inventory and real estate

Pricing Tips

- "The larger inns are selling for 8 (w/o seller financing) to 10 times (w/seller financing) S.D.E. Gross Rent Multiplier in the 4 to 5 range."
- "Smaller B&Bs (fewer than 8 rooms) are usually real-estate driven."
- "5 times gross room income; gross room income minus the net operating expenses (no debt service or management costs) = net operating income times 11 percent."

Expert Comments

"Buyers should have their home sold prior to buying a B&B. Contingent sale of a buyer home is not a very compelling offer. Sellers should have a thorough understanding of the inns for sale market. They should also realistically deal w/deal killers such as needing a new roof, windows, etc."

"Many of the larger inns have been selling in the 8 to 10 capitalization rate of net income, less any needed repairs and up to a 20% discount if seller financing is not involved. In the middle part of U.S., B&Bs are selling for $80K-$100K/guestroom on avg. The popular East & West Coast locations could be up to twice that amt. The larger the inn, the less value/guestroom. Values & Expenses vary greatly due to the non-standardized structure of the bldgs. & locale."

"B&B buyers must make both a lifestyle & financial purchase decision. Innkeeping is one of the few businesses that you want to live where you work! For the past 5+ years, we have had smaller B&Bs sold/converted back to homes than we've had homes being converted to inns! Start-ups are more difficult to accomplish today versus the mid-1980's primarily due to rising real estate values, high conversion cost, zoning restrictions, tougher lending practices, & a lack of market demand for innkeeping (during a strong economy). Some of the smaller inns in less popular areas were converted to alternative uses and a minority of inns closed for avoidance of taxes from capital gains and depreciation recapture."

Benchmark Data

Statistics (Bed & Breakfast & Hostel Accommodations)

Number of Establishments	7,531
Average Profit Margin	15.5%
Revenue per Employee	$113,200
Average Number of Employees	3.5
Average Wages per Employee	$20,329

Products and Services Segmentation

Bed & Breakfast	69.0%
Other—including Hostels	31.0%

Major Market Segmentation

Vacation travelers	58.2%
Family travelers	21.8%
Business travelers	12.0%
Other—including meetings	8.0%

Industry Costs

Profit	15.5%
Wages	18.0%
Purchases	21.2%
Depreciation	8.9%
Marketing	2.2%
Rent & Utilities	11.3%
Other	12.9%

Source: IBISWorld, June 2016

- "The larger inns are selling for 8 (w/o seller financing) to 10 times (w/seller financing) adjusted net operating income. The base real estate value of the smaller B&B contributes to a large part of the value. In small, supplemental income B&Bs, their value is typically $25,000 to $50,000 more than the base real estate value as a house or other real estate use. There are probably more supplemental income B&Bs than cash flow inns of the 20K+ U.S. B&Bs."

- "Profit (estimated) 40% to 45% of sales"

- "Many resort inns within three hours of a metro area can produce occupancy in the 40% to 50% range. Urban inns can produce 50% to 80% occupancy. Most non-urban inns below seven guestrooms provide to only supplemental income. It's kind of like owning a duplex; you can live in a better location & house than you could otherwise afford, but you don't give up your day job. About 50% of the U.S. B&Bs are this size."

- "Bed and Breakfast/Country Inn Statistics: The data below is from Studies and Surveys done by www.innkeeping.org—a very informative site.

Performance (in medians)

Occupancy Rate	43.7%
Average Daily Rate	$150
Revenue per Available Room	$58

- About the Inns
  Some interesting data from an Industry Study of Innkeeping Operations and Finance from the Professional Association of Innkeepers International (PAII).
  - ✓ 72% of B&Bs are run by couples
  - ✓ 79% of innkeepers live on premises
  - ✓ The typical B&B has between 4 and 11 rooms, with 6 guest rooms or suites being the average
  - ✓ The average B&B has been open for 15 years
  - ✓ The average age of the oldest part of a B&B building is 107 years

B - Rules of Thumb

- ✓ 29% of B&Bs were in rural locations, 23% were urban, 5% suburban, and 43% were village
- ✓ 94% of rooms have private baths
- ✓ 36% have achieved an "historical designation" by a local, state or national historic preservation organization
- ✓ 5,700 square feet is the average size for a B&B
- ✓ 93% offer free high speed wireless Internet
- ✓ Most B&Bs provide the following in common areas: Internet, magazines, hot/cold beverages, board games, fireplace, refrigerator, newspapers, telephone, cookies/cakes/candies/fruit, fresh flowers and televisions.
- ✓ Most B&Bs provide the following in guest rooms: Internet, television, luxury bed/linens, premium branded toiletries, robes, fireplaces, magazines and jetted tubs.

Expenses as a percentage of annual sales

Cost of goods	15%
Payroll/labor Costs	10%
Occupancy	10%
Profit (estimated pretax)	10%

Industry Trend

- "B&Bs primarily cater to affluent travelers and getaway couples. That market appears to be growing. This is also the market that the next generation of innkeepers is coming from."

Seller Financing

- "The typical $1M+ inn sale would typically have a buyer w/$200K down and the seller would typically offer a 2nd mortgage for the gap between that amount and 70% of the sale/appraised price. Conventional commercial lending would provide up to 70% of the sale. Recently, we've seen sellers doing all the financing for inn buyers. It's a better return on the loan than alternative investments. Additionally, the seller can receive a higher price by offering attractive, below-market loan terms."
- "Inns that are < $700K, conventional commercial financing is available. Over $700K, the seller and the SBA is usually involved. Typically it's buyer 10%, seller 25% and lender 65%."
- "7 years"
- "Seller is often 2nd 10 percent of sales price, 20-year term, 7-year balloon."
- "5 to 8 years; partial financing"

Questions

- "Can you show me how your B&B will work for me financially and in lifestyle?"

Resources

Websites

- Inns for Sale—This site has inns and B&Bs for sale and also offers educational programs: www.innsforsale.com
- Information for B & B owners: www.bedandbreakfast.com

Associations

- Michigan Lake to Lake Bed & Breakfast Association: www.laketolake.com
- Professional Association of Innkeepers International—a wonderful site, lots of good information: www.innkeeping.org

Bedding and Mattress Shops—Retail (See also Furniture Stores)		
SIC 5712-09	NAICS 442110	Number of Businesses/Units 9,227

Rules of Thumb

> 35 percent of annual sales plus inventory

Pricing Tips

- "More retail locations equal more favorable manufacturer pricing."

Expert Comments

"Bedding continues to be a needed product and the consumer now has a perceived need for enhanced comfort and a better night's rest."

Benchmark Data

Statistics (Bed and Mattress Stores)

Number of Establishments	9,227
Average Profit Margin	1.5%
Revenue per Employee	$254,800
Average Number of Employees	5.0
Average Wages per Employee	$30,227

Products and Services Segmentation

Traditional mattresses	49.3%
Specialty mattresses	23.1%
Frames and box springs	19.0%
Other, including bedding and pillows	8.6%

Industry Costs

Profit	1.5%
Wages	12.1%
Purchases	60.3%
Depreciation	0.5%
Marketing	6.7%
Rent & Utilities	7.0%
Other	11.9%

Market Share

Mattress Firm	20.9%
Select Comfort Corporation	9.8%
Sleepy's	7.2%

Source: IBISWorld, March 2015

- "Increased ticket % for same store sales for the same month as opposed to previous year."

Expenses as a percentage of annual sales

Cost of goods	25%
Payroll/labor Costs	10%
Occupancy	20%
Profit (estimated pretax)	45%

Industry Trend

- "Furniture and bedding retail sales increased an estimated 3.9% this year, reaching $102 billion. This is the first time sales have topped the $100 billion mark since before the housing collapse and the Great Recession began in 2007. Looking ahead, Furniture/Today and the statisticians from Easy Analytic Software Inc. predict overall furniture and bedding sales will grow by 19.6% over the next five years to a total of $122 billion in 2020."

Source: "Furniture and bedding sales projected to grow 19.6% by 2020," by Dana French, *Furniture Today*, February 16, 2016

Questions

- "What is the reason for selling? Where do you stand in terms of your relationships with the major bedding suppliers? What customer service issues might be pending?"

Resources

Trade Publications

- Bedding Today: www.furnituretoday.com/

Franchise

Beef 'O' Brady's Family Sports Pubs (See also Franchises)	
Approx. Total Investment	$631,000 to $1,073,000
Estimated Annual Sales/Unit	$1,000,000
NAICS 722410	Number of Businesses/Units 200

Rules of Thumb

➤ 25 percent of annual sales plus inventory

Resources

Websites

- www.beefobradys.com

Beer Distributorships/Wholesalers

SIC 5181-01	NAICS 422810	Number of Businesses/Units 4,601

Rules of Thumb

➤ $5.00 to $15 per case sold over the last 12 months; add hard assets & inventory. Multiple per case is dependent on brands sold—the popular ones command the higher multiples.

➤ "These types of distributing businesses are usually sold for the price of inventory at cost, plus the rolling stock, plus the land and improvements, if these are part of the sale, plus $1.00 for each case delivered per year, plus $1.50 for each keg delivered per year."

Pricing Tips

▪ "The two most important characteristics are (1) the brands carried, and (2) the territory. Brands vary considerably in market sales, and also vary regionally. Territories that are densely populated tend to be serviced more efficiently."

▪ 1 U.S. BBL (beer barrel) = 31 U.S. gallons = 13.778 = 24/12-oz. cases

Expert Comments

"Franchise restrictions are important constraints on resale."

Benchmark Data

Statistics (Beer Wholesaling)

Number of Establishments	4,601
Average Profit Margin	4.3%
Revenue per Employee	$555,400
Average Number of Employees	25.4
Average Wages per Employee	$50,539

Products and Services Segmentation

Cans of beer and ale	46.1%
Bottles of beer and ale	36.3%
Barrels and kegs of beer and ale	10.4%
Other malt beverages and brewing products	7.2%

Major Market Segmentation

Retail liquor stores	46.2%
Grocery stores and supermarkets	30.2%
Downstream wholesalers	15.6%
Restaurants, drinking establishments and hotels	7.4%
Other	0.6%

Industry Costs

Profit	4.3%
Wages	9.1%
Purchases	59.7%
Depreciation	1.0%
Marketing	4.7%
Rent & Utilities	3.0%
Other	18.2%

Enterprises by Employment Size

Number of Employees	Percentage
0 to 4	24.8%
10 to 19	10.8%
20 to 99	35.0%
100 to 499	18.0%

Source: IBISWorld, March 2016

- "97% of U.S. breweries produce less than 60,000 barrels per year
"93% of U.S. breweries produce less than 15,000 barrels per year
"91% of U.S. breweries produce less than 7,143 barrels per year
(Note: 7,143 barrels is a measurement the U.S. Alcohol and Tobacco Tax and Trade Bureau uses for a paperwork reduction rule for filing federal excise taxes.)"

Source: "Data Show Craft Brewers with Double Digit Volume Share of U.S. Beer Market," http://www.nbwa.org/news/america%E2%80%99s-beer-distributors-applaud-continued-growth-craft-beer 3/19/15

- "Market values for beer distributors tend to be discussed as a multiple of cases sold in the past 12 months. These often vary from $5 to $15 per case sold, for well-established brands and successful operations. Struggling brands and operations can be priced less. There is no comparable metric for wine or spirits."

Industry Trend

- "Craft brewers now represent more than 10 percent of the beer volume sold in the U.S. marketplace—the first time the craft segment has reached double-digit volume."

Source: "Data Show Craft Brewers with Double Digit Volume Share of U.S. Beer Market," http://www.nbwa.org/news/america%E2%80%99s-beer-distributors-applaud-continued-growth-craft-beer 3/19/15

- "The 'three-tier' system set up in most states after Prohibition is being challenged, at least on the edges, by interstate shipping of wine. Legal developments in this area will affect the value of wine distributors, although not beer distributors, over the next few years. Once you have a good operation in a decent area, this business will keep producing cash. Remember, the beer and wine business is over 2,000 years old."

Resources

Websites
- Beer Institute: www.beerinstitute.org

Trade Publications
- Beer Marketer's Insights: www.beerinsights.com

Associations
- The National Beer Wholesalers Association (NBWA)—an informative Web site: www.nbwa.org

Beer Taverns—Beer & Wine (See also Bars, Brew Pubs)

	NAICS 722410	

Rules of Thumb

➤ 6 times monthly sales plus inventory

➤ 1 to 1.5 times annual EBIT

➤ 55 percent of annual sales plus inventory

Pricing Tips

▪ "There are 1,980 ounces in a keg, less 10 percent waste, about 1,700 net ounces per keg. If there are 12 ounces (net) in a glass of beer, divide 12 ounces into 1,700 net ounces per keg to determine cost and number of glasses that should be poured from that keg. Determine what a 12-ounce glass of beer is selling for, then multiply that times the number of glasses that is poured from the keg. This will give you the total gross per keg."

Resources

Websites

▪ Beer Institute—has an excellent site: www.beerinstitute.org

Beer & Wine Stores—Retail (See also Liquor Stores/Package Stores)

SIC 5921-04	NAICS 445310	

Rules of Thumb

➤ 4 times monthly sales plus inventory

Benchmark Data

▪ For Benchmark Data see Liquor Stores

	Franchise
Ben & Jerry's Homemade, Inc.	
(See also Franchises, Ice Cream/Yogurt Shops)	
Approx. Total Investment	$188,485 to $485,800
Estimated Annual Sales/Unit	$300,000

SIC 2024-98	NAICS 722515	

Rules of Thumb

➤ 35 to 40 percent of annual sales plus inventory

	Franchise

Between Rounds Bakery Sandwich Café

(See also Franchises, Sandwich Shops)

Approx. Total Investment	$1,000,000 net worth
Estimated Annual Sales/Unit	$600,000

SIC 5461-01	NAICS 722513	Number of Businesses/Units 4

Rules of Thumb

➢ 40 to 45 percent of annual sales plus inventory

Resources

Websites

▪ Between Rounds: www.betweenroundsbagels.com

Bicycle Shops

SIC 5941-41	NAICS 451110	Number of Businesses/Units 4,130

Rules of Thumb

➢ 20 percent of annual sales plus inventory

➢ 1.5 times SDE plus inventory

Pricing Tips

▪ "Gross profit should be at a minimum in the 40-45% range. Inventory turns should 2.4x-2.7x. Check whether the business is over-inventoried. This is a common problem with bike shops. Also check to see that the inventory is current and sale-able. How much inventory is left over from last year? Will the buyer be able to retain the relationships with the manufacturers, ensuring a steady stream of product. Single brand shops have difficulty surviving in our market."

▪ "If shops don't repair as well as sell, they could lose most of their income. Need to have mechanic in store!"

Expert Comments

"Success or failure of bicycle shops is directly tied to the owner/operator. While brands and location can be a factor, it is the dedication of the owner to the bicycling industry and his/her participation in community events, industry shows, and local business organizations that makes a difference. In many ways, owners are subject to the whims of manufacturers and the changing tastes of the public. Inventory control is key and owners have to be quick on their feet and be able to respond to a constantly changing environment in the cycling industry."

Benchmark Data

Statistics (Bicycle Dealership and Repair)

Number of Establishments... 4,130
Average Profit Margin 4.2%
Revenue per Employee $198,300
Average Number of Employees 4.7
Average Wages per Employee $39,423

Products and Services Segmentation

Hybrid/cross bicycles 32.0%
Mountain bicycles 29.0%
Road bicycles 22.0%
Other bicycles 17.0%

Industry Costs

Profit 4.2%
Wages... 20.2%
Purchases 62.3%
Depreciation.. 0.9%
Marketing 3.0%
Rent & Utilities 7.7%
Other.. 1.7%

Source: IBISWorld, October 2015

- "According to the NBDA's 2015 Specialty Bicycle Retail Survey, the average bike store is now larger in both dollar volume (over $1 million per year, an all-time high), and physical size (6,461 square feet), than ever before. They are also improving in sales efficiency, with average sales of $185 per square foot, a record high for these surveys, and an increase of 3% from the previous year."
  Source: http://independentbikeblog.com/2015/07/17/survey-shows-rising-dealer-metrics-in-a-flat-market/

Average Expenses for Specialty Bicycle Retailers

(Expenses expressed as a percentage of gross annual sales)
Payroll Expenses 20.5%
Occupancy Expenses 7.7%
Advertising/Promotion.. 3.0%
Auto and Delivery 0.5%
Depreciation.. 0.9%
Insurance 0.8%
Licenses/Other Taxes 0.5%
Professional Services 0.5%
Office Supplies/Postage 1.2%
Telephone 0.6%
Travel/Entertainment.. 0.4%
Other operating expenses 1.3%
Total Operating Expenses.. 37.7%
Net Income before Tax.. 4.2%
Gross Margin on Bicycle Sales.. 36%
Gross Margin on Clothing Sales 43%
Gross Margin Other Equipment 48.1%

Source: "NBDA Cost of Doing Business Survey, 8/15/16"

Expenses as a percentage of annual sales

Cost of goods... 55%
Payroll/labor Costs... 0
Occupancy... 08%
Profit (estimated pretax) 08%

Industry Trend

- "2014 was a comeback year for the U.S. bicycle industry, with direct effect sales of $6.1 billion, including retail sales of bicycles, related parts and accessories, through all channels of distribution. This compares to $5.8 billion in sales in 2013. The source is the U.S. Bicycle Market 2014 report prepared for the NBDA by the Gluskin Townley Group."

  Source: http://nbda.com/articles/industry-overview-2014-pg34.htm

- "An emerging trend is the web-based, direct sale to consumer business model that has emerged in the past five years. It's the trickle down of the Amazon style of online selling that is being adopted by specific industries, such as bicycling, and it is a direct threat to the retail model. Shop owners have to be alert to this threat and need to be prepared to challenge it with excellent customer service and customer engagement."

- "The number of independent bicycle dealers is dropping, from a high of about 8,000 in the early 1980s to about 5,000 in early 2004. The bicycle retail industry typically loses about 1,000 bicycle dealers each year, mostly start-ups, but gains that many back because of even more start-ups. However, the overall number of storefronts has been declining in the last few years. Many people have lost their lives' savings in the retail bicycle business because they loved bikes but didn't have a similar zest for the art of retailing. Bike shops run by people who are only bicycle hobbyists, and not business people, typically find the going tough in today's competitive market.

  "Add all that to the overall slim profitability in the bicycle industry, and you can really get depressed. NBDA studies show the typical bicycle dealer needs about a 36% profit margin to cover the costs of doing business and break even financially. Studies also show the average realized profit margin on bicycles to be around 36%, which is a break-even proposition devoid of profit. Fortunately accessories products generally carry a higher profit margin than bicycles. Still, the average bike dealer's profit is less than 5% at year's end—about $25,000 for an average size store of $500,000 in annual sales.

  "The level of innovation and diversity has never been higher in 'dealer-quality' bicycle products. The number of entrepreneurial companies designing and manufacturing appealing products for the public is high, both in bicycles and accessories items. There isn't any part on a bicycle which hasn't been improved in the last five or so years. The bicycle is tied to health, vitality, fun and exercise. The bicycle is one of the least expensive transportation choices available, as well as a wonderful tool for fitness and fun. The bicycle affects people's lives in very positive ways, and its use contributes to the betterment of the environment.

  "Cycling participation is solid. There are approximately 45 million adult 'cyclists' today, and cycling ranks fifth on the list of most popular outdoor recreational activities."

  Source: NBDA

- "Mobile bike repair, e-bike dealers, and private label bikes are industry trends worth watching, according to Scott Chapin, bicycle industry risk specialist with

Marsh & McClennan Agency in Minneapolis. Here are some of the trends from Scott's position on the front lines of the bicycle insurance world:
- ✓ Mobile bike shops
- ✓ E-bike dealers
- ✓ Spin-off bike rental business
- ✓ Spin-off bicycle tour/guide services
- ✓ Online retailers
- ✓ Private labeling
- "The Internet Challenge—Competition from large Internet companies was rated as the biggest challenge facing independent retailers, with 71% ranking Internet competition as a very or extremely significant challenge. Among bike dealers, an emphatic 97% agreed.
  - ✓ "Pricing and Terms—Another issue was supplier pricing and terms that favor big competitors 'to use their market power to pressure suppliers.' 63% said regulators should more vigorously enforce antitrust laws against large and dominant companies.
  - ✓ "Insurance and Rent—High costs for health insurance were cited by many as a problem, as well as growing expenses for effective marketing. Bike dealers added two other challenges to the mix: high occupancy cost relative to sales, and competition from large brick-and-mortar stores."

Source: "The Independent Bike Blog," March 26, 2015

Seller Financing
- "Outside financing via the SBA is common, with some seller financing involved. Most buyers have to finance the purchase, since the value of inventory can be very high."

Resources

Trade Publications
- Outspoken: Published by the NBDA
- Bicycle Retailer & Industry News—an informative site: www.bicycleretailer.com

Associations
- Bicycle Product Suppliers Association—excellent site, well worth visiting: www.bpsa.org
- National Bicycle Dealers Association (NBDA): www.nbda.com
- People For Bikes: www.peopleforbikes.org

	Franchise
Big Apple Bagels (See also Bagel Shops, Franchises)	
Approx. Total Investment	$294,700 to $398,100
Estimated Annual Sales/Unit	$350,000
NAICS 722513	Number of Businesses/Units 100

Rules of Thumb
- ➤ 35 to 40 percent of annual sales plus inventory

Resources

Websites
- www.babcorp.com

Big City Burrito (See also Franchises)	Franchise
NAICS 722513	Number of Businesses/Units 9

Rules of Thumb

➢ 50%–55% of annual sales plus inventory

Resources

Websites
- www.bigcityburrito.com

Big O Tires (See also Auto Tire Stores, Franchises)	Franchise
Approx. Total Investment	$238,000 to $1,125,000
NAICS 441320	Number of Businesses/Units 361

Rules of Thumb

➢ 35 percent of annual sales plus inventory

Resources

Websites
- Big O Tires: www.bigotires.com

Billboard Advertising Companies (Outdoor Advertising)		
SIC 7312-01	NAICS 541850	Number of Businesses/Units 14,156

Rules of Thumb

➢ 12 times EBITDA

➢ 500 percent of annual sales

Pricing Tips

- "Billboards are bought and sold based on multiples of Net Revenue and Cash Flow, so these are the most common methods of valuation."
- "Values of billboard companies tend to be higher in large metropolitan areas, and lower in rural areas. Prices tend to be between 3 x and 6 x annual revenue."
- "EBITDA is normally 45% to 50%. Cap rates tend to be very low, usually more like real estate than an operating business. Acquirers prefer long-term leases at low rates for existing billboard locations."

- "Billboard companies are usually worth surprisingly high prices in the market. Buyers and sellers rely almost exclusively on market multiples that are widely recognized as the best measures of fair market value. Discount rates and capitalization rates in this industry are more closely aligned with real estate yields than returns on operating businesses."

    Source: "Appraising Billboard Companies" by Jeffrey P. Wright, ASA, CFA, Business Valuation Review

Expert Comments

"Industry growing, difficult to build new billboards"

"Revenue growth is up, while other advertising media are experiencing trouble. City, county and state rules controlling new billboard construction continue to tighten."

Benchmark Data

Statistics (Billboard & Outdoor Advertising)

Number of Establishments.. 14,156
Average Profit Margin 16.3%
Revenue per Employee $194,300
Average Number of Employees.. 3.0
Average Wages per Employee $42,344

Products and Services Segmentation

Billboards: bulletin.. 59.2%
Billboards: poster... 16.8%
Alternative and other leased displays 9.0%
Street furniture and other urban fixture displays.............................. 8.8%
Transit displays 6.1%

Major Market Segmentation

Other.. 22.7%
Miscellaneous retailers 14.5%
Financial, professional and real estate services 13.2%
Media and other entertainment companies 11.5%
Food and drink, including restaurants.. 11.1%
Nonemploying businesses and individuals....................................... 11.0%
Government and nonprofit advertisers 8.3%
Healthcare and pharmaceutical companies...................................... 7.7%

Industry Costs

Profit 16.3%
Wages.. 21.7%
Purchases.. 28.5%
Depreciation... 13.0%
Marketing 2.9%
Rent & Utilities 15.4%
Other.. 2.2%

B - Rules of Thumb

Market Share

Lamar Advertising Company	18.5%
Outfront Media Inc.	17.1%
Clear Channel Outdoor Holdings	15.2%

Source: IBISWorld, July 2016

- "Achieving cash flow margins of 35% or higher"
- "Net revenue multiples range from 3 to 8 times, and cash flow multiples range from 7 to 18 times."

Expenses as a percentage of annual sales

Cost of goods	05%
Payroll/labor Costs	05%
Occupancy	10%
Profit (estimated pretax)	45%

Industry Trend

- "'OOH's ability to augment mobile, online, and social media efforts is one of the many reasons the industry posted strong growth with both local and national advertisers in 2015,' said Stephen Freitas, OAAA chief marketing officer. 'The expansion of digital OOH formats provides advertisers with broader opportunities to engage with today's mobile consumers. These factors are the foundation for the positive outlook media analysts are projecting for OOH over the next few years.'"

Source: https://www.oaaa.org/NewsEvents/PressReleases/tabid/327/id/4437/Default.aspx

Seller Financing

5 years

Questions

- "Net revenue, cash flow, lease costs and occupancy levels"

Resources

Trade Publications

- BPS Outdoor: www.bpsoutdoor.com

Associations

- Outdoor Advertising Association of America: www.oaaa.org

Billiards (See also American Poolplayers Association)		
SIC 7999-12	NAICS 339920	

Rules of Thumb

➢ 50 percent of annual sales plus inventory

Industry Trend

- "Over the five years to 2014, revenue the Pool and Billiards Halls industry has steadily declined as a result of the recession and poor consumer sentiment. Because the industry is highly sensitive to changes in per capita disposable income, the subsequent decrease in the Consumer Confidence Index following the recession discouraged consumers from spending on leisurely activities such as pool and billiards. Furthermore, the industry faces fierce external competition from other bars and nightclubs that offer similar services to the casual pool player, as well as increasing alternative entertainment options such as video games and mobile technology."

Source: IBISWorld, May 2014

Resources

Associations
- Billiard Congress of America: http://home.bca-pool.com/

	Franchise
Blackjack Pizza (See also Franchises, Pizza Shops)	
SIC 5812-22 NAICS 722513	Number of Businesses/Units 45

Rules of Thumb
- ➤ 40% percent of annual sales plus inventory
- ➤ 3 to 4 times SDE (15% discount for cash) plus inventory

Resources

Websites
- Blackjack Pizza: www.blackjackpizza.com

	Franchise
Blimpie—America's Sub Shop (See also Franchises, Sandwich Shops)	
Approx. Total Investment	$130,450 to $359,050
Estimated Annual Sales/Unit	$185,000
SIC 5812-19 NAICS 722513	Number of Businesses/Units 360

Rules of Thumb
- ➤ 45 to 50 percent of annual sales plus inventory

Benchmark Data
- For Benchmark Data see Sandwich Shops

Resources

Websites
- Blimpie: www.kahalamgmt.com

Blood and Organ Banks

	NAICS 621991	

Rules of Thumb

➤ 51 percent of annual sales includes inventory

➤ 1.8 times SDE includes inventory

➤ 3 times EBIT

➤ 2.9 times EBITDA

Benchmark Data

Expenses as a percentage of annual sales

Cost of goods	13%
Payroll/labor Costs	01%
Profit (estimated pretax)	11%

Industry Trend

- "Profit expected to shrink, revenue is expected to grow, demand continues to grow."

Seller Financing

- "Outside financing"

Questions

- "Payor mix, market share, patient demographic data"

Resources

Websites

- America's Blood Centers: www.americasblood.org

Associations

- American Association of Blood Banks: www.aabb.org

Boat Dealers (See also Marinas)

SIC 5551-04	NAICS 441222	Number of Businesses/Units 118,243

Rules of Thumb

➤ 2 to 3 times SDE includes used boat inventory, parts and FF&E

➤ "Most dealerships finance their new boat inventory with flooring companies which are now requiring some type of industry background and/or experience. In most cases the new owner will take over the financing arrangements with the flooring companies for all current and future new boat inventory. The multiple can vary depending."

Pricing Tips

- "Boat dealerships in the Pacific Northwest typically sell for 2–3 times SDE which includes used boat inventory, parts and FF&E."

Benchmark Data

Statistics (Boat Dealership and Repair)

Number of Establishments	118,243
Average Profit Margin	5.9%
Revenue per Employee	$135,200
Average Number of Employees	1.3
Average Wages per Employee	$16,511

Products and Services Segmentation

New boats	56.5%
Parts and repair services	29.7%
Used boats	13.8%

Industry Costs

Profit	5.9%
Wages	12.2%
Purchases	63.6%
Depreciation	1.0%
Marketing	1.3%
Rent & Utilities	3.6%
Other	12.4%

Market Share

MarineMax Inc.	4.2%

Source: IBISWorld, July 2016

Industry Trend

- "Memorial Day weekend signals the start of the summer boating season, and today the National Marine Manufacturers Association (NMMA) reports boat sales are strong for the $35.9 billion U.S. recreational boating industry. An estimated 238,000 new powerboats were sold in 2015, an increase of 8.5 percent compared to 2014. NMMA anticipates sales of new powerboats to increase in 2016 as much as 5 to 7 percent.

  "'New boat inventories are at historically low levels and production is on the rise, driven by an acceleration in demand for new boats,' said Thom Dammrich, NMMA president. 'Summer is a heavy selling season for recreational boats, accessories and services throughout the U.S. and we anticipate sustained steady growth across most boat categories during the busiest boating months of the year.'"

  Source: "Boat Sales on the Rise Heading Into Summer," May 24, 2016, http://www.nmma.org/press/article/20566

- "The retail side of the recreational boating industry improved again this year, and we expect more of the same in 2016. Industry trends will continue to bode well for businesses and consumers. Boating participation remains strong for the fifth straight year. While new-unit sales are not exceeding pre-2007

performance, they are slowly rising into positive territory.
"Boat loan capacity will remain positive in 2016 as more lenders, both wholesale and retail, serve the needs of this important business space. The latest survey of key marine lenders reveals that boat loan underwriting guidelines are steady and boat loan bookings continue to increase.
"Marine lenders indicated they remain optimistic for new-loan volume in 2016. Consumer boat loan delinquency rates also remain low, as lenders project delinquency will remain stable in 2016."

Source: Jim Coburn, http://www.tradeonlytoday.com/features/industry-news/misc-news/outlook-2016/

Resources

Associations

- National Marine Manufacturers Association (NMMA): www.nmma.org

		Franchise
Boba Loca Specialty Drinks (See also Franchises)		
	NAICS 722515	Number of Businesses/Units 23

Rules of Thumb

➢ 30 percent of annual sales plus inventory

Resources

Websites

- Boba Loca Specialty Drinks: www.bobaloca.com

Book Stores—Adult		
SIC 5942-01	NAICS 451211	

Rules of Thumb

➢ 100 percent of annual sales includes inventory

Pricing Tips

- "Half down at closing; other half financed and used to prove gross sales (a kind of earnout schedule)"

Expert Comments

"Internet retail is driving down profits."

Benchmark Data

- "1,000 SF should equal $200k–$250k in gross sales."

Expenses as a percentage of annual sales

Cost of goods	20%
Payroll/labor Costs	n/a
Occupancy	12%
Profit (estimated pretax)	40%

Industry Trend
- "Slight drop but steady in some markets."

Book Stores—New Books

SIC 5942-01	NAICS 451211	Number of Businesses/Units 22,945

Rules of Thumb

➢ 15 to 20 percent of annual sales plus inventory

➢ 1.5 to 2 SDE plus inventory

Pricing Tips
- "The underlying lease is very important. The inventory turns should be between 4 and 5 times. It is important that the store is diligently returning new book inventory as allowed."
- "We don't use EBIT or EBITDA because the owner pretty much always works in the business. Normalizing for an industry standard expense would drive EBIT or EBITDA towards zero, making the multiple unrealistic. One note is that gift certificates outstanding need to be accounted for and treated as a liability. Lots of negotiation around this point."
- "Management should have an ongoing program to return new, unsold books to publishers. This keeps inventory fresh. Occupancy costs and lease terms are critical, of course. A store with lots of community involvement (school book fairs, author events, book groups) will do better than average. Best prices can be derived by 'going public' with availability, assuring an emotionally connected buyer. For stores with good reputations, buyers will be eager to engage."
- "Gross margin, occupancy costs, diversity of products (non-book items), frequency of community events are all important factors when considering the price of a book store."

Expert Comments

"An independent bookstore doing over $2,000,000 in an affluent, highly educated community can be sold."

"Anyone can open a bookstore, but many cannot succeed as they don't attract buyers. One needs to attract buyers by becoming part of the community. Many landlords like having bookstores, as they attract foot traffic."

27th Edition

Benchmark Data

Statistics (Book Stores)

Number of Establishments	22,945
Average Profit Margin	2.3%
Revenue per Employee	$127,000
Average Number of Employees	4.4
Average Wages per Employee	$15,040

Products and Services Segmentation

Other merchandise	33.5%
Textbooks	29.4%
Trade books	26.9%
Religious goods (including books)	5.3%
Magazines and newspapers	4.9%

Industry Costs

Profit	2.3%
Wages	11.9%
Purchases	59.7%
Depreciation	1.0%
Marketing	1.4%
Rent & Utilities	8.0%
Other	15.7%

Market Share

Barnes & Noble Inc.	27.5%
Follett Higher Education Group	7.5%

Source: IBISWorld, October 2015

- "One would like to see sales over $200 psf. Occupancy needs to be less than 10%. Cost of goods sold should approach 50%, unless it is a discounter, in which case it may be lower."
- "Sales per square foot need to be in excess of $200. Gross margin needs to approach 50% if not exceed this. Occupancy should be less than 8% of sales. A well-run café, even if outsourced, is a plus. A healthy sidelines business helps margins quite a bit."
- "Inventory turns of 3–4 times should be realized. Non-book sales should be at least 20% of overall sales. Store should be doing at least one event per week."

Expenses as a percentage of annual sales

Cost of goods	30% to 35%
Payroll/labor Costs	20% to 25%
Occupancy	06% to 10%
Profit (estimated pretax)	02% to 04%

Industry Trend

- "Online retail remained the top sales channel for publishers' revenue in the trade category, with 37.4% of the market. About 806 million units were sold online in 2015. Publishers saw increased revenue from trade book sales at physical retail stores for the second year in a row. In 2015, physical store sales grew 1.8% from $4.08 billion to $4.15 billion. More than 610 million trade book units were sold in 2015. Physical store sales comprise about 26.2% of publisher revenue.

"These sales channel numbers reflect how publishers get books into the marketplace, not retailers' revenue from consumers. While StatShot channel sales data can provide directional information about trends, the data is limited for trade books, as much of the business occurs through wholesale and distribution."

Source: "U.S. Publishing Industry's Annual Survey Reveals Nearly $28 Billion in Revenue in 2015," July 11, 2016, http://newsroom.publishers.org/us-publishing-industrys-annual-survey-reveals-nearly-28-billion-in-revenue-in-2015/

- "Independent businesses experienced healthy sales growth in 2015, buoyed by their strong community ties and growing public awareness of the benefits of locally owned businesses, according to the Independent Business Survey, released on Wednesday, February 10, by the Institute for Local Self-Reliance in partnership with the Advocates for Independent Business.

"The survey, now in its ninth year, gathered data from more than 3,200 independent businesses, including bookstore members of the American Booksellers Association. Respondents to the survey reported brisk sales in 2015, with revenue growing an average of 6.6 percent. Among independent retailers, who comprised just under half of survey respondents, revenue increased 4.7 percent in 2015, including a 3.1 percent gain during the holiday season. The survey report noted that these figures were in sharp contrast to the performance of many national retail chains, and overall holiday retail sales, which, according to the U.S. Department of Commerce, rose just 1.6 percent in December."

Source: "Survey Finds Indie Businesses Growing, But Policies Favor Large Companies," February 10, 2016, http://www.bookweb.org/news/survey-finds-indie-businesses-growing-policies-favor-large-companies

- "But the good news is that the indies are quietly resurging across the nation, registering a growth of over 30 percent since 2009 and sales that were up around 10 percent last year, according to the American Booksellers Association, the indies' main organization with more than 2,200 stores.

"'Existing stores are selling once more to a new generation of owners,' said Oren Teicher, the A.B.A.'s chief executive officer, noting that such stores could never be resold during the gloomiest years, when they were under threat from Barnes & Noble and then later, Internet sales."

Source: editorial by Francis X. Clines, *The New York Times*, February 13, 2016

- "Gradual growth in the number of independent bookstores, but the ones coming in are small. Owners of larger bookstores are aging out, but being replaced with relatively old owners (70+ selling to 50+). Competition will continue to increase from online sources, so the store has to be a community gathering spot to be successful."

Seller Financing

- "Usually, these stores are sold to wealthy buyers for cash. If there is any financing, it is typically from the sellers. Due to the high risk in the industry, seller financing is limited."

Questions

- "Sales trends, community standing, online sales, Website condition, staffing quality"

- "Tenure of staff, number of events, social media exposure, program of inventory returns, seasonality and is there a frequent buyer program in place."

Resources

Trade Publications
- Independent Bookselling Today-This site offers good information on opening a bookstore.: www.pazbookbiz.com
- Publishers Weekly: www.publishersweekly.com

Associations
- American Booksellers Association: www.bookweb.org

Book Stores—Rare and Used (See also Book Stores)		
SIC 5932-01	NAICS 453310	

Rules of Thumb

➤ 10 to 15 percent of annual sales plus inventory. In the case of rare books, the cost of the inventory would be based on some form of wholesale value or less the bookseller's standard markup.

Pricing Tips

- "Used book stores seem to be a vanishing business. Many owners of these stores have closed them and now offer their books online. Rare book stores would have the same multiple as used stores, perhaps a bit higher. The real value is the inventory."
- "In response to your question about a pricing rule of thumb [we had emailed our request for this to Susan Siegel of Book Hunter Press, and perhaps the leading authority on used bookstores in the U.S.], I'm not aware of any, but I doubt that even if one existed it would be helpful. But then, I must confess that I haven't been involved in buying or selling a business.

  "The reason for my skepticism: even among just-open shops, there is such a wide, wide range of inventory, that the same pricing mechanism could not automatically be used for all shops. Two shops may each have 10,000 books—but very, very different books in terms of wholesale or retail value.

  "The inventory in new bookstores is pretty homogeneous; this is not the case in a used bookstore. Even within a given store, there could be a range of value in the inventory with mass market paperbacks selling at one price point and hard-to-find hardcovers selling for $25-50+.

  "Stores with vastly different size inventories can have the same gross sales, depending on what types of books they are selling. In my humble judgment, one would have to arrive at a selling price based on the value of the inventory for that particular store, as well as that store's sales records.

  "One problem is that most dealers have only a small portion of their inventory computerized. And I have no idea of what type of pencil and paper records they keep for tax purposes on the cost of what they've bought.

  "Open shops that have gone out of business have disposed of their inventory in several different ways. Assuming that they can't sell the business to someone else who will continue it as a used bookstore (usually the first choice), some sell off their inventory to another, larger dealer. This may or may not involve donating the undesirable volumes to a library.

"Some dealers close their shops, sell off a portion of their inventory, and continue selling online with a smaller inventory, often, but not always, in a specialty area/s."

Source: Susan Siegel, Book Hunter Press

Benchmark Data

- "Three quarters of the dealers [open shops] sold an average of more than 200 books per month with 23% selling 200–499 books, followed closely by 21% selling 500–999 books a month. Sixteen percent of the open shops sold 2,000 or more books per month.

  "For shops in the most frequent open-shop size category (25,000–44,999 volumes), 31% of the dealers sold an average of 500–999 volumes per month, followed by 28% selling 200–499 volumes. Only 8% of the dealers within this size category sold fewer than 200 books per month and, at the other extreme, 16% sold 2,000 books or more."

  Source: *A Portrait of the U.S. Used Book Market*, published by Book Hunter Press. Note: A bit dated, but still valuable information and probably still very accurate.

Book Stores—Religious (See also Book Stores—New Books)

SIC 5942-11	NAICS 451211	

Rules of Thumb

➤ 15 percent of annual sales plus inventory

Resources

Associations

- The Association for Christian Retail: www.cbaonline.org

Bowling Centers

SIC 7933-01	NAICS 713950	Number of Businesses/Units 3,700

Rules of Thumb

➤ 160 to 180 percent of annual sales plus inventory

➤ "Maybe 2 times annual sales in highly exceptional situation"

➤ 5 to 6.5 times SDE plus inventory

➤ 5 to 6.5 times EBITDA

Pricing Tips

- "Going rate for sales of centers including the real estate is 1.6 to 2.0 times gross revenues and/or 5.5 to 6.0 times EBITDA. EBITDA runs about 25% to 30% of revenues depending on volume, product mix, etc."

- "Location, age of equipment, physical condition of facility and additional amenities are important factors."
- "All multiples if real estate included. If leased, 4–5 times EBITDA after lease expense."
- "$40,000 to $60,000 per lane for older centers. Newer centers up to $80,000 per lane (price must fit cash flow)."
- "Needed capital expenditures are a deduction."
- "Larger centers, metro markets and facilities in top physical condition each attract higher prices. Smaller centers, those in rural markets and/or those in need of capital get lower prices."

Expert Comments

"Owner needs attention to detail, focus on superior customer service, cater to specific demographics in local market."

"As the economy improves, most bowling centers are doing much better than in recent prior years."

"Location is critical factor. Demographics, access, size of population base are important."

"Bowling generally does well in tough times; cheap recreation close to home."

"Bowling centers are expensive to build."

"Historical trend, i.e., stability of performance, very important. Competition is not very important."

Benchmark Data

Statistics (Bowling Alleys)

Number of Establishments	3,700
Average Profit Margin	3.3%
Revenue per Employee	$53,200
Average Number of Employees	18.1
Average Wages per Employee	$13,934

Products and Services Segmentation

Restaurant	27.9%
Other	18.7%
Bowling—open play	13.3%
Bar/lounge	11.8%
Laser tag	9.7%
Bowling—league play	8.4%
Snack bar	7.2%
Shoe rental	3.0%

Industry Costs

Profit	3.3%
Wages	26.7%
Purchases	19.9%
Depreciation	5.4%
Marketing	2.2%
Rent & Utilities	17.4%
Other	25.1%

Market Share

Bowlmor AMFF 14.9%

Source: IBISWorld, March 2016

- Traditional sales per sq. ft. $60; BEC sales per sq. ft. $75

Gross Revenues per Lane per Year

Excellent	$40,000 or more
Good	$35,000 to $40,000
Average	$29,000 to $34,000
Inadequate	$28,000 or less

Controllable Expenses

Payroll—Bowling	30% of lineage revenues
Payroll—Bar	20% of bar revenues
Payroll—Food	25%–30% of snack bar revenues
Total Payroll	25%–28% of total revenues
Payroll Taxes	13% of total payroll
Employee Benefits	05%–07% of total payroll
Total Employee Costs	28%–33% of total revenues
Advertising & Promotion	03% of total revenues
Repair, Maintenance & Supplies	05%–06% of total revenues*
Utilities	05%–07% of total revenues

*Varies with age and condition of center, building and equipment

Operating Income** as % of Total Revenues

Above Average	Average	Below Average
30%–33%	25%–28%	20%–22%

**Operating Income is defined as the funds generated by an operation before interest, real estate rent, non-recurring expenses, principal payments, capital improvements, depreciation and owner's salaries (above normal limits) and fringe benefits.

Courtesy: Sandy Hansell & Associates, Bowling's Only Full-Service Brokers, Appraisers & Financial Advisors, (800) 222-9131, June 2015

- "The 2014 Experian Simmons National Consumer Survey found that the median income of a bowling household is over $76,000 per year. Over 28% of all bowlers have household incomes exceeding $100,000/year, and 64% of all bowlers are homeowners. The median age of all bowlers is 36. Almost 60% of bowlers earn their livings in professional fields (management, professional, sales, office, etc.) and the percentage of bowlers who have graduated college is significantly higher than in the population as a whole."

Source: "Overview of the Bowling Industry" by Sandy Hansell and Associates

Expenses as a percentage of annual sales

Cost of goods	25% to 35%
Payroll/labor Costs	25% to 30%
Occupancy	10% to 20%
Profit (estimated pretax)	20% to 30%

Industry Trend

- "Trending up for Bowling Entertainment Centers."
- "As of January 2016, approximately 4,800 bowling centers with about

95,000 lanes were operating in the United States. Of that group, over 4,200 facilities were commercial centers; the others were operated by the military, colleges, fraternal organizations and private clubs. Approximately 25% of the commercial centers are 32 lanes or larger in size. In addition, the industry also has about 175 duckpin and candlepin centers with approximately 2,800 lanes in the United States, mostly along the east coast. Bowling now ranks as the most popular participatory sport in America for those 18 and older."

Source: "Overview of the Bowling Industry" by Sandy Hansell and Associates

- "Most centers will add additional amenities/profit centers to attract a broader clientele. Examples include upgraded food operation, larger arcade, redemption, perhaps volleyball, laser tag, go carts, etc."
- "Well-run, well-promoted centers should do well—not much new competition"
- "Flat or declining revenues. Bowling is dependent upon customer's disposable income."

Seller Financing
- "Typically financed outside, many sales financed by SBA."
- "In few cases with seller financing, loans are short-term (3 to 5 years) with balloon"
- "15 years with 5–10 year call; not done very often, mostly all-cash sales"

Questions
- "Why selling, review each key staff."
- "What capital expenditures are needed? Quality of employees"
- "Time commitment, general business and management skills. Keep the facility in good shape, accurate accounting."
- "Makeup of local market, history of facility and equipment repairs and upgrades, league schedules."
- "Physical condition, necessary cap x, condition of equipment, life of lanes"
- "How much ready cash on hand? Experience in bowling?"
- "Are you open 365 days/yr.?"

Resources

Websites
- Sandy Hansell & Associates: www.sandyhansell.com

Trade Publications
- International Bowling Industry magazine: www.bowlingindustry.com

Associations
- Bowling Proprietors Association of America: www.bpaa.com

Brew Pubs		
	NAICS 722410	Number of Businesses/Units 4,346
Rules of Thumb		

➢ 40 percent of annual sales plus inventory

Benchmark Data

Statistics (Craft Beer Production)

Number of Establishments	4,346
Average Profit Margin	9.4%
Revenue Per Employee	$642,900
Average Number of Employees	2.2
Average Wages per Employee	$35,300

Products and Services Segmentation

IPA	20.4%
Seasonal	19.1%
Other	16.5%
Pale ale	13.9%
Lager	13.0%
Amber ale	8.8%
Wheat	5.5%
Fruit beer	2.8%

Industry Costs

Profit	9.4%
Wages	5.5%
Purchases	39.7%
Depreciation	4.7%
Marketing	5.2%
Rent & Utilities	6.9%
Other	28.6%

Market Share

D.G. Yuengling & Son Inc.	21.6%
Boston Beer Company	16.6%

Source: IBISWorld, August 2016

- "It's worth noting up front that some of the advantages of brewpubs stem from their ability as the manufacturer to sell a high-value-added product (aka beer) at better margins than a typical restaurant. In the latest Brewery Operations and Benchmarking Survey, smaller brewpubs (fewer than 1,000 barrels) derived 26.8 percent of their sales from house beers, and larger brewpubs (more than 1,000 barrels) derived 46.3 percent of their sales from house beers. In 2010, those percentages were closer to 35 percent for both groups. Regardless of the specific percentage, that means roughly a third of sales stems from a product that averages gross margins that can reach more than $800 per barrel depending on the business model and beer style.
  "These benefits don't come without risk. Brewpubs are betting heavily on their ability to sell their own beers, and not surprisingly, typically have a much lower percentage of their sales come from guest beers and other bar sales. Most people come to brewpubs looking to try the house beers, so if those beers don't meet the ever-increasing quality standards, there may be challenges. In addition, running a brewery inside a restaurant requires additional capital, expertise, staff, and more. So brewpubs are a step beyond the average restaurant on the classic risk-reward scale, with more invested, but greater

potential benefits. Given this basic tradeoff, what are the additional advantages that have allowed so many brewpubs to keep that balance firmly pointed toward reward?"

Source: "The Brewpub Advantage," by Bart Watson, February 17, 2016,
https://www.brewersassociation.org/articles/the-brewpub-advantage/

- "In 2014, craft brewers produced 22.2 million barrels, and saw an 18 percent rise in volume and a 22 percent increase in retail dollar value. Retail dollar value was estimated at $19.6 billion representing 19.3 percent market share."

Source: "Craft Brewer Volume Share of U.S. Beer Market Reaches Double Digits in 2014,"
Brewers Association, 3/16/15

Industry Trend

- "'Anyone who does want to sell, should be selling right now,' Hindy (Steve Hindy, founder of Brooklyn Brewery) told Reuters. 'Valuations are out of this world. There are people swarming all of us wanting to give us money.'

  "Merger & acquisition activity amongst top 50 craft breweries has accelerated considerably in the last two years and the list of prominent craft players that have sold all or parts of their companies is growing"

Source: http://www.brewbound.com/news/reuters-dozens-of-craft-breweries-for-sale

- "From the buy side, the craft beer business has never been hotter, with market share now approaching 8 percent by volume in the U.S. and margins that have gotten the attention of both big brewers and non-U.S. brewers alike."

Source: http://www.mwe.com/files/Uploads/Documents/Pubs/JFtnb15_GvtAffairs.pdf

- "Additionally, the number of operating breweries in the U.S. in 2014 grew 19 percent, totaling 3,464 breweries, with 3,418 considered craft, broken down as follows: 1,871 microbreweries, 1,412 brewpubs and 135 regional craft breweries. Throughout the year, there were 615 new brewery openings and only 46 closings."

Resources

Associations

- Brewers Association: https://www.brewersassociation.org

Bridal Shops		
SIC 5621-04	NAICS 448190	Number of Businesses/Units 46,758

Rules of Thumb

➢ 10 to 15 percent of annual sales plus inventory

Pricing Tips

- "Special-order gowns require deposits—many bridal stores don't put the deposits aside but co-mingle funds during the normal course of operations (a liability issue that could be deadly for a new buyer unless appropriate safeguards are in place). A bridal store's inventory is made of samples and the samples should be considered 'amortized over the ordering life of the gown style.'"

- "Bridal is not retail—to be successful in bridal, an owner has to treat it as a sales company and recruit and train salespeople. Traditional bridal is special-order and requires an excellent control system to monitor the progress of the customer's gown. Most bridal stores have 40 percent to 60 percent of their gown inventory tied up in 'one- of-a-kind' gowns. These are styles that are discontinued by the manufacturer and no additional orders can be placed. This severely curtails potential for a store. Some manufacturers are notorious for discontinuing their styles quickly. The bridal business is extremely sensitive to word-of-mouth; one horrendous experience and that bridal transaction will cost the company about $50,000 in sales over a period of 18 months, according to my estimations. Liquidation of our bridal inventory was 23 cents on the dollar—guaranteed."

Benchmark Data

Statistics (Lingerie, Swimwear & Bridal Stores)

Number of Establishments	46,758
Average Profit Margin	5.0%
Revenue per Employee	$109,900
Average Number of Employees	3.4
Average Wages per Employee	$14,563

Products and Services Segmentation

Lingerie	43.7%
Swimwear	23.0%
Bridal gowns	14.1%
Other	12.9%
Uniforms	6.3%

Industry Costs

Profit	5.0%
Wages	13.1%
Purchases	53.7%
Depreciation	1.1%
Marketing	2.9%
Rent & Utilities	9.3%
Other	14.9%

Market Share

L Brands Inc.	36.1%

Source: IBISWorld, June 2016

- "The average wedding cost in the United States is $25,200. Couples typically spend between $18,900 and $31,500 but, most couples spend less than $10,000. This does not include cost for a honeymoon."

Source: www.costofwedding.com

Franchise

Bruster's Real Ice Cream (See also Franchises, Ice Cream/Yogurt Shops)

Approx. Total Investment	$180,000 to $1,200,000
Estimated Annual Sales/Unit	$375,000

	NAICS 722515	Number of Businesses/Units 200

Rules of Thumb

➤ 40 to 45 percent of annual sales plus inventory

Resources

Websites
- Bruster's Ice Cream: www.brusters.com

Franchise

Budget Blinds (See also Franchises, Window Treatment/Draperies)

Approx. Total Investment	$89,240 to $187,070
Estimated Annual Sales/Unit	$700,000

	NAICS 442291	Number of Businesses/Units 800

Rules of Thumb

➤ 2 times annual EBIT plus inventory & equipment

➤ 50 to 55 percent of annual sales plus inventory

Resources

Websites
- www.budget-blinds-franchise.com

Franchise

Burger King (See also Franchises)

Estimated Annual Sales/Unit	$1,200,000

	NAICS 722513	Number of Businesses/Units 13,615

Rules of Thumb

➤ 35 percent of annual sales plus inventory

Resources

Websites
- www.bk.com

Bus Companies (Charter, School & Scheduled)

(See also Ground Transportation Companies)

SIC 4142-01	NAICS 485510	Number of Businesses/Units 18,891

Rules of Thumb

➤ 35 percent of revenues plus asset value of buses plus inventory

Benchmark Data

Statistics (Scheduled and Charter Bus Services)

Number of Establishments	7,950
Average Profit Margin	7.6%
Revenue per Employee	$93,900
Average Number of Employees	6.7
Average Wages per Employee	$25,907

Products and Services Segmentation

Scheduled bus services-interurban transit	31.5%
Long-distance charter bus services	31.0%
Local charter bus services	28.3%
Scheduled bus services-rural transit	9.2%

Major Market Segmentation

Private consumers-local	65.0%
Private consumers-long-distance	30.0%
Business travel	5.0%

Industry Costs

Profit	7.6%
Wages	27.7%
Purchases	27.0%
Depreciation	9.5%
Marketing	1.0%
Rent & Utilities	12.5%
Other	14.7%

Market Share

FirstGroup PLC	15.8%
Stagecoach Group PLC	11.2%

Source: IBISWorld, January 2016

Statistics (Public School Bus Services)

Number of Establishments	10,941
Average Profit Margin	6.2%
Revenue per Employee	$45,500
Average Number of Employees	19.8
Average Wages per Employee	$20,594

B - Rules of Thumb

Products and Services Segmentation

School busing for public schools	91.1%
School busing for private schools	5.0%
Employee bus services	2.6%
Other transportation and services	1.3%

Major Market Segmentation

Public schools	91.1%
Private schools	5.0%
Other	3.9%

Industry Costs

Profit	6.2%
Wages	45.2%
Purchases	21.0%
Depreciation	9.6%
Marketing	0.6%
Rent & Utilities	12.2%
Other	5.2%

Market Share

FirstGroup PLC	25.0%
National Express Group PLC	10.9%
Student Transportation Inc.	5.1%

Source: IBISWorld, October 2015

- "'The motorcoach industry continues to be a small-business success story, with small and medium-sized operators representing more than 98% of the total industry,' observed Peter Pantuso, President and CEO of the American Bus Association."

Source: American Bus Association Foundation's 2015 Motorcoach Census

Motorcoach Fleet Size	Carriers		Motorcoaches	
	Number	Percent	Number	Percent
100 or more	23	0.6%	8,799	24.1%
50 to 99	50	1.4%	3,278	9.0%
25 to 49	155	4.3%	5,378	14.7%
10 to 24	439	12.1%	6,724	18.4%
1 to 9	2,961	81.6%	12,342	33.8%
Industry Total	3,628	100.0%	36,520	100.0%

- Size and activity of the motorcoach travel industry in the United States and Canada for 2014

Highlights

U.S. Carriers	3,330
U.S. Motorcoaches	32,825
Passenger Trips	603.9 million
Passenger Trips per Motorcoach	16,500
Passenger Miles per Gallon of Fuel	199.4

Demographics

Students	22.0%
Seniors	26.6%
All Other	51.3%

Source: American Bus Association Foundation's 2015 Motorcoach Census

          Business Reference Guide **2017**

- "It is important to note that the motorcoach industry provides an average of 745 million passenger trips annually which is comparable to the domestic airlines and 25 times more than Amtrak."

Seller Financing

- 3 years

Resources

Trade Publications

- Bus Ride Magazine—another interesting site: www.busride.com

Associations

- American Bus Association: www.buses.org—a very informative site and their magazine, Destinations, is also very informative
- United Motorcoach Association—also an informative site: www.uma.org

---

Business Brokerage Offices (See also Real Estate Offices)		
SIC 7389-22	NAICS 531210	Number of Businesses/Units 2,610

Rules of Thumb

➢ "If you were to sell your business brokerage business, what multiple of SDE would you expect to sell it for?
   - ✓ Average 2.8 for 2012
   - ✓ Average 2.8 for 2013
   - ✓ Average 2.8 for 2014"
     Source: *Business Brokerage Press Survey* of the Business Brokerage Profession

➢ 50 percent of annual commissions

➢ 2 times SDE plus inventory

➢ 3 to 5 times EBITDA

Pricing Tips

- "Look at cash flow not annual gross sales. Bottom line is what the business is making; EBITDA."
- "There have been sales reported at 2 times SDE. If owner is active in production, then his or her production must be subtracted, unless they will be staying for a period of time. Even then, some discount must be applied to his or her sales, because after selling, their production will most likely drop off."
- "One school of thought on pricing a business brokerage office is to pay for fixed assets, and a certain amount for each year with the same phone number, as there is a goodwill factor for it. A ballpark figure might be $10,000 per year (area code change doesn't count). Then the 'house's' portion of the commissions received on the listings purchased by the new owner would be split between the new owner and the selling owner. For example: Take a $10,000 fee; the selling agent would receive $2,500, the listing agent would receive $2,500 and the remaining $5,000 would be split 50/50. This is one way to handle an earnout. This method would apply to all listings at the time of sale

---

and one renewal period. Deals in progress would be handled as follows: Offers signed both ways would belong to the selling owner and sales signed one way would belong to the new owner."

Expert Comments

➤ "There seems to be a 'falling out' of the part-time business broker, leaving the space open to full-time professionals."

➤ "The average number of associates/agents per office was six; the average number of businesses sold annually was 21.

Benchmark Data

Statistics (Business Brokers)

Number of Establishments	2,610
Average Profit Margin	7.8%
Revenue per Employee	$275,900
Average Number of Employees	1.5
Average Wages per Employee	$100,979

Products and Services Segmentation

Valuation	45.0%
Due diligence	25.0%
Other services	20.0%
Advertising	10.0%

Major Market Segmentation

Retail	33.4%
Service	23.8%
Restaurants	18.4%
Manufacturing	12.6%
Restaurants	11.8%

Industry Costs

Profit	7.8%
Wages	36.8%
Purchases	4.9%
Depreciation	1.5%
Marketing	2.8%
Rent & Utilities	8.3%
Other	37.9%

Market Share

Murphy Business & Financial Corp	5.8%
Sunbelt	4.6%

Source: IBISWorld, January 2016

Industry Trend

- "Increased business transactions with boomers nearing retirement or being laid off from corporate jobs."

Resources

Associations
- International Business Brokers Association (IBBA): www.ibba.org

Call Centers (Telemarketing)		
SIC 7389-12	NAICS 561421	Number of Businesses/Units 28,112

Rules of Thumb

➤ 10 to 12 times current monthly billings for larger services; may require earnout

➤ 5 to 7 times current monthly billings for smaller services; may require earnout

Pricing Tips

- "Annual rate increases are recommended. One of the most important formulas I use in evaluating a business is determining profitability, which comes down to your rate structure. I recently sold a medical service for over 14 times monthly billing, and the reason it sold for that multiple was the way the services were priced. It was very profitable, averaging $365 per client. The service had only 140 accounts but billed over $50K per month, producing a net profit margin of over 38%. Do not increase your rates just before selling your business to boost your monthly billing. A potential buyer will want to see a reasonable conversion history for the rate increase. I would also recommend going to a 28-day billing structure. This will give you an additional one month's billing per year, which should increase cash flow and your annual revenue.

"Buyers are interested in businesses with a good profit margin of at least 25% or better, that have advanced equipment with updated software, management in place and a history of growth. One of the first items buyers ask for after reviewing your listing information is a current financial statement along with at least one previous year's financials. Financials show historical growth as well as future potential.

"A telemessaging service with minimal profit and technology can sell for around 2.5 to 2.8 times annual net, whereas a highly profitable operation with the latest in technology, management in place, and located in a major market could sell for as high as four times annual net. If a hypothetical $30k per month business is averaging a 25% EBITDA, then it would most likely sell for between 3 and 3.5 times yearly net. For the sake of this particular example, let's assume that it is a 3.2 yearly net, which means the selling price would be $90,000 x 3.2, or $288,000 (which equals 9.6 times monthly billing)."

Source: Steve Michaels, TAS Marketing, tas@tasmarketing.com, an excellent site with lots of information on call centers. TAS Marketing is probably the nation's largest business brokerage firm specializing in answering services, call centers, etc.

Expert Comments

"Equipment—If you are six months away from selling your service then don't purchase new equipment or upgrade your software. You will not recoup your investment in that short period of time. If you sell, the buyer may also prefer a different brand of equipment or may buy only your accounts. You would then have to sell your equipment on the used market, which usually brings only pennies on the dollar. If you are two to three years from selling and have old equipment, then by all means consider either hosting or buying newer equipment. This enables you to keep up with technology and your competition by offering the same or more enhanced services.

"Automate—The biggest expense in the telephone answering service business is labor. Automating some of the functions required in the taking/delivering process can ultimately reduce your costs. Automating the messages delivery via email, fax, voice mail, text or cell phone will free up labor. You might also want to consider offering an automated attendant to increase call efficiency.

"Financial Record Keeping—Buyers are interested in businesses with a good profit margin of at least 25% or better, that have advanced equipment with updated software, management in place and a history of growth. One of the first items buyers ask for after reviewing your listing information is a current financial statement along with at least one previous year's financials. Financials show historical growth as well as future potential."

Source: Steve Michaels, TAS Marketing, tas@tasmarketing.com

Benchmark Data

Statistics (Telemarketing & Call Centers)

Number of Establishments	28,112
Average Profit Margin	15.0%
Revenue per Employee	$43,600
Average Number of Employees	17.4
Average Wages per Employee	$26,586

Products and Services Segmentation

Customer service	56.0%
Technical support	19.7%
Telemarketing	12.7%
Other	6.0%
Debt collection	5.6%

Major Market Segmentation

Telecommunications and IT	48.2%
Other	21.4%
Retail	17.6%
Banking and finance	12.8%

Industry Costs

Profit	15.0%
Wages	60.8%
Purchases	11.7%
Depreciation	1.8%
Marketing	1.7%
Rent & Utilities	6.0%
Other	3.0%

Market Share

West Corporation 10.1%
Convergys Corporation 7.9%

Source: IBISWorld, April 2016

Enterprises by Employment Size

Number of Employees	Number of Enterprises	Share
1 to 4	1,487	35.6%
5 to 9	543	14.4%
10 to 19	672	16.5%
20 to 99	839	20.6%
100 to 499	292	7.1%
500+	235	5.8%

Source: IBISWorld, November 2015

- "A well-run answering service can generate a 30% profit. Your labor should run you around 40%, with 10% going to phones and taxes, and 20% for administration. Utilizing a voice mail system along with faxing and email for message delivery should reduce your labor by at least 10% to 15%."
- "As of the beginning of 2014, there were 1,557 telephone answering services nationwide, billing $3.7 billion per year using 48,500 employees. Agents take approximately 41 calls per hour at 43 seconds each. The average revenue per minute is $1.09 and the revenue per call is $1.08."

Source: TAS Services, www.tasmarketing.com.

Industry Trend

- "Telephone answering services are evolving into the contact centers of tomorrow by offering a multitude of services including: telephone answering, voice mail, fax-on-demand, text messaging, order taking, customer service and support, product fulfillment, appointment making, referral locator, credit processing, and more."

Source: Steve Michaels, TAS Marketing, tas@tasmarketing.com

Resources

Websites
- TAS Marketing, Inc.—a telephone answering service brokerage firm: tasmarketing.com

Associations
- ContactCenterWorld: www.contactcenterworld.com
- International Customer Management Institute: www.icmi.com

Camera Stores

SIC 5946-01	NAICS 443130	Number of Businesses/Units 1,652

Rules of Thumb

➢ 10 to 15 percent of annual revenues plus fixtures, equipment & inventory

Benchmark Data

Statistics (Camera Stores)

Number of Establishments	1,652
Average Profit Margin	2.2%
Revenue per Employee	$347,700
Average Number of Employees	3.6
Average Wages per Employee	$38,098

Products and Services Segmentation

Cameras	47.2%
Photographic equipment and supplies	26.0%
Audio equipment	8.3%
Computer hardware, software and supplies	7.7%
Other merchandise	7.3%
Repairs	1.8%
Video cameras and gaming consoles	1.7%

Industry Costs

Profit	2.2%
Wages	11.0%
Purchases	56.5%
Depreciation	1.1%
Marketing	1.6%
Rent & Utilities	7.9%
Other	19.7%

Source: IBISWorld, May 2016

Establishments by Employment Size

Number of Employees	Share
0 to 4	43.6%
5 to 9	38.7%
10 to 19	13.9%
20 to 49	3.3%
50+	0.5%

Source: IBISWorld, April 2014

Industry Trend

- "The only remaining Cord Camera store, at 1132 W. 5th Ave., is scheduled to close on Wednesday. The once-thriving local chain fell victim to changing technology and the proliferation of digital cameras and smartphones. 'This is no longer a profitable industry,' said A.C. Strip, the attorney for Colfax Financial, owner of Cord Camera. 'Camera stores have gone the way of Kodak and Polaroid and manual typewriters.'

  "At its peak, Cord Camera had more than 30 shops in Ohio and Indiana. Cord closed six of its eight remaining stores in January. The Westerville store on Schrock Road closed last week. The company will not file for bankruptcy protection, Strip said. 'We hung on and hung on, but this is no longer an industry,' he said, adding that few people buy rolls of film or have them processed at stores such as Cord. 'We were competing with the big-box stores and Amazon (for equipment sales), and they sold the same cameras for the same price.'"

  Source: "Cord Camera closing last store on Wednesday," by Steve Wartenberg, *The Columbus Dispatch*, March 11, 2014, http://www.dispatch.com/content/stories/business/2014/03/10/cord-closing-last-store.html

- "As if smartphones hadn't already made the point-and-shoot camera, well, pointless, Nokia's NOK-0.25% new Lumia 1020—which has a full-featured camera jammed into its slim body—makes clear that soon few snapshots will be taken on devices that cannot also play Fruit Ninja.

"But while those who carry an iPhone or Android handset have little reason to reach for a point-and-shoot, smartphones still can't replace higher-end cameras. In fact, sales of SLRs are actually rising as photo sharing drives more consumers to seek out professional-level cameras for their personal use, says Chris Chute, a technology analyst at IDC.

"Consumers in the U.S. spent $1.9 billion on digital point-and-shoot cameras between June 2012 and May 2013—a 26% drop from the year before, according to The NPD Group's Retail Tracking Service. Yet Americans spent $2.1 billion on detachable lens cameras during the same period, up 5% from the previous year."

Source: "Smartphones aren't killing these cameras" by Maria LaMagna, MarketWatch, www.marketwatch.com July 15, 2013

Resources

Associations
- Photo Marketing Association (PMA)—good site: www.pmai.org

Campgrounds (See also RV Parks)		
SIC 7033-01	NAICS 721211	Number of Businesses/Units 14,790

Rules of Thumb
- 8.5 times EBITDA
- 8.5 to 8.9 times SDE; add store inventory

Pricing Tips

- "Often owners feel they need a 'lot of negotiating room.' This is not necessary. The astute prospective buyer will immediately recognize the value being correct, and may likely assume if they don't jump on this quickly, someone else will. Another common feeling is 'we can always come down in price, but we cannot go up.' Although this sounds very logical, with an unrealistic price tag you could be missing many qualified and cash buyers even viewing your business. Another negative could be the possibility of becoming 'market stale' and having prospective buyers wondering 'Why has this campground been for sale so long?'"
- "Typically 3–4 times SDE + value of Real Estate. 9–13% cap rates (depending on physical condition and location)."
- "'It's a relatively secure investment,' said Smith. 'When buying a house, you're really concerned about fluctuations in property values. But, when you buy a campground or RV park, the value of the property isn't as worrisome because much of the value of the business is based on the income it generates.'"As a result, values for campgrounds and RV parks never really went down. But, buyers wouldn't pay as much for them because they were getting such good deals on houses for the past several years, he explained.
"The capitalization rate for a business is best described as the ratio between the net operating income produced by the asset and its capital cost, either

the original price paid to buy the asset or its current market value. 'During the recession, buyers were paying an 8 to 12 cap rate,' said Smith. 'Now it's as low as 6. That means prices have gone up.' Interest rates on mobile home properties that also allow RVs, or permanent RV properties, is between 4.5 and 5 percent, he noted.

"'Never, in the 33 years I have been in the real estate business, have I seen interest rates this low,' he added. 'One client got 3.95 percent on a commercial property at a 5-year fixed rate.'

"There are also options, like seller financing, that help motivated buyers acquire properties. Some sellers have even agreed to accept a second mortgage on their properties, when working with the right buyers, Smith explained. 'Anyone who was close to retirement in 2007 and thinking about selling their campground or RV park, is really motivated to do so today,' he added. 'They've been waiting six or seven years.'"

Source: "Florida partnership aids campground buyers and sellers," March 27, 2014, http://rvdailyreport.com/campground/florida-partnership-aids-campground-buyers-and-sellers/

- "The above always includes real estate and, 65 percent of the time, owner financing and in good condition. In some areas, the real estate value may be much higher than the value as a campground. Rules of Thumb generally do not apply to the 'low end' or to large RV resorts. We have seen a lot of activity lately from investors who are trying to use cap rates and off-site management but this is primarily a business of owner managers."

- "Amenities sought after in both RV parks and campgrounds include large sites (nearly 50%), high ratings in a national camping directory, attractive landscaping and cooking areas, and quick check-in."

Source: National Association of RV Parks (ARVC)

- "You also need to be very careful about zoning and how well accepted the park is with neighbors. If they are operating on agricultural land with a special use permit and the area is surrounded by residences . . . look out! If they are on leased land, it might be impossible to expand or continue to lease if it expires."

Expert Comments

"Start 3 years with planning before selling. The price is directly tied to cash flow."

"Difficult start-up business due to lake shore and PCA regulations. Typically seasonal businesses."

"Sellers: Buyers are more sophisticated now and want to see credible valuation information to support the asking price and a business plan that shows the future. Have documentation about repairs and maintenance, permits and zoning and other issues that could limit the future. If you have a bank loan now, talk with your banker to see what they will require for a new owner.

"Buyers: You will need to work hard for the first few years but at a realistic pace. If the current owner is completely worn out, you may want to watch their labor costs and deferred maintenance. Financing can take time and the bankers will need to see plenty of working capital in addition to the down payment. Take time up-front to understand valuation before you get caught up in negotiating based on feelings. Leased property has a far lower value. The great locations will cost more but will also provide a much better future.

Different campgrounds will have a different type of customer too. Look for a location that caters to customers that you can relate to."

"We are seeing an increase in people wanting to own real estate based business that they can understand. It is very difficult and expensive to get permitting to build a new facility so replication is hard. The next 20 years should be good for the business as baby boomers retire and travel."

"Campgrounds are no more risky than a main street business. The one thing that gives them stability is the difficulty in building a new one, both from a cost standpoint and a land use standpoint."

Benchmark Data

Statistics (Campgrounds & RV Parks)

Number of Establishments	14,790
Average Profit Margin	16.8%
Revenue per Employee	$124,500
Average Number of Employees	3.5
Average Wages per Employee	$30,553

Products and Services Segmentation

Other unit accommodations and service fees	34.7%
Campground membership, tuition and long term fees	34.4%
RV and tent sites for travelers and others	30.9%

Industry Costs

Profit	16.8%
Wages	24.6%
Purchases	13.4%
Depreciation	8.3%
Marketing	2.1%
Rent & Utilities	9.2%
Other	25.6%

Source: IBISWorld, July 2016

- "A successful business will have operating expenses at 30% of GOI."
- "It is difficult to provide percentages for expenses because of the tremendous variety of operations. Cost of Goods for store sales should run 65% if they have a mix of groceries and souvenirs. Some facilities are much more labor intensive due to extensive landscaping and cabin cleaning. Food service can be a great amenity and help to separate yourself from the competition."
- "I do not believe in sales per employee or square foot in this business. My experience shows that there is too much variety in operations to make it accurate."

Expenses as a percentage of annual sales

Cost of goods	10%
Payroll/labor Costs	10%
Occupancy	40%
Profit (estimated pretax)	40%

C - Rules of Thumb

Industry Trend

- "When selecting which campgrounds to visit and stay, free Wi-Fi ranks as the third most important amenity, behind only clean bathrooms and a kid-friendly environment, and outpaces access to recreational activities such as a campground store, cabins and even safety lighting.

  "According to campers, reconnecting with nature (55%), reducing stress (54%), and spending more time with family and friends (49%) are the key reasons they camp. Economic and practical values were only identified as reasons for camping by less than 35% of those surveyed. Campers are likely to say that camping improves family relationships—in fact, 41 percent 'completely agree' with this.

  "Additionally, fully 4-in-10 campers (39%) suggest that camping has 'a great deal of impact' on allowing them to spend more time with family. Another third of campers say that camping has a positive impact on their relationships with family and friends (35%) and their emotional well-being (36%)."

  Source: RV Business, March 2015

Seller Financing

- "The majority of campgrounds are sold with a combination of owner and bank financing. When the closing date is set as it relates to their season can complicate things. If the closing is in the fall and the campground is closed for the winter, it could mean several months of payments without income. We often see delayed closings to make it realistic."
- 20 years

Questions

- "Will you carry a contract? Do you have a data base of customers? Age and condition of all utilities. We always would ask about: roof, sewer, property lines and permits."

Resources

Associations

- National Association of RV Parks and Campgrounds (ARVC): www.arvc.org

Camps		
SIC 7032-03	NAICS 721214	Number of Businesses/Units 3,050

Rules of Thumb

- ➤ 2 times annual sales plus inventory
- ➤ 5 to 8 times SDE plus inventory

Pricing Tips

- "Years in business. More years, the higher the multiple."

Expert Comments

"More and more moms and dads have to work today and that creates a need for child care in the summer months when the kids are out of school."

Benchmark Data

Statistics (Summer Camps)

Number of Establishments... 3,050
Average Profit Margin 8.4%
Revenue per Employee $124,600
Average Number of Employees... 7.7
Average Wages per Employee $35,593

Products and Services Segmentation

Overnight recreational camp tuition or fees 85.2%
Other services.. 8.4%
Food items prepared for immediate consumption 2.8%
Room or unit accommodation for travelers and others....................... 2.7%
Membership dues and fees 0.9%

Major Market Segmentation

Adolescents aged 10 to 17 .... 63.4%
Children aged 9 years and younger... 32.4%
Adults 18 and older.. 4.2%

Industry Costs

Profit 8.4%
Wages.. 28.7%
Purchases.. 34.0%
Depreciation.. 9.3%
Marketing 2.3%
Rent & Utilities 9.1%
Other.. 8.2%

Source: IBISWorld, August 2015

Resources

Associations
- American Camp Association: www.acacamps.org

Candy Stores		
SIC 5441-01	NAICS 445292	

Rules of Thumb

➤ 30 to 35 percent of annual sales plus inventory

➤ 1.7 times SDE plus inventory

Benchmark Data

- See Food Stores—Specialty for additional Benchmark Information
- "Candy proved its resilience last year, even in challenging economic times, by increasing sales across the board by 5.8 percent industrywide. Average sales per store rose 4.5 percent to $40,786."

- "Convenience stores remain the No. 2 confectionery source for consumers, ranking only behind supermarkets. (3.21 percent of in-store sales; 4.95 percent of in-store gross margin dollars).
  Source: "A Sweet year for Candy," Convenience Store News Market Research, June 2012

Expenses as a percentage of annual sales

Cost of goods	0
Payroll/labor Costs	55.6%
Occupancy	0
Profit (estimated pretax)	0

Industry Trend

- "Founded by candy veteran Jeff Rubin in 2006, this saccharine experience has become one of the largest and fastest growing specialty candy and gift retailers in the world. The IT'SUGAR Empire consists of over 70 retail locations in US hotspots such as New York, Las Vegas, Los Angeles, San Francisco, Miami, Scottsdale, Washington DC and Palm Beach, in addition to chic international destinations such as London, Dubai, and Grand Cayman.
  "With aggressive growth plans, IT'SUGAR sees a future where we are all 'twenty-something' years old and have access to the pure joy that comes from indulging in a world where life has no rules and the answer is always YES!
  "With retail locations ranging in size from 2,000 to 7,500 square feet, IT'SUGAR is a trendy sweets shop that lives at the intersection of attitude and fun. It's a place about joy, taste, color and sound. Sweet and sour, rich and creamy – that's how life should be, and that's how it is at IT'SUGAR."
  Source: http://www.itsugar.com/about-itsugar

- "A recent Nielson Report stated that consumers are calling for healthier choices from their food products. The question asked was would people really purchase their favorite candy, etc. if the manufacturers made them. The results as of September 2015 are that 67% of the respondents said Yes."
  Source: www.candyindustry.com

Resources

Trade Publications

- Candy Industry magazine—an excellent and informative site: www.candyindustry.com

Associations

- National Confectioners Association: www.candyusa.com

Card Shops (See also Gift Shops)		
SIC 5947-10	NAICS 453220	Number of Businesses/Units 64,066

Rules of Thumb

➤ [Note: We debated whether to leave card shops as a stand-alone business, but there are few, if any, pure card shops. However, card shops still have a SIC and a NAICS number, so someone feels that they are still a stand-alone business. On the other hand, we have seen few gift shops that didn't have cards. In either event, we suspect that the rule of thumb would be about the same for card shops.]

Benchmark Data

Statistics (Gift Shops & Card Stores)

Number of Establishments	64,066
Average Profit Margin	6.1%
Revenue per Employee	$102,900
Average Number of Employees	3.1
Average Wages per Employee	$14,593

Products and Services Segmentation

Souvenirs and novelty items	26.9%
Other	24.1%
Clothes, jewelry and costumes	17.4%
Seasonal decorations	15.0%
Greeting cards	8.8%
Kitchenware and home furnishings	7.8%

Industry Costs

Profit	6.1%
Wages	14.3%
Purchases	49.0%
Depreciation	0.9%
Marketing	1.6%
Rent & Utilities	11.4%
Other	16.7%

Market Share

Party City Holdings Inc.	7.1%

Source: IBISWorld, March 2016

Carl's Jr. Restaurants (See also Franchises, Restaurants—Limited Service)	Franchise
Approx. Total Investment	$1,318,000 to $1,814,000
Estimated Annual Sales/Unit	$1,300,000
SIC 5812-06 NAICS 722513	Number of Businesses/Units 1,356

Rules of Thumb

➤ 40 percent of annual sales plus inventory

Resources

Websites

▪ Carl's Jr. Restaurants: www.CKEfranchise.com

Carpet Cleaning

SIC 7217-04	NAICS 561740	Number of Businesses/Units 38,917

Rules of Thumb
➤ 60 percent of annual revenue plus inventory

➤ 1.5 times SDE plus inventory

Pricing Tips
- "It's also helpful to purchase a business that already has a presence among consumers in the area, which is why many people decide to buy a franchise. Franchising fees are fairly high in the industry, though, ranging from $20,000 to $50,000 on average."
  Source:http://www.iicrc.org/how-prepared-with-carpet-cleaning-business-for-sale-a-194.html
- "When you buy a business, one of the main things you are buying is the database. You want to insure that you have some previous happy customers to contact or else the business is worth very little. Find out how the database is maintained; this will give you an idea of the accuracy and worth of the database. What sort of information is in the database? Can you market to these people easily? Do you know what services the customers previously booked with the carpet cleaning business? Do you know who the commercial customers are as opposed to the domestic customers? If the business has no database at all, I would think twice about purchasing the carpet cleaning business."
  Source: http://jenadyco.com/2011/08/02/5-tips-to-help-you-decide-if-a-carpet-cleaning-business-is-worth-buying/
- "Probably one of the easiest formulas out there is multiplying your net income by 2–4 based on risk or maturity of the company.
  ✓ New company—2 x net profits
  ✓ Mature company—4 x net profits"
  Source: https://www.truckmountforums.com/threads/determining-market-value-of-your-carpet-cleaning-business-formula-by-rob-allen-March-2010.10958/

Benchmark Data

Statistics (Carpet Cleaning)
Number of Establishments	38,917
Average Profit Margin	9.6%
Revenue per Employee	$61,600
Average Number of Employees	1.8
Average Wages per Employee	$22,887

Products and Services Segmentation
Residential carpet and upholstery cleaning	42.9%
Commercial carpet and upholstery cleaning	28.9%
Other	17.3%
Offsite cleaning services	10.9%

Industry Costs
Profit	9.6%
Wages	37.2%
Purchases	21.8%
Depreciation	1.2%
Marketing	3.5%
Rent & Utilities	5.6%
Other	21.1%

Market Share

Chem-Dry Inc.	5.2%

Source: IBISWorld, January 2016

Resources

Websites

- Carpet and Rug Institute: www.carpet-rug.org

Associations

- Professional Association of Cleaning & Restoration (PACR): http:// professionalassociationofcleaningandrestoration.org/
- Restoration Industry Association: www.restorationindustry.org

Carpet/Floor Coverings

SIC 5713-05	NAICS 442210	Number of Businesses/Units 19,534

Rules of Thumb

➢ 20 percent of annual sales plus inventory

Benchmark Data

Statistics (Floor Covering Stores)

Number of Establishments	19,534
Average Profit Margin	3.6%
Revenue per Employee	$270,100
Average Number of Employees	3.9
Average Wages per Employee	$39,565

Products and Services Segmentation

Carpets and other soft-surface floor coverings	43.7%
Other hard-surface floor coverings	31.9%
Hardwood flooring	16.0%
Other services	8.4%

Major Market Segmentation

Do-it-for-me customers	38.3%
Do-it-yourself customers	25.7%
Building contractors	18.4%
All other establishments for resale	10.4%
Businesses for end use in their own operation	7.3%

Industry Costs

Profit	3.6%
Wages	14.8%
Purchases	60.8%
Depreciation	0.7%
Utilities	2.0%
Rent	5.1%
Other	13.0%

Source: IBISWorld, May 2016

Resources

Trade Publications

- Floor Covering Weekly: www.floorcoveringweekly.com
- Floor Covering News: www.fcnews.net/
- Floor Daily: www.floordaily.net

Franchise

Cartridge World (See also Franchises)	
Approx. Total Investment	$68,800 to $158,800
NAICS 424120	Number of Businesses/Units 1,000

Rules of Thumb

➤ 30 to 35 percent of annual sales plus inventory

Resources

Websites

- Cartridge World: www.cartridgeworld.com

Franchise

Carvel Ice Cream (See also Franchises, Ice Cream/Yogurt Shops)		
Approx. Total Investment		$35,100 to $354,550
SIC 2024-98	NAICS 722515	Number of Businesses/Units 434

Rules of Thumb

➤ 55 percent of annual sales or 20 to 25 times the number of gallons of liquid ice cream mix purchased plus inventory

➤ 2.25 to 2.5 times SDE plus inventory

Pricing Tips

- "Typically [priced] at $30 per gallon of ice cream mix used. Therefore, a 5,000-gallon store, which grosses approximately $250,000 would sell for $150,000 to $160,000 with SDE at about $65,000. The $150,000–$175,000 equates to approximately 60% of gross. Stores with disproportionate rental expense would be closer to 50% of gross or 2 times SDE. The exception is for the very few higher volume stores, above 8,000. These would sell for closer to $40 per gallon with SDE of 2.5."
- "Some franchised ice cream businesses with a positive history, updated facilities and verifiable sales numbers will move to 2.5 SDE. Conversely, a short lease and less than five years on franchise agreement will result in less than 2 times SDE."
- "Location drives price higher and typically has higher returns on product usage, therefore more profit. Free-standing buildings with volume in excess of 10,000 gallons, rule of thumb would be 60 percent of annual sales, with average lease of 7 years remaining."

Benchmark Data

- "Food cost percentage typically is equal to SDE unless rent is above $25 per sq. ft."

Expenses as a percentage of annual sales

Cost of goods	26%
Payroll/labor Costs	21%
Occupancy	11%
Profit (estimated pretax)	25%

Seller Financing

- 3 to 5 years

Resources

Websites

- www.carvelicecream.com

Car Washes—Coin Operated/Self-Service

(See also Car Washes—Full-Serve/Exterior)

SIC 7542-05	NAICS 811192	Number of Businesses/Units 14,616

Rules of Thumb

➤ Operations less than five years old generally sell for cost of original real estate, equipment, and improvement cost, plus negotiated figure 2 to 3 times EBIT.

➤ 4 times annual gross sales—"A good place to start"

Pricing Tips

- "Self-service value is derived by using a multiplier of 3 to 5 times the gross sales. Be advised the real estate is included in these basic values, and each wash has to be in business for at least three continuous years."
  Source: Roger Pencek, BRG Industry Expert
- "Identify the location by looking at the visibility and characteristics of the site, says the International Carwash Association. In terms of visibility, can the customer see the car wash easily while driving by? Does the car wash have pleasing architecture, good lighting and landscaping, and appropriate signage? As to characteristics, does the facility have wide, well-maintained driveways and sidewalks? Is the car wash in good shape? If it is not, you'll have the pay for renovations or, at least, negotiate a discount on the price based on expected repairs that will be needed.

  "Study the traffic pattern, says the International Carwash Association, including traffic speed—the slower the better in front of the car wash—and whether turns are easy or difficult to make. Also, look at the potential capture rate—the percent of cars driving by that are actually 'captured,' or stop to use the car wash.

  "According to a survey by 'Professional Carwashing & Detailing' magazine, capture rates range from 0.45 percent for exterior-only conveyor washes to

C - Rules of Thumb

0.52 percent for full-service washes. If 20,000 cars drive by the wash each day, that translates to 90 cars a day for a self-service wash (20,000 cars a day X .0045 capture rate = 90 cars). That may not sound like much, but over the course of 365 days in the year, that would translate to nearly 33,000 customers—if the car wash attracts that number each day.

"Also, ask the owner of the car wash you are considering purchasing for financial statements for the last three years. If the owner offers to provide only the past three months or so, that might not offer an accurate representation—as weather, for example, can greatly affect the number of customers who visit the car wash business. Only several years of financial statements will give you a full picture."

Source:http://smallbusiness.chron.com/buy-car-wash-business-44936.html

"Total cash business. Passive investment, almost labor free."

"90 percent of self-service car washes will have combination of self-service and automatic bays."

"98 percent of self-service/automatic car washes are sold with real estate, equipment and assets."

"Nearly impossible to sell business only"

"Takes 5 years to build new operation—gross annual sales volume to maturity."

Benchmark Data

Average gross revenue per car... $8.69
Average purchase price of the new property (land only) $642,000
Average cost of improvements (bldg., landscaping etc.)........................... $1,417,000
Average cost of equipment $550,000

Source: AutoLaundry News 2015 Exterior Conveyor Survey

Expenses (Operating Costs as Percentage of Total Monthly revenues)

2016 Report
Electricity 6.3%
Fuel (Gas, Oil, Etc.) 5.1%
Water 5.6%
Sewer.. 5.6%
Chemicals 6.5%
Vending Products... 1.1%
Softener Salt... 1.2%
Collection 1.6%
Attendant Labor 13.2%
Bookkeeping 2.3%
Replacement Parts (Normal Wear and Tear).. 5.1%
Replacement Parts (Vandalism) 1.8%
Refunds 0.5%
Pit Pumping 2.4%
Advertising & Promo... 2.0%

Source: AutoLaundry News, Self-Service Survey 2016, CarWashMag.com—a wonderful site. Check it out if you have any dealings in the car wash or car detailing industries. It has reports on Auto Detailing and Car Washes; it is a must see.

Self-Serve Statistics for a single operation (Wand or Coin-op Style)

Average monthly gross income per bay.. $1,652
Average monthly gross income per vacuum... $263
Average monthly gross income for vending.. $25

Source: Auto Laundry News, Self-Service Survey 2016

- "Competition in this industry is high."
- "Volatility medium (revenue fluctuations between 3 and 10 points)"
- "The life cycle stage is growth."
- "There are no major players in this industry."

Industry Trend

- "Consumers are increasingly turning to professional car washing, with those who wash their cars at home declining significantly over the last 10 years. Demographic and societal trends support a continuation, and likely an acceleration, in the use of professional car washing. It is estimated that total annual car wash sales revenue exceeds $24 billion."

Source: AutoLaundry News 2015 Exterior Conveyor Survey

Resources

Associations

- International Carwash Association: www.carwash.org

Car Washes—Full-Service/Exterior

(See also Auto Detailing, Car Washes—Coin Operated/Self-Service)

SIC 7542-01	NAICS 811192	Number of Businesses/Units 66,413

Rules of Thumb

- ➤ .80 to 1 times annual sales plus inventory
- ➤ 32 percent of annual sales includes inventory
- ➤ 3 times SDE includes inventory
- ➤ 23 times EBIT
- ➤ 3.75 to 4.75 times EBITDA
- ➤ 4 to 6 times owner's provable net income includes income

Pricing Tips

- "Full service is more complicated since there often are several profit centers that have differing profit margins. In general, however, full-service value is calculated by taking the EBIDTA (Earnings Before Interest, Depreciation, Taxes, and Amortization) and multiplying by between 5.8 and 6.8. Be advised the real estate is included in these basic values, and each wash has to be in business for at least three continuous years."

Source: Roger Pencek, BRG Industry Expert

- "Car Wash Industry in a 'Free Fall' past few years, 90% of our sales are with real estate, and that is almost the value of the transaction .I have just closed on two washes: Self Service bought for $990,000./7SS—3 Automatic. Bought in 2006....Closing Price today $330,000. Full Service Conveyor bought for $850,000.00 now sold for $130,000. Both operations sold with real estate. Most car washes are 'under water' with their financing."
- "The value of a car wash varies greatly from the East Coast to the West Coast. Weather conditions dictate the value vs. sales and earnings, as the West

Coast sees more sunshine and therefore more revenues on average."

- "Plus economic value of the land, plus inventory not attached to the carwash tunnel"
- "Mostly sold with real estate and is a cash business and not easy to verify income numbers."
- "Tax returns are not easily available and estimating is generally the rule; therefore using water bills, etc. to figure out the sales is one common method."
- "Key factors include current market conditions, owner salary, benefits, condition of equipment… these are just some of the typical costs and items buyers and sellers negotiate over."
- "4 times SDE without land; 2 times SDE + land & equipment"

Expert Comments

"A good high-volume car wash, $500k plus in annual sales with a good lease, brings forth a desirable business and good profit picture. The industry has slowed down some as the economy continues to struggle along with per household spending."

"Good weather brings forth more sales; summer is generally a better season than winter. There is some seasonality in this business; best time to purchase is early summer or late spring. Have working capital and cash flow in reserve for the winter months."

"Southern California market is saturated. Slow economy and increased labor costs are driving avg. performing full-service carwashes out of business. Express washes (fully automated, min. labor) are the new-trend car washes."

"Location, marketing, management, and visual appeal"

"In some areas replication is easy, and in others it's difficult due to the local restrictions on the usability of water and recycling it, plus the traffic problems."

"Expensive to build a new full-service facility."

Benchmark Data

Statistics (Car Wash & Auto Detailing)

Number of Establishments	66,413
Average Profit Margin	19.1%
Revenue per Employee	$49,800
Average Number of Employees	3.1
Average Wages per Employee	$16,159

Products and Services Segmentation

Conveyor car washes	49.7%
Detailing	17.7%
In-bay automatic car washes	11.4%
Self-service bays	10.8%
Hand washing	10.4%

Industry Costs

Profit	19.1%
Wages	32.3%
Purchases	21.3%
Depreciation	9.4%
Marketing	1.3%
Rent & Utilities	13.1%
Other	3.5%

Source: IBISWorld, April 2016

Operating Costs (As a percentage of total revenues)

Rent	9.0%
Equipment & Bldg. Maintenance	4.5%
Chemicals	5.5%
Labor	34.4%
Utilities	7.1%
Insurance	3.8%
Advertising & Promotion	3.0%
Equipment on Lease	2.5%
Customer Claims	0.7%

Source: AutoLaundry News 2015 Full/Flex Survey

Number of full-service carwashes	9,000
Number of exterior conveyor washes	10,500
Number of self-serve car washes	36,000
Number of in-bay automatics	58,000
Total number of carwashes	113,000
Total number of car wash employees	350,000
Number of cars washed annually	2.3 billion
Number of cars washed per day	8 million
Percent of car washes that also dispense gasoline	65%
Percent of car washes owned by small-business persons	90%
Estimate number of gallons of water used on each car	38 gallons
Average annual number of gallons of water lost per car wash	48,000

In-Bay Automatic Statistics for a single operation

Average number of cars washed annually	19,947
Average sale per vehicle	$6.34
Average profit per vehicle	$4.35
Average annual profit	$86,531
Average annual revenue	$139,000

Self-Serve Statistics for a single operation (Wand or Coin-op Style)

Average monthly revenue per bay	$1,489
Average annual revenue for a 2-bay operation	$41,000

Tunnel Carwash Statistics for a single operation

Average number of cars washed per year	45,750
Average price per carwash	$15
Average annual revenue	$686,250

Source: http://www.statisticbrain.com/car-wash-car-detail-industry-stats/ February 2, 2015

C - Rules of Thumb

- "Car washes typically have lower numbers if tied in with a gas station and will do much higher numbers if it's a stand-alone drive-thru."
- "Majority are sold with real estate."
- "$300 per sq. ft. is very good."
- "Car washes usually run at 1/3 profit from gross. Example: $90,000 gross = $30,000 net."

Expenses as a percentage of annual sales

Cost of goods..05% to 10%
Payroll/labor Costs...42.5%
Occupancy...10% to 20%
Profit (estimated pretax) 25%

Industry Trend

- "Consumers are increasingly turning to professional car washing, with those who wash their cars at home declining significantly over the last 10 years. Demographic and societal trends support a continuation, and likely an acceleration, in the use of professional car washing. It is estimated that total annual car wash sales revenue exceeds $24 billion."

Source: AutoLaundry News 2015 Exterior Conveyor Survey

Seller Financing

- "Virtually no outside financing or SBA available because of figures, and lack of bookkeeping."
- "Seller will generally carry 30–35% over five to seven years at 6% interest per annum."
- "20 percent down, 80 percent financing, 20 year amortization"

Questions

- "How many vehicles per month do they do, summer vs. winter, and the average ticket on each vehicle. Any environmental issues? The length of the lease and the rent factor. Is there at least one mgr.?"
- "You need to ask the seller the name of the equipment, the age of the equipment. Is the car wash brush or brushless, any problems with the system?"
- "Provable Gross and Net. Is all labor on the books. What percentage of gross income is cash. Average monthly car count and ticket price, all sources of income"
- "Water bills, proof of car counts and any other paperwork proving the stated numbers"
- "Are you clear with employees and are they all registered? Is there ground contamination? How are the tax records?"

Resources

Associations

- International Carwash Association: www.carwash.org

	Franchise
Car X Auto Service (See also Franchises)	
Approx. Total Investment	$214,000 to $326,000
Estimated Annual Sales/Unit	$750,000

	NAICS 811111	Number of Businesses/Units 164

Rules of Thumb

➤ 35 to 40 percent of annual sales plus inventory

Resources

Websites

▪ www.carx.com

Casinos/Casino Hotels		
SIC 7993-02	NAICS 713210	Number of Businesses/Units 732

Rules of Thumb

➤ Las Vegas Strip average: 8.1 times EBITDA

➤ Indian Gaming management contracts: 30 to 40 percent net (this is pulled from the top in "Operating Income" and should be calculated before debt service). 5 to 7 percent of gross used to be standard for Indian Gaming contracts. The NIGC must approve all contracts and agreements between management and tribal nations. The NIGC (National Indian Gaming Commission) is an independent federal regulatory agency of the United States. Management cannot own any part of the Indian casino. Contracts are typically five years with options to renew. The tribe will be responsible for paying down the debt service.

Pricing Tips

▪ "Casinos Only: Annual Revenue less than $3,000,000: 2.25 to 2.75 times verifiable annual cash flow (I would use a weighted average of the past three time periods). If the 'casino' doesn't own the slot machines, then the multiple would be less.

"Annual Revenue $3,000,000 to $10,000,000: 2.75 to 3.25 times verifiable annual cash flow (I would use a weighted average of the past three time periods). If the 'casino' doesn't own the slot machines, then the multiple would be less.

"Annual revenue over $10,000,000 (but not over $25,000,000): 3.00 to 4.00 times verifiable annual cash flow (I would use a weighted average of the past three time periods). If the 'casino' doesn't own the slot machines, then the multiple would be less.

"Remember the buyer must get a gaming license. In Nevada, that could run: 6–7 months and $5,000 in cost for a 'Restricted License.' This allows the licensee to operate not more than 15 slot machines, not table games, etc. This is common in what we call 'Tavern Licenses.'"

Benchmark Data

Statistics (Casino Hotels)

Number of Establishments.. 403
Average Profit Margin 18.1%
Revenue per Employee $142,700
Average Number of Employees... 1,053.3
Average Wages per Employee $33,912

Products and Services Segmentation

Gambling machines 52.7%
Other... 16.3%
Gaming tables... 12.8%
Accommodations 11.9%
Alcoholic beverages... 4.3%
Admissions to live performances 2.0%

Industry Costs

Profit 18.1%
Wages... 23.9%
Purchases... 19.6%
Depreciation.. 6.8%
Utilities 3.5%
Rent 7.9%
Other... 20.2%

Market Share

MGM Resorts International... 11.6%
Caesars Entertainment Corporation 6.9%

Source: IBISWorld, June 2016

Statistics (Non-Hotel Casinos)

Number of Establishments.. 329
Average Profit Margin 15.8%
Revenue per Employee $161,800
Average Number of Employees.. 344.1
Average Wages per Employee $32.513

Products and Services Segmentation

On-premises gaming (riverboat and barge casinos)......................... 69.3%
Off-track betting (riverboat and barge casinos)................................ 14.7%
Cruise casinos 7.0%
Food and non-alcoholic beverages (riverboat and barge casinos)...... 4.8%
Alcoholic beverages (riverboat and barge casinos).......................... 2.2%
Arcades and video games (riverboat and barge casinos) 2.0%

Industry Costs

Profit 15.8%
Wages... 20.0%
Purchases... 5.0%

Depreciation	5.6%
Marketing	8.5%
Rent & Utilities	3.4%
Other	41.7%

Market Share

Penn National Gaming Inc.	6.9%
Caesars Entertainment Corporation	3.9%

Source: IBISWorld, August 2016

Industry Trend

- "It's become a truism of the U.S. gaming industry that slots will be in trouble if millennials don't get in the game—and fast. Certainly, younger players are not likely to sit on a row of clanging one-armed bandits like their parents and grandparents. But slots can be maximized with the right product and delivery. Hence, the rise of third-party content providers. Their specialty: games built for the mobile generation.

  "'For the millennial generation, it's all about entertainment, connectivity and immediacy,' says Kent Young, game designer and founder of Reno-based Spin Games. 'For pre-millennials, the social component wasn't as important. But these kids are used to jumping on their phones and playing on Xbox; they don't have the patience to put $10 worth of coins in a slot machine. Their experience needs to be seamless, quick and easy.'"

  Source: http://ggbmagazine.com/issue/vol-14-no-12-december-2015/article/ten-trends-for-2016

  "Oxford's study found that the U.S. gaming industry:
  - ✓ Contributes $240 billion—nearly a quarter-trillion—to the U.S. economy, which is equivalent to the total state budgets of New York and Texas combined;
  - ✓ Supports more than 1.7 million jobs—more than double Washington, D.C.'s total employment—and nearly $74 billion in income;
  - ✓ Generates $38 billion in tax revenues to local, state and federal governments—enough to pay more than half-a-million teachers' salaries."

  Source: http://www.gettoknowgaming.org/news/groundbreaking-new-research-reveals-impressive-magnitude-us-casino-gaming-industry 9/30/14

- "Legalization of Internet betting in several U.S. states is turning the gaming industry on its head and turning some states, like New Jersey, into a case study for the promise and pitfalls inherent in Internet disruption of status quo businesses. New Jersey's gaming companies have emerged as pioneers in online gaming—Nevada and Delaware are the only competition—but the Garden State's big online bet is still stuck somewhere between cutting-edge technology and desperation in what has been a slowly dying market."

  Source: "For casinos, baby steps on a virtual Atlantic City boardwalk," by Nia Hamm, www.cnbc.com January 21, 2014

Resources

Websites

- Interactive Gaming Council: www.igcouncil.org
- North American Association of State & Provincial Lotteries: www.naspl.org
- Indian Gaming: www.indiangaming.com

Trade Publications
- World Casino News: https://news.worldcasinodirectory.com/
- World Casino News: https://news.worldcasinodirectory.com/

Associations
- National Indian Gaming Association: www.indiangaming.org
- American Gaming Association: www.americangaming.org

Caterers/Catering

SIC 5812-12	NAICS 722320	Number of Businesses/Units 123,231

Rules of Thumb
➢ 35 to 40 percent of annual sales plus inventory

Benchmark Data

Statistics (Caterers)
Number of Establishments	123,231
Average Profit Margin	7.8%
Revenue per Employee	$35,600
Average Number of Employees	2.1
Average Wages per Employee	$10,771

Products and Services Segmentation
Food served at events on customer's premises	37.3%
Food served at events on caterer's premises	31.4%
Other services	10.0%
Food dropped off at the customer's event	8.0%
Food prepared for immediate consumption	10.0%
Alcoholic and nonalcoholic beverages	2.6%
Food prepared for customer pick-up	2.1%

Industry Costs
Profit	7.8%
Wages	30.2%
Purchases	39.5%
Depreciation	2.0%
Marketing	1.5%
Rent & Utilities	9.1%
Other	9.9%

Source: IBISWorld, June 2016

Resources

Trade Publications
- Cater Source Journal: www.catersource.com

Associations
- The National Association of Catering Executives (NACE): www.nace.net
- International Caterers Association: www.internationalcaterers.org

Catering Trucks

(See also Food Trucks, Ice Cream Trucks, Route Distribution Businesses)

	NAICS 722330	Number of Businesses/Units 61,557

Rules of Thumb

➢ 40 percent of annual sales plus inventory

Benchmark Data

Statistics (Street Vendors)

Number of Establishments.. 61,557
Average Profit Margin 6.8%
Revenue per Employee $36,100
Average Number of Employees... 1.1
Average Wages per Employee $7,279

Products and Services Segmentation

Traditional street vendors 45.0%
Mobile food preparation vehicles.. 37.0%
Industrial catering vehicles 18.0%

Major Market Segmentation

Street locations and corners... 55.0%
Other locations, venues and events 18.0%
Industrial or construction worksites.. 15.0%
Shopping malls 12.0%

Industry Costs

Profit 6.8%
Wages.. 20.0%
Purchases.. 40.6%
Depreciation... 2.4%
Marketing 1.3%
Rent & Utilities 6.6%
Other.. 22.3%

Source: IBISWorld, October 2015

- "This type of business will be largely cash intensive, since most individuals purchasing items from a mobile vendor pay in cash. Accordingly, gross receipts will be the main focus for the examination. The examiner will expect to see large cash deposits to the business bank account. To verify all cash is deposited or accounted for, the examiner must analyze the markup percentage. The examiner should expect to see a consistent markup percentage of about 100% on cold foods sold and about 200% on hot foods sold. For example, if an item is purchased for $0.50, it will generally sell for $1 or more."

Source: Internal Revenue Service Retail Industry Audit Technique Guide (ATG)

Cellular Telephone Stores

	NAICS 443112	

Rules of Thumb

➤ 4 percent of annual revenues plus inventory

➤ "Most cell-phone stores receive a small percentage of the usage fees based on the sale of the plan purchased by the customer with the telephone."

Resources

Associations
▪ Cellular Telecommunications & Internet Association (CTIA): www.ctia.org

Cemeteries

SIC 6553-02	NAICS 812220	Number of Businesses/Units 8,308

Rules of Thumb

➤ 6 times SDE includes real estate

➤ 8 times EBIT includes real estate

➤ 6 times EBITDA includes real estate

Pricing Tips

▪ "Valuations will vary depending on the strategic fit of the buyer. A local funeral home is generally the best strategic fit and should, therefore, be willing to pay the most."

Benchmark Data

Statistics (Cemetery Services)

Number of Establishments	8,308
Average Profit Margin	9.5%
Revenue per Employee	$107,900
Average Number of Employees	4.1
Average Wages per Employee	$37,940

Products and Services Segmentation

Sale of graves, plots and other spaces	28.0%
Interment services	24.8%
Sales of funeral goods	22.5%
Cemetery maintenance services	10.1%
Cremation services	7.1%
Pre-burial services	6.7%
Other	0.8%

Industry Costs

Profit	9.5%
Wages	35.0%
Purchases	15.2%
Depreciation	3.5%
Marketing	2.1%
Rent & Utilities	4.1%
Other	30.6%

Market Share

Service Corporation International	25.2%
StoneMor Partners LP	5.3%

Source: IBISWorld, March 2016

- "Funerals are expensive. Today, the average funeral costs over $8,000 but often exceed $10,000. By comparison, funeral costs averaged $708 in 1960, which in today's dollars would be about $5,600. Opting for cremation can lower a funeral cost to around $3,500, which is one reason why cremations are becoming more popular.
"Cremation rates in the United States:
  - ✓ 2000: 26%
  - ✓ 2005: 32%
  - ✓ 2012: 43%
  - ✓ 2020: 55%
  - ✓ 2030: 70%"

Source: http://foresthill.williamcronon.net/geography-of-death/an-overview-of-the-death-careindustry/

Industry Trend

- "The cemetery's trustees celebrated the groundbreaking of their new columbarium, which will house cremated remains. It is a building that represents what is increasingly becoming the future of death. 'People are looking for alternatives to in-ground burials,' said Michael Lally, office manager of Lowell Cemetery. 'They can be any nationality, any religion.'
"In Massachusetts, 45 percent of all deceased persons will be cremated in 2015, according to the National Funeral Directors Association, and the rate has been steadily increasing for decades. The Bay State is closely following the nationwide trend, which saw just 3.5 percent of Americans choose cremation in 1960 but nearly 50 percent today. Maine and New Hampshire are near the top of the pack, with cremation rates higher than 70 percent."

Source: "With cremations on rise, Lowell Cemetery decides to build a home for all those ashes," by Todd Feathers, *Lowell Sun*, 05/04/2015

Questions

- "Trust fund information is critical. What are the liabilities? Are they properly funded? Is there a successful sales organization/program in place?"

Franchise

CertaPro Painter(See also Franchises)

Approx. Total Investment	$129,000 to $161,500
Estimated Annual Sales/Unit	$741,000

SIC 1721-01	NAICS 238320	Number of Businesses/Units 420

Rules of Thumb

➢ 45 percent of annual sales plus inventory

Resources

Websites

- www.certapro-franchise.com

Check Cashing Services (See also Ace Cash Express, Payday Loans)

SIC 6099-03	NAICS 522390	

Rules of Thumb

➢ 75 percent of annual revenues

➢ 2 times SDE

Pricing Tips

- "The check cashing business is growing; every state has its own rules and regulations. Lease terms and whether a franchise or independent will affect pricing."

Benchmark Data

- See Payday Loans for additional Benchmark Data.

Services/Products Offerings & Volumes

Check Cashing	96%
Money Orders	96%
Money Transfers	96%
Bill Payments	96%
Prepaid Debit Cards	88%
Payday Advances	58%
Travelers Checks	04%
Installment Loans	25%
Other Financial Products	63%

Source: Financial Service Centers of America, www.fisca.org

- "Check cashing should provide the owner with 1% of total gross sales as owner's discretionary income."

Expenses as a percentage of annual sales

Cost of goods	99%
Payroll/labor Costs	01%
Occupancy	01%
Profit (estimated pretax)	01%

Resources

Websites
- Financial Service Centers of America - an excellent site with lots of information: www.fisca.org

---

	Franchise
Cheeburger Cheeburger Restaurants	
(See also Franchises, Restaurants—Limited Service)	

Approx. Total Investment	$230,000 TO $585,000

SIC 5812-19	NAICS 722513	Number of Businesses/Units 69

Rules of Thumb

➢ 35 to 40 percent plus inventory

Resources

Websites
- www.cheeburger.com

	Franchise
Chick-fil-A (See also Franchises, Restaurants—Limited Service)	

Estimated Annual Sales/Unit	$3,500,000

SIC 5812-06	NAICS 722513	Number of Businesses/Units 1,750

Rules of Thumb

➢ 60 to 70 percent of annual sales plus inventory

Resources

Websites
- www.chick-fil-a.com

Children's and Infants' Clothing Stores		
(See also Family Clothing Stores)		

	NAICS 448130	Number of Businesses/Units 17,946

Rules of Thumb

➢ 25 to 30 percent of annual sales plus inventory

27th Edition

155

C - Rules of Thumb

Benchmark Data

Statistics (Children's & Infants' Clothing Stores)

Number of Establishments	17,946
Average Profit Margin	5.3%
Revenue per Employee	$100,900
Average Number of Employees	5.5
Average Wages per Employee	$12,054

Products and Services Segmentation

Girls' clothing	54.8%
Boys' clothing	20.8%
Infants' and toddlers' clothing	14.1%
Other	10.3%

Industry Costs

Profit	5.3%
Wages	11.8%
Purchases	66.6%
Depreciation	0.9%
Marketing	1.9%
Rent & Utilities	6.0%
Other	7.5%

Market Share

Carter's Inc.	16.1%
The Children's Place Retail Stores Inc.	16.1%
The Gymboree Corp.	12.6%
Ascena Retail Group Inc.	10.9%

Source: IBISWorld, August 2016

- "The average family spends $107.28 on children's clothing -- $123.79 for each girl, $90.77 for each boy. Spending varies dramatically depending on household income and age of the primary householders. Households with an income under $10,000 spend an average of $24.67 on boys' clothes and $49.75 on girls' clothes, while households that earn $70,000 or more spend an average of $167.04 on boys' clothes and $216.57 on girls' clothes."

Source: http://www.companiesandmarkets.com/News/Textiles-and-Clothing/
Children-s-wear-market-value-to-hit-173-6-billion-by-2017/NI3785

Industry Trend

- "The global children's wear mark is estimated to hit a value of US $173.6 billion by 2017. Developed regions within Europe and North America are considered traditional leaders and account for a principal share of the global children's wear market. Asia-Pacific, spurred by rapidly escalating markets in India, China, Korea, Thailand, Taiwan and others is poised to deliver the fastest growth rate of 5.3% through to 2017."

Source: "Children's wear market value to hit $173.6 billion by 2017," by Matt Bodimeade,
http://www.companiesandmarkets.com/News/Textiles-and-Clothing/
Children-s-wear-market-value-to-hit-173-6-billion-by-2017/NI3785

Children's Educational Franchises

(See also FasTracKids, Floppy's Mouse Club, Franchises, Huntington Learning Center, Kumon, Montessori Schools, Sylvan)

Rules of Thumb

➢ 2.5 times SDE

➢ 2 times EBIT

➢ 2 times EBITDA

Pricing Tips

- "The typical learning center with sales of up to $300k and EBITDA of $85k will sell at approximately a 2.5 multiple. While deals are done for more than that, it should not be the expectation of the seller."

Benchmark Data

- "$250/sq. ft."

Expenses as a percentage of annual sales

Cost of goods	20%
Payroll/labor Costs	25%
Occupancy	20%
Profit (estimated pretax)	25%

Industry Trend

- "Demand is increasing as schools are having a difficult time keeping up with the curriculum changes mandated by the states. As a result, the perception of parents is that they need to invest in their children's supplemental education in order to help them succeed in school."

Seller Financing

- "Seller financing is common but with the more recent loosening of the lending practices by banks outside financing is also becoming more prevalent."

Questions

"Buyer needs to know the retention rate of the business, the demographics of the area, the average length of stay for the clients. How often has franchisor changed the royalty structure in the past."

Chiropractic Practices

SIC 8041-01	NAICS 621310	Number of Businesses/Units 70,061

Rules of Thumb

➢ 55 to 60 percent of annual sales includes inventory

➢ 1 to 2.5 times SDE includes inventory

➢ 1.5 to 2 times EBITDA

C - Rules of Thumb

Pricing Tips

- "The value of chiropractic practices is generally at an all-time low. Decisions regarding what, where, when and how to practice are influenced by numerous factors, including: personal preferences, market forces, state and federal policies and programs, and institutions that constitute the health care system. Increasing retirement, plus the trend toward shorter working hours, increases the supply of practices for sale, and decreases the available FTE workforce available as buyers. The increasing rate of boomer retirement contributes to a reduction of value of practices for sale. Of particular concern when determining value of a chiropractic practice accepting Medicare payments is ensuring not only that the purchase price is Fair Market Value, but also that the valuation method does not take into account the volume or value of referrals that the selling chiropractor has made or may make to the purchaser, such that the purchase price could be challenged as a kickback or inducement. The OIG has provided guidance on the question of how to value a practice. The ailing economy is leading many Americans to skip doctor visits, and put off X-rays. The results of the Income Approach of valuation identifying 'dividends' [(SDE minus market rate compensation of one working owner) x 1.5-1.7 (ie 65-75% Cap rate)] is becoming more important. 'Percentage of annual gross sales' or SDE multiplier as valuation Rules of Thumb are obsolete, if ever valid. Growth Rates are available through the Congressional Budget Office reports; rarely above 2% historically. Chiropractic practice is riskier —and demands higher Cap rates—than other professional practices like accounting, law, architecture and engineering which are not subject to clinical malpractice risks, or subject to Medicare or insurance company changing reimbursement limitations or denials. The impact of FTE work-schedule and leverage of employed licensed providers is profound. Medicare is continually reducing reimbursement, which impacts other insurances which often base their payment on a percent of Medicare (i.e., 80-120% of Medicare), so dependence on insurance reimbursement is an important consideration in value. In addition; changes to Workers' Compensation laws have further reduced reimbursement and profits during the past decade. Cash practices are usually worth more since there is a higher profit for less work, and often provide a better lifestyle. You may hear from sellers or buyers that chiropractic practices sell—or sold—for a lot more than that, which is true. There was a flurry of sale of practices in the 1990s–2000s wherein the buyers then later failed, and defaulted on their loans, because they paid more than the business-income could sustain. My practice-purchase lenders tell me that many banks have quit lending—or now require much bigger down payments—to chiropractors because of that. Accounts Receivable represent past gross charges for services rendered and as yet uncollected or adjusted-off. These receivables must be discounted to reflect both insurance company reimbursement disallowances, plus the decreasing value over time due to difficulty in collections of past due accounts. In other words, the historic collection ratio of the practice does not yet include the 'standing wave' of uncollectable accounts at practice end, or at a particular point in time, as in a valuation at a particular date."

- "Patient records are not a true 'asset' of the practice since they can't be put on the balance sheet as an asset using the Asset Approach valuation methodology. Patient record valuation is only used to specifically allocate intangibles, assuming they exist at the time of the valuation. The doctor has the physical record, but usually cannot legally sell or dispose of it without the patient's consent (per state statutes), only transfer 'custodianship.' So the doctor is basically a 'custodian' of the record rather than an owner of an asset with independent value. When paper charts are involved, I have come to the opinion that the value of the chart is zero because of the attendant custodianship liability costs. With EMR, a digital record may need to be converted from one digital platform to another either by custodianship transfer or technology succession, in which case a printout and re-entry may be required, probably exceeding in labor costs any physical value to the original digital chart."

- "Most chiropractors take insurance and Medicare, and so are subject to the same equity valuation multiples as medical physicians."
- "Depends on hours worked. Value of equipment can vary considerably depending on techniques/technology. Equipment value for solo practice may range from $20k to $150k+ so this can affect value quite a bit. Price usually does not include A/R and sold as asset sale."
- "Cash practice is worth more than insured practice."
- "Are you and the doctor a compatible personality match? Is the personality of the selling doctor vivacious and outgoing, while the 'new' doctor is a little reserved? Is your chiropractic technique compatible with the seller's? Every instance of non-compatibility may mean one fewer patient will remain with you.

"With compatibility being addressed, I value the practice and goodwill to be equal to one-year net income. This figure will be corrected based upon a few factors:

   ✓ Blend of patient financial classes
   ✓ Insurance dependency/non-dependency
   ✓ Selling doctor's philosophy (pain practice/wellness practice)
   ✓ Percentage of actual overhead (high overhead lowers value)
   ✓ "Purchasing a practice is a very smart thing to do. I would always look for a practice to buy rather than start fresh."

Source: From an article by Bruce A. Parker, D.C. in *Today's Chiropractic*. For more information, go to www. bruceparkerconsulting.com.

Expert Comments

"Most states limit ownership to chiropractors or physicians. Don't try to use boilerplate broker contracts to sell chiropractic practices, as it is easy to violate state or federal regulations; have all the paperwork and terms done by a medical practice transaction specialist attorney."

"It's easier to become a chiropractor than an MD or DO, so competition is often higher, and compensation lower."

"Fairly easy to start a solo practice in many underserved communities. Many communities are over-served. Many chiropractors are located in small communities. However, the distribution of chiropractors is not geographically uniform. This occurs primarily because new chiropractors frequently establish their practices in close proximity to one of the few chiropractic educational institutions. Growth in this sector mirrors demand by the increasingly health-conscious consumer who seeks alternatives to prescription drugs and invasive surgical procedures. Benefit coverage of chiropractic care is an important trend and continues to increase. Currently, coverage is offered in Medicare, Medicaid, Federal Employees Health

Care Benefits Programs, Federal Workers' Compensation, Departments of Defense and Veterans Affairs, approximately three quarters of employer health programs and all state workers' compensation programs. Job prospects for new chiropractors are expected to be good, especially for those who enter a multi-disciplined practice, consisting of, for example, a chiropractor, physical therapist, and medical doctor. Multi-disciplined practices are cost effective and allow patients to remain in-house. Should a patient be referred to a medical doctor, they may use the 'in-house' doctor or one of their own choosing. Chiropractors usually remain in the occupation until they retire and few transfer to other occupations, so replacement needs arise almost entirely from retirements."

"Insured practices subject to more risk"

Benchmark Data

Statistics (Chiropractors)

Number of Establishments	70,061
Average Profit Margin	20.1%
Revenue per Employee	$86,500
Average Number of Employees	2.4
Average Wages per Employee	$30,044

Products and Services Segmentation

General chiropractic care	42.4%
Sports and rehabilitation chiropractic care	17.9%
Family chiropractic care	17.8%
Retail	7.2%
Diagnostics	6.5%
Other patient care	6.3%
Other	1.9%

Major Market Segmentation

Private health insurance	34.2%
Patients paying out-of-pocket	33.5%
Medicare and Medicaid	14.4%
Auto insurance	10.9%
Workers' comp	3.6%
Other	3.4%

Industry Costs

Profit	20.1%
Wages	34.8%
Purchases	5.1%
Depreciation	2.2%
Marketing	2.5%
Rent & Utilities	10.8%
Other	24.5%

Source: IBISWorld, March 2016

- "High variability in practice settings, from solo docs with no staff, to highly leveraged multi-specialty institutions."

- "There are many subspecialty modalities, often described by chiropractors as 'straights' versus 'mixers', i.e., straights do just spinal manipulation, mixed add other modalities; so benchmarks vary."
- "65%–75% overhead"

Components of Chiropractic Practice

Direct patient care 52.9%
Documentation 18.9%
Patient education 15.1%
Business management 13.2%

Source: National Board of Chiropractic Examiners

Reimbursement Categories, Managed Care, and Referral

Private Insurance... 21.5%
Private pay/cash 21.2%
Managed care 19.4%
Personal injury 13.6%
Medicare 10.8%
Workers' Comp 07.8%
Pro Bono 03.9%
Medicaid 01.8%

Source: National Board of Chiropractic Examiners

Expenses as a percentage of annual sales

Cost of goods.. 05% to 14%
Payroll/labor Costs.. 05% to 15%
Occupancy... 04% to 08%
Profit (estimated pretax) .... 25% to 50%

Industry Trend

- "Competition continues to increase; consolidation has slowed the growth of business entities; increased demand, lower profitability."
- "Fast Company, Forbes, Career Cast, and other organizations repeatedly name chiropractic as a top job. Aside from the personal satisfaction of helping people, a chiropractic career is in demand; the Bureau of Labor Statistics has reported that the employment of chiropractors is expected to increase faster than the average for all occupations through the year 2022. Because chiropractors emphasize the importance of healthy lifestyles, chiropractic care is appealing to many health-conscious Americans. Projected job growth for the chiropractic profession stems from increasing consumer demand for a more natural approach to health care."

Source: "Chiropractic profession has the best job security, according to Market Watch, April 3, 2015

- "High exit of boomers increases practices for sale. Lousy insurance reimbursement and control of patient referrals under PPACA ACOs is a big concern."
- "High provider saturation keeps values up due to difficulty getting patients from scratch"
- "Up as boomers' health deteriorates"
- "Ancillary product revenue is increasing trend (nutrition, pillows, ointments, orthotics, exercise, etc.)."

Seller Financing

- "Outside financing"
- "Bank financing up to 80% is pretty common."
- "75% SBA guaranteed financing is generally available."
- 2–5 years

Questions

- "Payor mix, market share, patient demographic data"
- "Source of new patients, wait list, insurance impact, ancillary services or providers, ratio of established and returning patients ('once a back patient, always a back patient')"
- "Any regulation/law changes in recent years (or planned) that may significantly impact revenue? % income from professional services versus product sales. Hours worked, number of patient visits/week, payer mix/insurance reimbursement."
- "If the buyer is not a licensed chiropractor, the buyer should inquire of the state if a non-chiropractor is allowed to own a chiropractic practice or employ a chiropractor in that state."
- "Is the practice set up to support the way you want to work? If you want to run a family practice, and most of the clientele are work-related injury or PI (personal injury) patients, you will have to start from scratch to attract families to your practice. If your technique is notably different from the previous doctor's, you will have a difficult time transitioning the patients.

"Is the practice located in the right place? If the practice is in a town you want to move to and live in for a long time, you can proceed knowing that you will be buying a business you can stay with for years. If the practice is not exactly where you want to be located, you will probably be better off finding a town you like and starting your own practice.

"Is the price reasonable? Many doctors will inflate the prices of their practices for two reasons: 1. They want to get paid for their years of work, and 2. They have been counting on using the proceeds of the practice sale to fund their retirement.

"A practice in which the doctor has only been working a few days a week might seem like a steal, but if the selling doctor won't come down in price, you could end up paying too much for the practice.

"Can you get a non-compete from the doctor? The last thing you want is to buy a practice and have the selling doctor open up down the street and take back all of his or her former patients. Some states (like California) do not uphold non-compete agreements, and you will have to pay a reasonable amount of money for a non-compete as part of the purchase price.

"If you don't think you can get a good non-compete, or you don't think it will be upheld in court, the practice may not be for you. Make sure that you know the actual reason the doctor is selling. If your instincts tell you that you're not getting the whole story, be cautious.

"How long will it take you to make a living from the practice? If the price is too high, if there is no strong patient base, or if you are going to have to start effectively from scratch, you might be better off going down the street and opening your own practice.

"Finally, trust your instincts. If the offer sounds too good to be true, it probably is. If everything looks great and you have a good feeling about the practice and the location, it could be a wonderful lifelong investment for you."

Source: Jean Murray, PhD, who has been counseling small business owners since 1974 and is currently helping chiropractic students and graduates who want to start their own practices.

Resources

Trade Publications
- Chiropractic Economics: www.chiroeco.com

Associations
- American Chiropractic Association: www.acatoday.org
- National Society of Certified Healthcare Business Consultants: www.nschbc.org
- National Board of Chiropractic Examiners—an excellent site: www.nbce.org
- Medical Group Management Association: www.mgma.com

		Franchise
Closet Factory (See also Closets by Design, Franchises)		
Approx. Total Investment		$182,500 to $310,000
	NAICS 238390	Number of Businesses/Units 60
Rules of Thumb		
➢ 45 to 50 percent of annual sales plus inventory		

Resources

Websites
- Closet Factory: www.closetfactory.com

		Franchise
Closets by Design (See also Closet Factory, Franchises)		
Approx. Total Investment		$124,900 to $278,400
SIC 1521-20	NAICS 238390	Number of Businesses/Units 30
Rules of Thumb		
➢ 45 percent of annual sales plus inventory		

Resources

Websites
- Closets by Design: www.closetsbydesign.com

Clothing Stores—Used		
(See also Consignment Shops, Resale Shops, Used Goods)		
SIC 5932-05	NAICS 453310	
Rules of Thumb		
➢ 20 percent of annual sales plus inventory unless it is on consignment		

Benchmark Data

- "The online clothing resale industry is a $34 billion opportunity, created by the quantity of unworn clothing and accessories in American closets and the rate at which people add to their wardrobes every year.

  "More Americans will visit a resale store than an outlet mall this year. Where Are Americans Shopping?
    - ✓ Thrift Store: 16–18%
    - ✓ Consignment Shop: 12–15%
    - ✓ Factory Outlet Mall: 11.4%
    - ✓ Apparel Store: 19.6%
    - ✓ Major Department Store: 21.3%"

Source: https://www.thredup.com/resale

Resources

Associations

- The Association of Resale Professionals (NARTS)—a good site: www.narts.org

Cocktail Lounges (See also Bars)		
SIC 5813-03	NAICS 722410	

Rules of Thumb

➢ 40 percent of annual sales plus inventory

➢ 3 to 4 times monthly sales; add license (where applicable) and plus inventory

➢ 1.5 to 2 times SDE; add fixtures, equipment and inventory

➢ $ for $ of gross sales if property is included, 40 percent of annual sales for business only plus inventory

Benchmark Data

- "Sales price 2½ to 3 times the annual liquor sales. Rent should never exceed 6 percent of the gross sales."
- "When buying liquor, only purchase what you can sell. Ignoring this simple rule has put many bars out of business...The only way to maintain a profitable operation is to establish a firm system of liquor control, and usage, that lets you know, to the penny, exactly how much each drink costs, and how much liquor is poured...Each dollar tied up in inventory is a dollar not working for you. And cash flow is the name of the game. So keep your inventory lean.... If you sell one-ounce drinks for $2 each, a quart bottle can generate 32 drinks, and $64 in revenues. If the quart bottle costs you $12, your gross profit will be $52. Subtract about $15 to cover labor and overhead, and you should clear $37.... However, if your bartender 'free pours' liquor, and his shots average 1 1/2 ounces, the number of drinks you get from a quart will be cut from 32 to 21. This will cut your revenue from $64 to $42. And your gross profit will fall from $52 to $30. And, if your bartender also gives away 4 free drinks out of the same bottle, your gross profit will drop to $22, minus your $15 in labor and overhead, which will leave you with just $7. That's why your liquor should be guarded like cash."

Source: "Eleven Tips to Owning a Profitable Bar," Specialty Group, Pittsburgh, PA

Expenses as a percentage of annual sales

Cost of goods	Food—30% to 40%; Beverages—18% to 22%
Payroll/labor Costs	25%
Occupancy	08%
Profit (estimated pretax)	10%

Industry Trend

- "Demand for this type of business seems to be declining."

Coffee Shops

(See also Coffee Shops (Specialty), Restaurants—Limited Service)

SIC 5812-28	NAICS 722515	Number of Businesses/Units 76,801

Rules of Thumb

➤ 3.5 to 4 times monthly sales plus inventory

➤ 35 to 40 percent of annual sales plus inventory

➤ 2 to 2.2 times SDE plus inventory

Pricing Tips

- "It is rare in business to discover a product where consistently offering 100% quality is the best commercial decision you can make. . . Promote multiple sales. A coffee shop will never make enough money to pay the bills from coffee sales alone. . . Coffee may be the prime motivator for customers coming to the business, but they must leave with multiple sales if you are going to be successful. As a target, coffee should be no more than 40% of your weekly sales and two item sales per customer transaction means you are getting it about right."

Source: "What's The Secret To A Successful Food Business" by Peter Baskerville, Founder of 20 Cafes and Food Businesses, www.forbes.com

- "Trend of sales; owner's compensation including benefits, net profit, lease terms"

Expert Comments

"Ease of entry; unsophisticated owner/operators; personal use of products"

Benchmark Data

Statistics (Coffee and Snack Shops)

Number of Establishments	76,801
Average Profit Margin	6.7%
Revenue per Employee	$57,900
Average Number of Employees	9.1
Average Wages per Employee	$14,912

C - Rules of Thumb

Products and Services Segmentation

Coffee beverages	51.0%
Food	36.0%
Other beverages	9.0%
Other	4.0%

Industry Costs

Profit	6.7%
Wages	25.8%
Purchases	38.5%
Depreciation	3.7%
Marketing	3.5%
Rent & Utilities	11.1%
Other	10.7%

Market Share

Starbucks Corporation	39.8%
Dunkin' Brands Inc.	21.9%

Source: IBISWorld, May 2016

- "Whether you're buying or selling, your rent shouldn't be more than 10% to 15% of your monthly gross sales. If it is, it has to be renegotiated or you'll be working to pay the landlord."
  Source: http://www.bizben.com/blog/posts/coffee-shop-tips-christina-lazuric-110209.php
- "Food costs should not exceed 30%–33% of sales."

Expenses as a percentage of annual sales

Cost of goods	28% to 32%
Payroll/labor Costs	25%
Occupancy	08% to 12%
Profit (estimated pretax)	16% to 20%

Industry Trend

- "While 82 percent of coffee drinkers nationwide report having at least one cup a day, according to Zagat's *Third Annual Coffee Drinking Survey*, coffee culture and drinking protocol have changed. Some consumers are seeking out boutique coffee shops with painstaking preparation methods, while others are focused on expanding their coffee experiences—trying new brewing or dispensing methods."
  Source: "Category Spotlight: The New Coffee Culture," by Nicole Potenza Denis, January 11, 2016, https://www.specialtyfood.com/news/article/category-spotlight-new-coffee-culture/
- "The NCA's 2015 National Coffee Drinking Trends© (NCDT) also finds that 59% of Americans say they drink coffee each day, while 71% reported partaking at least once per week. For 2015, total coffee consumption remained steady within the study's margin of error. Past-year consumption came in at 78% versus last year's 79%, past-week at 71% versus 73% and past-day at 59% versus 61%."
  Source: "Coffee is Americans' Favored Daily Beverage Next to Water," 3/13/15 http://www.ncausa.org/i4a/pages/index.cfm?pageID=1062
- "Frequent openings, frequent closings. Independents lose out to franchises."

Questions

- "Why are you selling? What problems have you had with employees, landlord, vendors, municipal officials, etc.? Do company records show all income? (unlikely)."

Coffee Shops—Specialty

(See also Coffee Shops, Restaurants—Limited Service)

| SIC 5812-28 | NAICS 722515 | |

Rules of Thumb

➤ 40 percent of annual sales includes inventory

➤ 2.2 times SDE includes inventory

➤ 3 times EBIT

➤ 2.5 times EBITDA

Pricing Tips

- "The value of a coffee house is repeat business from a loyal customer base. Ensure that all vendor contracts will convey or transfer."
- "Recognize that profitability is key to determining overall value of the operation. A well-run, mature coffee house can net to the owner in excess of 20 percent of gross revenue."

Expert Comments

"While it is relatively easy to start a coffee house business, especially in relation to other types of food establishments, it can be a higher risk type of business due to the perceived simplicity of the business. Historically, specialty coffee establishments have participated in a high-growth industry segment and consequently have greater than average interest from potential buyers who are looking for a business."

"Opening a coffee house is relatively easy relative to other food and beverage businesses, however understanding the unique dynamics of the coffee house business can be a challenge. Is your location on the correct side of the road? Is your wholesale coffee pricing and quality up to par? How are you going to differentiate your location from the ubiquitous Starbucks?"

Benchmark Data

- "Consumers appear to be shifting to gourmet coffee options, according to the NCA National Coffee Drinking Trends (NCDT) market research study. Daily consumption of gourmet coffee beverages is up to 34% of American adults over 2013's 31%, while daily non-gourmet coffee drinking is down to 35% from last year's 39%.
"Released during today's preview of research findings at the NCA annual convention, NCDT data also reveal that espresso-based beverages accounted for the increase in gourmet coffee beverage consumption. Daily consumption of espresso-based beverages came in at 18% of American adults versus last year's 13%, while gourmet coffee was flat at 19%. Gourmet coffee beverages

consist of espresso-based beverages and regular coffee made with gourmet coffee beans."

Source: Consumers Shifting to Gourmet Coffee Options, Says New NCA Market Research 3/22/14, ncausa.org

- "Specialty coffees represent 37% of U.S. coffee cups and are considered the highest quality in the world. The retail value of the U.S. coffee market is estimated at $30–$32 billion, with specialty comprising approximately a 37% volume share but nearly 50% value share."
- "Drink COGS should not be higher than 28% inclusive of all paper-goods costs."

Expenses as a percentage of annual sales

Cost of goods	28%
Payroll/labor Costs	25%
Occupancy	10%
Profit (estimated pretax)	20%

Industry Trend

- "31% of consumers aged 18+ drank specialty coffee yesterday, compared with 34% in 2014, 31% in 2013 and 2012, 25% in 2011, and 24% in 2010."

Source: http://scaa.org/?page=resources&d=facts-and-figures

- "Among demographic specific data, NCDT findings indicate that those 25–39 years of age are the strongest consumers of gourmet coffee beverages, with 42% who say they consume daily, as compared with about one-third among consumers aged 18–24 and those 40–59, and just one-quarter of those 60+. "Daily consumption of gourmet coffee beverages is also strongest among Hispanic-Americans, 48% of whom said they drink gourmet coffee beverages daily, as compared with 42% of Asian-Americans, 32% of Caucasian-Americans and 23% of African-Americans."

Source: Consumers Shifting to Gourmet Coffee Options, Says New NCA Market Research, March 22, 2014, ncausa.org

Seller Financing

- 3 years

Questions

- "What is your average ticket sale? What marketing efforts are currently in place? Have you measured customer loyalty? Are your employees cross trained?"

Resources

Associations

- National Coffee Association of USA: www.ncausa.org
- Specialty Coffee Association of America: www.scaa.org

Coin Laundries

SIC 7215-01	NAICS 812310	Number of Businesses/Units 22,706

Rules of Thumb

➤ 100% to 125% of annual sales plus inventory

➤ 1 to 1½ times annual sales plus inventory

➤ 3 to 5 times SDE includes inventory (higher multiple for newer equipment and long lease)

➤ 4 to 5 times SDE plus inventory—assumes long-term lease (10+ years) and newer equipment (3–5 years old).

➤ 3 to 6 times EBIT

➤ 3 to 6 times EBITDA

Pricing Tips

▪ "You must buy value; which means you need to understand exactly what you are buying, being very careful not to pay too much. One of several major keys to price is gross sales. In fact, it is fair to say that a 10% misrepresentation as to gross sales can impact the overall value of a coin-laundry business by some 20%, and maybe considerably more; therefore, you must ask the right questions, and be able to assess the accuracy of the answers."
Source: http://laundromatadvisor.com/

▪ "The average-size laundromat will cost you in the neighborhood of $200,000 to $500,000—whether you choose to purchase an existing laundry or build one in a retail space."
Source: http://www.entrepreneur.com/article/190424

▪ "A laundry is not a re-locatable asset. These factors require a strong lease. When possible, it is always better to purchase the property."
"That said, it is obvious that the length, quality and terms of the lease must be looked at carefully before entering into any laundry purchase. It is often necessary to re-negotiate the lease during a transaction. In many cases there are some issues that need to be modified, extensions required and rental rates or terms adjusted. It is recommended that you have an Industry Expert look at the lease; as well as your attorney."
"The equipment, condition and age all have considerable value to the purchase decision; but not as much as you might think. In a new laundry, the cost of equipment is typically only about 55% of the total price, less in many cases. The cost of providing the services (sewer, water, mechanical work, fees, plans, permits and construction) accounts for the rest. In a laundry with equipment that is 7 years or older, you should anticipate making equipment changes as a part of your acquisition planning."
Source: http://www.bizben.com/blog/posts/buying-a-coin-laundry-051209.php

▪ "Most Laundromats in our market sell for 1 to 1.5X gross sales depending on the age and condition of the equipment. Their sales trend and lease also come in to play on the value."

▪ "Coin Laundry operations consist of three basic areas:
✓ Janitorial
✓ Maintenance
✓ Money Handling (Collecting & Loading Coin Changers)"
Source: Laundry Industry Overview, Coin Laundry Association, www.coinlaundry.org

- "One ill-advised means of independent verification, which is commonly promoted by coin-laundry touts (both on-line and as half-learned authors of books on the subject), is the comparison of claimed revenue to water usage. "I consider it ill-advised for several reasons. Firstly, it is a relatively inexpensive method by which a seller can perpetrate a fraud by simply running-off water. Secondly, issues such as leaking water and mineral deposits within water meter mechanisms (water meter maintenance tends to be neglected by water providers) can significantly affect the accuracy of an analysis. Thirdly, many commercial washers now offer surreptitious programing which can significantly impact water usage (e.g., Wascomat 'Generation 6' washer can be adjusted to utilize 1.2 to 1.9 gallons of water per lb. of laundry—a maximum differential of 58.3%!)."

  Source: An excellent article by Gary Ruff, an industry consultant who is also an attorney.
  Gary Ruff can be reached via his informative Web site: www.laundromatadvisor.com
  or at (212) 696-8502 or (631) 389-280. He maintains two offices;
  if you need advice or legal services in the coin laundry business—he knows his stuff.

- "Depending on the location, competition and most of all the lease, % of rent to sales and age of equipment."

- "Coin laundries normally sell for a multiple of their net earnings. The multiple may vary between three and five times the net cash flow, depending on several valuation factors. The following primary factors establish market value:
  - ✓ The net earnings before debt service, after adjustments for depreciation and any other nonstandard items including owner salary or payroll costs in services.
  - ✓ The terms and conditions of the real estate interest (lease), particularly length; frequency and amount of increases; expense provisions; and overall ratio of rent to gross income.
  - ✓ The age, condition and utilization of the equipment, and leasehold improvements; the physical attributes of the real property in which the coin laundry is located, particularly entrances/exits, street visibility and parking.
  - ✓ Existing conditions, including vend price structure in the local marketplace.
  - ✓ The demographic profile in the general area or region
  - ✓ Replacement cost and land usage issues.

- "This resale market standard assumes an owner/operator scenario, with no allocation for outside management fees. Marketing time for store sales averages 60 to 90 days, depending on price, financing terms and the quality and quantity of stores available at the time of sale. Coin laundry listings are generally offered by business brokers who charge a sales commission of 8 percent to 10 percent. Many coin laundry distributors also act as brokers. The accepted standard of useful life for commercial coin laundry equipment is as follows:
  - ✓ Topload Washers (12 lbs. to 14 lbs.): 5–8 years
  - ✓ Frontload Washers (18 lbs. to 50 lbs.): 10–15 years
  - ✓ Dryers (30 lbs. to 60 lbs.):15–20 years
  - ✓ Heating Systems: 10–15 years
  - ✓ Coin Changers: 10–15 years"

  Source: Laundry Industry Overview, Coin Laundry Association, www.coinlaundry.org,
  an excellent and informative site

- "Determine the age and condition of the equipment. Inspect the water heating systems, as this is many times the most expensive single component to replace. These two observations will go a far way in determining an asking price, or variance from the standard of 100% of gross revenue as an asking price. Another great metric is determining water usage. Quite often water companies will sell water in HCF or Hundred Cubic Feet Units. 7.48 gallons of water is equal to one cubic foot of water, so 748 gallons of water equals a Hundred Cubic Feet. A standard top loader uses 30 gallons of water, and the 30 and 50 pound units are multiples of the top loader. The dryer revenue should equal at least half of the washer revenue, up to 100% of the washer revenue."

- "Location is very important. Good locations are in densely populated areas with high percentage renters and low-to-mid income."

- "The good news is that, although banks want buyers to meet the same requirements for existing laundries, they can purchase a lower risk opportunity that requires less cash, because existing laundries, in most all cases, cost far less for the investor.

"Existing laundries often have leaseholds grandfathered in, so buyers end up paying three to four times the net cash flow for an up-and-running business and save tons of money. Let's say that a laundry has a net cash flow of $75,000. You'll likely pay $225,000 to $300,000, and the bank would need 30% of these numbers. This saves more than two-thirds of the cash out of pocket compared to the new laundry scenario.

"If you lose your lease, it is very expensive to set up in a new location: machine pad construction (far more expensive if there is a basement); sufficient gas supply for dryers; lawful wastewater egress; plumbing (including sufficient water supply); three-phase and single-phase electrical layouts; dryer venting system; flooring, ceiling, and counter space. Accordingly, laundromats need to have a long and easily assignable lease."

Source: Gary Ruff, www.laundromatadvisor.com.

- "Location and demographics. It's important to study the surrounding area for city planned changes or housing changes that may affect business performance."

- "Larger multiplier number used for newer equipment & long-term lease"

Expert Comments

"The establishment of a new facility to compete with an existing store is very expensive. An existing store is established and for the most part a better investment than building a new competing facility."

"Review the utility bills and match those up to the monthly sales. Review the lease rate and terms, especially future increases upcoming."

"Obtaining permits to build can be quite challenging"

"Larger, bigger stores 5,000–10,000 sq. ft. with more services and larger washers and dryers. More 'card' stores."

"Competition in this category is not a significant concern, as most of the establishments have found their population niche. Therefore the amount of risk is not significant relevant to new Laundromats opening. At the same time the amount of growth is limited by the same geographic and population element, and so while the business is consistent, the potential for growth is limited. Locations are usually in economic areas that would support this type of business, and the facilities for the most part are average. Marketability spreads quickly by word of mouth. So, if you have a clean store with working machines and good lighting, you can be assured to be in the game. The trend in the industry has been and will remain consistent. While card-operated and automated machines have made some inroads, basic coin operation still leads the pack. While not difficult to replicate, the cost of replication is significant. And therefore the calculated return on the investment is long term."

Benchmark Data

Statistics (Laundromats)

Number of Establishments	22,706
Average Profit Margin	8.9%
Revenue per Employee	$96,000
Average Number of Employees	2.2
Average Wages per Employee	$16,152

Products and Services Segmentation

Washer services	53.3%
Dryer services	34.1%
Other	6.2%
Self-service dry cleaning	5.0%
Commercial laundry services	1.4%

Major Market Segmentation

Renters using laundromats	38.6%
Renters using on-site laundry facilities	22.4%
Commercial, industrial, service industries and routes	16.9%
Colleges and universities	13.1%
Homeowners	9.0%

Industry Costs

Profit	8.9%
Wages	16.9%
Purchases	16.5%
Depreciation	8.9%
Marketing	0.8%
Rent & Utilities	25.3%
Other	22.7%

Market Share

CSC ServiceWorks	19.4%

Enterprises by Employment Size

Number of Employees	Share
0–4	89.7%
10–19	1.9%
20–99	0.6%
100+	0.01%

Source: IBISWorld, June 2016

- "Self Service Laundry Basic Info:
  - ✓ The cost of buying an existing vended-laundry ranges from less than $100,000 to over $1 million, depending on size, age, and net income.
  - ✓ Laundries typically occupy between 1,500 and 4,000 square feet of

retail space, however, some go up to 6,000 square feet, depending on market size, the density of the trade area, and the quality and number of competitors.

✓ Most laundries occupy retail space that is rented on a long-term lease (10-25 years). Negotiating a satisfactory lease is the single most important part of developing a new laundry, or purchasing an existing one. PWS is an expert in this area and handles lease negotiations for all new stores we develop."

Source: http://www.pwslaundrywest.com/p-12525-industry-overview.html

- "ATTENDED OR UNATTENDED?

Approximately 39% of respondents say their stores are fully attended, down 5% from last year's survey. Roughly 26% say their stores are partially attended, while 34.2% say their stores are unattended.

Overall, 65.8% of operators currently employ one or more attendants at their stores. Unlike last year, respondents this year were asked to provide a range of how many people they employ across all of their stores.

An even 12% of respondents only have one employee, while 44.0% employ two to three. The remaining 44.0% say they have four or more employees.

"UTILITIES COST

Operators were asked about their utilities cost (as a percentage of gross). The responses ranged from 10% to 42%.

At the time of our survey in February, operators were paying an average of 21.4% for utilities (as a percentage of gross), down slightly from 22.6% last year. The most common response was 30%, up from last year's figure (a tie between 22% and 25%).

Utilities account for the largest store expense for the majority of respondents (63.2%), while insurance is the smallest expense (47.4%).

"COIN OR CARD?

Approximately 66% of respondents operate coin-only stores, 7.9% operate card-only stores, while 26.3% offer both.

"Here are the most popular top-load prices, followed by the percentage of respondents using them:

1. $2 (31.0%)
2. (Tie) $1.75, $2.25 or $2.75 (13.8% each)
5. $1.50 (10.3%)

"The most popular prices for some of the small front loaders are:

✓ 18 pounds: $2
✓ 20 pounds: $2.25
✓ 25 pounds: $3.50"

Source: "2014-2015 State of the Self-Service Laundry Industry Report," by Carlo Calma, April 13, 2015, https://americancoinop.com/articles/2014-2015-state-self-service-laundry-industry-report-conclusion

- "A self-service laundry that is well laid out and with equipment to handle most garments should create a gross revenue of $70 per square foot per year."

- "The amount of money you can make from a laundry varies tremendously. According to the Coin Laundry Association's Brian Wallace, the annual gross income from one store can range from $30,000 to $1 million. The expenses incurred while running a store range between 65 and 115 percent of the gross income. That means that for a store grossing $30,000 per year, at best it nets $10,500 and at worst it loses $4,500. For a store grossing $1 million per year, the profit could be as high as $350,000, or there could be a loss of up to $150,000, depending on expenses. Wallace says these profit margins have less to do with the size of the store than with its owner. An owner who runs his or her store well—who keeps it clean, repairs its equipment quickly, uses energy-efficient systems and offers good customer service—will see profit margins of about 35 percent."

Source: www.entrepreneur.com

- "Varies a lot depending if it's attended or unattended and what type of location it's in."
- "Cleanliness tops all; working equipment; neighborhood business (quarter to half mile needs 15,000–20,000 population, predominance of renters and incomes from $15,000–$49,000 per annum.)"

Expenses as a percentage of annual sales

Cost of goods	0%
Payroll/labor Costs	09% to 12%
Occupancy	14% to 25% (40% to 55% including utilities)
Profit (estimated pretax)	25% to 35%

Industry Trend

- "The trend for housing is smaller as opposed to what we had experienced in the past. More and more families will enjoy the convenience of self-service laundries."
- "I see these businesses becoming more in demand, as many people are retiring but still want something to do that makes a good income without a full-time work load."
- "As more and more people become renters, the industry should prosper."
- "The trend will continue to pace or follow history. The need or demand for the industry is not changing, so I would conclude a bright future."
- "Large facilities will drive out smaller facilities. Successful operations will provide a wide range of services and customer assistance including pickup and delivery."
- "Laundromats adding some other services: children's play areas, sales of ancillary items, video rentals and more."

Seller Financing

- "Most use seller financing, although we have financed 4 with SBA funding recently."
- "Seller, if any"
- 5 to 10 years

Questions

- "Books and records: are they available?"
- "What is the percentage of utility cost to your represented income?"
- "Occupational license? Water and sewer impact (connection) fees? Organizational skills?"
- "Area crime rate. Review utility bills. New development in trade area. New competition in trade area."
- "I would request copies of utility bills for at least 12 months. Request model

numbers and age of washers and dryers, and ask for maintenance records. Especially request information on water heating systems, as this is probably the one single point of failure that can easily be the most costly repair item."

- "Age & condition of equipment. Is equipment mix suitable for market area? Are they taking in wash & fold or dry cleaning? Is store attended? Easy loading and parking? Environmental compliance and local government fees and restrictions? Length of increase value of business. Typically, the lease should be at least 10 years or more."

Resources

Trade Publications
- American Laundry News: www.americanlaundrynews.com
- Coin-Op Magazine: www.americancoinop.com
- Laundry and Drycleaning News International: http://www. laundryandcleaningnews.com/

Associations
- Drycleaning & Laundry Institute: www.dlionline.org
- Coin Laundry Association: www.coinlaundry.org

	Franchise
Cold Stone Creamery (See also Franchises, Ice Cream/Yogurt Shops)	

Approx. Total Investment	$261,125 to $404,525
Estimated Annual Sales/Unit	$285,000

SIC 2024-98	NAICS 722515	Number of Businesses/Units 1,039

Rules of Thumb
- ➢ 30 percent of annual sales plus inventory
- ➢ 1.5 to 2 times SDE plus inventory

Expert Comments

"Product is unique, large machinery investment is required, thus difficult to duplicate without industry knowledge and sizeable investment ($250,000) in equipment."

Benchmark Data

- "Food cost is low at 20%, rent is typically above 10% since it is location dependent. Leases must be at least 15 years to provide value and time for ROI long term."

Expenses as a percentage of annual sales

Cost of goods	20%
Payroll/labor Costs	22%
Occupancy	12%
Profit (estimated pretax)	22%

Questions

- "Will you finance, how is the store managed, do you have a production staff, separate from your counter staff? Are there any wholesale or outside accounts?"

Resources

Websites

- www.kahalamgmt.com

Collectibles Stores (See also Retail Stores (Small Specialty), Used Goods)

| SIC 5947-05 | NAICS 453220 | |

Rules of Thumb

➢ 20 percent of annual sales plus inventory

➢ Note: Inventory of collectibles is difficult to price. It is normally the cost that the seller paid for it (wholesale price), not the current retail price. However, with collectible inventory, it is quite possible that the current "wholesale price" has increased (or even decreased). The offer or letter of intent should cover how the inventory is to be handled.

Benchmark Data

- For Benchmark Information see Retail Stores (Small Specialty)

Industry Trend

- "The growth of Websites competing with retail shops has forced many retail shop owners to close their doors and offer their inventory just on the Web."
- "Although hard sales data have been difficult to come by, the general consensus in the industry is that after a down period, sales of collectibles are slowly on the upswing."

Source: "Crazy About Collectibles" by Randall G. Mielke, www.giftshopmag.com

---

Collection Agencies

| SIC 7322-01 | NAICS 561440 | Number of Businesses/Units 9,592 |

Rules of Thumb

➢ For agencies with revenues of $1 million +, 75 percent to 125 percent of annual revenues

➢ 100 percent of annual revenues includes inventory

➢ 4 to 6 times EBIDTA

Pricing Tips

- "Collection agencies are typically priced on a recast EBITDA income stream which includes earnings before interest, taxes, depreciation, and amortization and should add shareholders' salaries, perks and non-recurring expenses and then subtract a replacement salary for the shareholders. The valuation multiple typically ranges between 4 and 6 times EBITDA. The primary determinant of the multiple is the size of the company."

- "Adjustments are made for non-recurring expenses to arrive at adjusted EBITDA."
- "Debt collection agencies have contracts with clients that are usually only for 30 days or less. In addition, client concentration is a major force as well."

Expert Comments

"Sustainability of profits is important."

"Collection agencies typically have 30-day contracts with clients, whereby a client can pull back accounts in 30 days if performance is not meeting expectations."

Benchmark Data

Statistics (Debt Collection Agencies)

Number of Establishments	9,592
Average Profit Margin	11.1%
Revenue per Employee	$102,600
Average Number of Employees	14.2
Average Wages per Employee	$40,192

Products and Services Segmentation

Contingent-fee servicing	54.5%
Portfolio acquisition	32.0%
Fixed-fee servicing	5.9%
Other	4.0%
Collateral recovery and repossession services	3.6%

Major Market Segmentation

Financial services	34.5%
Telecommunications	22.1%
Other	14.0%
Healthcare	10.6%
Retail and commercial	10.2%
Government	8.6%

Industry Costs

Profit	11.1%
Wages	39.5%
Purchases	7.3%
Depreciation	1.5%
Marketing	1.4%
Rent & Utilities	7.5%
Other	31.7%

Market Share

Expert Global Solutions	10.5%
Encore Capital Group	5.4%

Source: IBISWorld, July 2016

Expenses as a percentage of annual sales

Cost of goods	10%
Payroll/labor Costs	40% to 50%
Occupancy	05% to 10% (Varies by area)
Profit (estimated pretax)	15% to 20%

Industry Trend

- "Profitability should rise as unemployment improves."

Questions

- "Tenure of existing clients, percent of revenues from clients, any change in commission rates and placement volumes, tenure of the collection staff and management, pipeline of business opportunities."

Resources

Trade Publications

- Collection Advisor: www.collectionadvisor.com

Associations

- International Association of Commercial Collectors: www.commercialcollector.com

Comic Book Stores		
SIC 5942-05	NAICS 451211	

Rules of Thumb

➤ 12 to 15 percent of annual sales plus inventory

Benchmark Data

- "It's difficult to say what average sales are because very few stock only comics. We would guess that the average store turns $150,000 to $200,000 in comics, but again, that is not likely to be all that any of them sell."

Industry Trend

- "Technically, you can talk about the North American comics industry without mentioning Marvel and DC Comics. It'd just be an exercise in futility. While other publishers have seen rapid growth recently, these two still comprise more than half the industry, and can send shockwaves through comics with relatively little effort."

  Source: "The Rising Tide: The State of the Comics Industry in 2015" by Chase Magnett 07/05/2015

Computer Consulting		
SIC 7379-05	NAICS 541512	Number of Businesses/Units 500,050

Rules of Thumb

➤ 50 to 65 percent of annual sales plus inventory

Pricing Tips

- Note: Many consulting businesses are one-man operations or are headed by someone who has the contacts and may basically be "the business." This person may be the goodwill, and without his or her presence the business may not be worth much. If this person stays while the business is slowly being transferred and an earnout is in place, the value may still be there.

Benchmark Data

Statistics (IT Consulting)

Number of Establishments	500,050
Average Profit Margin	6.5%
Revenue per Employee	$175,800
Average Number of Employees	4.5
Average Wages per Employee	$87,635

Products and Services Segmentation

Computer application design and development	24.3%
IT infrastructure and network design services	20.8%
Other services	18.3%
Computer systems design, development, and integration	13.4%
IT technical support services	12.2%
IT technical consulting services	11.0%

Major Market Segmentation

Financial services	24.5%
Federal and state governments	22.5%
Manufacturing and retail	17.6%
Communications an technical	13.1%
Healthcare	11.9%
Other sectors	10.4%

Industry Costs

Profit	6.5%
Wages	48.2%
Purchases	18.6%
Depreciation	0.8%
Marketing	2.0%
Rent & Utilities	3.0%
Other	20.9%

Market Share

International Business Machines Corporation	7.9%

Source: IBISWorld, April 2016

- "Of those that run multi-person businesses, most have fewer than three owners. Corporations have two to three non-owner employees. Almost 90% of firms earned $500,000 or less, while 4.4% earned a million or more. 75% of ICCA Consultants have over 15 years of experience in their field."

Source: Independent Computer Consultants Association, (ICCA), www.icca.org

Industry Trend

- "The number of IT jobs grew 0.2 percent sequentially last month to 5,074,900, according to TechServe Alliance, the national trade association of the IT & Engineering Staffing and Solutions industry. On a year-over-year basis, IT employment grew by 3.8% since February 2015 adding 186,500 IT workers. "Enginerring employment was essentially flat up only 0.02 percent sequentially to 2,530,500. On a year-over-year basis, engineering employment grew by an anemic 0.6% since February 2015 adding 15,700 engineering workers— continuing to underperform the overall workforce."

    Source: http://tsa.prod2.classfive.com//files/Index%20Release%20March.%202016MBR.pdf

Resources

Associations

- Independent Computer Consultant Association: www.icca.org
- TechServe Alliance: www.techservealliance.org/

Computer Services		
SIC 7378-01 NAICS 811212		Number of Businesses/Units 60,775
Rules of Thumb		
➢ 55 percent of annual sales, plus fixtures, equipment and inventory		

Benchmark Data

Statistics (Electronic & Computer Repair Services)

Number of Establishments	60,775
Average Profit Margin	7.0%
Revenue per Employee	$137,200
Average Number of Employees	2.4
Average Wages per Employee	$39,412

Products and Services Segmentation

Other electronic equipment (including medical equipment) repairs	41.6%
Computer and office machine repairs	36.9%
Communications equipment repairs	16.6%
Consumer electronics (including radio, TV and VCR) repairs	4.9%

Major Market Segmentation

Small and medium businesses	48.9%
Large companies	23.0%
Households	12.1%
Federal government	6.4%
Nonprofit organizations	4.8%
State and local governments	4.8%

Industry Costs

Profit	7.0%
Wages	26.9%
Purchases	36.6%
Depreciation	1.4%
Utilities	1.6%
Rent	4.6%
Other	21.9%

Source: IBISWorld, December 2015

Computer Stores

SIC 5734-07	NAICS 443120	Number of Businesses/Units 16,072

Rules of Thumb

➤ 30 percent of annual sales plus inventory

Benchmark Data

Statistics (Computer Stores)

Number of Establishments	16,072
Average Profit Margin	3.5%
Revenue per Employee	$330,500
Average Number of Employees	5.6
Average Wages per Employee	$39,993

Products and Services Segmentation

Laptop computers	35.0%
Desktop computers	32.0%
Printers, scanners and supplies	11.0%
Peripherals and other hardware	10.0%
Software	8.0%
Storage devices	4.0%

Major Market Segmentation

Households	59.2%
Businesses	22.3%
Educational institutes	12.5%
The government	6.0%

Industry Costs

Profit	3.5%
Wages	12.1%
Purchases	65.0%
Depreciation	0.5%
Utilities	1.7%
Rent	5.0%
Other	12.2%

Source: IBISWorld, November 2015

Computer Systems Design		
SIC 7373-98	NAICS 541512	

Rules of Thumb

➤ 50 percent of annual sales plus inventory

➤ 2 to 4 times SDE plus inventory

➤ 3 to 6 times EBIT

➤ 3 to 7 times EBITDA

Pricing Tips

- "Very work-force intensive. Make sure the business can prosper without the owner. Contracts are important."
- "System design firms are often classified as 'programming' firms. More work is being done by temporary employment firms, renting IT professional staff."
- "Highly variable valuations. Biggest component of valuation is the management structure. Midmarket companies with excellent management structure can get very good multiples but a small operation which is highly owner driven may get very little. Having contracts with large customers can improve valuation significantly."

Expert Comments

"Talented people can easily leave and start their own gig. Contracts with a very wide customer base can be very important. Corporate clients are more valuable than consumer clients."

"Design firms are being acquired by the large consulting houses. May be attractive for strategic reasons, such as industry niches and/or package familiarity."

"Highly knowledge driven industry. Risk can be very high depending on the importance of the role played by the current owner. If the owner's role is non-critical, then the business can be very lucrative."

Benchmark Data

- "$100,000 or more in revenues per technician and $200,000 or more per engineer"
- "Revenue and profit growth is more important than stability of earnings. Sales per employee is a key metric."

Expenses as a percentage of annual sales

Cost of goods	20%
Payroll/labor Costs	50% to 55%%
Occupancy	05%
Profit (estimated pretax)	20%

Industry Trend

- "Continuing growth as technology and tools become indispensable for businesses and individuals."

Questions

- "Reasons for the exit. Strategic growth plans. Customer retention plans. Employee specific compensation issues."
- "Who is (are) the key employee(s) who drives the sales? Are there any critical technical roles?"

Concrete Bulk Plants (Ready-Mix)		
SIC 5032-30	NAICS 32732	Number of Businesses/Units 5,333

Rules of Thumb

➢ 30 to 35 percent of SDE plus fixtures, equipment and inventory

Benchmark Data

Statistics (Ready-Mix Concrete Manufacturing)

Number of Establishments	5,333
Average Profit Margin	4.0%
Revenue per Employee	$356,500
Average Number of Employees	15.1
Average Wages per Employee	$54,904

Products and Services Segmentation

Standard ready-mix concrete	65.0%
Specialty ready-mix concrete	35.0%

Major Market Segmentation

Public works construction and other infrastructure	35.0%
Road and highway construction and maintenance	25.0%
Residential construction	20.0%
Private nonresidential	5.0%
Other	2.0%

Industry Costs

Profit	4.0%
Wages	15.5%
Purchases	52.2%
Depreciation	3.5%
Marketing	0.1%
Rent & Utilities	2.2%
Other	22.5%

Market Share

Cemex SAB de CV	5.9%

Source: IBISWorld, March 2016

Consignment Shops

(See also Clothing Stores—Used, Resale Shops, Used Goods)

SIC 5932-04	NAICS 453310	

Rules of Thumb

➤ 15 to 20 percent of annual sales

➤ Note: Consignment shops are just that. They very seldom purchase inventory; rather, they place it on the sales floor and have agreements with the owner regarding price, and generally a schedule in which the price is reduced every month or so for a set period of time. After this period, the goods are usually returned to the owner. The shop works on essentially a commission or fee only if the goods sell.

Benchmark Data

- For additional Benchmark Data see Used Goods
- "What sells: clothing, bookcases, cookbooks. costume jewelry, kitchen gadgets, golf clubs. What doesn't sell: collectible dolls, fur coats, large paintings, vintage dinnerware, needlepoint art."

Source: National Association of Resale and Thrift Shops

Industry Trend

- "Resale or retail? Can you tell the difference? Probably not! Today's resale shops look the same as mainstream retailers... except for one big difference—they sell high quality goods at lower prices! The resale industry offers 'Quality at a Savings'!

"While many businesses close their doors every day, resale remains healthy and continues to be one of the fastest growing segments of retail. With new stores entering the industry and current establishments opening additional locations, the industry has experienced a growth—in number of stores—of approximately 7% a year for the past two years. This percentage reflects the estimated number of new stores opening each year, minus the businesses that close. NARTS is proud to say that future owners who look to the Association for education prior to opening, then continue their education through NARTS membership, are very successful. Many resale shops don't survive that critical first year because the owners did not do their 'homework' and had no idea where to begin or what expect. There are currently more than 25,000 resale, consignment and Not For Profit resale shops in the United States.

"Resale is a multi-billion dollar a year industry. First Research estimates the resale industry in the U.S. to have annual revenues of approximately $17 billion including revenue from antique stores which are 13% of their statistics. Goodwill Industries alone generated $5.37 billion in retail sales from more than 2,000 Not For Profit resale stores and online sales in 2014. Longtime NARTS member, Crossroads Trading Co., based in Berkeley, CA, rang up over $20 million in sales 2012. They have 32 locations, 375 employees and plans to add additional locations. Add to this the many thousands of single location shops, hundreds of multi-location chains, franchises and Not For Profit stores and you begin to realize the vast scope of this growing industry."

Source: 2016 NARTS: The Association of Resale Professionals (This is an excellent site)

Resources

Associations

- The Association of Resale Professionals: www.narts.org

Construction—Buildings		
	NAICS 236	Number of Businesses/Units 199,545

Rules of Thumb

➤ 20 to 30 percent of annual sales plus inventory

➤ 1 to 2 times SDE plus inventory

➤ 1 to 3 times EBITDA

Pricing Tips

- "With very small companies with 1 or 2 employees the norm lately has been to look at FMV of assets as bottom line for pricing purposes."
- "Value in construction trades business is dependent on many factors not normally associated with small business valuation."
- "In many instances in a challenging economy it is not unusual to sell one of these companies for the fair market value of their assets."

Expert Comments

"Small companies have been hit really hard in the economic downturn we have been in for the last few years."

"Make sure you understand the sales and marketing side of the business and how feasible it will be to remove the owner from the business without a serious decline in new and referral business."

Benchmark Data

Statistics (Home Builders)

Number of Establishments	199,545
Average Profit Margin	5.3%
Revenue per Employee	$180,000
Average Number of Employees	2.3
Average Wages per Employee	$23,358

Products and Services Segmentation

Vinyl siding exterior homes	29.7%
Brick exterior homes	22.7%
Stucco exterior homes	22.6%
Other exterior homes	19.3%
Wood exterior homes	5.2%
Aluminum siding exterior homes	0.5%

Major Market Segmentation

Private-sector clients - property developers	81.1%
Private-sector clients - households	16.6%
State or locally funded projects	1.2%
Federally funded projects	1.1%

C - Rules of Thumb

Industry Costs

Profit	5.3%
Wages	13.0%
Purchases	72.1%
Depreciation	0.4%
Marketing	0.4%
Rent & Utilities	1.7%
Other	7.1%

Market Share

DR Horton Inc.	13.6%
Lennar Corporation	13.3%
PulteGroup Inc.	9.3%
NVR, Inc.	7.6%

Source: IBISWorld, May 2016

- "In the final analysis, a construction business should always be worth the FMV of its hard assets."

Expenses as a percentage of annual sales

Cost of goods	20% to 30%
Payroll/labor Costs	25%
Occupancy	05% to 10%
Profit (estimated pretax)	25% to 45%

Industry Trend
- "The surviving companies will be slow to recover."
- "Stagnant"

Questions
- "What would happen to this company if we plucked you out of here today for 1–3 months? Would the business operate effectively?"

Construction—Excavation (Site Preparation)

NAICS 238910	Number of Businesses/Units 26,313

Rules of Thumb
- 25 percent of annual sales plus inventory
- 2.2 times SDE plus inventory
- 1.8 times EBIT
- 2 times EBITDA

Pricing Tips
- "Adjust for age/condition of equipment."

Benchmark Data

Statistics (Excavation Contractors)

Number of Establishments... 26,313
Average Profit Margin 6.1%
Revenue per Employee $229,900
Average Number of Employees... 10.0
Average Wages per Employee $60,079

Products and Services Segmentation

Earthmoving, excavation work, land clearing (Non-Residential Bldg.)............... 41.0%
Earthmoving, excavation work, land clearing (Residential Bldg.)....................... 32.5%
Foundation Digging.. 10.6%
Nonbuilding construction excavation 8.7%
Trenching contractor 7.2%

Major Market Segmentation

Nonresidential building market 41.0%
Residential building market... 32.5%
Nonbuilding construction market 26.5%

Industry Costs

Profit 6.1%
Wages... 26.1%
Purchases... 42.5%
Depreciation... 3.6%
Marketing 0.5%
Rent & Utilities 3.7%
Other... 17.5%

Source: IBISWorld, May 2016

Expenses as a percentage of annual sales

Cost of goods.. 25%
Payroll/labor Costs.. 40%
Occupancy.. 10%
Profit (estimated pretax) 25%

Industry Trend
- "The construction industry is tied to the economic recovery."

Questions
- "Customer lists, future contracts, condition of equipment and any lawsuits?"

Construction—In General
Rules of Thumb

➢ 20 to 30 percent of annual sales plus inventory

➢ 1.5 to 2.5 times SDE plus inventory

> ➤ 2 to 3.5 times EBIT
> ➤ 2 to 4 times EBITDA
> ➤ Note: "Some construction firms own significant equipment and some are run from storefronts, so Rules of Thumb are misleading. The business history is very important, as is the value of signed contracts to be completed, and understanding how a company bills its work in progress. Accounts receivable can average over 45 days, increasing the working capital required and decreasing the business value. Rules of Thumb are not very useful."

Pricing Tips

- "Pricing a construction company is tough for several reasons. The involvement of the current owner (seller) is a key issue; if the owner is crucial to the getting of new jobs and maintaining levels of revenue, then this will decrease the price of the business. The buyer would have to discount the business relative to the loss of earning potential. Further, if there is a problem in transferring the existing or establishing a new license, such as occurs when the buyer is not qualified to obtain a license, and the seller must remain in the business in order to continue as usual, this may affect the buyer's ability to afford the business. In addition, there are significant differences in the various types of construction firms or license classifications. Therefore, Pricing Tips here are very general in nature and may not apply to all types of construction companies."
- "Rule of thumb on gross revenues is very difficult as the gross profit and net profit range wildly for this industry. Consideration for the following must also be taken: revenue that is recurring by long-term contracts vs. repeat clients that still require quotes vs. amount of business that is quoted fresh to new clients."
- "Many times businesses in this sector will end up selling for the fair market value of their assets not including cash, receivables, or investments. When pricing these businesses you must consider the fair market value of the assets."
- "Good supply of buyers for firms doing over a million dollars in EBIT with 20 percent or better profit margins. Smaller ones are fairly difficult, and the best practice is to merge with a larger company that doesn't have a presence in that area. Important for owner to stay after transaction. Individual to individual transactions are the most difficult."
- "Determining the sale price of a contracting or service-related business is difficult at best. One must consider how dependent the business is on the ongoing involvement of the owner, does the business have an established client base that produces repeat business that will continue post acquisition, does the business have a systematic sales and marketing function that will continue to produce new business without the owner present, and, does the fair market value of the equipment exceed the rule of thumb price?"
- "Stock vs. assets, employment agreements."
- "Construction companies are relatively hard to sell, with the exception of ones that have been established many years and enjoy an established name and reputation. These should be [priced at] depreciated value of fixtures and equipment and rolling stock, plus 10 percent of the sale price for goodwill, plus 25 percent of the part of the business period which has already been contracted for."

Expert Comments

"Keep the books solid and up-to-date. Contractors are notorious for not keeping good books and letting things slip. Again, this is much more common in the smaller operations. Make sure the equipment is in good working condition, including vehicles."

"The competition follows the profitability, and vice versa. As one goes up, so goes the other. The industry is definitely stronger and more predictable in recent months than it was a few years ago. Construction tends to follow the economy very closely, so there's not much immunity from the inevitable rise and fall."

"Construction and service-related businesses have a low cost of entry and require a minimum investment to start. Many of these businesses are centered around the owner's reputation and do not have a sales and marketing plan in place to develop new sales on a regular basis."

"It takes a special buyer to take on a contracting or service-related business. Your most likely buyer on some occasions might be a competitor from another market that wants entrance into your market. In some fields the fact that a contractor is union is actually a plus because the contractor only needs to have the journeymen on payroll when they are on the job, and therefore ongoing payroll costs are reduced and profit is increased. Additionally, the union contractors get a significant amount of support from the union that translates into additional business and growth opportunities."

Benchmark Data

Statistics (Municipal Building Construction)

Number of Establishments	48,900
Average Profit Margin	3.2%
Revenue per Employee	$496,400
Average Number of Employees	5.2
Average Wages per Employee	$72,973

Products and Services Segmentation

General contracting services	52.5%
Construction management services	20.7%
Remodeling contracting services	15.6%
Other construction activities	11.2%

Major Market Segmentation

Education sector	53.8%
Healthcare sector	25.3%
Recreation sector	13.1%
Public safety sector	5.6%
Religion sector	2.2%

Industry Costs

Profit	3.2%
Wages	14.5%
Purchases	73.0%
Depreciation	0.4%
Marketing	0.1%
Rent & Utilities	1.5%
Other	7.3%

Source: IBISWorld, June 2016

- "Many service-related contracting businesses will charge at least 2 times their direct costs as their hourly fee for service."

Expenses as a percentage of annual sales

Cost of goods	25%
Payroll/labor Costs	30% to 40%
Occupancy	05% to 10%
Profit (estimated pretax)	25%

Industry Trend

- "I see a steady increase in jobs and sales over the next few years. This is partly due to the general lift in the economy, plus the gradual increase in home values, making better economic sense to build new homes. Home remodeling has seen a significant uptick in recent months. Of course, all the specialty trades follow the growth path of general building."

- "The industry in general seems to be doing a repeat of 15 years or so ago. Companies start small and as the economy grows, so do they. Lots of small startups in the market place right now; these businesses struggle more than their high revenue, big outfit competitors."

- "Most construction and specialty contracting firms were founded by skilled technicians, not by general business managers... they had to learn their trade first then become managers. Because the values of their businesses are so high, a typical technician would not be in a financial position nor the mindset to purchase the business. Hence, new owners are business managers that can run the business, but need skilled technicians as managers or supervisors. The current owners are still so heavily involved in the day-to-day operations that they must be replaced when they exit the business. Most buyers recognize this and ask the seller to stay on board for up to a year— which is not preferred by the seller. I advise sellers to start replacing themselves sooner in the selling cycle—they must start training a manager to cover their operational duties. The trend in this industry will be that more buyers will appear with less knowledge in the industry—so middle to upper managers will be in higher demand."

- "10 construction industry trends to watch in 2016:
  1. Skilled labor shortage will continue to plague construction companies
  2. Prefab/offsite construction methods will become more popular
  3. Construction companies will be more cautious about project selection
  4. BIM will become a necessity, and owner interest in the technology will grow
  5. Green building will grow in commercial and residential sectors
  6. Jobsite accidents and criminal indictments on the rise
  7. Booming multifamily sector will slow down as single-family sector picks up steam
  8. Laser scanning technology will gain popularity
  9. Remodeling will have a strong year, especially in the luxury market
  10. Homebuyers will seek out simple, walkable communities"
  Source: http://www.constructiondive.com/news/10-construction-industry-trends-to-watch-in-2016/411402/

Seller Financing

- "Outside financing is tough in this industry. I work closely with an SBA lender who specializes in construction, and he has a very detailed and rigid approach to the financing of anything construction related. It can be done, but it's not normally simple."

- "Seller financing works very, very well here. One of the reasons for this is the frequency of sellers staying on for time to train or qualify a license. This is a natural fit for seller financing."

- "I typically see a seller carrying back a note with a qualified buyer for 3 to 5 years, at 2–3 points above the prime rate. Most buyers pay off early, so there is normally no prepay penalty."

▪ "Most typical is outside financing of 50 to 75% with approximately 10 to 25% seller financing (per each deal). Less than 10% of the companies sold would be cash down payment and seller financing of approximately 50%."

Questions

▪ "How involved are you in the business? Does the business rely on your presence to keep new jobs coming in? How much work do you currently have on the books? Is this business influenced heavily by season changes?"

▪ "If for some reason you were unable to work for the next 6–12 months, what would happen to this business? Where do you get your business from? What systems do you have in place to generate new sales?"

Resources

Associations

▪ National Association of Home Builders: www.nahb.com

Construction—Specialty Trades

SIC 1799-99		

Rules of Thumb

➤ 50% of Annual Gross Sales plus inventory

➤ 2 times SDE plus inventory

➤ 2 to 3 times EBIT

➤ 1 to 2 times EBITDA

Pricing Tips

▪ "Like most services businesses, the key is in the existing relationships. Two times SDE is fair as long as there is evidence that the relationships will transfer smoothly to the buyer."

Expert Comments

"Customers don't care about the provider's location and facilities, just that the job can be done at a reasonable cost. These businesses can be hard to market because specific experience—or a good amount of mentoring—is paramount to who runs the business next."

"This is a highly competitive business that is typically dependent on the owner's goodwill."

Benchmark Data

▪ "Service businesses will set hourly rates at 2 to 3 times their direct cost per employee per hour to cover overhead and markups."

Expenses as a percentage of annual sales

Cost of goods	25%
Payroll/labor Costs	40%
Occupancy	10%
Profit (estimated pretax)	25%

Seller Financing

- 2 years

Questions

- "Reason for selling. What he/she does on a daily basis. Employee census. Worker's comp mode rate. Upside potential."
- "How do you get new jobs? Do you have a sales and marketing plan that generates new work on a consistent basis?"

Contract Manufacturing (See also Job Shops, Machine Shops)		
SIC 3999-06	NAICS 332710	

Rules of Thumb

➢ 4 times EBIT

➢ 3 to 5 times EBITDA plus reasonable owner's compensation

➢ 2 to 4 times SDE plus inventory

Pricing Tips

- "Mark down for concentration of majority of revenues coming from one to three customers. Mark down for old equipment. Mark down if owner is key production or engineering employee. Smaller shops get lower multiples. Premium for larger shop with many customers—especially large company customers, newer equipment of high quality brands, ISO9000, management team, outside sales employees, current IT technology, online ordering, automated QC department. Also premium price if all contract manufacturing services are integrated under one company: metal fab, machining, painting, plating, PCB assembly, cable & harness assembly, box build, testing, fulfillment."

Expert Comments

"Most contract manufacturing businesses are capital intensive and require a crew of skilled and semi-skilled employees. On the business side, the company needs professional organization and infrastructure with current enterprise management software and systems, ISO9000 and Mil Spec certifications plus an experienced management team. You can't just rent an industrial space and get this sort of business up and running in a few months. It takes years to develop the infrastructure, employees and management team, build customer relations, obtain the needed certifications and manage the operation profitably. This creates goodwill when achieved so that the business is worth much more than the value of the tangible assets."

"Competition is high and the key to gross profit margins is using technology to be low-cost manufacturer."

Benchmark Data

- "$300,000 revenue per employee"

Expenses as a percentage of annual sales

Cost of goods	45% to 60%
Payroll/labor Costs	20%
Occupancy	05% to 15%
Profit (estimated pretax)	10% to 20%

Industry Trend

- "Work presently contracted offshore is moving back to the U.S. As costs rise in Asia, the U.S. becomes more competitive."

Seller Financing

- "Outside financing is readily available for profitable, well-established contract manufacturing businesses. Also, the business equipment is usually valuable collateral. It is critical that the buyer have industry experience."
- "5 years max with a due on sale provision."

Questions

- "Customer concentration and who has technical skill to operate"
- "Discuss the outlook for the company. What opportunities exist for the buyer and why the seller isn't pursuing them."

Contractors—Masonry

SIC 1741-01	NAICS 238140	Number of Businesses/Units 91,416

Rules of Thumb

➢ 27 percent of annual sales includes inventory

➢ 1 to 2 times SDE includes inventory

Pricing Tips

- "Commercial masonry is worth more than residential masonry."
- "Home masonry will go for 1X SDE, and B-2-B will go for 1.5X SDE."

Expert Comments

"Relationships with your builders help getting the contracts for work."

"The industry is changing to foreigners and they are bidding lower to get jobs."

"When home building is doing well, so is this industry; when the home building industry slows down, so does this industry."

Benchmark Data

Statistics (Masonry)

Number of Establishments	91,416
Average Profit Margin	4.5%
Revenue per Employee	$117,100
Average Number of Employees	2.3
Average Wages per Employee	$35,583

Products and Services Segmentation

Masonry contracting using brick, block or concrete	68.4%
Other (including work with slate, marble and granite)	12.0%
Pointing, cleaning, and caulking	9.2%
Stucco contracting	6.6%
Stone contracting	3.8%

Major Market Segmentation

Residential construction market	41.2%
Commercial construction market	28.0%
Municipal construction market	23.8%
Other	7.0%

Industry Costs

Profit	4.5%
Wages	30.8%
Purchases	39.8%
Depreciation	0.7%
Marketing	0.3%
Rent & Utilities	4.4%
Other	19.5%

Source: IBISWorld, August 2016

Expenses as a percentage of annual sales

Cost of goods	20%
Payroll/labor Costs	50%
Occupancy	10%–15%
Profit (estimated pretax)	15%–20%

Industry Trend
- "Flat"

Questions
- "What % of bids do they get?"
- "Union or non-union labor?"
- "Relationships to the customers, are the contracts assignable, and when will you introduce the buyer to customers before closing?"
- "Make sure they have good foremen in place to run the crews going forward with a new buyer."
- "Understand the builders' contracts in place."

Convenience Stores (See also Gas Stations/Mini-Marts)

SIC 5411-03	NAICS 445120	Number of Businesses/Units 43,726

Rules of Thumb

➤ 10 to 20 percent of annual sales plus inventory

➤ 2 to 2.5 times SDE plus inventory

➤ 2 to 3 times EBITDA plus inventory—C-store only

➤ 6 to 8 times EBITDA plus inventory—real estate + business

➤ 5 times EBITDA less cosmetic renovation to receive a national brand of fuel; inventory is separate and above

Pricing Tips

- "Additional revenue sources such as: ATM machines, game machines, fresh fruits and increased deli items, Lotto sales, money orders and even check cashing have become increasingly more important to convenience store retailers with the industry trending toward lower margins and increased competition over the past several years. Many stores are also offering petroleum product discounts to their customers if paying cash rather than using credit cards. This helps the retailer with cash flow as well as saving approx. 2% (or more in some cases) in credit card processing fees which is substantial especially in high-volume gasoline sales locations selling millions of gallons of petroleum products annually."
- "Always check the profit margins carefully other than overall sales."
- "Location of business. Competition in the immediate area. Types of products sold. Lottery commissions helpful."

Expert Comments

"Inside profit margins are not as sensitive as in other food operations. Folks shop for convenience, not price."

"The fact that this is mostly a cash business, relatively less risky, easy to learn and replicate make this business appealing to many people. Some areas are obviously saturated and avoidable. In general, the industry is very marketable if and only if: seller has substantiating books and records for current 3 years and that daily inside sales are minimum $1,000–$1,500 (excluding extraneous revenues). Importance of location, traffic count and trading area demographic to this industry is no different than to any other retail business. Industry growth has been very stable."

"Easy to start up a convenience store location. Some areas are saturated with this type of business."

Benchmark Data

Statistics (Convenience Stores)

Number of Establishments	43,726
Average Profit Margin	1.3%
Revenue per Employee	$193,500
Average Number of Employees	3.3
Average Wages per Employee	$16,057

27th Edition

Products and Services Segmentation

Tobacco products	35.9%
Food service	19.4%
Packaged beverages	15.4%
Other	11.4%
Candy and snacks	10.6%
Beer	7.3%

Industry Costs

Profit	1.3%
Wages	8.3%
Purchases	78.7%
Depreciation	0.9%
Marketing	1.1%
Rent & Utilities	3.4%
Other	6.3%

Market Share

7-Eleven Inc.	30.7%

Source: IBISWorld, June 2016

- "Overall, 80.7 percent of convenience stores (124,374 locations) sell motor fuels."
- "The average convenience store is 2,744 square feet. New stores are bigger, with 3,590 square feet, with about 2,582 square feet of sales area and about 1,008 square feet of non-sales area.

"An average store selling fuel has around 1,100 customers per day, or more than 400,000 per year. Cumulatively, the U.S. convenience store industry alone serves nearly 160 million customers per day, and 58 billion customers every year."

Source: nacsonline.com

Convenience Channel Market Share by Category

Cigarettes	88.43%
Packaged beverages	52.93%
Other tobacco products	91.60%
Liquor	15.60%
Packaged ice cream/frozen novelties	15.52%
Salty snacks	25.81%
Candy and gum	38.89%
Wine	7.17%
Health & beauty care	5.89%
Beer/malt beverages	60.59%
Fluid milk products	14.92%

Source: http://www.csnews.com/research-and-data/results-reports-central/c-stores-gaining-cross-channel-category-showdown

Expenses as a percentage of annual sales

Cost of goods	60% or less—Good Store
Payroll/labor Costs	20% +/- (Owner operator will lower)
Occupancy	07% to 15% +/- (Rent or mortgage payment)
Profit (estimated pretax)	10% to 15%; gasoline profit should cover rent/mortgage

Industry Trend

- "The number of U.S. convenience stores continues to rise, with store-count growth in the past year again dominated by single-store operators.
"The number of U.S. convenience stores increased nearly 1 percent year over year to 154,195 stores as of Dec. 31, 2015, up from 152,794 stores as of Dec. 31, 2014, according to the 2016 NACS/Nielsen Convenience Industry Store Count.
"Single-store operators represented 74.3 percent of the industry's store-count growth in 2015 and now account for 63.1 percent of all U.S. convenience stores (97,359 single stores in total), reported NACS, the Association for Convenience & Fuel Retailing, and Nielsen.
"By comparison, single stores accounted for 83.5 percent of the industry's 2014 store-count growth and represented 60.3 percent of all c-stores in the nation (96,318 in total) last year at this time.
"On a state-by-state basis, Texas continues to lead in c-store count with 15,607 stores. The rest of the top 10 states for convenience stores are: California (11,540 stores), Florida (9,909), New York (8,446), Georgia (6,765), North Carolina (6,330), Ohio (5,605), Michigan, (4,880), Illinois (4,732) and Pennsylvania (4,706)—the same top 10 as the previous year."

Source: "U.S. C-store Count Rises on Increase in Single Stores," January 28, 2016
http://www.csnews.com/research-and-data/market-research/us-c-store-count-rises-increase-single-stores

Seller Financing

- "Seller financing for businesses is usually limited to 5 years. If real estate is involved, seller financing is usually limited to 10 years."
- "5 years all due and payable with 15-year amortization"
- 5 to 7 years

Questions

- "Have your margins been shrinking over the past five years?"
- "Do you have accurate books so I can go to a bank for a loan?"
- "Any previous environmental issue, current leak test result, 3 years' tax return, lease agreement. Do you want to sell or test the market?"
- "Ask for 3 years of tax returns. Don't base buy decision on under-the-table numbers."
- "Amount of gross that's tobacco related. Lottery sales, any employee or customer thefts?"
- "Location, location, location; traffic count and number of rooftops dictate the best locations, along with traffic patterns, red lights, curb cut access, etc. Age and condition of petroleum and other equipment are important; environmental issues must be dealt with prior to closing. Phase I and II reports are almost always required for financing and property transfer. What is the mixture of sales? How do your sales break down concerning gas, merchandise/cigarettes, beer, grill, deli? Have all of your EPA requirements been completed? How many robberies have you had since you bought the store? Do you have key people? Who supplies your gasoline? Who owns the gasoline equipment? Who is your wholesaler that supplies the majority of your groceries? Are there any convenience stores being built within two miles of the store?"

Resources

Websites
- CS News Online: www.csnews.com

Associations
- National Association of Convenience Stores—excellent site, lots of valuable information: www.nacsonline.com

		Franchise
Cost Cutters Family Hair Care (See also Barber Shops, Beauty Shops, Fantastic Sam's, Franchises, Great Clips, Hair Care)		
Approx. Total Investment		$94,495 to $210,295
SIC 7241-01	NAICS 812112	Number of Businesses/Units 480
Rules of Thumb		
➢ 55 to 60 percent of annual sales plus inventory		

Resources

Websites
- www.costcutters.com

Country/General Stores		
SIC 5399-02	NAICS 452990	
Rules of Thumb		
➢ 20 percent of annual sales plus inventory		

Coupon Books (See also Direct Mail—Advertising, Franchises, Valpak)		
	NAICS 541870	
Rules of Thumb		
➢ 2 to 4 times EBITDA		

Seller Financing
- "Not usually seller financed. If financed, 2 to 3 years."

Court Reporting Services		
SIC 7338-01	NAICS 561492	
Rules of Thumb		
➢ 30 to 35 percent of annual revenues includes inventory		

Benchmark Data

- "There are no major players in this industry."
- "According to the AOC study, which was done by the staff of the National Center for State Courts, the average state-employed court reporter earns $53,000 in salary and $1.25 for every page of a court record transcribed."

Source: "N.C. weighs necessity of court reporters; 'it's all about the money' by Michael Gordon, *Charlotte Observer*, February 10, 2014

Industry Trend

- "Of the more than 50,000 court reporters in the United States, more than 70 percent work outside of the courtroom, according to the National Court Reporters Association."
- "Statistics project that jobs in this field will grow more than 18 percent between 2008 and 2018—a good deal faster than the average for all occupations."
- "'Court reporting is forecasted by the U.S. Department of Labor to grow at the rate of 14 percent between now and 2020. With the present workforce so competitive, it is important that students learn about this unique and age-old profession that can take as little as two years to enter and one that offers a full-time average salary according to the U.S. Department of Labor Bureau of Statistics of $62,000 nationwide and upwards of $83,000 in the New York area' said Stuart M. Auslander, the school's director."

Source: http://www.ncra.org/News/newsdetail.cfm?ItemNumber=15025 April 2, 2014

Resources

Associations

- The U.S. Court Reporters Association: www.uscra.org
- American Association of Electronic Reporters and Transcribers: www.aaert.org
- National Court Reporters Association: www.ncraonline.org

Franchise
Coverall Health-Based Cleaning Systems (Commercial Cleaning) (See also Franchises)

Approx. Total Investment	$16,839 to $49,505
NAICS 561720	Number of Businesses/Units 7,966

Rules of Thumb

➤ 2 to 3 times monthly volume

➤ Master/Area developer—sell for 3 to 5 times earnings plus some blue sky for size and potential of market (some cases).

➤ 4 times EBITDA

Pricing Tips

- "The four basic components of determining the value and price of a Master Franchise of Coverall include the collective principal amount of Franchisee Notes outstanding, the value of the exclusive rights to the population territory inclusive of the number of businesses with 5 or more employees, the value of the business structure (number of commercial accounts serviced and the number of franchisees) and the cash flow of the territory."

Expenses as a percentage of annual sales

Cost of goods	80%
Payroll/labor Costs	04%
Occupancy	01%
Profit (estimated pretax)	10%

Resources

Websites
- www.coverall.com

	Franchise

Culligan International—Franchise/Dealership (See also Franchises)

Approx. Total Investment		$35,000
	NAICS 422490	Number of Businesses/Units 586

Rules of Thumb
➤ 80 to 120 percent of gross annual sales—dependent on several things: market size, current penetration rental base, water quality, etc.

Seller Financing
- "Frequently 7 to 10 years"

Resources

Websites
- www.culligan.com

	Franchise

Curves (See also Fitness Centers, Franchises)

SIC 7299-06	NAICS 713940	Number of Businesses/Units 5,122

Rules of Thumb
➤ 1.5 to 2 times SDE includes inventory
➤ 30 percent of annual sales includes inventory

Pricing Tips
- "1.5 to 2 times SDE. The number of monthly check drafts and club size and location are important value factors along with membership trends."
- "Most clubs need 175–200 members to break even. 90% EFT is typical."

Expert Comments

"Acquisitions of existing franchises are generally excellent investments as a result of expected return on investment, market potential, and ongoing franchisor investment and research in the fitness industry."

"Other franchisors using the '30-minute-circuit' program have entered the marketplace with very mixed results. Current Curves locations have closed in market areas which were saturated."

Benchmark Data

- "1.5 employees per $100K sales"
- "It takes about 125 members to break even."
- "Usually owner-operated facilities are run at minimal expenses."

Expenses as a percentage of annual sales

Cost of goods	05%
Payroll/labor Costs	20% to 25%
Occupancy	10% to 15%
Profit (estimated pretax)	25% to 30%

Seller Financing

- 3 years

Questions

- "What was your highest membership number? Review monthly membership history for last 3–5 years. Why do members join your club? Why do/don't they renew yearly membership? Explain club safety/parking lot issues if any. Review lease. Any complaints from adjoining tenants concerning music/noise issues? What are the nearest Curves Clubs to you? Other competing franchise clubs?"

	Franchise
Dairy Queen (See also Franchises, Ice Cream/Yogurt Shops)	
Approx. Total Investment	$1.077,225 to $1,833,125
Estimated Annual Sales/Unit	$775,000
SIC 2024-98 NAICS 722513	Number of Businesses/Units 6,511

Rules of Thumb

➤ Price = 1.1 to 1.2 times annual sales for stores w/real estate

➤ Price = .45 times sales for leased facility. Rent = variable item

➤ "Walk-up"— two windows with real estate—1.24 (+/-) times annual sales

➤ Without real estate —.5 (+/-) times annual sales

➤ Full Brazier— with real estate—1.15 (+/-) times annual sales

➤ Without real estate—.5 (+/-) annual sales"

Pricing Tips

- "Dairy Queens: With Real Estate = 1.1X sales. IDQ leaning toward 'Corporate' type ownership, moving away from 'Ma & Pa' owners."

Expert Comments

"Many players in this market"

Expenses as a percentage of annual sales

Cost of goods	31%
Payroll/labor Costs	25%
Occupancy	08%
Profit (estimated pretax)	15%

Seller Financing

- "Rarely seller financed"
- "5 years with balloon payment."
- "SBA financing—17 to 18 years with real estate; 7 to 10 years without real estate."

Questions

- Questions to ask seller: "Leased facility—rent important; owned facility—loan & taxes important"

Resources

Websites

- www.dairyqueen.com

Data Processing Services		
SIC 7374-01	NAICS 541513	Number of Businesses/Units 68,567

Rules of Thumb

➤ 15 percent of annual sales plus inventory

➤ 2.2 times SDE plus inventory

➤ 2 times EBIT

➤ 2.2 times EBITDA

Pricing Tips

- "The Data Processing and Hosting Services industry has a medium level of capital intensity. For every $1.00 spent on wages, an estimated $0.19 is allocated toward capital expenditure in 2015. Although investment in capital has remained stable during the past five years, wages' share of revenue has risen. As a result, the industry's capital intensity level has declined during the five years to 2015.

"The industry is labor-, skill- and knowledge-intensive but with significant need for computing and software-related equipment. Labor costs are the largest expense for industry operators, representing an estimated 43.0% of revenue in 2015."

Source: IBISWorld, January 2015

- "A proprietary software component could raise the multiple to as much as 10 x."

Benchmark Data

Statistics (Data Processing & Hosting Services)

Number of Establishments 68,567
Average Profit Margin 14.6%
Revenue per Employee $221,000
Average Number of Employees 9.3
Average Wages per Employee $87,929

Products and Services Segmentation

Application service provisioning 23.8%
Other services 22.2%
Business process management and data processing 18.4%
Data storage and management services 11.1%
Website hosting services 10.1%
IT technical support services 9.1%
IT computer network and network management services 5.3%

Major Market Segmentation

Non-financial enterprises 41.3%
Resellers 27.5%
Financial firms 17.0%
Content Providers 7.4%
Government organizations 6.8%

Industry Costs

Profit 14.6%
Wages 39.8%
Purchases 11.3%
Depreciation 8.2%
Marketing 3.6%
Rent and Utilities 3.2%
Other 19.3%

Market Share

International Business Machines Corp. 10.8%
Hewlett-Packard Enterprise Company LP 8.5%

Source: IBISWorld, March 2016

- "Location is not important. Skill sets and experience of employees is the key to larger contracts. Annual maintenance contracts based on number of 'seats' is more valuable than service contracts."

D - Rules of Thumb

Expenses as a percentage of annual sales

Cost of goods	n/a
Payroll/labor Costs	35%
Occupancy	n/a
Profit (estimated pretax)	40%

Industry Trend

- "The pullback in information technology (IT) spending immediately following the recession resulted in a slowdown of industry growth rather than a decline in revenue. The Data Processing and Hosting Services industry's performance will improve over the next five years due to renewed IT spending and increased outsourcing by nonindustry companies seeking to trim IT costs. Consolidation within other industries will likely push more companies to a level of complexity in which the outsourcing of their IT needs is more convenient and affordable than maintaining those services in-house. Meanwhile, the increasing prevalence of internet-based media and services has continued driving this industry's revenue beyond prerecessionary highs."

Source: IBISWorld, January 2015

- "More maintenance contracts vs. service contracts"

Questions

- "Ask for resumes of employees and meeting with a few top customers during due diligence."

Dating Services

SIC 7299-26	NAICS 812990	Number of Businesses/Units 5,740

Rules of Thumb

➤ 30 to 35 percent of annual sales

Expert Comments

"Regulators across the world have sought to regulate dating services, as they try to protect the growing number of individuals that use them. Mainstream sites such as eHarmony and Match.com, alone, have 20 million and 17 million worldwide users respectively."

Source: "Online dating: growth, regulation, and future challenges" by Elena Magrina, Policy Analyst at Inline Policy, 9/8/14

Benchmark Data

Statistics (Dating Services)

Number of Establishments	5,740
Average Profit Margin	13.0%
Revenue per Employee	$291,700
Average Number of Employees	1.5
Average Wages per Employee	$81,515

Products and Services Segmentation

Online dating	48.7%
Mobile dating	26.2%
Matchmakers	14.2%
Singles events	6.7%
Other	4.2%

Major Market Segmentation

Consumers 25 to 34 years old	33.3%
Consumers 35 to 44 years old	25.8%
Consumers 18 to 24 years old	15.2%
Consumers 45 to 54 years old	12.1%
Consumers 55 to 64 years old	9.1%
Consumers 65 years and older	4.5%

Industry Costs

Profit	13.0%
Wages	28.0%
Purchases	13.7%
Depreciation	3.4%
Marketing	17.1%
Rent & Utilities	4.2%
Other	20.6%

Market Share

Match Group Inc.	25.7%
eHarmony Inc.	11.9%

Source: IBISWorld, April 2016

Online Dating Statistics

Total number of single people in the U.S.	54,250,000
Annual revenue from the online dating industry	$1,249,000,000
Average spent by dating site customer per year	$239
Percent of users who leave within the first 3 months	10%
Percent of male online users	52.4%
Percent of female online users	47.6%
Percent of marriages in the last year in which the couple met on a dating site	17%

Source: Reuters, *Herald News, PC World, Washington Post*, January 1, 2014

Industry Trend

- "1. Online dating has lost much of its stigma, and a majority of Americans now say online dating is a good way to meet people.

  2. Online dating has jumped among adults under age 25 as well as those in their late 50s and early 60s.

  3. One-third of people who have used online dating have never actually gone on a date with someone they met on these sites.

  4. One-in-five online daters have asked someone else to help them with their profile.

  5. 5% of Americans who are in a marriage or committed relationship say they met their significant other online."

Source: "5 facts about online dating," by Aaron Smith and Monica Anderson, February 29, 2016, http://www.pewresearch.org/fact-tank/2016/02/29/5-facts-about-online-dating/

- "With the industry expected to grow by another $100 million every year through 2019, analysts say the dating game is increasingly becoming a battle of the ages, with both sides hoping their age-based gambles yield the most profit from those looking for love.

  "It's not clear that the young and perky are the best market for corporate matchmakers. Two-thirds of the singles and fling-seekers in America's online-dating market are older than 34, IBISWorld data show. Pew Research surveys show 45-to-54-year-olds in America are just as likely to date online as 18-to-24 year olds, either because they're divorced or far from the easier dating scenes of college campuses and first jobs."

  Source: "Online dating's age wars: Inside Tinder and eHarmony's fight for our love lives," by Drew Harwell, April 6, 2015, https://www.washingtonpost.com/news/business/wp/2015/04/06/online-datings-age-wars-inside-tinder-and-eharmonys-fight-for-our-love-lives/

- "The Internet and dating will continue to be a match made in heaven. With consumers using the Internet more than ever before, demand for online dating services is on the rise. In particular, demand from niche dating networks and baby boomers is increasing, and a new wave of smartphone applications will bring the industry to more people."

  Source: IBISWorld, April 2015

Resources

Trade Publications

- Online Dating Magazine: www.onlinedatingmagazine.com

Day Care Centers/Adult (See also Assisted Living, Nursing Homes)		
SIC 8322-10	NAICS 624120	Number of Businesses/Units 5,984

Rules of Thumb

➤ 70 to 75 percent of annual sales

➤ 2.5 times SDE plus inventory

Pricing Tips

- "The mix of payers is important. What is the % of private pay vs. Medicaid vs. VA vs. County programs... The higher the private pay component, the higher the value, as the business is not subject to governmental pricing changes. If an adult day care center also provides in-home non-medical care for their clients, this adds to the value of the enterprise. If an adult day care center has their own transportation available to clients, this adds to the value of the enterprise."

Expert Comments

"This is a great industry to invest in as the growth trendline is positive and the margins are solid if the operation is run properly. Not unlike any other Main Street business."

"The major risk is similar to any other business—under capitalization. It takes a long time to reach breakeven, as it takes time to bring clients into the program and keep up with those leaving the program (inevitable due to aging...) at the same time as they need higher levels of care at assisted living facilities or nursing homes."

"The time to reach breakeven is relatively long as this is still a relatively new segment of senior healthcare. The majority of adult day care centers are run by non-profit entities. The challenge for adult day care owners is to build a payer mix that is not dependent upon governmental programs (i.e., Medicaid) and to focus on the private pay client. Unlike the in-home non-medical care business, this is a 'bricks & mortar' investment with significant initial build-out cost but has a staffing model that is perfect for an absentee owner or an owner/operator."

Benchmark Data

Statistics (Adult Day Care)

Number of Establishments	5,984
Average Profit Margin	7.5%
Revenue per Employee	$48,800
Average Number of Employees	24.9
Average Wages per Employee	$21,864

Products and Services Segmentation

Social and medical model	44.0%
Social model	33.0%
Medical model	23.0%

Industry Costs

Profit	7.5%
Wages	44.5%
Purchases	17.6%
Depreciation	2.3%
Marketing	2.3%
Rent & Utilities	7.1%
Other	18.7%

Source: IBISWorld, June 2015

Expenses as a percentage of annual sales

Cost of goods	0
Payroll/labor Costs	25% to 35%
Occupancy	12% to 20%
Profit (estimated pretax)	20% to 25%

Industry Trend

- "With the portion of the population 65 and older growing significantly, the demand for adult day care will rise well above the overall GDP growth rate for at least another decade. This is a superior alternative to the only other option for seniors to stay in their home: the non-medical in-home care providers."

Seller Financing

- "Similar to other Main Street businesses, there is a mix of outside financing and seller financing. Typically Sellers will carry a small percentage (10–20%) of the transaction value."
- "Yes, usually for three (3) years."

Questions

- "What is your mix of payors? What is your employee to participant ratio? Should be 1 to 5 or less to ensure good service is provided...
- How do clients get to the center? Your own transportation, regional senior transport, adult children or spouses dropping participants off at the center?"

Resources

Associations

- National Adult Day Services Association: www.nadsa.org

Day Care Centers/Children (See also Schools)		
SIC 8351-01	NAICS 624410	Number of Businesses/Units 816,343

Rules of Thumb

➤ 50 to 55 percent of annual sales includes inventory

➤ 2.5 to 3.5 times EBIT

➤ 3.5 to 4.5 times EBITDA

➤ 2 times SDE includes inventory. Most childcare centers are acquired with the real estate. The 2 multiple of SDE is after the debt service required to buy the real estate.

Pricing Tips

- "State regulations significantly impact value."
- "National or large regional operators will pay 3–5X EBITDA for centers licensed for 125+. Smaller centers will sell to owner-operators for 2.5–3X SDE. Inventory is typically not an issue. Quality of the center facility is very important to achieve higher multiples."
- "Rent including CAM needs to be below 20%."
- "Licensed capacity is key—centers over 125 sell for higher multiples."
- "Facility layout is important, as room size dictates staff:child ratio efficiency."
- "Staffing is key to profitability/value. Staff costs need to be under 50%, preferably under 40%."
- " . . .industry experts say operating a child day care business can be an ongoing struggle to balance expenses with parents' ability to pay. Regulations can add to costs—sometimes before operators are able to recover the increase through higher fees."
- "Percentage of Annual Revenue—30% to 45% of annual revenue for the business value only

  Percentage of Annual Revenue—140% to 300% of annual revenue for the value of the real estate and business together

  Multiple of Sellers Discretionary Cash Flow (SDCF) for the business value only—For centers licensed for under 100 children: 1 to 2 times annual SDCF; for centers licensed for 100 to 250 children: 2 to 2.5 times annual SDCF; for very profitable centers licensed over 250 children: 2.5 to 3.5 times annual SDCF. SDCF is also referred to as Adjusted Profits. It is calculated as: EBITDA + the Owner's Compensation.

Multiple of Earnings before Interest, Taxes, Depreciation, & Amortization (EBITDA) for the business value only—3 to 4 times annual EBITDA
Based on licensed capacity—$1,000 to $2,500 per child for the business value only
Based on licensed capacity—$6,000 to $14,000 per child for the real estate and business together"

- "Businesses with EBITDA of less than $100,000 will generally sell at a much lower multiple say 2–3 times, where an EBITDA of $300,000 will be 3.5–4 times. Building type, location, occupancy levels play a more important role in sale price than just the profit; centers with daily fees of under $60 per day per child will struggle to sell at any price; centers with a license of 50–80 children are the most; sort out sizes."

- "State regulations play a major role in the valuation of a child care business. As a general rule, higher degree of regulation often leads to higher quality of child care and lower business value due to cost of regulatory compliance. Child care market rates are not keeping pace with the cost to meet state regulations."

- "Site location is critical; curb cuts and ease of access in/out of center is very important; proper side of road for traffic flow during rush hour; tenure of center, tenure of teachers and their level of secondary education; strong director/mgr very important; quality centers with consistent earnings achieve price points in the higher end of the price range than other centers."

Expert Comments

"Buy a business that the owner is retiring from and has run for a long time, or is moving out of state or area. Look at two areas: payroll should be between 40 and 50%, and rent/mortgage no more than 20%."

"Run it like a business—not as an educator or on passion."

"Cleaner centers tend to do better and keep a higher enrollment while smaller, dirtier centers are closing their doors. Bottom line—reinvest in the business. Keep the doors and walls free of used tape and staples."

"Replication more difficult in states with high regulatory compliance"

"It would take 6–12 months to start from ground up, dealing with DCF licensure, health department, fire department, etc."

"Be careful to make sure that the seller isn't being taxed twice on any reimbursements from any governmental agencies."

"While it is relatively easy to replicate a child-care business, value can be created in a center that has a track record and has been in existence for decades."

"Newer facilities will command a higher service cost. Make sure the educational program keeps pace with changes in the educational sector. Some businesses have dual licenses and are licensed by the Department of Education."

"Very expensive to start a medium to large center from the ground up"

"Many variables here; location is key factor; strong operators/directors can achieve 22%–28% EBITDA depending on location, state & federal programs, level of income in area, etc."

"Depending upon growth rate of young population base, the better the curriculum the more difficult the business is to replicate."

"Other than 'occupancy costs' all other expenses are pretty proportional to enrollment or gross revenues and are easily managed as such. If rent can be tied to enrollment, then risk is greatly reduced (example: 10% of gross receipts for rent)."

"Real estate can be the largest value in a day-care transaction. Rent should be adjusted to reflect Fair Market Value (FMV) rent based on a) comparable information available or, b) a percentage of the real estate appraisal value and, c) cross-checked by making sure, if financed, that the rent will cover the debt services (and a return on the down payment)."

Benchmark Data

Statistics (Day Care)

Number of Establishments	816,343
Average Profit Margin	9.7%
Revenue per Employee	$29,000
Average Number of employees	2.1
Average Wages per Employee	$14,331

Products and Services Segmentation

Child day-care services	58.7%
Preschool programs	19.2%
Government contributions	13.1%
Other services and receipts	9.0%

Industry Costs

Profit	9.7%
Wages	49.4%
Purchases	13.1%
Depreciation	2.5%
Marketing	0.5%
Rent & Utilities	14.3%
Other	10.5%

Source: IBISWorld, July 2016

- "All operating ratios depend on each state's level of regulations. Heavy regulated states with low student-to-teacher ratios are significantly less profitable. There are no common, national benchmarks accurate across all states."
- "Revenue should be minimum $10K per unit of licensed capacity however this may vary due to practical capacity that is lower than approved capacity (due to ratios of quality limit). Size is important. Most desirable size is 125+ capacity. 75–125 is acceptable. Difficult to profit on less than 75."
- "Small centers (under 100) need to have an owner/operator to realize a profit. Over 100 and it can be run by an absentee owner. Any rent above $10–$12 a square foot is too much."
- "State's license based upon square footage per child. Physical layout combined with rent is a large factor in determining profitability of a business."
- "Easier to sell small and large centers, harder to sell medium-size centers."

Expenses as a percentage of annual sales

Cost of goods	10%
Payroll/labor Costs	40% to 55%
Occupancy	10% to 20%
Profit (estimated pretax)	10% to 18%

Industry Trend

- "Child care is evolving, and most care providers and parents agree the changes are for the best. What are some of the latest trends in child care and what should parents be looking for when making an all-important child care decision?
  - ✓ Child Care Is Catering to Budget-Minded Families
  - ✓ Child Care is Now Early Education
  - ✓ Drop-In Child Care is More Common
  - ✓ Corporate Child Care is Raising Quality Bar
  - ✓ Technology is Changing Provider/Parent Connection
  - ✓ Most Child Care is Becoming Safer
  - ✓ More Child Care Options Exist
  - ✓ The Internet Can Help You Find Child Care
  - ✓ Communications Are More Frequent, More Useful
  - ✓ Child Care Caters to Time-Crunched, Working Parents
  - ✓ Vacation Destinations, Kid-Friendly Hotels Offering On-Site Care
  - ✓ After-School Programs and Care Provide Child Care Flexibility"
  Source: by Robin McClure, April 19, 2016, https://www.verywell.com/top-trends-in-child-care-616937
- "Average growth; declining profits with increased regulations; labor shortages of qualified teachers."
- "If people have children, this business will be forever. This is a need business: food, gas, childcare, home."
- "Stable, however there is volatility related to employment. Child care spending is usually first expense cut when unemployed."
- "Will follow general economy."
- "Federal health officials proposed to overhaul 500,000 child care centers across the country, beefing up safety standards including background and fingerprint checks for employees and requiring states to better monitor the facilities."
- "Roughly 1.6 million U.S. children attend child care centers on subsidies—paid in the form of vouchers to families—from the federal government."
- "Continued growth, especially in some ethnic groups. Pricing schedules will not increase due to economy. Parents will seek out alternative, less expensive child care options."
- "Number of centers will stay flat. Cost to open is high."
- "Solid growth; education requirements becoming more important and required"
- "Regional and national chains will continue buyouts."

Seller Financing

- "Most if not all sales are financed with an SBA program. If the seller helps with a note, the SBA loan will not allow the seller to get a payment for some time as it is on full standby."
- "Depends on size—more seller financing with smaller centers."
- "5% to 10% seller financing; the rest of the financing is from SBA loans."

Questions

- "Occupancy records, look at competitors' occupancy as well. The future is more important than the past!"
- "Capacity, enrollment, rates, revenue, estimated profitability, facility. Does business owner or closely related 3rd party entity own the real estate? Detailed info on staff (hire dates & their credentials). Center's distinguishing characteristics. Describe local competition (reputation/rates/size/enrollment as % of capacity/advantages/disadvantages). Reason for sale?"
- "Are you on the food program? Subsidized care? Gold Seal?"
- "Does the provider have a contract with the children's parents? If yes, ask for the contract. Does the provider have a rate schedule? Is the same schedule used for all children or do some have a special rate? Determine which children have a different rate and the amount. If the provider does not have the rate schedule for the year in question, ask for the current rate schedule and then ask how it differed in the tax year under exam. Does the provider furnish year-end statements to the parents as to how much they paid in the tax year?"
- "Any state subsidies? Review price schedule. Listing of all licenses—NAEYC accredited? Any claims against center? Confirm enrollment counts. Discuss curriculum. Education/experience of staff."
- "What local, state & gov. programs are you getting funding from & how much per age group... then go & verify from the state & counties how much of this money you will NOT be getting during the 6–8 month probationary period post closing & what the risks are of losing this funding ST & LT. Be sure you properly calculate this loss into your working capital needs & be prepared for it post closing. Consult with state & verify playground has adequate square footage for licensed capacity stipulated on license (they do not always match)."
- "Licensing compliance, working ratios, teacher education qualifications, rates in terms of competition, private pay vs. government-supported care."

Resources

Websites
- Childcare Brokers: www.childcarebrokers.com

Associations
- National Association for Family Child Care: www.nafcc.org
- National Child Care Association: www.nccanet.org/
- National Association for the Education of Young Children: www.naeyc.org
- Association for Early Learning Leaders: www.earlylearningleaders.org

	Franchise
Deck the Walls (See also Franchises)	
Approx. Total Investment	$112,500 to $202,000
NAICS 442299	Number of Businesses/Units 200+

Rules of Thumb

> 35 percent of annual sales plus inventory

OK

Resources

Websites
- www.dtwfraninfo.com

Delicatessens (See also Restaurants)

| SIC 5812-09 | NAICS 445110 | |

Rules of Thumb

- 40 percent of annual sales plus inventory
- 2 times SDE plus inventory
- "If the deli is open five days a week, it's 50 percent of annual sales; if it's open six days a week, it's 40 percent of annual sales; and, if it's open seven days a week it's 30 percent of annual sales."
- Retail: 40 percent of annual sales plus inventory
- Industrial: 50 percent of annual sales plus inventory
- Office Buildings: 50 percent of annual sales plus inventory

Pricing Tips

- "It's important to recognize the distinction between sandwich shops and a real delicatessen. A real deli sells cold cuts plus many other traditional deli items; it usually does make and sell sandwiches, but it represents only a portion of their business. A sandwich shop is like a Subway or Quiznos."

Resources

Associations
- International Dairy-Deli-Bakery Association: www.iddba.org

Delivery Services (Courier Services)

| SIC 4212-05 | NAICS 492210 | Number of Businesses/Units 177,276 |

Rules of Thumb

- 70 percent of annual sales plus inventory (if any)
- 3 times SDE including Inventory
- 2 times EBITDA for businesses under $1 million
- 3 times EBITDA for businesses from $1 to $5 million
- 4 times EBITDA for businesses over $5 million

Pricing Tips

- ". . . FedEx has more pricing flexibility because its deliveries are handled by independent contractors while UPS employs unionized drivers."

Expert Comments

"It is worthy to note that the Frontier study (Frontier Economics, London) did research on 'why' businesses use and value express delivery for global shipments. Here are the value points for the global customer according to the study:

- ✓ Global Reach—ability to send items anywhere
- ✓ Reliability—knowing the items arrive on time
- ✓ Transparency—being able to track the items
- ✓ Speed—ability to reach destination quickly
- ✓ Security—knowing the items move in a secure supply chain."

Benchmark Data

Statistics (Courier and Local Delivery Services)

Number of Establishments	177,276
Average Profit Margin	13.7%
Revenue per Employee	$122,100
Average Number of Employees	4.1
Average Wages per Employee	$34,360

Products and Services Segmentation

Ground deliveries	70.2%
International air transit deliveries	12.5%
Domestic air transit deliveries	12.4%
Messengers and local deliveries	4.9%

Major Market Segmentation

Retail trade	30.0%
Households	20.0%
Finance and insurance	15.0%
Other	15.0%
Government departments	10.0%
Healthcare	10.0%

Industry Costs

Profit	13.7%
Wages	28.5%
Purchases	9.9%
Depreciation	4.8%
Marketing	0.4%
Rent & Utilities	2.2%
Other	40.5%

Market Share

United Parcel Service Inc.	43.8%
FedEx Corporation	29.9%

Source: IBISWorld, February 2016

- "Of the online retailers profiled in the Top 500 Guide, 184 list UPS as their shipping carrier, 139 FedEx and 107 USPS, according to Top500Guide.com"

Expenses as a percentage of annual sales

Cost of goods.. 42%
Payroll/labor Costs... 30%
Occupancy... 0%
Profit (estimated pretax) 28%

Industry Trend

- "The US courier and parcel delivery services industry consists of about 7,500 companies both large and small, which have combined annual revenue of about $90 billion. The industry has seen steady growth in the last few years. A major chunk of the industry is held by its two key players, FedEx and United Parcel Services."

Source: by Ally Schmidt, July 17, 2015,
http://marketrealist.com/2015/07/key-trends-shape-courier-industry-2015/

- "Overall ecommerce will continue to account for larger share of world trade. For example, the ecommerce share of trade volumes of developed countries could reach 40% in 2025 and up to 30% in emerging markets. In China alone, according to a MasterCard study, cross-border online sales reached $2.92 billion in 2012 and their projection for 2015 is $8.11 billion. Finally, total ecommerce global is expected to grow by 20% the next two years and reach $2.3 trillion in 2017."

Source: "The Huge Growth for the Express Delivery Industry" 3/23/15 http://expressassociation.org/delivery_
and_logistics_news/THE_HUGE_GROWTH_FOR_THE_EXPRESS_DELIVERY_INDUSTRY_194.asp

Seller Financing

- "Cash purchase"

Resources

Associations

- Express Delivery & Logistics Association: www.expressassociation.org

		Franchise
Del Taco (See also Franchises)		
Approx. Total Investment		$847,700 to $1,815,500
Estimated Annual Sales/Unit		$1,200,000
	NAICS 722513	Number of Businesses/Units 247

Rules of Thumb

➤ 70 percent of annual sales plus inventory

Resources

Websites

- www.deltacofranchise.com

Dental Laboratories		
SIC 8072-01	NAICS 339116	

Rules of Thumb

➢ 45 percent of annual sales plus inventory

➢ 1 times SDE plus equipment and inventory

➢ 2 times SDE includes equipment & inventory

Benchmark Data

- "Let's start with the premise that for most laboratories labor is the largest single cost item, typically running between 45% and 60% of revenues. Keep this important concept in mind. Increasing the productivity of your technicians is not just the number of units you ship to clients. It requires increasing output without increasing the time the technicians spend working. If they build 40 units of porcelain in a 40-hour week, building 50 units in a 50-hour week is not increased productivity. It's actually worse because you are now paying overtime. Increasing productivity requires producing 45 units in that 40-hour week. If you are a crown and bridge lab, your goal should be to produce 3.75 complete finished units per technician per day. Removable labs should shoot for 3.25 units. A five-technician crown and bridge lab should average 18.75 per day."

  Source: "Higher Productivity = Bigger Profits" by Chuck Yenker, www.dentalproductsreport.com. March 2010. (dated, but still of interest)

- "Industry Asks FDA to Improve Regulation of Dental Restorations to Protect Patient Safety in $5.5 billion U.S. dental-restoration products industry. Most domestic dental laboratories are exempt from registering with the FDA, and most typically employ just 3.5 people."

  Source: National Association of Dental Laboratories and www.businesswire.com

Industry Trend

- "The Top 5 Dental Lab Trends of 2014:
  - ✓ The gap between practice and lab grew even smaller
  - ✓ Labs of every size realized they could handle more case types than they thought
  - ✓ 3D printing continued to march forward
  - ✓ All-digital started to be more than a marketing slogan
  - ✓ Creativity still mattered"

  Source: "The Top 5 Dental Lab Trends of 2014" by Ryan Hamm 12/19/2014
  http://www.dentalproductsreport.com/lab/article/top-5-dental-lab-trends-2014

- "Nevertheless, as the number of people with private health insurance slightly increased at an annualized rate of 1.3% during the five years to 2014, demand for industry services propelled forward. Additionally, rapid technological changes, such as new filling, bonding and implant compounds, such as all-ceramic restorative systems; cutting edge computer-aided design and computer-aided manufacturing (CAD and CAM systems); and computer imaging, stimulated demand for industry services."

- "The Dental Laboratories industry is highly fragmented and has a low level of concentration. No company generates more than 5.0% of industry revenue, and the largest industry firm, National Dentex Corporation, accounts for about 3.6% of revenue. 'In 2014, the largest four players generate less than 10.0%

of industry revenue,' says Turk. Over the five years to 2014, concentration has been stable; the number of industry firms has remained relatively flat, increasing at an estimated average annual rate of 0.2% to 6,850. Further, many industry players belong to regional and national dental laboratory associations, such as the National Association of Dental Laboratories, which prevents one operator from strengthening their market share."

Source: www.PRWeb.com, February 28, 2014

Dental Practices

SIC 8021-01	NAICS 621210	Number of Businesses/Units 187,652

Rules of Thumb

➤ 50 to 65 percent of annual sales includes inventory

➤ 1.3 to 2 times SDE includes inventory

➤ 3 to 4 times EBIT

➤ 2 to 4 times EBITDA

➤ 50 to 70 percent of annual collections subject to how weighted practice is towards managed care versus private fee for service (cash pay) and condition of equipment

Pricing Tips

▪ "Performing a valuation on a dental practice, or any business for that matter, involves looking at more than one variable. You have to look at the adjusted net income, the equipment market value and the risk attributes of a practice. A simple rule of thumb may be 65% of gross annual sales, but what if the practice has poor margins? Then, the rule of thumb goes out the window. The best valuation would be to use a net income approach, a book value method and a capitalization method. Taking a weighted average of these three approaches will provide an accurate value of a practice."

▪ "Age of equipment, quality of three-party payer contracts, quality of location in terms of patients."

▪ "What should I scrutinize when looking at a practice? Look at the gross production of the office to determine if you can produce or have produced that amount of dentistry. Also look to see if collections are close to the level of production, what the overall overhead of the office is and what makes up that overhead. For the physical office, look to be sure the location is in an area that will support your vision of your practice and that the building is in good condition. Within the office, note the quality and age of the equipment and whether anything is in major disrepair. Eventually, you will review patient charts and reports to verify statistics like new patient flow and the amount of active patients. You will want to get some idea of what kind of treatment patients are accustomed to and what has been done for them. Despite the importance of working equipment, do not over-emphasize its value. You are primarily purchasing goodwill, or the ongoing patient flow and production of the office. Equipment is easily, and affordably, replaceable. A quality patient base, skilled staff and working office systems are not."

Source: Buying a Practice—FAQs, www.towniecentral.com/Dentaltown/Article

D - Rules of Thumb

- "A 'must' purchase is the American Dental Association's "Valuing a Practice: A Guide for Dentists." http://www.adacatalog.org/. Read it, learn it and memorize it!"

Expert Comments

"The industry is evolving with consolidation occurring. Corporate practices are growing. Sellers have trouble selling to corporate buyers. Insurance companies are also changing the industry. Many doctors sell directly to an employee in the practice, eliminating the need for a broker."

"Expensive set up for new practice with high office renovation, plumbing and other construction costs. Easy financing available through many sources. Banks are very accommodating to dentists. There appear to be fewer dentists exiting dental schools who are interested in practice ownership."

"Dental practices are most marketable in desirable suburban areas and least in rural areas. Good profit for time practicing, typically 40% to 45% of gross, depending on practice."

"Fewer dentists from schools, trend to aggregate dental practices."

"Fee-for-service or insurance-based practice will cause multiples and marketability to increase/decrease."

Benchmark Data

Statistics (Dentists)

Number of Establishments	187,652
Average Profit Margin	19.7%
Revenue per Employee	$127,400
Average Number of Employees	5.4
Average Wages per Employee	$47,447

Products and Services Segmentation

Restorative dental services	22.3%
Preventative services	16.3%
Dental consultations and diagnostic services	15.9%
Other	15.1%
Prosthodontics (fixed and removable)	9.4%
Orthodontics	9.3%
Surgical oral and maxillofacial services	7.0%
Nonsurgical endodontic services	4.7%

Industry Costs

Profit	19.7%
Wages	34.3%
Purchases	11.5%
Depreciation	2.4%
Marketing	1.6%
Rent & Utilities	4.7%
Other	25.8%

Source: IBISWorld, July 2016

- "$25,000 per employee per month in revenues. $25,000 per operatory per month in revenues. National average margin of 35%. National average overhead of 65%."

✓ "Male dentists are practicing an average of 34 hours per week, while female dentists practice 27 hours per week.

✓ There will be 15 new dental schools opening in the coming years.

✓ Since 2005, dentists have experienced a 13% decline in their average annual income, even though spending on dental care by patients has increased each successive year.

✓ By the year 2020 (just 6 years away), the majority of practicing dentists will be women, and over the next 10-20 years, this increased influx of women into the field of dentistry may be one of the most defining forces in the entire make-up, culture and practice organization in dentistry.

✓ 60% of practicing dentists under the age of 44 are women.

✓ The market for chairside milling is slowly, but steadily, increasing, with an expected compound annual growth rate (CAGR) of 10.5% between 2012 and 2019, which will increase the approximately 12,650 chairside milling units in use in the United States in 2012 to an estimated 22,087 by 2019.

✓ Most graduating dentists are coming out of dental school with anywhere from $150K–$300K worth of student loan debt, and 41% of all graduating dentists say this debt load influences their practice choice (the reason many join a group practice as opposed to establishing a solo practice).

✓ The average retirement age for dentists is now 68.3 years"

Source: "Trends in Dentistry, Forces impacting the dental industry's course in 2014 and Beyond," Inside Dental Technology

Expenses as a percentage of annual sales

Cost of goods	07% to 14%
Payroll/labor Costs	30% to 40%
Occupancy	04% to 09%
Profit (estimated pretax)	30%

Industry Trend

▪ "The demographic profile of dentists has changed significantly over time as well. In 1975, dentists were generally young and male. Fifty-seven percent of all dentists were younger than 45 years old, and almost all of them (98%) were male. The past 40 years have seen a lot of change. In general, the dentist population is now older, and there is a much larger representation of females. Today, 42% of dentists are at least 55 years old, and only 31% are younger than 45 years old. The differences are even greater when gender is considered. More than half of the male dentists (52%) are at least 55 years old. 56.2% of female dentists, on the other hand, are younger than 45 years old.

"Major changes have occurred in the number and distribution of dental personnel over the past 60 years. We have moved from a model typically comprised of one dentist and one assistant per practice to one with a much larger and more diverse group of personnel. In 1950, there were approximately 155,000 dental personnel, which included dentists, dental hygienists, dental assistants, and other staff (e.g., receptionists, office managers, bookkeepers, sterilization assistants, laboratory technicians). Just over 50% of these individuals were dentists. By 2012, the total number of dental personnel had risen to almost one million, nearly a sixfold increase. Over the next decade (2015-2024), many of these dentists will retire. As they sell their practices, the degree to which these practice sales go to corporate entities could have a major impact on the proportion of private practices in the marketplace.

"The second demographic challenge comes in the next decade (2025-2035) with the aging of the baby boomer patients. As retirees on fixed incomes, will they continue to demand the same level of dental services? In addition, there will be some population loss in this age group as well. The loss of these patients or a reduction in their demand for dental services could have a major impact on the profile of dental services provided and the aggregate amount of income going into dentistry. Once again, a more competitive marketplace will provide a challenge to the private practitioner."

Source: "Dental workforce trends and the future of dental practices," by Eric Solomon, DDS, MA; February–April 2015, www.dentaleconomics.com

- "Consolidation of practices as baby boomers start to retire. Few solo practices and more corporate practices. Insurance companies reduce reimbursements causing downward pressure on profitability."
- "As the economy improves, patients will have more dentistry done."
- "Increasing due to the Health Care Reform allowing millions of disadvantaged persons in"
- "Dentistry remains a good profession. Excellent profit potential for those willing to work hard. Technology and new cosmetic procedures should keep productivity and demand high."
- "Growing demand. Trend to add more ancillary services (i.e., teeth whitening, cosmetics) to improve profitability."
- "Dependent on insurance coverage allocated to dental practices"
- "Improvements in technology, quality of materials, and education of consumers regarding services available and transparency in pricing will continue to accelerate."

Seller Financing
- "Banks love dentists as the failure rate is under 1%. Bank financing is readily available."
- "Very good 3rd-party financing available—sometimes even 100 percent."

Questions
- "What procedures are done? What is your philosophy on treatment? Is your practice digital? How do you market for new patients? Why are you selling? Would you be willing to stay on and work for a while?"
- "Patient demographics, Revenue per patient, hygienist revenue, employee turnover, recall system"
- "Ask about: What are the revenues comprised of? What 3rd party payer sources exist? Age and condition of equipment. How they market."
- "Besides all the typical questions, how many active patients do they have; do they want to stay on or leave; and if they own the real estate (50%–60% do), do they want to rent or sell it."
- "Age of practice and equipment, demographics of practice, call-back programs, average annual billing per patient."
- "Type of practice, hours worked, amount of hygiene revenue, number of operatories, type of procedures commonly performed, payer mix, insurance contracts"

Resources

Trade Publications
- Dental Economics: www.dentaleconomics.com

Associations
- American Dental Association: www.ada.org

Diagnostic Imaging Centers

	NAICS 621512	Number of Businesses/Units 17,231

Rules of Thumb
- ➢ 100 percent of annual sales includes inventory
- ➢ 3.25 times SDE includes inventory
- ➢ 4 times EBIT
- ➢ 5 times EBITDA

Pricing Tips
- "May be necessary to include A/R in the price for working capital needs. Age and type of equipment very important."

Expert Comments
"Highly competitive and constant change taking place with reimbursement rates via Medicare."

Benchmark Data

Statistics (Diagnostic Imaging Centers)
Number of Establishments	17,231
Average Profit Margin	13.3%
Revenue per Employee	$184,000
Average Number of Employees	6.1
Average Wages per Employee	$61,184

Products and Services Segmentation
Computed tomography (CT) scanning	27.5%
Magnetic resonance imaging scans	27.1%
All other diagnostic imaging	21.4%
Ultrasound imaging	10.8%
Radiographic imaging (Including x-rays)	10.0%
Other services	3.2%

Major Market Segmentation
Private insurance payments	40.6%
Medicare and Medicaid payments	20.2%
Other	12.3%
Health practitioner payments	11.6%
Hospital payments	9.1%
Out-of-pocket payments	6.2%

Industry Costs

Profit	13.3%
Wages	33.2%
Purchases	37.6%
Depreciation	5.5%
Marketing	0.9%
Rent & Utilities	5.4%
Other	4.1%

Source: IBISWorld, November 2015

Expenses as a percentage of annual sales

Cost of goods	10%
Payroll/labor Costs	25%
Occupancy	05% to 10%
Profit (estimated pretax)	40%

Industry Trend

- "Here are five trends we expect to have a vital impact on medical imaging in 2015:
  - ✓ 3D mammography. Digital breast tomosynthesis (DBT) has been a frequent topic in trade publications for a few years.
  - ✓ Multimedia enhanced radiology reporting (MERR). Text-only reports are fading away.
  - ✓ Wider adoption of cloud technologies. Radiology, along with the rest of the healthcare sector, is moving to the cloud, and it is happening fast.
  - ✓ Centralization of clinical data. Collaboration is a must for health facilities. No department can be left out of the patient experience equation.
  - ✓ Telemedicine. The global telemedicine market in 2016 is predicted to be $27 billion, with virtual health services accounting for nearly 60% of the total."

  Source: "The Top Medical Imaging Trends of 2015," January 25, 2015, http://www.carestream.com/blog/2015/01/29/top-medical-imaging-trends-2015/

- "Uncertainty. While the need for scans (CT, MRI, X-ray) will continue to go up, reimbursements will likely fall."

Dialysis Centers		
	NAICS 621492	Number of Businesses/Units 40,037

Rules of Thumb

➤ 5 to 10 times EBITDA

Pricing Tips

- "Patient mix (types of payer sources) is key; geography is also important given differences in reimbursement in different areas and regulations."

Benchmark Data

Statistics (Emergency & Other Outpatient Care Centers)

Number of Establishments	40,037
Average Profit Margin	16.0%
Revenue per Employee	$150,400
Average Number of Employees	16.8
Average Wages per Employee	$58,495

Products and Services Segmentation

Other outpatient care centers	45.5%
Freestanding ambulatory surgical and emergency centers	25.3%
Kidney dialysis centers	21.1%
HMO medical centers	8.1%

Major Market Segmentation

Government	36.4%
Private insurance	28.6%
Other	18.1%
Contributions, gifts and grants	12.4%
Patients (out-of-pocket)	4.5%

Industry Costs

Profit	16.0%
Wages	38.7%
Purchases	14.1%
Depreciation	2.6%
Marketing	0.5%
Rent & Utilities	5.6%
Other	22.5%

Market Share

Fresenius Medical Care AG & Co. KGaA	12.0%
DaVita HealthCare Partners Inc.	9.3%

Source: IBISWorld, April 2016

- "Often owners will hear estimates based on amounts 'per patient' which can be inaccurate, as they may be based on very different types of programs in different areas with different payer groups."

Expenses as a percentage of annual sales

Cost of goods	13%
Payroll/labor Costs	06%
Occupancy	0
Profit (estimated pretax)	05% to 15%

Industry Trend

- "For 400,000 people across the country with failed kidneys, dialysis care is a matter of life and death. It is also a lucrative business, in part because Medicare pays for such treatment regardless of age. But as for-profit clinics and chains have grown to control about 85 percent of the dialysis market over the last decade, researchers have documented starkly higher mortality rates in centers owned by for-profits compared with nonprofits."

Source: "Hospitals' Dialysis Plan Is Under New Scrutiny," by Nina Bernstein, www.nytimes.com February 12, 2014

Questions

- "Whether they are the medical director, and what relationships they have with patient referral sources; whether they would continue to work in the unit post transaction, etc."

		Franchise
Dick's Wings & Grill (See also Franchises)		
Approx. Total Investment	$100,000 per restaurant + a net worth of $500,000	
	NAICS 722513	Number of Businesses/Units 22

Rules of Thumb

➤ 35 percent of annual sales

Resources

Websites

- www.dickswingsandgrill.com

Diners (See also Restaurants)		
	NAICS 722511	

Rules of Thumb

➤ 30 to 35 percent of annual sales plus inventory

Direct Mail—Advertising (See also Coupon Books, Valpak)		
SIC 7331-05	NAICS 541860	Number of Businesses/Units 2,691

Rules of Thumb

➤ 40 to 50 percent of annual revenues plus inventory

➤ 2 to 2.5 times SDE not including inventory

Pricing Tips

- "Valpak used to be the gold standard for this industry at a multiple of 3. Considering new technology and the economy most have been selling at 2 X SDE or slightly less."

Expert Comments

"Online coupon technology has hurt this industry."

"Marketability is high. Location and facilities are solid because this biz thrives in metropolitan areas and can be run out of your home."

Benchmark Data

Statistics (Direct Mail Advertising)

Number of Establishments	2,691
Average Profit Margin	5.5%
Revenue per Employee	$246,500
Average Number of Employees	18.0
Average Wages per Employee	$51,277

Products and Services Segmentation

Full direct mail services	51.8%
Printing and fulfillment services	18.7%
Other services	13.5%
Lettershop services	12.9%
Mailing list support services	3.1%

Major Market Segmentation

Retail Stores	34.5%
Other	19.8%
Finance, banking and insurance institutions	18.0%
Restaurants and travel companies	15.7%
Business-to-business market	12.0%

Industry Costs

Profit	5.5%
Wages	21.0%
Purchases	32.3%
Depreciation	1.2%
Marketing	6.9%
Rent & Utilities	6.1%
Other	27.0%

Market Share

Valassis Communications Inc.	11.8%

Source: IBISWorld, February 2016

Expenses as a percentage of annual sales

Cost of goods	65%
Payroll/labor Costs	05% to 10%
Occupancy	05%
Profit (estimated pretax)	20% to 25%

Industry Trend

- "7 Trends to watch:
    - ✓ Oversized mailings
    - ✓ Adding a soft-touch varnish to increase tactile appeal
    - ✓ Luxury marketers who are doubling down on direct mail
    - ✓ Loyalty program support and acceleration
    - ✓ Power use of direct mail by selected market segments
    - ✓ The vanishing reply form
    - ✓ Smaller quantities"

Source: "7 Trends to Watch in Direct Mail Marketing," by jeangianfagna, July 20, 2015

Questions

- "How many recurring agreements are in place? How large is your biggest client?"
- "How many active clients? What is your average net profit?"

Resources

Associations
- Direct Marketing Association: www.the-dma.org

Direct Selling Businesses		
SIC 5963-98	NAICS 4543	Number of Businesses/Units 706,380

Rules of Thumb

➢ 4.5 to 5 times EBITDA

Pricing Tips

- "It all depends on who is buying and who is selling. Buyer and seller motivation is key. If the seller is very successful and getting in the way of larger companies, that would tend to dramatically increase the price."

Benchmark Data

Statistics (Direct Selling Companies)

Number of Establishments	706,380
Average Profit Margin	6.9%
Revenue per Employee	$50,100
Average Number of Employees	1.1
Average Wages per Employee	$8,882

Products and Services Segmentation

Home and family care products	30.9%
Wellness and personal care products	30.8%
Other products and services	19.3%
Leisure and educational products	10.0%
Clothing and accessories	9.0%

Industry Costs

Profit	6.9%
Wages	17.8%
Purchases	63.5%
Depreciation	0.7%
Marketing	2.6%
Rent and Utilities	4.3%
Other	4.2%

Source: IBISWorld, August 2016

- "$150,000 annual sales per employee"

Expenses as a percentage of annual sales

Cost of goods... 60%
Payroll/labor Costs.. 01%
Occupancy .... 01% to 04%
Profit (estimated pretax) .... 07% to 10%

Industry Trend
- "Increasing consolidation"

Seller Financing
- "Both are common, many times it is a combination of the outside financing and seller financing."

Questions
- "You need to have detailed information on all the customers. See what the trends have been the last 3 years. Who are the suppliers? Many times the key supplier is the buyer. About the employees, how long they have been there and their roles in the company. Need to see all financial information including tax returns for the last 3 years. What equipment is being included, like trucks, forklifts and warehouse equipment? Are the bottles, racks, water coolers, and coffee brewers in good shape? What is the age of this equipment? What about accounts receivable? Need A/R aging reports, totals and for each customer."

Distribution/Wholesale—Durable Goods		
	NAICS 423	

Rules of Thumb
- ➢ 4 times EBITDA
- ➢ 2 to 2.5 times SDE plus inventory
- ➢ 4.5 times EBIT

Pricing Tips
- "Inventory (durable or non-durable) is critical to the sale and must be current, well managed with appropriate controls and real time valuation processes in place."
- "Worth approximately one-half of sales volume; watch out for large, stale inventory."
- "% of annual gross sales is a poor guide to follow. EBITDA drives ROI and ability to service debt."
- "Add cost of replacing current ownership with professional management to SDE, and then multiply this number by 4 to 6 to get price. variance is for security of earnings, competition, assets, etc."

Expert Comments
"There are significant competitive cost barriers to entry into this industry, where size does matter along with quantity and quality of product lines,

adequate logistical distribution channels, good supplier pricing and terms, adequate facilities sizing and location. Solid, well-diversified customer base mitigates risk and wards off competitive challenges."

Benchmark Data

- "Distribution costs are sensitive to energy prices. Direct competition from manufacturers is increasing which creates a challenge for many distributors and a need to find service and delivery differentiation for the clients."
- "Cost of goods should be less than 74%, with 70% as ideal; operating expenses of less than 20%; sales/assets ratio of 3.0; W/C ratio of 13% to 15% of revenues; current ratio of 3.0 or greater; A/R turnover ratio of 12.0; inventory turns of 6.0 or greater; sales per employee greater than $250,000; sales per sq. ft. in excess of $300,000."

Expenses as a percentage of annual sales

Cost of goods	70% to 80%
Payroll/labor Costs	10% to 20%
Occupancy	03% to 08%
Profit (estimated pretax)	08% to 15%

Seller Financing

- "Banks like the industry and will generally provide SBA 7(a) credit to qualified buyer and where consistent cash flow is evident."

Questions

- "Does the business belong to any distributor buying groups/co-ops?"

Resources

Associations

- National Association of Wholesaler-Distributors: www.naw.org

Distribution/Wholesale—Electrical Products

NAICS 423610	Number of Businesses/Units 14,875

Rules of Thumb

➢ 35 percent of annual revenues plus inventory

Benchmark Data

Statistics (Electrical Equipment Wholesaling)

Number of Establishments	14,875
Average Profit Margin	4.2%
Revenue per Employee	$828,700
Average Number of Employees	13.6
Average Wages per Employee	$69,563

Products and Services Segmentation

Other electrical equipment	34.5%
Wiring	21.7%
Lighting fixtures and light bulbs	16.1%
Relay and industrial controls	8.1%
Switchgear and switchboard apparatus	7.8%
Motors and generators	6.4%
Power and distribution transformers	5.4%

Major Market Segmentation

Industrial users	39.0%
Construction	32.0%
Utility	15.0%
Commercial, institutional and governmental	14.0%

Industry Costs

Profit	4.2%
Wages	8.5%
Purchases	80.6%
Depreciation	0.5%
Marketing	0.2%
Rent & Utilities	2.1%
Other	3.9%

Market Share

WESCO International Inc.	2.9%

Source: IBISWorld, June 2016

Distribution/Wholesale—Grocery Products/Full Line

SIC 5141-05	NAICS 424990	Number of Businesses/Units 5,785

Rules of Thumb

➢ 3 to 4 times SDE

➢ 4 times EBIT

➢ 4 to 4.5 times EBITDA

Pricing Tips

- "Use 25%–30% of GPM [gross profit margin] times 4 to arrive at goodwill price including all F F & E. To this number, add the dollar amount of net working capital, if any, to be included in the sale."

Benchmark Data

Statistics (Grocery Wholesaling)

Number of Establishments	5,785
Average Profit Margin	2.8%
Revenue per Employee	$1,292,400
Average Number of Employees	27.0
Average Wages per Employee	$57,148

27th Edition

Products and Services Segmentation

Other	23.5%
Fresh meat and meat products	20.0%
Canned food	17.7%
Frozen food	13.0%
Dairy products	10.0%
Specialty food	6.0%
Fresh fruits and vegetables	5.4%
Paper and plastic products	4.4%

Major Market Segmentation

Food service outlets	51.3%
Supermarkets and other grocery retailers	36.5%
Other wholesalers	9.0%
Other	3.2%

Industry Costs

Profit	2.8%
Wages	4.4%
Purchases	87.4%
Depreciation	0.4%
Marketing	0.6%
Rent & Utilities	1.6%
Other	2.8%

Market Share

SYSCO Corporation	22.3%
C&S Wholesale Grocers Inc.	16.1%
US Foods	11.9%
Performance Food Group	8.0%
Wakefern Food Corporation	6.7%

Source: IBISWorld, April 2016

- "$285,000–$300,000 sales per employee would be a good benchmark for a successful wholesale distributor."

Expenses as a percentage of annual sales

Cost of goods	80% to 83%
Payroll/labor Costs	12%
Occupancy	05%
Profit (estimated pretax)	07% to 08%

Questions
- "Stability of gross profit margins?"

Distribution/Wholesale—Industrial Supplies

	NAICS 423840	Number of Businesses/Units 10,623

Rules of Thumb

➢ 50 percent of annual revenues plus inventory

➢ 4 to 5 times EBITDA

Pricing Tips

▪ "Many distributorships for larger equipment do not order high dollar inventory until they receive a request from a customer to order that equipment. Therefore, inventory levels may not be extremely high as they try to not hold excess inventory. If the business you are evaluating is not operated this way and there is a large amount of inventory, you may need to consider that in your working capital calculations."

Expert Comments

"Companies that represent quality lines of products are desired. Contracts with customers to consistently provide their equipment or supplies or maintenance are a major plus."

Benchmark Data

Statistics (Industrial Supplies Wholesaling)

Number of Establishments	10,623
Average Profit Margin	5.5%
Revenue per Employee	$734,700
Average Number of Employees	9.3
Average Wages per Employee	$64,203

Products and Services Segmentation

Abrasives, strapping and tape	30.8%
Industrial containers	19.0%
Other supplies	16.5%
Mechanical power transmission supplies	15.4%
Industrial valves and fittings	14.4%
Welding supplies	3.9%

Major Market Segmentation

Industrial users for production inputs	49.0%
Other wholesalers for resale	25.7%
Businesses for end use	10.3%
Other	7.0%
Retailers for resale	5.0%
Building contractors	3.0%

Industry Costs

Profit	5.5%
Wages	8.5%
Purchases	74.7%
Depreciation	0.6%
Marketing	0.4%
Rent & Utilities	1.0%
Other	9.3%

Source: IBISWorld, June 2016

Questions

▪ "Who are your distributor agreements with? What restrictions do you have regarding geography and other products? How many additional products can your current sales force add to their sales book?"

D - Rules of Thumb

Resources

Associations
- Industrial Supply Association: www.isapartners.org

Distribution/Wholesale—In General

Rules of Thumb
- ➤ 65 percent of annual sales plus inventory
- ➤ 2.75 times SDE plus inventory
- ➤ 3.2 times EBIT
- ➤ 3 times EBITDA

Pricing Tips
- "Distribution companies that are profitable with a strong history and diversified customer base can command high multiples."
- "Assumes SDE in excess of $500K. Where less than $500K, lower multiples; where over $1M, multiples exceed 3 and escalate as SDE increases."
- "Suppliers, how many, and will that continue for a new owner, under the same or better terms. Current contracts with customers and account concentration issues all of high importance in determining value."
- "Debt service will have great impact on ultimate rule of thumb multiple considering 'living wage' necessary by locality after debt is serviced."

Expert Comments

"Sellers—Start preparing for your sale as much as five years in advance. Selling a business is very complex and you need to develop a good team of advisors. Five years in advance is not always possible but I recommend the seller hire an exit planner with experience in this industry to help with the complexities of the process. I also suggest you hire an experience investment banker. They have sold many businesses and understand they types of advisors required (Tax and Audit CPA, Transaction Attorney, Financial Advisor and more - all should have M&A experience, if you have an important advisor without the experience let them help you find one to augment their skills and experience). No matter how much the advisors cost they should easily pay for themselves many times over.

"Buyers—Assuming you know the industry please put a high quality team of advisors together as mentioned above. You will need a forensic CPA (audit), a good tax CPA, transaction attorney and more. "

"However it does take a lot of capital (inventory) to get started and depending on the technology (high tech vs. low tech) the costs to support customer can vary."

"Easy to market with use of the Web. For a savvy new owner with more technical abilities, an existing wholesale/distribution business can market to the world."

"Can be easy to replicate; the sales force is often key to success."

"Distributor with large, developed customer base is difficult to duplicate, thus enhancing the value. Seller-based financing is essential with the limitation on SBA financing where the major business asset is inventory."

Benchmark Data

- "The occupancy costs can vary considerably depending if the seller is the landlord or not."
- "High margins for the most part"
- "Low rent can be easy to achieve for these types of 'warehouse' businesses."
- "Cost of goods sold varies from 60%–70% depending on product."

Expenses as a percentage of annual sales

Cost of goods	70%
Payroll/labor Costs	15% to 19%
Occupancy	05%
Profit (estimated pretax)	10% to 15%

- "High-tech distribution and value add services distributors will continue to grow and outperform competition. Those that have figured out a recurring revenue model (30 to 50% of revenue) are appraised at considerable higher multiples."
- "When marketing to the wholesale distribution industry, it is important to have a firm understanding of the current wholesale distribution market. With annual sales of about $5 trillion (down from $6 trillion in early 2011), the US wholesale distribution industry includes about 300,000 companies. For the period between 2010 and 2015, the output of the US wholesale distribution industry is forecast to grow at an annual compounded rate of 6 percent. A respected industry overview cited the industry's growth over the last decade as having been 'above average' as compared to other industries. If this sounds less than enthusiastic, here's the reality check they provide: during that 10-year period, while distributor revenue grew nearly 50%—with computers, electrical goods, and machinery leading the pack—retailers showed 40% growth, and the US economy saw 30% growth. Considering that the decade in question included the 'ugliest financial disaster since the Great Depression,' and that the US economy still managed to show 30% growth on average, we'd say 'above average' works well enough."

  Source: http://www.thefrantzgroup.com/industry-marketing-experiences/
  wholesale-distribution-industry-overview/

- "Wholesaler-distributors should plan on economic expansion in 2015, though generally at a milder pace than was evident in 2014. Wholesaler-distributors closer to the consumer side of the economy will likely see stronger growth than those in the business-to-business market. A faster rate of growth in the U.S. economy, and thus a great demand on wholesaler-distributors, should be anticipated for 2016."

  Source: "State of the Wholesale Distribution Industry" by Alan Beaulieu,
  http://www.naw.org/about/industry.php

- "Growing industry, particularly over the Internet"
- "Highly competitive . . . unless a unique product, specifically manufactured. Margins are declining as competition increases."

Seller Financing

- "If a good quality firm then outside financing is traditional along with some seller financing (the banks like to see the seller share a little risk)."

Questions

- "What other products or lines can they distribute, are there any restrictions given by current suppliers?"
- "Get financials for past 3 years and year-to-date. What has changed in your industry? Do you sell to distributors? If so, what are the margins? What is the source of your product and is there an agreement to assure continued supply?"
- "What is the current method of finding and keeping customers? How do they expect the current sales to grow? Does China or overseas production cause any future issues for the current products sold?"
- "How many clients do you have and how many are 'regularly' serviced?"

Resources

Trade Publications
- Modern Distribution Management: http://www.mdm.com/

Associations
- National Association of Wholesaler-Distributors: www.naw.org

Distribution/Wholesale— Janitorial	
NAICS 423850	Number of Businesses/Units 2,656

Rules of Thumb

➢ 30 to 40 percent of annual sales plus inventory

Benchmark Data

Statistics (Cleaning & Maintenance Supplies Distributors)

Number of Establishments	2,656
Average Profit Margin	3.5%
Revenue per Employee	$301,400
Average Number of Employees	12.1
Average Wages per Employee	$31,651

Products and Services Segmentation

Paper and plastics products	54.4%
Chemical supplies	27.0%
Janitorial supplies and accessories	8.1%
Power equipment	7.1%
Other janitorial products	3.4%

Major Market Segmentation

Others	19.3%
Healthcare Centers	14.9%
Industrial buildings	14.6%
Janitorial service companies	14.5%
Schools, colleges and universities	13.7%
Government buildings	8.4%
Retail outlets, malls, department stores, grocery stores and other	7.9%
Commercial buildings	6.7%

Industry Costs

Profit	3.5%
Wages	10.5%
Purchases	72.9%
Depreciation	0.6%
Marketing	0.6%
Rent & Utilities	4.9%
Other	7.0%

Market Share

United Stationers Inc.	15.7%

Source: IBISWorld, November 2015

Distribution/Wholesale—Medical Equipment & Supplies

NAICS 42145	Number of Businesses/Units 12,952

Rules of Thumb

➤ 50 percent of annual revenues plus inventory

Pricing Tips

- "Pricing on medical equipment tends to be a higher percentage of sales than medical supplies. While the percentage of annual sales price might be a bit higher than the multiple in the Rule of Thumb above, the price based on percentage of annual sales for medical supplies could be lower."

Benchmark Data

Statistics (Medical Supplies Wholesaling)

Number of Establishments	12,952
Average Profit Margin	5.7%
Revenue per Employee	$817,500
Average Number of Employees	16.2
Average Wages per Employee	$105,895

Products and Services Segmentation

Surgical, medical and hospital instruments and equipment	53.4%
Surgical, medical and hospital supplies	24.1%
Orthopedic and prosthetic appliances and supplies	10.4%
Dental equipment, instruments and supplies	6.5%
Other	4.2%
Pharmaceuticals, cosmetics and toiletries	1.4%

Major Market Segmentation

Hospitals	62.3%
Clinics	22.0%
Alternate care providers	10.8%
Dentists	4.9%

Industry Costs

Profit	5.7%
Wages	12.7%
Purchases	74.4%
Depreciation	0.8%
Marketing	0.7%
Rent & Utilities	0.7%
Other	5.0%

Market Share

Cardinal Health Inc.	7.1%
Owens & Minor Inc.	5.4%

Source: IBISWorld, April 2016

Distribution/Wholesale—Paper

	NAICS 425120	Number of Businesses/Units 1,474

Rules of Thumb

➤ 3 to 4 times SDE plus inventory

➤ 4 to 5 times EBIT

➤ 5 times EBITDA

Pricing Tips

- "Use 25–30% of GPM [Gross Profit Margin] times 4 to arrive at goodwill price including all FF&E. To this number, add the dollar amount of net working capital to be included in the sale."

Benchmark Data

Statistics (Paper Wholesaling)

Number of Establishments	1,474
Average Profit Margin	2.2%
Revenue per Employee	$2,201,400
Average Number of Employees	8.6
Average Wages per Employee	$71,825

Products and Services Segmentation

Printing and writing paper	59.8%
Fine roll paper	21.0%
Paper and plastic products	8.8%
Other	7.6%
Newsprint	2.8%

Major Market Segmentation

Paper Converters	30.0%
Other industries	29.6%
Book and magazine publishers	26.5%
Commercial printing	8.9%
Newspaper publishers	3.0%
Exports	1.9%

Industry Costs

Profit	2.2%
Wages	3.3%
Purchases	79.6%
Depreciation	0.2%
Marketing	0.5%
Rent & Utilities	1.1%
Other	13.1%

Market Share

Xpedx	36.7%

Source: IBISWorld, January 2016

Expenses as a percentage of annual sales

Cost of goods	70% to 75%
Payroll/labor Costs	10%
Occupancy	04%
Profit (estimated pretax)	08% to 10%

Industry Trend
- "Stable"

Questions
- "Stability of gross profit margins, number of inventory turns per year. Percentage of slow moving inventory and the need for adjustments thereof."

Distribution/Wholesale— Tools

	NAICS 423171	Number of Businesses/Units 8,193

Rules of Thumb

➤ 55 percent of annual sales includes inventory

➤ 3.7 times SDE includes inventory

Pricing Tips
- "Higher multiples for the higher net profit industries"

Expert Comments

"Location is not typically important since there is not much drop-in traffic."

D - Rules of Thumb

Benchmark Data

Statistics (Tool and Hardware Wholesaling)

Number of Establishments... 8,193
Average Profit Margin 4.7%
Revenue per Employee $668,300
Average Number of Employees..11.5
Average Wages per Employee $58,370

Products and Services Segmentation

Bolts, nuts, rivets and other fasteners (excludes nails) 55.7%
Hand tools and power tools 29.7%
Miscellaneous hardware 8.0%
Plumbing and hydronic heating equipment.. 6.6%

Major Market Segmentation

Retailers.. 43.7%
Other wholesalers... 19.8%
Manufacturing and mining industries 13.6%
Building contractors and heavy construction 12.0%
Businesses and others for end use 10.9%

Industry Costs

Profit 4.7%
Wages... 8.8%
Purchases... 58.7%
Depreciation... 0.5%
Marketing 1.0%
Rent & Utilities 3.5%
Other... 22.8%

Market Share

Stanley Black & Decker Inc. 8.1%
Ace Hardware Corp. 7.8%

Source: IBISWorld, July 2016

- "Very hands-on with the key customers. Must maintain knowledge of the products they need to service their clients."

Expenses as a percentage of annual sales

Cost of goods...74%
Payroll/labor Costs...08%
Occupancy...01%
Profit (estimated pretax) 15%

Industry Trend
- "Good"

Questions
- "Do you need a mechanical background or inclination to be successful?"

Business Reference Guide **2017**

Document Destruction

	NAICS 561990	

Rules of Thumb

➤ 150 percent of annual sales includes inventory

➤ 4 times SDE includes inventory

➤ 6 times EBIT

➤ 6 times EBITDA

Pricing Tips

- "Prices range from 1.25 to 2.0 times gross revenues"
- "Mobile shredding operations include price adjustments to compensate for the age of the fleet."

Expert Comments

"In a world of daily data breaches, identity theft and privacy concerns, ensuring the protection of information is dire. Companies are looking for better protection in regard to the secure destruction of their private documents as confidentiality and security top businesses' list of importance."

"High revenue growth rates have attracted new market competition."

"This is a high growth industry, with low technology requirements and relatively few barriers to entry."

Benchmark Data

- "Well-run businesses can generate $250K–$300K revenue per vehicle in fleet."
- "EBITDA margins should exceed 30% for mobile operations and 35% for plant-based operations."

Expenses as a percentage of annual sales

Cost of goods	40%
Payroll/labor Costs	25%
Occupancy	05%
Profit (estimated pretax)	30%

Industry Trend

- "Industry revenues should continue to grow. Consolidation has reduced the number of larger independently owned businesses."
- "Revenue trends exceed 20% growth due to heightened awareness of confidentiality and identity theft concerns. Many state regulations require shredding of confidential information."
- "Shredding Ahead: business booms as market demands document destruction"

Source: www.ezy-waysecurityshredding.com.au

Questions

- "Age of fleet and the output of plant facilities are important. Industry standard equipment is a must."

D - Rules of Thumb

- "What % of the business is recurring versus one-time purge service revenues? Is the service provided on-site at the customer location via a mobile shredding truck or destroyed in a plant environment off-site?"

Resources

Trade Publications
- Storage and Destruction Business: www.sdbmagazine.com
- Security Shredding and Storage News: www.securityshreddingnews.com

Associations
- National Association for Information Destruction: www.naidonline.org/nitl/en

Dog Kennels (See also Pet Grooming)		
SIC 0752-05	NAICS 812910	

Rules of Thumb
- ➤ 1 times annual sales plus inventory
- ➤ 2 to 3 times SDE plus inventory
- ➤ 2.7 times EBIT

Pricing Tips

- "Annual Gross Multiplier not accurate reflection, comparable sales range from 0.2 to 1.2, would not advise using. SDE multiplier the most consistent method of establishing value and it varies from 2 to 3.3. Low end multiplier for more risky businesses; ie. high owner dependency and large amount of revenue from grooming or training. Higher end multiplier for facilities with management, less owner dependency, well trending revenues, long term lease or property owned by seller."
- "Multiplier can be anything from 1 to 3.5, most sold comps support a range of 2 to 3. Issues affecting multiplier selection are: longevity, occupancy rates for boarding kennels (similar to hotel/motel analysis), seller involvement, financing ability, state of facilities, location, etc. Grooming salons are in the 1 to 2 times multiplier; if seller is the groomer and no staff, there is no business goodwill."
- "Careful consideration of multiplier of 'add backs,' revenue trend, geographic location."
- "American Boarding Kennel Association (ABKA) uses 1 to 1.5 times gross sales plus real estate. These transactions can be very real estate intensive and often business does not support debt service. That needs to be taken into consideration when pricing. Location and zoning influence pricing considerably."
- "Multiplier depends largely on 1) type of facility (old/new), 2) geographic area (how difficult is licensing and zoning), 3) growth of business in the past 5 years, 4) how involved/important is the seller in the operation, 5) how large is real estate component (if high, price gets inflated, so business is priced for less)."
- "One way of calculating the market value of a boarding kennel would be to figure the present market value of just the real estate and add to that 1 or 1½ times the annual gross. Now, the difference between 1 and 1½ times would be

determined by the area. For example, if the kennel is in a growing area, you would be more inclined to go 1½ times. If the kennel is in an area that is static, and there is reason to feel that the kennel will continue to do more business, then you could use one times the annual gross."

Expert Comments

"There are limited barriers to entry except the cost of facilities. No professional licenses required, kennel license requirement varies by state, county and city (typically easy to obtain). Risk factors are mainly centered around the seller's involvement in business; this is a highly loyalty & trust based industry. High profit industry if properly managed, SDE typically 25% to 30% of gross revenue. Often seller owns the real estate, so Rent expense needs to be adjusted to FMV of rent (some owners don't charge rent at all so a recast needs to account for that negative adjustment). Industry trending very strongly upwards."

"Competitors not only include other facility (i.e., real estate) based businesses, but an animal owner's friends, relatives, etc. that often 'watch the pet' cheaper. In home petsitters are gaining popularity, so they need to be considered in competition analysis. 'Barriers to entry' include zoning and land use laws, which are getting stricter raising the value of existing, properly zoned facilities. Industry itself continues to grow and has survived the recession fairly well. Very marketable business, but lots of unqualified buyers. Risk can be high, especially to a buyer with no prior industry experience. Lending can be challenge due to mixed-use properties. Seller's personal goodwill needs to be measured carefully against real business goodwill; high customer loyalty to seller causing a risk for buyer. If seller is the groomer, buyer can expect the grooming income to diminish drastically upon purchase. Often a real estate holding company (owned by the seller as well) owns the real estate and the business (operating company owned by the seller) pays rent to the holding company. When recasting, it's imperative to substitute that rent for Fair Market Rent in the area; sometimes this leads to an add-back, sometimes to a deduction. The business must be valued based on SDE that INCLUDES occupancy cost. One can't add back all the rent and then value based on that SDE; there is a cost for the real estate the business uses to generate income."

"Multiplier depends on the following factors: 1. Geographic location (determines marketability and desirability) 2. Seller's role and risk assessment of transfer 3. Historical revenue trends 4.Type and age of facility (older facilities are less desirable/not many buyers willing to buy 5. Real estate value (if high, business will most likely not generate enough to support debt service, hence fetches a lower valuation to still stay within a price range that it can actually be sold)."

"Dog daycares are experiencing heavy growth and thus competition, easy to replicate. Older boarding kennels with outdated facilities are difficult to market/sell, resort styles attract more buyers. Industry is growing, profit margins are historically high and continue as such. Zoning restrictions are growing limiting entry in some states. The smaller the business, the higher the risk for new owner. Customers tend to be very loyal to the owner, and do not deal with change in ownership well. Grooming salons are very high risk, as most customers will leave with the seller. The less the seller is involved in the business, the lower the risk. This is a personal service industry, and needs to be assessed as such."

"Barriers to entry depend largely on zoning and licensing. In some states it's very easy, some states very restrictive. Seller is the highest risk for buyer due to the personal nature of the business. Lots of interested buyers, financing the deal can be difficult. Industry growing as a whole; the trend is more toward the resort style/ communal play facilities. Older facilities are hard to market, small buyer pool."

Benchmark Data

- "Too varied. Payroll should be below 35% of gross revenue."
- "Occupancy! A successful facility should have a year-round occupancy level of at least 50%. Per-run revenue can be measured; but, as many facilities also provide grooming and daycare services, not a reliable benchmark. Payroll below 40% of Gross Income. Overall, SDE should be close to, or above, 30% of Gross Income."
- "Boarding kennels: Year-round occupancy should be minimum of 50%, preferably over 55%. Average annual income per run/enclosure around $3500. Dog daycares: average number of dogs per day around 1 dog per 75 SF of (inside) area."
- "Analyze like a hotel, based on occupancy. Statistically, a decent operation should have at least a 50% occupancy (yearly). SDE should be 24% to 30% of gross sales, if business well managed."

Expenses as a percentage of annual sales

Cost of goods	03%
Payroll/labor Costs	35% to 40%
Occupancy	17%
Profit (estimated pretax)	30%

Industry Trend

- "Growth."
- "Industry continues to grow, new services are being added. Customers spend more and more money on their pets, that have been elevated to a family member status."
- "Growth, more franchises, more 'resort' style facilities, more competition."

Seller Financing

- "Combination of both. SBA loans are readily available if business cash flow is sufficient."

Questions

- "Investigate owner involvement with customers. Verify licenses, zoning, allowed use. If seller grooms or trains, except that income to be eliminated with a sale."
- "1. What are your day to day duties at the business? (how much does the customer base rely on the seller) 2. Verify zoning and land use from the county department directly. 3. How much of the income do you produce personally

(grooming, training, etc.)? 4. Staff and what level of authority do they have? 5. How do you think the clientele will react when they learn that you've sold? 6. Get confirmation on any septic, well, etc. issues. 7. Which licenses are required (besides regular business license) to operate?"

- "1. Determine if a successful kennel or not. 2. Pricing in comparison to competition and how often they are raised (industry notorious for not raising prices regularly) 3. Real estate issues: septic, water, inspections, set-backs, neighbors, noise ordinances, etc."

- "How involved is seller in day-to-day operations and with clients? License/zoning/inspections. Relationship with neighbors and veterinary clinics. Longevity of staff. If grooming is a part of the business, is it a groomer or the seller doing the work? How does the facility stand out from the competition in the area?"

Resources

Associations
- International Boarding and Pet Care Services Association: www.ibpsa.com
- National Association of Professional Pet Sitters: www.petsitters.org

		Franchise
Dollar Discount Stores (See also Dollar Stores, Franchises)		
Approx. Total Investment		$99,000 to $195,000
	NAICS 452990	Number of Businesses/Units 140

Rules of Thumb
➢ 20 percent of annual sales plus inventory

Benchmark Data
- For Benchmark Data see Dollar Stores

Resources
Websites
- dollardiscount.com

Dollar Stores		
	NAICS 452990	Number of Businesses/Units 42,754

Rules of Thumb
➢ 15 to 20 percent of annual sales plus inventory

➢ 2 to 2.5 times SDE plus inventory

➢ 2 to 2.5 times EBITDA

➢ 1.5 to 2 times EBIT

D - Rules of Thumb

Pricing Tips

- "With the increase in competition, margins must be looked into carefully."
- "Sells easily, as mom-and-pops are moving in, and it's day hours only."
- "Very competitive market. More diversification and the astute marketers are moving to the $1–$5 spread."
- "There seems to be a downward pressure on profitability but the dollar stores are expanding into higher priced and higher margin items."

Expert Comments

"Stores do better in a down economy."

"Not too difficult to replicate; needs a large amount of inventory; the larger the store, the better the variety and the sales."

Benchmark Data

Statistics (Dollar and Variety Stores)

Number of Establishments	42,754
Average Profit Margin	5.2%
Revenue per Employee	$182,200
Average Number of Employees	9.5
Average Wages per Employee	$16,843

Products and Services Segmentation

Groceries	26.6%
Others	21.1%
Soaps, detergents, cleaning supplies and paper related products	17.6%
Drugs, health aids and beauty cosmetics such as lipsticks	12.7%
Cosmetics such as moisturizers, and hygiene products	9.1%
Men's and womenswear, and other textile products	7.0%
Kitchenware and home furnishings	5.9%

Industry Costs

Profit	5.2%
Wages	9.2%
Purchases	69.0%
Depreciation	1.0%
Marketing	0.4%
Rent and Utilities	4.7%
Other	10.5%

Market Share

Dollar General Corporation	30.9%
Dollar Tree Stores Inc.	24.1%
Big Lots Inc.	7.5%

Source: IBISWorld, August 2016

- www.buckstore.com/store-development is an excellent site and we suggest if more information about size, investment dollars, etc. is needed, this is the site to visit. In fact if you are even visiting dollar stores, don't miss this site.
- "Prices at Dollar General for the same item tend to be 30 to 40 percent cheaper than a typical drugstore, and 15 to 20 percent cheaper than a standard grocery store, MacDonald said. Most of Dollar General's items are priced below $10, with about 25 percent of goods selling for $1 or less.

Family Dollar's average transaction is about $10, with about 30 percent of merchandise priced at $1 or less, according to the companies."

Source: www.buckstore.com/dollar-stores by Chelsey Livingston, Staff Writer, May 2, 2014

Expenses as a percentage of annual sales

Cost of goods	70% to 75%
Payroll/labor Costs	15% to 17%
Occupancy	10%
Profit (estimated pretax)	20% to 25%

Industry Trend

- "Marshal Cohen, chief industry analyst for NPD, noted that shoppers visit dollar stores with the intent to buy something, not to browse, adding that 'dollar store traffic has been increasing over the past few years because they have expanded their selection of products, making the channel even more useful and pleasing to price-savvy consumers.'

  "Three-quarters of all shoppers in the dollar store channel purchase one or more items during each visit, and the amount they spend is up 3 percent on average since last year. Additionally, in the past two years, the dollar store channel shopper has become younger, with 50 percent under 45 years of age, compared to 42 percent two years ago."

  Source: "Dollar Store Traffic Up 14% Despite Brick-and-mortar Decline," by Kyle Shamorian, September 25, 2014

- "Showing that many Americans are still pinching pennies, the largest dollar store chains are planning to open more new stores nationwide in 2014 than they have since the economic recession started.

  "Dollar General Corp., which operates 11,061 stores in 40 states, wants to open 700 more of its yellow stores in the coming year. Plans are to also remodel or relocate another 525, said company spokesman Dan MacDonald. Competitor Family Dollar Stores Inc. runs 8,000 storefronts in 46 states, said spokesman Josh Braverman. Plans are to open 525 more stores and close 80 locations nationally in fiscal year 2014. The company's fiscal year started in September. Family Dollar says its average customer is a female head-of-household in her mid-40s earning $40,000 a year.

  "Seventy percent of Dollar General stores are in communities with populations of less than 20,000, according to the company. Family Dollar in the past has looked to open in strip shopping centers, in urban and suburban areas. Now Family Dollar prefers to build new stores to suit, company officials said."

  Source: Dollar Stores, Chelsey Levingston, www.buckstore.com/dollar-stores, May 2, 2014

- "Next to supercenters, dollar stores remain the fastest growing channel among food, drug, and mass retailing. No-frills stores, low prices, and a small, easy-to-shop and easy-to-access format gives shoppers a convenient option to big box discount retailers, like Wal-Mart. 'Dollar stores combine pricing power, efficient operations, and small stores to make the model work,' comments Skrovan."

  Source: www.retailindustry.about.com/od/seg_dollar_stores/a/bl

Questions

- "Tax returns and all invoices"
- "Paperwork, and sit and observe"
- "Margins and vendor contacts"

Resources

Websites

- Dollar$tores: www.buckstore.com—a must see site

	Franchise
Domino's Pizza (See also Franchises, Pizza Shops)	
Approx. Total Investment	$119,950 to $461,700
Estimated Annual Sales/Unit	$925,000

SIC 5812-22	NAICS 722513	Number of Businesses/Units 9,942

Rules of Thumb

➢ 45 percent of the first $400K in annual sales, 50 percent of the next $100K ($400 to $500K) in annual sales, then 55 percent of the next $250K of annual sales (from $500 to $750K)

Resources

Websites

- www.dominosbiz.com

Donut Shops (See also Dunkin' Donuts, Restaurants—Limited Service)		
SIC 5461-05	NAICS 722515	Number of Businesses/Units 23,701

Rules of Thumb

➢ 45 to 50 percent of annual sales plus inventory (and can go much higher for a great store)

➢ 2 to 2.5 times SDE plus inventory

Pricing Tips

- "Higher coffee sales (60 percent of sales) produce higher value. Very low coffee sales produce lower values."
- "Length & cost of lease? Retail vs. wholesale business? Percentage of business that is coffee (the higher the percentage of coffee sales, the higher the price)"

Benchmark Data

Statistics (Doughnut Stores)

Number of Establishments	23,701
Average Profit Margin	6.4%
Revenue per Employee	$66,200
Average Number of Employees	9.2
Average Wages per Employee	$16,803

Products and Services Segmentation

Donuts in bulk 25.0%
Coffee 20.0%
Other beverages 18.0%
Other items 18.0%
Yeast donuts 10.0%
Mini donuts and donut holes.. 5.0%
Other donuts 4.0%

Industry Costs

Profit 6.4%
Wages... 25.4%
Purchases... 38.8%
Depreciation... 3.3%
Marketing 3.4%
Rent & Utilities 12.5%
Other.. 10.2%

Source: IBISWorld, March 2016

Expenses as a percentage of annual sales

Cost of goods...21% food (+ 4.2% paper goods)
Payroll/labor Costs..20% to 23%
Occupancy 10%
Profit (estimated pretax) 0

Industry Trend

- "Doughnut sales from quick service restaurants, like Krispy Kreme and Dunkin' Donuts, are up for the third straight year, after several years in decline, according to data from NDP CREST, a New York-based market research firm.

- "'This is not a breakfast business,' said Will Slabaugh, managing director at financial services firm Stephens. 'This is much more of treat business than a breakfast business.'"

Source: "People tried to eat healthier. Instead, doughnut sales went up," by Jacob Bogage, June 11, 2015, https://www.washingtonpost.com/news/wonk/wp/2015/06/11/people-tried-to-eat-healthier-instead-doughnut-sales-went-up/

- "Over the past few years, Americans have become far more concerned with healthy eating than ever before. So as you might expect, demand for foods that are high in sugar and saturated fats has plummeted. But there are a few notable exceptions to the rule—such as donut shops, in particular. Demand for donuts is rising, benefiting donut shops across the country. There are a number of interesting trends that are impacting donut shops and the donut industry as a whole.

  ✓ Rise in Gourmet Donut Shops
  ✓ Fewer Independent Donut Shops
  ✓ Increased Need for Technology
  ✓ Greater Need for Originality
  ✓ Healthy Options Will Be More Prevalent"

Source: "Hmmmm, Donuts—Today's Trends in Donut Shops," by Joe Stanton, August 24, 2015

D - Rules of Thumb

Franchise

Dream Dinners (See also Franchises)	
Approx. Total Investment	$273,200 to $418,000

	NAICS 445299	Number of Businesses/Units 87

Rules of Thumb

➤ 40 percent of annual sales plus inventory

Resources

Websites
- www.dreamdinners.com

Drive-in Restaurants (See also Restaurants)		
	NAICS 722513	

Rules of Thumb

➤ 40 to 45 percent of annual sales plus inventory

➤ 5 to 6 times monthly sales plus inventory

Drive-In Theaters (See also Movie Theaters)		
	NAICS 512132	Number of Businesses/Units 595

Rules of Thumb

➤ 2 percent of annual sales plus equipment and real estate

Benchmark Data

- "In 2015, there were 595 drive-ins in the U.S., up from 366 in 2012."
  Source: natoonline.org—an interesting web site

Industry Trend

- "It's likely that few young people today have attended a drive-in movie. Half a century ago, the gigantic outdoor screens were everywhere—in the 1950s there were more than 4,000 drive-ins in the U.S.—but the current figure is well under 10 percent of that peak.

  "Yet one has to admire what back in the '50s would have been called the moxie. Johnny Rockets seems to be betting that, with all the world's troubles, what will draw moviegoers back isn't more of the 3-D Imax experience. It's the old-time family-and-date-night, sit-in-the-car experience. Other investors, too, seem to think that the time has come to give the drive-in another shot."
  Source: "Future of the Movies Is in the '50s," by Stephen L. Carter, October 30, 2014, http://www.bloombergview.com/articles/2014-10-30/future-of-the-movies-is-in-the-50s

- "Drive-ins and small-town movie theaters have been challenged in the past few years since the movie industry has been phasing out film prints and implementing the use of digital protection. Adapting to digital, however, can cost theater owners $70,000–$80,000 per projector."

Resources

Associations

- National Association of Theatre Owners: http://www.natoonline.org/
- United Drive-in Theatre Owners Association: www.driveintheatre-ownersassociation.org

	Franchise
Dr. Vinyl (See also Franchises)	
Approx. Total Investment	$44,000 t0 $69,500

	NAICS 325211	Number of Businesses/Units 170+

Rules of Thumb

➤ 75 percent of annual sales plus inventory

Resources

Websites

- www.drvinyl.com

Dry Cleaners		
SIC 7212-01	NAICS 812320	Number of Businesses/Units 36,784

Rules of Thumb

➤ 1 times to 1.2 times annual revenues. The larger dry cleaners, over $500,000 with a cash flow of 40% or more command higher prices. Typically, a dry cleaner doing $1 million or more in revenue annually will sell for 1.1 to 1.2 times revenue.

➤ 70 to 80 percent of sales plus inventory. Plants with on-site laundry equipment will get a higher multiple. Plants with over-the-counter sales of $35,000 will receive higher multiples.

➤ 2.5 to 3 times SDE plus inventory

➤ 2 to 3 times EBIT

➤ 2.5 to 3 times EBITDA

Pricing Tips

- "I personally don't rely on gross revenue; that is a starting point. I form my opinion of value based on SDE, and I take a consideration for the dry cleaner machine. There is a big price difference if the dry cleaner plant has a perc. machine vs. hydrocarbon or wet machine, for example. Front assigned parking is critical for dry cleaners, the location etc."

D - Rules of Thumb

- "There are several formulas to determine selling price. Most of them work on some version of a multiple of net profit over the last three years, giving more preference for recent years. This profitability factor translates to what the business is worth, and is used to assess the 15% to 30% rate of return a buyer wants to achieve. So, if a buyer wants to achieve a 15% rate of return, and the business churns out a $30,000 net profit per year, the buyer will not pay more than $200,000 for the business (because a $200,000 investment will return exactly a 15% return of $30,000, which is the current profitability)."

  Source: https://americandrycleaner.com/articles/right-way-sell-your-drycleaning-business-conclusion

- "Business that has good equipment and has its own shirt machine and does mostly retail business and is not a discount store will always be in high demand."

- "Dry cleaners grossing under $500,000 sell for about 1X gross sales, 2.5X cash flow. Dry cleaners grossing over $500,000 sell for about 3X cash flow. Dry cleaners with a cash flow over $500,000 can sell for 4X cash flow."

- "Dry cleaning machine and shirt machine play a big key role in pricing. There will be a significant price difference between a dry cleaner plant with an extra large size and good brand hydro carbon machine and very good condition shirt machine vs. dry cleaner with perc machine and no or older type shirt machine. Perc dry cleaner machine will be obsolete in 2020, therefore it has no value; it's the same with a shirt machine, if the owner does it with old press machine, creative old way vs. newer shirt machine. A good brand 60-lb. hydro- carbon dry cleaning machine and shirt machine will run approximately $80,000 to $100,000 after delivery and installation, and configuring, plumbing and electrical. Other important equipment overlooked are all pressers and the boiler—are they installed correctly and are they up to the current code?"

- "Dry cleaner plant with high volume over-the-counter (retail vs. wholesale) will get more SDE multiple. Ample parking is very important with 1 or 2 assigned parking spaces in the front."

- "Owner who is involved and works in the business will get lower SDE multiple vs. owner who only oversees the business and has all employees in place including front counter."

- "Location, age of equipment and is the equipment state of the art."

- "The price has a lot of qualifications. Larger revenues command higher multiples, age of equipment, location, type of dry cleaning done—discount or full price, delivery, fire restoration, etc."

- "There are many factors that will determine value. In order of importance are verified retail sales, lease terms, equipment condition, breakdown of how sales occur (wholesale, discount, full retail, shirts vs. dry cleaning etc.). We also look at competition, tenant mix, parking, signage, customer lists and more."

Expert Comments

"Do lot of research before buying a dry cleaners; the buyer should know all state and local environmental restrictions, and have to be ready to work hard."

"Buyer: the age of the dry-cleaning unit, condition of the equipment, and don't overpay."

"Seller: have an expert/business valuator give you a price for the business, not your accountant or business broker who has no expertise of the industry."

"Dry cleaners are fairly easy to replicate, however location is most important. The dry cleaning industry trend is very good, but there are more and more dry cleaners being built constantly."

"Dry cleaners with plants are very costly, with all the environmental and state and city requirements. Landlords who rent to dry cleaners are very careful about contamination, especially the dry cleaners with perc. machines that have the history of causing contamination. All the perc. machines will be replaced with hydrocarbon, wet dry cleaner machines, etc."

"Age of the equipment and the care of it is very important. The trend is for dry clean business owners to eliminate the use of perchlorethylene as the cleaning solvent. Buyers should take into consideration the cost of a new dry cleaning machine that will use the environmentally friendly solvents."

"Competition is driven by services. Amount of risk is low if services are high and a clean store is maintained"

"Dry cleaning is not difficult, just a lot of hard work!"

"Competition in the dry cleaning industry is very high and reputation and location are very important factors."

"Dry cleaning is a long-term business with not a lot of drastic ups and downs."

Benchmark Data

Statistics (Dry Cleaners)

Number of Establishments	36,784
Average Profit Margin	7.8%
Revenue per Employee	$61,400
Average Number of Employees	4.0
Average Wages per Employee	$20,119

Products and Services Segmentation

Retail dry cleaning and laundry services	63.2%
Commercial full-service laundry	16.0%
Commercial dry cleaning services	12.4%
Other	8.4%

Industry Costs

Profit	7.8%
Wages	32.8%
Purchases	16.0%
Depreciation	5.4%
Marketing	2.8%
Rent & Utilities	17.8%
Other	17.4%

Source: IBISWorld, March 2016

- "COGS above in expenses as a % of annual sales is for dry cleaner agencies; the plants will have way less COGS, but the labor cost will be higher."
- "Dry cleaner agencies have higher COGS because the garment will be picked up and delivered by dry cleaner plants."

D - Rules of Thumb

- "Typical breakeven for a dry cleaning store is approximately $150,000 annual sales. Average is $250,000"
- "Location with drive-thru"
- "Keep agency work to a minimum."

Expenses as a percentage of annual sales

Cost of goods.. 30%
Payroll/labor Costs............................... 25% (lower figure with owner working full time)
Occupancy.................... 11% to 15% + RE Taxes & CAM (top locations MA)
Profit (estimated pretax) .... 15% to 25%

Industry Trend

- "Lot of dry cleaner plants with perc. machine will go out of business especially those with lower revenue because of environmental AQMD law; all perc. machines will be removed by end of 2020."
- "This industry is very stable if the following is applied: customer relationship and quality of service is the key."
- "Dry cleaners are consolidating. Individual owners are owning more than one location."
- "Dry cleaners with perc. machines will be closing down unless they are in a great location and their volume is high. More and more bigger cleaners will be replacing the little cleaners, including discount cleaners. It is very difficult for discount cleaners to make a profit in a high-cost area like California."
- "Sales will be up as more and more employees are trending to looking and feeling good about how they present themselves."
- "Tide is already known as a laundry detergent. Now, the brand is being expanded into a chain of franchised dry cleaners, with the first location in Minnesota now open in Apple Valley. The location touts its drive-thru and 24-hour service, including a dropbox where customers can leave laundry at any time along with 24-hour lockers where customers can pick up their dry cleaning anytime. Procter & Gamble owns the Tide brand. The franchise is being developed in conjunction with Procter & Gamble's wholly owned subsidiary, Agile Pursuits Franchising Inc."
  Source: http://www.twincities.com/business/ci_28020131/business-briefing-tide-dry-cleaners-opens-franchise, April 30, 2015
- "Dry cleaning industry in general is consolidating. Larger dry cleaners are taking over market share from the smaller cleaners and offering discounting small dry cleaners cannot compete with."
- "I believe we are in the beginning of a growth phase. Consumer confidence, fabrics, clothing costs and economy are some of the reasons. It's easy to copy but hard to replicate a successful operation. Our industry is very detailed in nature. The removal of small stains, professional pressing, replacing missing or cracked buttons are all fairly easy tasks but you need someone on staff that will actually look for and complete. It is this consistency of quality and caring that will build your sales. Customer service is the primary reason people either stop coming or continue to become loyal customers."
- "In metropolitan areas, business will decline. In high-income areas, it will grow."

Seller Financing

- "Seller financing is very typical, usually 3 to 5 years depend on the loan amount, and the monthly payment. The seller has to be reasonable with the monthly payment when they structure the deal."

- "Seller financing with 40% down."
- "Dry cleaners sell with SBA financing 30% of the time, seller financing 30% of the time, all cash or 401k rollovers 40% of the time. SBA loans are 10 yrs., seller financing 3 to 5 yrs."
- "Seller financing is a must, usually 50 to 60% down and the rest will be carried by the seller for 4 to 5 years with 5% to 7% interest depending on the monthly payment."
- "Combination of bank and seller carry financing."
- "Bank financing is difficult to get for dry cleaners although not impossible. Seller financing is preferred although a lot of sellers do not want to provide any financing."
- "In my experience existing stores sell using some percentage of seller financing. New plants with expensive equipment are typically leased or bank financed."

Questions

- "Always the first question I ask for plants is what type of dry cleaner machine do they have? Do they have a shirt machine, what type and the brand? Do you have computerized POS system to verify the sales? Ask the seller if he knows about any EPA problems. Are they a discount cleaner or a full-price cleaner? How many hours the seller or family member works in the cleaner. Who does the alterations? This is a very important question that is overlooked by the buyers."
- "Do you have computerized cash registers so verification of the sales can be made?"
- "Make sure that the store doesn't have any EPA problems."
- "How much does a seller actually work in the business?"
- "Buyer should ask for all the brands and sizes of all the equipment including laundry machines and determine if the capacity will be enough in case of growth. Number of slots on conveyor line, discount or full service, prices for garment, delivery retail or wholesale. If they do delivery is the van included in the price? Tailoring—if so, who does it? How to handle work in process/ accounts receivable."
- "Books and records, age of equipment and what solvent is being used."
- "Who are the biggest competitors?"
- "The age of the boiler and the dry cleaning machine. Anything newer than 10 years is good."
- "How has his business been trending in the last 3 years?"
- "Contamination from PERC"
- "Monthly sales important, any environmental issues, will landlord renew lease?"

Resources

Trade Publications

- National Clothesline: www.natclo.com
- American Dry Cleaner: www.americandrycleaner.com

Associations
- National Cleaners Association: www.nca-i.com
- Dry Cleaning and Laundry Institute: www.dlionline.org

Dry Cleaning Pickup Outlets/Stores (See also Dry Cleaning)		
SIC 7212-01	NAICS 812320	

Rules of Thumb
- 25 to 50 percent of annual sales
- 30 times weekly sales

Dry Cleaning Routes (See also Dry Cleaning)		
SIC 7212-01	NAICS 812320	

Rules of Thumb
- 15 to 40 percent of annual revenues

		Franchise
Dry Clean USA (See also Dry Cleaners, Franchises)		
Approx. Total Investment		$300,000 to $750,000
SIC 7212-01	NAICS 812320	Number of Businesses/Units 45

Rules of Thumb
- 55 percent of annual sales plus inventory

Resources

Websites
- Dry Clean USA: www.drycleanusa.com

		Franchise
Dunkin' Donuts (See also Donut Shops, Franchises)		
Approx. Total Investment		$240,100 to $1,667,750
Estimated Annual Sales/Unit		$920,000
SIC 5812-06	NAICS 722515	Number of Businesses/Units 11,400

Rules of Thumb
- 60 to 100 percent of annual sales plus inventory
- 4 times SDE plus inventory
- 5 times EBITDA

> ➤ "Prices typically run 5 times EBITDA on groups of 3 or larger. Rule of thumb, which is still very strong in the marketplace, is about 1.25 times annual sales in very high coffee sale areas of New England. It is closer to 1 times sales in the Mid-Atlantic where coffee sales are still very good, but not as high as in New England. Where coffee sales are much less, values run about .75 times annual sales. These numbers can be affected (up and down) by unusually low or high rents, and/or the requirement to undergo a major remodel in the near future."

Pricing Tips

- "The higher values are ascribed to units with a greater percentage of coffee sales."
- "Dunkin' Donuts' minimum cash required is $750,000 with a net worth of at least $1,500,000. Minimum 5-store development required."

Source: Dunkin' Donuts

- "The value is decreased if the unit or units require substantial remodeling in less than 4–5 years."
- "Sufficient length of leases and franchise agreements, percentage of businesses coming from coffee/beverages."

Expert Comments

"It is a well-known franchise, but there is stiff competition from Starbucks and McDonald's."

"The marketability is not as high as one would expect for such a profitable and growing business. The reason is that the franchisor has very strict requirements to approve a buyer."

Benchmark Data

- "Fourth quarter highlights include:
  - ✓ Dunkin' Donuts' U.S. comparable store sales growth of 1.4%
  - ✓ Added 260 net new restaurants worldwide including 141 net new Dunkin' Donuts in the U.S.
  - ✓ Revenue increased 5.5%
  - ✓ Adjusted operating income increased 8.4%; adjusted operating income margin of 50.1%
  "Fiscal year 2014 highlights include:
  - ✓ Dunkin' Donuts U.S. comparable store sales growth of 1.6%
  - ✓ Added 704 net new restaurants worldwide including 405 net new Dunkin' Donuts in the U.S.
  - ✓ Positive Baskin-Robbins U.S. net store growth
  - ✓ Revenue increased 4.9%"

Source: 2/5/15 http://www.dunkinbrands.com/news/dunkin-brands-reports-fourth-quarter-fiscal-year-2014-results

- "How the Donut Divides" ... back-of-the-envelope financial estimates for running a shop that does about $87,000 in sales a month, which he says is about average in New England. Rent on retail space—10%; payroll—22.5%; miscellaneous costs (mortgage payments for the franchise, which can go for $1.5 million around here in New England) plus taxes, utilities, maintenance, etc.—19.1%; food and paper supplies—27.5%; fees to Dunkin Brands split between shared advertising fund and franchise fees)—10.9%; profit (if the shop runs efficiently)—10%.

E - Rules of Thumb

"Estimated sales breakdown is beverages—65%; sandwiches, bagels, and other products—27%; and donuts—8%."

The above is from a very successful franchisee of Dunkin' Donuts with many stores. It is from an article in the *Boston Sunday Globe* written by Neil Swidey, "Time to Make the Empire," September 21, 2014.

- "Food cost can be in the low 20's, as well as labor costs."
- "Food costs 20% to 24% or less, depending on business mix."

Expenses as a percentage of annual sales

Cost of goods	23% to 24% + 4% supplies (paper)
Payroll/labor Costs	22%
Occupancy	08% to 10%
Profit (estimated pretax)	15% to 20%

Industry Trend

- "Dunkin Donuts on Wednesday opened its first store in Reykjavik, Iceland, drawing crowds eager for a taste of the chain's baked goods and coffee. . . .Drangasker, the franchise holder, has the right to open as many as 16 restaurants in the country over five years, chief executive Arni Petur Jonsson said. Dunkin's parent company, Canton, Mass.-based Dunkin' Brands Group, signed a deal in January to open more than 1,400 shops in China over the next two decades, plus 100 more in Mexico. Worldwide, the company has 11,000 locations in 36 countries."

  Source: *Bloomberg News* as reported in *Boston Globe*, 8/6/15

- "Dunkin' Donuts plans to double its locations in the United States over the next 20 years, the company announced Wednesday. The coffee and doughnut chain currently operates nearly 7,000 stores nationwide. Each new store adds an average of 20 to 25 new employees, both full and part time a Dunkin' spokeswoman said."

  Source: "Dunkin' Donuts to double U.S. locations" by Annalyn Censky, CNNMoney

Seller Financing

- "7 years—usually are bank/SBA financed."

Questions

- "When are remodels due? Lease details are critical, and length of time remaining on the franchise agreements. Does the seller have expansion rights in adjacent areas?"
- "What percent of sales is beverages?"

Resources

Websites

- www.dunkinfranchising.com

	Franchise
Eagle Transmission Shop	
(See also AAAMCO Transmissions, Auto Transmission Centers, Franchises)	
Approx. Total Investment	$194,000 to $292,500
SIC 7537-01 NAICS 811113	Number of Businesses/Units 27

Rules of Thumb

➤ 40 percent of annual sales

➤ 2.5 times SDE

➤ This franchise is primarily Texas based, but is expanding.

Benchmark Data

- "Cost to get to breakeven is the same as AAMCO—approx. $200,000 (this is my targeted bottom sale price)."
- "Franchises with an owner overseeing a manager in the expenses are still selling for 2.5 to 3 X SDE."
- "Franchised shops with SDE of at least $100,000 with high percentage retail are very marketable."
- "Franchised shops that historically are not breaking even with a manager in the expenses are very hard to sell."
- "If the location seems OK, the price seems to bottom out at about $125,000. Small independents are getting more and more difficult."

Resources

Websites
- www.eagletransmission.com

E-Commerce (Internet Sales)		
SIC 5731-24	NAICS 454111	Number of Businesses/Units 154,409

Rules of Thumb

➤ 30 percent of annual sales includes inventory

➤ 2 to 4 times SDE includes inventory

➤ 3 to 6 times EBITDA

Pricing Tips

- "Gross sales are not necessarily important to determine value because of tendency for very high gross margins. A business with little or no inventory is more valuable. Businesses with very high inventory are very difficult to value and sell; the business is the inventory."
- "High inventory businesses will be harder to sell. Higher multiples with SDE over $100K are more easily sold. The ease of the operation will determine marketability. Many are too complicated for the average buyer."
- "The more niche-related the product, the higher the multiple."
- "Typically, an e-commerce website will sell for 2.75x SDE. However, there are variables that may increase the multiple or decrease the multiple. The more automated the website and if capable of drop shipping, the multiple increases closer to 4x. Also, if there is inventory involved and additional staff is needed, the multiple decreases."
- "Prices vary depending on age of business...at least three years is excellent...12 months is usually necessary."

27th Edition

- "Must understand and quantify Internet traffic, search engine rankings (organic vs. ppc), and which sites they sell product through (i.e., eBay, Amazon, internal Website, etc.)"

Expert Comments

"Internet storefronts can easily be replicated. Finding a good source for product will always help reduce risk."

"The business will be more valuable if it is harder to replicate."

"Online shopping continues to grow, but so does the competition, so being able to differentiate oneself is a major coup."

"A unique product with aggressive marketing will usually succeed."

"Internet companies can be replicated structurally, but very difficult to replicate from an SEO stand point."

Benchmark Data

Statistics (E-Commerce & Online Auctions)

Number of Establishments	154,409
Average Profit Margin	6.2%
Revenue per Employee	$815,700
Average Number of Employees	2.5
Average Wages per Employee	$46,224

Products and Services Segmentation

Other merchandise	31.5%
Computer hardware	18.4%
Clothing, footwear and accessories	18.2%
Furniture and home appliances	9.1%
Medication and cosmetics	7.8%
Sporting goods, toys, hobby items and games	7.2%
Office equipment and supplies	5.5%
Food, beverages and alcohol	2.3%

Industry Costs

Profit	6.2%
Wages	5.6%
Purchases	56.1%
Depreciation	0.8%
Marketing	4.2%
Rent & Utilities	4.3%
Other	22.8%

Market Share

Amazon.com Inc.	19.9%

Source: IBISWorld, June 2016

- "Always look at current market comps when pricing as conditions may be subject to change."

- "On average, the gross margin is 20%. The expenses tend to be very low because many internet businesses are relocatable and do not require an office or warehouse."
- "Profits can be as high as 50–90%"
- "Because of the low overhead and ease of operations, many of these businesses have returns of 30%–40%."
- "Average conversion rate would be anything around 1% (that is 1% of all visits turn into orders). Anything over 2% is excellent."
- "Sales per square foot is the key. Sales divided by the square foot."

Expenses as a percentage of annual sales

Cost of goods	20% to 50%
Payroll/labor Costs	0% to 50%
Occupancy	0% to 10%
Profit (estimated pretax)	50% to 60%

Industry Trend

- "By 2015 the online share of total retail sales reached 10.6% excluding fuel and auto sales and restaurants and bars. This represents a 75.8% increase in online sales from $194.3 billion in 2011 to $341.7 billion in 2015."
  Source: U.S. Department of Commerce, Internet Retailer
- "E-commerce sales are expected to grow to more than $400 billion in the next several years, with Forrester Research estimating $414.0 billion in sales in 2018 and eMarketer estimating $491.5 billion in 2018."
  Source: eMarketer, Forrester Research
- "As more B2B buyers choose to do much of their purchasing online, the number of sales reps in the United States will decline rapidly over the next several years. By 2020, the number will drop by 1 million, a decrease of 22% between 2012 and 2020. Sales reps that offer extra services to assist the purchasing of complex products for big companies will fare better."
  Source: Forrester Research Inc.
- "Upward trend"
- "Unlimited growth potential for the next 3–5 years."
- "Online shoppers in the United States will spend $327 billion in 2016, up 45% from $226 billion this year and 62% from $202 billion in 2011, according to a projection released today by Forrester Research Inc. In 2016, e-retail will account for 9% of total retail sales, up from 7% in both 2012 and 2011, according to the report, 'US Online Retail Forecast, 2011 to 2016,' by Forrester analyst Sucharita Mulpuru. That represents a compound annual growth rate of 10.1% over the five-year forecast period.
  "The steady growth in the number of web shoppers also is helping to boost e-commerce sales. Forrester says that 192 million U.S. consumers will shop online in 2016, up 15% from 167 million in 2012. But the bigger factor in driving e-commerce growth is that each shopper will spend more on average, the report says. U.S. consumers in 2016 will each spend an average of $1,738 online, up 44% from $1,207 in 2012.
  "Many consumers will prefer the Web to bricks-and-mortar retailers in large part because of online deals, the report says—70% of holiday shoppers last year said they made purchases online rather than in stores because online retailers offered better deals."
  Source: "E-retail spending to increase 62% by 2016" by Thad Rueter, Senior Editor, Internet Retailer

Seller Financing
- "Recently it's buyer financing"
- 1–5 years

Questions
- "Ask the sellers before you analyze numbers if all the revenues generated are from products that either do not require a license to be sold, or, if they do require a license or some kind of special permission, that it transfers or can be transferred to a new owner. Look at 3 year trends in annual sales. Why are you selling? Ask to see payment gateway record for the past 3 years to help verify financials, i.e., company PayPal Account or other merchant gateway. Is all of the income shown on the company Payment Gateway Record only from income generated from that particular company?"
- "Do they have tracking information—Google Analytics, or other? What platform is the website built on? Is the website part of a brick and mortar business? If so, are funds co-mingled."
- "How does the business or system operate? Do you stock inventory? How easy and long does it take to learn the operation?"
- "Does the seller inventory the product? Who does the credit card processing and what are their fees? Who does the Web hosting and how much traffic can the Web site handle? How do they maintain their Internet rankings? What are they doing to increase their Web presence?"
- "How easy is it for a buyer to learn the business?"
- "Any repeat business? Percentage of revenue budgeted for advertising?"

Resources
Trade Publications
- Internet Retailer: www.internetretailer.com
- E-Commerce Times: www.ecommercetimes.com/

Electricians		
	NAICS 238210	Number of Businesses/Units 206,399

Rules of Thumb
> ➢ 2 times SDE plus inventory

Pricing Tips
- "Strong order book is essential. Wide range of customers."

Expert Comments
"Underpricing of bids is a serious risk but may be used to increase order book in preparation for sale. Good demand for sound business. Location is relatively unimportant."

Benchmark Data

Statistics (Electricians)

Number of Establishments	206,399
Average Profit Margin	4.8%
Revenue per Employee	$148,800
Average Number of Employees	4.5
Average Wages per Employee	$52,937

Products and Services Segmentation

Electric power and systems installation and servicing	66.7%
Other services	9.5%
Telecommunications installation and servicing	9.2%
Electronic control system installation and servicing	7.5%
Fire and security system installation and servicing	7.1%

Major Market Segmentation

Commercial buildings	35.9%
Institutional, educational, and civic organization buildings	18.2%
Nonbuilding construction	14.4%
Industrial buildings	13.9%
Single-family homes	12.5%
Multifamily housing (e.g. apartment buildings)	5.1%

Industry Costs

Profit	4.8%
Wages	35.5%
Purchases	38.5%
Depreciation	0.8%
Rent & Utilities	0.2%
Marketing	3.3%
Other	16.9%

Source: IBISWorld, April 2016

Expenses as a percentage of annual sales

Cost of goods	50%
Payroll/labor Costs	30%
Occupancy	n/a
Profit (estimated pretax)	06%

Industry Trend
- "Directly dependent on construction industry but can work related areas if necessary to cover slack period."

Questions
- "1. Details of job costing, current and bids 2. List of staff, experience, and time with business 3. Usual financial and due diligence."

Electric Motor Repair

SIC 7694	NAICS 811310	

Rules of Thumb

➢ 33 percent of annual sales plus inventory

➢ 3 times SDE plus inventory

➢ 5 times EBIT

➢ 4 times EBITDA

Pricing Tips

"Condition of equipment and customer concentration are significant factors."
"Industry is always a mix of repair of customer motors and resale of new
motors and related products. Rule of thumb for pricing is one-third of annual
repair sales plus 15% of annual product sales, plus inventory. Most successful
buyers for smaller businesses in the industry have electric motor background.
Condition of equipment and extent of machine shop tools is important."

Expert Comments

"This is a mature industry. The repair market (higher margins) is stable
to declining slightly as increased costs force higher horsepower standard
motors to be replaced (lower margins) rather than repaired. Other
technological factors and the shift to more offshore manufacturing have
resulted in no net growth and eroding profits. Successful shops have either
good niche customer markets and/or services or a long- term approach
to partnering with customers to reduce customer's motor operating costs.
Sales growth for individual companies usually comes from taking sales
away from competitors."

Benchmark Data

- $150,000 sales per employee is an average for companies with approximately
2/3 repair, 1/3 new sales.

Expenses as a percentage of annual sales

Cost of goods	25%
Payroll/labor Costs	25%
Occupancy	10%
Profit (estimated pretax)	05%

Industry Trend

- "Repair lags general industry trends. Emphasis on power generation and
distribution including wind energy."

Questions

- "Technical strengths of shop employees? Concentration of customers? Where
is future growth coming from?"
- "Buyer needs to establish the repeatability and retainability of current
customers after change in ownership."

Embroidery Services/Shops

SIC 7389-42	NAICS 314999	

Rules of Thumb

➢ 55 to 60 percent of annual sales plus inventory

Engineering Services

	NAICS 54133	Number of Businesses/Units 139,037

Rules of Thumb

➢ 40 to 45 percent of annual revenues; add value of fixtures & equipment; may require earnout

Benchmark Data

Statistics (Engineering Services)

Number of Establishments	139,037
Average Profit Margin	19.9%
Revenue per Employee	$198,700
Average Number of Employees	7.6
Average Wages per Employee	$85,602

Products and Services Segmentation

Other projects and services	30.9%
Industrial and manufacturing projects	21.1%
Energy projects	10.8%
Project management services	10.3%
Commercial, public and institutional projects	10.2%
Transportation projects	9.3%
Municipal utility projects	3.8%
Hazardous and industrial waste projects	3.6%

Major Market Segmentation

Private businesses	49.1%
Government bodies	30.0%
Engineering firms	6.1%
Architectural firms	5.6%
Construction firms	5.1%
Individuals	3.3%
Nonprofit organizations	0.8%

Industry Costs

Profit	19.9%
Wages	42.7%
Purchases	14.0%
Depreciation	1.8%
Marketing	0.4%
Rent and Utilities	3.6%
Other	17.6%

Market Share

AECOM...5.0%
Fluor Corp. 2.7%

Source: IBISWorld, July 2016

Environmental Testing		
	NAICS 541380	

Rules of Thumb

➤ 60 percent of annual sales plus inventory

➤ 2 to 2.5 times SDE plus inventory

Pricing Tips

- "SDE must at least be equal to new debt service using a 1.5 ratio, owner's salary and any capex requirements, or it's priced too high."
- "Be sure the accounting is on the accrual method so there is no confusion as to how values are arrived at."

Expert Comments

"Owner and his contacts are more the driving, networking force than the location or the facilities."

Benchmark Data

- "It can be a roll-up-your-sleeves kind of business."

Expenses as a percentage of annual sales

Cost of goods..02%
Payroll/labor Costs...30%
Occupancy..03%
Profit (estimated pretax) 16%

Industry Trend

- "The environmental testing market is driven by the rising concern for environment degradation and increasing regulations regarding environment protection. The environmental testing market is projected to grow at a CAGR of 6.4%, valued at $9.5 Billion by 2019. The market in Asia-Pacific is projected to grow at the highest CAGR due to the increasing industrial activities and rising concern for environmental pollution."
  Source: http://www.marketsandmarkets.com/PressReleases/environmental-testing.asp
- "Steady, but real estate activities have a big influence."

Questions

- "Why did you get in the business and why are you getting out at this time?"

Resources

Websites

- Environmental Business International: www.ebionline.org

	Franchise

Environment Control (Commercial Cleaning Services)
(See also Franchises)

Approx. Total Investment	$55,000 +$150,000 net worth

	NAICS 561720	Number of Businesses/Units 50

Rules of Thumb
➢ 42 percent of annual sales plus inventory

Pricing Tips
▪ The firm has 50 units in 19 states. Go to their Web site for more information: www.environmentcontrol.com

Resources

Websites
▪ www.environmentcontrol.com

Event Companies

SIC 7389-44	NAICS 812990	Number of Businesses/Units 224,031

Rules of Thumb
➢ 3 times EBITDA plus asset value

Pricing Tips
▪ "Are there events on the books going forward? How many repeat clients?"

Benchmark Data

Statistics (Trade Show and Conference Planning)
Number of Establishments	4,978
Average Profit Margin	5.3%
Revenue per Employee	$159,700
Average Number of Employees	17.9
Average Wages per Employee	$37,890

Products and Services Segmentation
Exhibit sales and design services	43.6%
Registration, analytics and show services	24.1%
Sponsorships, entertainment and advertising sales	21.4%
Shipping, logistics and other services	10.9%

Major Market Segmentation

Other	34.8%
Consumer goods, sporting goods, travel and other consumer services	18.2%
Medical and healthcare	18.1%
Business services	10.5%
Communications and information technology	9.2%
Producers of commodities, chemicals and engineered materials manufacturers	9.2%

Industry Costs

Profit	5.3%
Wages	23.9%
Purchases	29.7%
Depreciation	0.5%
Marketing	19.1%
Rent & Utilities	6.2%
Other	15.3%

Market Share

The Freeman Companies	13.3%
Viad Corp.	5.2%

Source: IBISWorld, March 2016

Statistics (Party & Event Planners)

Number of Establishments	219,053
Average Profit Margin	9.8%
Revenue per Employee	$20,800
Average Number of Employees	1.0
Average Wages per Employee	$6,016

Products and Services Segmentation

Corporate social events	41.6%
Weddings	28.7%
Birthday parties	16.0%
Other	13.7%

Industry Costs

Profit	9.8%
Wages	28.2%
Purchases	21.0%
Depreciation	2.5%
Marketing	6.0%
Rent & Utilities	6.7%
Other	25.8%

Source: IBISWorld, September 2015

Industry Trend

- "Top predictions for 2016:
    - ✓ Attendee Engagement
    - ✓ Security
    - ✓ Participant Matchmaking
    - ✓ Streamlined Tools
    - ✓ Bespoke event locations"

Source: "2016 Meeting and Event Trends for Event Planners" by Al Wynant, December 9, 2015, http://hel-loendless.com/2016-meeting-and-event-trends-for-event-planners/

- "The event industry has been an extremely exciting place to be over the last few years, and 2016 looks to be no different, with plenty of innovations lining up to expand and change the face of the industry:
  - ✓ Revenue re-think
  - ✓ Changing employee roles
  - ✓ New technology
  - ✓ Evaluating events
  - ✓ Versatile venues
  - ✓ Keynote know-how
  - ✓ Multi-sensory experiences"
  Source: "Top Trends to Look Out for in the Event Industry in 2016" by Tina Benson, January 26, 2016

Seller Financing
- 2 ½ years

Fabric Stores		
SIC 5949-02	NAICS 45113	Number of Businesses/Units 24,003

Rules of Thumb
➤ 3 times monthly sales plus inventory

Benchmark Data

Statistics (Fabric, Craft & Sewing Supplies Stores)
Number of Establishments 24,003
Average Profit Margin 14.6%
Revenue per Employee $78,500
Average Number of Employees 2.7
Average Wages per Employee $10,715

Products and Services Segmentation
Fabrics 40.0%
Sewing and craft supplies 33.0%
Other 12.0%
Seasonal decorations 8.0%
Fabric home decor 7.0%

Industry Costs
Profit 14.6%
Wages 13.7%
Purchases 59.0%
Depreciation 0.9%
Marketing 2.2%
Rent & Utilities 6.0%
Other 3.6%

Market Share
Michaels Stores Inc. 47.0%
Jo-Ann Stores Inc. 25.0%
Hobby Lobby Stores Inc. 18.0%
Source: IBISWorld, July 2016

Industry Trend

- "Question: What happened to fabric stores? Answer: Good women's clothes made from beautiful fabrics became cheaper as more people were making money on cheap labor, so there was less sewing going on. Also, a lot of stores that have gone were family-run businesses. The younger generation had no interest in continuing to run them."

Resources

Websites

- The Fabric Shop Network—an online resource: www.fabshopnet.com

---

Family Clothing Stores (See also Women's Clothing)

SIC 5651	NAICS 448140	Number of Businesses/Units 45,197

Rules of Thumb

➤ .75 to 1.5 times SDE plus inventory

➤ 2.4 to 2.8 times SDE includes inventory

➤ 40 to 45 percent of annual sales includes inventory

Pricing Tips

Women's Apparel— "try 23 percent of annual sales + inventory and/or 1.1 times SDE."

Benchmark Data

Statistics (Family Clothing Stores)

Number of Establishments	44,921
Average Profit Margin	5.0%
Revenue per Employee	$134,400
Average Number of Employees	17.1
Average Wages per Employee	$15,401

Products and Services Segmentation

Other women's wear	25.7%
Women's casual wear	25.5%
Men's casual wear	15.0%
Other men's wear	13.1%
Women's formal wear	8.9%
Children's wear	7.8%
Men's formal wear	4.0%

Major Market Segmentation

Generation X	35.5%
Baby boomers	24.5%
Generation Y	22.5%
Seniors aged 65 and over	10.0%
Children aged nine and under	7.0%
Commercial buyers	0.5%

Industry Costs

Profit	5.0%
Wages	11.4%
Purchases	59.9%
Depreciation	1.0%
Marketing	2.0%
Rent & Utilities	6.0%
Other	14.7%

Market Share

The TJX Companies Inc.	14.9%
Gap Inc.	12.2%
Ross Stores Inc.	10.5%

Source: IBISWorld, February 2016

Expenses as a percentage of annual sales

Cost of goods	46% to 52%
Payroll/labor Costs	14% to 18%
Occupancy	06% to 10%
Profit (estimated pretax)	12% to 15%

Seller Financing
- 5 to 10 years

Family Entertainment Centers

	NAICS 713120	

Rules of Thumb
- 3 times EBITDA

		Franchise

Fantastic Sam's (See also Barber Shops, Franchises, Great Clips)

Approx. Total Investment		$136,100 to $247,100
	NAICS 812112	Number of Businesses/Units 1,143

Rules of Thumb
- 35 to 40 percent of annual sales plus inventory

Resources

Websites
- www.fantasticsams.com

Fast-Fix Jewelry and Watch Repairs (See also Franchises)

Approx. Total Investment		$170,000 to $498,000
SIC 7631-01 & 7631-02	NAICS 811490	Number of Businesses/Units 159

Rules of Thumb

➤ 80 to 85 percent of annual sales plus inventory

Resources

Websites
- www.fastfix.com

Fast Food (See also Restaurants—Limited Service)

	NAICS 722513	

Rules of Thumb

➤ 35 to 45 percent of annual sales plus inventory

Industry Trend

- "Fast food had been thought to be largely recession proof, and indeed the industry did not suffer nearly as much as other discretionary spending sectors. In fact, there was some increase in consumer visits as people choose cheaper fast food options over fast casual or traditional restaurant choices. But overall, the recession hurt spending, and consumers overall purchased less with each trip. Fast food franchises fared reasonably well but still felt some pain."

  Source: https://www.franchisehelp.com/industry-reports/fast-food-industry-report/

Resources

Websites
- Nation's Restaurant News: www.nrn.com

Associations
- National Restaurant Association: www.restaurant.org

FastFrame (See also Franchises)

Approx. Total Investment		$105,800 to $150,300
SIC 7699-15	NAICS 442299	Number of Businesses/Units 128

Rules of Thumb

➤ 32 percent of annual sales

Resources

Websites

- www.fastframe.com

FasTrackKids	Franchise
(See also Schools—Educational/Non-Vocational, Children's Educational Franchises)	
Approx. Total Investment	$48,717 to $203,517

	NAICS 624410	Number of Businesses/Units 270

Rules of Thumb

➤ 45 percent of annual sales plus inventory

Resources

Websites

- www.fastrackids.com/

Fast Signs (See also Franchises, Sign Companies)	Franchise
Approx. Total Investment	$168,812 to $308,830

SIC 3993-02	NAICS 541890	Number of Businesses/Units 630

Rules of Thumb

➤ 42 to 46 percent of annual sales plus inventory

Resources

Websites

- www.fastsigns.com

Fire Suppression Systems Sales & Services

	NAICS 238220	

Rules of Thumb

➤ 80 percent of annual sales plus inventory
➤ 2.2 times SDE plus inventory

Pricing Tips

- "Business does not have to be profitable to obtain price, but must have good accounts, preferably with contracts in place."
- "The value of the customers can depend on whether the owner is the primary contact or the employees."

- "Most of these businesses are small and run by a family. There are larger companies that are actively seeking to roll up smaller companies. Their primary interest is retaining the current customers and the pricing of the products and services. They are more focused on gross sales than SDE or EBITDA."

Expert Comments

"Location of the business is not important as long as it is central to its customer base. In general these are not retail businesses and do not have walk-in traffic. They test/service/refill fire extinguishers and do installation and service of fire suppression systems. This has been a 'mom-and-pop' industry with businesses that have revenues of less than $1 million. There are several companies like Simplex Grinnell who are big players. It is an industry that is ripe for roll-up to increase revenues by adding customers, and consolidation is occurring in many markets."

Benchmark Data

- "Typical benchmarks are sales per customer. These range from $100 to a $1,000 per year. Customer concentrations can be of big concern. A large quantity of smaller companies and customers that represent less than 5% of revenue are preferred."

Expenses as a percentage of annual sales

Cost of goods	20%
Payroll/labor Costs	24%
Occupancy	05% to 06%%
Profit (estimated pretax)	15%

Industry Trend

- "The fire protection systems (FPS) market revenue market is expected to grow from $33.58 billion in 2013 to $79.18 billion in 2020 at a CAGR of 11.53%. The global fire protection systems market exhibits a lucrative growth potential for the next six years. The growth of the market is propelled by the government mandates and political support, increased fire protection expenditure from the enterprise segment, and technological innovations in equipment and networking. The lack of integrity in system interfaces and higher initial investments for the fire protection systems' installation are restraining the growth of fire protection systems globally.

"Some of the major players in this market include Gentex Corporation (U.S.), Halma PLC (U.K.), Hochiki Corporation (Japan), Honeywell International Inc. (U.S.), Johnson Controls (U.S.), Robert Bosch GmbH (Germany), Siemens AG (Germany), Tyco (Switzerland), United Technologies Corporation (U.S.), VT MAK (U.S.)."

Source: "Fire Protection Systems (FPS) Market worth $79.18 Billion by 2020,"
http://www.marketsandmarkets.com/PressReleases/fire-protection-systems.asp

- "Smaller businesses will be purchased by larger businesses."
- "Increasing NFPA requirements for portable extinguishers is driving the sale of new models with an opportunity to increase service. Businesses have to stay compliant with NFPA standards for insurance purposes."

Questions

- "Revenue per customer? Are there contracts in place for service? Employees interact with customers, so questions about their capabilities are important. Ask questions about relationships with local fire marshals and fire departments which can be very important. You want them on your side because they are often the enforcement arm for fire safety compliance."
- "Questions about customer concentration. There should be lots of small accounts as measured by revenue ($500–$1,000 per year). Large accounts suggest risk in transfer for the buyer."

Resources

Associations

- National Fire Sprinkler Association: www.nfsa.org
- National Fire Protection Association: www.nfpa.org
- Fire Suppression Systems Association: http://www.fssa.net/

Fish & Seafood Markets

	NAICS 445220	Number of Businesses/Units 4,607

Rules of Thumb

➢ 20 to 25 percent of annual sales plus inventory

Benchmark Data

Statistics (Fish and Seafood Markets)

Number of Establishments	4,607
Average Profit Margin	2.4%
Revenue per Employee	$185,500
Average Number of Employees	2.9
Average Wages per Employee	$21,604

Products and Services Segmentation

Fresh and frozen fish	82.4%
Fish meal and fish oil	13.7%
Canned fish	2.9%
Cured fish	1.0%

Major Market Segmentation

Consumers	68.6%
Single-location restaurants	16.5%
Chain restaurants	14.9%

Industry Costs

Profit	2.4%
Wages	11.7%
Purchases	69.3%
Depreciation	1.6%
Marketing	0.7%
Rent & Utilities	4.7%
Other	9.6%

Source: IBISWorld, January 2016

F - Rules of Thumb

Industry Trend

- "LONDON, Dec. 30, 2015 /PRNewswire/ -- In the last five years, the demand for fish and seafood has been witnessing a steady growth. Technavio's market research analyst expects the global fish and seafood market to multiply, growing at a CAGR of more than 4% during the forecast period. One of the major factors leading to the rise of the fish and seafood market is the increasing demand for processed seafood. Time-strapped consumers prefer processed seafood, which is not only healthy but also convenient and saves a lot of time and effort as they are already available in ready-to-cook packaging. "Aquaculture, which is the fastest-growing food production process globally, is an emerging trend that is expected to drive the fish and seafood market in the next five years. In terms of volume production, aquaculture method has overshadowed most other food-sourcing methods such as traditional agricultural practices and wild fish harvesting."

  Source: "Global Fish and Seafood Market 2016-2020," *Report Buyer*, December 30, 2015

- "The world seafood market, which encompasses fresh, canned and frozen seafood products, is expected to excess $370 billion by 2015, according to Global Industry Analysts. It is predicted the market will be fueled by a rising global population, increased discretionary incomes, and technological advances such as packaging and improved transportation. Demand will be particularly strong in developing regions including Latin America and Asia-Pacific. The overall market for aquaculture and fisheries is predicted to exceed 135 million tons by 2015, reports Global Industry Analysts."

  Source: "Fish and Seafood Markets," www.reportlinker.com/ci02030/fish-and-seafood.html

- "Going forward, the pace and robustness of the recovery will determine how overall sales improve for fish and seafood and which of the various categories will enjoy the highest growth. Packaged Facts projects that the retail market for fish and seafood will grow to $17.1 billion by 2017, with the overall compound annual growth rate for the retail fish and seafood market projected at 3.1% for the period."

  Source: www.packagedfacts.com/Fish-Seafood-Trends-7649917/

Fitness Centers		
SIC 7991-01	NAICS 713940	Number of Businesses/Units 113,729

Rules of Thumb

➢ 70 to 100 percent of annual sales plus inventory

➢ 2 to 3.5 times SDE plus inventory

➢ 4 to 5 times EBIT

➢ 3 to 5 times EBITDA

➢ "One year's annual revenues, usually reduced (or pro-rated) by memberships already contracted and paid for"

Pricing Tips

- "With the small to medium size clubs a significant amount of profit is often used to support the owner's lifestyle. This discretionary spending needs to be calculated and added back to give a clear picture of the net benefit to ownership."

- "Gyms are priced as a function of SDE, and the typical range is 1.8–2.2X SDE. Gyms will sell at the high end of the range if membership is growing with a large percentage of recurring revenue."
- "This is a capital intensive business, so first break apart tangible and intangible assets. Sadly, the market value of used fitness equipment is generally low, so the primary value will be from cash flow; however, it will be easier to break this out first to better value large from smaller facilities. For intangible value average the cash flow quantity and quality. Use 2x SDE for intangible quantity and average that with 10x monthly contract revenues to reflect the quality (or dependability) of that cash flow. Finally, calculate the value of outstanding paid-in-full contracts and subtract that from the consideration."
- "Pricing varies by size. Smaller fitness studios with little infrastructure may sell for 3X EBIT. Larger businesses, with multiple locations, upscale clientele and solid management team, will be much higher."
- "If the business model is based on member's paying monthly through pre authorized payments this business can be very stable. Most facilities have a good value in assets if the owner takes care in maintaining the equipment. The greatest challenge is often from rising occupancy cost so if an owner can purchase the building they occupy or secure a long term favourable rental agreement, they can ensure their continued profitability. Many facilities have gone with great success to a model that includes multiple revenue streams (personal training, group fitness, nutritional consultation, juice bar, pro shop, etc.) to provide a better and more even cash flow."
- "Drivers are quality of equipment and facilities. 5% of annual revenues needs to go into CAPEX annually so best driver of value is EBITDA minus CAPEX (Capital Expenditures). Facilities get a lot of wear and tear and they need to be updated regularly. Retention also drives multiple and value. Facilities with excellent retention (better than 80%) will garner higher multiples and valuations than those at 60% or less. 60% is usually average retention rate for a quality facility 50% or less for poorer run facilities."
- "Be wary of value of smaller storefront facilities/franchises. Many are often upside down, meaning a multiple of EBITDA doesn't justify the original purchase price on the business."
- "Multiples vary by size of the business. A small yoga or Pilates studio would likely generate a 3 times multiple of adjusted EBITDA, whereas a multi-location larger chain could generate a 5x multiple, or up to 1x revenue, assuming a 20% profit margin. Multiples will be lower if the owner teaches personally."

Expert Comments

"The most significant factor in whether a location will be profitable is the cost of occupancy in the area."

"Sellers should be able to articulate a reasonable growth strategy. Buyers should be able to understand the skills of each staff member, trainer and understand all aspects of revenue—how much is subscription, one time, etc."

"The fitness/health club industry is a very competitive one as barriers to entry are low, member retention is always an issue, and business models and the focus of gyms tend to change every few years. The group fitness concept is quickly emerging at the expense of one-size-fits-all gyms like Bally and 24 Hour Fitness. In addition, members are more likely to be interested in paying on a class-by- class basis as opposed to annual subscriptions."

"Never get into fitness center ownership because of your knowledge of fitness alone. Be sure you have adequate sales and marketing resources to survive."

"Fitness is enjoying a lot of popularity right now, which has brought in a great deal of competition. It is about sales production, and often people get into it thinking it is about fitness, Because of their failures, the equipment, while expensive, isn't worth that much although recurring revenues from contracts in place are worth a great deal."

"The media spends a lot of time promoting fitness and diet. This is a business that isn't going away."

"In the CrossFit space specifically, competition is increasing to keep up with consumer demand, which has grown several fold over the past 5 years. Gyms can command a premium if they: have established themselves deeply in the local market and build strong brands; have trainers that have built large and engaged followings; have sent delegates to compete in the CrossFit games; and are in Tier 1 locations (but not crippled by rent)."

"This is a competitive industry with a lot of different segments; low-cost, low-service to high-touch, high-cost facilities. You need to understand where a facility fits in its competitive landscape."

"The biggest risk to fitness center business is capitalization. It takes 12–18 months to get to breakeven. They get hurt if they don't adequately capital their companies. Once you get to breakeven, 70–90% of the next dollar flows to the bottom line, so depending on its profitability trend, bringing a little bit of growth can be very accretive."

"These are excellent businesses to sell. It's a fun industry and fun business. There are lots of buyers."

"Building from scratch or greenfielding operations has much more risk associated with it."

"Location in affluent areas is key for successful Pilates or yoga studios. A long-term lease is also key. Private sessions are significantly more profitable than group classes, so a studio with a higher percentage of privates will be more profitable than one that focuses on group classes. Industry is highly fragmented, with few large industry players."

"There are a few big publicly held competitors in the marketplace which have a big effect on market areas that are densely populated. There are increasing numbers of franchise systems filling niche areas of the fitness industry. Though there is more competition, health club membership enrollment by the general population is still well below 20% nationwide. This, coupled with the increasing awareness of the need for regular exercise, bodes well for continued industry growth."

Benchmark Data

Statistics (Gym, Health & Fitness Clubs)

Number of Establishments	113,729
Average Profit Margin	10.3%
Revenue per Employee	$47,800
Average Number of Employees	5.8
Average Wages per Employee	$16,434

Products and Services Segmentation

Membership fees	60.4%
Other	19.9%
Personal training services	8.2%
Guest admission sales	2.9%
Athletic instruction (excluding personal training services)	2.7%
Meals and beverages	2.2%
Merchandise sales	2.0%
Spa services	1.7%

Industry Costs

Profit	10.3%
Wages	34.6%
Purchases	5.4%
Depreciation	5.9%
Marketing	1.1%
Rent & Utilities	7.3%
Other	35.4%

Source: IBISWorld, May 2016

- "Health and Fitness Center Satisfaction Rankings:
  - ✓ Gold's Gym (836) ranks highest in customer satisfaction, performing particularly well in the equipment condition, variety of classes offered and safety factors.
  - ✓ Capital Xsport Fitness (835) ranks second, performing particularly well in equipment condition and variety of classes.
  - ✓ Planet Fitness (828) ranks third and performs well in price and cleanliness.
  "Key Study Findings:
  - ✓ Overall satisfaction with health and fitness centers is 813.
  - ✓ More than four in 10 (43%) members indicate they receive free or discounted membership.
  - ✓ Despite relatively high levels of satisfaction, there is significant room for improvement, as only 47 percent of members say they 'definitely will' recommend their club to a friend, relative or colleague."

  Source: "J.D. Power 2015 Health and Fitness Center Satisfaction Report,"
  http://www.jdpower.com/press-releases/2015-health-and-fitness-center-satisfaction-report
- "Having the majority of the clients on preauthorized payment for membership fees is critical to the long-term success and salability of the club."
- "Contract sales should be at least 75% of total revenues in a healthy sales environment."
- "Good benchmark numbers to look at are the total number of active members (paying monthly) and the average amount each of those member pay. Member growth and attrition over a three-year period can be a good indicator as to future performance."
- "Urban is $200 per square foot; suburban is $100 per square foot. Occupancy costs of 15% average; 20% OK but high; less than 10%, excellent. Location is key; need highly visible, easily accessible locations."

Expenses as a percentage of annual sales

Cost of goods	05%
Payroll/labor Costs	23% to 30%
Occupancy	20% to 25%
Profit (estimated pretax)	15% to 20%

Industry Trend

- "'The International Fitness Industry Trend Report provides real-world feedback on what fitness club operators and professionals are actually utilizing in the marketplace,' said IHRSA President and CEO Joe Moore. 'The report provides an in-depth analysis of niche, emerging, and mature trends based on comprehensive responses from leading club operators and fitness professionals.'

  "The key findings from the report include:
    - ✓ Personal training has the highest adoption rate of any program or service in the fitness industry.
    - ✓ Traditional functional fitness equipment and accessories (medicine balls, BOSU, stability balls) and flexibility/mobility equipment (foam rollers, stretch trainers and myofascial release devices) proved to be today's hottest equipment.
    - ✓ Boot-camp training, small-group training, HIIT group exercise classes and functional resistance training have all achieved a high level of adoption and continue to show above average growth.
    - ✓ Social media is the only well-adopted technology trend. The industry has yet to fully embrace technology as a means to enhance the member/client experience and improve productivity and efficiency. Technology opportunities such as online pricing transparency, online registration and reservations for programs, selling memberships online, virtual training and club mobile applications all have opportunity to gain significantly greater adoption with the industry.
    - ✓ Senior fitness programs are among the top ten most frequently adopted industry trends.
    - ✓ Treadmills and elliptical trainers have experienced resurgence in growth in the past two years.

  Notably, a significant majority of the trends across all three categories fell into either the emerging or niche categories."

  Source: "Fitness Industry Trends Around the Globe," September 15, 2015
- "Smaller locations with higher service"
- "Trend is positive for group fitness. The massive success of CrossFit and Spinning classes have introduced the world to the many benefits of group fitness, and I expect many new group fitness concept to emerge in the upcoming years."
- "Remember Curves, very hot when it was introduced and now they are difficult to give away. Similar fitness centers models built on a program grow rapidly and will then collapse. They can be very profitable if you get in early and then get out after growing a number of units. Generic facilities will have greater staying power."
- "Physical inactivity is growing in the United States despite health club memberships growing, too, according to the Physical Activity Council's (PAC) 2015 Participation Report released Thursday. The report showed physical inactivity has reached a six-year high even though health club memberships across the country have grown during nearly the same period. According to

Business Reference Guide **2017**

a media release from the PAC, 82.7 million Americans (28.3 percent) were physically inactive in 2014, an increase of 0.7 percent from 2013."

Source: "PAC Report: American Physical Inactivity Reaches Six-Year High, Club Memberships Increase" by Eric Stromgren, www.clubindustry.com April 23, 2015

- "Growth! As the population becomes older, there is an increased need to maintain fitness levels to maintain overall health."
- "The trend in the industry is towards smaller facilities that are providing a much higher level of service (Personal Training Studios). These facilities are able to change significantly more that the old barn style facility due to the extra service and don't suffer as much by the rise in the value of real estate."
- "Yoga is becoming segmented by type within larger markets. When considering competitors, focus on competitors that offer a similar type of yoga. Pilates is much smaller industry, but growing rapidly."

Seller Financing

- "Usually I see a 1/3, 1/3, 1/3 scenario whereby the buyer has 1/3 cash and borrows a 1/3 from a lending institute, the final third is provide by the seller as vendor financing with the seller taking the second position behind the bank on the security (equipment)."
- "Conventional lenders see fitness centers like restaurants, assets that are not worth much if they have to be liquidated. It will require a solid history of cash flows to attract one to finance a deal. Because of this, seller financing is often used in creative ways."
- "These businesses usually sell with some form of vendor financing up to 35% of the purchase price."
- "Outside financing more common"
- "If you have a large chain, there is little seller financing needed. If you have one facility, you may need to provide significant financing."
- "Some banks will provide financing."

Questions

- "Recurring revenue, opportunities for growth, lease transferability, value and state of equipment, potential deferred maintenance"
- "Do you use Mind Body Online for scheduling? How are instructors paid? Are the instructors on payroll (which they should be) vs. 1099s?"
- "What is your retention rate of members and employees? Employee retention drives member retention."
- "Match bank statements with monthly remits and request supervised access to the membership software."
- "What is the attrition level? How many members are on long-term contracts? Request the monthly remit amounts for trailing 12-month period."
- "Do you know of or have you heard of any rumors about any potential competition coming within 15 miles of this club? Why selling?"

Resources

Websites

- Club Industry: www.clubindustry.com
- HealthClubs.com: www.healthclubs.com

Associations
- IDEA Fitness: www.ideafit.com
- International Health, Racquet & Sportsclub Association: www.ihrsa.org

Flower Shops (Florists)		
SIC 5992-01	NAICS 453110	Number of Businesses/Units 35,611

Rules of Thumb

➢ 30 to 35 percent of annual sales includes inventory

➢ 2 times EBITDA

Pricing Tips

- "Review the Profit and Loss Statement to determine if wire service revenues and expenses (FTD, Teleflora, etc.) are tracked on separate line items to ensure that the sales are not overstated and cost of goods is not understated."
- "A premium should be given for stores with a significant number of commercial accounts (especially if there is a credit card on file for ease of billing) which helps protect revenues from big box stores that also sell flowers and plants."
- "Florists with a significant number of weekly or house accounts are very attractive in the marketplace and can command slightly higher multiples. Below market rent can also justify higher multiples. Conversely, shops located near grocery stores with large floral departments or near big box discounters should expect lower multiples."

Expert Comments

"Owning a flower shop continues to be a desirable lifestyle business for creative entrepreneurs who wish to provide an artistic and meaningful contribution to their community."

"The floral industry has been deeply affected by the economy and online 'orders.' Grocery stores and discount warehouses have also taken market share from retail florists."

Benchmark Data

Statistics (Florists)

Number of Establishments	35,298
Average Profit Margin	3.2%
Revenue per Employee	$69,800
Average Number of Employees	2.3
Average Wages per Employee	$14,779

Products and Services Segmentation

Arranged cut flowers	57.6%
Giftware and other	18.9%
Potted plants	11.8%
Unarranged cut flowers	11.7%

Industry Costs

Profit	3.2%
Wages	21.2%
Purchases	45.1%
Depreciation	1.6%
Marketing	2.4%
Rent & Utilities	9.6%
Other	16.9%

Source: IBISWorld, December 2015

Statistics (Online Flower Shops)

Number of Establishments	313
Average Profit Margin	4.0%
Revenue per Employee	$842,800
Average Number of Employees	10.8
Average Wages per Employee	$48,112

Products and Services Segmentation

Arranged cut flowers	28.5%
Potted Plants	23.5%
Unarranged cut flowers	22.7%
Giftware and others	19.0%
Floral Network Services	19.0%

Industry Costs

Profit	4.0%
Wages	5.4%
Purchases	62.9%
Depreciation	1.2%
Marketing	15.5%
Rent & Utilities	3.9%
Other	7.1%

Market Share

1-800-Flowers.com Inc.	35.5%
FTD Companies Inc.	31.9%

Source: IBISWorld, August 2016

- "Robin and David Heller, owners of Flowers by David in Langorne, Pa., and Florists For Change members, know they can't compete with $5 bouquets at supermarkets, whose cut-flower market share is 32 percent, or the order-gatherers, who have 12 percent. (Independent florists like the Hellers still claim 40 percent.)"

  Source: "Small florists struggle for differentiation from Internet middleman" by Virginia A. Smith, *Philadelphia Inquirer*, May 3, 2014

- "For a florist to be profitable, the rent should not exceed 15% of gross sales."
- "Local business is generally more profitable than wire-service-generated income."

F - Rules of Thumb

Expenses as a percentage of annual sales

Cost of goods	33%
Payroll/labor Costs	20%
Occupancy	10%
Profit (estimated pretax)	20%

Industry Trend

- "Consumers will continue to purchase industry products from e-commerce sites and supermarkets rather than florists over the next five years. To maintain favorable profit margins, many florists will increasingly specialize in creative, individualized arrangements, allowing them to stand out from competitors and increase prices. As a result, profit is expected to increase slightly despite falling revenue. Demand from wedding services and funeral homes is anticipated to account for an increasing percentage of sales because these services are less sensitive to pricing and convenience concerns. Overall, industry revenue is expected to decline at an annualized rate of 0.3% over the five years to 2020, totaling $5.7 billion as external competition continues to drain revenue from industry operators."

    Source: http://clients1.ibisworld.com/reports/us/industry/industryoutlook.aspx?entid=1096

- "Floral departments ranked 6th in growth among all supermarket departments."

Seller Financing

- 2 to 5 years

Questions

- "Percentage of local business versus wire service?"

Resources

Websites

- Some free information, but lots of data available for a fee: www.aboutflowers.com

Trade Publications

- Florists' Review: www.floristsreview.com

Associations

- Society of American Florists—for members only: www.safnow.org
- Wholesale Florist & Florist Supplier Association: www.wffsa.org

Food Processing & Distribution		
	NAICS 233310	

Rules of Thumb

➤ Processing:
  Branded—5 to 7 times EBIT
  Non-Branded—4.5 to 6 times EBIT
  Distribution:
  Branded and Non-Branded—4 to 5 times EBIT

Pricing Tips

- "Rate of growth; gross margins—higher is better; customer concentration—high is a threat; management continuity, high synergies."

Food Service Contractors	
NAICS 722310	Number of Businesses/Units 55,746

Rules of Thumb

➤ 40 to 45 percent of annual sales plus inventory

➤ 2.5 to 3 times SDE plus inventory

➤ 3 to 3.5 times EBIT

➤ 3.5 times EBITDA

Pricing Tips

- "Location. Location. Location. A rule of thumb: 1 person will occupy a building for every 200 sf of total building space. This number is very important to calculate a frequency rate depending on the building usage/mix (customer count and average ticket is key); also if there are multiple buildings in the center, assume 1 person for every 450 sf of buildings more than 25 yards away from primary building will frequent the shop."
- "A better operator can create 25% to 40% more sales quickly. You can still sell potential in this industry."

Expert Comments

"More and more operators are getting as close to office and workforce personnel as possible with smaller units. This will create pressure on price and profit."

"There is a low amount of competition for drinks, snacks, light & quick meals, but over the years there have been many franchises, lunch delivery & catering operations fighting for this market. The building owners see the shops in their buildings as an amenity in small buildings and are very accommodating. Large buildings, however, see this as a revenue source. As markets change so do the value and view of these type of shops change for the building owners & managers. When you find an accommodating landlord, take advantage of it because the odds are the tides will turn and the lease could be working against you."

Benchmark Data

Statistics (Food Service Contractors)

Number of Establishments	55,746
Average Profit Margin	5.6%
Revenue per Employee	$68,600
Average Number of Employees	11.9
Average Wages per Employee	$20,346

F - Rules of Thumb

Products and Services Segmentation

Cafeteria dining services	30.0%
Retail outlets and concessions	26.0%
Food and nutrition services	13.0%
Other	12.0%
Catering and banquet	11.0%
On-site restaurants	8.0%

Major Market Segmentation

Business and industry	28.5%
Educational institutions	27.5%
Healthcare	23.3%
Sports and entertainment	12.6%
Other	6.0%
Airlines and airports	2.1%

Industry Costs

Profit	5.6%
Wages	29.9%
Purchases	41.5%
Depreciation	2.3%
Marketing	0.7%
Rent & Utilities	7.9%
Other	12.1%

Market Share

Compass Group PLC	22.5%
Aramark Corporation	17.1%
Sodexo	16.6%
Delaware North Companies Inc.	5.0%

Source: IBISWorld, May 2016

- "Keep occupancy cost under 10% • get all food service in the building and if possible the inter center • operation should be set up to run with a very low amount of employees • food cost will be higher because customers are expecting a discount for their loyalty; not willing to pay for the convenience as you would expect. • get the vending in the center for all the building."

Expenses as a percentage of annual sales

Cost of goods	31% to 39%
Payroll/labor Costs	16% to 25%
Occupancy	04% to 10%
Profit (estimated pretax)	12% to 20%

Industry Trend

- "The Food Service Contractors industry will continue to benefit from increased consumer spending and higher corporate profit over the next five years. As unemployment rates decline and incomes rise, consumers will increasingly spend on luxuries such as eating out. Various private and public institutions and facilities will recognize the benefits of outsourcing foodservices to professionals that can deliver quality and consistent food options. Over the five years to 2021, industry revenue is projected to climb 2.3% per year on average to $50.5 billion."

Source: http://clients1.ibisworld.com/reports/us/industry/industryoutlook.aspx?entid=1681

- "This industry has nice potential over the next few years as landlords struggle to fill empty office & industrial space, but the secret is out so there will be more operators interested in these smaller spaces."

Seller Financing

- "There is very little outside financing the sales, and lack of increased sales volume prohibits banks from participating in the financing. Will most likely be owner financing."
- "3 to 5 years is common with about 30% down."
- "Finance no longer than the current lease term. 3 to 5 years is average."

Questions

- "#1) The lease is very important (get a copy and read it slowly). #2) Agreement with company is very important (get a copy and read it slowly). #3) What are the sales trends for the last 2 years? #4) What improvements or repairs are needed? #5) Count the people in the building. #6) Get information on employees. #7) Make a spreadsheet of the compatible operations. #8) Outside setting is a big value. If they don't have it, can you add outside set? #9) Do you like the food they sell? #10) What equipment will you need and is there room for it? #12) Make sure the common areas are kept up nicely. #13) How many hours does the owner work? #14) Call health department for inspection ASAP. #15) Can you increase the hours? #16) Equipment age is important. #17) When is the last time seller had a price increase?"

Food Service Equipment and Supplies		
	NAICS 423440	

Rules of Thumb

- ➢ 45 percent of annual sales plus inventory
- ➢ 2.5 times SDE plus inventory
- ➢ 4.5 to 5 times EBIT
- ➢ 5 to 6 times EBITDA

Pricing Tips

- "10 times EBITDA for dealerships"
- "All assets saleable? Obsolete equipment?"

Benchmark Data

- "Operators 2016 Foodservice Equipment and Supplies Budget by Product Category:

  Primary cooking equipment 18.13%
  Refrigeration and ice machines 11.27%
  Warewashing and safety equipment 5.17%
  Food preparation equipment 8.05%
  Serving equipment 8.67%
  Storage and handling equipment 4.59%
  Smallwares 11%

Tabletop items.. 3.59%
Furnishings 4.3%
Paper goods/disposables 15.4%
Janitorial/sanitation supplies.. 9.89%"

Source: "Foodservice 2016 Forecast: Chugging Along," August 31, 2015,
http://fesmag.com/research/industry-forecast/12891-foodservice-2015-forecast-chugging-along

- "It comes as no surprise that anticipated labor pressures will have an effect on a foodservice operator's bottom line, rippling out to other aspects of the business. In fact, 80 percent of the operators surveyed report they have changed their purchasing behaviors in the past year due to the business concerns outlined above. Along those lines, 41 percent of operators altered their approach to food purchases, 38 percent changed their approach to purchasing foodservice equipment and 34 percent say they altered their approach to procuring supplies."

Source: "Food Service Equipment & Supplies," fesmag.com/research/industry-forecast/11581-2014

Expenses as a percentage of annual sales

Cost of goods... 30%
Payroll/labor Costs.. 30%
Occupancy .... 05% to 07%
Profit (estimated pretax) 10%

Industry Trend

- "Cautious consumers and mixed economic indicators combined with the impact of a harsh winter will result in the foodservice industry experiencing a moderate 2014 but point to a somewhat promising 2015."

Source: "2015 Equipment and Supplies Industry Forecast: Balancing the Salty with the Sweet" by Joseph M. Carbonara, www.fesmag.com 9/2/14

Resources

Trade Publications
- Food Service Equipment & Supplies Magazine:: www.fesmag.com
- Foodservice Equipment Reports: www.fermag.com

Food Stores—Specialty	
NAICS 44529	Number of Businesses/Units 84,022

Rules of Thumb

➤ Food Stores—Specialty consists of several types of retail food stores including:

➤ Candy Stores—30 to 35 percent of annual sales plus inventory

➤ Bakeries—40 to 45 percent of annual sales plus inventory

➤ Dairy Stores—25 percent of annual sales plus inventory

➤ Other—35 to 40 percent of annual sales plus inventory

Pricing Tips

- "This category also includes the following retail businesses: confectionery products, gourmet foods, organic and health foods, packaged nuts, spices and soft drinks."
- "In general, these businesses will sell for 30 to 35 percent plus inventory."

Benchmark Data

Statistics (Specialty Food Stores)

Number of Establishments	54,074
Average Profit Margin	5.2%
Revenue Per Employee	$70,200
Average Number of Employees	2.4
Average Wages per Employee	$13,520

Products and Services Segmentation

Candy, chocolate and snacks	28.7%
Bakery products	23.1%
Other	17.9%
Refrigerated/frozen meats and eggs	9.4%
Coffee and tea	8.8%
Dairy products	6.1%
Gourmet prepared foods	6.0%

Industry Costs

Profit	5.2%
Wages	19.1%
Purchases	49.2%
Depreciation	2.0%
Marketing	1.6%
Rent & Utilities	10.4%
Other	12.5%

Source: IBISWorld, July 2016

Statistics (Ethnic Supermarkets)

Number of Establishments	29,948
Average Profit Margin	2.4%
Revenue per Employee	$28,500
Average Number of Employees	5.0
Average Wages per Employee	$19,347

Products and Services Segmentation

Other food items	38.9%
Meats	16.5%
Produce	14.0%
Non-food items	9.7%
Beverages (including alcohol)	9.3%
Dairy items	7.4%
Frozen foods	4.2%

F - Rules of Thumb

Industry Costs

Profit	2.4%
Wages	8.9%
Purchases	71.5%
Depreciation	1.3%
Marketing	1.1%
Rent & Utilities	6.5%
Other	8.3%

Source: IBISWorld, November 2015

Industry Trend

- "Sales of specialty foods have been increasing worldwide as demand for ethnic foods has continued to grow. In part, the increase comes from immigrant consumers seeking out foods from their own cultures. In the US, Hispanic consumers command about $1 trillion in buying power, and some experts expect this figure to double within a decade, according to Datamonitor. Nielsen projected in 2013 that Asian-American buying power would reach $1 trillion by 2017. As consumers worldwide see higher wages and travel increases, interest in other ethnic cuisines such as Filipino, Pakistani, and Peruvian is expected to rise.

  "The US specialty food store industry includes about 23,000 establishments (single-location companies and units of multi-location companies) with combined annual revenue of about $22 billion. Retail specialty food sales grew 19% from 2012 to 2014, growth that far surpassed the modest 2% gain for food sales overall during the period, according to the State of the Specialty Food Industry 2015 report from the Specialty Food Association, which drew upon on data from consumer research firm Mintel. Sales of specialty food account for nearly 15% of all US retail food sales."

  Source: http://www.firstresearch.com/Industry-Research/Specialty-Food-Stores.html

- "The popularity of organic food in recent years has led many large food companies to acquire small organic businesses. The past year alone saw a surge in specialty food business acquisitions, with sales including Annie's Homegrown to General Mills, Mom Brands to Post, and Rudi's Organic Bakery to Hain Celestial.

  "Some in the industry believe consumers are being fooled into thinking their favorite organic brands are not connected to food giants and that these larger businesses are hurting a movement that is based on avoiding conventional foods. While these mergers have led to wider access to organic foods and lower prices, some analysts predict organic standards will weaken as a result."

  Source: https://www.specialtyfood.com/news/article/should-large-companies-run-organic-food-businesses/

Resources

Websites

- Specialty Food: www.specialtyfood.com

Food Trucks (See also Catering Trucks)		
	NAICS 722330	Number of Businesses/Units 4,318

Rules of Thumb

➢ 25 to 30 percent of annual sales plus inventory

Pricing Tips

- "A big difference between food trucks and catering trucks is that the food truck is many times named after a restaurant or recognizable chef. This is often difficult to transfer and most likely neither the restaurant nor chef will be willing to allow a stranger to operate under their name. In other words a good portion of the value (and goodwill) is the name. If franchises such as Chili's or one of the steakhouse franchises get into the food truck business—that would be transferable with franchisor approval. Some food trucks do not use a well-known name, but rather specialize, such as the grilled cheese sandwich truck that did so well on a TV show. A food truck specializing in a particular food category would be transferable, again with permission."
- "Food trucks might be a fad, but they may also be a very successful business model."

Benchmark Data

Statistics (Food Trucks)

Number of Establishments	4,318
Average Profit Margin	9.0%
Revenue per Employee	$58,900
Average Number of Employees	3.5
Average Wages per Employee	$22,107

Products and Services Segmentation

American	38.3%
Latin American	24.6%
Asia and Middle Eastern	18.1%
Other	9.6%
Dessert	9.4%

Industry Costs

Profit	9.0%
Wages	37.3%
Purchases	36.0%
Depreciation	1.4%
Marketing	1.8%
Rent & Utilities	8.9%
Other	5.6%

Source: IBISWorld, September 2015

- "The mobile food industry is in its seventh year of consistent growth and the 2015 food truck industry statistics are here prove it. While food trucks may not be the new kid in the food service industry, the fact remains that the food truck segment is still growing. The best part is that there is still plenty of room for additional growth. Many cities across the country are still trying to determine how to regulate the industry, but many of them have started leaning towards fair ordinances that allow vendors to flourish."

2015 Food Truck Industry Statistics	Data
Annual food truck revenue	$1,200,000,000
Industry revenue increase over the past five years	12.4 %
Total number of food trucks in U.S.	4,130
Average revenue generated per food truck	$290,556
Average spending per order at a food truck	$12.40
Average cost of food truck	$85,000

F - Rules of Thumb

2015 Food Truck Location Market Segments	Percent of Sales
Street locations / corners	55 %
Other locations / venues / events	18 %
Industrial / construction work sites	15 %
Shopping malls	12 %

2015 Food Truck Expense Breakdown	Percent of Expenses
Food and Beverage for resale	27 %
Insurance, repairs and maintenance, licenses, fuel	26 %
Employee wages	18 %
Other	29 %

2015 Food Truck Startup Costs	Average Cost
Food truck (includes wrap & equipment)	$85,000
Total Startup Cost	$90,300

Source: "2015 Food Truck Industry Statistics show worth of $1.2B," by Richard Myrick, http://mobile-cuisine.com/trends/2015-food-truck-industry-statistics-show-worth-of-1-2b/

Outfitting a Truck/Major Expenses	
Medium used truck price	$43,000
Truck decals	$5,000
Electronics	$500
Permits	$500

- Most Common Truck Specialties
  1. Cheeseburgers
  2. Mexican/Tacos
  3. Desserts
  4. American Classics
  5. Sandwiches

Source: Matthew Twombly, NGM Staff Sources; Todd Schifeling, University of Michigan; Daphne Demetry, Northwestern University, Roaming Hunger; National Restaurant Association

Industry Trend

- "Top 10—2016 Food Trends
  Locally sourced meats and seafood
  Locally grown produce
  Hyper-local sourcing
  Natural ingredients/minimally processed food 6 Environmental sustainability
  Healthful kids' meals
  New cuts of meat
  Sustainable seafood
  House-made/artisan ice cream
  Ethnic condiments/spices
  Authentic ethnic cuisine"

Source: "Top Food Truck Trends 2016," by Richard Myrick, http://mobile-cuisine.com/trends/what-2016-food-trends-mean-for-your-food-truck/

- "The Food Trucks industry is in the growth phase of its life cycle. Although growth has tempered slightly over the past two years, revenue is still growing at a much faster rate than the broader food-service sector. Food trucks have fared better than their food-service counterparts primarily due to the budget-friendly characteristics of their products and the rising trend of consumers seeking experimental food concepts. Furthermore, the industry continues to evolve and new establishments are still entering the industry with new concepts. Over the 10 years to 2020, industry value added (IVA), which measures an industry's contribution to GDP, is expected to grow at an average annual rate of 6.4%. By comparison, GDP is anticipated to grow at an annualized rate of 2.5% over the same period."

Source: http://clients1.ibisworld.com/reports/us/industry/industryoutlook.aspx?entid=432

- "The food truck business has grown 80% since 2009, and it's on the way to becoming a billion-dollar industry by 2020."

Source: Matthew Twombly, NGM Staff Sources; Todd Schifeling, University of Michigan; Daphne Demetry, Northwestern University, Roaming Hunger; National Restaurant Association

- "The food truck industry has fared well over the past five years, but over the five years to 2019, industry associations will need to work closely with city governments and other restaurateurs to resolve issues related to city regulations, increased competition and low profit margins if food trucks are to play a bigger role in the country's food-services sector.

"The food truck industry has only grown in strength over the past five years and is one of the best performing segments in the broader food-service sector. The industry's remarkable rise began in 2008, just as the recession hit, as hundreds of new vendors recognized changing consumer preferences favoring unique, gourmet cuisine."

Source: http://foodtruckjobs.mobile-cuisine.com/food-truck-industry-growth-trends/

- "According to research firm IBISWorld, in the past five years, food-truck sales nationwide grew at an annual rate of 9.3%, to $857 million, as the trend spread to cities from Los Angeles to Boston."

Source: "Meal Impact" by Alice Park, *Time*, June 1, 2015

- "Emergent Research expects food trucks to generate between 3 and 4 percent of total restaurant revenue—about $2.7 billion—by 2017, a fourfold increase from 2012. In other words, food trucks are not a fad but a viable market segment with significant competitive advantages over quick-serve, fast-food and take-out food vendors. To delve deeper into the trend, Emergent Research recently interviewed a cross section of food truck operators and their customers."

Source: www.network.intuit.com

Resources

Websites
- Mobile Cuisine: mobile-cuisine.com

Franchise

Foot Solutions (See also Franchises, Shoe Stores)	
Approx. Total Investment	$200,000 to $225,000
NAICS 448210	Number of Businesses/Units 150

Rules of Thumb
➢ 60 to 65 percent of annual sales plus inventory

Resources

Websites
- www.footsolutions.com

		Franchise
Framing & Art Centre (See also Franchises, Picture Framing)		
Approx. Total Investment		$118,200 to $179,400
SIC 5999-27	NAICS 442299	Number of Businesses/Units 50

Rules of Thumb

➤ 60 percent of annual sales plus inventory

➤ Note: This is a Canadian franchise company

Benchmark Data
- For Benchmark Data see Picture Framing

Resources

Websites
- www.framingartcentre.com

Franchise Food Businesses (See also Franchises)		
	NAICS 722	

Rules of Thumb

➤ (This category is dominated by McDonald's, Burger King, Wendy's, KFC, Domino's, Pizza Hut, Arby's, Dairy Queen, Taco Bell & Denny's—others are Subway, Blimpie, Baskin Robbins & Schlotzsky's)

➤ 52 to 60 percent of annual sales plus inventory

➤ 2.5 SDE plus inventory

➤ 4 times EBIT

➤ 3.5 times EBITDA

➤ Asset value plus 1 year's SDE plus inventory

Pricing Tips
- "Franchise resales can skew these metrics higher depending on the quality of the franchise or the current 'hotness' of the franchise concept."
- "Rule of thumb: will list for 60% of gross and sell for 60% of list. Add cost of franchise fee on top of selling price . Non-traditional sites ... very lease dependent!"
- "Establish seller-adjusted cash flow and multiply times 2.5 to 3.5"
- "The multiples are a bit above the level for the industry in which the franchisee participates."

- "Stability of income, down payment & quality of franchisor"
- "Labor costs typically represent 15 to 20 percent of gross food sales. Food costs generally run from 28 percent to a high 40 percent for red meat on the menu. Pizza shops run about 28 to 30 percent. Rent should not exceed 10 percent."
- "Check the franchise agreement. Who pays transfer and training fees? Does the franchisor have the first right to purchase the business? Will the transition require the facilities to be upgraded to franchisor's current standards? If yes, the upgrade cost can be substantial."

Benchmark Data

- "Food Costs 25%–30% of sales. Labor Costs 25%–28% of sales. Rent (total occupancy including CAMS, taxes and insurance) 8%–10% of sales"
- "QSR 25–30 % food cost"
- "$600 to $800 per sq. ft. is respectable."

Expenses as a percentage of annual sales

Cost of goods	30%
Payroll/labor Costs	19%
Occupancy	07%
Profit (estimated pretax)	22%

Seller Financing

- "5 to7 years; however, SBA loans up to 10 years can be obtained."

Questions

- "What would you do to improve sales? Would you do it again?"

Resources

Websites

- We Sell Restaurants Blog: http://blog.wesellrestaurants.com/

Franchise Resales

Pricing Tips

- "Omitting a step, or even performing a step late, could have disastrous effects on the resale transaction. For example, franchisors often require upgrades and enhancements at time of transfer (costing thousands of dollars). If detailed information is not provided to both seller and buyer prior to executing an agreement, buyers—typically the party responsible for upgrades—may decide to walk away from the transaction. To make matters worse, this often occurs right before the closing table. Surprises like that may not always kill the transaction, however corporate will receive stressful, time-consuming phone calls from frustrated buyers unaware of the upgrades required of them.
"If the seller gets tied into a listing agreement with a local broker who does not educate the seller on proper pricing techniques, the franchisee will be tied into a one-year listing agreement to find their overpriced, or mispriced, business

never sells. Therefore, their sales and profits decrease; royalties decrease; the business is worth less; or they are in jeopardy of going dark. It is critical that sellers are educated on the pricing of their business, and the steps involved to properly value their business prior to market."

Source: Jon Franz, *Franchise Times*, http://digitaledition.qwinc.com/display_article.php?id=935202

Resources

Trade Publications
- Franchise Times: www.franchisetimes.com

Franchises		
		Number of Businesses/Units 784,000 +

Rules of Thumb

➤ We have listed franchises with a "quick" rule of thumb, or range, usually expressed as a percentage of sales. For many of them we have based it on quite a few actual sales; others may have been based on just a few; and in some cases just one where we felt it was appropriate. They can be a good starting point for pricing the business.

➤ Many of the franchises are well known while others are very new with just several units. By the time this goes to press, some of the franchises may have folded, sold or merged. We try to keep this as up-to-date as possible. We could use your help. To contribute to our ever-growing list, just go to our Web site and click on Franchise Update. Complete the form that will show up and email to us at tom@bbpinc.com. Also if you find that a franchise has disappeared or merged, etc., please let us know. Obviously the big changes such as Mail Boxes to UPS Stores will be caught by us or by our researchers (hopefully).

➤ Keep in mind that Rules of Thumb are just that. Every business is different and Rules of Thumb will never take the place of a business valuation or even an opinion of value. But, they will give you a quick ballpark idea of what the business might sell for everything else being equal. A rule of thumb will tell you whether a seller is in the ballpark when he or she tells you what they think their business is worth or what they want to sell it for.

➤ For up-to-date information and for those companies where the number of units is not shown, track down their Web site. Read the footnotes where indicated. Also, additional information is usually available under its own listing in this Guide. We have listed many of the franchises listed below, and others where information was available, by itself alphabetically by name within the Rules of Thumb section. In some cases, there is the Estimated Annual Sales per Unit and the Approximate Total Investment.

➤ Remember that Rules of Thumb are not intended to create a specific value or to be used for an appraisal. They supply a quick "ballpark" price range. They can provide a starting point for pricing a business or a sanity check after performing an informal valuation. Read the How to Use Section of the Guide, in the front, to gain some insight on how to make some adjustments to make the rule of thumb a bit more accurate.

➤ Several other factors can greatly influence the selling price of a franchise. One is the question of the transfer fee levied by the franchisor and who pays it. This amount can be substantial, so find out the information on this prior to going to market. The second is the franchisor requiring a major change in outside appearance and a change in the interior of the unit -- or both. This should also be investigated before attempting to sell it. The costs involved in either requirement can be substantial.

Name of Franchise	Selling Price as a % of Sales
AAMCO Transmission	40%–42%
A & W Restaurants	45%
Ace Cash Express	1.25%
Ace Hardware stores (1)	45%
Adam and Eve Stores	35%
Aero Colours	70%
All Tune & Lube	20%–25%
Allegra Printing	70%
AlphaGraphics	60%–65%
American Poolplayers Association (2)	1.4 SDE
Andy on Call	25%
Anytime Fitness	2.5 SDE
Atlanta Bread Company	25%–30%
Baskin-Robbins Ice Cream	46%–56%
Batteries Plus Bulbs	30%–35%
Beef O'Brady's	25%
Beltone Hearing Aids	50%
Ben & Jerry's	35%–40%
Between Rounds Bagel Deli & Bakery (3)	
Big Apple Bagels	35%–40%
Big City Burrito	55%–60%
Big O Tires	35%
Blackjack Pizza	40%
Blimpie	45%–50%
Boba Loca	30%
Bruster's Ice Cream	45%–50%
Budget Blinds (4)	50%–55%
Burger King	35%
Carl's Jr.	40%
Cartridge World	30%–35%
Carvel Ice Cream/Restaurants	55%
Car X Auto Service	35%–40%
CertaPro Painters	45%
Cheeburger Cheeburger	35%–40%
Chick-Fil-A	60%–70%
Closet Factory	45%–50%
Closets by Design	45%
Cold Stone Creamery	30%
Cost Cutter's Family Hair Care	55%–60%
Coverall North America (5)	2–3 times mo. sales
Culligan Dealerships	80%–120%
Curves for Women (6)	30%
Dairy Queen	45%
Deck the Walls	35%
Del Taco	70%
Dick's Wings and Grill	35%
Domino's Pizza	45%–50%
Dream Dinners	40%

Dr. Vinyl... 75%
Dry Cleaners USA.. 55%
Dunkin' Donuts (7) 60%–100%
Eagle Transmission Shops (8).. 40%
Environment Control 42%
Fantastic Sam's (9)... 35%–40%
Fast Fix (Jewelry) 80%–85%
Fast Frame 32%
FasTrac Kids.. 45%
Fast Signs... 42%–46%
Foot Solutions.. 60%–65%
Framing & Art Centre 60%
Friendly Computers 30%
Friendly's Restaurant.. 40%
Gatti's Pizza.. 30%–35%
Geeks on Call 60%
General Nutrition Centers 40%
Godfather's Pizza 25%–30%
Goin' Postal.. 30%–35%
Goodyear Store (Business Opportunity).. 35%
Grease Monkey International... 58%
Great Clips.. 1–1.5 SDE
Great Harvest Bread Co. (10)
Great Steak... 55%–60%
Grout Doctor 85%–90%
Harley-Davidson Motorcycles (11)...................................... 85%–90%
Home Helpers.. 40%–45%
Home Team Inspection 35%
Honest-1 Auto Care 70%–75%
House Doctor... 24%
Hungry Howie's Pizza & Subs 35%
Huntington Learning Center.. 60%
i9 .... 65% to 70%
Iceberg Drive Inn 40%–45%
Jani-King.. 25%–30%
Jersey Mike's Subs... 50%
Jiffy Lube... 45%–50%
Jimmy John's 65%–70%
Johnny Rockets 70%–75%
Jon Smith Subs... 20%
Juice It Up 20%–25%
Kentucky Fried Chicken (KFC) 30%–35%
Kumon Math & Reading Centers 80%–90%
Kwik Kopy (printing).. 50%–60%
Lady of America 45%–50%
Laptop Xchange.. 80%–85%
Lenny's Subs 15%–20%
Liberty Tax Service.. 45%–50%%
Li'l Dino Subs (12) 64%
Little Caesar's Pizza 55%
Logan Farms (honey-glazed hams).. 30%
MAACO Auto Painting and Bodyworks.. 40%
MaggieMoo's Ice Cream (13).. 25%
Maid Brigade... 45%
Mama Fu's 30%
Marble Slab Creamery 45%
Martinizing 55%–60%
McGruff's Safe Kids ID System... 52%
Meineke Car Care Center 30%–35%

Merry Maids	45%
Midas Muffler	30%–35%
Minuteman Press	65%
Miracle Ear Hearing Aids	60%
Molly Maid	40%
Money Mailer	40%–45%
Mountain Mike's Pizza	27%
Moto Photo	72%
Mr. Jim's Pizza	35%–40 %
Mr. Payroll	130%
Mr. Rooter Plumbing (14)	1–4 times SDE
Mrs. Fields Cookies	40%
Murphy's Deli	50%
Music Go Round	40%
My Favorite Muffin	30%–35%
Nathan's Famous	85%–90%
Nature's Way Café	45%
Natural Chicken Grill	25%–30%
Once Upon A Child	25%
Orange Julius	32%
Original Italian Pie	35%–40%
OXXO Care Cleaners	60%
Pak Mail	50%
Panera Bread	35%–40%
Papa John's Pizza (15)	35%–40%
Papa Murphy's Pizza	35%–40%
Parcel Plus	25%
Petland	50%
Pillar to Post—Home Inspection	25%–30%
Pizza Factory (16)	30%–35%
Pizza Inn	45%
Planet Beach	35%–40%
Play It Again Sports	40%–45%
Precision Tune Auto Care	35%–40%
Pump It Up	30%
Purrfect Auto	45%
Quaker Steak & Lube	45%
Quizno's Classic Subs (17)	25%
Red Robin Gourmet Burgers	30%–35%
Renaissance Executive Forums	70%
Rocky Mountain Chocolate Factory	50%–55%
Rita's Italian Ice	80%–130%
Roly Poly Sandwiches	35%
Safe Ship	40%
Samurai Sam's Teriyaki Grill	45%
Sarpino's Pizza	50%
Sears Carpet & Upholstery Care	35%
Senior Helpers	40%–45%
ServiceMaster Clean	55%–60%
Servpro	90%–95%
Signarama	55%–60%
Sir Speedy (printing) (18)	55%–60%
Smartbox Portable Self Storage	45%–50%
Smoothie King	40%–45%
Snap Fitness	40%
Soup Man (Original)	30%
Subway (19)	50%–60%
SuperCoups	40%–45%
Swisher (restroom hygiene service)	50%

F - Rules of Thumb

Sylvan Learning Center ....1.7 X SDE
Synergy Home Care 30%–35%
Taco John's 30%
TCBY 40%–45%
The Maids 40%–45%
Togo's Eatery 60%
Tropical Smoothie Café 50%–55%
Two Men and a Truck 40%–45%
UPS Stores 35%–40%
U-Save (auto rental) (20) 10%
Valpak Mailers 40%–45%
Valvoline Instant Oil Change 50%
Wienerschnitzel 30%–35%
Wild Birds Unlimited 30%–35%
Wine Kitz (Canada) 55%
Wingstop Restaurants 30%–35%
Wireless Toyz 45%–50%
Worldwide Express 50%–55%
Your Office USA 60%
You've Got Maids 60%
Ziebart International (auto services) 42%
Zoo Health Club 20%

(1) Sales seem to indicate that smaller sales bring a higher multiple (50% +) than stores with sales over $1 million, which seem to bring lower multiples. Price is plus inventory which may be the cause of lower multiples for larger stores. (2) $1,000 to $1,800 per team in sales; selling price: $2,000 to $2,500 per team (3) 3–4 times earnings (4) 2 times annual EBIT, plus inventory & equipment (5) Master/Area developer—Sell for 3 to 5 times earnings plus some blue sky for size and potential of market (some cases). (6) Prices for Curves for Women seem to be all over the place. Some sales have been reported at 75+% of sales. One sale reported was 1.31 times sales for four units. (7) Dunkin Donuts shops now sell for 75–125% of annual sales, depending mainly on geography. It's about 125% in New England, 100% of sales in the Mid-Atlantic States, and lower in the South and Midwest. There really is not a Dunkin' Donuts market in the West, however they are now moving into the West Coast market. A sale in Colorado was reported that sold for 22% of sales. (8) Eagle is a Texas-based franchise www.eagletransmission. com. They are the strongest transmission franchise in the Dallas area with 21 locations and are a minor player in Houston and Austin. The attraction is the royalties at 4% in Dallas and 6% in Houston and Austin, and the training is "hands on" locally. (9) These stores sell for maximum 2 times SDE versus $120,000 to $150,000 + for new. 10 to 12 sales have been reported at 2 times SDE for absentee owner stores (most are) and 2 times SDE + manager's salary of owner operated. (10) 3.3–3.4 times SDE (11) Netted $2,100,000 and seller retained 20% of ownership (12) One sold for 80% of sales, but it was located in an office building with vending rights. (13) One MaggieMoo's Ice Cream & Treatery sale was reported at 92%, three years old, great location, growth at 15% approx. a year; but only 15% down payment (14) 1–4 times SDE plus hard assets. The number between 1–4 depends on several factors such as the owner operating a truck, etc. (15) The only sale reported of Papa John's was a 3-store chain which sold for $475,000 with $150,000 down and grossed $1,191,700. (16) Pizza factory has approximately140 units in the 10 western states. (17) Quiznos, which has struggled as a higher-priced

alternative to Subway, has closed an estimated 1,000 of its U.S. shops (the company won't confirm the number) and has begun putting mini-stores in gas stations in a bid to boost sales—from www.msn.com April 2011 (18) One sale was reported at 70% of sales. (19) "As a former multi-unit Subway franchisee and a Development Agent, now a business broker for Subway stores, there are many different formulas I have seen. 30 to 40 weeks' sales, or 60 to 70% of sales is a popular one. Actual sales price depends on supply and demand and is closer to 70% of sales in So. CA." "On stores with gross sales of $300,000 to $500,000, multiple of 40% of annual sales. On stores with sales of $500,000+, multiple of 50% of annual sales. Franchisor would like 30% as a down payment on resales." (20) Price does not include cost of vehicles, and revenues do not include auto sales.

Pricing Tips

- "Rule of thumb for the Franchise Industry varies with the sub-industry. Typically you will find that franchise concepts trade for 1x to 2x above the rule of thumb for the specific sub industry. i.e., if an independent Auto Repair shop trades for 3x, a franchise concept can trade for 4x to 5x. The determining factor for whether a franchise concept trades for 1x over the sub industry or 2x depends on the strength of the franchise system."
- "Middle Market can vary wildly depending on size of the system and industry."
- "'When I started and you talked about the value of a franchisee, people talked about 4.5 to 5.5 times EBITDA,' said Bill Kraus, senior managing director of GE Capital, Franchise Finance. 'That might still be true. But for consolidators that have a lot of scale, prices are in the 7s now.'"
- "Presumes profitability on top of market-rate wages to the owner(s) for the time spent working in and on the business. I have observed about 90 business categories of franchised enterprises. It is hard to generalize about 'franchised enterprises' in general. Other considerations can be time left on the license and franchiser transfer fees. Still another consideration can be the history and SIZE (number of units regionally—nationally) reflecting the strength of the brand."
- "Varies depending on the type of franchise, the revenues, net income or SDE, age of business, and several other possible factors."
- "Branded businesses tend to sell at higher prices than non-franchised businesses. Example—Maid Services, 10% to 20% higher. Has everything to do with the track record of the franchiser. Some franchisers fail, at least 25% to 40%. This can vary based on the category. Some new franchisers will take anyone's money anywhere in the U.S. Some potential franchisees get impressed with an idea at a trade show and walk away from their background. Ethics vary."
- "Pricing the franchise resale obviously depends on the franchise. Is the franchise value added or—as in some cases—value subtracted? Does franchising add value to the business or would the same business— independent of a franchise label—bring as high a price in the marketplace? When calculating a multiple of annual sales, is it before subtracting the royalty fees, or are they included in the annual sales? After all, 6 percent of just $500,000 in annual revenues is $30,000, but just $12,000 at 40 percent of annual sales. The $12,000 probably doesn't have much of an impact on pricing unless the sales are really astronomical.

"McDonald's has always been the franchise that everyone compares others to, but that has changed recently. However, it probably hasn't hurt the price of a McDonald's—it is still a very strong brand. One disadvantage of franchising is that, like Burger King, the company gets sold several times, and the direction of the new owners can play havoc with operational support, advertising and growth of the company. In most cases, franchisees have no control over this. The strength of a franchise is the success of the brand name and the reputation created in the marketplace. Many franchises have been able to create that brand-identity and awareness to add a lot of value to the price of one of the units. And, if you want to buy a very popular franchise in a particular geographical marketplace, you have to pay the going rate.

"Some prospective business buyers like the security and the support of a franchise. Still others want the independence of owning and controlling their own business. Buying an independent business provides just that. No answering to the franchisor, no royalties and no heavy advertising fees, no forced purchasing from certain suppliers—and no politics. Owning your own independent business also allows you to expand, change, add or delete products and/or services. Independent businesses can be very quick to adjust to changes. Franchises, especially large ones, are very cumbersome and slow to adapt to new trends and ideas.

"The choice is a personal one. Some very strong independent operators have chosen, after years of independence, to buy a franchise, while some franchisees felt stifled and changed to an independent business.

"As for pricing a franchise, we don't see much of a difference between an independent business and the franchised one, except for the very big players, where the franchise label probably adds a lot of value, maybe 10 to 20 percent, based on the same gross. On the other hand, the fledging franchise with just a few units has some real problems on the resale side. If it's fairly new, there are plenty of new units available, the name doesn't really mean anything yet, and the age old question is asked—why is the business for sale? In cases like this, the percentage multiples might be reduced by the same figure as is added for the well-known brand name—most likely lower.

"Despite what the franchise industry would like us to believe, not all franchises are successful. What has always struck us as strange is the buyer who is very number- oriented and turns down a very good business due to some slight anomaly in the financial statement from two years ago, but will be the same buyer who purchases a franchise (a new one) where he has seen no books and records and has no idea whether the location will work out or not."

Source: *The Business Broker* (Business Brokerage Press)

- **Key Considerations When Pricing a Franchise**
    - ✓ "Lease Terms—If the lease doesn't contain a provision for at least 10 years remaining, the price can be affected accordingly.
    - ✓ "Franchise Rights—If there aren't at least 10 years left in the franchise agreement, a price adjustment downward should be made. This may not be applicable in those states where the franchisor may not terminate the agreement unless there is a default.
    - ✓ "Territorial Rights—If the franchise agreement does not provide for territorial rights, this could be a minus. In other words, if the franchisor can open additional units in the immediate area, the value of the existing franchise could be diminished. However, if the franchisee has additional territorial rights then the value may be increased.
    - ✓ "Business Mix—If the bulk of the sales is in low-profit items, value may

be diminished; whereas if high profit items make up a substantial part of the business, value may be increased. Is there wholesale business? Do one or two customers make up a majority of the business? Business mix should be considered.

✓ "Remodel Requirements—Does the franchise agreement state that the business has to be remodeled periodically? How often and how much remodeling? The value of the business may be reduced by the cost of the remodeling, depending on when it has to be done.

✓ "Hours of Operation—Does the franchisor require specific hours and days open? Some franchisors, especially food related, donuts/convenience stores, may state that the business has to be open 24 hours a day, seven days a week. The shorter the hours, the better the price.

✓ "Location—Obviously, the better and more desirable the location, the better the price.

✓ "Cash Flow—The price of a small business may be based on its sales history rather than on reported profitability. Some businesses are just not operated efficiently from a cash management point of view. Certainly, strong cash flow benefits the price asked, but a poor cash flow coupled with strong historical sales does not necessarily detract from the price."

Excerpted from a presentation to the American Institute of Certified Public Accountants by Bernard Siegel, Siegel Business Services, Philadelphia, PA.

Expert Comments

"Industry stats show continued growth for the franchise industry over the next couple of years, on top of the growth it's seen in the past few years. Corporate America is changing and more and more skilled executives are looking to be business owners but they need a plan, a system, a structure. They don't want to reinvent the wheel and franchises offer them what they need (over-used phrase but I'll say it anyway: be in business for themselves but not by themselves)."

"Franchises are operated under the terms of a franchise agreement which requires a buyer to utilize a competent franchise attorney and accountant. In addition certain franchisors require a location to be remodeled upon a sale. This could cost the buyer more capital than anticipated. Most importantly, be sure the terms of the new franchise agreement, which a buyer must execute, don't contain higher royalties which will distort the financial statements the buyer is relying on."

"People in general, regardless of industry, are choosing to use/consume from a brand name more each year, moving away from independent companies more. That trend is not expected to change anytime soon."

"Call other franchisees in the system to validate. Speak with both those who are successful and those who might be struggling to get a realistic expectation."

"Regarding the ease of replication—typically it's difficult because one must develop a concept, develop the business structure, develop the systems, and prove the model in multiple locations before expanding thru franchising. It takes a lot in the beginning but it offers great value down the road to investors looking for such proven models!"

"A franchisee must be committed to following the franchise system. Franchisees that sway from the franchise standards seem to struggle. The learning curve for a franchise is much, much quicker than a typical business with systems, controls and procedures normally in place. This makes is much simpler for the franchisee to expand the business in size and/or locations"

"Besides brand strength, the business system of the franchiser has a lot to do with success. Franchisees (new & re-sales) have to follow the business system."

Benchmark Data

- Franchise metrics vary depending upon the category. Fast food tends to have higher margins but is more labor intensive with higher occupancy costs. Service franchises tend to produce less revenues with lower operational costs. In addition, a number of franchises are now home based which results in much lower expenses."
- "This varies greatly depending on the business and the specific industry it's in within the franchise industry. I can't really generalize since so many various industries are included in franchising."
- "I value most business based on multiple of SDE plus assets."

Industry Trend

- "Top 10 trends in franchising today:

10. Increased technology in franchising
9. Increasing minorities and women in franchising
8. Internationalization of franchises
7. Franchising in 'faster than fast' food
6. Franchisors buying litigation insurance
5. Crowdfunding in franchising
4. Franchising in fitness gyms
3. Franchising in home health care
2. Multi-unit franchisees
1. Franchising in fast casual restaurants"

Source: by Tomas H. Lucero, July 06, 2015,
http://www.businessreviewusa.com/top10/5031/Top-10-trends-in-franchising-today

- "1. The franchise categories, that led the industry in 2015, will continue to dominate franchising in 2016:
  ✓ QSR—look for more specialty and ethnic based franchise concepts.
  ✓ Personal Services—especially the home care and children services sectors will remain vibrant. The wellness and fitness sectors will remain strong.
  ✓ Lodging—fueled by a stronger U.S. economy and lower oil prices, more people will travel and use lodging services in 2016.
  ✓ Residential and Commercial Services—will continue to grow and will benefit from an aging population of home owners that seek home maintenance services, as well as a resurgence of the residential housing market.

2. Any increase in interest rates such as the recent ¼ point increase by the Federal Reserve will tighten credit for small businesses and franchising.

Look for third party lenders that specialize in the franchise industry to grow in popularity.

3. There will be continued acquisitions and mergers by private equity firms in 2016. The favorable returns and scalability that franchising offers will increase the amount of investment in franchise companies by financial firms.

4. The Joint Employer issue promulgated by recent NLRB decisions, especially the Browning-Ferris Industries ruling, will cause the most vulnerable franchisors to increase their oversight and increase control over their franchisees by tweaking their franchise contracts to avoid direct and immediate control over franchisee employment. Franchising will continue to seek relief from the further NLRB decisions regarding Joint Employer rulings through congressional action.

5. Politicians will remain divided and polarized over particular issues regardless of the 2016 election outcomes.

6. Item 19 disclosures will increase in use and detail, as Financial Performance Representations become a significant competitive issue.

7. The franchise industry will continue to experience positive growth.

8. Franchisors, especially in the QSR sector, will adapt to increases in minimum wages by increasing the use of technology."

Source: "Franchise Know How" by Ed Teixeira

- "Strong growth market"
- "Franchise resales are increasingly popular while independent sales are tougher. There are pockets of the country (California for example) where a combination of the new minimum wage laws, occupancy costs and cost to build are rendering restaurants almost impossible to resell. The East Coast is not as affected."
- "Younger investors/owners (new college grads who aren't finding the jobs they expected); more passive/semi-absentee investors who may still have a corporate job but are planning ahead for that next lay-off or that simply want to diversify their income with multiple revenue streams to help them plan for their retirement years."
- "Franchising will continue to grow especially in the home care, children's services and fitness categories."
- "'Our forecast for the franchise sector continues to be presented with a note of caution because recent employment actions by the National Labor Relations Board create a cloud of uncertainty over the franchise sector, which could impede the growth of the number of franchise businesses, and thus franchise employment and output,' said James Gillula, managing director, IHS Economics.

"Highlights from the forecast include:

Projected growth of the number of franchise establishments in 2015 is projected to reach 781,931 an increase of 1.6 percent, matching the pace of growth in 2014.

"As employment growth economy-wide continues to strengthen, employment in the franchise sector will continue to outpace growth in businesses economy-wide, as it has in each of the last four years. Franchise employment is expected to reach 8,820,000 jobs, a 2.9 percent increase, while total private nonfarm employment will increase 2.7 percent.

"The 2015 forecast for economic output of franchise businesses in nominal dollars continues to show an increase of $890 billion or a 5.4 percent increase–

ahead of the $845 billion (5.0 percent) gain in 2014. The gross domestic product (GDP) of the franchise sector will increase by $521 billion or 5.2 percent in 2015, an increase over the $496 billion generated in 2014. "This will exceed the growth of U.S. GDP in nominal dollars, which is projected at 4.2 percent. The franchise sector will contribute approximately 3 percent of U.S. GDP in nominal dollars."

- "Franchise businesses will continue to increase and create jobs at a faster pace than the overall economy in 2015, as it has in each of the last four years, the International Franchise Association said today. According to the quarterly update of the Franchise Business Economic Outlook prepared by IHS Economics, employment and output growth for the franchise sector will increase over the previous year, echoing the yearly forecast released in January."

Source: "Franchise Employment Growth Continues to Outpace Economy-Wide Hiring" by Jenna Weisbord, http://www.franchise.org/franchise-employment-growth-continues-to-outpace-economy-wide-hiring 4/10/15

- "More than half of franchisees struggle to make a decent living, and nearly two-thirds wouldn't recommend investing in their franchise system, according to a new survey sponsored by a coalition of unions pushing to reform the franchise business model. In addition, 42 percent of franchisees surveyed were dissatisfied with their franchise system. The survey was conducted for the coalition Change to Win by FranchiseGrade.com, which surveyed more than 1,100 operators over a one-month period in February and March."

Source: "Survey: Franchisees struggle to make a living" by Jonathan Maze, *Nation's Restaurant News*, 5/4/2015

- "The franchise industry solicits studies regularly and the most recent (2015) shows the franchise industry growth to continue this year in the 4–5% range. It also shows that the franchise industry produces more jobs in the U.S. than any other industry."
- "Over the course of 25 years, while the establishment of new franchise locations has been relatively flat, the share of new locations has increased through the efforts of franchise brokers."
- "It is getting harder to start an 'unbranded' business. It is easier to open multiple locations with a branded business. Franchising is being driven on a commercial & consumer level. Despite the economy, new franchisers are entering all markets—everywhere nationwide."
- "Continued growth and interest as confidence in corporate jobs decreases."

Seller Financing

- "For franchise resales, we almost always see banks lending at 10 year terms with 6% rates with 20% down. We are also getting identical terms for independent restaurants. Seller financing is more common for independent sales and there we see 30% or so held on a note payable in typically three years or less."
- "Outside financing for the majority, but sellers seem to be carrying part of the deal lately."
- "In the sale of an existing franchise, it is usually a combination of personal funds, outside financing and seller financing. In the sale of a new unit or location, there is no seller financing."
- "Most franchises, especially existing profitable franchises, can be financed."
- "Combination of both as in an SBA loan and a seller carryback."
- "Outside financing for new locations, both for resales."

Questions

- "What do you wish you had done differently in the last six months, three year, five years? Where do you feel better controls over the business could be put in place?"
- "It's important to use the services of professionals Be sure to understand the terms of a new franchise agreement, study most recent sales trend. Review who franchise competes against. Ask if a remodel of the building and location is due. Meet the franchisor staff so as a buyer you will know who you'll be dealing with."
- "Would you invest in this opportunity if you had it to do again?"
- "The same questions that apply to any business for sale, plus: Have you reached your financial expectations that you had when you purchased the franchise? How long have you owned the franchise? Have you had problems or issues with the franchisor? Has the franchisor provided the support and services they agreed to? How many new franchises have been sold in the past 2 years?"

Resources

Websites

- Entrepreneur 2014 Franchise 500: www.entrepreneur.com/franchise500
- Franchise Gator: www.franchisegator.com
- FranNet: www.frannet.com
- FranchiseKnowHow: www.franchiseknowhow.com
- Franchise Grade: Franchisegrade.com

Trade Publications

- Franchise Times: www.franchisetimes.com
- Blue MauMau: www.bluemaumau.org

Associations

- International Franchise Association: www.franchise.org
- American Association of Franchisees & Dealers: www.aafd.org
- American Bar Association—Forum on Franchising: www.americanbar.org/groups/franchising.html

Freight Forwarding

SIC 4731-04	NAICS 488510	Number of Businesses/Units 47,213

Rules of Thumb

➤ 50 percent of annual sales
➤ 2.6 times SDE

Expert Comments

"Just sold a niche market, owner plus one employee freight forwarder, for $1.1 million at these figures."

Benchmark Data

Statistics (Freight Forwarding Brokerages & Agencies)

Number of Establishments	47,213
Average Profit Margin	4.8%
Revenue per Employee	$431,500
Average Number of Employees	6.3
Average Wages per Employee	$57,640

Products and Services Segmentation

Domestic freight transportation arrangement services	51.9%
International freight forwarding and customs brokerage services	35.1%
Non-vessel operating common carrier services	9.2%
Other	3.8%

Major Market Segmentation

Manufacturers	41.4%
Wholesalers	23.4%
Exporters	18.2%
Importers	17.0%

Industry Costs

Profit	4.8%
Wages	13.4%
Purchases	47.7%
Depreciation	0.6%
Marketing	0.9%
Rent & Utilities	4.1%
Other	28.5%

Source: IBISWorld, April 2016

Questions
- "Do you need a customs license?"

	Franchise
Friendly Computers (See also Franchises)	
Approx. Total Investment	$56,980 to $109,480
NAICS 811212	Number of Businesses/Units 260

Rules of Thumb
➢ 30 percent of annual sales plus inventory

Resources

Websites
- www.friendlycomputers.com

	Franchise
Friendly's (See also Franchises)	
Approx. Total Investment	$482,200 to $1,959,600
Estimated Annual Sales/Unit	$1,150,000

	NAICS 722511	Number of Businesses/Units 144

Rules of Thumb

> ➤ 40 percent of annual sales plus inventory

Resources

Websites
- Friendly's Restaurant: www.friendlys.com

Fruits and Vegetables (Wholesale)

SIC 5148-01	NAICS 424480	Number of Businesses/Units 7,549

Rules of Thumb

> ➤ 25 percent of annual sales plus inventory

> ➤ .50 to 1 times SDE plus inventory

> ➤ .75 times EBIT

> ➤ .75 times EBITDA

Pricing Tips

- "What is the average 'per basket or package' profit the company normally charges/expects?"
- "How much commission/profit does wholesaler charge its customers per basket/box? It usually is about $2.50 to $3 per . . . anything less makes the wholesaler merely a shipping company."
- "Actual gross sales achieved is not an important analysis tool . . . since there is usually an inverse relationship between sales volume and amount of profit that may be achieved (for instance, the more a box of tomatoes costs, the less profit may be added on). Better to determine how many packages/boxes of product are handled weekly and what 'profit per unit' is achieved."

Expert Comments

"It is perhaps one of the least expensive businesses to start and operate, but just as easy to destroy without a strong paying customer base. One can grow this business through adding of multiple delivery trucks and yet not even have to rent warehouse space."

F - Rules of Thumb

Benchmark Data

Statistics (Fruit & Vegetable Wholesaling)

Number of Establishments	7,549
Average Profit Margin	4.1%
Revenue per Employee	$763,500
Average Number of Employees	14.1
Average Wages per Employee	$46,198

Products and Services Segmentation

Vegetables	44.3%
Bananas	15.6%
Apples	14.3%
Watermelons	6.7%
Grapes	6.4%
Strawberries	5.3%
Oranges	4.5%
Peaches	2.9%

Major Market Segmentation

Other wholesalers	42.1%
Retailers	33.7%
Foodservice providers	15.2%
Others	9.0%

Industry Costs

Profit	4.1%
Wages	6.1%
Purchases	88.0%
Depreciation	0.6%
Marketing	0.2%
Rent & Utilities	0.5%
Other	0.5%

Source: IBISWorld, August 2016

- "How much is profit per package/box? Is a buyer used?"
- "Is there adequate storage area for holding buy-in/specials?"

Expenses as a percentage of annual sales

Cost of goods	40% to 50%
Payroll/labor Costs	30%
Occupancy	10%
Profit (estimated pretax)	10% to 20%

Industry Trend

- "Little is expected to change in the next five years for the fruit and vegetable wholesaling industry. Revenue growth will remain sluggish, and wholesale bypass will continue to reduce the number of industry operators. Per capita fruit and vegetable consumption will also remain stagnant and, therefore, demand is not expected to significantly increase. Consequently, industry revenue is forecast to increase at an annualized rate of 0.7% over the five years to 2020 to total $81.9 billion, including an increase of 1.5% in 2016."

Source: http://clients1.ibisworld.com/reports/us/industry/industryoutlook.aspx?entid=978

- "If the 'hothouse effect' is a reality for our environment and fuel prices continue an upward trend, the produce business will be adversely affected."

- "Smaller wholesalers either going out. . . or taking on additional food lines."
- "Large food distributors/club stores are a constant source of competition . . . so the only way to keep a customer base is through providing personalized service. This is the current and future trend."

Seller Financing

- "Both outside financing and seller financing, depending on what the corporate tax returns look like and the amount/age of equipment owned by the company."

Fruit & Vegetable Markets (Produce)	
NAICS 445230	Number of Businesses/Units 12,471

Rules of Thumb

➤ 35 to 40 percent of annual sales

Benchmark Data

Statistics (Fruit and Vegetable Markets)

Number of Establishments	12,471
Average Profit Margin	4.1%
Revenue per Employee	$149,000
Average Number of Employees	2.4
Average Wages per Employee	$17,305

Products and Services Segmentation

Vegetables	54.4%
Fruit	32.8%
Meat, fish, seafood and poultry (including prepackaged meats)	4.9%
Dairy products and related foods (including milk, eggs and cheese)	3.9%
Frozen foods (including frozen packaged foods)	2.1%
Delicatessen items (including deli meats)	1.9%

Industry Costs

Profit	4.1%
Wages	11.6%
Purchases	68.6%
Depreciation	0.9%
Marketing	1.7%
Rent & Utilities	5.6%
Other	8.5%

Source: IBISWorld, May 2016

Industry Trend

- "Conflicting factors will impact performance for the fruit and vegetable market industry over the five years to 2020. On one hand, an increased focus on healthy eating habits will continue to underpin higher demand for farm-fresh fruits and vegetables. At the same time, mounting competitive pressure from supermarkets, grocery stores and mass merchandisers that fall outside the scope of the industry, such as Walmart and Target, will pull consumers away from fruit and vegetable markets. As a result, revenue growth is anticipated to remain subdued over the five years to 2020, rising at a forecast 1.2% annualized rate to reach $4.7 billion."

Source: http://clients1.ibisworld.com/reports/us/industry/industryoutlook.aspx?entid=1045

Resources

Trade Publications
- The Packer: www.thepacker.com

Fuel Dealers (Wholesale)	
NAICS 424720	

Rules of Thumb
➤ 1.5 times SDE plus inventory
➤ 1.5 EBITDA

Pricing Tips
- "Wholesalers/distributors are large-volume, low-margin operators; therefore the price is 1–2 times EBITDA."

Benchmark Data
- "Typical wholesaler does $30 million in annual sales."

Industry Trend
- "Due to fuel prices and consumption falling from a peak demand situation during the unusually harsh winter in early 2014, as well as the ongoing downward spiral in oil prices, the price of industry products fell, and industry revenue is expected to decline by 0.2% in 2016 to $38.4 billion."

Source: http://clients1.ibisworld.com/reports/us/industry/industryoutlook.aspx?entid=1115

Resources

Trade Publications
- Butane Propane News: www.bpnews.com

Associations
- National Propane Gas Association: www.npga.org

Funeral Homes/Services		
SIC 7261-02	NAICS 812210	Number of Businesses/Units 29,881

Rules of Thumb
➤ 200 percent of annual sales includes inventory and real estate
➤ 1.5 to 3 times SDE
➤ 5 to 6 times SDE includes inventory and real estate; 4 times SDE without real estate
➤ Under 75 funerals per year, 3 to 4.5 times EBITDA; 75 to 150 funerals, 4 to 5 times EBITDA; and 150 + funerals, 4.5 to 6 times EBITDA
➤ 6 to 6.5 times EBITDA if real estate is included. If real estate is not included, long-term triple net lease is a must (8 to 10 percent of sales); purchase price would be 4 times EBITDA or approx. 1 times trailing 12 months sales
➤ 6 times EBIT includes real estate

Pricing Tips

- "The standard within the industry is to use a multiple of the historical EBITDA to determine a purchase price. The current multiple of EBITDA is a range between 4 to 6 times and includes all the assets including the real estate. A percentage of the total purchase price needs to be in the form of a non-compete agreement."
- "The standard within the industry is to use a multiple of EBITDA, typically 4.5 to 6 to determine a purchase price for everything including real estate. When determining EBITDA make sure to adjust the earnings by subtracting out the Cash Advance Items as they are a pass through and can inflate the earnings figure. These are things that are provided to families at cost—such as obituaries, flowers, cemetery expense, etc. As to what multiple to use, that is where the 'art' comes in, but some things to consider: condition of building, age of vehicles, is it the only one in town or is there a lot of competition, how much is in the prepaid funeral accounts, has revenue been increasing, decreasing or flat, what about market share. A funeral home that has been updated, has newer vehicles, is the only one in town that has 3–5 years annual revenue in prepaid accounts with flat to increasing revenue and market share would be closer to a 6. One that has not been updated since the 70s, with 10-year-old vehicles, and declining revenue in an area with a lot of competition would obviously get a much lower multiple."
- "Funeral homes that are larger in size and have more traditional funeral services are slightly more valuable than the standard Rules of Thumb."
- "Valuations can be negatively affected by high cremations or eroding market share. Valuations can be positively affected by strong real estate values, high growth areas, or increasing market share."

Expert Comments

"The historical profit trend is declining with the rise in the number of families choosing cremation which is a lower priced service. Marketability is fair to good, as a fairly priced funeral home should sell. It is typically hard for a new funeral home to enter an established market, as it is a relationship based business, and it is expensive to build a new funeral home, so the ease of replication is hard to very hard."

"1. 200 percent of annual sales includes inventory and real estate

"The rule of thumb has been around for a long time, but it always used to be a range of '1.5 to 2 times annual sales including inventory and real estate,' plus the math of 2X is easier the 1.5X to do in your head).

"There are two big issues with this method. First, it does not take into account cash advance items. These are items that the funeral home purchases for the family and puts on the contract, but there is no mark up. These items are easily identified in a contract analysis, or if the funeral home has accurate P&L's as they should be line items.

"Things like obituaries, flowers, death certificates, opening/closing the grave, crematory fee, required permits, etc. These can add up to between $1,000 and $2,000 per service. Since there is no profit to the funeral home, there should be no mark-up/multiple assigned to these items when trying to value a funeral home. If anything, a slight discount should be applied, because many funeral homes give families 30 days to pay, so they are giving an interest fee loan to the families served.

"As an example, most industry participants use a multiple of EBITDA to value a funeral home, if we compare the two, here is what we get. (assuming we already subtracted out cash advance items):

revenue is $1,000,000 so 2 times sales would be a value of $2,000,000.

"However, using EBITDA it would be $1,800,000 (A funeral home can be run at a 30% EBITDA, so in this case $300,000 and the average multiples used are 4 to 6, so 6 times $300,000= $1,800,000). While it is only 10% over-priced using this method, if cash advance items are not subtracted first, it can be 20–30% overpriced.

"If we used the 1.5 times sales, we would be at $1,5000,000 and since EBITDA multiples are 4–6 most of the time we use a multiple of 5, since it is in the middle of the range. A $300,000 EBITDA x 5= $1,500,000. We have a match!! This is the area that 90%+ of the deals actually get done.

"2. 5 to 6 times SDE includes inventory and real estate, 4 times SDE without real estate

"The issue with this rule of thumb as it is written is that is also the same (or even higher) as the EBITDA method listed in the guide and since the SDE method adds back all the owners earnings and the EBITDA method allows for a reasonable owners salary, obviously one of the methods in the guide is wrong.

"The one that is wrong here is the SDE as it overinflates the value of the funeral home, and since most general business brokers use the SDE method, it is causing a lot of funeral homes to be listed, but not being sold. If we stick with the fictional funeral home doing $1 million in revenue, it would not be out of the question for an owner or manager to have a salary of $90,000/year and use of a company car. So, if using SDE that $90,000 is added back in and say $10,000 for use of a car, we would be adding back in $100,000 which could increase the sale price by up to $600,000 or more above the EBITDA method.

"If we stick to the fictional funeral home we have been using in the previous example, the EBITDA was $300,000 and at a multiple of 6 would value the funeral home at $1,800,000 a multiple of 4 would be $1,200,000. The SDE method would add back the $100,000 owner's compensation/benefits and give us a figure of $400,000. Based on that, to arrive at a similar valuation as the EBITDA method you are looking at an SDE multiple between 3 and 4.5 times. (3 x $400,000=$1,2000,000 and 4.5 x $400,000 = $1,800,000). This range would bring it in line with the EBITDA method, allow general business brokers to arrive at a realistic value and get deals done.

"3. Under 75 funerals per year 3 to 4.5 times EBITDA; 75 to 150 funerals, 4 to 5 times EBITDA; and 150+ funerals, 4 to 6 times EBITDA

"These numbers are pretty close, the lower multiples for the smaller businesses are because nobody really wants a firm under 100 services per year as there is typically not enough money to hire another licensed funeral director, so the buyer is really buying a job and may be better off to just stay working somewhere else and making about the same amount of money, getting some time off, and having no financial risk.

"4. 6 to 6.5 times EBITDA if real estate is included. If real estate is not included, a long-term triple net lease is a must (8 to 10 percent of sales); purchase price would be 4 times EBITDA or approx. 1 times trailing 12 months' sales.

"Obviously, this one is on the high end of the EBITDA range. Because this is the top of the range, the real estate, furniture, fixtures, equipment, vehicles better be in pristine condition, if not, the cost to update repair or replace these items should be subtracted from the valuation arrived at.

"Also, while a long-term lease is a must, the difference between a gross lease and a triple net lease depends on if you are the buyer of seller, although the 8–10 of net sales is about the right percentage.

"5. 6 times EBIT includes real estate

"Again, top of the range. Competition is average, as most families continue to use the same funeral home as they have in the past. However, there is a bit more competition from low-cost Internet based cremation companies starting to affect the industry. I rank the risk as average since this is a fairly stable industry. The profit trends have been declining sharply with the rapid rise in cremation versus traditional burial. This has resulted in a drop in revenue and profits which in turn has lowered values of the businesses themselves. Location and facilities I ranked as good; most funeral home real estate is well cared for and most people know where the funeral home in there town is. Marketability I ranked as good, there are buyers for fairly priced funeral homes and the SBA is typically willing to finance them. I ranked the industry trend as poor, only because it is rapidly changing from traditional funeral/burial to cremation. Owners will have to adapt to the changing preferences of the baby boomers, or they will find other options such as having a memorial service and or luncheon at a banquet facility and not involve the funeral home. I ranked ease of replication as very hard, as it is very expensive to start a funeral home and often zoning issues can be a challenge. In addition most funeral homes allow families to pre-plan their funeral; once this is done people rarely use a different funeral home."

Benchmark Data

Statistics (Funeral Homes)

Number of Establishments	29,881
Average profit Margin	11.4%
Revenue per Employee	$126,500
Average Number of Employees	4.2
Average Wages per Employee	$31,799

Products and Services Segmentation

Traditional pre-burial services	31.3%
Merchandise sold	28.7%
Other	23.0%
Body preparation services	7.5%
Direct cremation services	5.6%
Transportation	3.9%

F - Rules of Thumb

Industry Costs

Profit	11.4%
Wages	24.8%
Purchases	25.7%
Depreciation	3.0%
Marketing	2.5%
Rent & Utilities	4.2%
Other	28.4%

Market Share

Service Corporation International 11.7%

Source: IBISWorld, April 2016

- "A typical single location funeral home can be run at an EBITDA in a range of 28–32%. Any more than that, and they are likely not putting money back into the facility and equipment."
- "Employment of funeral service workers is projected to grow 12 percent from 2012 to 2022."

Expenses as a percentage of annual sales

Cost of goods	20%
Payroll/labor Costs	28% to 30%
Occupancy	10% to 20%
Profit (estimated pretax)	28% to 35%

Industry Trend

- "The rise in nontraditional funeral services and cremation has resulted in lower revenue per call and less cash flow to the business. This in turn has lowered the values of funeral homes, and in some cases, the drop in revenue has resulted in some businesses falling behind on their debt. This trend will continue, and if interest rates increase, a lot of funeral homes purchased in the last 10 years or so will be in trouble with their lenders as most have a variable interest rate and are operating on thin margins currently. There will be continued consolidation in the industry on both a regional and national basis.

  "The other trend that is gaining momentum is funeral homes putting in banquet facilities or even building a separate banquet center on their property if space allows. These facilities not only allow families to have a funeral luncheon after a service, but they can also be used for other community events.

  "According to the NFDA the U.S. Cremation Rate was 43% in 2012—an approximate 65% increase above the cremation rate in the year 2000. If that trend continues, the U.S. will be at 71% cremation by 2024."
  Source: http://connectingdirectors.com/articles/44929-what-to-consider-before-selling-your-funeral-busines
- "5 Funeral Trends to Watch out for in 2016:

  Trend #1: Liquor licenses transform funeral homes into event centers

  Trend #2: Holographic eulogies let your families speak at their own funeral

  Trend #3: 3D Printing meets personalized urns

  Trend #4: Less products, more connection

  Trend #5: Bringing the funeral back home

  "While the idea of reinventing your funeral business might make your chest tight with anxiety, it's worth thinking about the fact that one day your business may be mobile or multifunctional. And if you're smart, both."
  Source:http://blog.funeralone.com/grow-your-business/unique-services/funeral-trends-to-watch-for-in-2016/

- "The rise in nontraditional funeral services and cremation has resulted in lower revenue per call and less cash flow to the business. This will result in lower valuations and some firms will need to close or merge with competitors as they will not need to have as large of a building in the future. Firms will need to adapt to these changes and focus on educating the public on the importance of honoring and celebrating a life lived by having a service. These services will be nontraditional and more of a celebration; they may be held at the funeral home or offsite. Successful funeral directors in the future will become more like event planners."

Seller Financing

- "The standard is outside financing for 75-80% of the purchase price, with the seller carrying back the balance in the form of a non-compete agreement over several years. Since this is a relationship based business, the non-compete helps to protect the buyer and helps to insure the seller will assist in transitioning the relationships in the community to the new buyer."
- 10–15 years
- "15–20 percent of purchase price for 10 years"
- 7–10 years

Questions

- "Why are you selling? Are you going to stay in the community? How long are you willing to stay on? Will you introduce me to the local clergy?"
- "Ask if the firm has ever been cited by the state regulators for anything, ask if they have ever been cited by the FTC. Ask to see copies of the facility license from the state and make sure it is current."
- "Make sure to ask about the prepaid funeral accounts and the last time they were audited. Make sure your attorney has a clause in the purchase agreement that states you are only assuming the prepaid funeral liabilities specifically disclosed and that can be verified. Get advice from someone experienced in the business."
- "Why is seller selling? How long has seller owned the business? How many competitors are there in the market? What are the demographics in the market? Are there any key employees in the business?"
- "Check volume trends and average sales trends for at least 5 years."

Resources

Associations

- International Cemetery, Cremation & Funeral Association: www.iccfa.com
- National Funeral Directors Association: www.nfda.org

Furniture Refinishing		
SIC 7641-05	NAICS 811420	Number of Businesses/Units 23,450

Rules of Thumb

> 50 percent of annual sales plus inventory

Benchmark Data

Statistics (Furniture Repair & Reupholstery)

Number of Establishments.. 23,450
Average Profit Margin 9.7%
Revenue per Employee $51,500
Average Number of Employees 1.5
Average Wages per Employee $18,841

Products and Services Segmentation

Office and institutional furniture repair 55.8%
Upholstery repair of household furniture.. 18.9%
Wooden household furniture repair... 13.3%
Other furniture repair services 12.0%

Major Market Segmentation

Households... 51.7%
Businesses 44.3%
Government 4.0%

Industry Costs

Profit 9.7%
Wages.. 36.8%
Purchases.. 30.2%
Depreciation.. 1.7%
Marketing 1.5%
Rent & Utilities 7.7%
Other.. 12.4%

Source: IBISWorld, July 2016

Industry Trend

- "Over the past five years, the influx of low-cost imported furniture into the United States has created problems for furniture repairers and reupholsters. Instead of paying to have their existing furniture fixed, consumers are increasingly favoring purchasing new items at marginally higher prices. Unfortunately for the industry, this trend is expected to continue through 2020, and will slowly starve the industry of demand."

Source: http://clients1.ibisworld.com/reports/us/industry/industryoutlook.aspx?entid=1713

Furniture Stores		
SIC 5712-16	NAICS 442110	Number of Businesses/Units 37,450

Rules of Thumb

➢ 60 percent of annual sales includes inventory

Pricing Tips

- "Analyze gross profit margin & ratio of repeat clientele to new customers."

Benchmark Data

Statistics (Furniture Store)

Number of Establishments	37,450
Average Profit Margin	5.0%
Revenue per Employee	$273,000
Average Number of Employees	5.9
Average Wages per Employee	$34,707

Products and Services Segmentation

Living room furniture	49.6%
Bedroom furniture	18.9%
Other furniture	17.9%
Dining room furniture	13.6%

Industry Costs

Profit	5.0%
Wages	12.8%
Purchases	57.5%
Depreciation	0.8%
Marketing	3.2%
Rent & Utilities	8.8%
Other	11.9%

Market Share

Inter IKEA Systems BV	9.9%
Ashley Furniture Industries Inc.	6.2%

Source: IBISWorld, May 2016

Expenses as a percentage of annual sales

Cost of goods	30%
Payroll/labor Costs	15%
Occupancy	20%
Profit (estimated pretax)	35%

Industry Trend

- "Leather upholstery sales reached $11.74 billion in 2015 and accounted for 38% of the upholstery category, including stationary sofas, motion sofas, sectionals and recliners. All told, 19% of consumers will spend $1,000 or more on a 100% leather sofa; 29% will spend between $500 and $999 more; 23% are willing to shell out an additional $300 to $499 more; and 29% of consumers will pay up to $300 for a leather covered sofa.

  "Three-fourths of leather upholstery buyers purchase through furniture stores, including traditional stores, manufacturer-branded stores and lifestyle stores, such as RH and Pottery Barn. Bestselling price points in furniture stores are a median of $1,599 for a leather stationary sofa; $3,699 for a sectional sofa; $1,549 for a motion sofa; and a median of $899 for a leather recliner."

  Source: "Gen X and the affluent willing to spend the most on leather," by Dana French, *Furniture Today*, April 26, 2016

- "Imports from China accounted for 57% of the total furniture imported into the United States last year, reaching $13.68 billion. That represented an 11.9%

increase over the country's 2014 shipments of $12.23 billion.

"5 largest source countries of U.S. household furniture imports in $ millions:

	2015	2014	% change from 2014
China	$13,678.4	$12,226.3	11.9%
Vietnam	$3,142.6	$2,620.2	19.9%
Canada	$1,248.4	$1,118.8	11.6%
Mexico	$1,197.0	$1,086.4	10.2%
Italy	$715.7	$641.0	11.7%

"U.S. furniture imports, 2015 by source country:

China	57%
All other countries	17%
Vietnam	13%
Canada	5%
Mexico	5%
Italy	3%

Source: "Furniture imports climb 11.9% in 2015," by Dana French, *Furniture Today*, April 11, 2016

- "Consumers are likely to resume purchases of furniture as the economy strengthens. IBISWorld expects per capita disposable income to rise at an average annual rate of 2.4% over the five years to 2021. Consumer sentiment is also expected to increase, encouraging customers to purchase goods from furniture stores."

Source: http://clients1.ibisworld.com/reports/us/industry/industryoutlook.aspx?entid=101

Questions
- "What is the reason for selling? Will the purchaser assume ownership of the client base? Is there already a fully functional Website?"

Resources
Trade Publications
- Bedding Today: www.furnituretoday.com/

Garage Door Sales & Service		
SIC 5211-02	NAICS 444190	Number of Businesses/Units 839

Rules of Thumb
➤ 25 percent of annual sales plus inventory

Benchmark Data

Statistics (Garage Door Installation)

Number of Establishments	839
Average Profit Margin	5.2%
Revenue per Employee	$101,400
Average Number of Employees	1.6
Average Wages per Employee	$36,972

Products and Services Segmentation

Retrofits and upgrades 68.0%
Repair and maintenance work 20.0%
Installation in new residential construction 10.0%
Installation in new commercial construction 2.0%

Major Market Segmentation

Homeowners 62.0%
Garage door merchants 26.0%
Construction firms 12.0%

Industry Costs

Profit 5.2%
Wages 36.5%
Purchases 34.4%
Depreciation 1.1%
Marketing 1.1%
Rent & Utilities 3.7%
Other 18.0%

Source: IBISWorld, December 2015

Garden Centers/Nurseries

(See also Landscaping Services, Lawn Maintenance and Service)

SIC 5261-04	NAICS 444220	Number of Businesses/Units 22,526

Rules of Thumb

➤ 3–5 times Seller's Discretionary Earnings plus inventory

➤ 25 percent of sales plus inventory

Pricing Tips

▪ "Customer database indicating the amount of recurring revenue per customer"

Expert Comments

"This is a maturing industry but the right business location and a good marketing and management of finances makes all the difference. Affluent customer base is necessary to compete effectively with mass merchants. A service component of the business is helpful but increases risk."

Benchmark Data

Statistics (Nursery and Garden Stores)

Number of Establishments 22,526
Average Profit Margin 3.3%
Revenue per Employee $302,100
Average Number of Employees 6.1
Average Wages per Employee $28,647

Products and Services Segmentation

Equipment... 51.4%
Grain and animal feed 19.1%
Chemicals 17.2%
Plants... 8.3%
Tools and other supplies 4.0%

Major Market Segmentation

Consumers aged 55 and older 29.5%
Consumers aged 35 to 54 .... 27.1%
Consumers aged 34 and younger 25.4%
Farmers 10.0%
Corporate entities 8.0%

Industry Costs

Profit 3.3%
Wages... 9.6%
Purchases.. 66.6%
Depreciation... 1.3%
Marketing 1.3%
Rent & Utilities 2.9%
Other.. 15.0%

Source: IBISWorld, December 2015

- "Greenhouse Grower's 2016 State Of The Industry Survey included separate questions for growers and for suppliers. Of our 358 respondents, 103 were suppliers, 111 were grower-retailers, 109 were wholesale growers, and 35 were young plant growers. Among growers, 57% indicated their operations were small (less than 100,000 square feet), 21% were medium-sized (100,000 to 399,999 square feet), and 22% said they were large growers (400,000 square feet or larger).

"Annual Sales Volume:
Less than $100,000 .... 31%
$100k to $249,999 .... 13%
$250k to $999,999 .... 13%
$1 million to $4.99 million 14%
$5 million to $9.99 million 11%
$10 million to $19.99 million 08%
$20 million to $29.99 million 04%
$30 million to $39.99 million 03%
$40 million to $49.99 million 01%
More than $50 million .... 02%"

Source: "Growers And Suppliers Move Forward With Cautious Optimism In 2016," by Laura Drotleff, January 18, 2016, http://www.greenhousegrower.com/business-management/growers-and-suppliers-move-forward-with-cautious-optimism-in-2016/

Expenses as a percentage of annual sales

Cost of goods.. 48%
Payroll/labor Costs.. 28%
Occupancy... 05%
Profit (estimated pretax) 04%

Industry Trend

- "I still have reason to believe that the most successful greenhouse and nursery firms in 2016 will be those that are well-positioned with their customers in the marketplace, not overleveraged, and clearly articulating their value proposition. We will likely see continued structural changes across the industry supply chain as we morph into the more compact and efficient industry of the next decade. This will not only mean further consolidation in the industry, but deeper, more strategic relationships among those left from the transition. The green industry in the next decade will not look the same as the last decade."

    Source: "Green Industry Is Set For Continued Growth In 2016," by Charlie Hall, January 21, 2016, www.greenhousegrower.com/business-management/green-industry-is-set-for-continued-growth-in-2016/

- "'Labor is one of the biggest concerns in our industry. Although we have a good resource in H-2A that is volatile due to government regulations,' said Danny Gouge of Willoway Nurseries. 'Quite frankly, if the minimum wage went up to $10 an hour, I would be out of business. How can a small owner deal with this issue? You can only raise prices so much,' said Ara Lynn of Amazing Flower Farm.

    "Top concerns going into 2016 for growers are the economy (26%), production costs (23%), government regulation (17%), and (the always constant) weather (12%)."

    Source: "Growers And Suppliers Move Forward With Cautious Optimism In 2016," by Laura Drotleff, January 18, 2016, http://www.greenhousegrower.com/business-management/growers-and-suppliers-move-forward-with-cautious-optimism-in-2016/

- "The highly anticipated trends report, published annually since 2001, finds that gardening goes hand-in-hand with a healthy lifestyle. People see both outdoor and indoor spaces as extensions of themselves and are making conscious decisions to use plants and garden products as 'tools' to increase their overall well-being and lead a sustainable lifestyle. In 2015, the report says brands are being held to ever higher standards, as customers demand that products are not only reliable but have a positive impact on the planet. Brands that help consumers make positive environmental, personal and community impacts will pull ahead.

    "According to the report, the idea of 'going green' takes on a dual meaning in 2015. As more states decriminalize marijuana, consumers will also invest time in 'growing their own.' 'First it was "eat your garden." Then it was "drink your garden." Now, it's "smoke your garden,"' says McCoy. 'Marijuana is going to become a great ornamental plant as people continue to customize their garden and outdoor space to meet their needs.'

    "What are some of the components that are fueling this sustainable lifestyle and contributing to eco-friendly gardens and outdoor spaces? Garden Media identified nine new trends driving major industry shifts:
    - ✓ The new consumers
    - ✓ Wellbeing
    - ✓ Garden-tainment
    - ✓ Bite-sized decadence
    - ✓ Rebel-hoods
    - ✓ Color pops
    - ✓ Portable gardening
    - ✓ Bed head style
    - ✓ Smoke your garden"

    Source: http://www.gardenmediagroup.com/clients/client-news/435-gmg-releases-2015-trends

- "Landscape Firms Scale Up To Remain Competitive
    Landscape service trends appear to be improving. In fact, according to First

Research, the output of the U.S. landscaping industry is forecast to grow at a compounded annual rate of 4 percent through 2016, indicating steady growth in the longer term. I made an informal tally of the mergers and acquisitions over the last three years and they filled up three pages single-spaced! About 80 percent of those were in the landscape sector, reflective of the fact that regional landscape firms are rapidly scaling up to achieve the economies of scale necessary to compete with the behemoth created by the Brickman's and Valley Crest merger."

Source: "2015 State Of The Industry: Current Green Industry Trends" by Charlie Hall, http://www.greenhousegrower.com/business-management/2015-state-of-the-industry-current-green-industry-trends/ 1/19/15

Seller Financing

- 5 to 15 years

Questions

- "Here are some key questions to get answered in analyzing garden centers:
    - ✓ How many months are you open for business (determine season)? If not open all year, which months are you open?
    - ✓ What method do you use to value your ending inventory (e.g., cost)?
    - ✓ What makes up your inventory in the winter months?
    - ✓ How are obsolete/damaged goods accounted for?
    - ✓ What is your policy regarding returns and allowances for plants?
    - ✓ Do you have a slow season? Which months? What other sources of income do you have during the slow season?
    - ✓ Who are your major suppliers (any related parties)?
    - ✓ What services do you provide? (landscaping, lawn service, delivery, plant rental, etc.?)"

Source: The above is excerpted from an IRS Audit Technique Guide (Market Segment Specialization Program—MSSAP)

- "What am I not seeing in your numbers? Is unaccounted cash being removed from the business? How current and complete is your customer database?"

Resources

Websites

- Today's Garden Center: http://www.todaysgardencenter.com/

Trade Publications

- Garden Center Magazine: http://www.gardencentermag.com/

Gas Stations—Full-and/or Self-Serve

(See also Gas Stations with Convenience Stores/Mini Marts)

SIC 5541-01	NAICS 447190	Number of Businesses/Units 12,892

Rules of Thumb

➤ 10 to 15 percent of annual sales plus inventory

➤ 2.5 to 3 times SDE plus inventory

➤ 2.5 to 3.0 times EBIT

➤ 2.5 to 3.5 times EBITDA (business only)

Pricing Tips

- "Buyers are looking for high volume gas stations; the norm is the higher the gasoline volume per month the more attractive the business becomes. That being said you also need to be aware of the margin on each gallon of gas sold. Find out if the tanks underground have been inspected in the last year and meet or exceed EPA and local standards. Ask if any leaks or hazardous waste has been found/detected on the premises in the last ten years. If the gas station has a convenience store associated the value is higher, if there is a car wash the value increases again."

- "Margins are getting squeezed in some areas, therefore must be taken into consideration."

- "3 to 4 times EBITDA including the real estate is a common rule. Location, traffic count, brand, and population are important considerations."

- "Age of tanks; does station have canopy (is it cantilever or mech. attached); is it clean (environment); location, location, location."

Expert Comments

"Major oil companies are getting out of owning properties and managing labor. More and more newer immigrants are getting into locations as owners across the country. Oil companies primarily want to be in the fuel supply business as their core profit driver."

"It is getting very expensive to build a new ground-up facility. Average does cost close to $2 million, therefore it is not that easy to replicate. Not to mention the uphill battle with most urban zoning requirements which causes lengthy delays and adds to the soft costs."

"Gas stations are easy to market, especially with the real estate. Competition is declining, since some stations choose to close rather than face environmental upgrades. Profit trends downward on gasoline, with gas profit paying some to most of costs only. Marts/snack shops/stores are major moneymaking factors."

Benchmark Data

Statistics (Gas Stations)

Number of Establishments	12,892
Average Profit Margin	1.6%
Revenue per Employee	$799,700
Average Number of Employees	8.3
Average Wages per Employee	$22,164

Products and Services Segmentation

Diesel	49.2%
Gas	41.8%
Other	5.6%
Nonautomotive fuel	1.8%
Automotive services (e.g. repairs, car washes and general parts)	1.6%

Major Market Segmentation

Consumers	68.8%
Businesses	26.1%
All other	5.1%

Industry Costs

Profit	1.6%
Wages	2.9%
Purchases	82.3%
Depreciation	0.7%
Marketing	1.5%
Rent & Utilities	2.6%
Other	8.4%

Market Share

Royal Dutch Shell PLC	9.7%

Source: IBISWorld, May 2016

Expenses as a percentage of annual sales

Cost of goods	75%
Payroll/labor Costs	08% to 10%
Occupancy	05% to 10%
Profit (estimated pretax)	03% to 05%

Industry Trend

- "The Gas Stations industry is expected to grow over the five years to 2020. Operators will experience more competition from retail sites in the Gas Stations with Convenience Stores industry while demand for gasoline will decline due to the growing popularity of fuel-efficient vehicles. However, a mild rebound in the world price of crude oil over the next five years is expected to enable industry operators to moderately raise prices for fuel. Higher per capita disposable income will mitigate these price increases somewhat, by allowing consumers to opt for the most convenient retail sites, despite higher prices, and by raising demand for diesel fuel and premium grades of gasoline. As a result, IBISWorld anticipates industry revenue to grow at an annualized 1.8% to $116.0 billion during the five years to 2020."

  Source: http://clients1.ibisworld.com/reports/us/industry/industryoutlook.aspx?entid=1063

- "Steady growth. Even if the type of fuel changes from gasoline to another product it will be still sold through a fuel station of sorts, therefore the business model is stable."

Seller Financing

- "3 years, on average 8 percent interest per annum."
- "As much as 50 percent of sales price could be financed—3 to 5 years typical."
- "Franchise—2 to 3 years (5 to 10 percent)"
- "Property—10 to 15 years (8 to 11 percent)"

Questions

- "5 years' financial and gallonage history; phase I & II environmental reports"
- "Any new competition? Security & safety? Road construction? Introduction to vendors."

- "Gallons history, margins history, both for last four years; plot against spot prices to see how tight street pricing gets on that street."
- "Some Key Questions:

  A buyer would want to ask the current owner if the oil company owns the property or if the land is leased to the oil company. The value of the business will be less if the land is leased from another entity. The reason is that when the lease expires, even if there are options, the oil company may decide not to renew. Make sure the oil company owns the property; worst case make sure the lease for the station runs at least for another 10 years (when the oil company does not own the land). Buyers should also be concerned about the types of tanks that are underground—are they steel or fiberglass? If the owner has steel tanks, find out why the tanks have not been replaced with fiberglass. Ask the current owner if there have been any leaks or contamination. If the answer is yes, find out when and to what extent. Has the problem been corrected?

  "One should also find out who is responsible for any and all contamination that lies above or below the surface of the site. Always require, in an offer to purchase agreement, a clause that states that the buyer will perform as part of the due diligence a Phase I report by an accredited environmental or chemical engineer who has a license to do so, with the results approved to the buyer's satisfaction. If a Phase II or III report is required, it is strongly suggested that it be done as well."

Resources

Trade Publications
- National Petroleum News: www.npnweb.com

Gas Stations w/Convenience Stores/MiniMarts

(See also Convenience Stores, Gas Stations)

SIC 5541-01	NAICS 447110	Number of Businesses/Units 110,254

Rules of Thumb

- 20 to 25 percent of annual sales plus inventory
- 80 percent of annual sales with real estate plus inventory
- 4.0 to 4.5 times SDE plus inventory, when a full service car wash is included (min. $250k SDE)
- 3 to 5 times EBIT
- 2.5 to 3.75 times EBITDA (business only)

Pricing Tips

- "1) What type of gas supply agreement is in place; rack deal gets a high price; dtw (dealer tank wagon) average price; commission agent low price. Buy a commission agent gas station only if there is a 10 or more year lease.

  2) Gas volume and pool margin on gas

  3) Convenience store gross profit preferred 30% or higher

4) Independent or brand name. Independent are valued at a higher price.

5) If it has a car wash it has a higher value.

6) Low rent high value.

7) If diesel is also sold, higher value as pool margin on diesel is high

8) The more the revenue stream, the higher the price."

- "Location, years history of proven growth, modern facility and, attention to competition."

- "The number and breadth of variables makes ROT pricing invalid, and largely misleading—we don't use it."

- "1) Valuation is 2–3 times net income for owner-operated gas stations and for absentee owned 3–4 times.

2) Potential buyers must consider rent, pool margin on gas, mechanics on salary or commission.

3) Age of the car wash equipment. Most car washes last 10 years.

4) Land owned by the oil company is a plus; if third party owns the land, check the underlying lease between the oil company and the landlord.

5) Check transfer fee and security deposit charged by the oil company"

- "Age and condition of the petroleum equipment and environmental issues are important considerations in selling and buying these businesses. A phase I & II report are required for both purchased and leased sites. Standard SBA loans are becoming more challenging as we all are aware; find the bank or lending institution in your area that provides the best opportunity for a bank/SBA loan for gas stations and convenience stores."

- "Some factors that detract are small lot size and access issues."

- "The most valid pricing comes from capitalizing adjusted cash flow, or SDE. If the gas station acquisition includes the real estate, this either needs to be broken out and priced in addition to the business, or digested in the capitalization calculation. Severely reduced transaction volume, little or no new construction, and poorly defined interest rate scale to define risk (& CAP rates) due to government intermediation make the standard approaches to pricing uncertain."

- "Gasoline volume and gasoline margin are key indicators of value; beer/wine license receives a higher price; store size greater than 1000 sq. ft. gets a higher price; length of time and type of fuel contract; franchised vs. independent impacts price, but depends on area."

Expert Comments

"Be conservative on growth forecast and be ready to invest in upgrades, when needed, to the facility and promotion of the business."

"To Buyers:

Work in a station for a minimum 6 months before buying one.

Make sure you have 2–3 months working capital after the purchase

To Sellers:

Start preparing two years prior to selling so you have clean financials. Not having proper financials will lead to lower valuation.

Prepare a good management/employee team so the station is on auto pilot."

"Gas stations are a retail business with a very high barrier to entry. Same inventory keeps changing hands as opening a new location is tough due to zoning laws and regulations and it costs over $2 million to get a new one started. It's a recession free business. You don't need a lot of employees, mostly one, unless you have a great hot food program."

"Municipalities dictate barriers to entry. Licensing (privileged licenses) are provided to qualified applicants only."

"This industry is dominated by large national and regional players with deep pockets."

"Use a broker, and find a specialist for the market you're going into. Business standards of practice, jobber relationships, environmental regulations, etc., vary greatly among regions of the country and the various states."

"The overall appetite for profitable businesses in this class is trending upward."

Benchmark Data

Statistics (Gas Stations with Convenience Stores)

Number of Establishments...110,254
Average Profit Margin...2.1%
Revenue per Employee...$419,600
Average Number of Employees...7.5
Average Wages per Employee...18,468

Products and Services Segmentation

Regular gasoline...58.9%
Groceries...12.8%
Mid-grade and premium gasoline...12.1%
Other...10.7%
Diesel...5.5%

Industry Costs

Profit...2.1%
Wages...4.4%
Purchases...85.8%
Depreciation...1.0%
Marketing...0.2%
Rent & Utilities...3.3%
Other...3.2%

Market Share

Alimentation Couche-Tard Inc....8.3%

Source: IBISWorld, February 2016

- "It's often said that 80 percent of a convenience store's sales come from just 20 percent of its customers."
- "CGS, operating expenses, and net profit as a percent of sales varies greatly as a function of fuel-to-store sales, and the price of fuel. Also, the revenue centers in the store, whether there is a QSR, a carwash, or mechanical service

as part of the non-fuel sales mix provides too much variance to make simple comparisons meaningless."

- "Looking at demographics, drivers aged 18 to 34 are most likely to visit c-stores this summer, according to the NACS survey. Seventy-eight percent of consumers surveyed in this age group expect to purchase a snack while traveling this summer; 74 percent plan to buy a drink; 73 percent will use the bathroom; and 40 percent will buy a sandwich or meal."
  Source: http://www.csnews.com/product-categories/fuels/more-summer-vacationers-will-take-road?cc=1

- "Average profit pretax is about 10%. Gas volume should be minimum 1.2 million gallons per year. $600,000 in convenience store sales with 30–40% gross profit. Car wash must do minimum $100–$150k per year"

- "Case by case, customer count to average sale $12.00+ per transaction."

- "Gross profit % of in-store sales is an important metric, and many of the major players will use gasoline as a lost leader to get you in the store."

- "Benchmarks for success depend upon revenue centers on the property and the sales mix among the centers, most easily illustrated by considering fuel and c-store. Fuel sales for a metro station might be 60-80% of sales with a profit margin of 2–4%, and the balance under-the-roof at 30% gross margin. (Fuel margins are expressed in pennies/gallon, called blended or pooled margin—easily converted into percent.) Rural stations tend to function more as a grocery store where fuel is the convenient item. These might do 80–90% under the roof and 10–20% or so in fuel. Store margins in rural settings can approach 40%, and fuel pooled margins $.30/gal. (vs., currently, $.12-.18/gal. in metro settings) Additional products and services also are a factor in this evaluation, e.g., carwash, alcohol sales, QSR (franchised or not), quick lube, etc."

- "Gross Profit margins in C-Stores should not be less than 30%, for delis not less than 50%, car wash GP margins 90%. Gasoline pool margins should be a min. of $.15/gallon."

- "There are 123,289 convenience stores selling fuel in the United States, and these retailers sell an estimated 80% of all the fuel purchased in the country. Overall, more than 58% of the convenience stores selling fuel are single-store operators—more than 70,000 stores across the country."
  Source: www.nacsonline.com/Research/FactSheets

Expenses as a percentage of annual sales

Cost of goods	65% to 80%
Payroll/labor Costs	08% to 15%
Occupancy	06% to 16%
Profit (estimated pretax)	04% to 10%

Industry Trend

- "Continuing trend to food service in the store. In AZ, not a great amount of alternative fuels emerging yet. We have started seeing more electronic charging stations showing up at non-gas station retail, e.g., fast food restaurants, larger shopping centers (malls)."

- "The performance of the Gas Stations with Convenience Stores industry will depend heavily on trends in gasoline sales and prices. Consequently, as gasoline prices rise, industry revenue is anticipated to follow suit. Meanwhile, sales of convenience store merchandise are expected to grow more solidly, as operators continue to refine their product selections and consumer spending on discretionary items increases. Merchandise sales are expected to help sustain some revenue stability, while oil prices remain subject to external factors. Meanwhile, purchases of fuel-efficient cars will continue to pose a threat to the success of the industry, as these vehicles require a smaller volume of fuel per mile. Therefore, revenue growth for the industry is forecast to be moderate over the next five years, averaging 4.1% per year to reach $395.7 billion in 2021."

Source: http://clients1.ibisworld.com/reports/us/industry/industryoutlook.aspx?entid=1062

- "Small owner/operators will continue to be taken over by larger operations."
- "Freedom to choose where to stop was cited by 59 percent of those stating they will travel by car this summer, also a 7-percent jump. Once consumers do stop, c-stores are certain to benefit. Three-quarters (76 percent) of vacationers on the road this summer plan to stop to use the bathroom; 69 percent expect to get gas; and 67 percent expect to get food or drinks, reported NACS. Those in the 18-to-34 age group are expected to visit c-stores the most."

Source: http://www.csnews.com/product-categories/fuels/more-summer-vacationers-will-take-road?cc=1

- "High competition amongst major convenience retailers. Bigger and better stores, more varieties and add-ons."
- "But, by far, the key message across most of the speaker programs was how the nation's changing demographics will impact business in the years ahead. The demographics of aging baby boomers, digitally-connected millennials and a larger multicultural population will have a profound effect on c-stores."

Source: "Don't Put All Your Eggs in the Millennials' Basket" by Don Longo, *Convenience Store News*, 4/17/15

- "The trend is towards the larger, modern stores with more inside sales offerings including fast food, and multiple fueling locations outside."
- "Continued improvement and profitability with reasonable reduction in risk."

Seller Financing

- "Outside financing is more typical. If Seller financing is available, only a small portion of the sales price and for a short term that is secured with a personal guarantee."
- "The most common financing is only for inventories for merchandise in the convenience store and fuel in the tanks. It normally will not exceed six months and will require some guarantee."
- "A combination of seller financing and outside financing recently. Less amount today for request of seller."
- "If real estate is part of the seller's assets, outside financing. If it's the business only with a lease, you can still get SBA financing, but often times the seller will need to provide 'filler' or 'gap' financing."
- "70% of the purchase price plus inventory paid by the buyer at closing and 30% seller financing for 2–4 years at 6–7% interest rate."

Questions

- "When do you know it's time to sell?"
- "How much financing can the seller do? What is your gas pool margin? Do you have a supply agreement with an oil company or are you independent? What is the gross profit on your convenience store sales? How old is the car wash equipment? If repair, how old is the equipment in the bays? Do you have

emission/inspection? Do you have any fleet contracts for gas? Do you own the ATM or is it leased? What is your lotto commission? If buying real estate also: how old are the tanks, any road widening plans, how much insurance premiums does he pay. What is the workers comp insurance premium especially if there is a repair shop with the gas station? Who is the nearest competitor?"

- "Ask for 5 years' financial statements and tax returns; petroleum equipment detail; environmental assessments."
- "1) Potential buyers must consider rent, pool margin on gas, if mechanics are on salary or commission.

2) Age of the car wash equipment. Most car washes last 10 years.

3) Land owned by the oil company is a plus; if third party owns the land, check the underlying lease between the oil company and the landlord.

4) Check transfer fee and security deposit charged by the oil company."
"What would you do different to enhance sales?"

Resources

Websites
- American Petroleum Institute: www.api.org

Trade Publications
- Retail Business Review: www.conveniencestoresgasstations.retail-business-review.com
- Fuel Oil News: fueloilnews.com
- Convenience Store News: www.csnews.com
- Convenience Store/Petroleum News: www.cspnet.com

Associations
- New York Association of Convenience Stores: www.nyacs.org
- PA Petroleum Association: www.ppmcsa.org
- National Association of Convenience Stores: www.nacsonline.com
- Arizona Petroleum Marketers Association: www.apma4u.org
- Gasoline & Automotive Service Dealers Of America: www.gasda.org

	Franchise
Gatti's Pizza (See also Franchises, Pizza Shops)	
Approx. Total Investment	$511,975 to $3,430,445
Estimated Annual Sales/Unit	$1,000,000
SIC 5812-22 NAICS 722513	Number of Businesses/Units 77

Rules of Thumb
➤ 30 to 35 percent of annual sales plus inventory

➤ Company also offers a larger restaurant: GattiTown—$2,900,000 to $3,200,000

Benchmark Data

- Size—3,000 to 8,000 sq. ft.
- GattiTown—18,000 to 25,000 sq. ft.

Resources

Websites
- www.gattispizza.com

		Franchise
Geeks on Call (See also Franchises)		
Approx. Total Investment		$53,350 to $82,150
	NAICS 811212	Number of Businesses/Units 123

Rules of Thumb

➤ 60 percent of annual sales plus inventory

Resources

Websites
- www.geeksoncall.com

		Franchise
General Nutrition Centers (See also Franchises)		
Approx. Total Investment		$165,000 to $200,000
SIC 5499-04	NAICS 446191	Number of Businesses/Units 935

Rules of Thumb

➤ 40 percent of annual sales plus inventory

Resources

Websites
- www.gnc.com

Gift Shops (See also Card Shops)		
SIC 5947-12	NAICS 453220	

Rules of Thumb

➤ 30% to 40% of annual sales plus inventory

➤ 2.5 to 3.5 times SDE includes inventory

➤ 3 to 4 times EBITDA

➤ Inventory @ cost + FF&E + 1 to 2 times SDE

Pricing Tips

- "Specialty Stores; boutique w/ exclusive lines; location is important."
- "If the store has a good location, has a customer tracking system and a good Website that is providing at least 10% of annual sales, the values above will hold. Fortunately, most buyers believe that they could run and manage a retail gift business. It is a 'fun' business; most folks don't go into a gift shop 'unhappy.' It is a 'feel good' business."
- "Inventory should be valued separately and include any costs associated with shipping inventory to the point of sale and preparing it for sale. Example: beads are bought in bulk. They are heavy and require extra costs to ship and require time and cost to re-package and weigh into smaller sellable units."
- "1. Location weighs heavily. 2. Products are very important in relation to value. Is the store a card + gift shop? Does it carry high-end American crafts and upscale gifts, gifts + toys? The mix is important along with profit margins."

Expert Comments

"The buyer needs to feel comfortable that they can manage and run the business; and they need to feel comfortable with the vendor/ trade-show sourcing of inventory."

"Competition from Internet shopping/on-line shopping expansion."

"Gifts make people smile. An owner needs to be able to have joyous empathy with their customers—especially those looking for that 'special gift' for someone special to them. And, you need to have good taste for what your customers may want. Providing services such as gift baskets and shipping can add to the business, especially with developing corporate sales."

"For smaller stores, unreported cash sales may exist. For larger stores, management, location and experienced buyers are key. Volume/type of products sold is very important. Merchandise buyers can make or break profitability, image, etc."

"Relatively easy to get into a craft business but difficult to obtain and maintain profitability. Smaller independently owned stores tend to be operated by owners with a passion for the craft rather than a passion for business."

Benchmark Data

- For additional Benchmark Data see Card Shops
- "Needs 'high traffic area' location"
- "The open hours make for a long work day. Most successful stores are owner run to keep wages in balance. Also, most stores use part-time help to keep the hours at lower wages."

Expenses as a percentage of annual sales

Cost of goods	48% to 55%
Payroll/labor Costs	08% to 18% (larger stores)
Occupancy	06% to 08%/mall stores 08% to 12%
Profit (estimated pretax)	20% to 25% sole proprietor; larger 05% to 10%

Industry Trend
- "Location will remain important; however, building a loyalty client program and customer contact & relationships with customers will continue to be critical to success."
- "More use of good Websites to sell more to repeat customers that do not have to actually come back into the store. Also, building up customer list with reminders and specials."
- "While spending on gifts, greeting cards and souvenirs will pick up over the next five years due to revived income levels, industry revenue will continue to decline. Competition from free virtual outlets like social networking sites and online greeting cards websites will constrain the industry's growth over the next five years. Furthermore, more consumers will shop at discount retailers instead of specialty stores, further cutting into revenue growth."

Source: IBISWorld, March 2014
- "I don't have the statistics, but I believe there are fewer gift shops in business every year. The successfully operated gift stores appear to be in tourist locations and affluent communities. It is extremely difficult to secure unique gift products to sell, and many gift products are available at major retailers and discounters nationally at often discounted prices, making it virtually impossible for small stores to compete."
- "Survival is extremely difficult."
- "Large stores have survived recession, etc. Small stores are becoming extinct due to rising costs, difficulty in obtaining knowledgeable/motivated employees, the inability to buy with volume discount, difficulty moving old inventory, poor buying decisions."

Seller Financing
- "Seller financing, five years."
- 3 to 7 years

Questions
- "Why selling. Require the seller to attend at least one industry trade show with introductions to vendors and other sources of inventory."
- "Look for a business that you would like to own and be proud to say that you owned it. The decision should be a blend of #1) what the seller has been doing for the last 3 years and #2) what ways do you see to improve and grow the business."
- "Any unusual trends, seasonal or one-time hot selling items included in gross sales revenue? Explain the competition in detail. Discuss thoroughly the theft and/or shrinkage issues. Any convictions recently? Who is really responsible for purchasing duties?"
- "For small stores—What are your cash sales and are any expenses paid with cash? What do you 'love' and 'hate' about owning this store? Both answers may surprise you!!"

Resources
Associations
- Craft and Hobby Association—a good site: www.craftandhobby.org

	Franchise

Godfather's Pizza (See also Franchises, Pizza Shops)

Approx. Total Investment $100,000 to $300,000 depending on business model	
Estimated Annual Sales/Unit	$384,000
SIC 5812-22	NAICS 722513	Number of Businesses/Units 600

Rules of Thumb
> 25 to 30 percent of annual sales

Resources
Websites
- www.godfatherspizza.com

	Franchise

Goin' Postal (See also Franchises, Mail & Parcel Centers)

Approx. Total Investment	$48,865 to $139,500
SIC 7331-01	NAICS 561431	Number of Businesses/Units 350

Rules of Thumb
> 30 to 35 percent of annual sales plus inventory

Resources
Websites
- www.goinpostal.com

Golf Carts—Sales & Service (See also Golf Courses, Golf Shops)

SIC 5571-02	NAICS 441228	

Rules of Thumb
> 25 to 30 percent of annual sales plus inventory

Golf Courses

SIC Private: 7997-06; Public: 7992-01		
	NAICS 713910	Number of Businesses/Units 11,776

Rules of Thumb
> Rule of Thumb (Private): 2.5 to 5 times SDE plus inventory
> Rule of Thumb (Public): Net income multipliers—8 to 11, typically 9 to 10
> 4 times golf-related income (green fees, golf carts, driving range—does not include pro shop or food & beverage)

Pricing Tips

- "Real estate value big determinant in price of a golf course"
- "Personal property + equipment (FF&E) usually accounts for 3 to 10 percent of the purchase price depending on the amount of equipment leased and type of operation (daily fee vs. private). From 4 to 7 percent of price is typical."
- "Due to weather-related conditions, a 5-year average for cash flow should be used— capital reserves of 5 percent should always be accounted for."
- "Add to price for additional assets such as development land. Also check rounds of golf, P&L and type of facilities."
- "Be careful to look at non-golf income for 'normal' distribution."

Expert Comments

"Golf is a nearly $70B U.S. industry, impacting 2 million jobs w/ an annual wage income of $55.6B."

"'The industry is adapting to provide shorter golf experiences—such as six or nine holes—and non-traditional forms of the game, like FootGolf, while still upholding the integrity and rules of golf. USGA handicaps now allow for nine-hole scores. This will help to increase participation among those seeking a more time-sensitive experience.'"

Source: quote from Steve Mona, CEO of World Golf Foundation,
www.forbes.com/sites/darrenheitner/2015/04/04/the-state-of-the-golf-industry-in-2015/2/#2cb4bf701ce6

"Further, golf courses are a breeding ground for lawsuits. Golf and legal issues can be found in every square inch of a golf facility. From defective golf carts to improperly designed fairways; from wetlands to wrongful serving of alcohol to minors. Are all entitlements in place? Are all liquor licenses proper? Will the new buyer inherit some old tax problems?"

Source: http://www.hospitalitynet.org/news/4063485.html

Benchmark Data

Statistics (Golf Courses & Country Clubs)

Number of Establishments	11,776
Average Profit Margin	1.0%
Revenue per Employee	$74,000
Average Number of Employees	26.3
Average Wages per Employee	$30,139

Products and Services Segmentation

Golf course green use	33.9%
Memberships	30.4%
Food and beverages	30.1%
Other sales and services	3.9%
Equipment rentals and sales	1.7%

Industry Costs

Profit	1.0%
Wages	40.9%
Purchases	19.0%
Depreciation	9.5%
Marketing	1.4%
Rent & Utilities	6.6%
Other	21.6%

Source: IBISWorld, June 2016

- "However, despite the price tag, fungicide spending doesn't rank as a top budgetary concern. In fact, "chemical spending" ranks fourth among all respondents' top-five concerns, and breaks onto the list only in the Midwest and South.
  "'Labor' and 'equipment replacement' held the No. 1 and No. 2 spots respectively except for in the Midwest where they were flipped. With regard to equipment replacement spending, the budget numbers indicate that superintendents are budgeting less on mowing and cultivation equipment in 2015 than they did in 2012 ($31,300 vs. $37,644, respectively), which may contribute to this anxiety. The biggest difference, according to the data, is the nearly $13,000 drop in spending among private courses."

  Source: 2015 State of the Industry Report, January 14, 2015

Expenses as a percentage of annual sales

Cost of goods	20%
Payroll/labor Costs	45%
Occupancy	15%
Profit (estimated pretax)	20%

Industry Trend

- "Private courses, according to the data, experienced the greatest boost in their average operating budget over the last three years, reporting an increase just over $91,000. Regionally, Midwest supers were below the overall average, with budgets of around $553,000; and those in the Northeast fared the best with budgets around $800,000, followed by those in the South ($771,000) and the West ($740,000), according to the data. And when compared to the previous year, 61 percent of private courses plan to work with a larger budget, as well as 60 percent of courses out West. On average, that increase is between 1 percent and 9 percent, according to the data."

  Source: "2015 State of the Industry Report," January 14, 2015

- "A separate Sports and Fitness Industry Association report, citing a Physical Activity Council study, said golf participate rate dropped 2.5% last year to 24.7 million players on a golf course, and has seen an average annual decline of 2.8% the past five years."

  Source: "If you want a bargain on golf equipment, now's the time to buy" by Andria Cheng, http://blogs.marketwatch.com/behindthestorefront/2014/05/20/dicks-sporting-goods-troubles-mirror-golf-industrys-challenges/ 5/20/14

- "Once the go-to activity for corporate bonding, the sport is suffering from an exodus of players, a lack of interest among millennials and the mass closure of courses. The tangled personal life of Tiger Woods, who for years was golf's biggest ambassador, also hasn't helped. All that has taken a toll on the companies that make and sell golf equipment, including Dick's Sporting Goods Inc. and Callaway Golf Co.
  "About 400,000 players left the sport last year, according to the National Golf Foundation. While almost 260,000 women took up golf, some 650,000 men quit. A severe winter on the East Coast worsened the situation this year by delaying the start of golfing season for many. Slow sales of clubs and other gear dragged down results for Dick's this week, sending its stock on the worst tumble since the retail chain went public in 2002.
  "There also are fewer places to play golf these days. Only 14 new courses were built in the U.S. last year, while almost 160 shut down, the National Golf

Foundation said. Last year marked the eighth straight year that more courses closed than opened."

Source: "Golf Market Stuck in Bunker as Thousands Leave the Sport"
www.bloomberg.com/news/articles/2014-05-23/golf-market-stuck-in-bunker-as-thousands-leave-the-sport

Seller Financing
- 5 to 7 years
- 20 years

Questions
- Questions to ask seller: "Is there adjoining acreage that could be used for golf community homes? This can greatly increase value of the golf course."

Resources

Websites
- Golf Course Industry: www.golfcourseindustry.com

Trade Publications
- Analysis and Valuation of Golf Courses and Country Clubs: http://www.appraisalinstitute.org/analysis-and-valuation-of-golf-courses-and-country-clubs/

Associations
- National Golf Course Owners Association: www.ngcoa.org

Golf Driving Ranges & Family Fun Centers

SIC 7999-31	NAICS 713990	Number of Businesses/Units 53,817

Rules of Thumb
➤ Golf Driving Ranges—70% to 75% of annual sales including inventory

Benchmark Data

Statistics (Golf Driving Ranges & Family Fun Centers)
Number of Establishments	53,817
Average Profit Margin	4.9%
Revenue per Employee	$87,300
Average Number of Employees	2.3
Average Wages per Employee	$21,129

Products and Services Segmentation
Other	31.6%
Amusement and recreation services	30.5%
Coin operated games and rides	14.0%
Amateur sports teams and club services	6.7%
Meals and beverages	5.5%
Fitness and recreational sport center services	5.1%
Registration for sports tournaments and matches	3.8%
Golf course and country club services and memberships	2.8%

G - Rules of Thumb

Industry Costs

Profit	4.9%
Wages	24.7%
Purchases	26.0%
Depreciation	2.7%
Marketing	3.0%
Rent & Utilities	9.5%
Other	29.2%

Source: IBISWorld, February 2016

Industry Trend

- "The future of FECs from a physical plant perspective seems to be the inclusion of multiple experiences under one roof. We see this now in concepts, including our new brand Pinstack where we've put bowling, full-service dining, a ropes course, bumper cars, rock wall, laser tag, and more than 100 games. Guests are gravitating toward one-stop shopping, which is also reflected in the movie theater, dining, bowling, and game concepts."

Source: "Multiple Experiences Under One Roof," by Brian Cohen, VP of Operations, Entertainment Properties Group Inc., www.iaapa.org/news/funworld/funworld-magazine/family-entertainment-centers---May-2015

Golf Shops (See also Golf Courses)		
	NAICS 451110	

Rules of Thumb

➤ 30 percent of annual sales plus inventory

Benchmark Data

- "The specialty golf channel is now dominated by the national chains. 76% of all square footage and 34% of the door counts are owned by multi-door retailers with store footprints over 10,000 square feet."
- "Key findings from research done by the Longitudes Group in 2014:
    - ✓ 47% of the gear sold last year in the US golf market flowed through the off-course channel including $2.28 in apparel/soft goods and $2.98 in hard goods.
    - ✓ Total square footage of off-course retail increased by 1.9% to 8.6M square feet, while the number of total off-course stores decreased by 8.6% to 869 stores."

Source: "2015 Off-course retail report shows a mixed bag of growth & contraction" by Longitudes group, 2/19/15

Industry Trend

- "The expansion of the global golf equipment industry is forecast to reach 1.9% p.a. in the coming years. Between 2008 and 2014 the market increased with an average annual growth of 0.3%. Currently, golf clubs account for 50.5% of the global demand while the remaining market share is divided between golf balls (18.1%) and other golf equipment (31.4%).

"China, Japan, South Korea, the United Kingdom and the United States represent the largest golf equipment markets while the strongest annual growth is forecast to occur in Ecuador (12.3%), Moldova (10.9%), China (5.8%), Morocco (4.9%) and Malaysia (4.5%)."

Source: March 2, 2015, http://www.prnewswire.com/news-releases/golf-equipment-markets-in-the-world-to-2019---market-size-trends-and-forecasts-300044039.html

Questions

- "Is the seller willing to allow the buyer a 10% rejection on the inventory (or some other fixed amount)?"

Resources

Websites

- National Golf Foundation: www.ngf.org
- Professional Golfers Career College: http://www.golfcollege.edu/

Goodyear Tire Stores (See also Tire Stores)

	NAICS 441320	

Rules of Thumb

➤ 35 percent of annual sales plus inventory

Gourmet Shops (See also Food Stores—Specialty)

SIC 5499-20	NAICS 445299	

Rules of Thumb

➤ 20 percent of annual sales plus inventory

Benchmark Data

- For Benchmark Data see Food Stores—Specialty

Grease Monkey (See also Auto Lube/Tune-up, Other Lube Franchises)
Franchise

Approx. Total Investment		$190,000 to $300,000
	NAICS 811191	Number of Businesses/Units 240

Rules of Thumb

➤ 50 percent of annual sales plus inventory

Resources

Websites

- www.greasemonkeyfranchise.com

Great Clips (See also Barber Shops, Fantastic Sam's, Franchises)
Franchise

Approx. Total Investment		$114,150 to $216,000
	NAICS 812112	Number of Businesses/Units 3,700

Rules of Thumb

➤ 1 to 1.5 times SDE plus inventory

Resources

Websites

▪ www.greatclipsfranchise.com

		Franchise
Great Harvest Bread Company (See also Franchises)		
Approx. Total Investment		$192,411 to $313,919
	NAICS 311811	Number of Businesses/Units 200

Rules of Thumb

➢ 3.2 to 3.4 times SDE plus inventory

Resources

Websites

▪ www.greatharvest.com

			Franchise
Great Steak (See also Franchises, Restaurants—Limited Service)			
Approx. Total Investment			$146,600 to $439,050
Estimated Annual Sales/Unit			$425,000
SIC 5812-19	NAICS 722513		Number of Businesses/Units 63

Rules of Thumb

➢ 50 to 55 percent of annual sales plus inventory

Resources

Websites

▪ www.kahalamgmt.com

Green Businesses		
	NAICS 541620	

Pricing Tips

▪ "My expertise is in what I call an 'industry horizontal.' Environmentally sustainable businesses can exist in virtually any industry. I've sold a furniture company, a toy manufacturer, a retail store, a recycled product manufacturer, a body care product company, etc. The multiples and Rules of Thumb for those are the same as the industries they are a part of, the difference being that their environmental sustainability makes them value at the higher end of the range than average."

Industry Trend

- "The U.N. report, which the Support Team on Climate Change wrote, identified five 'inflection points' that it said reveal a deep shift in the way companies are doing business.
  - ✓ New commitments to low-carbon business
  - ✓ The rise of the green bond
  - ✓ The use of internal carbon prices
  - ✓ Nervous investors
  - ✓ Proactive insurance companies"

  Source: "5 signs the private sector is stepping up on climate change," by Ben McCarthy, October 29, 2015, https://www.greenbiz.com/article/5-signs-private-sector-stepping-climate-change

- "Continued growth especially in sectors such as renewable energy and organic food products. Organic body care products and natural and organic clothing are up and coming in this space as well."

Resources

Websites

- GreenBiz: https://greenbiz.com

Ground Transportation (See also Bus Companies)		
	NAICS 484110	

Rules of Thumb

➤ 50% of Annual Gross Sales plus inventory

➤ 2 to 3 times SDE plus inventory

➤ 3 times EBITDA plus vehicle value for small to midsize operations; 4 times EBITDA plus—for over 15 vehicles

Pricing Tips

- "You must look at ODCF before you use a multiple. It is important to know if the vehicles are owned, leased or financed. Depreciation will not be a total add back because you must factor in the life of the vehicle so that only a portion of depreciation is added back. You must reduce Fair Market Value by outstanding debt."
- "Maintenance records? Facility?"
- "Who controls the groups? The quality of the drivers and how long have they been with the company? Are the groups preformed or do they sell into them? Condition of equipment counts."

Expert Comments

"It is a business with low barriers to entry. Now that the economy is improving, this is a discretionary expenditure that has started to increase."

Benchmark Data

Statistics (Airport Shuttle Operators)

Number of Establishments	4,022
Average Profit Margin	7.7%
Revenue per Employee	$61,900
Average Number of Employees	2.6%
Average Wages per Employee	24,944

Products and services segmentation

Local shuttle services for business	53.5%
Local shuttle services for leisure	41.6%
Long-distance shuttle services	3.2%
Other	1.7%

Industry Costs

Profit	7.7%
Wages	40.1%
Purchases	29.1%
Depreciation	4.5%
Marketing	1.1%
Rent & Utilities	4.6%
Other	12.9%

Source: IBISWorld, March 2015

- "Driver earnings vary by city. For example, in New York City, median UberX drivers make between $26 and $30 per hour. In Chicago, that average is closer to $16 per hour. UberBlack drivers earn more per hour—except in New York, where UberX is slightly ahead.

  "Overall, median hourly earnings for Uber drivers tend to be higher than hourly wages for other taxi and chauffeur jobs, and are sometimes 50–100% higher. However, Uber contractors are not reimbursed for driving expenses like gasoline, depreciation, or insurance, while employed drivers often are."

  Source: "The Numbers Behind Uber's Exploding Driver Force" by Brian Solomon,http://www.forbes.com/sites/briansolomon/2015/05/01/the-numbers-behind-ubers-exploding-driver-force/ May 1, 2015

Expenses as a percentage of annual sales

Cost of goods	30% to 40%
Payroll/labor Costs	30%
Occupancy	10%
Profit (estimated pretax)	20%

Industry Trend

- "Global consumers are increasingly spending their disposable income on experiences rather than material goods. And consumers' desire for these life experiences is spurring a growth in luxury travel that is outpacing the rest of the travel industry, according a new report commissioned by global travel technology company, Amadeus. The report, Shaping the Future of Luxury Travel, reveals the fresh challenges and opportunities that the luxury travel market will face over the next decade. Some key findings from the report include:

  ✓ We have entered a new age of luxury travel, where luxury is curated, real-time and experience-led

  ✓ North America and Western Europe account for 64% of global outbound luxury trips, despite only making up 18% of the world's population

  ✓ From 2011-2025, Asia Pacific's luxury travel market will see faster overall

growth than Europe's, but this growth will decelerate from 2015-2025
- ✓ India's luxury market CAGR of 13% is higher than any of the other BRIC nations, and is the highest of the 25 countries explored in this report
- ✓ A human desire for more rewarding experiences provides an essential catalyst to evolve and improve travel industry quality and service standards
- ✓ A hierarchy of luxury travel needs is identified, ranging from 5-star quality and service standards to exclusive VIP privacy and security"

Source: "Luxury travel outpaces the rest of the travel industry, according to new Amadeus report," May 18, 2016

- "Uber's active driver base has grown from basically zero in mid-2012 to over 160,000 at the end of 2014. The number of new drivers has more than doubled every six months for the last two years. Most of that exponential growth has come from the cheaper UberX service, which in most areas lets drivers use their own cars to pick up riders. UberBlack, the commercial-licensed black car service, has seen steady but not exponential growth.

"On average, Uber drivers are younger, more educated, more white, and (slightly) more female than the rest of U.S. taxi workers. 49.2% of Uber drivers are under 40 years old, vs. 28.4% of taxi drivers. Yet nearly 37% have college degrees, and 10.8% have postgraduate degrees too (vs. 14.9% and 3.9% of taxi drivers, respectively).

"More than 40% of Uber drivers self-identify as White non-Hispanic, vs. 26.2% for taxi drivers. Women make up nearly 14% of Uber drivers, more than the 8% of female taxi drivers, but much less than their 47.4% portion of the rest of the U.S. workforce. Women also work fewer hours, on average, than male drivers."

Source: "The Numbers Behind Uber's Exploding Driver Force" by Brian Solomon, http://www.forbes.com/sites/briansolomon/2015/05/01/the-numbers-behind-ubers-exploding-driver-force/ May 1, 2015

Seller Financing
- "Based on the price of the vehicle and the down payment, the term should be 5 to 7 years."

Questions
- "What has been your biggest frustration?"

Resources
Trade Publications
- Limousine, Charter, and Tour: www.lctmag.com

	Franchise
Grout Doctor (See also Franchises)	
Approx. Total Investment	14,405 to $37,415
NAICS 811411	Number of Businesses/Units 70

Rules of Thumb
➤ 85 to 90 percent of annual sales plus inventory

Resources
Websites
- www.groutdoctor.com

Guard Services (See also Security Services/Systems)

| SIC 7381-02 | NAICS 561612 | |

Rules of Thumb

➤ 30 percent of annual sales plus inventory

➤ 3 times SDE includes inventory

➤ 3 times EBITDA

Pricing Tips

- "Non-union are worth more"
- "If guards are 1099's, business is worth less."

Expert Comments

"As crime increases, so does security."

"It is easy to lose a client if you have to go to bid every year."

Benchmark Data

- For additional Benchmark Data see Security Services/Systems
- "Cost is different for an armed guard, for an event security, or 24-hour security service."

Expenses as a percentage of annual sales

Cost of goods	05%
Payroll/labor Costs	70%
Occupancy	05% to 10%
Profit (estimated pretax)	15% to 20%

Industry Trend

- "Despite growing concerns over a potential global economic slowdown, the outlook for the Private Security Services industry in the U.S. and abroad continues to be upbeat. As security concerns continue to escalate, government and private entities are expected to increase spending to improve all aspects of their security programs.

  "The following statistics and trends suggest that the Private Security Services Industry is poised for continued growth in 2016:

  ✓ Worldwide annual spending on private contract security services is predicted to climb to $244 billion this year, according to a report from the Freedonia Group. The report finds that the U.S. will remain the biggest consumer of security services, accounting for 26% of overall global private contract security services spending. U.S. spending on such services is estimated to rise 5% to $68 billion annually by 2019.

  ✓ The Freedonia Group report also notes that security guard services will attract the largest share of overall U.S. security spending through 2019, highlighting the continued importance of having skilled, qualified personnel to conduct security system monitoring and incident response. Despite the proliferation of security technology, highly trained security guards remain the best way to provide an adequate deterrent to potential unauthorized incursions and coordinate effective responses to unexpected events.

✓ The U.S. Bureau of Labor Statistics anticipates "excellent" overall job opportunities for security guards through 2024, with employment growing at about 5% during the period. The BLS expects the number of people employed as security guards in the U.S. to reach 1.15 million by 2024.

✓ IBISWorld's Security Services market research report predicts an annual growth rate of 2.4% for the security services sector over the next 10 to 15 years. According to IBISWorld, U.S. spending on security services has surged over the past five years in tandem with the economic recovery and increased investment in commercial, residential and public construction projects.

✓ Fiscally strapped municipalities are increasingly turning to contract security services providers as an alternative to expanding their more expensive police forces, notes a research report from Robert H. Perry & Associates. Contracted private security guards services will increasingly replace traditional in-house guard services at government-run schools, hospitals, parking facilities and other municipal properties.

"As always, people will remain the key to effective security services, even in an age of proliferating technology. The increasing adoption of ever more advanced security technology will only spur the need for well-trained security officers, who are able to monitor and work with complex systems."

Source: "Looking Forward: Security Industry Trends and Outlook for 2016 and Beyond," January 21, 2016, http://www.summitsecurity.com/looking-forward-security-industry-trends-and-outlook-for-2016-and-beyond/

- "'Formal training of the nation's one million-plus private security officers is widely neglected, a surprising finding when contrasted with other private occupations such as paramedics, childcare workers, and even cosmetologists,' said Mahesh Nalla, lead investigator and MSU professor of criminal justice.

"The research also states that security guards say they're unprepared to handle problematic people and physical altercations and to protect themselves. It strongly endorses the need for systematic and standardized training in the $7 billion-a-year industry.

"'It's reasonable to conclude that private security continues to be an under-regulated industry despite the increase in the roles private security guards play in people's lives and the fact that they greatly outnumber sworn police officers in America,' Nalla said."

Source: "Security guard industry lacks standards and training," www.gsnmagazine.com, 6/9/14

Questions
- "Most guard companies have major clients; explain anything over 20%, could become an earnout event."
- "Relationship to customers?"

Gun Shops and Supplies		
SIC 5941-29	NAICS 451110	Number of Businesses/Units 6,490

Rules of Thumb

➢ 30 to 35 percent of annual sales plus inventory

Benchmark Data

Statistics (Gun & Ammunition Stores)

Number of Establishments	6,490
Average Profit Margin	15.4%
Revenue per Employee	$123,700
Average Number of Employees	4.0
Average Wages per Employee	$25,819

Products and Services Segmentation

Ammunition	25.0%
Pistols	24.0%
Rifles	22.0%
Equipment and accessories	15.0%
Shotguns	8.0%
Revolvers	6.0%

Industry Costs

Profit	15.4%
Wages	21.2%
Purchases	38.9%
Depreciation	3.7%
Marketing	1.2%
Rent & Utilities	5.1%
Other	14.5%

Source: IBISWorld, October 2015

- "While NSSF (National Shooting Sports Foundation) sells copies of the entire report, here are the highlights:
    - ✓ 84 percent of retailers surveyed reported that overall sales in 2012 exceeded sales from the previous year.
    - ✓ 76.9 percent of retailers surveyed said sales of AR-style modern sporting rifles in 2012 exceeded sales from the previous year (60.1 percent), the largest increase in the firearms category.
    - ✓ Retailers surveyed said that 25.8 percent of their customers were first-time firearm buyers in 2012 compared to 25 percent in 2011 and 20.8 percent in 2010.
    - ✓ For the third year in a row, the number of female customers increased. For the year 2012, 78.6 of retailers surveyed said more women came to their stores, compared to 72.8 in 2011 and 61.1 in 2010.
    - ✓ Firearms most often purchased by women were a semiautomatic handgun followed by revolvers, modern sporting rifles, shotguns, traditional rifles and muzzleloaders."
    Source: "National gun dealer survey shows unique buying trends for ARs, women," by Lee Williams, *Herald-Tribune*, May 17, 2013 A bit dated, but still of interest)

Average Annual Firearm Production (U.S.)

Weapon	Production
Rifle	1,425,500
Shotgun	777,125
Revolver	352,625
Pistol	889,125
Total Average Yearly Production	3,444,375

Firearm Sales Statistics

Guns and ammunition manufacturing annual revenue $11,000,000,000
Number of weapons and ammunition manufacturers in the U.S. 465
Number of retail gun dealers 50,812
Number of background checks for gun purchases in 2013 17,000,000
Percent of U.S. households that own a gun 32%
Annual number of Americans who used a firearm for protection 645,000
Percent who felt laws limiting gun ownership
    infringe on the public's right to bear arms.. 49%

Source: www.statisticbrain.com, research date: January 1, 2014

Industry Trend

- "In spite of the fact that gun ownership is becoming increasingly restrictive due to government legislation in both the United States and Canada, opening and operating a retail business that buys, sells, and trades guns still has the potential to be profitable. In addition to gun sales you can also sell ammunition and hunting-related products as well as offer a gun repair service. Promote the business by establishing alliances with gun clubs and shooting ranges as well as firearm instructors, as these clubs and individuals can refer your business to others. Starting this type of business will require a substantial investment and you will also have to clear a few legal hurdles before you can open. A well-promoted and operated gun shop could return the owner a six-figure yearly income."

Source: "Gun Shop—Business At A Glance" www.entrepreneur.com

- "Months after the shooting that killed 26 at a Connecticut elementary school, General Electric (GE, Fortune 500) has halted its lending programs for purchases from gun shops, the company said Wednesday. GE Capital, which provides consumer financing services, had previously provided lending services to gun shops to help consumers finance firearm purchases. Earlier this year, the company sent letters to shops notifying them that the program would be terminated for future purchases. It will not affect financing for guns bought at major retailers like Wal-Mart (WMT, Fortune 500) and Dick's Sporting Goods (DKS, Fortune 500), which sell guns along with a range of other items."

Source: "GE Capital halts lending for gun shop purchases" by Melanie Hicken, www.money.cnn.com April 24, 2013

Resources

Associations
- National Shooting Sports Foundation: www.nssf.org

Hardware Stores (See also Ace Hardware, Home Centers, Lumberyards)

SIC 5251-04	NAICS 444130	Number of Businesses/Units 19,617

Rules of Thumb

➢ 45 to 50 percent of annual sales plus inventory

➢ 3 to 3.5 times SDE plus inventory

➢ 3.5 times SDE includes inventory

H - Rules of Thumb

Expert Comments

"Stores with revenues below $600k are very difficult to sell. Profits provide low incomes to the owner. Stores should be franchised to gain any advantage in this market."

"Stores in good locations will still bring premium prices. Rural locations are often insulated from the effects of big boxes."

"Reasonably profitable hardware stores sell very quickly."

"Heavy industry consolidation by the big boxes means that small operators must be aligned with a major franchisor. Local dealer advertising groups are also a must. Plenty of help on the store floor, convenient parking, knowledgeable staff, and quick service are far more important to today's hardware shoppers than price. Therefore, small neighborhood stores that possess those characteristics will survive the big boxes quite well."

Benchmark Data

Statistics (Hardware Stores)

Number of Establishments	19,617
Average Profit Margin	4.3%
Revenue per Employee	$173,000
Average Number of Employees	7.7
Average Wages per Employee	$25,696

Products and Services Segmentation

Hardware, tools, plumbing and electrical supplies	57.7%
Lumber and other building materials	16.3%
Lawn, garden and farm supplies	9.2%
Other	9.1%
Paint and sundries	7.7%

Major Market Segmentation

Do-it-yourself consumers	49.0%
Contractors	21.5%
Other	16.4%
Do-it-for-me consumers	8.1%
Businesses	5.0%

Industry Costs

Profit	4.3%
Wages	15.0%
Purchases	68.4%
Depreciation	1.0%
Marketing	1.4%
Rent & Utilities	3.4%
Other	6.5%

Market Share

True Value Company	24.0%
Ace Hardware Corp.	22.4%
Do It Best Corp.	19.1%

Source: IBISWorld, May 2016

- "Should turn their inventory 2.5 to 3 times per year. Fixtures and equipment should not exceed 16 percent of the average stock carried per year. These stores are sold for fixtures and equipment at depreciated value plus the inventory at wholesale cost. Markup runs from 35 to 40 percent."

Expenses as a percentage of annual sales

Cost of goods	50% to 60%
Payroll/labor Costs	12% to 15%
Occupancy	05% to 08%
Profit (estimated pretax)	01% to 03%

Industry Trend
- "Computerization, renovation, innovation. Do or die."

Seller Financing
- "A good, qualified buyer should bring at least 25% down to the table. In such cases a ten-year amortized note is fairly common."

Questions
- "Have you increased the markup on your merchandise in the last two years? Sellers often begin increasing prices just before they sell a business to pump up the bottom line. The increased prices makes it look like revenues are increasing from one year to the next, when in fact, it is just because merchandise is being sold at a higher price. It often takes a year or two before the customers finds out that prices were increased and decide to shop elsewhere. If you bought such a store based on the pumped up bottom line in the current year, you might find that your customer base disappears the next year."
- "How do you value your ending inventory on the books? Is there concealed inventory or understated inventory? How often do you do a physical inventory? Is your cash register point-of-sale system read barcodes? Are your inventory counts computerized? "

Resources

Websites
- Home Channel News: www.homechannelnews.com/section/hardware-stores

Associations
- National Retail Hardware Association: www.nrha.org

Harley-Davidson Motorcycle Dealerships
(See also Motorcycle Dealerships)

SIC 5571-06	NAICS 441228	

Rules of Thumb
- 2.5 to 3x SDE plus net assets plus inventory
- 1 to 4 times EBITDA

27th Edition

H - Rules of Thumb

Benchmark Data

- For Benchmark Data see Motorcycle Dealerships

Industry Trend

- "2015 has seen the U.S. dollar grow strong against local currencies in international markets, where macroeconomic volatility has had a harsh impact on business activity. However, this set in motion a domino effect, which, in turn, has had a negative effect on the financials of one of the most beloved and iconic American multinationals, Harley-Davidson. The motorcycle manufacturer has suffered at the hands of stiff competition from European and Japanese competitors, due to their pricing advantage, as the dollar continued to grow strong. Harley, on the other hand, looked to protect its premium brand image and profitability, and maintained high model prices. Millennials are typically more price conscious, and the loss in price competitiveness for Harley shows through its results for the first three quarters.

  "Harley is aiming to increase its reach and availability. In the last quarter alone, the company put up 14 dealerships internationally, a rise of 2% in its overall international dealerships. Over the next five years, Harley is looking to open 150 to 200 new dealerships internationally, representing a 20% to 25% increase in its international dealerships."

  Source: "Harley-Davidson Is Taking Steps To Reverse Its Declining Sales Trends," December 9, 2015, http://www.forbes.com/sites/greatspeculations/2015/12/09/harley-davidson-is-taking-steps-to-reverse-its-declining-sales-trends/#2c4e5f164793

Questions

- "Why are you selling? What are the strengths and weaknesses of your business? Are there any add-backs? What is your reputation in the marketplace? What is the upside potential?"

Resources

Websites

- www.harley-davidson.com

Health Care Center

Rules of Thumb

- 51 percent of annual sales plus inventory
- 1.8 times SDE plus inventory
- 3 times EBIT
- 2.9 times EBITDA

Benchmark Data

Expenses as a percentage of annual sales

Cost of goods	13%
Payroll/labor Costs	01%
Profit (estimated pretax)	11%

Health Food Stores (See also General Nutrition Centers)

SIC 5499-01	NAICS 446191	Number of Businesses/Units 90,602

Rules of Thumb

➤ 1 to 1.5 times SDE plus inventory

➤ 40 percent of annual sales plus inventory

Benchmark Data

Statistics (Health Stores)

Number of Establishments	90,602
Average Profit Margin	6.1%
Revenue per Employee	$124,600
Average Number of Employees	2.1
Average Wages per Employee	$24,934

Products and Services Segmentation

Vitamin and mineral supplements	26.6%
Orthopedic equipment	24.5%
Sports nutrition products	12.6%
First-aid products	12.2%
Other	12.2%
Convalescent care products	11.9%

Industry Costs

Profit	6.1%
Wages	19.9%
Purchases	57.0%
Depreciation	1.3%
Marketing	3.7%
Rent & Utilities	5.2%
Other	6.8%

Market Share

General Nutrition Centers Inc.	7.3%
Vitamin Shoppe Inc.	5.2%

Source: IBISWorld, January 2016

Industry Trend

- "Global sales of healthy food products, in fact, are estimated to reach $1 trillion by 2017, according to Euromonitor. While the health fads and trends have come and gone (remember oat bran in the 1980s or low-fat everything in the 1990s?), this time the category appears to have serious stamina. Consider Nielsen's 2015 Global Health & Wellness Survey that polled over 30,000 individuals online and suggests consumer mindset about healthy foods has shifted and they are ready to pay more for products that claim to boost health and weight loss. Some 88% of those polled are willing to pay more for healthier foods.

  "All demographics—from Generation Z to Baby Boomers—say they would pay more for healthy foods, including those that are GMO-free, have no artificial coloring/flavors and are deemed all natural. Functional foods—including foods high in fiber (36%), protein (32%), whole grains (30%) or fortified with calcium

(30%), vitamins (30%) or minerals (29%)—that can either reduce disease and/ or promote good health also are desirable."

Source: "Consumers Want Healthy Foods—And Will Pay More For Them," by Nancy Gagliardi, February 18, 2015, http://www.forbes.com/sites/nancygagliardi/2015/02/18/consumers-want-healthy-foods-and-will-pay-more-for-them/#46b45bcb144f

- "These healthy foods and drinks are on track to hit $1 trillion in sales by 2017, predicts Euromonitor International, spurring innovative new products in nearly every industry sector. This even holds true for the confectionery sector, where companies are touting healthier-for-you snacks such as whey-protein energy gummies, gluten-free licorice and countless dark chocolate, fruit and nut combinations, notes Candy Industry magazine.

Source: "Healthy Food Trends Drive New Products," by Brian Kennell, October 1, 2015, http://www.huffingtonpost.com/brian-kennell/healthy-food-trends-drive_b_8222388.htm

- "'On-the-go convenience has replaced all-in-one convenience for grocery-buying consumers,' Webster (Justin Webster, Hillphoenix Design specialist) explained.' Increasingly, consumers would rather make more frequent trips to smaller stores where they can pop in and out with ease.' That's one of the drivers behind drug stores netting 54 percent of quick-trip shopping experiences, according to Chicago-based market researcher IRI. Small-format dollar stores claim 46 percent of those short shopping trips, IRI reported—compared with 25 percent of traditional grocers. The bottom line: Conventional grocery stores have lost 15 percent of their market share in the last five years to competing warehouses, dollar stores and drugstores, Phil Lempert, a Santa Monica, Calif.-based grocery and retail analyst told USA Today.

"Aided by store-based nutritionists, shoppers will look for fresher and healthier options, even on the go, so sales of fresh juices and pre-cut produce will keep climbing. 'Ready, fresh, now is on the minds of millennials looking for instant gratification in healthy, fresh alternatives that are also convenient,' Webster explained."

Source: http://supermarketnews.com/store-design-construction/consumer-driven-trends-center-convenience-health-and-smaller-stores-2015-0

Resources

Associations
- Specialty Food Association: www.specialtyfood.com

Health Practitioners—Offices of Miscellaneous Others

Rules of Thumb
➢ 51 percent of annual sales plus inventory
➢ 1.8 times SDE plus inventory
➢ 3 times EBIT
➢ 2.9 times EBITDA

Benchmark Data

Expenses as a percentage of annual sales

Cost of goods	26%
Payroll/labor Costs	11%
Profit (estimated pretax)	11%

Industry Trend
- "Competition is high and steady, growth is expected for the next 5 years, fragmentation should remain relatively constant."

Seller Financing
- "Outside financing"

Questions
- "Payor mix, market share, patient demographic data."

Hearing Aid Clinics

SIC 5999-79	NAICS 446199	Number of Businesses/Units 4,544

Rules of Thumb

➢ 40 to 45 percent of annual revenues plus inventory
➢ 4 times EBITDA

Pricing Tips
- "Larger practices with multiple offices and support infrastructure sell at higher multiples. The more trained audiologists and dispensers that a practice maintains, the more stability the practice will offer to purchasers."
- "Transition agreements for long periods are common."

Expert Comments
"Market for audiology and hearing aids is expanding as baby boomers enter the market. Franchises such as Miracle Ear (1,300 franchised units) and Beltone reduce obstacles to entry and increase ease of replication."

Benchmark Data

Statistics (Hearing Aid Clinics)
Number of Establishments ... 4,544
Average Profit Margin ... 12.9%
Revenue per Employee ... $185,700
Average Number of Employees ... 2.6
Average Wages per Employee ... $44,372

Products and Services Segmentation
Digital hearing aids ... 50.0%
Analog hearing aids ... 33.0%
Batteries and accessories ... 14.8%
Other ... 2.2%

Major Market Segmentation
Consumers older than 65 ... 41.9%
Consumers aged 55 to 64 ... 25.6%
Consumers aged 45 to 54 ... 14.0%
Consumers aged 18 to 34 ... 7.0%
Consumers aged 35 to 44 ... 7.0%
Consumers younger than 18 ... 4.5%

Industry Costs

Profit 12.9%
Wages 23.9%
Purchases 44.4%
Depreciation 1.6%
Marketing 3.1%
Rent & Utilities 6.3%
Other 7.8%

Market Share

Starkey Hearing Technologies 18.4%
Amplifon USA 10.3%
Sonova 7.6%
William Demant Holding AS 6.0%

Source: IBISWorld, March 2016

Expenses as a percentage of annual sales

Cost of goods .... 30% to 35%
Payroll/labor Costs 20%
Occupancy .... 05% to 10%
Profit (estimated pretax) .... 18% to 20%

Industry Trend

- "Following are five trends to follow in the New Year:
  - ✓ Awesome New Products: More powerful digital processing technologies, improved integration of wireless features, constant improvements in sound processing software, and integration with mobile phones will continue to result in fantastic new products.
  - ✓ Consumers in the Driver's Seat: As the new products get new markets of customers excited, the 'consumerization' of the hearing business will accelerate.
  - ✓ Hot Competition/Lower Prices/Lower Margins: More choices mean more competition for manufacturers.
  - ✓ Bigfoot and Big Brother: Big Brother in the form of federal governments providing various subsidies to consumers will play an even larger role in driving demand for hearing aids.
  - ✓ The Audiologist Squeeze—Adapt or Die: Audiologists, hearing-aid dispensers and other hearing health professionals have been the heart and soul of the hearing products business since its inception. But in the past several years, direct-to-consumer Internet sales and the big-box-retail 'Costco phenomenon' have squeezed the profits of private independent audiologists and started to undermine their base of patients."

  Source: "2015 Hearing Industry Outlook: Only The Strong Survive," by David Copithorne, December 31, 2014, http://hearingmojo.com/2015-hearing-industry-outlook/

- "Continuing to increase as baby boomers enter market and stigma of wearing hearing aids decreases."
- "The market, driven by technological advancements in cochlear implants, bone-anchored hearing-aids and the introduction of wireless Bluetooth capability from Starkey, GN Resound and Cochlear America, is expected to touch almost $8 billion in annual sales by 2018."

Source: headsets.tmcnet.com

Seller Financing
- "Manufacturers offer financing if customers commit to purchasing their products. Many acquisitions require an earn-out based on sales and/or profit." "3 years"

Questions
- "Is this business free from liens/encumbrances with vendors that would prohibit the sale of the practice?"
- "Are any loyalty agreements or right of first refusals in place?"

Heating Oil Dealers		
	NAICS 454310	

Rules of Thumb
➤ 25 percent of annual sales plus inventory

➤ 2.5 times SDE plus inventory

➤ 3 to 3.5 times EBIT

➤ 3 to 4 times EBITDA.

Pricing Tips
- "Purchase price is typically based on FMV of assets plus retained gallonage."
- "Gross profit per gallon is the main value driver....the higher the better."
- "Most of these businesses are bought on a retained gallonage basis, typically around 1 X gross profits plus assets. Location, customer mix, automatic vs. will call delivery are important issues. Impacted by weather."
- "There is slow turnover in this industry, as most dealers are 2nd or 3rd generation in the business."
- "Industry buyers used to price on the basis of gallons delivered, especially automatic gallons. They now price at 4 to 5.5 times EBITDA, based upon number of automatic vs. 'will call' customers, margins per gallon, location, competition from discounters, condition of equipment, etc."
- "Low margin, high risk business since there is credit risk involved."
- "Most industry buyers want to acquire on the basis of 'retained gallons,' where the buyer offers a limited amount of cash up front and pays only for customer gallons that actually get delivered over a period of time. This puts the risk on the Seller and often requires the Seller to remain in the business for some period. It also, however, allows the Seller to get top dollar for his business due to the 'no risk' nature of the deal to the Buyer. Industry buyer will also pay cash up front, but only for customers who are on some type of automatic delivery (automatic, service, and budget customers). These customers are less price sensitive and will typically stay through any transition in ownership."
- "It depends on the amount of hard assets. Gross profits generally drive the value of these businesses. The higher the gross profit, the higher the value. Gross profit per gallon is a key ratio. Some things that detract from value are high real estate values (land & bldgs.), and other outdated petroleum bulk plants, & petroleum equipment. Any environmental problems are a concern."

Expert Comments

"Consider the risk involved in getting into this industry as it is a mature industry on the decline."

"Mature industry; customers are switching to other fuels; environmental concerns, industry image."

"Customers switching to other fuels due to high price of product; environmental concerns; industry image old."

"Customer satisfaction/loyalty is inversely proportional to price of fuel oil."

"Mature industry with significant environmental regulations. Price spikes similar to summer of 2008 hurt the industry. Growth generally comes through acquisitions. More consolidation for the future."

"Competition is relatively high due to: 1. Discounters; 2. Overcapacity of oil to be delivered, trucks, personnel in a mild winter and every summer; 3. The consolidation in the industry."

"Replication is easy at an entry level if the entrant is near a distribution point and sells on a 'cash on delivery' basis. Otherwise, it takes years to develop a strong customer base on automatic delivery."

Benchmark Data

- "As heating oil prices rise, savings from switching to gas heat grow—PSE&G's average customer would pay $1,122 for the year beginning last October, the company announced when it set its yearly rate last May. It would take 757 gallons of oil to produce the same amount of heat as gas."
- "Gross profit per gallon is a key benchmark. The higher the better."
- "Less desirable companies (discounters) are very difficult to sell."
- "EBITDA is the most common benchmark. Another would be number of automatic gallons x margin per gallon x a multiple of 1 to 1.5 but in the end, industry buyers will look at EBITDA."

Expenses as a percentage of annual sales

Cost of goods	60% to 70%
Payroll/labor Costs	10% to 15%
Occupancy	02% to 05%
Profit (estimated pretax)	05% to 10%

Industry Trend

- "The sensational drop in oil prices—below US$40 per barrel at the end of 2015, down more than 60 percent from their high in the summer of 2014—reflects rampant supply and weak global demand amid concerns over slowing economic growth around the world, especially in China. This imbalance is only going to worsen this year. Saudi Arabia continues to pump at full tilt, less concerned about propping up oil prices and more intent on securing market share, hoping to drive out marginal producers, particularly in the United States. As early as the second quarter of 2016, the flow of Iranian oil is likely to increase, adding to the glut. Even Middle East instability, such as the tension that erupted between Russia and Turkey in Syria toward the end of 2015, has not budged crude prices. Consequently, we expect oil prices to remain low for the near future, although it would not surprise us if volatility returns."

Source: "2016 Oil and Gas Trends," by Viren Doshi, Andrew Clark, and Adrian del Maestro, http://www.strategyand.pwc.com/perspectives/2016-oil-and-gas-trends

- "Slow decline as customers switch to other fuels."

Seller Financing

- "Outside financing for the assets; seller financing for retained gallonage/ intangible value."
- "We typically get cash at closing for fixed assets, and finance the intangibles over 2 to 5 years."
- 2 or 3 years
- 5 to 7 years

Questions

- "Are there any environmental concerns; compliance with government regulations?"
- "5 years' financials and gallonage history; customer base breakdown by class of customer and type of delivery (automatic or will call); asset listing; phase I & II environmental reports."
- "How many gallons do you deliver? What are your average margins per gallon? How many gallons delivered are to automatic customers, service customers, budget plan customers, and 'will call' customers?"

Resources

Websites
- American Petroleum Institute (API): www.api.org

Trade Publications
- Oil & Energy Magazine: www.nefi.com/oilandenergy.php

Associations
- Petroleum Marketers Association of America (PMAA): www.pmaa.org
- PA Petroleum Association: www.ppmcsa.org
- Empire State Energy Association: http://www.eseany.org/index.php

Heavy Equipment Sales & Service		
	NAICS 811310	

Rules of Thumb

➢ 50 percent of SDE plus fixtures, equipment and inventory

Pricing Tips

- "Value is based upon Fair Market Value of balance sheet including real estate. Low ROI based upon required 40% equity."

Expert Comments

"Buy quality name on the sign."

"Suppliers want large, professionally managed dealerships. Move is towards multi-unit operations. Size does matter."

Benchmark Data

- "Have to look at how numbers are assembled. Manufacturers can supply specific targets as well as how they see your client. Balance sheet composition has a great deal to do with profitability."

Industry Trend

- "Strong. Many of the manufacturers are worldwide companies and industry leaders."

Seller Financing

- "Minimal seller financing. Manufacturer may want up to 40% equity in the deal."

Questions

- "What are issues with the local manufacturer representative?"

Hobby Shops (See also Toy Stores)		
SIC 5945-08	NAICS 451120	Number of Businesses/Units 21,351

Rules of Thumb

➤ The Hobby and Toy category in IBISWorld also includes: Craft Supplies, Hobby Goods, Traditional & Electric Games, and Magic Supplies (See Benchmarks for percentages of each). The percentage of annual sales and the multiple of SDE would be about the same as listed below plus inventory.

➤ 20 percent of annual sales plus inventory

➤ 1.5 times SDE plus inventory

Pricing Tips

- "Don't buy too much inventory. In the hobby business, October through January are the busiest sales months while many find February, March, August and September are slower. When approaching a heavy selling season, you need to increase inventory. When it ends, you need to move whatever seasonal or outdated inventory that did not sell out the door as quickly as you can."

Source: www.nrhsa.org

Benchmark Data

Statistics (Hobby & Toy Stores)

Number of Establishments	21,351
Average Profit Margin	6.9%
Revenue per Employee	$137,600
Average Number of Employees	6.8
Average Wages per Employee	$15,845

Products and Services Segmentation

Hobby, craft and art supplies	34.3%
Toys	27.5%
Other	15.3%
Kitchenware and home furnishings	14.2%
Games (including electronic and video games)	5.8%
Seasonal decorations	2.9%

Industry Costs

Profit	6.9%
Wages	11.6%
Purchases	54.4%
Depreciation	0.8%
Marketing	2.4%
Rent & Utilities	9.5%
Other	14.4%

Market Share

Michaels Stores, Inc.	21.7%
Toys"R"Us Inc.	15.8%
Hobby Lobby Stores Inc.	10.6%

Source: IBISWorld, May 2016

- "The gross profit margin for the average hobby shop is around 35 percent, before expenses and taxes. Net profit margins are usually less than 10 percent."

Source: National Retail Hobby Stores Association

Industry Trend

- "HobbyTown, the franchisor of the largest chain of independently owned and operated retail hobby stores in the U.S., is pairing with AMain Performance Sports & Hobbies, which specializes in radio-controlled products and is one of the top ecommerce companies in the hobby retail industry. With this partnership, HobbyTown hopes to expand its website and grow its online sales while AMain increases its brick-and-mortar presence by franchising stores under the AMain name."

Source: "HobbyTown is teaming up with AMain Performance Hobbies," April 28, 2016, http://modelretailer.com/en/The%20Industry/Industry%20News/2016/04/HobbyTown%20is%20teaming%20 up%20with%20AMain%20Performance%20Hobbies.aspx

- "Continuing a trend from the past five years, independent hobby and toy stores will find it increasingly challenging to compete with mass merchandisers and department stores, which offer lower prices and convenience. Over the next five years, changing consumer preferences will create tough market conditions for industry operators, as children begin to demand more adult-focused products, like electronics and media players. Still, greater demand from baby boomers and increasing disposable incomes will benefit the industry."

Source: IBISWorld, April 2014

Resources

Trade Publications

- Model Retailer Magazine: www.modelretailer.com

Associations

- Craft & Hobby Association: www.craftandhobby.org/eweb/
- National Retail Hobby Stores Association: www.nrhsa.org

Home-Based Businesses

Rules of Thumb

➢ The best way to price a home-based business is to first find out if the business is dependent on the owner. If so, it may be impossible to price, as it may have little or no value. However, if the business is transferable it may have value. Prepare an SDE figure and then create a multiple (see Introduction for more information on SDE and a corresponding multiple) to arrive at an approximate price. If the business corresponds to a business listed in this Guide, see if the information there helps.

Pricing Tips

- "The primary objective that you need to accomplish when selling your home business is to come up with a fair price for it that you are willing to take and a reasonable buyer will be willing to pay. Setting a realistic price early on will allow you to negotiate more easily down the line.

  "Be ready to show your potential buyers all your assets, liabilities and cash flow. These will be your convincing reasons for an interested buyer to buy.

  "All figures must be absolutely honest. Never fudge on your figures. Nothing will chase away an interested buyer faster than this. Count on them checking everything closely. If they see you are well prepared their interest will rise real fast."

  Source: http://www.streetdirectory.com/travel_guide/22035/home_businesses/
  when_and_how_to_sell_your_home_business.html

- "Run your business without getting too involved: When you are ready to sell your business, make sure that your business is able to operate without you. If a single-person business is totally dependent on its current owner for smooth operation, then the business will be a hard sell. Potential buyers will be unwilling to purchase such business because there's no value without the current owner. Buyers have to be assured that, new staff and technology alone can run the business. A fully functional home-based business, regardless of the owner will get a higher selling price.

  "Offer to stay with the business for a certain period: One major problem with home-based service businesses is that the whole business revolves around the existing owner. The current owner can offer to stay with the business for a certain period. This offer will lower the risks and thus add value to the selling price. Current owners can stay and ensure a smooth transition."

  Source: http://exitadviser.com/seller-status.aspx?id=sell-homebased-business

Industry Trend

- "After 37 years of following small and home business launches, the National Mail Order Association (NMOA) predicts a new explosion in people starting a business because of layoffs and fears of salary reductions. 53 percent of small (businesses with one or more owners but no paid employees) businesses in the U.S. are 'home-based' businesses."

Home Centers (See also Hardware Stores, Lumberyards)

NAICS 444110	Number of Businesses/Units 9,051

Rules of Thumb

➢ 40 to 45% percent of annual sales includes inventory

➢ 2 times SDE plus inventory

Pricing Tips

- "Tend to be asset value sales"
- "Sales indicate that smaller sales bring higher multiple than stores with sales over $1 million. Price is plus inventory."
- "Home centers are a hybrid hardware/lumberyard. Typically they will do 50% lumber and 50% hardware. They focus primarily on the do-it-yourself customers, although they will also deal with the pro contractors. Home centers will usually have little higher prices in lumber than a pro lumberyard. However, they are usually in nicer locations and well-defined commercial areas. Lumberyards need much more yard space and therefore are often located in areas where acreage is cheap, i.e., in the more undeveloped areas. Home centers will usually have retail store space in the 10,000 to 20,000 sq. ft. range with a modest sized outdoor lumber area."

Expert Comments

"The high capital costs for inventory and fixtures and the lack of good locations are significant barriers to entry."

Benchmark Data

Statistics (Home Improvement Stores)

Number of Establishments	9,051
Average Profit Margin	9.6%
Revenue per Employee	$235,600
Average Number of Employees	79.0
Average Wages per Employee	$27,398

Products and Services Segmentation

Lumber and other building and structural materials	32.7%%
Household appliances, kitchen goods and housewares	29.6%
Hardware, tools and plumbing and electrical supplies	23.3%
Lawn, garden and farm equipment supplies	14.4%

Major Market Segmentation

Professionals (commercial projects)	42.0%
Professionals (do-it-for-me consumer projects)	40.0%
Do-it-yourself customers	18.0%

Industry Costs

Profit	9.6%
Wages	11.6%
Purchases	70.3%
Depreciation	1.0%
Marketing	1.2%
Rent & Utilities	2.5%
Other	3.8%

Market Share

The Home Depot Inc.	49.7%
Lowe's Companies Inc.	35.1%
Menard Inc.	5.6%

Source: IBISWorld, July 2016

- "Sales per square foot of retail space should be greater than $250. Margins should be greater than 33%; payroll should be less than 17%–18% to be profitable. Must have well-defined marketing programs in place. Should have advertising greater than 2% of sales, preferably 3% or more."
- "A good home center may do $300–$400/sq. ft. per year in sales."

Expenses as a percentage of annual sales

Cost of goods...65% to 70%
Payroll/labor Costs..12% to 15%
Occupancy...05% to 06%
Profit (estimated pretax) ....10% to 15%

Industry Trend

- "Steady if you have the labor available to compete service wise with the big box stores."
- "Home centers have been less impacted than lumberyards during the last two years. The primary reason is that profits come mostly from the hardware side of the business, which has been 'hit' less hard than lumber sales."

Questions

- "How do you compete with the competition? Is it through franchise type buying power?"
- "Why are you selling? Are there any potential franchise or refurbishment costs that may be included in the sale?"
- "Does any one contractor represent more than 10% of your lumber business? This is a personality business. If the old owner goes, the customer might leave too."

Home Health Care—Care-Giving

(See also Home Health Care—Equipment & Supplies)

	NAICS 621610	Number of Businesses/Units 469,718

Rules of Thumb

➤ 50 percent of annual sales plus inventory

➤ 2 to 4 times SDE plus inventory

➤ 4 to 6 times EBIT

➤ 3 to 5 times EBITDA

Pricing Tips

- "Current agency I am selling includes two franchise agreements valued at $115,000. Seller will pay franchise transfer fee of $50,000. That is $165,000 of value regardless of SDE. Seller will keep AR. These must be factored into pricing. A good agency generating over $1 million revenue will produce a return of 15–17%. Very important to plot at least 3 year growth track. This franchise has over 300 successful agencies that can provide great stats."
- "The range of multiple for home care companies ranges from 2.5X to 3.5X.

What allows for a higher valuation are several factors including: 1) Revenues over $1MM, 2) Growth in revenues and profit year over year, 3) Sustainability, i.e., number of referral sources, key personnel in place, role of the owner, demographics of the territory covered, 4) types of clients, etc. 5) if a franchise, the brand."

- "Businesses that have $600K to $1M of SDE tend to sell for 4x SDE. The multiple gradually goes lower with less than $600 SDE. The multiples are the same for both franchises and non-franchises. However, it's easier to sell franchises because of the additional support, branding and marketing. Businesses with $2M+ in revenue are easier to sell."
- "Businesses with $2M+ in revenue often turn down business because of a lack of caregivers. Recruiting and retaining caregivers is the industry's biggest challenge."
- "Health care and related service businesses such as home health care, doctor's offices, PT clinics, personal transportation, etc. can vary slightly. Each is considered on a case by case basis due to the complexities and variables of each owner and their business. I do not use hard and fast numbers on health related businesses without meeting with an owner first."
- "Must be aware of reimbursement"
- "A good business should have at least a 20-point margin. If not, the business may be a lot more valuable to a seasoned acquirer than the numbers show."
- "Need to watch for employee and customer related litigation."

Expert Comments

"Sellers should have a sales force in place. The owner will participate in the sales process but must not be the face of the business. Most agencies have excellent financial records and sellers should make sure they are up to date at all times. For buyers you must understand the sales process and be willing to follow the franchise business model. There are many opportunities in specialized areas and buyers should be prepared to look for these opportunities."

"There are several national franchises operating in this space. Each has its benefits. Starting an agency is a relatively high-risk process because it takes a long time to reach profitability. Many startups are under-capitalized. All of the agencies I have worked with show great growth and this industry will continue to grow with the aging of baby boomers. Marketability is OK, but it takes a special buyer to operate these agencies and financing the purchase for a relatively new agency is extremely difficult."

"The home-care industry has exploded with the aging population. Today, with 10,000 Americans turning 65 every day, the demand for senior care is ever increasing. The U.S. senior population currently sits at approximately 50 million and by 2030, it is expected to swell to 81 million (Source: U.S. Census Bureau). An estimated 70 percent of people over 65 will require home-care services at some point in their lives."

"Sell Side—Work with a broker who really understands the industry and has a proven track record. Buy Side—Both franchises and non-franchises are valued with similar multiples—so buying a franchise gives you much more bang for the buck (support, marketing, branding....)"

"Very tough to start a successful new business because of the chicken and egg dilemma (you need caregivers to recruit clients and you need clients to recruit and retain caregivers)."

"It is easy to start a home health company but difficult to get past the critical point of $1 million–$2 million in sales. Businesses past that point see a lot less competition than the smaller ones."

Benchmark Data

Statistics (Home Care Providers)

Number of Establishments	458,995
Average Profit Margin	6.2%
Revenue per Employee	$47,600
Average Number of Employees	4.3
Average Wages per Employee	$23,589

Products and Services Segmentation

Traditional home healthcare and home nursing care	57.3%
Home hospice	22.6%
Home therapy services	9.1%
Homemaker and personal services	6.1%
Other	4.9%

Major Market Segmentation

Medicare	41.5%
Medicaid	36.5%
Private insurance	8.6%
Out-of-pocket	8.2%
Other	5.2%

Industry Costs

Profit	6.2%
Wages	49.0%
Purchases	10.6%
Depreciation	1.0%
Marketing	0.7%
Rent & Utilities	3.1%
Other	29.4%

Source: IBISWorld, May 2016

Statistics (In-Home Senior Care Franchises)

Number of Establishments	10,723
Average Profit Margin	13.5%
Revenue per Employee	$61,200
Average Number of Employees	19.5
Average Wages per Employee	$26,318

Products and Services Segmentation

Homemaker and personal services	6.1%
Home hospice (end of life) care services	22.6%
Other services	4.9%
Traditional home healthcare and home nursing care	57.3%
Home therapy services	9.1%

Major Market Segmentation

Medicare	21.9%
Private Insurance	13.0%
Out-of-pocket	40.2%
Medicaid	17.8%
Other sources	4.7%
Other government (e.g., Veterans Affairs, Indian Affairs, etc.)	2.4%

Industry Costs

Profit	13.5%
Wages	43.0%
Purchases	8.5%
Depreciation	3.1%
Marketing	4.5%
Rent & Utilities	3.2%
Other	24.2%

Market Share

Home Instead Inc.	7.1%
Interim HealthCare Inc.	5.9%

Source: IBISWorld, April 2015

- "Gross Profit over 40% indicates an agency with pricing power."
- "Net profits closer to 20% margin"
- "Price should generate a 50%+ gpm on direct labor costs."
- "When comparing terminations and ceased operations, home care franchises were only 4.9% compared to 6% for the franchise industry.
- "The Top 10 Home Care Franchises Based upon Number of U.S. Locations
    - ✓ Comfort Keepers
    - ✓ Home Instead Senior Care
    - ✓ Visiting Angels
    - ✓ Right at Home
    - ✓ Home Helpers
    - ✓ Interim HealthCare
    - ✓ BrightStar Care
    - ✓ Senior Helpers
    - ✓ Synergy HomeCare
    - ✓ Griswold Home Care

"A Profile of Home Care Franchises

Item	Average	Median
Min. Initial Franchise Fee	$37,736	$42,087
Max. Initial Franchise Fee	$39,500	$41,250
Royalty	06%	05%
Min. Franchise Investment	$91,729	$70,875
Max. Franchise Investment	$172,958	$123,945
Initial Term	9 years	10 years
Renewal Term	8 years	10 years
VetFran Participants	12 Franchises	

"Over a period of four years the home care franchise industry has experienced net growth of 1,757 locations, or a 47% increase."

Source: Home Care Franchise Industry Update 2015

Expenses as a percentage of annual sales

Cost of goods	05% to 09%
Payroll/labor Costs	50% to 56%
Occupancy	05%
Profit (estimated pretax)	20% to 27%

Industry Trend

- "Personalized medical assistance is a cost effective measure to control treatment expenditure and acts as major driver for the industry. According to the U.S. Bureau of Labor Statistics (USBLS), personal care and healthcare assistance in a home-setting environment is anticipated to reach a value of USD 13 million by 2020, an increase of 70% from 2010 to 2020.

  "The home healthcare industry is anticipated to be majorly driven by the huge aging population volume which is highly prone to various diseases such as venous stasis ulcers, diabetic ulcers, and pressure ulcers. According to WHO, the global volume of population falls under the age group of 60 years and above has reached 841 million in 2014 and is expected to reach 2 billion by 2050.

  "Therefore, rising global aging-population along with the statistics that approximately 70% of home healthcare patients belong to 65 years and above age group, is anticipated to fuel demand in the near future.

  "According to the PRB (Population Reference Bureau), at present, approximately 50 million citizens of North America are over 65 years and the number is projected to reach to 89 million by 2050."

  Source: http://www.cbs8.com/story/32054427/north-america-home-healthcare-market-being-driven-by-personalized-medical-assistance-facility-for-geriatric-population-till-2022-grand-view-research

- "Agencies that offer medical and non-medical care will continue to grow as baby boomers age and the cost of healthcare rises."
- "Very positive trend due to aging population"
- "Demand continues to grow as the senior population increases. Many seniors prefer to age in place as long as they can."
- "For example, from 2010 to the present, the number of home care franchise systems has increased by 24 and the number of franchisees in the United States has increased from 4,038 to 5,522 from 2010 to 2013. The franchise home care sector will continue its growth as the U.S. population continues to grow in size and age. Home care services properly administered are less costly compared to the cost at long-term care facilities. By 2020 it is projected that there will be 5 million people in the U.S. 65 years or older."

  Source: Home Care Franchise Industry Update 2015

- "Home Health Care Industry Focus—In 1994, approximately one in eight Americans was age 65 and older. But by 2030, one in five Americans will be a senior citizen. From 2010 to 2030, the number of baby boomers age 65 to 84 will grow by an estimated 80 percent while the population age 85 and older will grow by 48 percent. In addition, between 1994 and 2020, the nation's population of 85 years and older is projected to double to 7 million, and then increase to between 19 and 27 million by 2050. So it's easy to see why those in the home health care industry see another boom on the horizon—one of ever-increasing demand for services."

  Source: www.missouribusiness.net/iag/focus

Seller Financing

- "A mature agency can probably be purchased with SBA financing. The agencies I have sold are relatively new (under 5 years) and the licensing process and historical numbers make SBA nearly impossible."

- "SBA financing is the norm (75%) for 10 years. 10% seller financing with a 3 year hold back period (8 years in total)."

Questions

- "Who are the referral sources? What are the roles of the key employees? What is the Workman's Comp rate and Experience Mode? Where do you get your clients mostly from?"
- "Past caregiving incidents? Owner's roles and responsibilities? # of clients driving 10%, 50% of revenue? 3-year monthly trend of revenue?"
- "Be prepared to be fully invested and do whatever it takes for your clients. What do you worry about the most and how can I grow this?"
- "Is the business a franchise, is there restricted territory, is there a fair amount of outstanding AR, are the employees 1099 or W-2, etc. All items can be addressed and resolved."
- "Who runs the operations (i.e., people) and will they be staying post acquisition?"

Home Health Care—Equipment and Supplies

(See also Home Health Care Rental)

SIC 8082-01	NAICS 532291	

Rules of Thumb

➢ 85 percent of annual sales plus inventory

➢ 4 times EBITDA excluding rental equipment depreciation

➢ 4 times EBIT

➢ 4 times SDE plus inventory

Pricing Tips

- "Know the payer source—% of Medicare. Know the product mix—# of respiratory patients. Know the referral concentration—# of referring physicians. Know the monthly new-patient setups."
- "Payer mix rental vs. sales"
- "Depends on type of contracts (Medicare-Medicaid, private pay, nursing home, etc.) and length of contracts."
- "The age of the equipment may make it subject to obsolescence. A careful inventory of equipment located in patient homes must be made and evaluated by an expert."
- "Multiples of EBITDA range from 3 to 5. Much of the pricing depends on product mix, e.g., respiratory, DME, infusion, sleep apnea, etc."
- "Competition is high because the market is huge and growing. Risk is low because established businesses have patient referral sources. Profits are slightly down due to more third-party 'paperwork' requirements. Marketability is high, since many large companies are growing by acquisition. Industry is growing due to an aging population."

H - Rules of Thumb

Expert Comments

"Substantial pressure on margins due to Medicare implementing cost controls and national competitive bidding."

Benchmark Data

- See additional Benchmark Data under Home Health Care (care-giving and nursing)
- "20% + EBITDA margins. Need to show annual growth in sales and profits. Stable referral sources."

Expenses as a percentage of annual sales

Cost of goods	35%
Payroll/labor Costs	20%
Occupancy	05%
Profit (estimated pretax)	35%

Industry Trend

- "Medicare sees significant cost savings when it preserves spending on home medical equipment, according to a new study unveiled at The VGM Group's Heartland Conference this week. The study, conducted by Brian Leitten of Leitten Consulting, found, for example, that for every $1 that Medicare pays for mobility equipment, it saves $16.78 in treatment for avoided falls. 'The message is clear: HME does save Medicare money and helps beneficiaries live where they want to be—at home,' said John Gallagher, vice president of government relations for VGM, in a press release.
  "Other examples from the study: For every $1 Medicare spends on supplemental oxygen therapy, it saves $9.62 in treatment for COPD-caused medical complications; and for every $1 Medicare spends on CPAP therapy, it saves $6.73 for the treatment of OSA-related complications."

Source: "Medicare saves with HME, study says," www.hmenews.com, 6/12/14
- "Continued consolidation due to competitive bidding."
- "Declining profits because of Medicare pricing pressures"

Questions

- "Any outstanding Medicare audits? Are they accredited?"

Resources

Websites

- www.hmenews.com

Home Health Care Rental

(See also Home Health Care—Equipment and Supplies)

SIC 5999-20	NAICS 532291	Number of Businesses/Units 7,826

Rules of Thumb

➤ 4 times EBITDA

Pricing Tips

- "Payor mix (Medicare, Medicaid, commercial, etc.). How many 'capped' patients?"

Expert Comments

"Industry demand is growing but margins continue to decline as CMS (Center for Medicare & Medicaid Services) reduces reimbursement to providers."

Benchmark Data

Statistics (Home Medical Equipment Rentals)

Number of Establishments	7,826
Average Profit Margin	6.4%
Revenue per Employee	$133,100
Average Number of Employees	5.4
Average Wages per Employee	$41,828

Products and Services Segmentation

Oxygen and respiratory therapy equipment	65.0%
Mobility aid equipment	23.3%
Diabetic therapy equipment	5.9%
Other medical equipment	5.8%

Major Market Segmentation

Medicare insured individuals	42.8%
Other insured individuals	28.2%
State and local governments	14.6%
Out-of-pocket individuals	14.4%

Industry Costs

Profit	6.4%
Wages	31.2%
Purchases	11.7%
Depreciation	27.8%
Marketing	1.2%
Rent & Utilities	6.2%
Other	15.5%

Market Share

Lincare Holdings Inc.	8.6%

Source: IBISWorld, July 2016

Expenses as a percentage of annual sales

Cost of goods	10%
Payroll/labor Costs	20%
Occupancy	04%
Profit (estimated pretax)	18%

Industry Trend

- "The global medical equipment rental market was recorded at US$33,417.4 million in 2013 and, at a CAGR of 5.8% during the forecast period of 2014 to 2020, will reach a value of US$49,112.8 million by 2020. According to device type, the global medical equipment rental market is segmented into home/personal care equipment, surgical equipment, electronic/digital equipment, durable medical equipment, and storage and transport equipment. Durable medical equipment is currently the leading sector in the market and is expected to grow at a 6% CAGR during the forecast period. By end user, the global medical equipment rental market is divided into institutional medical equipment rental and personal/home care medical equipment rental. Personal/home care medical equipment rental is presently the leading sector and is anticipated to grow at a CAGR of 5% during the forecasting horizon.

  "Though the global medical equipment rental market is expected to grow steadily, the lack of appropriate regulatory framework and poor pricing flexibility is expected to hamper growth of this market."

  Source: December 30, 2014   http://www.transparencymarketresearch.com/medical-equipment-rental.html

- "Continued pricing pressures and uncertainty of Medicare reimbursement rates. Implementation of competitive bidding will further erode profit margins."

		Franchise
Home Helpers (See also Franchises, Home Health Care—Care-Giving)		
Approx. Total Investment		$65,750 to $106,000
	NAICS 621610	Number of Businesses/Units 627

Rules of Thumb

➢ 40 to 45 percent of annual sales plus inventory

Resources

Websites

- www.homehelpershomecare.com

Home Inspection		
	NAICS 541350	Number of Businesses/Units 24,622

Rules of Thumb

➢ 45 percent of annual sales includes inventory

Benchmark Data

Statistics (Building Inspectors)

Number of Establishments	24,622
Average Profit Margin	19.2%
Revenue per Employee	$86,700
Average Number of Employees	1.6
Average Wages per Employee	$33,063

Products and Services Segmentation

Home inspection services	28.3%
Other	24.6%
Specific element inspection services	21.2%
Commercial building inspection services	20.4%
New home construction inspection services	5.5%

Major Market Segmentation

Commercial and other markets	33.8%
Home buyers and sellers	31.2%
The government	21.2%
Contractors	13.8%

Industry Costs

Profit	19.2%
Wages	38.0%
Purchases	10.5%
Depreciation	2.7%
Marketing	2.6%
Rent & Utilities	4.0%
Other	23.0%

Source: IBISWorld, October 2015 (latest available)

- "While it is difficult to scientifically predict your market potential, there are some general guidelines which you might find useful. As a rule of thumb, roughly 15,000 existing homes are sold annually per 1,000,000 population size, or 1.5%. Calculating the percentage of these homes, the percentage that are inspected can be as high as 95% in major cities and along the East and West coasts, and as low as 10%–25% in more rural areas. Try to obtain from local officials and real estate salespeople the figures for the population in your region and the percentage of homes there that are inspected. Then apply the following formula to estimate your current home inspection business opportunity: (Population x .015) x % of homes inspected = # of home inspections conducted per year.

  "For example, if (1) one million people live in your area and you determine that roughly (50%) fifty percent of the homes sold are inspected, then you can estimate that about (7,500) seven thousand five hundred inspections are conducted annually. This is a minimum figure, because it does not include inspections of newly built homes and, as the market and consumer awareness grow, the number of home inspections overall will grow as well.

  "Now check your local Yellow Pages to determine the number of home inspectors working in your area, and divide the number of annual home inspections by that figure. Twenty (20) inspectors in our example above would mean that each inspector would average about three hundred seventy five (375) inspections per year. This is only a general picture, however, since multi-inspector firms account for a larger market share, while part-time inspectors will do fewer. The average home inspection fee nationally is $240, and so a home inspector in this scenario could project to earn an annual gross income of $90,000. It is quite feasible, however, for well-trained inspectors to earn well over $100,000."

  Source: International Society of Home Inspectors, http://www.ishionline.org/

Resources

Trade Publications

- Home Inspector Magazine, published by the Organization of Real Estate Professionals: http://www.workingre.com/home-inspector-magazine-news/

Associations

- National Association of Home Inspectors—a good site: www.nahi.org
- International Society of Home Inspectors—An excellent site with lots of good information: www.ishionline.org

Homeland Security

Rules of Thumb

➢ 100 percent of annual sales includes inventory

➢ 3.5 times SDE includes inventory

➢ "Defining a company as Homeland Security is tricky. Government contractors are typically more Homeland Security companies than traditional security companies. Since this industry is already in the hundreds of billions, and is expected to grow exponentially over the next decade, I would recommend a new category."

Pricing Tips

- "Funded contracts are worth a minimum of 1x revenue."
- "There is a tremendous difference between backlog and funded backlog. Funded backlog should receive a very high premium on that number. If customer is Federal Government, and you are supplying them with a unique technology, there is a tremendous amount of value, even after the life of the product, in parts. This will add longevity to any product pipeline."

Expert Comments

"As the government grows, the industry will grow exponentially."

"The Homeland Security industry is experiencing consolidation. Therefore competition is increasing in certain areas where companies have historically not seen any. Companies with proprietary technology, particularly technology currently being used by the government, are greatly increasing in value."

"The recent government funding for Homeland Security products has made this a growing industry for many years to come. Large Homeland Security contractors, many who are also defense contractors, are seeking small companies with patented products to be able to capture more government products."

"Location is irrelevant. It is important to have a plan for foreign sales."

Benchmark Data

- "A patented product with a history of orders can realize as much as 30x earnings."

- "Multiple of earnings for funded contracts is typically 7–8x's."
- "1 to 3 times revenue"

Expenses as a percentage of annual sales

Cost of goods	30%
Payroll/labor Costs	20%
Occupancy	10%
Profit (estimated pretax)	25%

Industry Trend

- " There is a steady demand for security products and technology for well into the future. The trend is clearly toward exponential growth."
- "Growing, but a lot going to the larger industry players."

Questions

- "Can you export this service or technology? Are you an 8a company? How do you market this product? (Most do not, and have a few key contacts)."
- "How much of his orders are funded? How much is coming from GSA schedule? Can you see an invoice? Does the government pay him promptly?"
- "What is the amount of your funded backlog? How much of your equipment is rejected each year? Do you know how many pieces of your equipment are deployed and actively used? What patent or market protection do you have?"

Resources

Trade Publications
- Government Security News: www.gsnmagazine.com

Home Nursing Agencies (See also Home Health Care—Care-Giving)		
	NAICS 621610	

Rules of Thumb

➢ 4 times EBITDA

➢ 2 to 4 times Seller's Discretionary Earnings plus inventory

Pricing Tips

- "Very stable pricing. Depends on contracts and customer types"
- "Multiples of EBITDA commonly used for home nursing agencies run from as low as 1 to 5 times 12 month trailing EBITDA."

Expert Comments

"This is part of the growing healthcare segment. As the population gets older, the need for in-home services grows."

Benchmark Data

"With the aging of America, and the growing need for health care services, this is a growth industry. Low cost of entry equals a competitive environment."

Expenses as a percentage of annual sales

Cost of goods	0
Payroll/labor Costs	50% to 60%
Occupancy	10%
Profit (estimated pretax)	15% to 20%

Seller Financing
- "10%–20% seller financed; 2 to 5 years"

Questions
- "Percentage of business under contract; percentage of business under long-term care"

Resources

Associations
- National Association for Home Care and Hospice: www.nahc.org

	Franchise

Home Team Inspection Service (See also Franchises, Home Inspection)

Approx. Total Investment	$37,400 to $70,600

SIC 7389-96	NAICS 541350	Number of Businesses/Units 160

Rules of Thumb
➤ 35 percent of annual sales plus inventory

Benchmark Data
- For Benchmark Data see Home Inspection

Resources

Websites
- www.hometeam.com

	Franchise

Honest-1 Auto Care (See also Franchises)

Approx. Total Investment	$169,975 to $457,975

	NAICS 811111	Number of Businesses/Units 43

Rules of Thumb
60 to 65 percent of annual sales plus inventory

Resources

Websites
www.honest-1.com

Hospital Laundry—Supply (See also Uniform Rental)

	NAICS 812331	

Rules of Thumb

➤ 50 percent of annual sales plus inventory

Pricing Tips

- An industry expert states that for laundry with hospital contracts a rule of thumb is 50 percent of gross annual sales. This is because that market is a very competitive one.

Benchmark Data

- For additional Benchmark Data see Uniform Rental
- "The size in value of the laundry market, including: healthcare, hospitality, and federal government is $10.5 billion annually, as follows:

Total Laundry Market Size and Value by Segment

Segment	Percent
Healthcare	45.9%
Hospitality	52.8%
Federal Government	1.3%
Total	100.0%

- "As indicated, the size of the federal government market is small compared to the total laundry market. The statistics related to this market are as follows: healthcare—hospitals: 4,915, 823,560 beds; healthcare—nursing homes:17,000, 1.6 million beds; hospitality—hotels: 53,500 rooms; and federal government—1,231 locations."

Source: "Competition in the Laundry Industry," www.sourceamericalaundry.mindtouch.us/

- The Textile Rental Services Association (TRSA) estimates the following costs that hospitals spend for on-premise laundry services:
  - ✓ fringe benefits, taxes, insurance—12%
  - ✓ fuel oil, natural gas—07%
  - ✓ depreciation—02%
  - ✓ maintenance—02%
  - ✓ water and sewer—01%
  - ✓ electricity—01%
  - ✓ interest on investment, administration, and support—05%

Source: www.trsa.org

Resources

Associations

- Textile Rental Services Association (TRSA): www.trsa.org

Hospitals—Medical and Surgical

	NAICS 622110	

Rules of Thumb

- ➢ 51 percent of annual sales plus inventory
- ➢ 1.8 times SDE plus inventory
- ➢ 3 times EBIT
- ➢ 2.9 times EBITDA

Pricing Tips

- "Tremendous variation in types of hospitals today. Substantial due diligence is required to determine appropriate EBITDA multiples for a particular hospital at a particular point in time."

Expert Comments

"Due diligence is essential!"

"Tremendous variation in types of hospitals today. Some are profitable and growing, some are bankrupt and closing. Some have excellent state of the art facilities, while others are closing due to failure to meet required standards."

Benchmark Data

- "The American Hospital Association provides an annual survey with basic statistics. Levin Associates tracks publicly announced transactions. The Healthcare Financial Management Association provides industry statistics and surveys."

Expenses as a percentage of annual sales

Cost of goods	08%
Payroll/labor Costs	03%
Profit (estimated pretax)	06%

Industry Trend

- "Tremendous changes in technology and the business model. More services will continue to move out of the inpatient setting. Value-based payment will continue to push focus to the full continuum of care. More personalized medicine will rely on genomics."
- "Revenue is expected to grow, demand expected to grow, consolidation expected to continue, profit expected to decrease."

Seller Financing

- "Outside financing"

Questions

- "Payor mix, market share, patient demographic data."

Resources

Websites

Levin Associates: www.levinassociates.com

Associations

- American Hospital Association: www.aha.org

Hospitals—Medical and Surgical (Non-Profit)

Rules of Thumb

➤ 51 percent of annual sales plus inventory

➤ 1.8 times SDE plus inventory

➤ 3 times EBIT

➤ 2.9 times EBITDA

Benchmark Data

Expenses as a percentage of annual sales

Cost of goods	08%
Payroll/labor Costs	03%
Profit (estimated pretax)	06%

Hospitals—Psychiatric and Substance Abuse

	NAICS 622210	

Rules of Thumb

➤ 51 percent of annual sales plus inventory

➤ 1.8 times SDE plus inventory

➤ 3 times EBIT

➤ 2.9 times EBITDA

Benchmark Data

Expenses as a percentage of annual sales

Cost of goods	09%
Payroll/labor Costs	03%
Profit (estimated pretax)	06%

Industry Trend

- "Demand expected to grow, revenue projected to grow, consolidation expected to continue, costs projected to increase."

Seller Financing

- "Outside financing"

Questions

- "Payor mix, market share, patient demographic data"

Resources

Associations

- National Association of Psychiatric Health Systems: www.naphs.org

Hospitals—Specialty

Rules of Thumb

➤ 51 percent of annual sales plus inventory

➤ 1.8 times SDE plus inventory

➤ 3 times EBIT

➤ 2.9 times EBITDA

Benchmark Data

Expenses as a percentage of annual sales

Cost of goods	08%
Payroll/labor Costs	03%
Profit (estimated pretax)	06%

Industry Trend

- "Further consolidation, revenue projected to increase, profit projected to grow, demand expected to increase."

Seller Financing

- "Outside financing"

Questions

- "Payor mix, market share, patient demographic data"

Resources

Associations

- American Hospital Association: www.aha.org

Hotels & Motels

SIC 7011-01	NAICS 721110	Number of Businesses/Units 90,112

Rules of Thumb

➤ 250 to 300 percent of annual sales plus inventory

➤ 8 times SDE

➤ 8 to 10 times EBITDA

➤ 2.0 to 3.5 times annual room revenues—average 2.5

➤ Outside corridors—2.0 to 2.5 times annual room revenues

➤ Inside corridors—2.5 to 3.0 times annual room revenues

➤ Seldom seen—3.5 times annual room revenues

➤ $20,000 per room

➤ 10 to 12 percent cap rate

Pricing Tips

- "Independents 1.5–2 x room revenue; budget franchise 2–3 x room revenue; higher end franchise 4–5 x room revenue; larger full service propitious 10 cap rate."

- "In addition to basic financials, buyers should be sure to check fundamental business metrics such as the occupancy rate of the hotel, as well as room rates. To put the business fundamentals in better perspective, potential buyers should investigate the room rates at nearby hotels for comparison. If possible, interested buyers should also stay at the hotel as a guest for a few days before approaching the seller to get a first-hand look at hotel operations, customer satisfaction, and occupancy rates. All this takes a lot of time, but it's essential."

  Source; http://www.bizjournals.com/bizjournals/how-to/buy-a-business/bizbuysell/2012/12/buying-a-hotel-3-tips.html?page=all

- "Now take the asking price and subtract what you will pay in the equity down payment. Consider if your offer will include a request that the seller finance some improvements. You might be able to negotiate this up to an amount equal to your down payment as the money will be going directly back into the hotel."

  Source:http://www.hotel-online.com/Trends/Payne/Articles/SoYouWanttoBuyaHotel.html

- "Hotel Valuations are hybrid deals as they are between business and real estate. Each asset varies in the valuation method."
- "Lease arrangements, age of equipment, management in place, length of existence."
- "Most hotel buyers look at a multiple of room revenue. One of the few industries that is not based on EBITDA. On very large properties a cap rate is sometime used."
- "Large capital investment on front end makes the property susceptible to new, better-located competition. Need ongoing reserve for replacement of FF&E."
- "Location and franchise make a great difference. Also, we must consider extended-stay motels."
- "Check contracted room business and QA score if franchised."
- "We use several approaches to establish value. One is the Performance Index Method—developing a valuation table showing (a) cap rate (b) economic value (c) value per room (d) multiple of room revenue and (e) multiple of total revenue. One can then determine economic value by using either desired cap rate (best method), per room rates, X gross or Y total revenue. We also use discounted future earnings, discretionary cash flow, book value, market value and rule of thumb. We usually provide a range of values based on profitability, income risk, desirability, business type, business trend in location, competition, industry, terms of sale, along with a few other factors."
- "Our general analysis using a high and low range utilizes several approaches to value (1) the income approach (2) excess earnings (3) discounted future earnings (4) discretionary cash (5) book value (6) market value (7) rule of thumb—then we have value comparisons and then a correlation and final opinion of value range and finally an opinion of value. We base the above on: profitability, income risk, desirability, business type, leasehold, and product exclusivity. A factor is assigned to each of the above for both high and low range."
- "Room revenue multiplier (2x to 6x), net operating income multiplier (6x to 12x). The multiplier you choose determines the capitalization rate."
- "Location—highway changes—age—obsolescence—market conditions—affiliation."

H - Rules of Thumb

Expert Comments

"Look and compare several properties."

"High cost of entry."

"One must be aware of trends but be careful it is not a fad. Location is a key ingredient, items like parking, traffic lights, visibility. Highly competitive for some, so locating near target audience is crucial."

"Buy low, sell high. Market is good. Money is still cheap, multiples are still down. Try to find a property 5 years old or less selling at the right price and you will score yourself a win in the buyer markets."

"Mid-market and nice economy franchises are in demand as well as independent properties. Less need for pools and restaurants on site. Most people are busy and just need a nice clean place to lay their heads and be on their way."

"Constant upgrades and increased same class competition can strangle cash flow."

Benchmark Data

Statistics (Hotels and Motels)

Number of Establishments	88,052
Average Profit Margin	16.2%
Revenue per Employee	$104,300
Average Number of Employees	18.8
Average Wages per Employee	$25,993

Products and Services Segmentation

Guest room rentals from properties with between 75 and 299 rooms	42.7%
Guest room rentals from properties with under 75 rooms	19.7%
Meals, nonalcoholic drinks and other items for immediate consumption	9.8%
Guest room rentals from properties with over 500 rooms	8.3%
Conference room and venue space rentals for events	6.7%
Guest room rentals from properties with between 300 and 500 rooms	6.7%
Alcoholic beverages served for immediate consumption	3.1%
Other services (meals for catered events, laundry services, parking)	3.0%

Major Market Segmentation

Domestic leisure travelers	50.0%
International leisure travelers	19.5%
Business travelers	18.2%
Meeting, events and incentive travelers	12.3%

Industry Costs

Profit	16.2%
Wages	25.0%
Purchases	26.9%
Depreciation	9.7%
Marketing	2.0%
Rent & Utilities	8.2%
Other	12.0%

Market Share

Marriott International Inc. 14.7%
Hilton Worldwide Holdings Inc. 13.8%
InterContinental Hotels Group PLC 7.4%
Source: IBISWorld, July 2016

Statistics (Boutique Hotels)

Number of Establishments.. 2,060
Average Profit Margin 16.2%
Revenue per Employee $118,500
Average Number of Employees... 30.3
Average Wages per Employee $31,071

Products and Services Segmentation

Lodging 69.0%
Food and beverages.. 24.5%
Spa and wellness services 6.5%

Major Market Segmentation

Domestic leisure travelers 50.0%
Business travelers 30.5%
International leisure travelers.. 19.5%

Industry Costs

Profit 16.2%
Wages... 26.3%
Purchases... 27.9%
Depreciation... 9.7%
Marketing 2.3%
Rent & Utilities 8.2%
Other... 9.4%

Market Share

Starwood Hotels & Resorts Worldwide Inc. 16.8%
InterContinental Hotels Group PLC 14.6%
Source: IBISWorld, August 2016

- Price per unit varies upon condition, location, brand and type of hotel
- Penn State Index of U.S. Hotel Values (2017)

	Value Per room	Annual % Change
Overall	$136,015	5.5%
Luxury	$422,594	4.1%
Upper Upscale	$218,934	4.5%
Upscale	$158,499	3.9%
Upper Midscale	$121,226	5.8%
Midscale	$76,851	5.8%
Economy	$41,938	6.9%

Source: "Penn State Index of U.S. Hotel Values, The Pennsylvania State University

- "Hotels are based on many things, since you just don't buy a hotel business. You have real estate attached 100% of the time. Revenue per available room, occupancies, average daily rates play important parts. In general, a hotel would sell according to the amount of rooms built. Usually use a rule of thumb from 2.0 to 3.0 of gross sales. In extreme cases, up to 3.5 - 4.0 for excellent franchised property. Age and condition of property as well as FF&E makes a difference. We use several approaches to actual valuation of a property. Adequate (approx. 5%) for reserves. RevPAR (Revenue per Available Room) seems to be the thing today, not always room revenues."

Expenses as a percentage of annual sales

Cost of goods	01% to 10%
Payroll/labor Costs	20% to 30%
Occupancy	50% to 60%
Profit (estimated pretax)	10% to 22%

Industry Trend

- "MMGY Global predicts a record number of vacations and new highs in vacation spending among American travelers in the next 12 months. The market's intention to vacation during the next 12 months represents a 10-year high that surpasses the pre-recession record.
  - ✓ 28 percent of travelers indicated an intention to take more vacations, while only 14 percent reported that they plan to take fewer, resulting in a 14-point net positive variance.
  - ✓ Vacation spending has fully recovered from the Great Recession and spending intentions have soared well above the pre-recessionary levels in recent quarters.
  - ✓ In 2016, travelers reported having spent an average of $5,048 on vacations in the previous 12 months – an impressive 30 percent increase from 2010, and a 12 percent increase from an already-strong 2015.
  - ✓ Travelers are planning to spend an average of $5,182 in the next 12 months – an astonishing 23 percent increase in only four years, and a nine percent increase in the past year."
    Source: "Leisure travel and vacation spending will achieve record levels in the next 12 months," http://www.hotelnewsresource.com/article89709.html

- "Times might feel uncertain, but the industry is still positive. Following Bank of America's decision to downgrade hotels due to threats like soft corporate demand, increased popularity in homesharing services, and an onslaught of supply, pessimism from analysts outside the industry ramped up. Though some outside market reports may be indicating the end of a golden era for hotels, many hoteliers still appear to feel optimistic about the rest of 2016. Top executives from companies like Hilton Worldwide, FelCor Lodging Trust, Host Hotels & Resorts, Hersha Hospitality Trust, and Marriott International all see reasons to stay positive about this year's industry outlook."
    Source: "Despite Outside Concerns, Hotel Execs Maintain Positive Outlook," May 25, 2016, http://lodgingmagazine.com/lodgingdailynews/

- "In less than a decade Airbnb, the San Francisco-based home-sharing platform worth an estimated $25.5 billion, has become one of the biggest disruptors in the travel space. And the industry for whom Airbnb has been the most disruptive — hospitality — is keeping a very close watch on the company's every move. Every day, there seems to be a new headline suggesting the hospitality industry's demise at the hands of short-term rental sites like Airbnb."
    Source: "What Americans Really Think About Airbnb and Home-Sharing," by Deanna Ting, May 20, 2016, https://skift.com/2016/05/20/what-americans-really-think-about-airbnb-and-homesharing/

- "Foreclosure caused price decrease over the last few years and prices are slowly coming back."
- "High number of rooms under construction that raises the bar for older properties to compete."
- "Lots of short sales and foreclosures brought the market values down but the properties are making a resurgence. Very few rundown franchises any more. Punch list requirements keeping properties above board. If not they convert to an independent."

Seller Financing

- "Outside financing with a small portion of owner financing 10-15%, sometimes decreed for 2 years, 20-30 year amortization from most lenders."
- "Mostly outside financing...but many times deals are made with extremely creative and sophisticated financing models."
- "Outside financing since there is a large asset in the real property included. Any owner financing is 10–20% at tops. If a seller is willing to finance more than that, be very leery."
- 20 years
- 5 to 10 years

Questions

- "PIP requirements? STAR reports?"
- "ADR, occupancy, RevPar, punch list, recent inspection reports"
- "Are there capital expense items that need attention? How much contracted room business do they have? How much room business do they have on the books and for how long a period of time? What was their last QA score if it is a franchise hotel? Do they know of any new highways being constructed in the future that may divert traffic to or away from the hotel? Any new competition coming up in the area?"
- "Contract on the brand franchise? Age of equipment? Age of property? And all paperwork?"

Resources

Websites

- Hotel Management: www.hotelmanagement.net
- Hotel Business: www.hotelbusiness.com

Trade Publications

- Hotels and Motels: Valuations and Market Study, published by the Appraisal Institute: www.appraisalinstitute.org
- Lodging Magazine: www.lodgingmagazine.com

Associations

- American Hotel & Lodging Association: www.ahla.com

Franchise

House Doctors (See also Franchises)

Approx. Total Investment	$89,300 to $124,450
NAICS 236118	Number of Businesses/Units 54

Rules of Thumb

➤ House Doctors is a handyman service specializing in minor home repairs
24 percent of annual sales plus inventory

Resources

Websites
▪ www.housedoctors.com

Franchise

Hungry Howie's Pizza & Subs

(See also Franchises, Pizza Shops, Sandwich Shops)

Approx. Total Investment	$219,700 to $371,500
Estimated Annual Sales/Unit	$635,000
NAICS 722513	Number of Businesses/Units 550

Rules of Thumb

➤ 35 percent of annual sales plus inventory

Benchmark Data
▪ For Benchmark Data see Pizza Shops & Sandwich Shops

Resources

Websites
▪ www.hungryhowies.com

Franchise

Huntington Learning Center (See also Franchises)

Approx. Total Investment	$99,000 to $204.000
NAICS 611691	Number of Businesses/Units 218

Rules of Thumb

➤ 60 percent of annual sales

Resources

Websites
▪ www.huntingtonfranchise.com

HVAC—Heating, Ventilating & Air Conditioning

	NAICS 238220	Number of Businesses/Units 112,344

Rules of Thumb

➢ 25 to 40 percent of annual sales plus inventory

➢ 2 to 3 times SDE plus inventory

➢ 3 to 4 times EBIT

➢ 2.75 to 3 times EBITDA

Pricing Tips

- "If you're looking to exit your business or acquire another company, there are two ideas to think of in terms of the value of that business. The reality value of the business would be 3 to 6 times its EBITDA, but the opportunity value, as Cassel points out, can be much higher. 'Most financial people will tell you that profit is king, but I'll tell you the phone number is king,' said [Lon] Cassel. 'No matter how you value your business, you'll have to find a buyer for it. Make sure you find someone who really knows the opportunity value of a residential service call, so both buyer and seller receive a fair return on their investment of time and money,' instructed Cassel.

  "Cassel also emphasized the importance of planning for your exit. 'The fact is that everyone is going to exit their business someday, and, depending on how you exit, it could be with a lot of money or very little money. Some may value your company on profits and some may value it on service calls or both. Just make sure it is a fair value,' he concluded."

  Source: http://www.achrnews.com/articles/90302-what-8217-s-your-hvac-plumbing-business-worth

- "1) Residential service companies that have a healthy list of ongoing annual preventative maintenance agreements command higher multiples.

  2) Residential new construction companies that install for 'cookie cutter' homes are riskier, unless they were smart enough to secure installation locations for future service.

  3) Commercial contractors with healthy list of ongoing service agreements are more valuable than those that merely install and move on."

- "Higher percentage of business associated with residential 'service work' drives value. Number of active residential service (maintenance) agreements holds value. Heavy dependence on new construction depletes value. Commercial service work helps value, if ongoing activity by commercial accounts can be proven. Certain HVAC contractors are involved in energy conservation services, which are not proven popular (or sustainable) in all states at this time."

- "Mix drives value. There is an enormous range of pricing based on the mix of business. Prices for these businesses range from under 10% of revenue to over 100% of revenue. This is an enormously fragmented industry and therefore every company mix, set of controls, recurring nature, and margins will drive value."

Expert Comments

"Look for high number of service agreements."

"Although there has been an increasing separation between the 'haves' and the 'have nots' over the past few years, 2015 offered some hope for those in the middle."

"The value of qualified HVAC companies (and trade companies in general) are on the rise, due to the lower number of people interested in becoming HVAC technicians/tradesman. The average cost of this service will rise significantly over the next 10 years, making this industry prime for consolidations, mergers and buyouts."

"Competition: highly fragmented, over 50,000 contractors. Risk: a required recurring market. Historic profit trend: as varied as there are contractors. Location: proximity to market important, but not a driving factor as services provided off-site. Marketability: tough to carry sustainability based on typical owner influence. Growth: somewhat mature, slow-growth industry. Ease of replication: these businesses are easily replicated."

Benchmark Data

Statistics (Heating and Air-Conditioning Contractors)

Number of Establishments	112,344
Average Profit Margin	3.4%
Revenue per Employee	$185,500
Average Number of Employees	4.1
Average Wages per Employee	$49,829

Products and Services Segmentation

New construction HVAC installations	51.7%
HVAC maintenance and repairs	31.8%
Existing structure HVAC installations (i.e., replacements)	10.6%
Refrigeration system installations, maintenance and repairs	5.9%

Major Market Segmentation

Single-family homes	25.6%
Manufacturing and industrial buildings	12.7%
Other	12.5%
Office buildings	11.6%
Retail and storage spaces	11.6%
Healthcare and public safety buildings	10.4%
Educational buildings	9.2%
Apartment buildings, dormitories and barracks	6.4%

Industry Costs

Profit	3.4%
Wages	26.8%
Purchases	46.6%
Depreciation	0.8%
Marketing	0.7%
Rent & Utilities	2.0%
Other	19.7%

Source: IBISWorld, June 2016

- "Sales per employee, including administrative:
  High = $250,000
  Medium = $225,000
  Low = $175,000

"Sales per Service Truck:
High = $350,000*
Medium = $300,000
Low = $250,000

*Accessory sales are a must for higher service sales per truck. (i.e., surge protectors, compressor savers, UV lights, filtration, etc.)"

"Sales per Field Technician Employee:
Optimal = $350,000
Average = $250,000
Poor < $175,000

"Field Techs to Inside Support Ratio:
Optimal = 5/1
Average = 3/1
Poor = 2/1"

Expenses as a percentage of annual sales

Cost of goods	35% to 65%
Payroll/labor Costs	10% to 22%
Occupancy	02% to 03%
Profit (estimated pretax)	05% to 15%

Industry Trend

- "Continued consolidation, especially if/when the economy slows again."
- "Consolidation will occur over next ten years, due to added cost of retaining qualified employees."
- "Wider spread between 'haves' and 'have nots.' Larger and stronger are consuming the mid-size and weaker. Home energy services are on the rise, but spotty acceptance per state. Home energy services have high barriers to entry, due to high certification and equipment costs."
- "Here's what's happening:
  - ✓ Plumbing companies moving into the HVAC business
  - ✓ HVAC companies adding plumbing to their service offerings
  - ✓ Contractors adding specialty services to their businesses. Some examples include irrigation, lawn fertilization, water softeners, bottled water, geothermal market, water-well drilling
  - ✓ Business scope changes—large, residential new-construction contractors change to primarily commercial
  - ✓ Single-family home contractors beginning to do multi-family condos
  - ✓ Service and repair contractors entering the single-family market
  - ✓ Single-family specialists moving into multi-family construction
  - ✓ Radiant work is becoming more marketable in upscale homes, particularly in the Northeast. It's used in just under 25% of homes in Canada, and the trend is moving south."

Source: "An Industry Forever Changing" by Eddie Hollub, Contracting Business, www.contractingbusiness.com

Seller Financing

- "Mix of outside financing and seller financing. When consolidation occurs, key owners/managers are retained for 6–24 months to aid transition."
- "Combination of both. Outside financing is accepted, as this can be recession proof business. Sellers willing to finance, if they know the customer base is solid. (good amount of preventative maintenance agreements and recurring business)"
- "Seller financing is more common, because most sellers have not properly prepared to sell, leaving themselves in a vulnerable position."

Questions

- "Review list of active customers over previous three years, to see if service trends are solid."
- "Ask for no less than five years of tax returns or financials. Ask for proof of PMA's. Ask for employee descriptions and longevity. Ask for list of recurring customers."
- "Number of service agreements. Number of active accounts over 5–10 years. Are equipment (HVAC system) warranties held 'in house,' or are they held by manufacturer(s)? What is/are the manufacturer's policies regarding transfer of business ownership as it relates to warranties? List of key employees and why they are key? (easy for one key man to buy a truck and start installing/servicing to feed himself). Are there any employee agreements in place?"

Resources

Trade Publications
- Air Conditioning Refrigeration News: www.achrnews.com
- HVACNews.com: www.hvacnews.com

Associations
- Kentucky Association of Master Contractors: www.kyamc.com
- The Indoor Environment and Energy Efficiency Association: www.acca.org

	Franchise
i9 Sports (See also Franchises)	
Approx. Total Investment	$44,900 to $69,900
NAICS 713990	Number of Businesses/Units 125

Rules of Thumb

➢ 65 to 70 percent of annual sales plus inventory

Resources

Websites
- www.i9sportsfranchise.com

Iceberg Drive Inn (See also Franchises)	Franchise
Approx. Total Investment	$132,500 to $556,000
NAICS 722513	Number of Businesses/Units 16

Rules of Thumb

> 40% to 45% of annual sales plus inventory

Resources

Websites

- www.icebergdriveinn.com

Ice Cream Trucks (See also Catering Trucks)	
NAICS 722330	

Rules of Thumb

> 1 times SDE plus fair market value of the truck(s) plus inventory

Pricing Tips

- "Today, ice cream trucks are owned by small regional companies that rent to independent drivers, or individuals who go it alone. Some, including Tanner, buy a fleet and rent to drivers such as Phillips, who take home 35 percent of their daily sales—minus the $12 daily truck rental fee and gas costs. Tanner gets the other 65 percent to cover operational and stocking costs: he supplies 64 varieties of ice cream from various suppliers to every truck. Phillips said that, so far, her best day netted more than $400 in sales. She's been working six days a week, now aiming for $500."
  Source: *Boston Globe*, August 18, 2005. (dated, but still informative.)

Benchmark Data

- For Benchmark Data see Catering Trucks
- "... While the profits don't quite cover tuitions, Toll (Taylor) says it's a huge help in paying for books and other expenses. She says the truck (ice cream) can rake in up to $1,000 on a good day."
  Source: "Paying for College with an Ice Cream Truck" by Gabrielle Karol, June 5, 2013, www.smallbusiness.foxbusiness.com/entrepreneurs

Industry Trend

- "Good Humor's trucks will soon be hitting the road again after a decades-long hiatus, but the iconic ice cream brand's fleet will be announcing its presence with tweets instead of clanging bells. Customers looking for an ice cream fix will be able to summon the classic Good Humor trucks by tweeting @GoodHumor. And, in another modern twist, the throwback trucks will be blasting pop music and rock songs instead of ringing their iconic chime bells."
  Source: "Good Humor's iconic ice cream trucks are making a big comeback" by Tom Huddleston, Jr., http://fortune.com/2015/06/23/good-humors-ice-cream-trucks/

Resources

Associations
- International Association of Ice Cream Distributors and Vendors (IAICDV): www.iaicdv.org
- International Dairy Foods Association: www.idfa.org

Ice Cream/Yogurt Shops (See also Baskin-Robbins, Carvel, etc.)		
SIC 5812-03	NAICS 722515	

Rules of Thumb

- ➤ 60 percent of annual sales plus inventory
- ➤ 2.2. times SDE plus inventory (franchised only)
- ➤ 3 times EBIT
- ➤ 3 times EBITDA
- ➤ 15 to 20 times weekly sales (independent only)

Pricing Tips
- "Length of lease a major factor and property ownership desirable"
- "Condition of premises, age of equipment, and location of shopping center critical to resale value."
- "2.5 x SDE applies to franchised ice cream stores with minimum 8+ year lease remaining with transfer fee included in the price. If less than 8 year lease or if seller requires buyer pay transfer fee, appropriate modifications need to be made. Non franchised ice cream businesses sell at 15-20x weekly sales assuming condition and lease (8+) years are acceptable."
- "Franchised ice cream operations have consumed the marketplace, and independent stores are virtually unsellable. Well-run franchised operations have good resale value, although seasonal in many marketplaces."
- "These stores are usually sold for a little less than one half year's gross sales. If it is a franchise store, such as Dairy Queen, Arctic Circle, or A&W, 15 percent can be added to the asking price. Net profit usually runs from 18 percent to 22 percent. Lease on the property should not exceed 6 percent (upper limit) of gross profit."

Expert Comments

"Location-driven business with increasing competition in the marketplace. Co-branding is an ideal situation for this concept to offset the seasonality and utilize the facility to a greater degree."

"Franchised operations protect many of the negatives, but increasing availability of premium desserts and ice cream limit expansion possibilities."

Benchmark Data
- For more Benchmark Information see Restaurants—Limited Service

Statistics (Frozen Yogurt Stores)

Number of Establishments	3,052
Average Profit Margin	11.5%
Revenue per Employee	$109,300
Average Number of Employees	6.0
Average Wages per Employee	$19,848

Products and Services Segmentation

Self-serve yogurt	68.9%
Full-service yogurt	18.1%
Toppings and other products	13.0%

Industry Costs

Profits	11.5%
Wages	18.5%
Purchases	37.7%
Depreciation	5.2%
Marketing	3.4%
Rent & Utilities	11.8%
Other	11.9%

Market Share

Menchie's	14.2%
Sweet Frog	12.7%
Yogurtland	11.2%
TCBY	9.8%
Orange Leaf Frozen Yogurt	8.1%
Pinkberry	5.9%
Red Mango	5.3%

Source: IBISWorld, December 2015

- "Product cost is lower in many franchises that manufacture product on site. However, those franchises typically have higher labor costs."
- "Limit retail operations to 1200 s/f or less."

Expenses as a percentage of annual sales

Cost of goods	28%
Payroll/labor Costs	22%
Occupancy	10%
Profit (estimated pretax)	05%

Industry Trend

- "It's not just frozen yogurt that's pulling away ice cream lovers—consumers are also enjoying gelato, Italian ice, custard, smoothies and other frosty concoctions."
- "Traditional ice cream sales have been slowly declining and seem poised to hit their lowest levels this year since the mid-1990s. Production of regular ice cream peaked in 2002 at about 14 quarts per person each year, according to government figures. That has fallen to 11.6 quarts per person, a 13% drop. Seven of the 10 biggest ice cream chains had fewer stores in 2012 than they had in 2011, according to research firm Technomic. Cold Stone Creamery has shuttered more than 100 stores since 2009. At Baskin-Robbins, revenue and store count have fallen every year since 2008."

Source: "The Decline of an All-American American Treat," finance.yahoo.com, 6/21/13
(dated, but still of interest)

- "Dramatically increasing product costs will strain profitability, increase in number of franchised concepts will cause competition unseen in the marketplace in its history."

Questions

- "Equipment servicing questions, employee history, historical sales"
- "Owner-operated or absentee? Any wholesale accounts?"
- "Sales by month to determine fluctuations; manager, if any, and salary, with benefits. Changes in product cost and related change in selling price of products. Sales trends, on a month-to-month basis. Must speak to company district manager, if a franchise, about his/her requirements of a new buyer."

Resources

Associations

- International Dairy Foods Association: www.idfa.org

Incentive Companies		
	NAICS 561520	

Rules of Thumb

➤ 3 to 5 times EBITDA—multiple expands as free cash flow number rises.

Pricing Tips

- "Is the future business under contract with cancellation clauses?
- "How many programs are on the books for the next 12 months? Are they serving various industries or concentrating on one sector? Diversity is better. Three types—travel, merchandise, debit card. Points tracking & redemption, etc. = big interest in online registration and digital offerings."

Industrial Safety and Health

Rules of Thumb

➤ Manufacturing—5 to 7 times recasted EBIT less debt

➤ Distribution—4 to 6 times recasted EBIT less debt

Information and Document Management Service Industries		
	NAICS 541513	

Rules of Thumb

➤ 4 to 6 times normalized EBITDA

Industry Trend

- "Over the five years to 2020, the Document Management Services industry is expected to post growth, with industry revenue forecast to rise at an annualized rate of 1.6% to total $5.9 billion. This includes projected growth of 2.0% during 2016. Industry growth will be supported by rising business formation and greater demand from healthcare institutions transitioning to electronic health records (EHRs)."

Source: http://clients1.ibisworld.com/reports/us/industry/industryoutlook.aspx?entid=5044

Information Technology Companies		
	NAICS 541512	

Rules of Thumb

➤ 100 to 150 percent of annual sales

➤ 2.5 to 4 times SDE

➤ 3 to 4 times EBIT

➤ 3 to 6 times EBITDA

Pricing Tips

- "Must understand vendor contracts, customer contracts, assignability, and how important employees are to the company having certain certifications."
- "The range of value varies widely by size of company and deal structure. Smaller companies (under $1 million in revenue) tend to see SDE multiples around 2.5 times SDE. Larger companies with more than $1 million EBITDA tend to see multiples of 4 times EBITDA, and are more likely to use EBITDA as the earnings metric. Companies in the middle of the foregoing range tend to be valued around 3 to 3.5 times SDE or EBITDA. Revenue is not a significant factor, except that most buyers will place a ceiling at 1 times revenue. Companies with recurring revenue and predictable earnings will be valued higher, such as IT Managed Service Providers, SaaS, DaaS, and hosted services with annual contracts and recurring income. Staff, technical capabilities, and sales team strength tend to be value drivers as well."
- "Might increase multiple if selling company has secured gov't contracts especially if in secured agency."
- "Consider any off-balance sheet value, i.e., IP, Gov't contracts, valued customer relationships, unique vendor relationships."
- "Is there an SLA (Software License Agreement) for each type/copy of software being used? Are the SLA's assignable? Has the vendor given written permission to assign them and under what conditions? Has the company been reported to the Software Consortium as a company using unlicensed software? Is the technology based on open standards and/or proprietary? Is there a complete inventory list of all software and hardware being used in the business? What 3rd parties are hosting applications and providing IT Services?"
- "Ask questions about client relationships that will remain, about product & market development, about other competitive advantages."

Expert Comments

"The world is becoming more computer and software dependent. Companies that address hardware, software, managed services, and data center storage are all poised to be in an industry that will experience vast growth into the future. Technology can get old very quickly, so companies must stay relevant."

"Overall the industry enjoys above average characteristics, but not necessarily the home-run characteristics of previous time periods. Overall the industry is trending up, but is more favorable to companies with modern methods of business. Older companies that continue to do business the way they did 5 years ago tend to suffer and see reduce valuation."

"Location makes very little difference. Novelty and future utility are the key growth factors."

"Historical profit trends are key. Also regarding the marketability is a factor if it has intellectual property value to sell."

Benchmark Data
- "Most important in the IT area would be sales growth trends"
- "Gross margin, utilization of consultants, percent recurring revenues"

Expenses as a percentage of annual sales

Cost of goods	05%
Payroll/labor Costs	75%
Occupancy	05% to 10%
Profit (estimated pretax)	15% to 20%

Industry Trend
- "Significant growth overall for hardware, software, services, and storage."
- "Managed Service Providers, SaaS, DaaS, and other fully hosted services and cloud-based services will continue to gain momentum. Old-line technology companies (break-fix, staffing, hardware support, etc.) will decline in popularity and valuation."
- "Budgets are still growing for IT. Sales revenue should grow."
- "Steady but moderate growth. Demand for Information Technology is ever increasing. Growing demand for additional storage and retrieval of data."

Seller Financing
- "While seller financing and earnout can be common, the industry tends to be a good fit for SBA 7(a) financing. This allows buyers to pay lower valuations in exchange for sellers receiving all cash at closing. When there is upside to be achieved or downside to mitigate, then revenue-based earnouts can be more effective here than other industries because fixed and variable expenses can often be more predictable."
- 3 years

Questions
- "Describe your streams of revenue and your contract lengths. Are your key salespeople operating with a non-compete agreement? Who has the primary contacts with your top 10 customers?"

- "Do you have contracts with your client companies? How many users are under contract? Is this hardware, software, etc...? How do your technical representatives work in your company? Where are they located? Do they have individual specialties? How are they paid? Who sells to the customers? Who takes care of client concerns? What do you use to back-up data? Where do you co-locate storage and back-up? Do you own all or part of a data center?"
- "Stability of staff, will owner(s) stay on for a reasonable period"
- "Why are they selling, revenue and earnings track record, size of customer's geographic footprint, who are their technology partners, etc...?"
- "Must have references and be able to demo product(s)"

Injection Molding

	NAICS 333249	

Rules of Thumb

➢ 4.5 to 6 times EBITDA

Inns (See also Bed & Breakfasts)

SIC 7011-02	NAICS 721110	

Rules of Thumb

➢ 8 times SDE including inventory

Pricing Tips

- "Firstly you should always know what your occupancy levels are, as well as ADR (Average Daily Rate) per room. Knowing these numbers will help you to stay focused on your budget, sales and marketing plans each year."
  Source: http://www.innconcierge.com/innkeeping-solutions/when-is-the-right-time-to-sell-your-inn/
- "The smaller the inn and lower the business income, the more the real value factor weighs heavy in the formula. The larger the inn and the higher the business income, the less weight this factor affects total value. Many of the larger inns have been selling in the 8 to 10 capitalization rate of net income, less any needed repairs, and up to a 20% discount if seller financing is not involved."
- "Must have private baths now. Operating expense can range from $3K to $10K per room depending on occupancy and size of building. Income is usually $5K to $20K per guest room depending on location (occupancy & room rate) and amenities."
- "Buyer should have a sense of good taste, common sense & hospitality ... cash flow is not great, it will mostly cover living expenses (mostly tax deductible) and there is real estate appreciation potential which you can retain tax free to the degree it is your primary residence. Future of business is excellent—has a great appeal to over-50, early-out, college-educated baby boomers; a lot of teachers. Buyer profile doesn't generalize to other typical businesses."

Benchmark Data

- "In the middle part of U.S., B&Bs are selling for $80K–$100K/guestroom on average. The popular East & West Coast locations could be up to twice that amount. The larger the inn, the less value/guestroom. Values and expenses vary greatly due to the non-standardized structure of the buildings and locale."
- "Operating expenses 40 to 50 percent"
- For additional benchmark information, see Bed and Breakfasts

Expenses as a percentage of annual sales

Cost of goods.. 15% (food, cleaning supplies & linens)
Payroll/labor Costs... 10% not including owner
Occupancy..07% to 10%
Profit (estimated pretax) 10%

Industry Trend

- "B&Bs primarily cater to affluent, baby boomer and millennial travelers. That market appears to be growing. This is also the market that the next generation of innkeepers is coming from."

Seller Financing

- "On inns that are < $700K, conventional commercial financing is available. Over $700K, the seller and the SBA is usually involved. Typically it's buyer 10%, seller 25% and lender 65%."
- "Most large inns are seller financed, typically with 20 percent down and terms @ 9 percent, 30-year amortization with a 7-year balloon."
- 5 to 10 years

Questions

- "Ask the broker/seller how their B&B will work for you w/the buyer's down payment."

Resources

Websites

- This is a Website offering inns for sale: www.bb-4-sale.com

Associations

- Professional Association of Innkeepers International: http://www.paii.com/
- Michigan Lake to Lake Bed and Breakfast Association: www.laketolake.com

Insurance Agencies/Brokerages		
SIC 6411-12	NAICS 524210	Number of Businesses/Units 428,675

Rules of Thumb

➢ 125 to 150 percent of annual sales includes inventory

➢ 150 to 200 percent of Commission Revenue

➢ 3 to 5 times SDE plus inventory

➢ 4 to 6 times EBIT

➢ 4 to 6 times EBITDA

Pricing Tips

- "Non-standard auto is approximately one times annual commissions. Standard agencies are currently selling for 2–2.25 annual commissions with increases for large agencies (more than $250,000 in annual commissions), desirable commercial policies and/or high-end homes."

- "The multiple increases the larger the insurance agency. Agencies with less than $1M in commissions have multiple ranging from 1.25 to 1.75 annual commissions. Once commissions reach over $1M they start selling for 2X until they get to $3M and any agency over that can sometimes go as high as 3X annual commissions."

- "Pricing as of the start of 2016 is well above the historical norm. Typical small agencies are selling for 2.0 times annualized commission revenue, with above average agencies selling for even more. Pricing for smaller agencies is usually based on a multiple of commissions, partially because the profitability of the book of business in the hands of the seller is much more relevant than its current profitability in the hands of the current owner."

- "There are really no Rules of Thumb. Each agency is so different; they each have their own valuations depending on many variables involved. Perhaps the average agency sells for 2x total revenues (without subtracting expenses), but 95% of agencies probably fall in the range of 1x to 3x revenues, depending on the quality of business, location and a number of other factors."

- "Although competition is high, there are significant barriers to entry. Personal expertise is essential, as is good sales ability. Gaining contracts from insurance companies (carriers) is essential, and difficult for someone starting an agency from scratch to do."

- "Don't confuse SDE with EBITDA with adjusted EBITDA. This is one of the biggest mistakes that I see made by other brokers. Many brokers also simply market an agency at 2 x revenue regardless of the quality of the book of business and available financing. There are many factors that can influence the market value such as the carriers, lines of business, client demographics and non-commission based income. Financing and deal terms are also critical to getting an agency sold and getting the highest price. Personal lines P&C agencies can be sold at fixed prices based on the low risk of a broad customer base. Commercial lines P&C and employee benefits agencies have larger accounts and are often structured with an earnout or retention-based payment on large accounts."

- "Niche agencies often receive higher value compared to main street agency."

- "Length of time in business, reputation, possible cross-selling opportunities in the future, etc."

- "Brand-name carriers, licensed personnel, revenue per client, revenue per employee, target accounts."

Expert Comments

"Sellers: clean books and records are your best friend."

"Because an agency's client base tends to stay with the agency in good times and in bad, the industry is less risky than most closely held businesses. Likewise, sale of independent agencies is easier than for most closely held businesses and demand for these agencies is high. It is currently a strong seller's market."

"Account retention by the buyer, post-sale, is critical. Sellers should be willing with account retention. Buyers should make sure the seller's employees are not likely to leave and compete with the new owner of the agency. If they do, account retention can suffer significantly."

"The insurance brokerage industry is very competitive, however there can be significant barriers of entry for new competition and the revenues are recurring."

"Existing brokers choose to grow their business by purchasing mature books of business from retiring brokers."

"Insurance agencies are generally very marketable. One reason is the ease with which one agency can often be consolidated with another."

"P&C personal lines independent agency competition is high due to direct writers Geico and Progressive, and profit margins continue to shrink due to carrier expense ratio pressures. Barriers to entry are relatively low if you buy into the industry, but high to start up a company from scratch due to appointment requirements by national carriers. Profitable and portable books of business are highly marketable at realistic multiples of EBITDA."

"Personal lines property/casualty premiums are increasing annually. Commercial lines property/casualty premiums are static or declining. Medical benefits premiums are increasing annually."

"Lot of competition in personal lines. Location is more important if the agency business is more personal lines. Commercial lines, location not much of a factor. What markets/contracts the agency has will limit them to the type of business the agency can focus on. Agencies are easy to sell to other agencies that want to expand. Larger insurance brokerages can absorb a book of business without much increase in overhead."

Benchmark Data

Statistics (Insurance Brokers and Agencies)

Number of Establishments	428,675
Average Profit Margin	12.3%
Revenue per Employee	$192,800
Average Number of Employees	1.8
Average Wages per Employee	$65,809

Products and Services Segmentation

Commercial P&C insurance	30.1%
Personal P&C insurance	27.6%
Health and medical insurance	14.4%
Other	12.2%
Life and accident insurance	9.4%
Annuities	5.0%
Insurance administration and risk consulting	1.3%

Major Market Segmentation

Businesses	65.6%
Individuals aged 45 to 54	7.1%
Individuals aged 35 to 44	6.7%
Individuals aged 65 and older	6.1%
Individuals aged 34 and younger	5.2%
Individuals aged 55 to 64	5.0%
Government	4.3%

Industry Costs

Profit	12.3%
Wages	34.2%
Purchases	1.9%
Depreciation	1.3%
Marketing	1.3%
Rent & Utilities	1.5%
Other	47.5%

Market Share

Aon Corporation	2.8%
Arthur J. Gallagher & Co.	2.7%
Marsh & McLennan Companies Inc.	2.6%
Willis Group Holdings	1.0%

Source: IBISWorld, August 2016

- "Above average agencies (top quartile) often put 25% of revenues on the bottom line, after adjusting for discretionary use of funds and reasonable owner's compensation. The best agencies often put around 40% of revenues on the bottom line. These agencies are highly sought after as acquisition targets. They usually have at least $5 million in annual revenues."

Expenses as a percentage of annual sales

Cost of goods	15%
Payroll/labor Costs	30% to 50%
Occupancy	05% to 12%
Profit (estimated pretax)	15% to 30%

Industry Trend

- "The Market is Softening
  Profit Margins Will Shrink
  National and Regional Brokers Aggressively Buying Independents
  Agency Value for Good to Great Firms Still High
  Internal Perpetuation is Difficult & Expensive
  Capital Gains and Ordinary Income Taxes May Go Higher
  Cluster Option for Smaller Agencies
  Producer Dilemma Continues"

Source: "8 Industry Trends to Exploit for 2016," by Catherine Oak, January 25, 2016,
http://www.insurancejournal.com/magazines/mindyourbiz/2016/01/25/395522.htm

- "Advanced analytics and customer centricity
  Digitization and portal development
  Cloud and software as a service
  Telematics and usage-based insurance
  Core modernization and innovation"

Source: "Here are 5 insurance tech trends you'll see this year,"
by Sreedhar Alavalapati and Krishna Prasad, January 18, 2016,
http://www.propertycasualty360.com/2016/01/18/here-are-5-insurance-tech-trends-youll-see-this-ye

- "As long as the stock market stays up, and the economy stays strong, these agencies will remain highly sought after acquisition targets. If the economy turns down, the seller's market may end, but they are likely to weather the storm better than the average small closely held business."
- "The current trend is the market continues to harden. This really began sometime in the second half of 2013. The past hard market was firmly in place

from about 2000 through 2003. Prior to this almost a whole generation had lived under soft market conditions! The current soft market has been in various lines in various regions for a number of years, since about 2007.

- "Managing the agency in a way that exploits these trends will lead the firm to success. With hard markets, there is a lot of work quoting for not a lot of reward in increased premiums and thus, commissions. In order to keep revenues up, agencies will still need to sell more – either cross sell or sell additional coverages to new customers. Value added services should be offered and a fee charged, to increase revenue."
- "The value of agencies is finally increasing because of today's improving economy and the ability to get credit lines from banks."
- "P&C—minimal growth; health—shrinking competition and revenues due to reduced compensation rates under PPAC (Obama's healthcare law)."
- "Standard agencies' revenue will improve as business revenue increases. Small standard agencies will be relegated to small business. Consolidation will continue with regional brokers acquiring strong local standard agencies."

Seller Financing

- "Cash is king. Outside financing is readily available."
- "Mostly both with the bank requiring the seller to have some 'skin in the game' of at least 10%."
- "There are about six or so specialty lenders who target this industry, and it's desirable to lenders."
- "Seller financing is very common when one independent agency buys another. If a national buyer is involved the upfront cash is often a large portion of the sale, with the balance in an earn-out. The earn-outs can be very hard to achieve in full."
- "Mostly a mix of the two with outside financing carrying the majority of the note."
- "Usually financed through Seller financing, however there are numerous cash buyers"
- "Most sales have some component of an earnout based on retained business (future commissions). May make it necessary for seller to stay on for a period of time after sale to increase likelihood business will stay with new ownership."

Questions

- "Is there any reason to expect carrier appointments not to transfer?"
- "Why is the agency for sale? Do your producers and other employees have employment contracts with some form of confidentiality and non-piracy provisions?"
- "What is your retention? How are your loss ratios? In your opinion, how likely is it that a new owner will be appointed by the carriers?"
- "Will you help with account retention post sale?"
- "Can I see your CSRP report? This is the agency report card."
- "Are you willing to remain with the business for 2 to 4 years?"
- "What insurance companies do you represent and what premium and loss ratio have you had with each for last 3 yrs.? Employees and date of hire? Persistency? Top 10 clients and commission revenue from each? Copies of all producer agreements? Cash or accrual basis tax payer? Itemized list of commission receivables and premium payables?"
- "What is the product mix? (personal lines, commercial lines, benefits, and general description of any specialization). 'S' vs. 'C' corp status. Have tax

issues been assessed? Will an asset sale generate tax issues for the seller? Are the employees subject to enforceable non-piracy agreements?"
- "Are you willing to do an earnout?"
- "Do your producers have vesting rights to their books of business?"
- "Size of book? Mix of book by product line? Expense ratio for agency? Loss ratio for P&C book? New business growth? Licenses held? Carrier appointments held? Written premium by carrier?"
- "Are your carriers A-rated?"
- "Copies of company's statements including production, loss ratios, possibility of transfer of appointments with insurance carriers, income taxes for last 3 years, how you get customers."

Resources

Websites
- Agency Equity: www.AgencyEquity.com
- Independent Insurance Agents and Brokers of America: www.independentagent.com
- Insurance Information Institute—lots of information and data: www.iii.org

Trade Publications
- American Agent and Broker: www.propertycasualty360.com/American-Agent-Broker
- Insurance Journal: www.insurancejournal.com/magazines

Associations
- American Association of Insurance Services: www.aaisonline.com
- Florida Association of Insurance Agents: www.faia.com
- Florida Association of Insurance Agents: www.faia.com
- Professional Insurance Agents: www.pia.org
- The Council of Insurance Agents and Brokers: www.ciab.com
- American Association of Insurance Management Consultants: www.aaimco.com

Insurance Companies (in general)

(See also Insurance Companies—Life, Property & Casualty)

	NAICS 524210	

Rules of Thumb
➢ 1 to 2 times capital and surplus

Pricing Tips
- "A couple of key metrics can be used to value insurance companies, and these metrics happen to be common to financial firms in general. These are price to book (P/B) and return on equity (ROE). P/B is a primary valuation measure that relates the insurance firm's stock price to its book value, either on a total firm value or a per-share amount. Book value, which is simply shareholders' equity, is a proxy for a firm's value should it cease to exist and be completely

liquidated. Price to tangible book value strips out goodwill and other intangible assets to give the investor a more accurate gauge on the net assets left over should the company close shop. A quick rule of thumb for insurance firms (and again, for financial stocks in general) is that they are worth buying at a P/B level of 1 and are on the pricey side at a P/B level of 2 or higher. For an insurance firm, book value is a solid measure of most of its balance sheet, which consists of bonds, stocks and other securities that can be relied on for their value given an active market for them."

Source: http://www.investopedia.com/articles/investing/082813/how-value-insurance-company.asp

- "A ton of information is required, beyond the company's financial statements and tax returns, such as reports submitted to the insurance department of the states the company does business in; actuarial reports on the adequacy of amounts in reserve to pay claims; rating of company by one or more insurers-rating organizations; status of any significant lawsuits pending against the company; its reputation in the industry; and its relationship with its sales force. Just getting an opinion as to value involves hundreds of hours of document review and analysis."

Resources

Trade Publications

- Insurance Networking News: www.insurancenetworking.com

Insurance Companies—Life (See also Insurance Agencies)	
NAICS 524210	Number of Businesses/Units 9,234

Rules of Thumb

➤ 1 to 2.5 times capital and surplus

Benchmark Data

Statistics (Life Insurance & Annuities)

Number of Establishments	9,234
Average Profit Margin	6.9%
Revenue per Employee	$2,552,700
Average Number of Employees	38.8
Average Wages per Employee	$101,975

Products and Services Segmentation

Variable deferred annuities	26.2%
Other	25.9%
Fixed rate deferred annuities	16.2%
Individual whole life premiums	10.1%
Group life premiums	6.2%
Individual term life premiums	6.0%
Individual universal life premiums	5.5%
Immediate annuities	3.9%

Major Market Segmentation

Individuals aged 45 to 54	23.5%
Individuals aged 35 to 44	22.2%
Individuals aged 65 and older	20.2%
Individuals aged 34 and younger	17.4%
Individuals aged 55 to 64	16.7%

Industry Costs

Profit	6.9%
Wages	4.0%
Purchases	61.5%
Depreciation	0.5%
Marketing	0.3%
Rent & Utilities	0.3%
Other	26.5%

Source: IBISWorld, June 2016

Insurance Companies—Property & Casualty

(See also Insurance Agencies)

	NAICS 524126	Number of Businesses/Units 14,814

Rules of Thumb

➢ ½ to 3 times capital and surplus

Benchmark Data

Statistics (Property, Casualty and Direct Insurance)

Number of Establishments	14,814
Average Profit Margin	13.1%
Revenue per Employee	$1,022,700
Average Number of Employees	40.6
Average Wages per Employee	$90,083

Products and Services Segmentation

Private passenger auto	36.3%
Other	17.2%
Homeowners multiple peril	15.1%
Other liability	8.7%
Workers compensation	8.5%
Commercial multiple peril	6.9%
Commercial auto	5.0%
Fire	2.3%

Major Market Segmentation

Other commercial market	42.3%
Private vehicle market	36.3%
Other private market	13.9%
Commercial vehicle market	5.0%
Other insurance carriers	2.5%

27th Edition

403

Industry Costs

Profit	13.1%
Wages	8.8%
Purchases	1.8%
Depreciation	1.2%
Marketing	1.3%
Rent & Utilities	1.4%
Other	72.4%

Market Share

State Farm Mutual Automobile Insurance Company	13.3%
Allstate Insurance Company	5.5%
Liberty Mutual Group Inc.	4.9%
The Travelers Companies Inc.	4.5%

Source: IBISWorld, April 2016

Questions

- "What is their stockholders' equity? What management do they have? What is their marketing ability?"

Internet Related Businesses

Rules of Thumb

➢ "Right now it's 2 times SDE maximum or asset liquidation value. ISP's are being sold for 3–6 times monthly gross sales."

➢ 80% of Annual Gross Sales

Pricing Tips

- "The market is growing, not only in terms of deals closed but demand from buyers. We are seeing around 10 buyers for every seller as a ratio. If you look at the total deals closed trends you can see that total deals closed went from $53 million to $112 million in 4 years. That is over a 100% increase. Our predictions, for 2016, is we will see another growth year again. As of writing this post we have 5 businesses listed and another 5 in the pipeline."
  Source: http://www.digitalexits.com/whats-your-online-business-worth/
- "It depends on if there is any profit. If there is, about 2 times SDE."
- "An important consideration during your search is the pricing of a potential web investment. According to Justin Gilchrist, a Manchester, England-based industry consultant and founder of FlipFilter.com, a website sales analysis tool, website buyers are typically paying between 12 and 24 months' revenue. You can usually expect to pay between $100,000 and $200,000 for an online business that is generating $100,000 in annual revenue."
  Source: http://www.entrepreneur.com/article/22342
- "Drop ship companies are worth more than one which requires inventory. Internet companies can sell for between 20% of sales and 50% of sales depending on how hands on the business is, if there is inventory or not, and what the growth potential is. "
- "Market values on Internet-based business vary based on so many different points; every deal is different."
- "Internet-based companies are currently trading at: 2.3–3.8 X the true net income of that company. Example: Business ABC has a net income of $100k/

year. That company would trade for somewhere in the ballpark of $230k–$380k, assuming there is no inventory included. Now remember each deal is different!"

Expert Comments

"When buying an Internet company, be sure to include enough training to understand the website and to maintain the SEO and ranking. Many buyers assume that websites are a cash cow, then they fail to maintain the website and the business begins to decline."

"A good Internet company with excellent SEO is hard to duplicate, as achieving high rankings and organic traffic in search engines can take years to develop."

Benchmark Data
- "Average gross margin is 20% of sales. Sales per square foot is difficult, as some drop-ship internet companies operate out of a very small commercial space or even a home office."

Industry Trend
- "There is a strong growth pattern as more and more people are using the internet."
- "The Internet is growing ever-so-fast! The trend over the few years is clearly on an upswing! Every single company/business out there needs an Internet presence, and if you don't have one, you're missing out on a major market share of your industry."

Seller Financing
- "Very short—2 to 4 years"
- "These business generally close with little or no bank financing. Most times, it is an all cash deal or 75% cash with 35% seller financing."
- "Currently the Internet Merger & Acquisitions space is an either all cash business or with a little seller financing thrown into the mix! Traditional banks are not at the point yet where they can evaluate how to protect their asset (the domain and its content). Unless you have free and clear real estate to put up as collateral, you're not getting a bank loan on an Internet company."

Questions
- "A buyer should ask to verify sales by using the credit card merchant account, as all online transactions are paid by credit card. Also, a buyer should ask if there is any product-specific knowledge needed to sell the product."

Investigative Services (See also Guard Services, Security Services/Systems)		
	NAICS 561611	

Rules of Thumb
➢ 70 to 75 percent of annual sales

Benchmark Data
- For Benchmark Data see Security Services/Systems

Investment Advice		
	NAICS 523930	Number of Businesses/Units 116,628

Rules of Thumb

➤ 1.5 times SDE

➤ 1 times annual sales

Pricing Tips

- "Contract persistency is critical to the continuation of fees. The demographics of the clientele base should be carefully analyzed. The range of valuation multiples is very wide and varies by the type of revenue stream and how it's paid. The numbers above are considered to be averages. Regulation violations by the owner can severely reduce the sales price."

Expert Comments

"Industry consolidation and company marketing efficiencies are promoting the move away from commissioned sales force."

Benchmark Data

Statistics (Financial Planning and Advice)

Number of Establishments	116,628
Average Profit Margin	22.5%
Revenue per Employee	$248,800
Average Number of Employees	1.7
Average Wages per Employee	$79,049

Products and Services Segmentation

Personal financial planning and advice	33.3%
Personal investment management	29.7%
Business and government financial planning and management	20.8%
Other Services	16.2%

Major Market Segmentation

Individuals and households	42.9%
Businesses	27.7%
Other clients	15.8%
Governments	13.6%

Industry Costs

Profit	22.5%
Wages	32.1%
Purchases	4.8%
Depreciation	1.2%
Marketing	1.7%
Rent & Utilities	2.8%
Other	34.9%

ADVERTISEMENTS

27th Edition

You're holding the essential guide to pricing businesses.

Now join the essential organization for business valuation and forensic accounting professionals.

AICPA®

Forensic and Valuation Services Section

We provide members with technical guidance, tools, checklists and education, in one convenient location.

Find out more at aicpa.org/FVS.

Copyright © 2014 American Institute of CPAs. 16286-326

27th Edition

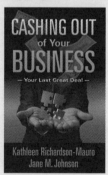

27th Edition

Market Share

Morgan Stanley Wealth Management... 17.9%
Wells Fargo & Company 13.7%
Bank of America Corporation 13.4%
Ameriprise Financial Inc. 4.9%

Source: IBISWorld, June 2016

	Franchise

Jani-King (See also Coverall, Franchises, Janitorial Services)

Approx. Total Investment		$8,170 to $74,000
	NAICS 561720	Number of Businesses/Units 11,000

Rules of Thumb

➤ 25 to 30 percent of annual sales plus inventory

Resources

Websites

▪ www.janiking.com

Janitorial Services (See also Coverall, Jani-King, Maid Services)

SIC 7439-02	NAICS 561720	Number of Businesses/Units 932,155

Rules of Thumb

➤ 45 to 50 percent of annual sales plus inventory

➤ 1.5 times SDE plus inventory

➤ 1 times one month's billings; plus fixtures, equipment and inventory

➤ 4 times monthly billings; includes fixtures, equipment and inventory

Pricing Tips

▪ "Basically, estimating value starts with adding up net annual sales and subtracting operating expenses to arrive at your annual operating profit. This number is then used to calculate how much the business is worth based on its future profit potential and by using a multiplier to arrive at an estimated value. The multiplier is based on the risk in the cleaning industry in general as well as in your business in particular, such as the number of long-term cleaning contracts."

Source: http://smallbusiness.chron.com/sell-janitorial-business-73876.html

▪ "1.5 to 1.75 times SDE including a working inventory for commercial janitorial service companies. 1.25 to 1.60 times SDE including a working inventory for maid service/residential businesses. Commercial companies with Gross Sales in excess of $3 million–$20 million could fetch a 3-6 time multiple of SDE. Companies with long terms (3-5+ years) client contracts have more weight. Fully staffed with supervision in place has more weight. Government contracts offer nice security for buyers but are difficult to transfer. Minority owned businesses carry less weight if client contracts are based on such ownership.

W-2 Employees carry more weight than 1099's. Quality of books and records are important."

- "Janitorial (Contract Cleaners)—1.5 times net, depending upon the amount of hired help. An industry evaluation is 3 to 5 times the monthly gross depending upon the equipment and the type of accounts; e.g., government vs. private . . . a very conservative approach which could vary widely on a monthly basis. Government contracts could offer more start-up security for a prospective purchaser."

Benchmark Data

Statistics (Janitorial Services)

Number of Establishments	932,155
Average Profit Margin	5.6%
Revenue per Employee	$28,780
Average Number of Employees	2.0
Average Wages per Employee	$14,255

Products and Services Segmentation

Standard commercial cleaning	59.1%
Other	20.3%
Residential cleaning	10.4%
Damage restoration cleaning	4.9%
Floor care services	3.0%
Exterior window cleaning	2.3%

Major Market Segmentation

Offices	32.9%
Educational facilities	22.5%
Retail complexes	12.3%
Residences	10.4%
Government	10.8%
Industrial plants	6.0%
Healthcare facilities	5.1%

Industry Costs

Profit	5.6%
Wages	49.3%
Purchases	19.1%
Depreciation	0.5%
Marketing	1.2%
Rent & Utilities	3.4%
Other	20.9%

Market Share

ABM Industries Inc.	5.3%

Source: IBISWorld, August 2016

Expenses as a percentage of annual sales

Cost of goods	03%
Payroll/labor Costs	45%
Occupancy	07%
Profit (estimated pretax)	40%

Industry Trend
- "The Janitorial Services industry will encounter promising conditions over the five years to 2020, due to an expected upswing that will be caused by the recovering economy. Operators will consequently benefit from the anticipated recovery in nonresidential construction and other industries that outsource cleaning activities. In particular, the education, health and medical industries, which outsource the majority of their cleaning requirements, will provide sustained growth for the industry."

  Source: http://clients1.ibisworld.com/reports/us/industry/industryoutlook.aspx?entid=1496

Seller Financing
- "SBA and private equity group financing is certainly an option. Most small units are sold with at least 80–90% cash down."

Resources
Trade Publications
- C M Cleaning & Maintenance Management—informative site based on the magazine: www.cmmonline.com

Associations
- International Sanitary Supply Association: www.issa.com
- Building Service Contractors Association International: www.bscai.org

	Franchise
Jersey Mike's Subs (See also Franchises, Sandwich Shops)	
Approx. Total Investment	$203,991 to $680,827
Estimated Annual Sales/Unit	$700,000
SIC 5812-19 NAICS 722513	Number of Businesses/Units 1020

Rules of Thumb
➢ 50 percent of annual sales plus inventory

Benchmark Data
- For Benchmark Data see Sandwich Shops

Resources
Websites
- www.jerseymikes.com

Jewelry Stores	
SIC 5944-09 NAICS 448310	Number of Businesses/Units 64,724

Rules of Thumb
➢ 4 to 6 times EBIT if inventory included
➢ None—too inventory intensive

Pricing Tips

- "What return on assets would be expected if current owner left city?"
- "A destination upscale jeweler has a much better 'chance' of being sold as a going business."
- "Highly capital intensive—inventory on hand most critical in pricing"
- "Price is based on amount of inventory, current value, years in business, and profit of operations now and after sale is completed."

Benchmark Data

Statistics (Jewelry Stores)

Number of Establishments	64,724
Average Profit Margin	6.8%
Revenue per Employee	$190,600
Average Number of Employees	2.7
Average Wages per Employee	$26,319

Products and Services Segmentation

Diamond Jewelry	42.0%
Other merchandise	20.7%
Watches	15.1%
Gold jewelry	9.6%
Pearl and other gemstone jewelry	8.1%
Loose gemstones, including diamonds and colored gemstones	4.5%

Industry Costs

Profit	6.8%
Wages	13.6%
Purchases	59.8%
Depreciation	0.8%
Marketing	2.9%
Rent & Utilities	8.8%
Other	7.3%

Market Share

Signet Jewelers Ltd.	17.1%
Tiffany & Co.	5.1%

Source: IBISWorld, April 2016

Expenses as a percentage of annual sales

Cost of goods	55% to 58%
Payroll/labor Costs	22%
Occupancy	n/a
Profit (estimated pretax)	06%

Industry Trend

- "The high-earners of the millennial generation will have a big impact on the fine jewelry market this year, according to YouGov's Affluent Perspective Global Study. The study is based on insights from 5,196 affluent respondents across 12 countries.

  "In the United States, respondents were divided into three categories: the base affluent ($150,000 to $199,000 in household income), middle affluent

($200,000 to $349,000) and upper affluent ($350,000 and over). Overall, the study found that fine jewelry purchases are expected to decrease 11 percent to $14.4 billion this year, while watch purchases are predicted to decrease by more than 3 percent to a market value of $6.7 billion in 2016.

"While spending on jewelry and watches is expected to drop, affluent millennials are expected to really step up their spending this year. According to the study, the generation's purchasing of fine jewelry could increase by as much as 22 percent in 2016, while spending on watches could rise by 10 percent."

Source: "Affluent Millennials Expected to Spend More on Fine Jewelry," by Brecken Branstrator, May 11, 2016, http://www.nationaljeweler.com/independents/retail-surveys/4228-affluent-millennials-expected-to-spend-more-on-fine-jewelry

Seller Financing
- "Not seller financed—inventory too portable—high risk"
- 3 years

Resources

Websites
- National Jeweler: www.nationaljeweler.com

Trade Publications
- Instoremagazine: www.instoremag.com

Associations
- Jewelers of America (JA): www.jewelers.org

Franchise

Jiffy Lube International
(See also Auto Lube/Tune-up, Other Lube Franchises)

Approx. Total Investment		$220,000 to $450,000
	NAICS 811191	Number of Businesses/Units 1,915

Rules of Thumb
➢ 45 to 50 percent of annual sales plus inventory

Resources

Websites
- www.jiffylube.com

Franchise

Jimmy John's Gourmet Sandwiches
(See also Franchises, Sandwich Shops)

Approx. Total Investment		$330,500 to $519,500
Estimated Annual Sales/Unit		$1,300,000
SIC 5812-19	NAICS 722513	Number of Businesses/Units 1,918

Rules of Thumb

➢ 65 to 70 percent of annual sales plus inventory

Benchmark Data

- For Benchmark Data see Sandwich Shops

Job Shops/Contract Manufacturing (See also Machine Shops)		
	NAICS 332710	

Rules of Thumb

➢ 1.5 to 2 times SDE plus inventory

➢ 3 to 5 times EBIT

➢ 4 to 5 times EBITDA

Pricing Tips

- "Customer concentration is an issue for most job shops and contract manufacturers. A customer over 30% or two customers over 50% is a major problem."
- "4 x EBITDA is just a rule of thumb. A range of 3 x to 8 x is realistic depending a range of factors (history, custom concentration, future prospects, etc."
- "Best rule of thumb in this industry to use as a barometer is FMV of FFE&M plus 1X EBITDA."
- "Job shops with full range of capabilities (turning, milling, grinding, stamping, etc.) are more desirable."

Expert Comments

"While some people consider ease of replication is easy they are wrong, wrong, wrong. The business might be easy to start but very difficult to get big-name customers until the company has established a track record."

"Competition is high and the key to gross profit margins is using technology to be low-cost manufacturer."

"Recent influx of orders from OEM's has contributed to better backlog. Receivable aging improving and more shops able to get 33%–50% deposits. Not as much used equipment in the field as prior years. Competitive edge goes to automated shops with palletized tool changing machining centers, wire EDM, etc."

"In some cases, the machinery & equipment has a higher value than the business."

Benchmark Data

- For additional Benchmark Data see Machine Shops
- "Revenues per man-hour can be all over the place because newer, numerical controlled machines are much more productive. The higher the revenues per man-hour the 'better' the business."
- "Most modern shops set up to have one employee service two machines."
- "Determine unused capacity. Buyers will want to determine potential without major capital investment."

Expenses as a percentage of annual sales

Cost of goods...40% to 50%
Payroll/labor Costs...25% to 28%
Occupancy...03% to 05%
Profit (estimated pretax) 12%

Industry Trend

- "Custom fabricators need to juggle highly variable demand cycles from myriad customers, and to do that they need capacity. Judging by the 2015 Capital Spending Forecast, they're building that capacity with more equipment. Projected capital spending growth has slowed from the dramatic rebound seen postrecession—2015 projections are up only 3.5 percent over 2014—but the spending has shifted.

Projected Operating Level by Plant Size

Employees	Higher	Lower	Same as 2014
1–19	59.8%	7.0%	33.2%
20–49	61.2%	3.1%	35.7%
50–99	68.0%	0.8%	31.2%
100–249	71.4%	6.7%	21.9%
250–499	65.3%	6.1%	28.6%
500–999	71.4%	3.6%	25.0%
1,000+	64.3%	14.3%	21.4%
Average	64.5%	5.2%	30.4%
2014 Average	57.1%	5.9%	37.0%
2013 Average	60.5%	7.0%	32.5%"

Source: "2015 metal fabrication forecast: Steady as she grows" by Tim Heston 12/8/2014
www.thefabricator.com/article/shopmanagement/2015-metal-fabrication-forecast-steady-as-she-grows-article
(A bit dated, but still of interest)

Seller Financing

- "Most deals to have some seller financing, usually 3 to 5 years at an interest rate between CD rates and bank loan rates. Our current experiences are interest rates in the 3% to 4% range."

Questions

- "Find out the seller's motivation. Could be issues related to hiring skilled machinists or constant battles with customers paying on time."
- "Discuss the outlook for the company. What opportunities exist for the buyer and why the seller isn't pursuing them."
- "Backlog, WIP, age, qualifications & tenure of staff, condition of equipment (look at line items for R&M closely to avoid machinery held together with band aids), need for CAPEX near and mid-term, etc.?"
- "Will the business be sustainable when owner leaves? Any known environmental issues?"

Resources

Trade Publications

- Design2Part Buyers Guide: www.D2PBuyersGuide.com

John Deere Dealerships

Pricing Tips
- "Rules of Thumb are totally inappropriate. If DOT then dealership has future but if not DOT, the days are numbered and must be acquired by an adjoining dealership. Market share is huge to JD and rebates reducing to those not DOT or not achieving market share objectives. Need 40% equity so forget about high leverage deals. Be careful and look at aging of inventory and losses hidden in leases and conditional sales contracts—dealers are exposed.
- "DOT is the term used for their Dealer of Tomorrow standards. The goal is to deal with $50 million plus dealers only. They no longer want 'Joe' who is a good salesman to be a dealer. They want organizations with sufficient size that they can afford to employ a full management team—general manager, controller/VP-Finance, sales manager, parts manager, and aftermarket manager. At $50 million, you can afford most of these people and at $100 million, you can afford better people and real economies of scale set in."

		Franchise
Johnny Rockets (See also Franchises)		
Approx. Total Investment		$539,525 to $975,575
Estimated Annual Sales/Unit		$1 million plus
	NAICS 722513	Number of Businesses/Units 337

Rules of Thumb
➢ 70 to 75 percent of annual sales plus inventory

Resources

Websites
- www.johnnyrockets.com

		Franchise
Jon Smith Subs (See also Franchises, Sandwich Shops)		
	NAICS 722513	Number of Businesses/Units 8

Rules of Thumb
➢ 20 percent of annual sales plus inventory

		Franchise
Juice It Up (See also Franchises)		
Approx. Total Investment		$152,144 to $377,821
	NAICS 722515	Number of Businesses/Units 83

Rules of Thumb
➢ 20 to 25 percent of annual sales plus inventory

Resources

Websites

www.juiceitup.com

	Franchise
KFC (Kentucky Fried Chicken) (See also Franchises)	
Approx. Total Investment	$1,300,000 to $2,500,000
Estimated Annual Sales/Unit	$950,000

	NAICS 722513	Number of Businesses/Units 4,199

Rules of Thumb

➢ 30 to 35 percent of annual sales plus inventory

	Franchise
Kumon Math & Reading Centers (See also Children's Educational Franchises, Schools—Educational/Non-Vocational)	
Approx. Total Investment	$64,187 to $134,000

	NAICS 611691	Number of Businesses/Units 2,123

Rules of Thumb

➢ 80 to 90 percent of annual sales plus inventory

Pricing Tips

- " ... franchisees say you have to have at least 200 [students] to make a center go."

  Source: "Branding Brawl" by Beth Ewen, *Franchise Times*, March 2013

Benchmark Data

- "By the Numbers:
  Change at Kumon North America centers since 2008
  Average selling price of existing center, to $106,000 from $86,000—up 24%
  Average enrollment, to 174 students from 145—up 20%
  Number of centers, to 1,514 from 1,305—up 16%"
- "They're requiring centers to locate in retail locations, not the church basements or community centers where they might have operated before. They are requiring operators to spend $600 per quarter on local marketing, and opening five days a week and eight hours a day, not the few part-time hours that centers used to do."

  Source: "Branding Brawl" by Beth Ewen, *Franchise Times*, March 2013 (Dated, but still of interest)

Industry Trend

- "Kumon, the world's largest after-school math and reading franchisor, has once again proven itself as a leader in the franchise industry. For the 14th consecutive year, Kumon has been ranked as the number one tutoring franchise in Entrepreneur magazine's annual Franchise 500 issue. The company, which has more than 375,000 students currently enrolled nationwide, has plans for continued growth throughout the United States, Canada, and Mexico in 2015."

Source: "Entrepreneur Magazine Ranks Kumon No. 1 Education Franchise for 14th Consecutive Year"

	Franchise
Kwik Kopy Business Center (See also Franchises, Quick Printing)	
Approx. Total Investment	$219,578 to $248,626
NAICS 323111	Number of Businesses/Units 18

Rules of Thumb

➢ 50 to 60 percent of annual sales plus inventory

	Franchise
Lady of America (See also Fitness Centers, Franchises)	
Approx. Total Investment	$9,250
NAICS 713940	Number of Businesses/Units 500

Rules of Thumb

➢ 45 to 50 percent of annual sales plus inventory

Resources

Websites
- www.loafitnessforwomen.com

Landscaping Services (See also Lawn Maintenance & Service)		
SIC 0782-04	NAICS 561730	Number of Businesses/Units 507,373

Rules of Thumb

➢ 45 to 50 percent of annual revenues plus inventory

➢ 1.5 times SDE; plus fixtures and equipment (except vehicles) & inventory

➢ 2 to 4 times EBITDA (may be higher for larger firms)

Pricing Tips

- "Multiples of EBITDA range from 2 to 6 depending on size, profitability and industry segment."
- "Landscape contractors need substantial capital investments for equipment. Startup costs of $100,000 are needed to compete in this industry. 'It's a difficult field unless you're a really large company' said Crabtree, who has been in the industry for over 15 years. Profit margins are typically 5%."

Source: www.urbanforest.org

Expert Comments

"Competition is fierce and ease of replication is as easy as owning a lawnmower and weed whacker. Much better once the company reaches several million in sales."

"Set yourself apart from the competition. Get long-term contracts. Focus on maintenance."

Benchmark Data

Statistics (Landscaping Services)

Number of Establishments	507,373
Average Profit Margin	7.3%
Revenue per Employee	$81,236
Average Number of Employees	1.9
Average Wages per Employee	$32,575

Products and Services Segmentation

Maintenance and general services-commercial	51.0%
Maintenance and general services-residential	31.0%
Design-build-installation services	13.8%
Arborist services and other services	4.2%

Major Market Segmentation

Residential markets	47.3%
Commercial markets	44.0%
Non-profit organizations and other	2.4%
Government and institutional markets	6.3%

Industry Costs

Profit	7.3%
Wages	40.2%
Purchases	42.0%
Depreciation	3.0%
Marketing	0.9%
Rent & Utilities	3.3%
Other	3.3%

Source: IBISWorld, July 2016

Expenses as a percentage of annual sales

Cost of goods	50%
Payroll/labor Costs	30%
Occupancy	05%
Profit (estimated pretax)	10% to 15%

Industry Trend

- "Labor Crisis Continues for Landscapers
  More Recruitment and Retention Programs for Landscapers
  Landscaping Businesses are going Mobile
  Landscapers Using Social Networks as a Business Tool

The Economy and Landscape Prices Continue to Correlate
A New Generation of Owners for Landscaping
Customer Experience at the Forefront for Landscape Contractors"

Source: "Landscaping Trends for 2016,"
https://getjobber.com/academy/resources/landscape-trends-of-2016/

- "In the coming five years, demand from residential and nonresidential construction markets will continue growing due to an increasing number of clients in need of landscape maintenance and installation. The number of housing starts and per capita disposable income are both expected to experience growth in five years to 2021, benefiting demand for industry services. However, IBISWorld expects the pricing structures that emerged in the years following the recession, including homeowners negotiating service contracts, operators offering free estimates and persistent (though lessening) price competition overall, to continue over the next five years. As a result, average industry profit margins, measured as earnings before interest and taxes, are forecast to remain stable at 6.9% in 2021, despite increasing demand for industry products."

Source: http://clients1.ibisworld.com/reports/us/industry/industryoutlook.aspx?entid=1497

- "Although tempered by the recent economic recession, and subsequent decline in consumer spending, residential housing and construction activity, the landscaping services market in the US is expected to recover and reach $80.06 billion by 2015.

  "The need to beautify commercial/residential property as a place for relaxation, entertainment or work, has long nourished the interest in landscaping. The worth added to the value of property by decorative structures, ponds, patios, and green-winding pathways too cannot be undermined. Keeping in view the growing popularity and importance of landscaping as an art, science, and commercial value proposition, it is of little surprise that landscaping services has now become one of the most important domains in the overall services industry."

Source: "2015: Landscaping Market to Hit $80 Billion,"
http://www.landscapeonline.com/research/article/13520

Seller Financing

- "Generally difficult to finance because of lack of assets."

Questions

- "Does the company have contracts with its clients? Are all employees legal? How many customers are built on relationships with the seller, and what will happen to them if he sells?"

Resources

Trade Publications

- Lawn and Landscape: www.lawnandlandscape.com
- Turf Magazine: www.turfmagazine.com
- Landscape Management: www.landscapemanagement.net

Associations

- National Association of Landscape Professionals: www.landscapeprofessionals.org
- Association of Professional Landscape Designers: www.apld.org

Land Surveying Services

SIC 8713-01	NAICS 541370	Number of Businesses/Units 18,805

Rules of Thumb

➤ 40 to 80 percent of annual fee revenues; plus fixtures, equipment and inventory; may require earnout

Benchmark Data

Statistics (Surveying and Mapping Services)

Number of Establishments... 18,505
Average Profit Margin 6.9%
Revenue per Employee $132,300
Average Number of Employees.. 3.2
Average Wages per Employee $51,282

Products and Services Segmentation

Property line, boundary and cadastral surveying................................ 24.8%
Topographical and planimetric surveying and mapping...................... 18.0%
Geospatial processing services 17.5%
Construction surveying 16.6%
Other services.. 13.2%
Enginerring services 4.6%
Subdivision layour and design services... 3.8%
Geophysical processing services 1.5%

Major Market Segmentation

Land subdivision and development firms.. 24.6%
Construction firms.. 22.6%
Professional technical firms 18.5%
Federal government departments and agencies 13.7%
Encrgy, utility and mining companies.. 12.3%
City, county and state surveying offices... 6.8%
Nonprofit firms 1.5%

Industry Costs

Profit 6.9%
Wages.. 39.1%
Purchases.. 19.6%
Depreciation... 3.3%
Marketing 0.6%
Rent & Utilities 3.1%
Other.. 27.4%

Source: IBISWorld, December 2015

Industry Trend

▪ "Overall employment of surveyors, cartographers, photogrammetrists, and surveying technicians is expected to grow much faster than the average for all occupations through the year 2016. The extensive availability and use of sophisticated technologies, such as remote sensing and GPS, will continue to increase the precision and productivity of these workers. Opportunities for surveyors, cartographers, and photogrammetrists should remain concentrated in engineering, surveying, mapping, building inspection, and drafting services firms."

Source: "Latest trends in the Economic Outlook for Land Surveyors," www.landsurveyor4hire.com

- "The executive director of the National Society of Professional Surveyors (NSPS) told members of a Congressional subcommittee that the U.S. Department of Labor's recent decision to categorize survey crew members as 'laborers and mechanics' was 'detrimental to the surveying profession,' and requested Congress' help in reversing DOL's decision."

Source: "Press Release from the National Society of Professional Surveyors concerning the Davis-Bacon Act," www.amerisurv.com, June 19, 2013

Resources

Trade Publications
- Professional Surveyor magazine: www.profsurv.com

Associations
- The National Society of Professional Surveyors: http://www.nsps.us.com/

	Franchise
Laptop Xchange (See also Computer Stores)	
Approx. Total Investment	$183,750 to $267,800
NAICS 443142	Number of Businesses/Units 20

Rules of Thumb
➢ 80 to 85 percent of annual sales plus inventory

Resources

Websites
- www.laptopxchange.com

Law Firms		
SIC 8111-03	NAICS 541110	Number of Businesses/Units 453,207

Rules of Thumb
➢ 90 to 100 percent of annual fee revenue; firms specializing in estate work would approach 100 percent; may require earnout.

➢ 4 times SDE includes inventory

➢ 3.5 times EBIT

➢ 3.5 times EBITDA

Pricing Tips
- "Many considerations go into a valuation. Even if you have a standardized multiple—which does not exist—the end results won't be the same. The

multiples I use by way of a shortcut valuation are .5 to three times the average annual gross revenue. That gives me a starting point. Then many factors comes into play, like the geography and history of the practice, the longevity of the earnings cycle, and whether the practice is ascending or descending in gross revenue. The final number will be based on the experience of the evaluator."

Source: http://www.lawpracticetoday.org/article/selling-your-practice/

"Valuing law practices vary widely depending on practice area, geographic location, systems and other key value drives. Transition plan is a key factor in the value of the practice."

- "A lot will depend upon the consultants, and how loyal they are to the firm."
- "Whether the multiplier is in the lower or the higher level of the range depends primarily on how much repeat business is expected, the nature of the law practice, the number of clients and the transferability of client relationships. If there is a great deal of repeat business and client loyalty that can be transferred, the multiplier will be higher. In the sale of a law practice, a portion of the clients will not stay with the practice by reason of the close personal relationship usually developed between client and attorney. This must be considered when determining the multiplier. The multiplier may then be raised or lowered depending on the stability of the flow of future revenue expected."

Source: "Valuing Professional Practices and Licenses"

Expert Comments

"Practices vary greatly depending on practice area, attorney and overall firm setup. Some fields would be on higher end of scale and some on lower."

"It is difficult to replicate, as the good businesses have reputations built over many years."

Benchmark Data

Statistics (Law Firms)

Number of Establishments	453,207
Average Profit Margin	19.1%
Revenue per Employee	$203,200
Average Number of employees	3.0
Average Wages per Employee	$77,302

Products and Services Segmentation

Commercial law services	43.6%
Other services	26.0%
Criminal law, civil negligence and personal injury	16.9%
Real estate law	8.1%
Labor and employment	5.4%

Major Market Segmentation

Business and corporate clients	66.1%
Households	29.1%
Government and not-for-profit clients	4.8%

Industry Costs

Profit	19.1%
Wages	38.1%
Purchases	1.8%
Depreciation	0.7%
Marketing	1.6%
Rent & Utilities	8.0%
Other	30.7%

Source: IBISWorld, March 2016

Expenses as a percentage of annual sales

Cost of goods	0
Payroll/labor Costs	0
Occupancy	0
Profit (estimated pretax)	30%

Industry Trend

- "The focus will shift to social media conversion.

  Law firms of all sizes will place a high importance on SEO (Search Engine Optimization).

  Microsites will become the preferred thought leadership platforms for practice and industry groups.

  Mobile will completely dominate desktop.

  Intelligent content will replace content marketing as the new content trend.

  Firms will focus on measuring ROI and actionable insight from their digital efforts.

  Multichannel marketing will become the key to a firm's marketing strategy.

  True marketing automation will emerge."

  Source: "The Top 8 Digital Marketing Trends for Law Firms in 2016," by Guy Alvarez, January 19, 2016, https://good2bsocial.com/the-top-8-digital-marketing-trends-for-law-firms-in-2016/

- "More consolidation and price competition for smaller practices. Attorneys looking to expand geographically, implement systems and software and become advisors as compared to transactions. As well, attorneys typically will work longer into retirement than other professionals and so many of the retirement age attorneys have delayed or have not planned for exit along with similar aged business owners."

- "Consistent with past practices, firms continued to raise their rates in 2014, albeit at a fairly modest level of 3.1 percent. And, also consistent with past experience, clients continued to push back, keeping strong pressure on firm realization rates. Over this ten-year period (2005 through November 2014), firms increased their standard rates by 35.9 percent from an average of $348 per hour to $473 (or an average increase of about 3.6 percent per year). At the same time, reflecting mounting client push back to these rate hikes, the collected rates achieved by law firms increased by a somewhat more modest 28.2 percent over the ten-year period, from an average of $304 per hour to $390 (or an average increase of about 2.8 percent per year). While the market for law for law firm services has clearly been impacted by external factors, there has also been an important shift in the internal dynamics of the market that has become increasingly apparent in recent years. Specifically, there is now strong evidence that the U.S. legal market has segmented into discernible categories of highly successful and less successful firms, and that the performance gaps between those categories has been steadily widening."

  Source: http://www.law.georgetown.edu/academics/centers-institutes/legal-profession/upload/FINAL-Report-1-7-15.pdf

Seller Financing

- "A mix, but mostly seller financing with small to medium practices. Max 50% down on practices with remaining being earnout or financed by seller."

Questions

- "Transition timeline. Claims history. Repeat clients. Systems. Key personnel. Key clients and ability to transition."
- "What is their backlog? Customer concentration?"

Lawn Maintenance & Service (See also Landscaping Services)		
SIC 0782-06	NAICS 561730	

Rules of Thumb

➤ 50 to 60 percent of annual sales plus inventory

➤ 2 to 2.75 times SDE plus inventory

➤ 1.7 to 3 times EBIT

➤ 2 to 4 times EBITDA

Pricing Tips

- "Multiples vary based on several factors, with the most important being the percentage of recurring revenues. Lawn care (fertilization & weed control companies) and landscape maintenance companies receive higher multiples than construction-oriented businesses. Larger companies (lawn care companies with revenues in excess of $1 million and maintenance companies with revenues in excess of $2.5 million tend to get higher multiples. Companies with EBITDA margins in line with industry benchmarks will usually get a higher multiple."
- "The age and condition of the fleet of vehicles and equipment used in the business may negatively impact the valuation if a buyer would expect to need a high level of capital expenditures."
- "Companies with a larger working capital requirement (more money tied up in accounts receivable) may receive a lower valuation."
- "Install/enhancement revenue does count...it is repetitive in nature."
- "Pre-billing or post-billing of clients....pre bill is more valuable."
- "Depending on size, 2–4 times EBITDA for large company, could be higher"
- "The baseline multiple of SDE for commercial landscape maintenance businesses is typically between 2.5 and 3 plus inventory. The range of the multiple depends on the customer concentration, type of customer, quality of equipment and management in place. Landscape construction and residential landscape maintenance businesses have much lower value compared to commercial landscape businesses. I have found that financial buyers typically pay more than strategic buyers since they are buying their way into the industry. The real value in landscape service companies relates to the recurring nature of the revenue including both the monthly maintenance fees and extras that are derived from the monthly maintenance customers."
- "Larger companies = higher value. Equipment Fair Market Value should be added to gross sales and SDE multiplier formulas."

Expert Comments

"Recognize the importance of both residential and commercial to cash flows due to terms."

"Landscape maintenance companies are marketable since the industry has been impacted less compared to other businesses in the current economy. Their margins have been reduced, but businesses still need to maintain their properties."

"Generally difficult to finance because of lack of assets"

"Maintenance is fairly easy to learn."

"Easy entry, many small companies and large companies. Those that are professionally operated are successful."

Benchmark Data

- For additional Benchmark Data see Landscaping Services
- "Many companies in this industry classify labor costs as a part of direct costs in calculating gross profit. Benchmark profit percentages: maintenance companies 10–15%, lawn care (fertilization and weed control companies) 15–30%, construction (design-build companies) 10–20%."
- "Enhancements can/should be around 20% of the gross service revenue annually. 2-man residential crew should max generate $150k annually."
- "Residential route can do up from $180,000 to $225,000 in revenue."

Expenses as a percentage of annual sales

Cost of goods	20% to 45%
Payroll/labor Costs	35% to 45%
Occupancy	02% to 05%
Profit (estimated pretax)	10% to 15%

Industry Trend

- "The industry weathered the Great Recession better than many observers expected. Business is recovering nicely and is expected to continue to expand as the construction sector strengthens. A robust merger and acquisition market has developed and is expected to continue in the near future led by high profile private equity transactions involving the industry's largest participants."
- "Continued growth, low barrier of entry going to allow for small companies to enter the market...limited financing will keep the industry fragmented"
- "Continued pressure on gross profits due to customer budget issues, increasing fuel costs and workers comp rates."
- "More smaller companies, easy entry."

Seller Financing

- "Smaller companies are usually sold with substantial seller financing, but transactions involving $2–$3 million purchase prices are often financed with SBA loans."
- "Seller financing...guarantees are not the norm despite the rumors otherwise"
- "Financing usually at the street value of the assets for 2 or 3 years"

Questions

- "The most important question is why are you selling. Multiples are relatively low and so the pay off from a sale is often limited compared to the cash flow experienced owners can generate. As a result, it is very important to understand why an owner is selling and is it a good reason."

- "What is your monthly service revenue? What types of properties do you do? (residential or commercial) What type of grass (blue, zosia, augustine, bahaia)? How many people in your crews? How many stops a day are they doing? Does your price per property include trimming, trees and shrubs (which drive labor)?"
- "Do they pre-bill or post-bill service? Is service billed monthly with cuts of 42 per year? What is the mix of service by commercial and residential? Density of the routes drives fuel and therefore labor and fuel consumption."
- "What % of revenue is maintenance versus new construction? Maintenance has much more value. What is the % of revenue from commercial maintenance versus residential maintenance? Commercial maintenance has more value. What is the customer concentration? Who maintains the relationships with the customers? What is the quality and maintenance history on the vehicles and equipment?"
- "What is the turnover of customers? How much business is the owner responsible for?"
- "What is your customer concentration? Who manages the customer accounts? Who holds the contractor's license? Will key employees agree to stay?"

Resources

Websites
- Lawn & Landscape: www.lawnandlandscape.com

Trade Publications
- Lawn and Landscape magazine: www.lawnandlandscape.com
- Landscape Management magazine: www.landscapemanagement.net
- Turf Magazine: www.turfmagazine.com

Associations
- National Association of Landscape Professionals: www.landscapeprofessionals.org
- AmericanHort: www.americanhort.org

	Franchise
Lenny's Subs (See also Franchises, Sandwich Shops)	
Approx. Total Investment	$216,500 to $369,000
SIC 5812-06	NAICS 722513	Number of Businesses/Units 150

Rules of Thumb
➢ 15 to 20 percent of annual sales plus inventory

Resources

Websites
- www.lennys.com

		Franchise
Liberty Tax Service (See also Accounting/Firms/Tax Practices, Franchises)		
Approx. Total Investment		$57,800 to $71,900
	NAICS 541213	Number of Businesses/Units 4,300

Rules of Thumb

> ➢ 45 to 50 percent of annual sales plus inventory

Resources

Websites
- www.libertytaxfranchise.com

		Franchise
Li'l Dino Subs (See also Franchises, Sandwich Shops)		
Approx. Total Investment		$47,400 to $240,800
	NAICS 722513	Number of Businesses/Units 15

Rules of Thumb

> ➢ 60 percent of annual sales plus inventory

Pricing Tips

- "One sold for 80 percent of sales, but it was located in an office building with vending rights."

Benchmark Data

- For Benchmark Data see Sandwich Shops

Limousine Services		
(See also Ground Transportation, Taxicab Businesses)		
SIC 4119-03	NAICS 485320	Number of Businesses/Units 137,306

Rules of Thumb

> ➢ 50 to 55 percent of annual revenues plus vehicles

> ➢ 2 to 2.5 times SDE plus vehicles

> ➢ 4 times EBITDA—companies with corporate accounts under contract plus vehicles.

> ➢ 3 times EBITDA plus vehicles

Pricing Tips

- "You need to look at Owner's Discretionary Cash Flow (also known as Seller's Discretionary Earnings). You also need to know whether the limousines are owned outright, financed or leased. Depreciation expense becomes an important consideration because the owned vehicles wear down rapidly and must be replaced to keep the business looking 'up to date.'"

- "A profitable business should net 15% to 20% because the margins are high."
- "The figure needs to be adjusted for the fair market value of the vehicles less the outstanding debt."
- Note: Depreciation is usually considered an "add-back" and is therefore part of the Seller's Discretionary Earnings/EBIT/EBITDA. However, in this type of business it should not be added back as it is a necessary business expense. Vehicles are the mainstay of the business and replacement is ongoing business.

Expert Comments

"Valuation Rules of Thumb

Limousine business owners commonly seek out a quick 'rule of thumb' to understand the value of their own business. Unfortunately, Rules of Thumb rarely apply to this industry. Relying on Rules of Thumb can be very misleading and very destructive if major financial decisions are based upon them. Depending on the size, profitability, location, and buyer of your business, a variety of valuation methods may be used to calculate the 'fair market value' for your business. Most likely, a combination of valuation methods will be applied and weighted accordingly to calculate the fair market value of your limousine business. When using an earnings valuation method, Seller's Discretionary Earnings (SDE) and Earnings Before Interest Taxes Depreciation & Amortization (EBITDA) are the most common formulas applied."

Source: http://www.limobusinessforsale.com/selling-limousine-business-101-part-1/

"No real barriers to entry. It is easy to finance vehicles and create a website."

"Any person can get started by buying one vehicle and building from there."

Benchmark Data

- "What percentages of your total gross revenues are devoted to the following business expenses?

Expenses	Small Operators (1–10 vehicles)	Medium Operators (11–50 vehicles)	Large Operators (51+ vehicles)
Payments	17%	14%	18%
Labor/wages/benefits	23%	31%	38%
Facilities mortgage or rent	07%	08%	07%
Technology/Systems	05%	05%	05%
Vehicle Insurance	15%	13%	09%
Vehicle Maintenance	11%	09%	09%
Fuel	16%	13%	10%
Marketing/advertising/PR0	06%	07%	06%"

Source: "2015–2016 LCT Fact Book Industry Survey"

- "Most respondents, 55%, were small fleet operators (1–10 vehicles); followed by medium-sized fleets 32% (11–50 vehicles); and large fleets, 13% (51-plus vehicles).

"The average operator/limousine company gross profit margin in 2014 was 20.7%, up from an average of 18.7% in 2013, an average of 16.7% in 2012 and 10% in 2011."

Source: "2015–2016 LCT Fact Book"

L - Rules of Thumb

Expenses as a percentage of annual sales

Cost of goods	30% to 35% (auto purchases)
Payroll/labor Costs	25% to 35%
Occupancy	05% to 10%
Profit (estimated pretax)	10% to 20%

Industry Trend

- "In 2015, there were 8,305 limo/chauffeured operators and 3,801 motorcoach/ charter and tour operators, for a total of 12,106. 65% were employed chauffeurs, and 35% were independent contractors."

- "Overall, the number of limousine operators held steady, year over year, due to two reasons we have observed anecdotally and heard from informed sources:

  1. The number of new limousine companies entering the industry has been growing, but,

  2. The number of mergers and acquisitions among established companies has risen as well.

  "Meanwhile the number of motorcoach operators stands about even as well, according to the American Bus Association, whose figures we cited."

  Source: "2015–2016 LCT Fact Book Industry Survey"

- "2014 Company Gross Revenues (all respondents)

$300,000 or less	44%
$301,000–$600,000	15%
$601,000–$1 million	12%
$1.1 million–$5 million	18%
$5.1 million–$10 million	05%
Over $10 million	06%

  2014 Gross Revenues for Small Operators

$300,000 or less	73%
$301,000–$600,000	19%
$601,000–$1 million	08%

  2014 Gross Revenues for Medium Operators

$300,000 or less	06%
$301,000–$600,000	14%
$601,000–$1 million	24%
$1.1 million–$5 million	49%
$5.1 million–$10 million	07%

  2014 Gross Revenues for Large Operators

$1.1 million–$5 million	20%
$5.1 million–$10 million	24%
Over $10 million	56%"

  Source: "2015–2016 LCT Fact Book Industry Survey"

- "Finding and hiring experienced professional chauffeurs has ranked consistently as a top priority among operators nationwide since the economy has rebounded. Since Uber launched in San Francisco in 2009 and spread widely starting in 2011, operators have been debating the on-demand company's effects on the industry, and more importantly, wrestled with allowing chauffeurs to participate as drivers for transportation network companies (TNCs).

"On the question, 'How have TNCs/Uber affected your ability to recruit chauffeurs overall' 'responses were mixed. A plurarlity (48%) said TNCs have not affected recruiting, 26% said TNCs have had some effect; 18% said it's made recruiting more difficult; and 7% said it's eased recruitment. Obviously, geography plays a part in the responses, as TNCs are mostly established in large cities and adjacent metro regions."

Source: "Exclusive Industry Study Reveals Uber Impact On Chauffeurs," by Tom Halligan, March 14, 2016, http://www.lctmag.com/industry-research/article/711184/exclusive-uber-industry-study-reveals-impact-on-chauffeurs

- ". . . estimates that iPads save the company up to 8% on annual fuel costs and up to 25% savings in paper costs. It also reduces chauffeur phone calls to operations by 20%. Moreover, there are many benefits that can't be tied to hard dollars, but operators know from feedback and observation that iPads are spurring better customer service, customer relations, and most importantly, customer satisfaction."

Source: "Touch & Go: Tablet Access Speeds Up Operations," www.lctmag.com/technology/article/107388

Seller Financing

- "Seller should expect 50% down and offer 10-year amortization with a 3-year balloon at 6% interest."

Questions

- "You will want to see the repair and maintenance records for all the vehicles. You will want to know if there have been any accidents. You will want to know if there is outstanding litigation or workmen's compensation issues. What background checks and drug tests are performed on new hires?"
- "Look at the maintenance logs; have a mechanic check all vehicles."

Resources

Trade Publications
- Limousine, Charter, and Tour: www.lctmag.com

Associations
- National Limousine Association—a lot of excellent information, with a study for members only: www.limo.org

Liquefied Petroleum Gas (Propane)

SIC 5984-01	NAICS 454312	

Rules of Thumb

- 130 percent of annual sales plus inventory
- 3 to 4 times SDE plus inventory
- 4 times EBIT
- 6 times EBITDA (Good double-check is 2.5 to 3.5 gross profit)

Pricing Tips

- "EBITDA multiples can range from 3.5 to over 7.0 X, depending on the specific characteristics of the company being sold; there are many variables to consider; multiple does not include inventory or A/Recs."

- "High % of company-owned tanks in the field, automatic delivery, high gross margin per gallon are all important factors in determining value."
- "Multiple of gallons 1–2X; multiple of gross margin 1–2.5X; add value .for high number of company- owned lease tanks, relatively new trucks (less than 5 years), high percentage of residential accounts, backup management and infrastructure, current safety programs, current equipment/storage controls."

Expert Comments

"Capital intensive business; supply displacements during peak winter season; high level of training and technical expertise required to install and maintain equipment in the field; CDL requirements for drivers and technicians."

"If the objective is to sell in three to five years, important factors to consider include:

- ✓ Increase profitability. Retail propane companies are typically valued, bought and sold based on applying a multiple to the EBITDA (earnings before interest, income tax, depreciation and amortization).
- ✓ Focus on developing good records (financial, operational, employee, safety, etc.).
- ✓ Book all revenues for a minimum of three years.
- ✓ Stop selling tanks to customers. Buyers like high company tank ownership for multiple reasons. It increases the ability to keep the customers, and it shelters income for the buyer as they can restart the depreciation schedule on acquired assets. If a customer leases a tank, make sure you have a signed lease (by the customer) on file for each tank in the field. (Goes back to record keeping).
- ✓ Increase other income where available, such as charging tank rent to the customers who lease a tank (which also helps confirm who owns the tank).
- ✓ Work on improving the trends of the company.
- ✓ If you are considering selling within the next 12 months, get your records in order. It may be too late to make changes to profitability, but have good records available for due diligence. Buyers won't pay you for what they can't see."

Source: http://www.lpgasmagazine.com/in-the-know-factors-to-consider-when-selling-a-propane-businesses/

"Large amount of capital needed for infrastructure & equipment, as well as for trucks and tanks; seasonal sales volume affects working capital requirements, depending on time of year."

"Hire a professional intermediary who has extensive experience in the propane industry as offers for these types of businesses vary widely."

"Even though the barriers to entry are increasing, smaller companies' marketability is decreasing."

"The propane industry is very capital intensive in that most companies want to own and control the tanks at customer locations. For this reason, the business is difficult to enter. Price spikes and supply displacements are also issues during the peak winter months. There is a high level of technical expertise needed to install and service propane equipment. Drivers and technicians must pass rigorous training programs and DOT requirements."

"Extremely mature industry with little innovation"

Benchmark Data

- "COGs and GP margins vary greatly from company to company, area by area; as such there is no real average. GP can vary from $.35 cents per gallon sold to well over $2.00 per gallon, depending on many factors. Net Income and EBITDA amounts and percentages can also vary greatly."
- "The business is a delivery business, so the more efficient the delivery, aka gallons per bobtail, the higher the profit."
- "Can vary considerably by company, depending on customer mix between residential, commercial, farm & industrial type customer."

Expenses as a percentage of annual sales

Cost of goods	40% to 50%
Payroll/labor Costs	15% to 25%
Occupancy	02% to 05%
Profit (estimated pretax)	15%

Industry Trend

- "ICF projects consumer propane sales to grow by about 800 million gallons (9 percent) between 2014 and 2025. Most of the growth will come from the propane engine fuel market, although lower propane prices associated with the growth in domestic propane supply and lower oil prices will also make propane more competitive in traditional propane markets, including residential and commercial space heating, and forklift markets."

  Source: http://www.afdc.energy.gov/uploads/publication/2016_propane_market_outlook.pdf
- "Tougher competition from natural gas, especially since natural gas pricing has gotten so much cheaper and more natural gas lines are being built."
- "Slow growth as customers shift away from heating oil in rural areas. Some upside potential in Autogas applications, particularly for fleets."

Seller Financing

- "100% all cash transactions typically (except for Invent & A/Recs which are paid within 90-180 days typically); non-compete allocations vary somewhat and these payments are sometimes tied to a payout period of 3–5 years"
- "Typically uses outside financing"
- "Typically cash at closing for fixed assets; intangibles are sometimes financed over five years."

Questions

- "5 years' financials and gallonage history; gross profit per gallon by segment of business; complete list of assets including tank inventory, bulk plants, trucks, etc.; real estate appraisal."
- "Customer concentration, competition, age of fleet, tenure/age of employees, reason for exit"
- "Company ownership of customer tanks & cylinders is an important consideration. Where the company owns most of the customer field equipment, and there are good gross profits, a much better value can be obtained."

Resources

Websites
- Propane Education & Research Council: www.propanecouncil.org

Trade Publications
- LP Gas Magazine: www.lpgasmagazine.com
- Butane/Propane News (BPN): www.bpnews.com
- Propane Canada: www.northernstar.ab.ca

Associations
- PERC—Propane Education & Research Council: www.propanecouncil.org
- National Propane Gas Association: www.npga.org

Liquor Stores/Package Stores (Beer, Wine & Liquor Stores)		
SIC 5921-02	NAICS 445310	Number of Businesses/Units 44,988

Rules of Thumb

➢ 35 to 45 percent of annual sales plus inventory

➢ 2 to 3 times SDE plus inventory

➢ 2.5 to 3.5 times EBITDA

➢ 3 to 3.5 times EBIT

Pricing Tips
- "Lottery Commission good indicator of area. Long hours and delivery reduce purchase price. Competition in area, parking big concerns."
- "Gross profit should be 24–39%, occupancy expense no more than 7.5%, and payroll expense 7% of revenue."
- "Stores doing less than $1MM are trading at a lower multiple."
- "Old inventory or lack of long, reasonable lease creates an un-marketable store."
- "The % to gross is between 40–50% depending on factors such as rent, payroll, gross profit. SDE will fluctuate as well between 2.5–3.25%."
- "Retail sales are more profitable and will drive a better selling price than wholesale sales."
- "Competition in area, employee benefits, hours of operation."
- "Location, rent, and payroll expense will be the first questions asked. Gross profit is right behind them. Be prepared."
- "Number of active licenses in town. Size and appearance of stores compared to competition. Lease terms, renewal clauses, options to buy. Lottery income."
- "Liquor stores are highly desired by buyers—particularly if they include real estate. The more inventory, the greater the value. If a big box competitor is already in place, and no new locations can open up, this is a positive if the store is making a profit."

Expert Comments

- "Be prepared to spend long hours in the store. Computerizing the business, if possible, will make running a successful operation much much easier."
- "Must buy existing liquor license in New Jersey. Talk of more BYOB restaurants possible."
- "Liquor store owners have a reputation in the business world for skimming cash and keeping poor books (a very easy habit for some owners to fall into when dealing with a cash-heavy business). Although credit/debit cards are being increasingly used, this affects the potential buyer because it may be impossible to determine the business's real profits. The seller may also factor unreported income into his asking price, and employees may be following the owner's lead and skimming cash as well. It may be necessary to reconstruct the financials, but the buyer must insist that the seller provide ample documentation to support the asking price. However, if the buyer is adept at keeping books, then better financials may be all the business needs to thrive more successfully than with the previous owner."

  Source: http://www.georgeandco.com/5-things-know-buying-liquor-store/
- "Ease of replication is restricted to local licensing rules."
- "Do your due diligence on competition and what big box stores could be coming into your geographic area that could impact business."
- "Good liquor businesses are in high demand. Far more buyers than sellers."
- "Work with the seller to verify sales. Pay attention to details; do not try to reinvent the wheel."
- "Location is very important, for the businesses success. In addition, multiple locations, allowing for larger case quantity purchases, will provide a better pricing and profit model for an owner. Thus, a buyer should provide for ongoing working capital to operate the store in order to take advantage of quantity case pricing. This is important to the success and ongoing survival of the store, particularly if there is a large-volume store close by, which is viewed as a competitor. Margins are shrinking in the industry at both the retail and wholesale levels. Hence, many small stores are struggling to survive, due to their occupancy cost being high, in relation to both their sales and margins. The lower margins drive the cost of occupancy up, which cannot be adjusted, when the owner is locked into a specific lease period. Hence, we are seeing many small operators, at best, buying a job. When they get into the business, they overlook the need for additional working capital and potential negative cash flow for an extended period of time, when starting a store, from 'scratch'".

Benchmark Data

Statistics (Beer, Wine & Liquor Stores)

Number of Establishments	44,988
Average Profit Margin	2.5%
Revenue per Employee	$280,100
Average Number of Employees	3.7
Average Wages per Employee	$20,451

Products and Services Segmentation

Distilled spirits, brandies and liqueurs	32.9%
Wine	32.3%
Beer	28.1%
Other	6.7%

Industry Costs

Profit	2.5%
Wages	7.3%
Purchases	74.8%
Depreciation	0.7%
Marketing	0.7%
Rent & Utilities	4.7%
Other	9.3%

Source: IBISWorld, March 2016

- "Rent as compared to Gross Sales must be below 7 percent. Must buy correctly to make money in this business. Small stores are usually not profitable."
- "9 stores sold over the past 30 months range from 25–47% of revenue."
- "Profit margin of 30% or higher typical to stores with high volume wine sales are very desirable and will trade at a higher multiple."
- "Gross margins on retail sales should be at least 25%."
- "Rental is a key component of the business. If the rent is too high a percentage of Gross Sales, business will not thrive."

Expenses as a percentage of annual sales

Cost of goods	65% to 80%
Payroll/labor Costs	05% to 12%
Occupancy	05% to 15%
Profit (estimated pretax)	08% to 15%

Industry Trend

- "Whether you prefer whiskey, vodka, gin, or rum, you may have noticed some recent shifts in the liquor business. In an international, incredibly broad industry, it's hard to know which trends are causing seismic shifts, and which are just blips on the radar. So, Business Insider turned to Gilles Bogaert, CFO of Pernod Ricard, the parent company of brands including Absolut and Jameson.

  "Here are three trends you need to know about that Bogaert believes are truly changing the liquor industry:

  1. 'Home-tainment' is a new way to drink.

  2. Consumers are getting more savvy.

  3. E-commerce is essential.

  "More immediately, social media and online marketing give the company a direct line to customers. Pernod Ricard can quickly respond to consumer habits and concerns, as well as meeting consumers where they already are. That, according to Bogaert, is an even bigger shift than any drinker's preference for whiskey or vodka."

  Source: "The liquor industry is experiencing 3 seismic changes," by Kate Taylor, February 26, 2016, http://www.businessinsider.com/3-biggest-trends-in-the-liquor-industry-2016-2

- "The smaller volume stores closing and selling the liquor licenses. Larger stores thriving with bigger Gross Sales."
- "Marketability should be good, but large grocery chains making a move in the state to obtain liquor licenses. The current law denies them from holding a liquor license."
- "The one-unit 'Mom & Pop' stores will diminish as state licensing laws change, allowing for more licenses. Additionally, the big box retailers, chains, and

supermarkets continue to break into the business. These large retailers with tremendous buying power will hurt the single unit liquor store as they will not be able to compete with pricing, forcing them to either sell or close their business."

- "Bad financial times equal more liquor store sales."
- "I expect the marketability to remain consistent, although multiple licensing bills in Maryland has made proprietors uneasy."
- "Some consolidation expected as larger stores are built to combat nationals like TotalWine."
- "Growing, more wine sales and specialty stores."

Seller Financing

- "Seller Financing required. Usually 1/3 to 1/2 half down payment plus the Inventory at cost."
- "Generally these transactions are SBA funded since there is little or no collateral. Two deals in the past 18 months were SBA funded at 6% amortized 120 months with 25% down."
- "Seller financing for inventory. Bank/Commercial financing for business acquisition."
- "Inventory cash at closing $ for $ at cost. Business 1/3 to 1/2 down, short-term seller financing only way to sell."
- "After 2008 seller financing was the only source, but within the last two years SBA has become more flexible."

Questions

- "Hours owner works? Delivery? Lottery? Employees' length of employment? Equip. maintenance records, compressors, HVAC etc."
- "Cash flow, gross profits, occupancy expense, payroll expense and category percentage mix."
- "Profit margin, category breakdown. How does the seller buy from the wholesalers?"
- "Review the sales and expenses over a two- or three-year period. See what trends are, up or down. Is theft a problem? Most sellers are either burnt out or not making money."
- "Rent expense, payroll, gross profit, category mix of gross and length of lease term?"
- "Seller—true margins, sales trends and mix; buyer—any experience in industry, reason for purchasing."
- "1. Lease terms and amount 2. Sales by year, for last 3 years 3. Margins and net profit. 4. Provide copies of all invoices and bank statements for a minimum of 2 years. 5. Will they be willing to owner finance a portion of the sale price. 6. Will they allow you to view the closing of the store each day, with regards to their bookkeeping, for 1–2 weeks. 7. Why are they selling the business. 8. What would they do to grow the business. 9. What 2 things do they not like about the business and how would they fix them, if they had the time and money. 10. How much time of a training period will the seller provide and would they be available, by phone, for additional support, up to one year, at an agreed upon day and time."
- "Blend of merchandise sales by wine, liquor and beer and by size of units sold. Special deals they receive from distributors. Under the table labor and vendors.

Is there a co-op to buy at best price?"

- "Closest competition, term of lease, payroll cost, how computer system controls inventory and ordering. Do they work on margins or markup? How do store margins compare to any stores within 2–3 miles? How did they arrive at selling price? How would they grow the business, and how long will they provide training and distance for a covenant not to compete?"

- "Is there an option on the property or is it owned by the seller? What competition is nearby? Are there any other licenses available in the town? Do you owe any back taxes or fees that would hold up the transfer of the liquor license?"

- "What are your sales tax numbers and are you current?"

- "Security/surveillance system in place? Theft/shrinkage."

- "How much income was derived from buying smart? Additional sources of revenue, if any and amount? Request copies of sales tax reports from state, to verify the numbers represented. How many suppliers are used and terms available if any? Has there been or is there any liquor store in the process of being opened in the area? What type of terms will the landlord provide, for a long-term lease with options? Does it justify being opened each day at 9:00 a.m. vs. 10:00 a.m. and what have the sales trends, by day, been during that extra hour? Obtain a certificate of good standing, from the state, relative to all taxes being paid and current, particularly the sales taxes. How does the buyer figure margins, markup, gross profit and/or product cost? Much confusion among individuals relative to this topic."

- "Ask to review bank statements, sales tax reports and purchase invoices to confirm unreported cash sales."

- "Why are they selling? Days and hours they work? Margins? Payroll paid off books? Case vs. broken-case pricing and what percentage of business is broken-case purchases? Cost of broken-case purchasing? Is this cost calculated before or after establishing margin on product sold? Also, any taxes paid on product purchases and are they, too, calculated before calculating margins or added

- on after this formula?"

		Franchise
Little Caesars Pizza (See also Franchises, Pizza Shops)		
Approx. Total Investment		$266,000 to $681,500
Estimated Annual Sales/Unit		$830,000
	NAICS 722513	Number of Businesses/Units 3,900

Rules of Thumb

➢ 55 percent of annual sales plus inventory

Resources

Websites

- www.littlecaesars.com

Lock & Key Shops

SIC 7699-62	NAICS 561622	Number of Businesses/Units 21,165

Rules of Thumb

➢ 40 to 45 percent of annual sales plus inventory

Benchmark Data

Statistics (Locksmiths)

Number of Establishments	21,165
Average Profit Margin	4.3%
Revenue per Employee	$56,700
Average Number of Employees	1.5
Average Wages per Employee	$19,268

Products and Services Segmentation

Nonresidential security system installation and repair	51.4%
Residential security system installation and repair	23.4%
Key cutting and duplication services	8.6%
Resale of locks and security merchandise	8.3%
Other services	4.4%
Residential and nonresidential system services with monitoring	3.9%

Major Market Segmentation

Businesses	52.7%
Households	30.6%
Government entities	10.9%
Not-for-profit organizations	5.8%

Industry Costs

Profit	4.3%
Wages	33.9%
Purchases	35.2%
Depreciation	1.6%
Marketing	2.9%
Rent & Utilities	5.0%
Other	17.1%

Source: IBISWorld, August 2015

Resources

Associations

- Institutional Locksmiths' Association: www.ilanational.org
- Associated Locksmiths of America: www.aloa.org

Logan Farms Honey Glazed Hams (See also Franchises)

Approx. Total Investment		$338,475 to $418,125
	NAICS 445210	Number of Businesses/Units 11

Rules of Thumb

➤ 30 percent of annual sales plus inventory

Resources

Websites

- www.loganfarms.com

Lumberyards (See also Home Centers)

SIC 5211-42	NAICS 444190	Number of Businesses/Units 46,791

Rules of Thumb

➤ 40 percent of annual sales includes inventory

➤ 4 to 6 times SDE includes inventory

➤ 4 times EBIT

➤ 4 to 6 times EBITDA

Pricing Tips

- "These comments would apply to lumberyards dealing with contractors, sometimes called 'ProYards,' not home centers (DIY business) . . . if profits (EBT) are 5%–10% of sales, the business would likely sell for 1.5 times book value; less profitable lumberyards sell for book value, or in an asset sale. In an asset sale, if profits are above 5% EBT, use lesser of cost or market on the inventory and FMV on equipment and real estate used in the business, plus one year's EBT for goodwill/non-compete."
- "The major buyers were offering to pay for the best yards 5.5 x EBITDA"
- "There are several types of lumberyards: the publicly traded 'big box' Home Depot, Lowe's types, whose value is daily shown on the NYSE; and the more prevalent independently owned 'Pro' type lumberyard, usually in or close to a metro area with sales in excess of $5 million, that has as its customers primarily professional contractors (most new-home builders), remodel/repair contractors, and commercial/industrial customers. These Pro yards have a minimum of 80% of their business with professionals and a maximum of 20% with DIYers. The smaller town lumberyards generally serve DIYers (60%) and Pro accounts (40%). The demand for lumberyards since 2006 has diminished to now be almost nonexistent. With the housing 'meltdown' and poor economy, there is little interest in a capital-intensive business with a large, expensive, slow-turning inventory, expensive equipment and large accounts receivable. The value of a lumberyard has also changed drastically. It used to be, prior to 2006, that a good, profitable Pro type lumberyard would bring 1.5 times its book value, or from 5–6 times EBIT. Now a good lumberyard, if still profitable, would likely sell for its book value and, maybe even less, its liquidation value. Even a strategic acquisition may bring only these prices. I do not see anything

on the horizon that would restore higher prices for these businesses. Home Depot and Lowe's are selling for about 50% to 60% of their highs of 2005–2006 so they too are showing signs of the tough economy."

Expert Comments

"Lumberyards are very difficult to duplicate. High dollar investment keeps most competition out of a market. It also requires a minimum of 2 acres to runs a $5 million lumberyard. Cost of land these days makes it impossible to start a new store. Most stores have been in existence for decades and have a very low cost basis on the facilities."

Benchmark Data

Statistics (Lumber & Building Material Stores)

Number of Establishments	46,791
Average Profit Margin	3.8%
Revenue per Employee	$308,000
Average Number of Employees	6.6
Average Wages per Employee	$46,307

Products and Services Segmentation

Lumber and other structural building materials	55.4%
Hardware, tools, plumbing and electrical supplies	22.1%
Doors and windows	9.9%
Flooring and roofing materials	8.4%
Other	4.2%

Major Market Segmentation

Professional Contractors	60.0%
Other	20.0%
Do-it-for-me customers	10.0%
Do-it-yourself customers	10.0%

Industry Costs

Profit	3.8%
Wages	15.2%
Purchases	60.4%
Depreciation	0.9%
Marketing	1.6%
Rent & Utilities	4.3%
Other	13.8%

Market Share

Builders FirstSource	5.5%

Source: IBISWorld, June 2016

- "Stores with 60% hardware and 40% lumber are considered home centers. If sales are 60% lumber or more and 40% hardware, it is a lumberyard. Lumberyards earn 20–23% margin on lumber compared to 23–26% for home centers. Lumberyards have very high levels of accounts receivable (60–80% of monthly sales). When housing starts are in decline, contractors are slow to pay their bills. Lumberyards will see their receivables jump from 30–45 day turnover to 50–60 day. That can add $200,000 to receivables very quickly and kill any cash flow the lumberyard has. Bad debt write-offs can quickly run into the tens of thousands of dollars. Lumberyard owner should have an unused line of credit equal to 50% of monthly sales. This will allow him to weather receivable increases, winter sales declines and so on."

- "Sales per employee vary from $200,000 to $400,000."
- "Sales typically are over $500 per square foot and $300,000 per employee for lumberyards with retail space of more than 8,000 sq. ft."

Expenses as a percentage of annual sales

Cost of goods	75%
Payroll/labor Costs	20%
Occupancy	03% to 05%
Profit (estimated pretax)	02% to 05%

Seller Financing

- "Very few sell on owner financing; the sales are generally to existing lumber dealers."

Questions

- "Why selling? Have audited 5 years' financials?"
- "Look carefully at profit, and if future earnings are possible."

Resources

Associations

- National Lumber & Building Material Dealers Association: www.dealer.org

---

Franchise

MAACO Auto Painting and Bodyworks (See also Franchises)	
Approx. Total Investment	$91,000 to $477,000
NAICS 811121	Number of Businesses/Units 457

Rules of Thumb

➢ 40 percent of annual sales plus inventory

Resources

Websites

- www.maacofranchise.com

Machine Shops (See also Contract Manufacturing, Job Shops)		
SIC 3599-03	NAICS 332710	Number of Businesses/Units 19,292

Rules of Thumb

➢ 50 to 65 percent of annual revenues includes inventory

➢ 2 to 3 times SDE plus inventory

➢ 4.5 to 7 times EBIT

➢ 3 to 5 times EBITDA

Pricing Tips

- "Valuation in this industry is tied to a multitude of factors: size of the shop, facilities list and type/condition of machinery, client concentration, industries served, age of machinists, backlog, WIP, etc. Multiples of gross sales are meaningless in this industry."
- "There are many factors that go into developing the EBITDA multiple, and here are just a few:

Position in a market. A company's position in a market, whether it is local, national or international, also has a bearing on its value. A market leader is likely to have a higher value, yet a company's rate of growth or decline in a market will also be a factor. For example, a relatively small market share can be viewed positively if the company has shown sustained growth, while a large market share might be viewed negatively if the share has been steadily eroding.

Products and services. Products and services offered can also impact value. New products and services may provide greater sales potential in the future, while mature products, although likely a major reason for past sales, may be at the end of their life cycle and unable to offer much in the way of sales growth. A company with an obvious lack of any new products or services could be viewed as lacking innovation and take a hit on its valuation. As with customers, the right mix of products and services is important. If a majority of sales comes from one or two products or services, there is more risk than if a wide variety of products contributes equitably.

Assets. A company with a great deal of new, updated equipment may have a higher value, especially if the equipment has demonstrated productivity or quality improvements. Buildings, land, solar panels and other energy-efficient and cost-saving systems can also increase a company's value.

Technology. How a company develops or utilizes technology can go a long way in increasing value.

Management team. An experienced, skilled management team also can increase a company's value. Of course, any positives associated with the management team can only last as long as the team remains intact."

  Source: http://www.mmsonline.com/columns/what-is-the-value-of-your-business
- "Client concentration remains an issue. Deduct 1X for any concentration over 50%. Proprietary processes and expertise in working exotic metals/materials, add 1–2 X. ISO and other certifications along with lean processes, add 1X. Five axis CAPEX adds 1–2X. Important to examine the excess earnings approach when valuing a machine shop. Retrofit Bridgeports and other more labor intensive equipment, deduct 1–2X. In general, the larger the shop the higher the valuation multiples."
- "Machine condition and level of technology are significant influences."
- "Wide range of customers a plus. Certifications extremely important most times."
- "Many are good solid businesses; important to remember work in progress when negotiating the transaction."
- "Strategic buyers tend to look for excess capacity."
- "Look for customer concentration. Determine sales mix between commercial and military/defense contractors. Age and type of equipment will affect valuation. Production capacity is important."

Expert Comments

"Like many industries, machine shops were affected by the recession but are rebounding with the automotive, medical and aerospace industries. CAPEX can be very expensive with pallet loading & auto tool changing 4+ axis machinery making barrier to entry higher than many industries. PE has a renewed interest in this industry especially those with excess capacity or a proprietary product(s). Shops producing 70%+ of capacity are considered healthy."

"Barrier to entry becoming higher as cost of high-tech equipment increases and good programmers are less abundant. OEM's are experiencing slightly better growth and accordingly machine shop's backlogs are increasing. Gross income per employee should be in the $200K per range. Does the shop do a lot of prototyping/short runs or is it more of a mid- to long-run shop? Cost savings realized from longer runs."

"Get involved with an industry association. Meet other owners. Stay abreast of new technology. Have equipment checked out as part of due diligence. Find out about quality issues with major customers. Focus on the retention of employees after the transaction is completed."

"Competition is dependent on capabilities. Niche marketing is common. Risk is high because of CAPEX. The industry is seeing a resurgence with the improving economy and 'some' products being re-shored. This has been a tough industry but on the mend. Profitability is up. Ease of replication is hard because of cost of equipment and the quality standards that many customers now require."

"Close attention should be paid to run rates per hour on machinery. Rent & labor will be split above and below COGS line. Percentages listed assume direct labor in COGS and admin; labor below the line."

"Industry requires significant capital expenditures. Sales tied closely to demand from OEMs. "

Benchmark Data

Statistics (Machine Shops)

Number of Establishments	19,292
Average Profit Margin	5.8%
Revenue per Employee	$175,100
Average Number of Employees	13.1
Average Wages per Employee	$50,285

Products and Services Segmentation

Milling	41.3%
Turning	24.4%
Other	20.0%
Grinding	9.3%
EDM and ECM	5.0%

Major Market Segmentation

Fabricated metal product markets	28.3%
Automotive, transportation and off-highway vehicle markets	23.7%
Industrial machinery and equipment markets (including components)	16.3%
Airline markets	15.9%
Medical markets	8.1%
Electronics and telecommunications markets	5.9%
Other markets	1.8%

Industry Costs

Profit	5.8%
Wages	29.2%
Purchases	34.1%
Depreciation	3.9%
Marketing	0.8%
Rent & Utilities	4.4%
Other	21.8%

Source: IBISWorld, May 2016

- "Smaller shops do not always put direct labor (machinists) or plant occupancy in COGS. Inventory is often stated for tax purposes. PE likes GP to be 70% or better. Capacity should be 70% or better. Backlog of orders tells a lot about the health (or lack thereof) of the shop."
- "Watch for inconsistencies in reporting of COGS, i.e., is all occupancy under the line? Is only production labor in COGS? Is inventory accurately represented? Total inventory value of raw material, WIP and finished goods should be 10–15%. Average growth last 5 yrs. has been 5–6%; watch for inconsistencies."
- "Geographic location is important to buyers since machinery is expensive to move."
- "Many shops like to get X dollars per hour per machine and then work towards 70%–80% capacity per machine or better."
- "There are no major players in this industry."

Expenses as a percentage of annual sales

Cost of goods	50% to 60%
Payroll/labor Costs	30% to 35%
Occupancy	03% to 08%
Profit (estimated pretax)	05% to 15%

Industry Trend

- "The trend has been upwards and other experts in the industry expect continued growth. Offshore competition in certain areas remains a threat."
- "Industry indications are growth through 2020."
- "'In large part, the decline in manufacturing technology orders is due to smaller manufacturers feeling a sense of economic uncertainty and therefore hesitant to make any kind of capital investment,' said AMT President Douglas K. Woods. 'In addition, the energy industry has curbed its spending, accounting for about half of the year-to-date decline in orders, and aerospace did not perform as well as expected in the first quarter. We expect the downturn to ease thanks to strong performance in the automotive and medical industries,

27th Edition

with industrial production and a stronger PMI also indicating resilience in manufacturing.'"

Source: by Bonnie Gurney, July 13, 2015

- "I see pockets of this industry doing very well and improving. There is some re-shoring going on where companies that moved their products to China (for example) are finding out the lead times and rising costs are not as lucrative as they once were."
- "As small shops leave the market, there will be opportunities for the medium to large shops."

Seller Financing
- "Rarely do we see much seller financing, however earnouts are common due to client concentration."
- "Generally it is a blend of seller financing and outside financing unless the business is asset heavy."

Questions
- "Backlog, client concentration, CAPEX, aging of receivables, organized labor, profit margins per category of equipment."
- "Any equipment need to be replaced, account concentration issues are very important to be informed of."
- "Personal salary & benefits, any unutilized or underutilized assets"
- "Will the owner stay on and will they finance, most important. Backlog and contracts also critical."

Resources

Associations
- Fabricators and Manufacturers Association, International: www.fmanet.org
- The Association for Manufacturing Technology: www.amtonline.org
- Precision Machine Products Association: www.PMPA.org

Franchise

MaggieMoo's Ice Cream and Treatery
(See also Franchises, Ice Cream/Yogurt Shops)

Approx. Total Investment		$225,000 to $375,000
Estimated Annual Sales/Unit		$200,000
SIC 2024-98	NAICS 722515	Number of Businesses/Units 159

Rules of Thumb
➤ 25 percent of annual sales plus inventory

Resources

Websites
- www.maggiemoos.com

		Franchise
Maid Brigade (See also Franchises, Janitorial Services, Molly Maid)		
Approx. Total Investment		$85,000 to $115,000
	NAICS 561720	Number of Businesses/Units 420

Rules of Thumb

> 45 percent of annual sales

Resources

Websites

- www.maidbrigadefranchise.com

Maid Services

(See also Janitorial Services, Maid Brigade, Molly Maid, etc.)

	NAICS 561720	

Rules of Thumb

> 35 to 40 percent of annual sales plus inventory

> 1.5 times SDE plus inventory

Benchmark Data

- For Benchmark Data see Janitorial Services
- "The Growing Residential and Commercial Cleaning Industry—The residential and commercial cleaning industry is a $94 billion market comprised of 500,000 companies, employing hundreds of thousands in labor force. The industry has enjoyed a 5.5% annual growth rate over the past five years and is projected to grow at a similar or greater rate over the next ten years.

   "Despite its extraordinary size and growth, the cleaning industry is largely dominated by family-owned, mom and pop operators. Over 80% of the cleaning services sector is comprised of small, family-owned business units that operate without a comprehensive set of standards and regulations.

   "According to Marketdata Enterprises, a research and analysis firm focused on the services sector, an average cleaning company employs five or less employees and grosses under $150,000 in annual revenue. The cleaning business is a 'low tech' business characterized by ease of entry. An individual cleaning company can be started with as little as $1000 in capital and be in operation a few days later. As such, most of the operators lack the necessary knowledge, experience and training to deliver a professional standard of service.

   "According to Marketdata Enterprises, the cleaning services sector has one of the highest customer loss rates, running as high as 45 percent per year. This translates into one of every two customers changing their cleaning provider at least once per year. Some studies indicate that more than 60 percent of building managers are not satisfied with their service provider. A recent survey conducted by the BSCAI Services Magazine identifies the 'low standard of quality' as the number one industry problem.

"One of the major reasons for the high customer dissatisfaction rate is the general lack of professionalism in the industry. The large majority of cleaning companies are small mom and pop¨ business units that lack the knowledge, training and experience demanded today. Frustrated with the low standard of quality, homeowners, renters, property management companies and commercial businesses are searching for a company that can offer them a service of uncompromising quality and professionalism."

Source: AW Cleaning Services, awcleaning.com.
Although this site is a bit self-serving for AW, it is very informative.

Industry Trend

- "According to a study by the investment bank Scott-Macon, the cleaning and janitorial industry is expected to grow faster between 2014 and 2020, at 4.3%, than it did in previous years (2.7% growth per year between 2010 and 2013). As a result, the market sector is expected to be worth nearly $60 billion in 2016, and to surpass that amount by 2017.

  "One of the reasons the cleaning services industry can undergo such growth is because of the low barrier of entry to start a successful cleaning company. In fact, the 4 largest companies in the industry account for less than 10% of the available market, with much of the rest taken up by smaller, often independent companies."

Source: http://www.slideshare.net/PSJanitorial/cleaning-industry-trends-for-2016

Mail and Parcel Centers (Business Centers)		
SIC 7389	NAICS 561431	Number of Businesses/Units 25,719

Rules of Thumb

- ➢ 40 to 45 percent of annual sales includes inventory, less direct cost of goods sold (pass-throughs, e.g., stamps, money orders, UPS charges)
- ➢ 2 to 3 times SDE for national franchises includes inventory
- ➢ 2.75 times EBIT
- ➢ 2.5 to 3 times EBITDA

Pricing Tips

- "Those netting up to $40,000 sell at a 1 multiple. Those netting $50,000 to $60,000 sell for a 1.5 multiple of provable net income. From $70,000 to $85,000 of provable net, the multiple is usually 2. Those netting $90,000 and up, the multiple is usually 2.25 to 2.5."
- "Pre-paid mailbox rentals will need to be prorated and credited back to the buyer unless negotiated out. Either way—it will affect value. Pass-throughs don't count toward annual sales."
- "Ratio of individual customers (only see them at Xmas) to business customers (regular, daily or weekly)."
- "The rental rate is very important to the valuation of mail and parcel centers. Some mail and parcel centers can be located off major streets because they are destination locations. Franchise businesses are usually worth more

than independent stores because of name recognition, brand value. These businesses are appealing to people who want flexible hours and no night hours. Also, most stores are open only a few hours on Saturdays. Sales are usually fairly predictable for mature stores."

- "Since it is a generally low barrier to entry, an established store that has well passed the breakeven is the best situation. An owner operator in this industry can see near 30% SDE so long as fixed costs are not too damaging."
- "Desirable cities demand higher prices because box rental customers will pay more."
- "Franchises will sell for higher % of annual gross sales. High-volume UPS stores sell for over 1x STR (Subject to Royalty)."
- "Rent is a very important factor, as it is a fixed cost. Stores below a certain minimum of sales diminish in value exponentially as they find it more and more difficult to cover the fixed costs."
- "Length of time in business, if sales are growing or declining, if competition is coming or going."

Expert Comments

"Easy to own and easy to operate."

"Risk can be high if owner does not audit the weekly Electronic Funds Transfers (EFT's) statements from the bank. The carriers make 'mistakes' in their favor that you must then call & argue with them to change."

"Perception of mail centers is they are easy to learn and easy to run."

"This is a good service business that is somewhat recession resistant."

"The main suppliers to the industry are the biggest competitors. They give out accounts like candy. You can only make it if you provide a real service along with the shipping."

"These businesses are proven concepts today; and generally, mail and parcel centers are lower risk than many other businesses."

"Competition is high—even from the suppliers (UPS, FEDEX) providing individual accounts to your customers."

Benchmark Data

Statistics (Business Service Centers)

Number of Establishments	25,719
Average Profit Margin	5.9%
Revenue per Employee	$109,000
Average Number of Employees	3.1
Average Wages per Employee	$29,231

Products and Services Segmentation

Copying and reproduction services	53.4%
Postal and shipping services and mailbox rentals	21.7%
Printing Services	11.6%
Other	11.0%
Packaging and labeling services	2.3%

27th Edition

Major Market Segmentation

Small Businesses	64.6%
Households	18.5%
Corporate clients	12.1%
Government	4.8%

Industry Costs

Profit	5.9%
Wages	27.0%
Purchases	39.3%
Depreciation	2.7%
Marketing	0.5%
Rent & Utilities	4.5%
Other	20.1%

Market Share

United Parcel Service Inc.	16.4%
FedEx Corporation	14.0%

Source: IBISWorld, June 2016

- "Must have an average 50% mark up on shipping (USPS, Fed Ex, UPS, etc.)"
- "There are a lot of startup stores or lower performing stores whose annual sales are under $200K. Be careful if it goes below $150K in annual sales, as fixed costs will eat up your profit."
- "Location is important, do not need a lot of SF. Keep the rent low."
- "Mailbox rentals should cover all operating expenses."
- "Most stores must be doing at least $150,000 in annual sales before they start showing any real profit. Advertising is very important; stores should not skimp on advertising. The client base is primarily within a radius of a few miles."

Expenses as a percentage of annual sales

Cost of goods	45% to 50%
Payroll/labor Costs	15% to 20%
Occupancy	10% or less
Profit (estimated pretax)	20%

Industry Trend
- "Trend toward more services—like opening, scanning and emailing mail to customers."

Seller Financing
- 3 years

Questions
- "What competition is nearby. Get a standard disclosure form completed."
- "Is the notary income being reported? If not, look at notary's journal to get idea of volume. Any accounts receivable (business accounts)? Any 'trade' for mail box rental? Do you want to slap customers who complain about you selling stamps for a penny or two more than the post office?"
- "Do they charge for packing labor? How much? If not, this is a pure profit area to explore! It does depend on their markup otherwise."
- "What services are offered? How many mailboxes do they have, how many are rented, how much are they rented for, and when was the last time they raised the rates?"

Resources

Associations
- Association of Mail and Business Centers: www.ampc.org

Mail Order		
SIC 5961-02	NAICS 454110	Number of Businesses/Units 48,887

Rules of Thumb
➢ 6 times EBIT

➢ 5 times EBITDA

➢ 80 percent of annual sales includes inventory

Pricing Tips
- "Valuation of firm typically based on house account quality (house database of customers) and EBITDA sustainability and growth"

Expert Comments
"Straightforward estimate of risk-reward. Margins declining, but from high past levels. Ease of replication reduces going concern values. Consolidation occurring."

Benchmark Data

Statistics (Mail Order)

Number of Establishments	48,887
Average Profit Margin	3.2%
Revenue per Employee	$586,700
Average Number of Employees	4.4
Average Wages per Employee	$42,455

Products and Services

Health and beauty products	62.2%
Other	15.4%
Computer hardware, software and office supplies	7.3%
Home furnishings	6.9%
Clothing, jewelry and accessories	5.8%
Sporting goods, toys, games and hobby items	2.4%

Industry Costs

Profit	3.2%
Wages	7.2%
Purchases	59.9%
Depreciation	0.8%
Marketing	3.9%
Rent & Utilities	4.0%
Other	21.0%

Source: IBISWorld, June 2016

Expenses as a percentage of annual sales

Cost of goods	60% to 67%
Payroll/labor Costs	01%
Occupancy	01%
Profit (estimated pretax)	09% to 10%

Industry Trend

- "The Mail Order industry has experienced slight contraction over the past five years, largely due to rising competition from online retailers and minimal improvements in disposable income among frequent mail order customers. While consumer sentiment and disposable income are expected to take a positive turn, individuals will turn to brick-and-mortar retail stores and internet stores for the majority of their purchases. More struggles are projected for the industry in the five years to 2019, as industry catalog mailers will likely struggle to tap into the growing percentage of consumers who favor e-commerce over traditional mail orders. Therefore, IBISWorld forecasts industry revenue to decline steeply in the next five years."

  Source: IBISWorld, October 2014

- "Over the past five years, the bulk of the industry's revenue has shifted from catalog to Internet sales."

  Source: www.firstresearch.com

Questions

- "What experience do you have in the catalog or direct marketing industry?"

Resources

Associations

- National Mail Order Association—an excellent site, loaded with information: www.nmoa.org

	Franchise
Mama Fu's Asian House (See also Franchises, Restaurants—Asian)	
Approx. Total Investment	$407,000 to $663,000
SIC 5812-08	NAICS 722513	Number of Businesses/Units 9

Rules of Thumb

➤ 30 percent of annual sales plus inventory

Resources

Websites

- Mama Fu's Asian House: www.mamafus.com

Management Consulting		
	NAICS 541611	Number of Businesses/Units 771,506

Rules of Thumb

➤ 2.5 times SDE

Pricing Tips

- "So What's My Firm Worth? That may be the question that popped into your head, so let's deal with it first. There are many factors involved in a valuation, however, in simple terms your firm is worth a multiple of the last 12 months profits.

"Of course, there are substantial variations in the numbers. For example, the average EBIT multiple may be 10, but the range goes from 4 to 40, and there are many other factors to consider for the particular circumstances of your firm. Also, as I'll go on to explain, the real value of your firm is in your ability to reliably predict your profits into the future."
Source: http://managementconsultingnews.com/article-paul-collins-1/

- "A firm with a track record of erratic revenues and profits sends a concerning message to buyers and investors, so if you can show sustained revenue and profit growth and high margins, you have an attractive proposition. Before you take your firm to market, you want to be able to demonstrate consistent growth over the last 3 years. Sales and profit growth is a reflection, or an output, of your performance in the other 7 levers."
Source: http://managementconsultingnews.com/article-paul-collins-2/

- "There are four key performance indicators that would be taken into account in a valuation:
    - ✓ Pipeline—A premium value would be placed on a firm with 75% of its pipeline as business booked over the next three months and 50% booked over the next six months
    - ✓ Sales Growth—15% consistent year-on-year growth would be viewed as strong, but 25% would win a premium valuation
    - ✓ Repeat Business—A firm with 80% repeat business would be seen as strong, and 90% would win a premium value
    - ✓ Client Relationships—Valuation would increase where long-term client relationships are prominent, and a discount would be applied if too many eggs are in one basket in terms of client concentration.

"The best time to sell is when the following three areas are in line and on the increase:
    - ✓ A peak in market activity (such as now)
    - ✓ A peak in your own profits
    - ✓ A peak in your market sector.

"If these three things coincide and you go to market at a time when you have an excellent sales track record and clients are singing your praises, then you stand a very good chance of getting the maximum value for your firm."
Source: http://managementconsultingnews.com/article-paul-collins-3/

Benchmark Data

Statistics (Management Consulting)

Number of Establishments	771,506
Average Profit Margin	9.8%
Revenue per Employee	$147,400
Average Number of Employees	2.3
Average Wages per Employee	$58,500

Products and Services Segmentation

Corporate strategy	38.5%
Marketing and sales	19.3%
Organizational design	13.0%
Process and operations management	9.4%
Human resources advisory	8.1%
Financial advisory	7.5%
IT strategy	4.2%

Major Market Segmentation

Financial services companies	23.8%
Consumer products companies	16.6%
Government organizations	14.6%
Manufacturing companies	11.0%
Technology and media companies	9.8%
Individuals and non-profit organizations	8.4%
Life science and healthcare companies	8.0%
Energy and utilities companies	7.8%

Industry Costs

Profit	9.8%
Wages	39.5%
Purchases	18.5%
Depreciation	0.7%
Marketing	1.7%
Rent & Utilities	3.2%
Other	26.6%

Market Share

Accenture PLC	2.9%
Deloitte Touche Tohmatsu	2.1%
McKinsey & Company	1.2%

Source: IBISWorld, May 2016

Manufacturing—Aluminum Extruded Products		
	NAICS 331318	

Rules of Thumb

➢ 50 percent of annual sales plus inventory

➢ 6 times SDE plus inventory

➢ 5 times EBIT

➢ 4 times EBITDA

Pricing Tips

▪ "Nature of contract with metal supplier; this is a low added value business."

Benchmark Data

▪ "At least a ratio of added value/salaries cost (total) of 2.0"

Expenses as a percentage of annual sales

Cost of goods	70%
Payroll/labor Costs	35%
Occupancy	05%
Profit (estimated pretax)	08%

Industry Trend
- "Growing"

Questions
- "Customer base, nature of metal contracts"

Manufacturing—Chemical		
SIC 2899-05	NAICS 32599	Number of Businesses/Units 1,763

Rules of Thumb

➤ .5 to 2 times annual sales includes inventory

➤ 4 to 9 times EBITDA

Pricing Tips
- "As the owner of a chemical manufacturing firm, you may want to begin evaluating your options and take advantage of this rare opportunity known as a 'Seller's Market' by planning ahead for your future and the future of your business. Every business owner should know the value of their business, even if they are not ready to sell, and we can tell you. To give you an idea of what formulas are used during the valuation process, we have provided some multiples below. Please keep in mind that many factors go into valuing a business and only a professional broker can tell you the true value."
- ".5–2x annual sales includes inventory; 4–9x EBITDA"
  Source: http://www.vikingmergers.com/blog/2015/how-to-sell-a-chemical-plant-for-the-best-price
- "Industry is very diverse (some businesses are state-of-the-art/cutting edge, some are very mature, and everything in between), therefore pricing depends on a variety of factors."

Expert Comments

"Chemical industry in U.S. on upward trend because of natural gas availability in the U.S., making for lower raw material costs in many cases"

Benchmark Data

Statistics (Chemical Product Manufacturing)

Number of Establishments	1,763
Average Profit Margin	8.1%
Revenue per Employee	$673,793
Average Number of Employees	33.4
Average Wages per Employee	$61,704

Products and Services Segmentation

Other chemical products and preparations	36.8%
Custom compounding of resins	28.3%
Photographic films, papers and plates	9.8%
Water treating compounds	8.9%
Photographic chemicals	6.0%
Automotive chemicals	5.4%
Evaporated salt, excluding table salt	2.7%
Gelatin, excluding ready-to-eat desserts	2.1%

Major Market Segmentation

Manufacturing sector	31.2%
Automobile industry	23.6%
Households	21.8%
Construction sector	18.7%
Other	4.7%

Industry Costs

Profit	8.1%
Wages	9.2%
Purchases	54.0%
Depreciation	1.7%
Marketing	0.1%
Rent & Utilities	2.1%
Other	24.8%

Source: IBISWorld, August 2016

- "EBITDA multiples are the most common benchmark, but exhibit wide variation"
- "Benchmarks are not common, given the diverse nature of the industry."

Expenses as a percentage of annual sales

Cost of goods	25%
Payroll/labor Costs	n/a
Occupancy	n/a
Profit (estimated pretax)	10%

Industry Trend

"North American chemical companies face workforce turnover issues, which if not resolved, could mean more unplanned operations disruptions, more hiring and training costs and more efforts to maintain safety — reports a new survey by Accenture (NYSE: ACN) and the American Chemistry Council (ACC). The survey was released today at the Council's annual business meeting.

"Chemical companies face a shortage of experienced workers and must replace a substantial number of retiring baby boomers in the coming years. More than 20 percent of the chemicals workforce is approaching retirement in the next three to five years, said 40 percent of respondents.

"If the aging workforce issue is not resolved in the next three to five years, 86 percent said the chemical industry's profitability will suffer significantly. This includes 49 percent of chemical companies that agree and 37 percent that strongly agree with this point of view at a time when industry expansion is expected to continue in North America."

Source: "Turnover of Millennials and Other Workers Challenge North American Chemical Companies as Retirement Surge Looms, New Survey by Accenture and American Chemistry Reports," by Guy Cantwell, Matt Corser, Patrick Hurston, June 7, 2016, https://www.americanchemistry.com/Media/PressReleasesTranscripts/ACC-news-releases/Turnover-of-Millennials.html

- "The Society of Chemical Manufacturers and Affiliates (SOCMA) on Friday celebrated President Obama's signing into law the American Manufacturing Competitiveness Act of 2016 (H.R. 4923), bipartisan legislation that would create a Miscellaneous Tariff Bill (MTB) process to eliminate tariffs on inputs and other products that aren't produced or available in the United States.

  "'This landmark victory finally ends years of unnecessary tax increases on U.S. specialty chemical manufacturers, many of whom are already paying higher prices for raw materials not domestically produced,' said William E. Allmond, SOCMA Vice President of Government and Public Relations."

  Source: "President's Signing of New MTB Law Huge Victory for Specialty Chemical Manufacturers," May 23, 2016, http://www.socma.com/article/id/2095/presidents-signing-of-new-mtb-law-huge-victory-for-specialty-chemical-manufacturers

- "Compared to June 2014, U.S. chemical production was ahead by 4.0 percent on a year-over-year basis, an improving comparison. Chemical production remained ahead of year ago levels in all regions."

  Source: "U.S. Chemical Production Activity Rebounded in June" by Patrick Hurston, July 21, 2015, http://www.americanchemistry.com/Media/PressReleasesTranscripts/ACC-news-releases/US-Chemical-Production-Activity-Rebounded-in-June.html

- "American chemistry is the global leader in production, providing over fifteen percent of the world's chemicals and representing twelve percent of all U.S. exports. It is also one of America's largest manufacturing industries, an $812 billion enterprise providing 793,000 high-paying jobs. For every one chemistry industry job, nearly 7.5 others are generated in other sectors of the economy, including construction, transportation, and agriculture, totaling nearly seven million chemistry-dependent jobs.

  "'2014 has proven to be another year of robust and sustained expansion for the American chemical industry, now larger than either the motor vehicle or aerospace industries,' said ACC President and CEO Cal Dooley. 'With continued access to abundant supplies of natural gas from shale deposits, the economics of shale gas continue to create a new competitive edge that is revitalizing the industry, and the U.S. is now the most attractive place in the world to invest in chemical manufacturing.'"

  Source: ad for American Chemistry Council's 2014 edition of the *Guide to the Business of Chemistry*, www.americanchemistry.com

Seller Financing

- 5 years

Questions

- "Normal due diligence type issues plus environmental/regulatory issues which are somewhat unique to the industry, and impact of overseas competition."

Resources

Trade Publications

- IHS Chemical Week: www.chemweek.com
- Chemical & Engineering News: cen.acs.org
- ICIS: www.icis.com

Associations

- The Society of Chemical Manufacturers and Affiliates (SOCMA): www.socma.com
- American Chemistry Council: www.americanchemistry.com

Manufacturing—Custom Architectural Woodwork and Millwork

	NAICS 337212	

Rules of Thumb

➤ 3 times SDE includes inventory

Pricing Tips

- "Growth and customer list affects multiple dramatically."

Expert Comments

"China is becoming a big factor."

Benchmark Data

Expenses as a percentage of annual sales

Cost of goods	50%
Payroll/labor Costs	30%
Occupancy	10%
Profit (estimated pretax)	10%

Industry Trend

"China will affect every aspect of this industry. Must have niche to prosper."
"Most owners are getting older, and the industry will consolidate."

Manufacturing—Electrical

	NAICS 33531	Number of Businesses/Units 2,177

Rules of Thumb

➤ 5 times EBITDA

Pricing Tips

- "Client relationships and strength of long-term contracts is a major factor. Patents and proprietary processes must be evaluated. Work force productivity factor, min. of $250K per man-year is essential."

Benchmark Data

Statistics (Electrical Equipment Manufacturing)

Number of Establishments	2,177
Average Profit Margin	5.9%
Revenue per Employee	$354,000
Average Number of Employees	51.2
Average Wages per Employee	$58,718

Products and Services Segmentation

Switches	30.6%
Motors and generators	28.0%
Relays and industrial controls	26.9%
Transformers	14.5%

Major Market Segmentation

Wholesalers	32.9%
Exports	32.5%
Retailers	11.9%
Utilities	11.7%
Downstream manufacturers	11.0%

Industry Costs

Profit	5.9%
Wages	16.7%
Purchases	49.8%
Depreciation	1.3%
Marketing	0.2%
Rent & Utilities	1.4%
Other	24.7%

Market Share

General Electric Company	11.1%
Eaton Corp.	9.8%
Schneider Electric SA	7.6%

Source: IBISWorld, July 2016

- "Use of third-party contract manufacturers continues to grow as more and more traditional manufacturers outsource."

Expenses as a percentage of annual sales

Cost of goods	64%
Payroll/labor Costs	07% to 08%
Occupancy	04%
Profit (estimated pretax)	12%

Seller Financing

- 5 years

Manufacturing—Electrical Connectors		
	NAICS 334510	

Rules of Thumb

➢ 3 times EBITDA

Pricing Tips

- "Transferring the customers and good accounting of inventory are very important."

- "Contract Mfg. companies sell for 3X SDE or under. Companies with proprietary products are 4–7 X SDE depending on growth."
- "The customer list and management talent are key."

Expert Comments

"The industry is very cyclical."

Benchmark Data

- "No customer bigger than 30%"

Expenses as a percentage of annual sales

Cost of goods	40% to 45%
Payroll/labor Costs	30%
Occupancy	10 to15%
Profit (estimated pretax)	10%

Industry Trend

- "Major consolidation"

Questions

- "How much engineering work do you do?"

Manufacturing—Food

	NAICS 311	

Rules of Thumb

➤ 4 to 7 times EBITDA

Pricing Tips

- "Pricing Tips include brand, years in business, strong customer base and length of relationship with customers, vendor certifications (i.e., certified organic, 100% natural, etc.)"
- "Earnings multiples depend heavily on: brand, customer concentration, size, recurring revenue, clientele, vendor certifications, working capital requirements, earnings stability, owner involvement, product category and differentiation, equipment age/condition (future CAPEX), and barriers to entry."

Expert Comments

"Food manufacturing businesses have high marketability"

"Generally there is little or no proprietary content."

Benchmark Data

- "Branded vs. private label, any notable long-term customers?"
- "Wide range, depending on product category, sales channel, branded vs. private label, etc."

- "Food manufacturing gross margins (after material costs and direct labor) should be at least 40%, and preferably at least 50%."

Expenses as a percentage of annual sales

Cost of goods	30% to 40%
Payroll/labor Costs	10% to 15%
Occupancy	05%
Profit (estimated pretax)	05% to 10%

Industry Trend

- "According to the 2016 annual U.S. Food & Beverage Industry Study, released Tuesday by WeiserMazars LLP, a leading accounting, tax and advisory services firm; most food and beverage companies anticipate a significant increase in sales this year.

  "Survey participants — which were drawn from over 200 companies across the food and beverage industry — are confident sales will increase 14% compared to 2015 and project net profits will rise by 10%. Respondents attributed this growth prediction to secular industry trends currently favoring both private label and healthy/nutritious foods."

  Source: "WeiserMazars' Annual US Food And Beverage Industry Study Shows Companies Anticipate Substantial Sales Increase In 2016," June 14, 2016

Seller Financing

- "Depends on the size of the deal. Average seller financing is 2–10 years"

Questions

- "Revenue, COGS, liabilities, owner involvement? Sales channel? Who are your customers? How long have you been supplying to these customers? Do you have contracts with clients? Any client that accounts for more than 10% of your sales? What is the production capacity? Type of equipment?"

Resources

Websites

- Food Manufacturing: www.foodmanufacturing.com

Trade Publications

- Food Engineering: www.foodengineeringmag.com/

Manufacturing—Furniture/Household

(See also Manufacturing—Wood Office Furniture)

SIC: 2599-01	NAICS 33712	Number of Businesses/Units 9,557

Rules of Thumb

➢ 4 to 7 times EBITDA

Pricing Tips

- "Size, growth, condition of plant, how profitable it is, place in the market, and management can play a part."

Benchmark Data

Statistics (Household Furniture Manufacturing)

Number of Establishments	9,557
Average Profit Margin	4.6%
Revenue per Employee	$190,600
Average Number of Employees	13.8
Average Wages per Employee	$38,119

Products and Services Segmentation

Upholstered household furniture	45.8%
Institutional furniture	22.1%
Nonupholstered wood household furniture	18.9%
Metal household furniture	10.1%
Other	3.1%

Major Market Segmentation

Wholesalers	36.8%
Contract outfitters	13.4%
Other retailers	12.5%
End users	10.4%
Exports	10.3%
Manufacturer-affiliated retailers	9.6%
Department and warehouse sales	7.0%

Industry Costs

Profit	4.6%
Wages	20.1%
Purchases	53.1%
Depreciation	1.0%
Marketing	0.6%
Rent & Utilities	2.1%
Other	18.5%

Market Share

Ashley Furniture Industries Inc.	8.4%

Source: IBISWorld, April 2016

Current U.S. Office Furniture Market Forecast

Year	Production	% Change	Consumption	% Change
2016	$10.3 billion	+1.0%	$13.4 billion	+3.9%
2017	$10.8 billion	+4.8%	$14.4 billion	+7.2%

Source: February 29, 2016, http://www.bifma.org/page/HistoricalData

Resources

Associations
- Business & Institutional Furniture Manufacturers Association: www.bifma.org

Manufacturing—General

SIC 3999-03		

Rules of Thumb

➤ 40 to 60 percent of annual sales includes inventory

➤ 2.5 to 3.5 times SDE (depending on size & quality) includes inventory

➤ 3 to 4 times SDE; must manufacture product; not be a job shop

➤ 3 to 5 times EBITDA

➤ 3.5 to 4 times EBIT

➤ Hard Assets + 1.5 to 2 times EBIT

Pricing Tips

- "4-8x depending upon barriers to entry and low customer concentration."
- "While it may prove worthwhile to target a 3.0 multiple, it's best to set the seller's expectations below 2.5."
- "The equipment included is a key factor in the valuation and sale of the business."
- "In terms of valuation, timing is less important than the EBITDA levels, growth prospects and quality of the underlying business. Companies that have patented products and proprietary methods will see a higher multiple. The transferability of the customer base will have a significant influence regarding price."
- "Important to understand finished product, parts, inventory and work in progress and exactly how much of each will or will-not be included in the purchase price."
- "Factors to look for: sales/profitability trends; years in operation; fixed asset value. Risk factors: technology, competition, and industry trends. Exclusive products and patents can raise the multiple."
- "Niche or proprietary products, processes, etc. require a premium. Repetitive long-term contracts generate a premium. ISO 2000 procedures in place deserve a premium. Discount for client concentration, labor unions and 'me too' products or services. Watch out for warranty exposure, product liability exposure, excessive WIP and old or obsolete inventory."
- "If the business is in a niche industry with a high barrier to entry it would likely see a higher multiple. Customer concentration can have a significant influence on the multiple, or may require a significant earnout. Exclusive products and patents can raise the multiple. How many competitors manufacture the same product? Companies facing little or no offshore competition will command a higher price. Values for job shops are lower than for companies with a product line."
- "Multiples are a starting point. Other variables are age and turnover of inventory, customer contracts or relationships in place for future revenues, age and quality of FF&E, ease of operations and learning curve, proprietary or niche products, market competition."
- "There has been increased demand for manufacturing businesses which is helping to push multiples higher."
- "Factors of importance: Is being an engineer critical to ongoing success?

What impact if any does Chinese manufacturing have on this business? Is the customer base spread out?"

- "Does it have solid and/or proprietary product lines? Can it be operated without the current owner? Are outside vendors/contractors used in the manufacturing process? Do they sell to large well-known companies or distributors? And are these relationships ongoing and transferable? Can it be relocated or folded into an existing company?"
- "Transferability of the customer base and maintenance capital expenditures are the two biggest issues to close a deal."

Expert Comments

"Capital ex is high in this industry but technology is not a barrier."

"Buyers: Surround yourself with talented people who are willing to be held accountable to growth goals. Sellers: Be prepared to transition out over a minimum of two months to a non-uncommon two years."

"In niche manufacturing, there is a great deal of interest on behalf of owner/operator buyers who value a high barrier to entry and the chance to outsell the competition."

"Focus on strong inside sales development."

"Location has no bearing on the business other than overall distance to ship to customers. International customers are difficult to have continuity with because the strength of the U.S. dollar negatively impacts sales internationally, especially Canada."

"Making strategic investments is essential for growth. Manufacturing technology is evolving faster than ever before and owners must lead with an eye toward that reality, and mot merely the current bottom line."

"The U.S. manufacturers have a structural cost disadvantage given the high corporate tax rates."

"Break the business down into categories and determine if there are any redundancies or efficiencies that can be integrated. Have a great sales team and take advantage of supplier discounts or credits. Have plenty of WC or a good LOC. Find a way to keep the seller around for a bit-as-added insurance that everything represented is what's expected."

"Location, rent and lease term must be clearly understood from the start. It can be difficult to replicate a running operation, therefore a business that may not currently be profitable may have substantial value to certain buyers."

"The burden of structural costs (corporate tax liability, employee benefits, tort litigation, regulatory compliance, etc.) is a competitive disadvantage relative to foreign competitors. The manufacturing sector's profitability is affected by cyclical movements in the economy. Profits, as a percentage of stockholders' equity, typically fall during a recession, but are coming back up. According to Fortune Magazine, private equity firms now have more than $1 trillion of available capital, which should mean more deals at higher prices."

"Barriers to entry can be the equipment, good employees, and customer base; it's critical to have a good understanding of these issues."

"As usual the seller will need to provide documentation on sales, distributors, vendors, operations and financials. The buyer will need to verify everything."

"Many of us believe that outsourcing to China and other places around the world will continue to slow down. We are seeing more manufacturing being brought back to the USA. These factors will have a positive impact on the value and sale of manufacturing businesses."

"Ease of replication is critical. Buyers tend to desire patents, sellers tend to have been too frugal to have incurred costs associated with patents."

"Profitability & sales trends important—FMV of equipment/machinery, inventory, real estate = financing."

"Unlike some industries, an unprofitable manufacturer may drive value due to its bolt-on capabilities. Overhead can be eliminated and capacity and customers can potentially be transferred to another company."

Benchmark Data
- "The goal is to see $300K–$350K per shop employee."
- "Successful manufacturers get significant amount of productivity from employees due to skills, training and efficiencies in automation. $150 K per employee in sales."
- "Employee/labor costs are on the rise along with insurance costs. Understanding where efficiencies can be put into play can be helpful for a buyer. Cost of goods sold also important to understand if current pricing for materials, etc. will continue and for how long."
- "3–4 x adjusted-verifiable net"
- "$1k sales per square foot, but it depends on what you are selling, power transmission products vs. electronics."
- "Proprietary products are most important."

Expenses as a percentage of annual sales

Cost of goods	45% to 60%
Payroll/labor Costs	15% to 20%
Occupancy	03% to 10%
Profit (estimated pretax)	05% to 10%

Industry Trend
- "Average...slow growth"
- "With assertive sales and marketing approaches, we should continue to see growth and even modest roll-ups among small manufacturers."
- "Challenging, because U.S. manufacturing is under intense pressure from foreign competition, currency exchange and the U.S. government as well as governments in the Northeast are anti-business and anti-manufacturing."
- "Manufacturing plants are going to be more data driven, where all internal and external activities are connected through the same information platform. This change is driven by:
  - ✓ The Internet of Things (IoT)
  - ✓ Robotics
  - ✓ 3D Printing"
- "Manufacturing seems to be a sought after industry from buyers in all price ranges."

- "According to IndustryWeek, the 'SMAC Stack' adoption will gain speed: A manufacturing comeback is being driven by SMAC—social, mobile, analytics and cloud. The SMAC Stack is becoming an essential technology tool kit for enterprises and represents the next wave for driving higher customer engagement and growth opportunities. The need to innovate is forcing cultural change within a historically conservative 'if it's not broke don't fix it' industry, and SMAC is helping early adopters in the manufacturing market increase efficiencies and change."
- "Growth including onshoring and manufacturing moving from China to U.S. and Mexico."
- "The trends should be upward based on: 1) natural gas costs have come down, 2) labor costs are going up in developing countries, and 3) new automation technology continues to increase productivity and require fewer skilled workers."
- "Small manufacturing seems to be holding its own."
- "For the company with the special products and customers the trend for success is positive."
- "Some key findings from the Manufacturing Institute:
    - ✓ Manufacturing is driving productivity growth in the U.S. economy, increasing at two and a half times the rate of the service sector.
    - ✓ Companies with under 100 employees make up over 94% of all U.S. manufacturers.
    - ✓ U.S. manufacturers invest a far greater percentage of revenue in research and development than other industries.
    - ✓ Manufacturing employees earn a higher average salary and receive greater benefits than workers in other industries.
    - ✓ U.S. manufacturers have reduced energy usage and emissions to below the level from 1990.
    - ✓ U.S. manufacturers are responsible for 47% of the total U.S. exports.
    - ✓ The U.S. is the number one destination for foreign direct investment by a wide margin.
    - ✓ The U.S. manufacturing sector is so huge that if it were its own country, it would rank as the tenth-largest world economy."

Source: www.themanufacturinginstitute.org

- "The strong have survived. Companies have made cuts so they are now more productive and efficient without some of the 'fat.'"

Seller Financing

- "We typically see a blend of down payment (25%), outside financing (60%), and a blend of a seller note and earn-out (15%)."
- "Some seller financing is typical for a business in this industry selling for less than a few million dollars."
- "Finance can include SBA bank finance with typically 25% down where the buyer may put down 15% and the seller carry the balance of 10%. The alternative is seller finance where a large percentage of transactions have been structured under. This typically involves 50% down with a personal guarantee and a lien on the assets of the business."
- "Primarily outside with some small seller participation."
- "Manufacturing companies with lots of (paid off) equipment and a good lease along with good financials may get a loan as long as the buyer is financially

strong and has direct industry experience. Seller financing is usually required to some degree, with or without a bank loan."
- "It's about 50/50 outside financing to seller financing."

Questions
- "Product line diversification by industry focus, i.e., not just products in the oil industry."
- "Why are you selling? What will this industry look like in 3–5 years? How hard is it to attract and retain talented staff?"
- "Can the training transition period last longer with a phase-out period and compensate the seller during transition?"
- "How much working capital is required? Who are your competitors? Do you have an up-to-date business plan? Who owns the working relationships with the customers? Are there any vendor concentration issues? Do you have many offshore competitors? What is your role in the business?"
- "Work in progress—how much and how it will be calculated. Inventory in both finished and unfinished product and how much included in the sale. Materials—how can they be accurately counted."
- "What is the quality of your management team, are your books and records audited by a national or large regional firm, are you a planner and can you show me your strategic plan vs. execution, etc."
- "Customer concentration. By whom are technical and sales relationships owned? Environmental? Quality control standards? ISO compliance? Risk of obsolescence? Competitive products/threats?"
- "Do you have a business plan? Who are your key employees? Will they stay? What skills/knowledge do I need to run this business successfully? How much working capital is required? Are any equipment upgrades needed in the near future? Is there any pending legislation you are aware of that may affect this industry? What is your customer concentration? What are the biggest challenges facing your business today? "
- "Raw materials-how much, will the current pricing continue? Long-term lease can be important; find out the status and if it is assignable or if a new one at the same or better rate is possible. Check the details carefully of all customer contracts."
- "Do they have patents on their products?"
- "Is your product certified and if so what kind of certification"
- "How is your business protected from off-shore competition?"
- "Insurance considerations—is the business properly insured?"
- "Value and margin of backlog; asset value and basis for value; product line breakdown & mix; 3 to 5 years P&L and balance sheets."

Resources

Associations
- The Manufacturing Institute: www.themanufacturinginstitute.org
- The National Association of Manufacturers: www.nam.org
- The Manufacturers Alliance for Productivity and Innovation: www.mapi.net
- The Association of Equipment Manufacturers: www.aem.org
- First Coast Manufacturers Association: www.fcmaweb.com

Manufacturing—General Purpose Machinery	
NAICS 3339	

Rules of Thumb

➤ 4.5 times EBITDA

Manufacturing—Guided Missile and Space Vehicle	
NAICS 336414	Number of Businesses/Units 131

Rules of Thumb

➤ 100 + percent of annual sales

➤ 3 to 4 times SDE plus inventory

➤ 6 to 10 times EBIT

➤ 5 to 8 times EBITDA

Pricing Tips

- "Pricing is heavily impacted by third-party lending criteria and formal appraisals/evaluations. Buyers and sellers are sensitive to industry standards and trends as well as a certain segment being sensitive to environmental issues and political correctness."
- "Usually need to sell as a stock sale due to the qualifications and licenses held by the seller."
- "Value increases with the company's ability to meet high quality controls and production deadlines as specified by military and military contractors. Extremely high barriers to entry in this industry keep values high."

Expert Comments

"Visual appeal of facility as well as the level of technology in equipment is very important."

Benchmark Data

Statistics (Space Vehicle & Missile Manufacturing)

Number of Establishments	131
Average Profit Margin	10.7%
Revenue per Employee	$375,000
Average Number of Employees	544.6
Average Wages per Employee	$121,994

Products and Services Segmentation

Missile systems	42.6%
Space systems	35.0%
Propulsion systems	12.3%
Other missile and space vehicle parts	10.1%

Major Market Segmentation

US military	56.7%
Domestic civilian market	31.8%
Exports	11.5%

Industry Costs

Profit	10.7%
Wages	32.1%
Purchases	36.2%
Depreciation	2.0%
Marketing	0.1%
Rent & Utilities	1.9%
Other	17.0%

Market Share

Lockheed Martin Corporation	31.4%
Raytheon Company	25.7%
The Boeing Company	10.1%
Orbital ATK Inc.	7.1%
Aerojet Rocketdyne Holdings	6.1%

Source: IBISWorld, May 2016

- "Quality of production is paramount in this industry along with on-time delivery."
- "There are no common benchmarks or Rules of Thumb. Most businesses in this industry are unique, requiring special detailed analysis."

Expenses as a percentage of annual sales

Cost of goods	31% to 35%
Payroll/labor Costs	50%
Occupancy	15%
Profit (estimated pretax)	20% to 21%

Industry Trend

- "The industry's future performance will remain dependent on the defense market. While US defense spending is expected to remain constrained, it is anticipated to stabilize. The Pentagon will continue to invest in missile defense systems, a new generation of stealthy and partially autonomous cruise missiles (i.e. LARSM) and new missiles for next-generation platforms such as the F-35. Continued defense investment, combined with growth in export sales, will lead industry revenue to increase at a projected annualized rate of 1.1% to $27.6 billion over the five years to 2020."

Source: "Industry Trends: Space Vehicle and Missile Manufacturing," February 22, 2016,
http://www.sme.org/MEMagazine/Article.aspx?id=8589938163

- "Uncertainty prevails due to government activity and controls. Economic uncertainty is still a lingering issue."
- "Trend is up due to war on terrorism."

Seller Financing

- "A mixture of 10% to 20% seller financing, a typical 20% and up buyer cash down payment, and 3rd party financing."
- "Five years at a premium over bank rates."

Questions

- "How are you going to pay for this business? If I carry back a note, what security are you going to provide and how many months of cash will you have at closing?"
- "Are the key employees willing to stay on post sale? Are qualifications and certifications up to current standards and valid?"

Manufacturing—Machinery		
	NAICS 333	

Rules of Thumb

➢ 100 percent of annual sales includes inventory

➢ 4 times EBIT

➢ 3 times EBITDA

Pricing Tips

- "Average of last 3 years' EBITDA plus stockholders comp, multiplied by 2 to 4 depending on profit history and market share."
- "Valuation method for work in process. Inventory turnover. Nature and situation of officer's account with business. Indebtedness. How easy for the firm to get bonded on basis of financial credibility."
- "A manufacturer of industry-specific machinery generally employs 50 to 500 people. A high price is 1 x sales figure (valid if market dominant worldwide). A good price is equal to total assets. A frequently observed price is twice net assets (Stockholder's Equity) or 5 times EBITDA for a firm in good standing. Multiple of net earning is meaningless since most owners minimize net earnings through various perks."

Expert Comments

"The machinery business is highly dependent on global market share (high), skills, reputation with customers based on customer service and availability of spare parts. Management predicament is: How to control a high global market share when you are a business with between 50 and 500 employees?"

"Any sales require customized engineering, manufacturing and assembly, plus installation and start-up which are always cursed with delays."

Benchmark Data

- "Take sales figure minus costs of raw materials and components, which is added value. Divide added value by total salaries cost including management. If result is consistently above 2.0, it is a well-managed business. Watch out: In figures in expenses below, we consider total salaries costs, not labor costs (meaningless)."
- "Added value/salaries cost >2. Added value/sales figure >50%. Sales per employee >$250,000. Identified competitors are few, and far away."
- "Sales per employee: $120,000 to $250,000; varies a lot as function of manufacturing integration. Our experience (300 clients during last 10 years)"

is that 80% of the world machinery industry is mismanaged because of lack of market focus and deficient customer service. The remaining can be highly profitable, and utilize market downturns to acquire competitors (most of our own business)."

Expenses as a percentage of annual sales

Cost of goods	60%
Payroll/labor Costs	25%
Occupancy	05%
Profit (estimated pretax)	10%

Industry Trend
- "It is moving to fast-growing economies where the biggest market is China, India, other NICs."
- "Favorable"

Questions
- "How many customers? Since when? How many customers amount to 50% of sales? How far away do they sell?"
- "Loans and advances to/from officers in balance sheet. Do they own their real estate (facility)? If so, is it undervalued in assets (historic value)?"

Manufacturing—Marine Products		
	NAICS 336612	

Rules of Thumb

➢ 85 percent of Annual Gross Sales plus inventory

➢ 2.1 times SDE

➢ 3.2 times EBIT

➢ 3.9 times EBITDA

Pricing Tips
- "EBITDA must be adjusted to show owner's discretionary cash flow. The multiple that is used varies by industry segments, geographical location, and specific business and must be determined in a subjective manner by one knowledgeable of current market conditions."

Expert Comments

"Niche products are key to success and to reducing competition."

"Only the strong survived during the recession, which was particularly difficult for the marine industry from 2008 thru 2012. The weaker competitors fell away so the last couple of years have experienced a sharp increase in business for the survivors."

"Location is also key. In order to control shipping costs it is important to be located in active boating areas. Marine related manufacturing is typically a complex business with extensive processes creating attractive barriers to entry."

"Manufacturing has been enhanced by technological systems which have greatly improved over the last 25 years. CADCAM systems and computerized equipment have greatly improved productivity in the industry."

Benchmark Data

- "Sales per employee with a strong management team in place: $120,000 to $180,000 depending on WIP production. A mix of customers is key with no one customer >20%."

Expenses as a percentage of annual sales

Cost of goods	32%
Payroll/labor Costs	25%
Occupancy	06%
Profit (estimated pretax)	21%

Industry Trend

- "With Memorial Day marking the kickoff to the summer boating season, the National Marine Manufacturers Association (NMMA) reported today healthy growth for the $35.4 billion U.S. recreational boating industry, with an estimated 171,500 new powerboats sold in 2014, an increase of 6.4 percent over 2013.

"The popular outboard boat segment, which includes pontoons, aluminum and fiberglass fishing boats, and small fiberglass cruising boats, comprised approximately 84.4 percent of the overall powerboat market. Outboard boats were the most popular type of new powerboat sold in 2014. In addition to new powerboats, new sailboats sold at retail increased 33.9 percent to 7,500 units and new personal watercraft sales increased 21.6 percent to 47,900 units.

"95% of boats on the water (powerboats, personal watercraft, and sailboats) in the U.S. are small in size at less than 26 feet—boats that can be trailered by a vehicle to local waterways. It's not just new boats Americans are buying, there were an estimated 940,500 pre-owned boats (powerboats, personal watercraft, and sailboats) sold in 2014."

Source: "Boat Sales Strong with Summer on the Horizon" May 19, 2015,
http://nmma.org/news.aspx?id=19879

Seller Financing

- "Depending on the records, banks are doing SBA deals recently. If not, 60% to 70% down with 30% to 40% seller financing is common."

Questions

- "Customer concentration and % of revenue from the top 10 customers"
- "Equipment needs to be up to date—updating equipment in this industry can be a large expense."
- "Are the contracts with manufacturers transferable to the new owner?"
- "Who is the competition?"
- "How is the business protected from offshore competition?"
- "Consider the WIP situation as these types of products can have significant amounts invested in work in progress."
- "Insurance considerations—is the business properly insured? Consider the value and margin of the backlog and make sure it is accounted for regarding insurance needs."
- "What are the capital expenditures required to maintain and grow the business?"

Resources
Associations
- Marine Industries Association of South Florida: www.miasf.org
- National Marine Manufacturers Association: www.nmma.org

Manufacturing—Metal Fabrication		
SIC 1791-04	NAICS 238390	

Rules of Thumb
➢ 70% to 80% of Annual Gross Sales plus inventory

➢ 4 to 4.5 times SDE plus inventory

➢ 5 to 6 times EBIT

➢ 4 to 6 times EBITDA

Pricing Tips
- "Products, type of metal fab and recurring revenue have material impact on value."
- "Equipment is a real expense so valuation will be dinged or improved based on how frequently seller updates equipment. Useful life of CNC equipment is typically 5–7 years depending on how hard it's used. CAPEX is a real expense of the business which keeps EBITDA multiples down. If they have any proprietary products, it improves value. Most contract manufacturers don't have proprietary products though."
- "Having spoken to over a hundred owners, I can attest that each is very unique. Confirm they don't have customer concentration and identify gross margins for their work. 40–50% gross margins are healthy."
- "Aerospace and defense fabrication typically garners better margins and multiples. It is common to have customer concentration in this space where one customer makes up 20–50% of sales. This brings value about a turn of EBITDA. Size matters too...$2M in EBITDA and below is limited to 5X and below. $2M–$5M is 5.5–6 and more than $10M of EBITDA 5.5–7X. 7X is very rich and that business will need a lot of other things going for it like heavy services (subassembly, kitting, supplier management, painting and e-coating, etc.)"
- "Adjustments to the multiple are: 1. Trend of revenues, gross margin and net . 2. Customer concentration. Anything over 10% is a deduct of 3%. Industry & geographic concentration. The more diversified the better 4. Number of products and services offered 5.Is the owner the business?"
- "Typical 3–7 times EBITDA depending on the business, industry and the buyer. 1.5 times gross profit plus net book value combined with the normal three valuation approaches."
  "EBITDA must be adjusted to show owner's discretionary cash flow. The multiple that is used varies by industry, geographic location, and specific business, and must be determined in a subjective manner by one knowledgeable of current market conditions."

Expert Comments

"There is significant variety in this industry. It's best not to rely on a rule of thumb, but focus on the specific attributes of the unique metal fabricator."

"The customers of these businesses regularly get competitive pricing from the market. It's not uncommon that you'll have a customer and lose a customer and get them back. The point is there is not a lot of pricing power for the owner."

"Pure welding and fabrication businesses that need less equipment are easier to sell than those that require more annual CAPEX spend."

"Proprietary products and processes can protect a company from competition, both domestic and overseas."

Benchmark Data

- For additional Benchmark Data see Manufacturing—Metal Stamping
- "5% of gross revenue goes into CAPEX each year. It is a real expense of the business. Gross margins from 30% to 55% are found depending on market and type of metal fabrication. Less than 30% GM is too commodity based and will trade for lower multiple (4 or less) 40–50% gross margin will trade 5X or above."
- "50 employees should generate $10M in revenues. You want to make sure you can pass commodity price increases along to customers."

Expenses as a percentage of annual sales

Cost of goods	30% to 40%
Payroll/labor Costs	24% to 30%
Occupancy	20%
Profit (estimated pretax)	15% to 20%

Industry Trend

- "More reshoring is going on in U.S. The trend for more metal parts fabrication domestically is growing."

Seller Financing

- "Outside financing unless there is customer concentration."
- "90% outside financing, usually 5%–10% seller financing. They're usually asset heavy so financing is readily available."
- 3 to 5 years
- 5 years

Questions

- "What are gross margins? What are quality systems? How many new clients do you get a year? What percent of revenues have gone into CAPEX the last three years? Is your scrap revenue on your income statement?"
- "Check on your ability to sell metal fabricated parts. Getting new sales is important. Often owners are very good at building and challenged at selling. This is competitive and it's hard to get someone to change suppliers if they are doing a good job. Therefore, you're looking for new part numbers from OEMs. Buyers should ask about their quality programs, operating team, safety record and sales/customer retention history."
- "Do you have any payment or performance bonds in place? Retainage? What is your backlog? Growing?"

Resources

Associations
- Precision Metalforming Association: www.pma.org
- Fabricators & Manufacturers Association Intl. (FMA): www.fmanet.org
- American Welding Society: www.aws.org
- The Society for Mining, Metallurgy and Exploration: www.smenet.org

Manufacturing—Metal Stamping		
	NAICS 332119	Number of Businesses/Units 2,381

Rules of Thumb
- ➤ 5 times SDE plus inventory
- ➤ 3 times EBIT
- ➤ 4 times EBITDA

Pricing Tips
- "Length of time in business. Customer base and spread of customer base by percentage."

Expert Comments
"Depending upon products being developed"

Benchmark Data

Statistics (Metal Stamping & Forging)
Number of Establishments	2,381
Average Profit Margin	5.2%
Revenue per Employee	$328,900
Average Number of Employees	44.5
Average Wages per Employee	$53,266

Products and Services Segmentation
Non-automotive stamping	33.1%
Ferrous forging	25.6%
Custom roll forming	24.0%
Nonferrous forging	8.7%
Powder metallurgy	6.0%
Other	2.6%

Major Market Segmentation
Aerospace	35.5%
Other	25.3%
Off-highway and agriculture markets	18.0%
Exports	11.9%
Ordnance markets	9.3%

Industry Costs

Profit	5.2%
Wages	16.3%
Purchases	53.4%
Depreciation	2.9%
Marketing	0.1%
Rent & Utilities	3.2%
Other	18.9%

Source: IBISWorld, June 2016

Expenses as a percentage of annual sales

Cost of goods	50%
Payroll/labor Costs	15%
Occupancy	15%
Profit (estimated pretax)	20%

Industry Trend
- "Lots of this work is going to China."

Questions
- "How long in business? Cost of goods sold? Lease and rent? How long have employees been there? Diversification of customer base?"

Manufacturing—Metal Valve and Pipe Fitting
(See also Manufacturing—Valves)

	NAICS 332919	

Rules of Thumb
- 7 times EBIT
- 100 percent of annual sales
- Assets plus 1 to 2 times EBITDA

Expert Comments
"High capital investment"

Benchmark Data
- "Four inventory turns, 50 percent gross margin"

Expenses as a percentage of annual sales

Cost of goods	50%
Payroll/labor Costs	20%
Occupancy	30%
Profit (estimated pretax)	15%

Manufacturing—Miscellaneous Electrical and Components

	NAICS 335999	

Rules of Thumb

➤ 8 times SDE

Pricing Tips

- "Customer concentration and special skills required by owner drive the price model."

Expenses as a percentage of annual sales

Cost of goods..50%
Payroll/labor Costs..25%
Occupancy..15%
Profit (estimated pretax) 10%

Manufacturing—Office Products

	NAICS 339940	Number of Businesses/Units 449

Rules of Thumb

➤ 5 to 8 times EBIT

➤ 1 times sales plus inventory

Pricing Tips

- "Key to higher valuation is the company's customer base. Does it include either:
  (a) One or more office superstores? (Staples, OfficeMax or Office Depot)
  (b) One or more national wholesalers? (United Stationers, etc.)
  (c) One or more contract stationers?"
- "Customer concentration—many office-product manufacturers have one major customers—a Staples, for example. This may impact valuation if too dependent. Manufactured vs. imported product—companies whose manufacturing base is not vulnerable to imports (from China or Taiwan) are more valuable than those who are."
- "There is no rule of thumb for the office products industry, but in general, pricing is affected by the size of the company. The larger the EBIT, i.e., over $5 million, then the higher the multiple. If a manufacturer of office products sells half to Staples et al and half to Wal-Mart et al, it is not a pure play in the office products business, so the price would be discounted accordingly. A better, more valuable, company would sell 100 percent to office product dealers, not 50 percent to mass merchants, 50 percent to office products. Other factors: breadth of product line, channels of distribution—how broad and complete is that industry, customer and supplier mix (80/20)? Dependency on family members means lower value; union is negative. Is M&E up to date? Growth rate correlation. Is company financeable, or only soft assets?"
- "1. Customer profile—are the products well-entrenched in the office superstore channel? 2. Uniqueness of product—are items basic commodities or are they unique or distinctive? If the latter, valuation may go up."

Benchmark Data

Statistics (Art & Office Supply Manufacturing in the U.S.)

Number of Establishments	449
Average Profit Margin	11.3%
Revenue per employee	$302,700
Average Number of Employees	18.2
Average Wages per Employee	$45,459

Products and Services Segmentation

Pencils and art goods	43.0%
Pens and mechanical pencils	22.0%
Carbon paper and linked ribbon	21.3%
Marking devices	13.7%

Major Market Segmentation

Wholesalers	31.0%
Other industries	25.4%
Retailers	24.0%
Exports	19.6%

Industry Costs

Profit	11.3%
Wages	15.1%
Purchases	53.2%
Depreciation	1.9%
Marketing	3.6%
Rent & Utilities	1.7%
Other	13.2%

Market Share

Newell Rubbermaid Inc.	19.3%
Crayola LLC	16.9%
ACCO Brands Corporation	15.3%

Source: IBISWorld, June 2016

Seller Financing

"Not very often. If it is a good company, it is a cash deal."

3 years

Manufacturing—Ornamental & Architectural Metal		
SIC 3446-04	NAICS 332321	

Rules of Thumb

➤ 3 to 7 times EBITDA depending on the company, industry and buyer.

Questions

"Do you have to pay union or David-Bacon linked wages for government work?"

Manufacturing—Personal Health Products

	NAICS 325412	

Rules of Thumb

➢ 5 times SDE plus inventory

➢ 6 times EBIT

➢ 5.5 times EBITDA

Pricing Tips

- "30% of GPM [gross profit margin] x 5 should roughly equal a fair valuation."

Benchmark Data

- "$200,000 sales per employee"

Expenses as a percentage of annual sales

Cost of goods	40%
Payroll/labor Costs	12%
Occupancy	05%
Profit (estimated pretax)	10% to 12%

Questions

- "Market share and stability of GPM [gross profit margin]"

Manufacturing—Pharmaceutical Preparation & Medicine

	NAICS 325412	Number of Businesses/Units 4,630

Rules of Thumb

➢ 75 percent of annual sales

➢ 5 times SDE

➢ 4 to 5 times EBIT

➢ 6 times EBITDA

Pricing Tips

- "Biotech, smaller pharma and R&D based companies are valued using a discounted cash flow of expected earnings less R&D expense and capital expenditures."
- "Depends on the market size and developmental maturity of products in the pipeline"
- "Because of products manufactured, it is important that the products are not on the FDA hit list."
- "Much of what the company is valued at will depend on how many products they manufacture, the concentration of clients to the gross revenues, the cost margin for each product, the number of short runs versus the number of long runs, and the opportunity for expansion through existing clients."

27th Edition

Expert Comments

"Seek outside advice for estimates of value. A thorough investigation of competing products is worth the effort. Consider taking an upfront retainer to cover some hard costs. Often when a company wants to sell it's because they are running out of cash. Therefore, it's critical to consider the company's burn rate alongside the length of the listing agreement."

"Value in this industry predicated on intellectual property, which means replication is or should be difficult. The industry has been riding a three-year upswing where values and multiples have gone up substantially dovetailing several significant successes. Profit trends are historically lower as many companies are purchased by larger companies prior to the launch of their products. Marketability can be good but is hampered but a limited pool of buyers. This is a very high risk industry but also high reward which can bring in competitors vying for the same treatment space."

Benchmark Data

Statistics (Brand Name Pharmaceutical Manufacturing)

Number of Establishments	3,179
Average Profit Margin	23.3%
Revenue per Employee	$1,014,200
Average Number of Employees	52.0
Average Wages per Employee	$88,233

Products and Services Segmentation

Other	45.7%
Oncological products	10.8%
Antidiabetes products	9.4%
Mental health products	9.2%
Respiratory agents	7.9%
Autoimmune products	6.9%
Lipid regulators	5.3%
Antihypertensives	4.8%

Major Market Segmentation

Chain pharmacies	37.3%
Exports	31.5%
Independent pharmacies	12.8%
Food and grocery stores	8.4%
Long-term care providers	5.5%
Mail service providers	4.5%

Industry Costs

Profit	23.3%
Wages	9.5%
Purchases	30.4%
Depreciation	2.2%
Marketing	0.9%
Rent & Utilities	2.1%
Other	31.6%

Market Share

Johnson & Johnson	11.5%
Merck and Co., Inc.	11.0%
Amgen	10.7%
Pfizer Inc.	9.0%
AbbVie Inc.	8.5%
Sanofi	6.3%

Source: IBISWorld, April 2016

Statistics (Generic Pharmaceutical Manufacturing)

Number of Establishments	1,451
Average Profit Margin	11.1%
Revenue per Employee	$947,900
Average Number of Employees	50.7
Average Wages per Employee	$87,634

Products and Services Segmentation

Nervous system disorders and antihypertensives	20.5%
Other	19.7%
Mental health and lipid regulators	18.5%
Pain and antibacterials	16.9%
Antidiabetics and respiratory	8.9%
Antiulcerants and thyroid	7.0%
Dermatologicals and hormonal contraceptives	4.7%
ADHD and anticoagulants	3.8%

Major Market Segmentation

Thid-party payers	53.1%
Medicare	25.7%
Medicaid	13.3%
Out-of-pocket	7.9%

Industry Costs

Profit	11.1%
Wages	9.2%
Purchases	31.9%
Depreciation	2.2%
Marketing	1.9%
Rent & Utilities	2.1%
Other	41.6%

Market Share

Mylan Inc.	12.4%
Teva Pharmaceutical Industries Ltd.	7.2%
Sandoz Ltd.	5.6%

Source: IBISWorld, April 2016

- "Biotech and R&D companies do not follow the same matrix as many other companies because they are typically pre-revenue companies. Nonetheless, they carry intellectual and enterprise value which can be significant, even the smaller companies, to the right buyer. Finding the right buyers/bidders is the key to realizing the full value of the selling company."

- "Development stage: number of drugs in pipeline, and the stage of development"
- "Pharmaceutical businesses are premium now that many trademarked items are available and companies are getting top dollar. FDA requirements are hard, and it can take months to get a company approved for manufacturing."

Expenses as a percentage of annual sales

Cost of goods	30% to 35%
Payroll/labor Costs	30% to 32%
Occupancy	15% to 20%
Profit (estimated pretax)	20% to 30%

Industry Trend

- "More and more U.S. companies are being sold outside the U.S. and this is expected to continue with the standardization of product approval requirements. This is driving values up, especially for many of the smaller companies. Yet it also is becoming more important to research competitors before selling a business in this industry because they are not just found in the U.S. Management should be able to tell you what the competitive landscape looks like and any knowledgeable buyer will want to know in pre-due diligence."
- "Consolidation of existing companies and emergence of many new entrants"

Seller Financing

- "Senior debt can be very hard to get as there is often very little in the way of hard assets and profitability"
- 5 years

Resources

Websites
- FiercePharma: www.fiercepharma.com

Manufacturing—Plastic and Rubber Machinery		
	NAICS 333249	

Rules of Thumb

➤ 9 times EBITDA

Pricing Tips

- "Look at customer concentration; determine age and condition of equipment; look at industry diversification."

Expenses as a percentage of annual sales

Cost of goods	50%
Payroll/labor Costs	12%
Occupancy	08%
Profit (estimated pretax)	15%

Manufacturing—Plastic Products

SIC 3089-10	NAICS 3261	Number of Businesses/Units 7,548

Rules of Thumb
3.5 times SDE

➤ EBITDA is 4X to 7X depending upon size, product mix (less for automotive or appliance, more for medical, and size of products produced (more for companies with larger products, less for smaller products).

➤ EBIT is 5X to 8X, depending upon same considerations as EBITDA

➤ Both totals assume customer amounts of Working Capital (inventory+A/R+other current minus A/P+Accruals) transfers with the business.

Pricing Tips

- "Multiples of EBITDA vary significantly based upon the seller's revenues, sales/employee, age/size of its equipment, and what industries are served. Companies supplying the automotive and appliance industries have lower multiples than those serving other industries. Companies supplying the medical industry have the highest multiples (especially if they have a clean room operation). Furthermore, if the company has value-added services this results in a higher valuation. Generally speaking, the EBITDA multiple range for the industry is 4.5x to 5.5x for companies with less than $2 million of EBITDA, 5.0x to 7.0x for companies with $2 to $5 million of EBITDA and 6.0x to 8.0x for companies with more than $5 million of EBITDA. Companies serving the medical industry will have higher multiple ranges. Companies focused purely on automotive and/or appliances will have lower ranges."

- "The larger the operation, the higher the multiple. Customer concentration is also a huge factor; dependence on large customers significantly lowers valuation expectations. Companies deriving more than 50% of their revenues from medical products/customers will command a significantly higher multiple. Companies that derive more than 50% of their sales from automotive or appliance customers have lower multiples. Also, for injection molders, general metric is EBITDA minus CapEx since these companies have to invest annually in equipment."

- "Good company should have net profits in the 15%–20% range. Multiples in the range of 5 to 7 times EBITDA are possible for good companies. Niche businesses can be very attractive. A model with some manufacturing in the U.S. and some in China also works well."

- "Pricing depends on whether molding company has proprietary products or is a custom molder. Any proprietary products enhance the value. Concentration of customers is critical. High concentration = high risk. Machines vary significantly in capacity and are very expensive. They should be well-maintained and no more than 15 years old, depending on hours of usage. Capacity utilization is a critical questions. With aging baby boomers, technical staffing is becoming an issue due to lack of apprenticeships. Mold makers are 'dying' out. Few millennials are interested in becoming mold makers or molders. If a company relies on an aging in-house mold maker, be cautious. ISO certification is becoming more important, not only as a process control, but also as a marketing tool. ISO certified companies command a premium. Labor and insurance costs are rising, as is off-shore competition, and therefore robotic systems for removing and packaging parts add efficiency and command a premium. Molding is price competitive. Secondary operations, such as sonic welding, stamping, painting and assembly, are often the most, or only, profitable operations. It's important to look the markets being served by the molder and whether the customers face production cycles or seasonal variations. Buyers should be knowledgeable in plastics operations. Otherwise, it's a very big learning curve."

- "Contract manufacturers are worth less than manufacturers of proprietary products. Value is also dependent upon the type of processes used by the manufacturer. In order of value, from lowest to highest, based on processes used, thermoformers are the lowest value range, then blow-molders, then extruders, then rotational molders, then injection molders. The size of the equipment also is a factor in value; manufacturers who only produce small parts are much less valuable than those who can produce large parts/products. Any company focused on the automotive industry will command less interest from acquirers."

- "Manufacturers who can produce their products from recycled materials also have an advantage."

Expert Comments

"A lot of consolidation in the U.S. With competition from China, it is becoming easy to lose business."

"Location matters. When shipping plastic products, most shipments 'dimension out' before they weigh out, which means most manufacturers are located within 500 miles of their customers. Many larger manufacturers build/buy factories near their larger customers. Also, 10 to 15 years ago, this industry suffered heavily from off-shoring manufacturing to Asia. However, most of the new work is staying in the USA, leading to a resurgence in the industry. Plus, the Great Recession wiped out many, many companies leaving those in operation today in a much better position than pre-2008."

"It is a competitive industry but there is high demand for a well-run company. Proprietary niches are attractive. General commodity products get very little attention or value."

Benchmark Data

Statistics (Plastic Products Miscellaneous Manufacturing)

Number of Establishments ... 7,548
Average Profit Margin ... 6.0%
Revenue per Employee ... $286,400
Average Number of Employees ... 46.7
Average Wages per Employee ... $47,403

Products and Services Segmentation

Consumer, institutional and commercial fabricated plastic products ... 23.1%
Fabricated plastic products for transportation applications ... 22.1%
Plastic packaging ... 18.2%
Fabricated plastic products for building applications ... 12.1%
Other plastic products ... 11.4%
Reinforced and fiberglass plastic products ... 5.5%
Plastic plumbing fixtures ... 3.9%
Fabricated plastic products for electrical/electronic applications ... 3.7%

Major Market Segmentation

Hardware and home improvement wholesalers 30.1%
Automotive manufacturers 26.7%
Other... 14.3%
Plumbing fixture wholesalers 4.8%
Electrical and electronic manufacturers.. 4.5%
Furniture and furnishing wholesalers.. 4.1%

Industry Costs

Profit 6.0%
Wages... 16.7%
Purchases... 49.1%
Depreciation.. 2.6%
Marketing 0.3%
Rent & Utilities 3.3%
Other... 22.0%

Source: IBISWorld, May 2016

Expenses as a percentage of annual sales

Cost of goods..60% to 74%
Payroll/labor Costs...08% to 20%
Occupancy...05% to 10%
Profit (estimated pretax) ....07% to 12%

Industry Trend

- "The industry continues to be hurt by overseas competition, especially for smaller parts."
- "Slow growth"
- "2015 to 2018 are expected to be very good years for plastics manufacturers."
- "Lots of niches and continued growth. Companies in fast-growing niches like drones, medical manufacturing do well."
- "Most molders serve a given niche. The industry will rise and fall with the general economy."

Seller Financing

- "Typically these businesses are financed with outside financing, especially senior debt. They are asset-laden businesses and customarily easy to finance."

Questions

- "Most plastics companies are terrible at marketing. Ask the owner how they sell/market their products. Also ask what makes them different from their competitors."
- "Customer concentration. Size, in tons, of equipment. How do they sell their products?"

Resources

Websites

- American Chemistry: www.americanchemistry.com
  Injection Molding ReSource: www.injection-molding-resource.org

---

27th Edition **483**

Trade Publications

- Plastics News: www.plasticsnews.com
- Plastics Technology Magazine: www.ptonline.com
- Plastics & Rubber Weekly: www.prw.com
- Plastics Engineering Magazine: www.plasticsengineering.org

Associations

- Society of the Plastics Industry: www.plasticsindustry.org
- Society of Plastics Engineers: www.4spe.org
- Manufacturers Association of Plastics Processors: www.mappinc.com

Manufacturing—Powder Metallurgy Processing		
	NAICS 332117	

Rules of Thumb

➢ 50 to 60 percent of annual gross sales includes inventory

➢ 5 times EBIT

➢ 4.5 times EBITDA

Pricing Tips

- "Price could vary widely depending on growth prospects."
- "If EBIT is 12% of sales, the multiple at 60% is 5X. Most of these businesses now are not bringing double digits down to the EBIT line, but they still have a lot of assets, most of which would be hard to sell."
- "Industry is under significant stress due to the concentration in the auto industry. Companies with less exposure are performing better and will be more marketable than businesses with auto exposure over 50%."
- "Prices vary widely by product type, primary customer markets, and gross margins achieved."
- "Industry and customer concentration is a major influence in transactions."
- "None have any merit due to profitability variations; sanity check at 80 percent of revenue."
- "Gross margins consistency and diversification of the customer base add value to PM business."
- "Value is and should be a function of projected future cash flow."
- "Investment value drives this and other manufacturing markets. 5 to 6 times EBITDA (adjusted for synergy) is typical, but never a firm rule."
- "Transactions are driven by technology fit, growth prospects, profitability and other attributes of the selling company. Other key factors are: management, technology & systems, markets, and equipment age & mix. Markets served may have an influence and older smelting furnaces may detract slightly."

Expert Comments

"Basic changes in the industry and individual company concentration will control the rate of recovery."

"The industry is 70% automotive based which has had a significant effect on companies with a high percent of sales in this market segment. Non-automotive PM manufacturers are experiencing much better results."

"Profit margins have been squeezed in recent years due to movement offshore and increased volatility in raw material costs. In addition, the cost of capital equipment has increased faster than industry sales growth"

"The current trend to move manufacturing to China and India is affecting the key customer groups of many PM companies."

Benchmark Data

- "Sales per employee = $125,000 (varies with primary materials in products delivered)."

Expenses as a percentage of annual sales

Cost of goods	30%
Payroll/labor Costs	40%
Occupancy	20%
Profit (estimated pretax)	10%

Questions

- "Percent breakdown of customer types by market segment. How large are the top 10 customers? What percent of sales do the top 10 account for? How large is the engineering and tooling staff? What experience does the technical staff have? How long have they been with the company?"
- "Customer trends; industry concentration; changes in key technical, management personnel and direct production supervisors."

Manufacturing—Prefabricated Wood Buildings	
NAICS 321992	Number of Businesses/Units 877

Rules of Thumb

➤ 100 percent of annual sales includes inventory

Pricing Tips

- "Modular plants sell at a premium. Log home companies sell at a discount."
  "Dealer network is important, or if selling direct, quality of sales staff."

Expert Comments

"Difficult to develop designs and engineering and establish a reputation, so it is not easy to start business from scratch."

"The log and timberframe industry has suffered more than the building industry in general because it is such a custom building market that has a higher unit cost than more traditional construction and has been adversely affected (log structures in particular) by tightening energy and building code requirements."

Benchmark Data

Statistics (Prefabricated Home Manufacturing)

Number of Establishments	877
Average Profit Margin	1.9%
Revenue per Employee	$192,700
Average Number of Employees	46.4
Average Wages per Employee	40,642

Products and Services Segmentation

Manufactured mobile homes	55.3%
Prefabricated wood buildings	33.6%
Nonresidential mobile buildings	11.1%

Industry Costs

Profit	1.9%
Wages	21.3%
Purchases	63.0%
Depreciation	0.7%
Marketing	0.5%
Rent & Utilities	1.5%
Other	11.1%

Market Share

Berkshire Hathaway Inc.	30.6%
Champion Enterprises Inc.	6.6%
Cavco Industries Inc.	5.0%

Source: IBISWorld, May 2016

- "Gross profit over 35%"
- "$1 million to $1.5 million sales per salesperson"

Expenses as a percentage of annual sales

Cost of goods	50%
Payroll/labor Costs	15%
Occupancy	03% to 05%
Profit (estimated pretax)	05%

Industry Trend

- "The U.S. wood product manufacturing industry includes about 14,000 companies with combined annual revenue of about $67 billion. Demand is closely tied to the level of home construction. The profitability of individual companies depends on efficient operations, because many products are commodities. Large companies enjoy economies of scale in purchasing. Small companies can often compete successfully by focusing on a local market."

Source: http://www.firstresearch.com/Industry-Research/Wood-Product-Manufacturing.html

Questions

- "Warranty policy and expense. How much warranty exposure is there? Does company have a favorable reputation for taking care of warranties?"

- "What is your backlog? How many leads have you received over each of the last 5 years? How do you sell your product —through a dealer network or direct or both? What patented processed do you have? Do you have challenges meeting energy or structural/building codes? What info do you have for your sales performance by region for the last 5 years? How many competitors do you have and where are they located? Do you sell internationally? Brand name, length of time in business and type of building system are extremely important."

Manufacturing—Products from Purchased Steel

| | NAICS 3312 | |

Rules of Thumb

➢ 3 to 5 times SDE includes inventory

Expert Comments

"Product line is the main importance along with the ability to deliver."

Benchmark Data

- "Payroll costs, equipment maintenance and age of equipment"

Expenses as a percentage of annual sales

Cost of goods	15%
Payroll/labor Costs	35%
Occupancy	20%
Profit (estimated pretax)	20%

Industry Trend

- "If you have a niche business, you will do well. If you are a job shop, chances are you will struggle."

Questions

- "How many customers does he have and what is the percentage of his business?

Manufacturing—Scientific Instruments

Rules of Thumb

➢ "Company value is 3 to 6 times EBITDA."

Pricing Tips

- "Where are the products in the life cycle? What new products are about to be introduced? Do they have strong patents? What is the competitive situation?"

Expenses as a percentage of annual sales

Cost of goods	50%
Payroll/labor Costs	25% to 30%
Occupancy	15%
Profit (estimated pretax)	10%

Manufacturing—Showcase, Partition, Shelving, and Lockers

	NAICS 337215	

Rules of Thumb

➢ 2 to 3 times SDE plus inventory

Pricing Tips

- "Customer concentration and any special skills required to operate can make for a big difference in pricing."

Expert Comments

"Economy changes the profitability very quickly here."

Benchmark Data

Expenses as a percentage of annual sales

Cost of goods	35%
Payroll/labor Costs	40%
Occupancy	15%
Profit (estimated pretax)	10%

Manufacturing—Signs (See also Sign Companies)

SIC 7389-38	NAICS 339950	Number of Businesses/Units 28,394

Rules of Thumb

➢ 45 to 50 percent of annual sales plus inventory

➢ 2 to 2.5 times SDE plus inventory

Benchmark Data

Statistics (Billboard and Sign Manufacturing)

Number of Establishments	28,394
Average Profit Margin	5.5%
Revenue per Employee	$147,200
Average Number of Employees	3.5
Average Wages per Employee	$36,579

Products and Services Segmentation

Traditional billboards and signs	44.1%
Digital billboards and signs	40.2%
Other	15.7%

Major Market Segmentation

Accommodation and food services	35.8%
Other retailers	15.5%
Outdoor advertisers	15.0%
Car dealers and gas stations	12.2%
Government	10.0%
Professional services	6.5%
Other	5.0%

Industry Costs

Profit	5.5%
Wages	25.0%
Purchases	40.4%
Depreciation	1.6%
Marketing	0.8%
Rent & Utilities	3.2%
Other	23.5%

Source: IBISWorld, July 2016

Industry Trend

- "The International Sign Association's initial ISA Sign Industry Market Monitor shows anticipated growth in large-format printers, dynamic digital signage, electric signage, and wayfinding signage throughout 2014 and into 2015. The ISA Sign Industry Market Monitor, sponsored by the National Association of Sign Supply Distributors (NASSD), assesses key drivers to compile data that shows changes in the market.

  "Large-format printers will enjoy stronger than average growth in both 2014 (.47) and 2015 (.59). Its growth will come largely as the manufacturing sector bounces back, posting anticipated growth of 4% in 2014 and 5% in 2015.

  "Dynamic digital signage also will grow in 2014 (.21) and 2015 (.48), thanks largely to hardware and software revenue. Display mounts are forecast to increase gradually each year, averaging 2.9% growth annually through 2017. All other cable and miscellaneous hardware revenue is expected to increase an average of 2.4% each year during the same time period. Installation (2.4%) and project management revenue (2.0%) also show growth.

  "Electric signage will experience a stronger year in 2014 (.74) but 2015 reflects a less aggressive growth rate (.48). Growth in this sector will largely will come from increases in out-of-home advertising, which is expected to grow 18% in 2014 and 15% in 2015. Other key factors include retail output, which is expected to increase 3% in 2014 and 4% in 2015; manufacturing output (3%, 2014 and 5% 2015); and professional services output (2% each year).

  "Wayfinding signage (.71 in 2014 and .45 in 2015) will find its growth driven by new construction of highways and streets, which increases by 3% in 2014 before flattening in 2015, as well as growth in manufacturing, retail and professional services sectors."

Source: ISA Sign Industry Market Monitor

Resources

Associations

- International Sign Association (ISA): www.signs.org

Manufacturing—Small (See also Manufacturing—General)

Rules of Thumb

➢ 4 to 5 times SDE plus inventory

Pricing Tips

- "For manufacturing companies with sales of $1 million to $5 million, a crude rule of thumb is 3 to 4 times SDE, assuming the company is reasonably well established and viable. As company size goes up, the multiple will go up."
- "Factors to look for: sales/profitability trends; SDE (and trends); industry trends; years in operation; fixed asset value, seller financing. Risk factors: technology, competition, industry trends."

Manufacturing—Specialty Vehicle

Rules of Thumb

➢ 4 times SDE includes inventory

Pricing Tips

- "Evaluate inventory closely as there is a tendency to accumulate difficult-to-use inventory."
- "Look for amount of booked business. Lead times from getting the order to shipping the finished vehicle can run 12 months or more."
- "Evaluate financials closely. Many in this industry do not know what their true costs are."

Expert Comments

"It is difficult to acquire the expertise to build these vehicles. Many can build them—few can build them well."

"Homeland Security issues make this a growth industry. It is fairly easy to replicate the 'physical facility,' but the real market advantage comes from experience in designing, building and using these vehicles."

Benchmark Data

- "Difficult to estimate sales per employee, but should probably be $175,000–$200,000 per hourly production employee."

Expenses as a percentage of annual sales

Cost of goods	55%
Payroll/labor Costs	25%
Occupancy	05%
Profit (estimated pretax)	10%

Industry Trend

- "Much of the business is tied to Homeland Security. If there are attacks on our soil, demand will increase. Otherwise budget cutbacks will dampen demand."
- "The market for mobile command centers, bomb trucks, SWAT trucks, etc.

will continue to be strong as long as the U.S. has to fight terrorists. Many corporations are developing mobile marketing vehicles which will also help drive demand."

Questions

- "Who has design experience in the company? Who has the mfg. experience in the company? How do you accurately cost jobs?"
- "What portion of the business is municipal, corporate, & private? Who are the key employees with industry experience? What is your marketing/sales plan? What is your backlog of business?"

Resources

Websites

www.vehiclesuccess.com/links

Manufacturing—Sporting Goods & Outdoor Products		
	NAICS 339920	

Rules of Thumb

➢ 4 to 7 times EBITDA

Pricing Tips

- "Brand and customer concentration are extremely important factors in valuing a manufacturer of outdoor and/or sporting products. These consumer products include hunting equipment, ammunition, fishing equipment, camping gear, sporting goods, outdoor apparel, etc. Patents are also an important value driver by increasing barriers to entry and making these consumer products harder to imitate. Customer diversity and relationships with key distributors are important. Brand awareness and time in the market place also add value. Many manufacturers outsource to contract manufacturers overseas to control costs and create a variable cost model. It's important to understand the sustainability of these supplier relationships."

Expert Comments

"Trade association reports show that consumers continue to spend money on sporting goods, even in tough economic times."

Benchmark Data

- "Gross margins tend to be very high for these manufacturers, well north of 50%, especially when they outsource manufacturing. Therefore, do not use revenue Rules of Thumb."
- "Cost of Goods—30% to 50%"

Manufacturing—Stainless Steel Food Service Fabrication		
	NAICS 333319	

Rules of Thumb

➢ 3 to 6 times EBITDA depending on the company, industry and buyer.

Questions
- "Are you a custom fabricator also? Do you install? Do you sell other food-service equipment? Do you sell to the cruise lines?"

Manufacturing— Turbine and Turbine Generator Set Units		
	NAICS 333611	

Rules of Thumb

➢ 8 to 10 times EBITDA

Pricing Tips
- "Use cap rate, similar to pricing commercial real estate."

Expert Comments

"This industry is, for a number of reasons, going to grow dramatically over the next decade. The economic model is very similar to that of commercial real estate—high upfront capital costs followed by extremely consistent cash flows, with upside appreciation potential. Smart money will get in early and ride the wave."

Benchmark Data
- "Revenue per kilowatt hour, capacity factor, PPA rate"

Industry Trend
- "The world market for turbines and related products (turbine-based engines, generators, and generator sets) is forecast to rise 6.4 percent annually to $162 billion in 2016. Wind turbines will remain the largest and fastest growing segment (albeit at a more moderate rate), while demand for gas combustion turbines will accelerate."

  Source: http://www.freedoniagroup.com/World-Turbines.html
- "Significant growth as the industry consolidates and becomes institutionalized."

Manufacturing—Valves		
	NAICS 332911	Number of Businesses/Units 1,337

Rules of Thumb

➢ 5 times EBITDA

Pricing Tips

- "Special consideration given for special products, market share, industry recognition."

Expert Comments

"A lot of competition with 'commodity' type valves; the more specialized, the less competition"

Benchmark Data

Statistics (Valve Manufacturing)

Number of Establishments	1,337
Average Profit Margin	7.2%
Revenue per Employee	$361,100
Average Number of Employees	72.2
Average Wages per Employee	$60,149

Products and Services Segmentation

Industrial valves	40.2%
Fluid power valves and accessories	31.1%
Other	16.0%
Plumbing fixture valves, fittings and trim	12.7%

Major Market Segmentation

Exports	37.5%
Construction	17.5%
Heavy manufacturing and mining	11.8%
Oil and gas	11.7%
General manufacturing	6.3%
Aerospace	5.6%
Utilities	5.5%
Other	4.1%

Industry Costs

Profit	7.2%
Wages	16.7%
Purchases	45.0%
Depreciation	2.4%
Marketing	0.3%
Rent & Utilities	1.3%
Other	27.1%

Source: IBISWorld, February 2016

Expenses as a percentage of annual sales

Cost of goods	60%
Payroll/labor Costs	20%
Occupancy	20%
Profit (estimated pretax)	15%

Industry Trend

- "For the first time since 2009, U.S. industrial valve shipments are predicted to have almost no growth in 2016, according to the annual forecast of the Valve Manufacturers Association (VMA). VMA's forecast indicates shipments will be up just $3 million over 2015 to be about $4.5 billion total.

  "'Our industry crested in 2008 at about $4 billion before taking a tumble from the recession. We've been slowly gaining ground ever since, but this is the first year we're predicting little to no growth,' says VMA President Bill Sandler.

  "'One of the reasons for the flatness from 2014 to 2015 is that the petroleum and power industries have encountered significant downturns, which affects our overall numbers,' he adds."

  Source: "Forecast for U.S. Valve Industry: No Growth Expected," by Judy Tibbs, February 16, 2016, http://www.valvemagazine.com/web-only/categories/trends-forecasts/7357-forecast-for-u-s-valve-industry-no-growth-expected.html

- "Trends toward specialization"

Seller Financing

- 5 years

Resources

Trade Publications

- Valve Magazine: http://www.valvemagazine.com/

Manufacturing—Wood Kitchen Cabinets and Countertops		
	NAICS 337110	

Rules of Thumb

➤ 2 to 2.5 times SDE plus inventory

Pricing Tips

- "Such companies are considered light manufacturing operations and since demand for manufacturing is at a premium, pricing may command higher multiples. Considerations must be put on how dependent on the amount of customization and specialty product the companies produce. Franchised operations are easier to assess if the owner is part of the production or part of marketing and sales. Franchised resale operations could be truly turnkey. If franchise resale, the territory scope could have a bearing on the multiples as its demographic plays a role in the profitability and scalability of the opportunity."
- "Some wood cabinet manufacturers have state-of-the-art equipment that increases the efficiency of the business. Analyzing and adding the value of the equipment is a component of the above."

Expert Comments

"Pricing the business accordingly will help sell the business quickly. A seller asking or waiting for a premium price might be coached to be prepared to get to closing. If the transaction is franchise resale, obtain and find out the resale process from the franchisor early in the process."

"Barriers to entry could be difficult unless someone has previous experience and a good handle on sales and marketing. Once established it could be 'auto pilot' as long as an ongoing marketing campaign is established. This industry sector is attractive to previous corporate executives and managers who have a penchant for light manufacturing operations."

"The sales trends are determined on the general economy of the geographic area. When housing starts are booming, demand is high."

Benchmark Data
- "The ability to buy supplies (melamine, hardware, etc) at a volume increases your profitability, as volume buy drives costs down."

Expenses as a percentage of annual sales
Cost of goods	25%
Payroll/labor Costs	35%
Occupancy	10%
Profit (estimated pretax)	0

Industry Trend
- "A steady trend for demand is expected. The millennial age group does have a tendency to rent versus buy homes. Most of the closet/cabinet/organizing industry lends to homeowners, but the ongoing home improvement of the baby boomer, coupled by high growth regions, will provide the steady growth. Not significant but steady."

Seller Financing
- "A high percentage will be eligible for SBA financing so most owners/sellers are able to walk away with a good amount of cash at closing. Seller financing 10% at a minimum."

Questions
- "How easy or difficult has it been to hire the production labor? What's your turnover rate in this area? Do you do the sales, are you in the production area or are you in the delivery area? How many vendors do you have to source the materials?"

Resources
Associations
- www.NAPO.net: National Association of Professional Organizers

Manufacturing—Wood Office Furniture		
SIC 2499-02	NAICS 337211	

Rules of Thumb
➤ 2.5 to 3 times SDE includes inventory

➤ 2.5 to 3 times EBITDA

Pricing Tips

- "Very cyclical business"
- "Rules of Thumb do not work well for an industry this diverse."
- "Customer list drives the value."

Expert Comments

"Really depends where you are on the food chain; these vary from high- to low-margin businesses."

"Very dependent on economic cycles and affected by China"

Expenses as a percentage of annual sales

Cost of goods	40%
Payroll/labor Costs	30%
Occupancy	20%
Profit (estimated pretax)	10%

Industry Trend

- "More consolidation and offshore competition"

Questions

- "How much design work and fashion trends?"

Resources

Associations

- Business and Institutional Furniture Manufacturers Association: www.bifma.org

	Franchise
Marble Slab Creamery (See also Franchises, Ice Cream/Yogurt Shops)	

Approx. Total Investment	$230,000 to $408,000
Estimated Annual Sales/Unit	$225,000

SIC 2024-98	NAICS 722515	Number of Businesses/Units 366

Rules of Thumb

➢ 45 percent of annual sales plus inventory

Resources

Websites

- www.marbleslab.com

Marinas (See also Boat Dealers)		
SIC 4493-06	NAICS 713930	Number of Businesses/Units 12,495

Rules of Thumb

➢ 10 to 12 times SDE plus inventory

➢ 10 times EBIT

➢ 11 to 12 times EBITDA

➢ 10 + times SDE plus inventory ("The real estate is included in the 10 + SDE figure. It is almost always owned. Very seldom is it leased, and then usually as part of a concession which has been bid out, say by the National Park Service or the TVA or something like that.")

Pricing Tips

- "Since the purpose of due diligence is to confirm the property's economic viability, the investor needs to know the property's probable expenses and income. Understanding the following can help to predict expenses and income:
  - ✓ capital costs required to make upgrades to the facility or to meet the investor's intended vision;
  - ✓ repair and maintenance costs associated with maintaining the facility such as maintenance dredging and periodic inspections of the structures;
  - ✓ operating and management costs for running the day-to-day business;
  - ✓ predicted income generated from slip rates;
  - ✓ slip mix occupancy and any seasonal fluctuations;
  - ✓ absorption; and
  - ✓ other services or products offered." (Dated, but still of interest)
    Source: http://www.ccim.com/cire-magazine/articles/159597/2012/03/
    unsinkable-investments/?gmSsoPc=1 (Dated, but still of interest)

- "This is a very complicated business. Estimating the selling price has many factors such as: dock leases, leases with resorts, years of operation, strength of mid-level management, survey of the vessels, competition, market, etc. Bottom line, it would be foolish to use a multiplier without a great deal of study."

- "Be very careful using multipliers as the price of waterfront land greatly distorts the valuation of a marina. The best rule of thumb is to ensure that slip rental and boat storage income will suffice to cover debt service, allowing the buyer to make a living off the other services offered by the marina."

- "Waterfront property makes the earnings multiple much higher than most businesses. That and the fact that marinas are very difficult to start from scratch anymore"

- "There are so many businesses within a marina that a % of gross is misleading at best. The pricing is driven by the real estate (waterfront property) and is usually at least 10 x EBITDA. The ROI is terrible. One is buying a lifestyle."

Expert Comments

"It is a tourist related industry. If the location requires costly travel and the economy is soft, the sales will be down."

"Location and facilities are critical but vary greatly."

"These businesses are notoriously hard to make a living at. They are hard work for very little return. I always tell purchasers they are buying a lifestyle and that they will probably work harder than they ever have. This is not a 'retirement' business."

Benchmark Data

Statistics (Marinas)

Number of Establishments	12,495
Average Profit Margin	15.3%
Revenue per Employee	$133,800
Average Number of Employees	3.0
Average Wages per Employee	$31,274

Products and Services Segmentation

Pleasure craft dockage, launching, storage and utilities services	40.6%
Fuel and merchandise sales	20.2%
Other	16.2%
Repairs and maintenance services	15.6%
Food and beverage sales	7.4%

Industry Costs

Profit	15.3%
Wages	23.5%
Purchases	31.9%
Depreciation	7.2%
Marketing	1.1%
Rent & Utilities	7.8%
Other	13.2%

Source: IBISWorld, May 2016

- "A marina is usually a combination of many businesses, each with its own benchmarks. You have a storage business, a service business, a gas station, boat sales, brokerage sales and sometimes a restaurant, all with different Rules of Thumb."
- "Slip rental income and storage fees should cover 100% of debt service. Owner compensation and other benefits would come from sales and service charges and appreciation of real estate value(s)."

Expenses as a percentage of annual sales

Cost of goods	60% to 65%
Payroll/labor Costs	20%
Occupancy	05% to 12%
Profit (estimated pretax)	05% to 10%

Industry Trend
- "Recreational boating will continue to be an expensive hobby, therefore demand for marinas depends on the amount of discretionary income consumers have for recreational activity. Per capita disposable income is forecast to rise in the next five years, encouraging consumers to purchase boats and marina memberships, given the increased financial security.

"The number of marina establishments is expected to grow an annualized 0.6% over the next five years, reaching 4,008 by 2020. The number of operators is forecast to increase at a similar rate of 0.5%, suggesting most businesses will enter the industry as a single marina operator, with some business expansion from existing marina operators."

Source: http://clients1.ibisworld.com/reports/us/industry/industryoutlook.aspx?entid=1654

- "With innovative design and consumer preferences for outboard power, many manufacturers are seeing the fishing boat replace the fiberglass I/O as the de facto family runabout.

  "'Reality is there are a lot of people that fish, [and] there are a lot of people that don't, but they want those dual consoles, they want those center consoles for the ease of boating' said Rob Parmentier, president and CEO of Larson Boat Group. 'You can put a lot of people on board, they have less canvas, they are easier to clean, a lot of them are easier to get in and out of. You can use them as kind of an SUV, and they have the technology of the outboard power, which has completely surpassed that of I/O.'"

  Source: "Market Trends: Family, outboard trends favor fishing boats" by Jonathan Sweet, 6/9/15
  http://www.boatingindustry.com/top-stories/2015/06/09/freshwater-phenomenon/

Seller Financing

- "It is extremely difficult to obtain bank financing, since the assets can literally float away. Large down payments and seller's financing is the rule."
- "Seller financing used as banks are loath to take any risks at all. They don't want foreclosure auctions which will only bring in a fraction of their loan."
- 15 years

Questions

- "Be ready for a lot of hard work. Ask about environmental history. Be careful of new boat sales as the floor plans/interest thereon will eat you up. Competition results in razor thin margins. Stick to brokerage if possible."
- "Why are you selling? Are you environmentally 'clean'? What would you do differently if you were starting again?"
- "The number 1 question would be to cover all environmental issues. A Phase 1 would probably be called for."
- "Do you have any environmental issues, are your storm water plans up to date?"

Resources

Associations

- Boat Owners Association of the U.S.: www.boatus.com
- National Marine Manufacturers Association: www.nmma.org
- American Boat Builders and Repairers Association: www.abbra.org
- Association of Marina Industries: www.marinaassociation.org

Marine/Yacht Services (Boat/Repair) (See also Marinas)	
NAICS 811490	Number of Businesses/Units 118,243

Rules of Thumb

- ➢ 100 percent of annual sales includes inventory
- ➢ 2.3 times SDE includes inventory

M - Rules of Thumb

Pricing Tips

- "Determine value of furniture, fixtures & equipment; any warranty work involved?"

Expert Comments

"The mega-yacht (80-foot to 180-foot boats) is a major growth industry, especially in south Florida."

Benchmark Data

Statistics (Boat Dealership and Repair)

Number of Establishments	118,243
Average Profit Margin	5.9%
Revenue per Employee	$135,200
Average Number of Employees	1.3
Average Wages per Employee	$16,511

Products and Services Segmentation

New boats	56.5%
Parts and repair services	29.7%
Used boats	13.8%

Industry Costs

Profit	5.9%
Wages	12.2%
Purchases	63.6%
Depreciation	1.0%
Marketing	1.3%
Rent & Utilities	3.6%
Other	12.4%

Market Share

MarineMax Inc.	4.2%

Source: IBISWorld, July 2016

Expenses as a percentage of annual sales

Cost of goods	30%
Payroll/labor Costs	15%
Occupancy	07%
Profit (estimated pretax)	40%

Industry Trend

- "Growth"

Questions

- "Customer base, length of time in industry, employee turnover, specific services performed"

	Franchise

Martinizing Dry Cleaning (See also Dry Cleaning, Franchises)

Approx. Total Investment		$305,000 to $593,700
	NAICS 812320	Number of Businesses/Units 422

Rules of Thumb

> Note: Also known as One Hour Martinizing

> 55 to 60 percent of annual sales plus inventory

Benchmark Data

- "He said a franchisee could open a store for anywhere from $293,500 to $476,000, including the franchise fee and purchase of in-house dry cleaning equipment. A typical investment for a franchisee to open a store would be $390,000."
- "Four percent of the sales from a franchised store's gross sales go back to the company."

  Source: "Martinizing Cleans Up" by Jeff McKinney, www.greenearthcleaning.com

Resources

Websites
- www.martinizingfranchise.com

	Franchise

McGruff's Safe Kids ID System

Approx. Total Investment		$7,995 to $9,995
		Number of Businesses/Units 26

Rules of Thumb

> 52 percent of annual sales plus inventory

Resources

Websites
- McGruff'sSafe Kids ID Systems: www.mcgruff-tid.com/

Meat Markets

SIC 5421-07	NAICS 44521	Number of Businesses/Units 9,600

Rules of Thumb

> 40 percent of annual sales plus inventory

> 2.5 times SDE includes inventory

> 5 times monthly sales plus inventory

Benchmark Data

Statistics (Meat Markets)

Number of Establishments	9,600
Average Profit Margin	3.4%
Revenue per Employee	$181,400
Average Number of Employees	4.4
Average Wages per Employee	$21,117

Products and Services Segmentation

Broilers	42.1%
Beef	25.8%
Pork	23.6%
Turkey	7.4%
Other red meat and fish	0.5%
Other chicken	0.6%

Industry Costs

Profit	3.4%
Wages	11.6%
Purchases	68.0%
Depreciation	1.7%
Marketing	1.7%
Rent & Utilities	5.0%
Other	8.6%

Market Share

Omaha Steaks International Inc.	6.8%

Source: IBISWorld, October 2015

Expenses as a percentage of annual sales

Cost of goods	50%
Payroll/labor Costs	15%
Occupancy	10%
Profit (estimated pretax)	15%

Industry Trend

- "Newspapers and news Websites have spent considerable ink (or kilobytes) this year talking about the rising prices of meat and poultry products, and some pundits questioned if there would come a price point where consumers had to stop buying meat altogether. If there is such a cliff, the market hasn't found it yet.

  "In reality, consumers bought meat at supermarkets or restaurants as much as they ever have. They may have reallocated their shopping dollars or switched proteins, but they kept meat on the plate more often than not. 'Everything that we see says that demand is holding up, so the consumer wants to buy beef,' says John Lundeen, executive director of market research for the National Cattleman's Beef Association."

  Source: http://www.preparedfoods.com/articles/115134-top-meat-and-poultry-trends-in-2015

- "As a result, Packaged Facts estimates that retail sales of meat and poultry products topped $85 billion in 2012, up from nearly $73 billion in 2008. Looking ahead, sales are projected to grow to $98.3 billion by 2017. Supporting that growth will be an economic recovery that, while it has been very slow, is underway and likely to pick up steam with each passing year."

Source: www.packagedfacts.com

- "Boutique butchers are now opening in cities across the country, from Brooklyn to Los Angeles, selling high-end, grass-fed meats to health-conscious consumers and foodies chasing trends, such as the charcuterie craze."

Source: "Family-run Denver butcher shop celebrates 90 years in business,"
www.denverpost.com/news May 25, 2013

Resources

Websites
- North American Meat Institute: www.meatami.org

Associations
- National Cattlemen's Beef Association: www.beef.org

Medical and Diagnostic Laboratories		
	NAICS 621511	Number of Businesses/Units 34,784

Rules of Thumb

➤ 1 times Annual Gross Sales

➤ 3 to 4 times SDE plus inventory

➤ 4 to 5 times EBIT

➤ 4 to 5 times EBITDA

Pricing Tips
- "Good diversity of accounts, good 3rd party payer contracts a must"
- "Multiple of SDE increases with profit levels."
- "Client concentration, market penetration and ability to expand"

Expert Comments

"It would take over four years to replicate a new diagnostic clinic and that long to obtain a good strong client base."

"Difficult to acquire accounts since physician groups don't like to make changes. 3rd party payer contracts are difficult to obtain"

"This is a marketing business. Location, ease of service, and networking with doctors and attorneys is a must."

Benchmark Data

Statistics (Diagnostic & Medical Laboratories)

Number of Establishments	34,784
Average Profit Margin	14.6%
Revenue per Employee	$186,300
Average Number of Employees	8.3
Average Wages per Employee	$60,423

Products and Services Segmentation

General pathology services	30.8%
Clinical pathology services	22.8%
Other	17.5%
X-ray/radiography imaging services	10.0%
Magnetic resonance imaging (MRI) services	9.9%
Anatomic pathology services	9.0%

Major Market Segmentation

Private insurance payments	41.3%
Medicare and Medicaid payments	20.5%
Health practitioners payments	10.9%
Hospital payments	9.7%
Other	6.9%
Patient out-of-pocket	6.0%
Outpatient care facility payments	2.5%
Other healthcare providers payments	2.2%

Industry Costs

Profit	14.6%
Wages	32.5%
Purchases	11.5%
Depreciation	3.8%
Marketing	0.4%
Rent & Utilities	4.2%
Other	33.0%

Market Share

Laboratory Corporation of America Holdings	18.1%
Quest Diagnostics Inc.	14.0%

Source: IBISWorld, May 2016

- "The purchase of your reagents and the building of your client list are the most important factors. This is a marketing business to some degree."
- "Sales are measured on a per-technician basis. Each MRI tech should produce a certain level of revenue."
- "Broad, even client base a big plus. Ability to expand beyond immediate geographical region without significant working capital requirements."

Expenses as a percentage of annual sales

Cost of goods	13% to 20%
Payroll/labor Costs	44% to 45%
Occupancy	03%
Profit (estimated pretax)	30% to 35%

Industry Trend

- "Heavy competition, steady growth for next 5 years, heavy regulation, low capital intensity."
- "Handheld ultra-sound scanners that are as 'cheap as a stethoscope' is the goal of a $100 million development project. Just as the clinical laboratory industry is seeing entrepreneurs pour hundreds of millions of dollars into

projects intended to create miniature medical laboratory testing devices, so also is radiology and imaging a target for ambitious entrepreneurs. The vision of biotechnology entrepreneur Jonathan Rothberg, Ph.D. is to have patients take a trip to their neighborhood drugstore rather than an imaging center the next time they need an ultrasound or MRI."

Source:" Biotech Entrepreneur Ready to Spend $100 Million to Design Cheap and Easy-to-Use Handheld Ultrasound Scanners that Can Be Used in Drugstores" by Andrea Downing Peck 8/3/15

- "Healthcare has been shifting from curative care to detection, prevention and personalized care over the past five years, which has benefited the diagnostic and medical laboratories industry. Moreover, the trend of preventive care stimulates demand for industry services, as more physicians monitor patients' blood and tissue, and test for health ailments with technology like MRI scans. However, the recession caused fewer individuals to have employer mandated health insurance and greatly limited industry revenue growth over the period. Nevertheless, during the next five years, the industry is expected to benefit from healthcare reform and the growing aging population, which will boost revenue. Geographic access to physicians has improved during the past five years, whereas laboratories have not diffused to rural areas as quickly."

Source: IBISWorld, April 2014

- "Flat to slightly growing"
- "More personal injury MRIs"

Seller Financing
- "Outside financing"
- "Yes, about 25% of the selling price can be seller financed over three to four years."

Questions
- "Payer mix, market share, patient demographic data."
- "Payer contracts, employee retention, distributor contracts for goods sold"

Resources
Trade Publications
- Clinical Laboratory and Pathology News and Trends: www.darkdaily.com

Associations
- American Society for Clinical Laboratory Science : www.ascls.org

Medical Billing		
	NAICS 541219	Number of Businesses/Units 3,940

Rules of Thumb
- 70 to 75 percent of annual sales plus inventory
- 3 times SDE
- 4 times EBIT
- 3 to 3.5 times EBITDA

Pricing Tips

- "When pricing a medical billing company, some factors to consider would be the client list, owner involvement, and the scalability of the operation."
- "Specialties of clients are a very important factor."
- "The value of medical billing companies is heavily dependent upon the billing rates they charge their clients and the length of the contract. Billing rates are typically in the 5% to 8% range for larger accounts, but can be as high as 15% and as low as 2%."

Expert Comments

"For someone looking to sell their medical billing business, I would recommend looking at ways to decrease expenses, such as outsourcing labor or working from home. For buyers, if you see a good opportunity, move quickly. The best opportunities sell quickly."

"Due to new rules and regulations relating to Obamacare, the medical billing industry has recently seen significant growth."

"Buyers should educate themselves on upcoming changes within the industry and find out the specific area of medicine that each client practices, example: surgeons, clinics, dialysis centers, etc."

"This is a highly competitive industry that has a strong financial outlook with the changes in the health care field and complicated coding and billing procedures."

Benchmark Data

Statistics (Medical Claims Processing Services)

Number of Establishments	3,940
Average Profit Margin	26.7%
Revenue per Employee	$131,900
Average Number of Employees	2.5
Average Wages per Employee	$48,013

Products and Services Segmentation

Claims processing	60.0%
Claims investigations	15.0%
Policy and claims examinations	15.0%
Back-office, administrative support and consulting	10.0%

Major Market Segmentation

Healthcare providers	60.0%
Private insurers	25.0%
Government insurers	15.0%

Industry Costs

Profit	26.7%
Wages	36.6%
Purchases	1.4%
Depreciation	1.7%
Marketing	1.0%
Rent & Utilities	2.4%
Other	30.2%

Market Share

HMS Holdings 33.9%
Source: IBISWorld, October 2015

- "Payroll typically runs 40-55% of revenue."
- "Sales per FT employee are typically around $100,000."

Expenses as a percentage of annual sales

Cost of goods.. 0
Payroll/labor Costs..45% to 50%
Occupancy 05%
Profit (estimated pretax) 25%

Industry Trend

- "I see an upward trend for this type of business over the next few years."
- "Very positive trend for the industry as a whole with larger companies looking to do roll-ups of smaller companies as the industry is consolidating."

Seller Financing

- "Seller financing is very common. However, the buyers for Chiropractically Yours were able to secure SBA financing. I believe future medical billing transactions will include outside financing due to the increase of SBA loans we are currently experiencing."

Questions

- "A good question for a buyer to ask a seller would be if there are any client concentration issues."

Resources

Associations

- Healthcare Billing and Management Association: www.hbma.org

Medical Practices (Physicians)		
SIC 8011-01	NAICS 621111	Number of Businesses/Units 463,300

Rules of Thumb

- 35 to 45 percent of annual gross sales includes inventory
- 1 to 3 times SDE includes inventory
- 1.5 to 2.5 times EBITDA
- 2.5 to 3.5 times EBIT

Pricing Tips

- "Price Rules of Thumb vary greatly (I mean a lot) based on practice type. Most primary care practices will sell in the 30%–35% range as percentage of gross. But can vary from zero % to 50% for small 1–4 doctor practices. Averages for specialty practices tend to be lower, perhaps in the 20%–25% range. Physical therapy and psychology/psychiatric higher in the 40%–45% range. Again these prices can vary greatly depending on number factors. Carefully examine discretionary earnings compared to industry compensation exceptions for that particular specialty. Compensation expectations vary dramatically for different types of doctors. $200K might be good for one type of doctor, whereas in other specialties new grads might commonly make $350K. Look at patient load and hours worked compared to industry norms for that specialty."

- "Industry sales dependent on the seller's role in the business, with a lower valuation going to extremely active owners and especially in the sale of practices."

- "Most medical practices are created and run to create high income for labor, not profit or EBITDA. There is an excess of jobs available driving up salaries and driving down profits, so driving down value. The Goodwill Registry on sale-data is helpful in some cases, but the often-quoted running-average 10-year median goodwill-value as a percentage of gross is irrelevant; as the average of many specialties reflects the midpoint of 10 years' steady decline. You need to acquire the full database and evaluate the underlying data to be useful; and look in particular at the Price:SDE data. The effect of the Medicare cuts which began in 2005 can distort the Registry summary statistics and need to be adjusted; and you need to remove results from court-valuations, divorces and other non-transactional data. The value of medical practices is generally at an all-time low. Decisions regarding what, where, when and how to practice are influenced by numerous factors, including: personal preferences, market forces, state and federal policies and programs, and institutions that constitute the health care system and medical education infrastructure. Increasing retirement, plus the trend toward shorter working hours, increases the supply of practices for sale, and decreases the available FTE workforce available as buyers. The increasing rate of boomer retirement and decreasing count of new physicians contribute to a reduction of value of practices for sale. A significant shortfall of physicians could develop over the next 15 or more years in the absence of increased output from U.S. medical schools, increased recruitment of foreign-trained physicians, or both. The American College of Physicians is concerned that the practice environment for those in medical practice has become so encumbered with regulation and practice hassles, at a time when reimbursement for care provided by physicians is declining, that physicians are finding it increasingly difficult to provide for their patients. Of particular concern when determining value of a medical practice is ensuring not only that the purchase price is Fair Market Value, but also that the valuation method does not take into account the volume or value of referrals that the selling physician has made or may make to the purchaser, such that the purchase price could be challenged as a kickback or inducement. The OIG has provided guidance on the question of how to value a physician practice or other healthcare provider. The ailing economy is leading many Americans to skip doctor visits, skimp on their medicine, and put off tests. Employment by hospitals is paying more, and insurance-reimbursement and gross income is often dropping, so the results of the Income Approach of valuation identifying 'dividends' [(SDE minus market rate compensation of one working owner) x 2 (i.e., 50% Cap rate)] is becoming more important for more specialties. 'Percentage of annual gross sales' or 'SDE multiplier' as valuation Rules of Thumb are obsolete, if ever valid. Growth Rates are available through the Congressional Budget Office reports; rarely above 2% historically. Medical practice is riskier—and demands higher Cap rates—than other professional practices like accounting, law, architecture and engineering which are not subject to clinical malpractice risks, or subject to Medicare or insurance company changing reimbursement limitations or denials. Many practices can't even sell at the value of the liquidated assets, since jobs pay more without asset purchase. The impact of specialty and location is profound, as is the FTE work schedule and leverage of employed licensed providers. Medicare is continually reducing reimbursement, which impacts other insurances which often base their payment on a percent of Medicare (i.e., 80–120% of Medicare), so dependence on insurance reimbursement is an important consideration in value. In addition, specific diagnosis and procedure ('ICD/CPT') billing-code reimbursement changes—like what has happened in dermatology, ophthalmology, allergy, cardiology, and other specialties—have further reduced reimbursement and profits during the past decade. Cash and cosmetic practices are usually worth more since there is a higher profit for less work, and often provide a better lifestyle, but even those can be difficult to sell. Many specialties are having trouble attracting new doctors no matter the income, so guaranteed wages are increasing, sales are becoming more difficult, and values are dropping. Make sure to read the 'white papers' on supply and demand available on many specialty professional association websites. The best overhead statistics are usually available at http://www.NSCHBC.org. The best market rate compensation stats are usually available at http://www.MGMA.com."

- "The rule of thumb in any of the medical fields (i.e., accepting Medicare) is 1.5 x dividends as defined by IRS RR59-60. (You can call it 1.5 x EBITDA, but that is slightly incorrect for non-capital, asset-heavy businesses). Includes normal inventory but not excess inventory. %-of-gross hasn't applied to medicine in decades since the doctor shortage began.

  "From SDE, I will subtract the estimate of the cost of employing one person at the same level of licensure, with the same work schedule, and with the same experience and sophistication as the current owner, at a market rate of compensation. This provides a perspective as if the owner was instead employed, and the balance was a return on investment to ownership. Another way to look at this is the result is the income available to the owner if the owner couldn't work and had to hire an equivalent replacement licensed professional to see the patients. This remainder income is equivalent to what the IRS defines as 'Dividends' in RR59-60. Dividends will be the income stream analyzed in the Income Approach."

- "If the practice is located near a hospital it will increase the value. Since there are so many specialties, a family practice might be easier to sell."

- "The payer mix (private insurance, Medicare/Medicaid and cash (fee for service) influences value. Practices heavy in Medicare or Medicaid reimbursements tend to have a lower valuation than those with a more balanced mix or are more heavily weighted in fee for service and/or private insurance. Revenue trends, condition of facility and site and the level of technology used in the practice also play a role in valuation."

- "Medical record charts are not a true 'asset' of the medical practice since they can't be put on the balance sheet as an asset using the Asset Approach valuation methodology. Medical record valuation is only used to specifically allocate intangibles, assuming they exist at the time of the valuation. The physician has the physical chart but usually cannot legally sell or dispose of it without the patient's consent (per state statutes), only transfer 'custodianship.'

So the physician is basically a 'custodian' of the medical record rather than an owner of an asset with independent value. When paper charts are involved, I have come to the opinion that the value of the chart is zero because of the attendant custodianship liability costs. With EMR, a digital record may need to be converted from one digital platform to another either by custodianship transfer or technology succession, in which case a printout and re-entry may be required, probably exceeding in labor costs any physical value to the original digital chart.

"The billing process in a medical practice is very complex, both in generating the charges using appropriate diagnosis and treatment codes, and in recording the payment and adjustments for uncollectable amounts. 'Accounts Receivable' represent past gross charges for services rendered and as yet uncollected or adjusted-off. These receivables must be discounted to reflect both insurance company reimbursement disallowances, plus the decreasing value over time due to difficulty in collections of past due accounts. In other words, the historic collection ratio of the practice does not yet include the 'standing wave' of uncollectable accounts at practice end, or at a particular point in time, as in a valuation at a particular date."

- "Don't try to use boilerplate broker contracts to sell medical practices, as it is easy to violate state or federal regulations; have all the paperwork and terms done by a medical practice transaction specialist attorney."
- "Adjusted expenses and adjusted SDE are critical to determining profit potential."

Expert Comments

"Healthcare experience is essential for your advisors, including valuation professionals, accountants, attorneys, and others."

"There is more variance than ever in healthcare providers and the way that they run their businesses. Some have excellent, state-of-the-art facilities and are extremely efficient. Others have poor facilities and outdated technology and business models. The regulatory environment is extremely challenging and ever changing."

"The market is mostly doctors selling to other doctors. Very few non-doctors buyers/sellers outside of hospitals/large groups, though in some states and practice types non-physician ownership is allowed and you will find investor buyers."

"Competition is relatively high for most locations. Competition from large health care systems and hospitals can eat into independent practices. Risk is fairly low. Most buyers will do pretty much the same as a seller. However be careful with specialty or referral based practices as transferring goodwill can be difficult and require significant overlap with seller staying on post sale. Profit trend in general is up modestly. Highly regulated industry. Some specialties are winners, other are losers, as government basically decides reimbursements as insurance companies follow government. Most doctors' offices are in professional office buildings or hospital complexes or standalone facilities. Generally decent buildings. Marketability varies a lot by specialty type, income, number of doctors, location, industry trends. Industry trend is up. People need medical care. Despite regulation, people will continue to need care. Very easy to replicate/startup. One of the reasons price multiples are so low compared to other business types."

"You have to go through medical school to get a medical license to legally be a buyer in most states, so hard replication."

"It's pretty easy to set up a medical practice from scratch in any underserved market, if you know how."

"Number of specialists per 100K population varies. Obamacare and healthcare reform is causing turmoil in industry. Industry is constantly evolving in response to government laws/regulations. Above-average practices can usually sell okay. Underperforming practices may have virtually no value and be unable to sell."

"Sell at Fair Market Value (FMV) to avoid the Anti-Kickback Statute or Stark Law. Ensure physician compensation is at FMV. Inquire as to the payor mix of the physician or physician practice to be bought and inquire as to any regulatory issues regarding the physician or physician practice to be bought."

"Managed care, political pressure on lowing reimbursements, regulatory pressures, uncertainties all are playing a part in valuation declines in the healthcare industry."

"Physicians are very smart but often choose their advisors poorly. Selecting a team of trustworthy advisors (legal, accounting, transactional) is key to success."

"Medicare reimbursements dropping. Many practices picking up cosmetic and other ancillary profit centers."

Benchmark Data

Statistics (Primary Care Doctors)

Number of Establishments	200,417
Average Profit Margin	12.7%
Revenue per Employee	$198,000
Average Number of Employees	6.6
Average Wages per Employee	$76,766

Products and Services Segmentation

Diagnosis of general symptoms	32.0%
Diagnosis, screening and preventative care	26.0%
Other	17.0%
Diagnosis of symptoms related to the musculoskeletal systems	12.0%
Disease treatment	7.0%
Diagnosis of symptoms related to the respiratory system	6.0%

Industry Costs

Profit	12.7%
Wages	38.9%
Purchases	14.3%
Depreciation	1.4%
Marketing	0.6%
Rent & Utilities	4.0%
Other	28.1%

Source: IBISWorld, April 2016

27th Edition

Statistics (Specialist Doctors)

Number of Establishments	262,885
Average Profit Margin	11.2%
Revenue per Employee	$174,500
Average Number of Employees	5.7
Average Wages per Employee	$89,757

Products and Services Segmentation

Other	52.5%
Psychiatry	10.2%
Anesthesiology	8.9%
Obstetrics and gynecology	8.9%
Emergency medicine	7.5%
Radiology and diagnostic medicine	6.2%
General surgery	5.8%

Industry Costs

Profit	11.2%
Wages	51.4%
Purchases	14.3%
Depreciation	1.4%
Marketing	0.6%
Rent & Utilities	4.0%
Other	17.1%

Source: IBISWorld, May 2016

- "Again all of these numbers vary dramatically with practice specialty type. Some px types like psychiatry have almost no tangible assets, but a cosmetic surgery or imaging center may have millions tied up in capital assets/equipment. For most smaller (1–2) doctor practices you should see owner discretionary earnings above 50% of gross collections. Doctor compensation, support staff ratios, expense ratios are all different by specialty type. Many professional organizations have good Benchmark Data for comparison. The price that hospitals will pay for practices often is 10–20 cents on the dollar compared to what another owner practitioner doctor will pay. Ability to transfer goodwill varies by practice type. Primary care transfers easier than specialty. Multi-doctor transfers easier than solo doctor."
- "Per bed, per full-time employee (FTE); per physician; per square foot; per machine; per member per month (PMPM)."
- "Physician salaries—Annual earnings from patient care

Highest paid specialties

Orthopedics	$421,000
Cardiology	$376,000
Gastroenterology	$370,000
esthesiology	$358,000
Plastic Surgery	$354,000

Lowest paid

Rheumatology	$205,000
Internal medicine	$196,000
Diabetes & endocrinology	$196,000
Family medicine	$195,000
Pediatrics	$189,000"

Source: "Precarious future for primary care," by R. Michael Rosenblum, *Boston Globe*, June 23, 2015

- "Practice benchmarks vary with specialty. Look up statistics/benchmarks for the practice type in question. A psychiatry practice may be a solo operation in

200SF with no support staff and almost no assets. A cosmetic plastic surgeon may have $500K in equipment and an in-house accredited surgical suite with a lot of staff. An oncology or allergy practice may have a great deal of value in drug inventory, whereas a pediatric practice may have no drug inventory. So for some practice types (e.g., psychiatry) the cost of goods sold is very small. Others have significant COGS. For most practice types expect a support staff ratio of 3–5 per full time doctor."

- "Profit for physician practices should be above 50%"
- "Revenue per procedure, cost per procedure, revenue per FTE physician, cost per FTE physician, revenue per work relative value unit (wRVU), cost per work relative value unit (wRVU) and compensation per work relative value unit (wRVU)"
- Note: www.healthcon.org is an excellent site and has a lot of data; however, one must purchase it, and non-members pay a lot more than members.

Expenses as a percentage of annual sales

Cost of goods... n/a
Payroll/labor Costs...25% to 40%
Occupancy ....05% to 10%
Profit (estimated pretax) ....10% to 20%

Industry Trend
- "More value-based payment as opposed to fee-for-service. More effective and efficient use of mid-level providers and technology."
- "General consolidation with hospitals and groups buying practices. But this varies by location. Some are buying, some are not. Some only want certain types of practices. The percentage of independent practice owners has decreased significantly in the last 10–15 years. Number of independent practices is about 30% of physicians."
- "Medical will continue to be in demand by buyers."
- "Under PPACA (Obamacare) hospitals are the main buyers, and can charge double what the acquired physicians could."
- "Increased merger & acquisition (M&A) activity, and steady growth in revenue."
- "Other important changes in physician practice arrangements that occurred between 2012 and 2014 include:
  - ✓ The share of physicians who were practice owners decreased from 53.2 percent to 50.8 percent.
  - ✓ The share of physicians who were in solo practice decreased 18.4 percent to 17.1 percent.
  - ✓ The share of physicians who were directly employed by a hospital increased from 5.6 percent to 7.2 percent
  - ✓ The share of physicians who were in practices that had at least some hospital ownership increased from 23.4 percent to 25.6 percent."

Source: http://www.ama-assn.org/ama/pub/news/news/2015/
2015-07-08-majority-americas-physicians-work-small-practices.page

- "Other types of practices hospitals have acquired include (in order of quantity):
  - ✓ Cardiology
  - ✓ Orthopedics
  - ✓ General Surgery
  - ✓ Endocrinology
  - ✓ Gastrointestinal
  - ✓ Urology
  - ✓ Oncology

M - Rules of Thumb

- "Hospitals report both offensive and defensive reasons for acquiring medical practices. These included:
  - ✓ Expanding service capabilities
  - ✓ Meeting community need
  - ✓ Insurance-related purposes
  - ✓ Increased efficiency and alignment
  - ✓ Increased Market Share
- "Other characteristics hospitals look for in an acquisition target include:
  - ✓ Reputation of the practice
  - ✓ Strategic value of the practice
  - ✓ Location of the practice
  - ✓ Quality of physician(s) in practice
  - ✓ Referral patterns
  - ✓ Existing relationships between hospital and practice"

Source: http://www.jacksonhealthcare.com/media-room/articles/physician-trends/physician-practice-acquisition-trends-2015/

- "The market trend is lower profits for the next few years."
- "A lot of turmoil due to regulatory changes. More practices trending to self-pay practices. Many doctors moving away from Medicaid and Medicare due to regulatory burden and low reimbursement. Still a very large part of the economy. Healthcare will still be strong in years to come. Likely to see more boutique practices and more capitation practices."
- "Demand for services and costs to provide services increasing while reimbursements decreasing."
- "Increasing competition; industry will tend to consolidate."
- "PPACA is driving physicians into employment, reducing available buyers."

Seller Financing
- "Seller financing is common, but outside financing is also available. Many hospitals are also purchasing medical practices."
- "Outside financing pretty common. Some seller carry."
- "100% financing is readily available through specialty bank departments."
- "Lenders look very favorably towards funding these deals. Many have special terms available for financing professional practices."

Questions
- "Obtain at least 5 years of tax returns, financial statements, productivity reports, aged accounts receivable. Carefully review leases, corporate agreements, employment agreements, payer agreements, etc. Many risks to be assessed."
- "Type of practice; hours worked per week; number of patient encounters per week; ancillary services % of revenue; types of procedures performed; drug inventory levels; in-house lab and equipment capabilities; industry trends for that particular specialty; number of providers; hospital/competition"
- "Historical productivity, payor mix. Unaudited financial statements are common in the industry."
- "An important fact is the type of medical practice, general or specialty! Number of Medicare and Medicaid patients? Billing process and whether in-house or farmed out."

- "Accounts receivable in collections amount should be under 25%. Insurance accepted and type of billing to insurance companies. Employee retention and turnover."
- "What are the ACO plans in this community? Is your ICD/CPT coding federally compliant? Are your provider employment and compensation plans and PECOS registrations state and federally compliant?"
- "History of staff, provider contracts, billing procedures type of patients"
- "Hours worked. Use of mid-level providers/physician extenders payer mix reimbursement trends up/down ancillary profit centers."
- "Sustainability of projected revenue stream, based on probability of patients remaining with practice, level of reimbursement yield, regulatory restrictions on ASTC, etc."
- "Atypical services, local hospital trends, specialty trends, insurance plans of note, % Medicaid, % Medicare, hidden income, technology and surgical obsolescence, if hospital will help recruit or is a potential buyer."
- "Why are you selling? Are you willing to recommend me to your patients, colleagues, and the community? Are you willing to provide full disclosure and transparency and assist to the fullest extent in transferring the value in the practice?"
- "Where do you get patients?"

Resources

Trade Publications
- Medical Economics: www.memag.com
- Physicians Practice: www.physicianspractice.com
- The BVR/AHLA Guide to Healthcare Valuation : www.amazon.com
- Medscape: www.medscape.com

Associations
- American Medical Association: www.ama-assn.org/ama
- Medical Group Management Association: www.mgma.com
- National Society of Certified Healthcare Business Consultants: www.nschbc.org
- American Academy of Family Physicians: www.aafp.org

Medical Spas		
	NAICS 812199	Number of Businesses/Units 23,175

Rules of Thumb
- ➢ 50% of Annual Gross Sales plus inventory
- ➢ 2.5 times SDE includes inventory
- ➢ 3.5 times EBIT
- ➢ 5 times EBITDA

27th Edition

Pricing Tips

- "Price varies according to the equipment as the industry is creating new treatments and new technologies every year. People are more aware of the newest treatments and the owners have to invest regularly in new equipment if they want to be able to keep the clientele.

  "More and more competitors are entering in this market because it's very profitable. Investors partner with doctors to create different types of spas, and business owners need to invest more money in marketing and social media to maintain their clientele. Clients are ready to invest a lot of money for their beauty, but they are becoming more demanding and look for the newest trends."

- "The most simple rule of thumb—with any legitimacy, limited as it is—is using a grossly simplified Income Approach, the primary approach per IRS Revenue Ruling 59-60. This approach looks at the return on investment (i.e., dividends) to the buyer after market-rate compensation of one working owner."

  Source: http://www.medicalpracticeappraisal.com/medspa-appraisal-valuation.html

- "1) It is critical to understand if the business had prepaid services as a liability. Many med spas have balance sheet complications due to large prepaid services that are paid in advance and delivered over a year or more. Any assumed liability by the buyer should be counted as consideration. 2) Because of equipment obsolescence, equipment leasing is common. 3.0 multiple assumes the seller pays off the leases or if the buyer assumes the leases, the assumed amount counts as consideration/purchase price. 3) Med spas with niche services such as hair replacement may bring a higher multiple, especially if they have a relationship with a well-known hair restoration/hair replacement surgeon."

Expert Comments

"To verify if the team is highly trained and experienced and how to secure the employees and clientele after the sale."

"Ease of replication is easy for new spas that don't have too much income, but very difficult to get the reputation and clientele built over the years; the number of good rated reviews on internet."

"Med spas provide a niche between spa/beauty treatments and invasive plastic surgery. With the aging population of baby boomers, more women and men are investing in non-invasive 'image enhancement.' Spending money on microdermabrasion, laser hair removal, Botox and other services is considered more acceptable than ever. Medical doctors see the category as attractive, as the services are almost always elective and do not involve insurance money and its associatedregulations."

Benchmark Data

Statistics (Health and Wellness Spas)

Number of Establishments	23,175
Average Profit Margin	10.6%
Revenue per Employee	$44,368
Average Number of Employees	16.6
Average Wages per Employee	$22,543

Products and Services Segmentation

Massage and bodywork treatments	35.6%
Skin-care treatments	24.1%
Hair and nail treatments	20.2%
Retail	10.8%
Other	9.3%

Major Market Segmentation

Adult women	52.7%
Seniors	18.9%
Adult men	18.1%
Teenagers and children	10.3%

Industry Costs

Profit	10.6%
Wages	50.7%
Purchases	15.7%
Depreciation	3.6%
Marketing	3.2%
Rent & Utilities	13.8%
Other	2.4%

Market Share

Massage Envy	9.0%

Source: IBISWorld, August 2016

Expenses as a percentage of annual sales

Cost of goods	05% to 10%
Payroll/labor Costs	30% to 35%
Occupancy	08% to 10%
Profit (estimated pretax)	25% to 30%

Industry Trend

- "The spas are intended to be more specialized in certain treatments for certain parts of the body or the face as so many new treatments and trends are appearing on the market. The spas would need more space and more equipment and qualified employees to be able to propose such a variety of treatments.

  "The trend is also to open larger spas with cafeteria, movement studio, retail accessories, beauty product store, and valet parking, to keep the clientele longer at the spa and to make them spend

  more money. So now the spa is becoming a leisure destination in itself"!
- "Eight biggest spa trends for 2015:
    - ✓ Wellness and preventive treatments
    - ✓ Specialty spas
    - ✓ Personalization
    - ✓ Treatments for men
    - ✓ Express, express, express
    - ✓ Social fitness
    - ✓ Expanded spa boutiques
    - ✓ Continued care"

27th Edition

- "'In the past, spas were trying to please everyone,' says Debra Koerner, co-founder of Well World Group, a spa consultancy firm. 'They were expanding their menus and offering an overwhelming number of services.' Fast forward to 2015. 'In the bigger cities, in particular, we're seeing more niche properties and new franchises open up that offer convenience and affordability, specializing in one thing— whether massages (Massage Envy now has 1,000 locations across 49 states.), brows, lashes, hair or feet.'"

  Source: http://www.marketwatch.com/story/8-biggest-spa-trends-for-2015-2015-01-14

- "One of the biggest factors influencing spa industry trends for 2015 is the Baby Boomers. The Baby Boomer generation in the U.S. will account for about 40% of all spending. That demographic of individuals, ranging from age 45 to 65, has a large focus on combating aging and slowing the process. In 2015, it is likely that there will be an increase of spa treatments to help with aging. Acupuncture is being more widely introduced into the Western world spas and while it is known to have positive mental health benefits, it can also rejuvenate skin! If you're able to get past nerves of needles, you should consider adding acupuncture as an offered service at your spa or wellness center."

  Source: http://www.floridaspaassociation.com/blog/spa-industry-trends-2015/

Seller Financing

- "We see in 80% of the cases seller financing—30% to 50%."
- 3 to 5 years

Questions

- "How did they get the clientele over the years, what the seller is intending to do after the sale, for how long the employees have been working in the business, their experience, and how do they get paid—on commission or fixed salary. How is the equipment: year, model, the maintenance? Is it all paid off? What are the nearest competitors in the area? Do a market search and go to the city hall or local business association to see if there are other projects for new spas that will open in the near future."
- "Revenue/service mix. Liability for prepaids. Equipment leases. Reason for selling."
- "1) Are there prepaids? 2) What unique services do you offer? 3) equipment leases 4) revenue/service mix 5) licensing/regulatory requirements 6) Do you need doctor/nurse to oversee operations? 7) Insurance"

Resources

Associations

- Day Spa Association (DSA): www.dayspaassociation.com

Medical Transcription	
NAICS 561410	Number of Businesses/Units 87,060

Rules of Thumb

➤ 75 to 80 percent of annual sales

➤ 3 to 3.5 times SDE

➤ 4.5 to 5 times EBITDA

Pricing Tips

- "MTSO's are almost always sold as a percentage of revenue with not too much attention paid to net profit but a great deal to gross profit. Most of the buyers are rolling up revenue and are therefore most concerned about the quality of the revenue and the cost of production (COGS.) MTSOs with revenue under $1.5M can generally expect to get about 75–80% of revenue as a purchase price, while those doing revenue of $1.5M plus can expect to see 80–100% of revenue.

  "The lower the risk profile of the customer base the greater the percentage of revenue one can expect. Customer concentration and risk of losing the customer to EHR are central to evaluating this risk profile. If the work is post EHR, that is the MTSO is working within the healthcare provider's EHR, then the buyer is going to perceive the revenue to be less at risk of loss to EHR.

  "Earnouts are virtually always a part of any MTSO transaction. Typically the buyer will come in with 50–60% cash and the seller will carry the balance on an 18–36 month earnout tied to ongoing revenue. A greater risk profile will equate to a larger earnout, a lower profile to less earnout.

  "Offshore, onshore or hybrid production models: The easiest MTSO to sell is where all the customers are U.S. based but most are OK with some or much of the production work being done offshore. If offshore production is allowed, many more buyers, especially from India, will come to the table with offers. Ideally the business has customers paying onshore rates but the buyers believe they can move much of the production off shore while keeping the customer pricing closer to onshore rates."

- "The market for Medical Transcription companies will vary according to several factors: the higher the 'price per line' the more a buyer is willing to pay; technology can influence price if the work is highly automated; the size of the service with regard to annual revenue and diversity of its customer base. These factors in combination can create a range of value from 75% of gross sales to 120% of gross."

Expert Comments

"The Medical Transcription industry has witnessed declines in revenue and profitability due to low-cost offshore labor, improvements in speech recognition technology and the government mandated adoption of Electronic Health Records."

"Three trends have significantly eroded medical transcription profitability and growth: offshore labor has brought line rates charged customers down from the heights of 16–18 CPL to 7–10 CPL; EMR vendors like EPIC and GE have taken much market share from traditional transcription; speech recognition technologies have resulted in turning many traditional transcriptionists into editors."

Benchmark Data

Statistics (Document Preparation Services)

Number of Establishments	87,060
Average Profit Margin	16.1%
Revenue per Employee	$35,100
Average Number of Employees	1.5
Average Wages per Employee	$16,049

Products and Services Segmentation

Document preparation services	48.0%
Typing services	40.0%
Other services	9.0%
Printing services	3.0%

Major Market Segmentation

Healthcare providers	48.0%
Other	27.9%
Small service-related business	12.1%
Federal, state and local government	7.6%
Individuals and households	4.4%

Industry Costs

Profit	16.1%
Wages	45.9%
Purchases	17.1%
Depreciation	1.4%
Marketing	2.0%
Rent & Utilities	4.9%
Other	12.6%

Market Share

Nuance Communications Inc.	8.4%

Source: IBISWorld, July 2016

- "Gross profit and EBITDA are very much tied to how much of the production is done offshore and or how much of the production is being processed via a speech engine. Use of technology and offshore labor will have a huge impact on how profitable the business is."
- "For work being produced through onshore labor, line rates should be 12–15 CPL with labor costs at 7–9 CPL and platform cost at about 1.5 CPL. Offshore production line rates are about 6 CPL, mostly in India followed by the Philippines. When production is done offshore, frequently the customer can get a line rate of 10–12 CPL. In hospitals speech recognition technologies are used to produce 70–80% of the work. In this case the customer may pay 10–12 CPL while cost of production (i.e., the editor plus the technology) might be more like 4 CPL for the editor/labor and 2–3 CPL for the speech engine."
- "Well-run MTSOs with only onshore operations can see gross profit margins in the 30–40% range; those with offshore operations can increase these margins by 10 points to the 40–50% range."
- "Medical transcriptionists continue to be an aging population. Part of this is impacted by the aging nature of the U.S. workforce overall. However, when compared to estimates of the 2006 age distribution of the U.S., the MT profession reflected in this survey trends older. This creates an immediate concern regarding the creation of not only a replacement workforce, but a workforce that can match the demands of the expanding healthcare industry."

Expenses as a percentage of annual sales

Cost of goods	50% to 70%
Payroll/labor Costs	0
Occupancy	0
Profit (estimated pretax)	15% to 20%

Industry Trend

- "Consolidation of smaller MTSOs by the large players, such as Nuance and lots of mid-sized regional/national players. More revenues will be lost to EHR and speech recognition technologies but the declines in revenue are tapering off from the big declines of the past few years of government incentivized EHR adoption."

Seller Financing

- "Occasionally for the smaller MTSO, the buyer will purchase with an SBA loan and the seller will hold a note for 15% of the transaction rather than the typical earn-out structure."
- "Transactions typically involve 50–60% cash down with the seller doing a 24–36 month earnout for the balance."

Questions

"Please describe each customer that accounts for more than 15% of your revenue. Have you or do you anticipate losing any business to EMR or to other competitors? Is your production being done onshore or offshore? Are you open to selling to someone with an offshore workforce? What platform, if any, are you using? Are your customer contracts assignable?"

Resources

Associations

- American Health Information Management Association: www.ahima.org
- The Association for Healthcare Documentation Integrity: www.ahdionline.org

	Franchise
Meineke Car Care Centers (See also Auto Mufflers, Franchises, Midas)	
Approx. Total Investment	$225,000 to $275,000
Estimated Annual Sales/Unit	$700,000
NAICS 811112	Number of Businesses/Units 975

Rules of Thumb

➢ 30 to 35 percent of annual sales plus inventory

Benchmark Data

- Average Meineke Center—Sales: $700,035

Cost of Goods Sold	26.5%	$185,509
Direct Labor (Inc. P/R Tax)	18.90%	$132,307
Variable Expenses	4.75%	$33,252
Fixed Expenses	14.40%	$100,805
Royalty	5.2%	$36,402
Advertising	7.6%	$53,203
Average earnings after		
Royalty and Advertising fees	22.65%	$158,558

Mental Health and Substance Abuse Centers (Outpatient)

	NAICS 621420	

Rules of Thumb

➢ 53 percent of annual sales plus inventory

➢ 2.1 times SDE plus inventory

➢ 11.3 times EBIT

➢ 1.7 times EBITDA

Benchmark Data

Expenses as a percentage of annual sales

Cost of goods... 12%
Payroll/labor Costs.. 05%
Profit (estimated pretax) 08%

Industry Trend

- "Moderate competition should remain steady, fragmentation should remain relatively constant, steady growth for next 5 years is expected."

Seller Financing

- "Outside financing"

Questions

- "Payor mix, market share, patient demographic data."

Resources

Associations

- www.naphs.org: National Association of Psychiatric Health Systems

Mental Health Physicians

	NAICS 621112	

Rules of Thumb

➢ 37 percent of annual sales plus inventory

➢ 1.3 times SDE plus inventory

➢ 3 times EBIT

➢ 1.7 times EBITDA

Benchmark Data

Expenses as a percentage of annual sales

Cost of goods... 07%
Payroll/labor Costs.. 05%
Profit (estimated pretax) 10%

Industry Trend
- "Consolidation has caused stagnation, however growth is expected as efficiency improves."

Seller Financing
- "Outside financing"

Questions
- "Payor mix, market share, patient demographic data."

Resources

Websites
- American Academy of Family Physicians (AAFP): www.aafp.org

Associations
- American Medical Association (AMA): www.ama-assn.org

Mental Health Practitioners (Except Physicians)

Rules of Thumb

➤ 45 percent of annual sales plus inventory

➤ 1.5 times SDE plus inventory

➤ 2.7 times EBIT

➤ 2.8 times EBITDA

Benchmark Data

Expenses as a percentage of annual sales

Cost of goods	07%
Payroll/labor Costs	01%
Profit (estimated pretax)	10%

Industry Trend
- "Increased consolidation, steady growth in revenue."

Seller Financing
- "Outside financing"

Questions
- "Payor mix, market share, patient demographic data."

Resources

Websites
- American Academy of Family Physicians (AAFP): www.aafp.org

Associations
- American Medical Association (AMA): www.ama-assn.org

	Franchise
Merry Maids (See also Franchises, Janitorial Services, Maid Services, etc.)	

Approx. Total Investment	$60,450 to $185,850

	NAICS 561720	Number of Businesses/Units 1,433

Rules of Thumb

> ➢ 45 percent of annual sales plus inventory

Resources

Websites

- www.merrymaids.com

	Franchise
Midas International (See also Auto Mufflers, Franchises, Meineke)	

Approx. Total Investment	$220,000 to $425,000
Estimated Annual Sales/Unit	$1 million +

	NAICS 811112	Number of Businesses/Units 2,000+

Rules of Thumb

> ➢ 30 to 35 percent of annual sales plus inventory

Resources

Websites

- www.midasfranchise.com

Middle Market Businesses (In General)

Rules of Thumb

> ➢ 2 to 5 times SDE plus inventory
> ➢ 3 to 5 times EBIT
> ➢ 3 to 5 times EBITDA

Pricing Tips

- "Only accept audited financials. Always retain qualified legal and accounting professionals early on in the process to uncover any 'hidden' issues that you may not discover on your own. Determine whether the industry sector of the business you are considering is trending up or down and what the long-term direction of the specific business's product line(s), within that industry, is projected to be. Determine what your exit strategy would be if you were to obtain control of the business."

Expert Comments

"Middle market businesses have very sophisticated competitors and are quite risky. Therefore, they are historically more profitable than smaller, main street operations. Because of the high cost of entry, there is a limited market for many of these businesses. Additionally, these companies tend to often be quite specific in their product line and hold a large market share in their respective geographic location."

Benchmark Data

- "Look for 'visionary' leadership and highly structured accounting and marketing departments. Look closely at employee costs and how 'deep' the middle management is, i.e., is middle management highly motivational or just high cost? Are all processes and procedures of the company in place or is everyone 'flying by the seat of their pants'? And which of these will be better for your given situation?"

Expenses as a percentage of annual sales

Cost of goods	20% to 30%
Payroll/labor Costs	25% to 30%
Occupancy	10%
Profit (estimated pretax)	30% to 40%

Questions

- "What are their companies' goals for the future and how have they prepared to make that a reality? Have they prepared a contingency plan in the event of unforeseen developments and what are their contingencies?"

		Franchise
Minuteman Press (See also Franchises, Print Shops)		
Approx. Total Investment		$100,000 to $150,000
	NAICS 323111	Number of Businesses/Units 940

Rules of Thumb

➢ 60 to 65 percent of annual sales plus inventory

Resources

Websites
- Minuteman Press: www.minutemanpress.com

Mobile Home Parks		
SIC 6515-01	NAICS 531190	

Rules of Thumb

➢ 3 to 8 times monthly income

M - Rules of Thumb

Pricing Tips

- "Before you decide to sell your manufactured home community/mobile home park there are several ways to increase the value of your investment and in doing so increase the value of the park and make it more saleable.
    - ✓ Submeter water, sewer and trash: By installing water meters at each mobile home and billing the residents back for water and sewer and trash, you are in effect increasing your bottom line.
    - ✓ Enforce rules and leases: By enforcing reasonable rules and regulations, your mobile home community will be regarded as a safe and comfortable environment. Get rid of problem tenants.
    - ✓ Buy manufactured homes for resale or rental. Buying used homes and placing them in your manufactured home community for resale or rental is another way to drastically increase the value of your community.
    - ✓ Increase the curb appeal: Encourage residents to clean up their yards and property. Hold cleanup days on a monthly basis. Have new and attractive signs installed at the entrances."

    Source: http://www.ebay.com/gds/Increasing-the-Value-of-your-Mobile-Home-Park-/
    10000000003154759/g.html

- Note: Mobile-home parks are generally real-estate-intensive—a real estate license is probably necessary to handle the sale.

Industry Trend

- "Such properties are not only good investments now but are set to become more so in the future, (Mark) Weiner said. Developers rarely build new ones anymore, and in particularly desirable communities, they're being closed to make the way for more lucrative housing instead. But Weiner said in California, demographic trends suggest both retirees and working-class residents will demand such communities as affordable options. 'We feel we meet the needs of low-income housing in every community we serve,' he said."

    Source: http://www.bizjournals.com/sacramento/news/2015/01/14/
    emerging-investment-trend-mobile-home-parks.html

Modeling Agencies

SIC 7363-01	NAICS 711410	Number of Businesses/Units 6,785

Rules of Thumb

➤ 20 percent of annual sales

Pricing Tips

- "Smaller agencies may be one-person businesses and the goodwill may be difficult to transfer. Earnouts may be necessary."

Benchmark Data

Statistics (Model Agencies)

Number of Establishments	6,785
Average Profit Margin	13.7%
Revenue per Employee	$91,000
Average Number of Employees	2.0
Average Wages per Employee	$41,136

Products and Services Segmentation

Commissions from model representation 60.1%
Performance or project related contract 25.8%
Other 9.6%
Product Licenses 4.5%

Major Market Segmentation

Advertising agencies 45.4%
Creative clients 30.2%
Other commercial clients 24.4%

Industry Costs

Profit 13.7%
Wages 45.2%
Purchases 21.6%
Depreciation 1.1%
Marketing 3.4%
Rent & Utilities 5.0%
Other 10.0%

Market Share

IMG Models 7.5%
Wilhelmina International Inc 7.1%

Source: IBISWorld, June 2016

	Franchise
Molly Maid (See also Franchises, Janitorial Services, Maid Services, etc.)	
Approx. Total Investment	$85,600 to $131,000
NAICS 561720	Number of Businesses/Units 620

Rules of Thumb

➢ 35 to 40 percent of annual sales plus inventory

Resources

Websites

- www.mollymaid.com

	Franchise
Money Mailer (See also Advertising Material Distribution Services, Franchises)	
Approx. Total Investment	$50,000 to $75,000
NAICS 541870	Number of Businesses/Units 190

Rules of Thumb

➢ 40 to 45 percent of sales plus inventory

➢ "If a cooperative direct mail business, such as Money Mailer or Supercoups is making $100,000, it could be sold for $150,000 to $225,000, and $250,000 if it was a perfect situation. Now, on the other hand, if it is a Valpak, I believe you could get up to 3 times what it is making because Valpak is the undisputed leader."

Resources

Websites
- www.moneymailer.com

Montessori Schools (See also Children's Educational Franchises)		
	NAICS 611110	

Rules of Thumb

➤ 35% of Annual Gross Sales plus inventory

➤ 1.5 to 2 times SDE

➤ 3 to 4 times EBITDA

Pricing Tips

- "The demographics profile—is it changing? Are the tuition rates within market—too low such that when increased will significantly affect enrollment and profits? Verify financials through due diligence by a knowledgeable CPA. Is the owner the director or simply the administrator overseeing operations? Are maintenance expenses being performed by the owner that would have to be assumed by the buyer? Is the enrollment going to change because of the personal goodwill of the owner and/or a director or key teacher who might leave? Why is the owner selling? Have there been any incidents or outstanding events that have not been disclosed. Verify continuation of enrollment due to possible aging of children in the area served. Is there a new school moving in or under construction nearby? Certifications of the teachers and their salaries. Teacher to student ratio. Are there foreseeable expenses in bringing the facility into code? What is the ethnic background of the owner/director and parents/students as compared to the buyer? Historic enrollment, actual enrollment, and maximum enrollment."
- "The larger schools with enrollment of 100 tend to sell for 3 times EBITDA, perhaps 4 times if the facility is in a location not easily replicated; the owners typically run them semi-absentee. Smaller schools are typically run by an 'owner/director' and are sold as a typical service business 1.5 to 2 times SDE."

Expert Comments

"Focus on why the facility is for sale and what the owner plans to do after sale."

"Most successful if enrollment is over 200 students, has a solid curricula with stable teachers in a high-income demographics"

Expenses as a percentage of annual sales

Cost of goods	n/a
Payroll/labor Costs	25% to 35%
Occupancy	30% to 45%
Profit (estimated pretax)	20% to 35%

Industry Trend

- "For an educational movement trying to use a century-old pedagogical method developed by an Italian Catholic, Maria Montessori, to teach Jewish tenets, mixing metaphors is the point. Arguing that the traditional Jewish day-school model they grew up with is outmoded and too clannish for 21st-century Judaism, a new generation of parents and educators are flocking to Montessori preschools and elementary schools that combine secular studies with Torah and Hebrew lessons.

  "Jewish Montessori schools, which began to catch on about 15 years ago, have also surged in popularity across the country. In Boca Raton, Fla., there are centrist Orthodox, Chabad Orthodox, Reform and Conservative Montessori preschools; Orthodox day schools have started Montessori programs in Houston and Cincinnati; and several New Jersey towns with large Jewish populations now have Montessori schools. The American Montessori Society says there are more than 4,000 Montessori schools in the United States; most are private (and secular, although some are associated with other religions) but a few are public. Ms. Petter-Lipstein said her group was tracking more than 40 Jewish Montessoris in North America and about 30 in Israel."
  Source: "Montessori Schools Surge in Popularity Among New Generation of Jewish Parents," by Vivian Yee, February 21, 2014, www.nytimes.com

- "Growing in areas where there are children in the pre-K through third grade. Trends down if they are above this level and there are good public schools. There is a very strong demand for special education for handicapped children"

Seller Financing

- "We have sold large facilities with enrollment of more than 200 students for 3X EBITDA. Smaller are more difficult and sell for about 2X."
- 5 years

Questions

- "Ethnic ratio of students and the owner/director. Qualification and tenure of teachers."
- "Are any of the teachers interns that will have to be replaced or higher paid later on?"

Resources

Websites
- www.montessori.edu
- www.montessori.org

	Franchise
MotoPhoto (See also Franchises)	
NAICS 81292	Number of Businesses/Units 16

Rules of Thumb
➢ 60 percent of annual sales plus inventory

Resources

Websites
- www.motophoto.com

Motorcycle Dealerships (See also Harley-Davidson Dealerships)

SIC 5571-06	NAICS 441228	Number of Businesses/Units 23,075

Rules of Thumb

➤ 12 to 14 percent of annual sales plus inventory

➤ 2 to 3 times SDE plus inventory

➤ 3 to 4 times EBITDA

Pricing Tips

- "It can be sold for a little higher, multiple of SDE because of the hobby aspect."
- "2x to 5x SDE; includes parts, garments, & accessories inventory (PG&A); can include used vehicles, but not new vehicles. High multiples for Harley dealerships, and lower multiples for Japanese or other brands."
- "The EBIT multiple above assumes that all new vehicle inventory is subject to floor plan financing that will be assumed by the buyer. Normal working capital acquired."
- "The actual value of the franchise type of cycle business is fixtures and equipment plus the price of used cycles that have been taken in (prior to shop work being done) at the used motorcycle book price, plus the new cycles, plus 5 years' to ¾ year's net profit. One note of caution: contact franchisor to determine what is exactly required to satisfy their requirements for opening or buying a dealership; e.g., flooring requirements and financial strength."

Expert Comments

"Several years ago motorcycle dealerships were easy to sell. Some regions of the country have experienced a downward trend in sales. The southeastern U.S. is still very strong. Currently, smaller dealerships can be very difficult to sell."

"The original equipment manufacturers (Honda, Harley-Davidson, Yamaha, Suzuki, Kawasaki, etc.) control the number of dealers permitted in a marketplace. An existing dealership can block the establishment of a competing dealership of the same brand within a geographical proximity to the existing dealership."

Benchmark Data

Statistics (Motorcycle Dealership and Repair)

Number of Establishments	23,075
Average Profit Margin	2.8%
Revenue per Employee	$319,000
Average Number of Employees	3.5
Average Wages per Employee	$32,463

Products and Services Segmentation

New motorcycles, motor scooters and motor bikes	53.5%
Motorized sports vehicles including all-terrain vehicles	24.5%
Used motorcycles, motor scooters and motor bikes	13.5%
Other	5.2%
Independent repairers (excluding dealerships)	3.3%

Major Market Segmentation

Male consumers	68.5%
Business	15.5%
Female consumers	15.0%
Government	1.0%

Industry Costs

Profit	2.8%
Wages	10.2%
Purchases	76.0%
Deprecation	0.6%
Marketing	1.2%
Rent & Utilities	2.8%
Other	6.4%

Source: IBISWorld, April 2016

Expenses as a percentage of annual sales

Cost of goods	77% to 85%
Payroll/labor Costs	05%
Occupancy	01%
Profit (estimated pretax)	02% to 03%

Industry Trend

- "Stable"
- "Sales are up again (slightly) and 2014 marks the fourth consecutive year of slight increases in U.S. motorcycle sales. The 2014 sales total for street bikes, dual-sport and off-road motorcycles is 483,526. That is up about 3.7% from the 465,783 total reported in 2013.

  "The largest increase in sales was for off-road motorcycles, which is rather surprising. Dual-sport bikes remain popular but scooter sales were down yet again. U.S. scooter sales in 2013 were reported down by 6,363 units, which would mean a decrease of -18.6% from 2012 and 2014 indicates another 3.5% drop. Harley-Davidson reported 47,149 motorcycles sold in Q4 2014. That includes 26,957 sold in the U.S., a 1.6% decrease from the previous year. 20,192 were sold outside the U.S., a 9.2% increase. 2014 has been a momentous year for the Husqvarna brand. Enjoying record figures in sales and turnover, a total number of 16,337 motorcycles were sold." (A bit dated, but still of interest)"

  Source: http://www.webbikeworld.com/motorcycle-news/statistics/motorcycle-sales-statistics.htm

Seller Financing

- "Seller financing, all cash."

Questions

- "PG&A inventory and new vehicle value requirements for a new buyer can be the most difficult and complex aspect to understand. A good deal of time should be spent understanding what inventory is there and how much is really needed. Inventory should turn on an average of 4x to 6X per year in a healthy dealership. Slower turns suggest the business is carrying too much inventory or is very seasonal."

Franchise

Mountain Mike's Pizza (See also Franchises, Pizza Shops)

Approx. Total Investment	$197,000 to $598,000
Estimated Annual Sales/Unit	$525,000

SIC 5812-22	NAICS 722513	Number of Businesses/Units 160

Rules of Thumb

➢ 30% of annual sales plus inventory

Resources

Websites

▪ www.mountainmikes.com

Movie Theaters

SIC 7832-01	NAICS 512131	Number of Businesses/Units 4,525

Rules of Thumb

➢ 4 times SDE

➢ 6 times annual adjusted earnings, 1000 plus seating

➢ 4 to 6 percent of annual sales; add fixtures & equipment

➢ 35 percent plus inventory for theaters with only one or several screens

Pricing Tips

▪ Concession sales usually make up 24 percent of movie-theater sales. It has been said that, without concession sales, the movie theater business would not be viable.

Benchmark Data

Statistics (Movie Theaters)

Number of Establishments	4,525
Average Profit Margin	12.9%
Revenue per Employee	$130,150
Average Number of Employees	26.6
Average Wages per Employee	$14,057

Products and Services Segmentation

Admissions	67.0%
Food and beverage sales	28.7%
Other	4.3%

Industry Costs

Profit	12.9%
Wages	10.9%
Purchases	39.0%
Depreciation	6.7%
Marketing	2.4%
Rent & Utilities	7.7%
Other	20.4%

Market Share

Regal Entertainment Group	21.0%
AMC Entertainment Inc.	19.6%
Cinemark Holdings Inc.	14.1%
Carmike Cinemas Inc.	05.4%

Source: IBISWorld, August 2016

Industry Trend

- "The strong growth in global box office would increase the proportion of the box office revenue to 42% of the total filmed entertainment revenue by 2017, from 40% in 2008. The shift is more evident in the emerging markets, while in the developed markets, the revenue share of box office to the total filmed entertainment sector is expected to rise only marginally.

  "The recent slate of films and lack of major blockbusters has hindered the growth of box office revenues over the past few years. However, there are numerous major titles scheduled for release in 2015 and 2016 which can potentially boost box office revenues in both developed markets and emerging markets as demand for blockbuster US content continues to increase with further globalization and access to content."

  Source: Cinema Operator Industry Report, www.redcapgroup.com

- "Wall Street usually shows little love for the movie business with its typically low, and unpredictable, profit margins. But in a combined look at the studio and exhibition businesses this morning, MoffettNathanson Research's Michael Nathanson and Robert Fishman tell Investors that it's time to take a fresh look—as long as they proceed with caution. They lowered profit estimates for major exhibition chains Regal and Cinemark, citing expectations for weaker domestic summer box office results vs 2013. They project a full-year decline of 1.6% to $10.7B followed by a 5% jump in 2015 to $11.3B and then a drop of 2.6% in 2016 to $11.0B."

  Source: "Film Business is Recovering, But It Won't Be Steady: Analysts," by David Lieberman, April 7, 2014, www.deadline.com

Resources

Websites
- Motion Picture Association of America: mpaa.org

Trade Publications
- "Business of Show Business: The Valuation of Movie Theaters," published by the Appraisal Institute: www.appraisalinstitute.org

Associations
- National Association of Theatre Owners: www.natoonline.org

M - Rules of Thumb

Moving and Storage

SIC 4214-01	NAICS 484210	Number of Businesses/Units 15,590

Rules of Thumb

➢ 50 percent of annual sales

Benchmark Data

Statistics (Moving Services)

Number of Establishments	15,590
Average Profit Margin	8.4%
Revenue per Employee	$161,500
Average Number of employees	6.8
Average Wages per Employee	$34,229

Products and Services Segmentation

Residential moving	60.5%
Commercial moving	16.5%
Other	12.3%
Warehousing services	10.7%

Major Market Segmentation

Consumers	67.0%
Corporate customers	23.0%
Government	10.0%

Industry Costs

Profit	8.4%
Wages	21.5%
Purchases	30.0%
Depreciation	2.1%
Marketing	2.8%
Rent & Utilities	8.6%
Other	26.6%

Market Share

UniGroup Inc.	9.3%
Sirva Inc.	5.6%
Atlas World Group Inc.	5.0%

Source: IBISWorld, April 2016

- "The combined storage space in all those 48,500 facilities we have equals 2.3 billion square feet. That's 78 square miles, or more than three times the size of Manhattan. To put it another way, there are 7.3 square feet of storage space for every single person—man, woman, and child—in the U.S. This means it is possible for everyone in the entire country to be standing inside a storage unit at the same time.

  "As of mid-2013, 87.4% of self storage units were occupied (percentage based on units rented per facility). Almost 9% of American households currently rent a self storage unit, even though 65% of them have a garage, 47% have an attic and 33% have a basement."

Source: "Important Self Storage Industry Trends Moving Companies Shouldn't Miss,"
http://blog.hireahelper.com/self-storage-industry-trends-for-movers/

Industry Trend

- "They are popping up all over, these garages-for-rent. The Self Storage Association will proudly tell you that self storage has been the fastest growing segment of the commercial real estate industry over the last four decades, while Wall Street analysts consider the industry to be recession-proof. There are 59,500 self storage facilities worldwide. Of these, 48,500 are in the U.S."

Source: "Important Self Storage Industry Trends Moving Companies Shouldn't Miss,"
http://blog.hireahelper.com/self-storage-industry-trends-for-movers/

Resources

Associations

- American Moving and Storage Association—an informative site: www.promover.org

		Franchise
Mr. Jim's Pizza (See also Franchises, Pizza Shops)		
Approx. Total Investment		$75,000 to $150,000
Estimated Annual Sales/Unit		$440,000
SIC 5812-22	NAICS 722513	Number of Businesses/Units 75

Rules of Thumb

➢ 35% of annual sales plus inventory

Resources

Websites

- www.mrjimspizza.net

		Franchise
Mr. Payroll (See also Franchises)		
Approx. Total Investment		$68,800 to $328,000
Estimated Annual Sales/Unit		$100,000 to $325,000
	NAICS 522390	Number of Businesses/Units 45

Rules of Thumb

➢ 130 percent of annual sales

Resources

Websites

- www.mrpayroll.com

	Franchise

Mr. Rooter Plumbing (See also Franchises)

Approx. Total Investment	$80,125 to $188,800
SIC 1711-05 | NAICS 238220	Number of Businesses/Units 241

Rules of Thumb

> ➢ 1 to 4 times SDE plus hard assets; the number between 1 and 4 depends on several factors, such as the owner operating a truck, etc.

	Franchise

Murphy's Deli (See also Delicatessens, Franchises)

Approx. Total Investment	Net worth of $200,000
NAICS 722513	Number of Businesses/Units 80

Rules of Thumb

> ➢ 50 percent of annual sales plus inventory

> ➢ Multiples have ranged from 40 percent to 60 percent

Resources

Websites
- www.murphysdeli.com

	Franchise

Music Go Round (See also Franchises)

Approx. Total Investment	$259,400 to $332,600
SIC 5736-08 | NAICS 451140	Number of Businesses/Units 33

Rules of Thumb

> ➢ 40 percent of annual sales plus inventory

Resources

Websites
- www.musicgoround.com

Music Stores (Record Stores, Musical Instruments)

SIC 5736	NAICS 451140	
Number of Businesses/Units Musical Instruments: 10,802; Record Stores: 4,416		

Rules of Thumb

> ➢ 25 percent of annual sales. Retail is generally higher, but the trend of this business is decidedly down, especially for the small independent store.

➤ 1 to 2 times SDE plus inventory. If just a record/CD store it may be difficult to sell period. Music is now being downloaded over the Internet and records/CDs are becoming almost obsolete. If the music store sells sheet music, musical instruments, etc. SDE multiple might be higher.

Pricing Tips

- "Inventory of tapes, CD's, DVD's at FMV (used) is in addition to the above."
- "Usually in a store of this kind inventory turns about twice a year. The store should be located in an area where rent will not exceed 4 percent of the gross sales. National average shows a gross profit of approximately 54 percent before expenses of wages, repairs, maintenance, advertising, bad debts, utilities, insurance, taxes, etc. National average net profit is approximately 10 to 18 percent."
- "The leading music retailers are now box stores (Walmart and Best Buy), and music-only stores are no longer a player in the industry."

Source: www.en.wikipedia.org

Expert Comments

"Independent brick and mortar locations are a dying breed."

Benchmark Data

Statistics (Musical Instrument and Supplies Store)

Number of Establishments	10,802
Average Profit Margin	2.0%
Revenue per Employee	$156,700
Average Number of Employees	3.3
Average Wages per Employee	$22,460

Products and Services Segmentation

Violins, drums, guitars, and other instruments	49.7%
Pianos and organs	16.2%
Instrument rentals	14.1%
Audio equipment, components, parts and accessories	12.3%
Sheet music	5.4%
Other goods (includes tapes, CDs and audiobooks)	2.3%

Major Market Segmentation

Hobbyists	52.1%
Professional	30.3%
Students	10.6%
Education	4.9%
Other	2.1%

Industry Costs

Profit	2.0%
Wages	14.4%
Purchases	50.3%
Depreciation	0.9%
Marketing	1.9%
Rent & Utilities	7.7%
Other	22.8%

Market Share

Guitar Center Inc.	32.9%

Source: IBISWorld, December 2015

Statistics (Record Stores)

Number of Establishments	4,416
Average Profit Margin	1.2%
Revenue per Employee	$108,000
Average Number of Employees	3.6
Average Wages per Employee	$15,678

Products and Services Segmentation

Compact discs, records, tapes & audio books	39.7%
Digital Video Discs (DVDs) and video tapes	33.6%
Other	16.6%
Toys, hobby goods & games	10.1%

Industry Costs

Profit	1.2%
Wages	14.7%
Purchases	63.1%
Depreciation	1.2%
Utilities	2.0%
Rent	7.7%
Other	10.1%

Market Share

Trans World Entertainment Corporation	18.4%

Source: IBISWorld, December 2015

Expenses as a percentage of annual sales

Cost of goods	35%
Payroll/labor Costs	25% to 30%
Occupancy	15%
Profit (estimated pretax)	20% to 25%

Industry Trend

- "CDs are dead. That doesn't seem like such a controversial statement. Maybe it should be. The music business sold 141 million CDs in the U.S. last year. That's more than the combined number of tickets sold to the most popular movies in 2014 (Guardians) and 2013 (Iron Man 3). So "dead," in this familiar construction, isn't the same as zero. It's more like a commonly accepted short-cut for a formerly popular thing is now withering at a commercially meaningful rate. And if CDs are truly dead, then digital music sales are lying in the adjacent grave. Both categories are down double-digits in the last year, with iTunes sales diving at least 13 percent."

Source: "The Death of Music Sales," by Derek Thompson January 25, 2015 http://www.theatlantic.com/business/archive/2015/01/buying-music-is-so-over/384790/

- "Bettendorf, Iowa—When Jim Foster opened his piano store 30 years ago, he had 10 competitors selling just pianos. When he closed Foster Family Music in late December, not one was still selling pianos in the Quad-Cities area of Iowa and Illinois. . . . Stores dedicated to selling pianos like Foster's are dwindling across the country as fewer people take up the instrument and those who do often opt for a less expensive electronic keyboard or a used piano. . . . But after gently falling over the years, sales have plunged more recently to between 30,000 and 40,000 annually."

Source: Associated Press as reported in the *Boston Globe*, January 3, 2015

Resources

Associations
- International Music Products Association: www.namm.com

		Franchise
My Favorite Muffin (See also Big Apple Bagels, Franchises)		
Approx. Total Investment		$254,300 to $379,628
	NAICS 722513	Number of Businesses/Units 70
Rules of Thumb		

> 30 to 35 percent plus inventory

Resources

Websites
- www.myfavoritemuffin.net

Mystery Shopping Companies		
	NAICS 561990	Number of Businesses/Units 700
Rules of Thumb		

> 50 percent of annual sales—the larger the company, the higher the percentage of annual sales over 50 percent.

Pricing Tips
- Large mystery service companies can sell for considerably more than 50 percent of sales.

Benchmark Data
- "How much can someone realistically expect to earn as a mystery shopper? Compensation for mystery shopping significantly varies depending on a number of factors, including the type of industry, the level of difficulty required to complete the assignment and the detail required by the mystery shoppers. Compensation for the typical shop ranges from $5 to $20. Some complex assignments, such as video mystery shop, can pay $75 or more.
"It is hard to find out more specifics on which companies get mystery shopped and how much shoppers are paid because shoppers are not allowed to divulge specific information, such as the name of the company they've shopped or how much they make per assignment. The shoppers are required to sign confidentiality agreements at the request of the mystery shopping providers and their customers."

Source: www.mysteryshop.org

Resources

Associations
- Mystery Shopping Providers Association (MSPA): http://www.mspa-na.org/

Nail Salons (See also Beauty Salons)

SIC 7231-02	NAICS 812113	

Rules of Thumb

> ➢ 25 percent of annual sales plus inventory

Pricing Tips

- "So, what records do you need to be able to provide? Kopsa provides the following list to get you started:
  - ✓ the last three years of tax returns
  - ✓ the last three years of the salon's accounting software records (such as QuickBooks or Sage 50)
  - ✓ the last three years of sales tax reports (to verify your retail sales)
  - ✓ the last three years to present day of your salon appointment records
  - ✓ a list of all employees, including how long they've been with the salon
  - ✓ the salon handbook (the new owner will likely need to carry over benefits, such as the number of vacation days, for employees who choose to stay with the salon)
  - ✓ the lease (which must be assignable to the new buyer)
  - ✓ the depreciation schedule"

Source: http://www.nailsmag.com/article/109714/sell-your-salon-with-savvy

Benchmark Data

- For additional Benchmark Data see Beauty Salons

Industry Costs (Hair & Nail Salons in the U.S.)

Profit	7.7%
Wages	23.2%
Purchases	21.0%
Depreciation	1.8%
Marketing	2.4%
Rent & Utilities	15.3%
Other	28.6%

Source: IBISWorld, August 2016

Nail Tech Demographics

Ethnicity	Percentage
Vietnamese	51%
Caucasian	40%
Black or African-American	05%
Hispanic or Latina	03%
Other	01%

Gender	Percentage
Male	03%
Female	97%

How many nail technicians work **at this location (including yourself)?**

Number of Technicians	Percentage
I am the only technician	43%
2 nail techs	22%
3 nail techs	12%
4 nail techs	09%
5 nail techs	04%
6 nail techs	03%
7+ nail techs	07%

Who are your clients?	Percentage
Girls under 12	01%%
Girls 12–15	01%
Girls 16–20	04%
Women 21–25	11%
Women 26–35	19%
Women 36–45	28%
Women 46+	33%
Men	03%

What percentage of your business is appointments vs. walk-ins?	Percentage
Regular appointments	39%
Standing appointments	25%
Walk-in appointments	25%
Other	11%

On Average what is your total weekly income?

Service Income	
$630	
Tip Income	$115
Incentives or earnings from retail sales	$82

Which best describes your current employment situation?	
Salon owner doing nails (not a booth renter)	31%
Nail technician (booth renter)	23%
Nail technician (employee)	14%
Cosmetologist	06%
Salon manager or nail dept. manager (doing nails)	02%
Student or apprentice	02%
Salon owner not doing nails	01%
Other	11%

What license(s) do you have?	
Nail technician/manicurist	79%
Cosmetologist/hairstylist	19%
Esthetician	10%
I am not licensed	06%
Barber	01%
Other	08%

- "49% of booth renters pay their rent weekly, and the average weekly rent is $117/week. 41% of booth renters pay their rent monthly, and the average monthly rent is $425/month."

  Source: 2015–2016 Nails Big Book, nailsmag.com

- "More experienced workers usually earn $50 to $70 per day, sometimes even $80. Their pay, though, still typically amounts to significantly less than minimum wage, given their long hours."

  Source: "High Price of Pretty Nails: Workers are Underpaid and Unprotected," *New York Times*, May 10, 2015

Industry Trend

- "As far as small businesses go, it is relatively easy to open a nail salon. Just a few thousand dollars is needed for things like pedicure chairs with whirlpool baths. Little English is required, and there are few licensing hoops to jump through. Many skip them altogether. Overhead is minimal: rent and some new bottles of polish each month—and the rock-bottom wages of workers. Beyond the law barriers for entry, manicurists, owners and others who have closely followed the nail industry are hard pressed to say definitively why salons have proliferated."

  Source: "High Price of Pretty Nails: Workers are Underpaid and Unprotected—A Boom In Nail Salons," *New York Times*, May 10, 2015

Resources

Trade Publications

- Nails Magazine—interesting and useful site, has an interesting survey of the nail salon business.: www.nailsmag.com

Franchise

Nathan's Famous (See also Franchises)	
Approx. Total Investment	$50,000 to $1,000,000

	NAICS 722513	Number of Businesses/Units 300

Rules of Thumb

➤ 85 to 90 percent of annual sales plus inventory

Benchmark Data

- Units range from 120 sq. ft. to 3,000 sq. ft.

Resources

Websites

- www.nathansfamous.com

Natural Chicken Grill		
	NAICS 722513	Number of Businesses/Units 14

Rules of Thumb

➤ 25 to 30 percent of annual sales plus inventory

➤ Note: This more of a business opportunity than a franchise. The initial fee is $20,000 in two payments of $10,000. There is also a $1,000-a-month charge after a unit has been open for three months. There is no royalty. The cost shown above is plus the build-out of the store. The cost includes training, set-up, consultation, etc. Units range from 1,500 sq. ft. to 3,500 sq. ft.

		Franchise

Nature's Way Café (See also Franchises)

Approx. Total Investment		$129,500 to $253,900
	NAICS 722513	Number of Businesses/Units 8

Rules of Thumb

➢ 45 percent of annual sales plus inventory

Resources

Websites
- www.natureswaycafe.com

Newspaper Routes

	NAICS 454390	

Rules of Thumb

➢ 90 to 100 percent of annual sales plus inventory

➢ $50 to $100 per daily/Sunday subscriber

Newsstands

SIC 5994-01	NAICS 451212	

Rules of Thumb

➢ 25 percent of annual sales plus inventory

Nursing Homes (See also Assisted Living Facilities, Retirement Homes)

SIC 8051-01	NAICS 623110	Number of Businesses/Units 33,845

Rules of Thumb

➢ 45 percent of annual sales plus inventory

➢ 2.5 times SDE plus inventory

➢ 3 times EBIT

➢ 4 times EBITDA

Pricing Tips

- "Percentage of revenue multiple is completely unreliable. This can range wildly from 1x to 2.5x depending on the performance of a facility. The best measure for value lies in a HUD 232 analysis that pins a CAP Rate to NOI (Net Operating Income). There is a specific set of calculations that adjust EBITDA to NOI before the CAP Rate is applied. This final number will be consistent with what nursing home specialist appraisers will come up with. Do not allow a general appraiser or even a commercial appraiser to conduct the appraisal. It must be done by a nursing-home or long-term care appraisal specialist."

- "Return on investment—cash on hand is the guiding rule. Cost per bed varies from $20,000 to $60,000. Cost of upgrading facility a strong factor."
- "In Florida (and other states) the licensing requirements have changed drastically, making entry into this industry very difficult, which in turn may raise the pricing multiple somewhat."

Expert Comments

"It really helps both sides if they have representation to assist them. Sellers absolutely should want and need a skilled broker assisting them. An honest review of the facility and suggested changes/improvements can be critical to the overall value. Buyers likewise would want assistance as to what to look for and to guide them through the lending process and due diligence."

"As it relates to nursing homes, the industry is very mature and many states have moratoriums on new licenses so new competition coming in is very limited. Assisted Living Facilities (ALFs) are much easier to gain approval for and thus new competition can come into any market rather easily. I have found the marketability of almost any size facility to be excellent. Strong census and profitability are key and go hand in hand."

"Licensing issues"

Benchmark Data

Statistics (Nursing Care Facilities)

Number of Establishments	33,845
Average Profit Margin	7.2%
Revenue per Employee	$75,500
Average Number of Employees	54.6
Average Wages per Employee	$30,587

Products and Services Segmentation

For-profit skilled nursing facilities	43.6%
For-profit nursing homes	33.0%
Nonprofit skilled nursing facilities	10.3%
Nonprofit nursing homes	7.8%
Government nursing homes and skilled nursing facilities	4.7%
Hospice centers	0.6%

Industry Costs

Profit	7.2%
Wages	40.8%
Purchases	18.4%
Depreciation	2.2%
Marketing	0.3%
Rent & Utilities	7.4%
Other	23.7%

Source: IBISWorld, March 2016

- "Long-term care facilities do not have the usual 'measures' as it relates to other industries. Long-term care facilities don't measure 'cost of goods' in the traditional sense and actually don't segment those out. There are categories consistent with the 'cost reporting' that is required that are split out between administration, nursing, plant operations, etc. Instead of the 4 items listed here you would need about 8 categories to reflect how the industry looks at certain matrixes."

- "With nursing homes the big thing is payor mix. Average to below average homes will run 90%+ Medicaid. An all-Medicaid home will not be extremely profitable. A good home must have some private pay, at least 10%, and a good mix of Medicare, say around 20%. If this is the case you'll have a home doing 15%+ bottom line EBITDA. Another good benchmark is to look at average Medicaid rate. If the average Medicaid rate for a year is $140/day that home is struggling to make ends meet (unless there is a ton of private pay/Medicare). If the average Medicaid rate is $185/day then that's a home getting higher acuity residents and they will be very profitable."

Expenses as a percentage of annual sales

Cost of goods	15%
Payroll/labor Costs	40% to 50%
Occupancy	10%
Profit (estimated pretax)	15% to 20%

Industry Trend

- "Very marketable. Nursing homes will continue to be under pressure with cuts to Medicare and families trying to hide money so that nursing homes can't get their private pay money. Medicaid itself is a losing proposition to all homes. If it wasn't for Medicare and private pay monies, most nursing homes would simply lose money with the Medicaid system as it currently is constructed. ALFs will continue to grow but this only serves the private pay market. We're seeing more in the way of alcohol rehab facilities popping up as states are allowing for fewer restriction to facility requirements for those facilities to exist (old homes can qualify). Population continues to age so there will be no end to the supply side for this business."

- "Skilled nursing facilities' occupancy rate continued to tick up in the first three months of 2014, while absorption flipped into positive territory for the first time in almost a decade, according to the latest quarterly figures from the National Investment Center for the Seniors Housing & Care Industry."

- "Nursing care occupancy reached 88.4% in the first quarter of this year, based on numbers gathered by NIC's MAP® Data and Analysis Service. This was an increase of 0.4 percentage points from the last quarter of 2013. The increase is in line NIC's forecast models, which predicted occupancy in seniors housing to exceed 90% this year, NIC President Robert Kramer told McKnight's recently.

- "The occupancy rate for independent living (90.2%) already has passed this benchmark, according to the data released Friday. Assisted living occupancy was at 89.1% in the first quarter."

Source: "Skilled nursing edges toward 90% occupancy, absorption rate makes first gain in nearly a decade, NIC data show," by Tim Mullaney www.mcknights.com April 14, 2014 (A bit dated, but still of interest)

- "The health care legislation includes a list of changes to nursing services for seniors and the disabled, including an infusion of federal funding to help state programs provide more care through home- and community-based settings, which, presumably, will result in a reduction in nursing home care. The industry is expected to experience lower demand, which will be moderately offset by an increase in the number of insured. Overall, sales are expected to grow by 1.5 percent on average per year through 2015, reaching $109.5 billion. This is slightly lower than the previous five-year average growth rate of 1.7 percent annually."

Seller Financing

- "Projects under $10 million can go SBA. Some seller financing is typical in these deals but not required unless the buyer needs help. HUD is a great option for the buyer, but expect a year to get a deal done with HUD lending. Make sure your seller client is prepared for this kind of wait. Any seller note in a HUD deal cannot be secured by the property, which means the seller cannot force the buyer to pay up if they fall behind. Seller needs to be aware of this."
- 10 years
- "SBA will allow a seller to be ballooned at 7 years (amortization can be 7 years or longer). HUD will allow seller financing (up to 50% of the amount buyer puts down - example: 20% down buyer and seller can contribute 10% each) but it MUST be a non-recourse loan, which makes it very difficult for the seller to collect if the buyer doesn't pay. If you're using SBA lending the seller note will have to be 7 years or longer."

Questions

- "You want to see the last 3 years' census by payor type by month. And, the last few surveys to review violations. What is their CMS rating? Any letters from CMS about violations? Any lawsuits in last 5 years? Last 3 rate sheets, whether that's Medicare, Medicaid or other state rate calculations (such as DTA, etc). Room types and how many beds per room. As an example, HUD will remove multi-bed rooms from the HUD 232 analysis, so if there are 3 or 4 beds in a room they will reduce that to 2 beds per room for revenue calculations. Usual questions regarding age of roof and other major building systems. Not as critical for SBA lending but very critical for HUD lending."

Resources

Associations
- American Health Care Association: www.ahca.org

Nursing—Skilled Nursing Facilities	
	NAICS 623110

Rules of Thumb

➤ 64 percent of annual sales plus inventory

➤ 1.0 times SDE plus inventory

➤ 1.3 times EBIT

➤ 1.3 times EBITDA

Benchmark Data

Expenses as a percentage of annual sales

Cost of goods	09%
Payroll/labor Costs	04%
Profit (estimated pretax)	07%

Industry Trend

- "Further consolidation, revenue projected to increase, profit projected to grow, demand expected to increase"

Seller Financing

- "Outside financing"

Questions

- "Payor mix, market share, patient demographic data"

Resources

Websites

- LeadingAge: www.leadingage.org

Associations

- www.ahcancal.org: American Health Care Association

Office Staffing and Temporary Agencies

(See also Staffing Services (Health Care))

SIC 7363-03	NAICS 561320	Number of Businesses/Units 70,049

Rules of Thumb

➤ 6 to12 times EBITDA

➤ 1 to 2 times annual sales plus inventory

➤ 3 times SDE plus inventory

➤ 2 to 5 times EBIT (smaller deals under $25 million)

➤ 5 to 7.5 times EBIT (larger deals over $25 million)

➤ 6 to 9 times EBIT (Information Technology)

Pricing Tips

- "One of the most common misconceptions I hear from staffing company owners is that the valuation of their business is directly tied to their annual revenue. While larger companies do tend to receive higher valuation multiples, staffing companies continue to be valued almost exclusively on a multiple of trailing 12-month (TTM) earnings before interest, taxes, depreciation and amortization (EBITDA), so growing the EBITDA of your business, not just its revenue, is the key to maximizing valuation.

"The misconception that the purchase price paid by buyers in staffing industry transactions is based on revenue rather than EBITDA is largely based upon the fact that for most publicly announced transactions, earnings information is simply not available. So in the absence of earnings information, observers may attempt to link the seller's annual revenue to the purchase price if the revenue of the business is disclosed. Further complicating transaction analysis, in the situations where EBITDA is publicly stated, information concerning any non-recurring expense adjustments are usually not disclosed, so the implied transaction multiple may be overstated and often misleading.

"Many buyers will also conduct a 'quality of earnings' assessment as a part of their transaction due diligence. Not only will this review include a confirmation of the annual or TTM EBITDA of the selling company, but factors such as the validity of the expense adjustments and the sustainability of the earnings will also be considered.

"The majority of companies in the staffing industry sell for between four to seven times their TTM EBITDA on a cash free, debt free basis, with the working capital of the seller (the receivables and payables) going to the buyer. In the rare cases where the seller keeps the working capital, then the purchase price is reduced by a comparable amount. Some fast-growing professional staffing companies may even sell for above seven times TTM EBITDA, while less differentiated and/or smaller commercial staffing businesses may trade for less than four times TTM EBITDA. Because this valuation range is so large and based upon a variety of factors, speaking with multiple potential acquirers is critical to achieving the best possible valuation.

"While staffing industry buyers may acquire for a variety of reasons, including access to new customers, expand the geography of their business, add a new service offering or bring additional management talent into their organization, they will almost always use EBITDA as their basis for valuation. Therefore, owners contemplating a future transaction should always be focused on the earnings line of their income statement, not revenue, in order to maximize the value of their staffing business in a sale."

Source: "EBITDA, Not Revenue, Drives Staffing Company Valuations," by John Niehaus, July 11, 2016, http://www.thestaffingstream.com/2016/07/11/ebitda-not-revenue-drives-staffing-company-valuations/?utm_source=feedburner&utm_medium=feed&utm_campaign=Feed%3A+TheStaffingStream+%28The+Staffing+Stream%29

- "Staffing companies that use the cash basis—only counting income or expenses when the money changes hands—for their accounting method will be at a significant disadvantage when approaching a transaction. Investment bankers, transaction attorneys and accountants agree that financial statements prepared using generally accepted accounting principles (GAAP) present a clearer and more easily understood snapshot of a company's financial health. GAAP uses an accrual basis which recognizes revenue when the services occur, regardless of when the money is received or paid. Because GAAP is consistently used by most companies, it is a powerful tool for ensuring a fair business valuation."

Source: http://wblcpa.com/maximize-your- staffing-business- value-now- eight-key-accounting-tax-and-finance- tips-to- prepare-your- staffing-business- for-sale/

- "Important to understand the gross margins, as sometimes even with what looks like a decent bottom line, if it is very low margin but high volume, the firm will typically not be very attractive.

"Attractiveness depends on a variety of factors including niche, geography, number of offices, next level of management in place etc."

- "Multiples based on SDE vary with segment, annual revenues, and growth. Location also influences multiple. Some examples:

  Light Industrial
  - ✓ $5 million minimum 2.5–3.25X
  - ✓ $10–$19 million 3–4X
  - ✓ $20 million plus (especially if multiple office locations) 4–5X

  IT
  - ✓ $5 million minimum 3.5–4X
  - ✓ $10 million 3.6–4.5X
  - ✓ $20 million 4–5 X (higher if strong gross profit and if in major metro market)
  - ✓ $50 million or higher 5–7X"

- "Pricing depends on industry sector, gross margin, client concentration, and size."

Expert Comments

"Seller—prepare well in advance and work with a business intermediary to recommend steps to improve the potential marketability. Buyer—spend time at conferences such as the American Staffing Association's Staffing World, or meetings of Staffing Industry Analysts to learn about the field and to meet people in the business before considering starting to evaluate potential acquisitions."

"Hire pros. Launch with clients you trust."

"Hire top recruiters, carefully interview temps, watch outstanding A/R with credit weak customers."

"Staffing valuations increase early in the economic cycle as their revenues increase when employers respond to increased demand with temporary personannel rather than adding to fixed overheads."

"Gross profit and A/R performance influence the multiple selection as does strength of locations (near bus lines). Factoring is common in this industry and net factoring expenses can impact profitability. Customer concentration issues require analysis with balanced weighting across several segments supporting higher valuations."

"Workers' comp., risk management, and mod factors affect light industrial staffing\PEO firms substantially."

"Profits are up in past two years as the general economy upticks but companies are reluctant to add overheads. Temp workers are utilized as a response to increased demand."

"Entry into the industry is relatively easy. Competition can be tough but the market is big. The industry has been on a strong upswing over the last couple of years but is very susceptible to economic conditions."

Benchmark Data

Statistics (Office Staffing & Temp Agencies)

Number of Establishments	70,049
Average Profit Margin	3.9%
Revenue per Employee	$45,302
Average Number of Employees	48.4
Average Wages per Employee	$32,655

O - Rules of Thumb

Products and Services Segmentation

Industrial staffing	34.1%
Office, clerical and administrative staffing	24.8%
Professional and managerial staffing	12.2%
Healthcare staffing	9.3%
Information technology staffing	8.5%
Other	7.6%
Engineering and scientific staffing	3.5%

Major Market Segmentation

Industrial	37.6%
Retail and other service-oriented sectors	21.1%
Other professional markets	13.4%
Technical sectors	12.2%
Healthcare	9.5%
Other	6.2%

Industry Costs

Profit	3.6%
Wages	70.3%
Purchases	14.9%
Depreciation	0.3%
Marketing	0.7%
Rent & Utilities	1.2%
Other	9.0%

Source: IBISWorld, August 2016

- "Profit margins play a major role in determining the value of an employment agency and job placement in specific industries can help you bring that profit margin up. If your firm is currently specializing in one area, you may want to consider branching out into other industries to help increase your profits. While most firms bring in profits a minimum of 9%, the average per industry is listed below.
  - ✓ Clerical, Light industrial: 16%
  - ✓ IT, Healthcare, Professional: 25%–28%"

  Source: http://www.vikingmergers.com/blog/2015/how-to- raise-the- value-of- a-staffing- agency

- "Typically a gross margin of lower than about 20% is not particularly marketable, with higher margins very desirable."
- "Hours billed per branch. Recruiting cost per employee. Workers Comp mod factor."
- "Multiple of SDE: 2 to 5; Gross Profit: 22% to 30%"

Expenses as a percentage of annual sales

Cost of goods	10%
Payroll/labor Costs	70%
Occupancy	10%
Profit (estimated pretax)	10%

Industry Trend

"The Office Staffing and Temp Agencies industry is in the mature stage of its economic life cycle. Industry value added (IVA), used to measure an industry's contribution to the overall economy, is projected to grow at an average annual rate of 4.6% over the 10years to 2021. In contrast, GDP is expected to grow an annualized 2.3% during the same 10-year period."

Source: http://clients1.ibisworld.com/reports/us/industry/industryoutlook.aspx?entid=1464

- "Declining as demand for variable labor and staff will decrease in a potentially softening economy. Potential upside in healthcare and IT (higher margin specialized areas)."
- "According to Teresa Carroll, senior VP and general manager, Global Talent Solutions for Kelly Services, these are the five types of free agents that exist today and the percentage of the global free agent population they represent; free agents may be represented in multiple categories:
  - ✓ Independent contractors (workers who perform independent work on a project-to-project basis): 64%
  - ✓ Freelance business owners (business owners with up to five employees who identify as both a freelancer and a business owner): 28%
  - ✓ Temporary workers (workers typically hired for a fixed duration, often through an agency): 24%
  - ✓ Moonlighters (workers who hold a primary, traditional job and also participate in free agency work on the side): 13%
  - ✓ Diversified workers (workers with multiple sources of income, derived from a mix of traditional and freelance work with the majority of their income derived from freelance work): 4%"

  Source: "Third of workers globally are 'free agents,' Kelly survey finds" staffingindustry.com, September 3, 2015
- "The U.S. temporary staffing industry is projected to grow 6% in 2015 to reach $115 billion and expand another 5% in 2016 to reach an all-time high of $121 billion, according to the U.S. Staffing Industry Forecast, a semi-annual report released recently by Staffing Industry Analysts. The report, based on staffing company revenues, serves as a benchmark for the staffing industry, charting the size and growth of temporary staffing skill segments.

  "Skill Segment Trends—The U.S. Staffing Industry Forecast is comprised of 10 different skill segments and all are forecasted for growth in 2015. Education, a relatively small and emerging segment, has the highest growth forecast at 15% as education continues to experience a surge in demand from K-12 school districts turning to staffing firms to hire substitute teachers. Engineering has the lowest growth forecast at 3% due to the lack of recovery in employment since the recession and a downturn in oil and gas exploration and production. Healthcare, IT, finance/accounting and marketing/creative all show 7% increases. The remaining segments of office/clerical, industrial, legal and clinical/scientific segments are also expected to grow.

  "While the likelihood of a recession occurring in 2015 or 2016 is low, an unexpected downturn in the overall economy remains the most severe risk to the forecasted growth rates of the industry, according to the report."

  Source: http://www.staffingindustry.com/About/Media-Center/Press-Releases/Staffing-Industry-Analysts-Projects-U.S.-Temporary-Staffing-Industry-Will-Reach-115-Billion-in-2015
- "Staffing is a leading economic indicator and moves early in the economic cycle. Reluctance by companies to add to overheads has directly benefited staffing business models. Watch Obamacare initiatives and their impact on the Staffing Industry."
- "These businesses will continue to consolidate and there will be continued gross margin pressures over the coming years. Businesses that can service multiple locations will attract higher multiples."
- "The industry is expected to grow significantly through 2024. This isn't a skill intensive business and many types of buyers are qualified to be owners."
- "Demand should remain strong as employers respond to rebounding economy and Obamacare uncertainties by hiring temps and avoiding adding to their overhead."

Seller Financing

- "For the more substantial transactions ($10million in sales and up) normally these are financed internally or with lines of credit for larger buyers. Smaller sellers, especially those with lower margins that are less desirable may be willing to consider seller financing."
- "50% or more owner financing common on transactions with less than $2 million in consideration. Owner financing declines to 20% level as transaction values climb over $5 million."
- "Outside financing is very common. Owner financing can be expected if there are client concentration issues."
- "This industry has an above average requirement for seller financing. Not uncommon for sellers to provide up to 50-70% financing."

Questions

- "Typical questions for any service business, customer concentration, staff non-competes, contracts with clients, ability to speak to next level of management when the time is right, historical growth, gross margins, etc."
- "Background. Financial strength. Industry experience."
- "Length of service by account. Gross Profit by account. Bad debt experience."
- "Who in the organization has the relationships with the clients? What is the gross margin? Which clients have vendor management systems in place? How frequently do they put these out to bid? What is the turnover of the recruiting and sales staff?"
- "Need to understand working capital requirements. Will sellers include some accounts receivable in seller price? Review client hiring patterns for past three years and match against their payment history."
- "What is concentration of sales for top five accounts? How long have you serviced these accounts? How many recruiters do you have? What is your bad debt experience for past two years?"
- "Closeness of relationships to clients; length of transition; recent changes to business or competition; staff retention."

Resources

Websites

- Staffing Industry Analysts: www.staffingindustry.com

Associations

- National Association of Personnel Services: www.naps360.orgPUBS
- American Staffing Association: www.americanstaffing.net

Office Supplies and Stationery Stores		
SIC 5943-01	NAICS 453210	Number of Businesses/Units 10,724

Rules of Thumb

➢ 25 percent of annual sales plus inventory

➢ 1.5 times SDE plus inventory

➢ 12 percent times EBIT

Pricing Tips
- "Check inventory levels and FF&E carefully. Owners of these types of businesses tend to hide cash flow in excessive inventory and FF&E."

Benchmark Data

Statistics (Office Supply Stores)

Number of Establishments	10,724
Average Profit Margin	2.2%
Revenue per Employee	$181,400
Average Number of Employees	7.2
Average Wages per Employee	$20,023

Products and Services Segmentation

Office supplies and equipment	44.6%
Office machines	28.5%
Technology	13.0%
Services	8.2%
Office furniture	5.7%

Major Market Segmentation

Small businesses	27.8%
Households for education purposes	22.5%
Large businesses	16.8%
Households for general purposes	15.3%
Other	8.5%
Households for satellite work	7.2%
Federal, state and local government	1.9%

Industry Costs

Profit	2.2%
Wages	11.0%
Purchases	59.5%
Depreciation	0.8%
Marketing	1.9%
Rent & Utilities	5.5%
Other	19.1%

Market Share

Office Depot Inc.	37.2%
Staples Inc.	36.3%

Source: IBISWorld, April 2016

- "Historical sales against same store performance would be a good measurement. Adequate advertising budget (5% of gross is desirable). Gross sales per square foot of $200/year would be good, $250/year would be very good, $300/year or more would be excellent."

Industry Trend
- "Office-supply retailers are grappling with controlling costs as they battle increased competition and technological shifts that are reducing demand for traditional supplies such as pens, paper clips and paper. Profitability among

privately held office-supply, stationery and gift retailers (NAICS 4532) declined between 2012 and 2013, according to recent data from Sageworks, a financial information company. In fact, preliminary estimates from Sageworks' financial statement analysis of 2013 data show net profit margins swung from positive to negative in 2013. Office-supply retailers are typically one of the least profitable retail industries anyway, according to Sageworks, but last year they saw overhead expenses and costs of goods sold increase relative to sales.

"'There's a big shift in the landscape within this industry, particularly because there's less need for these office products now that everyone's going digital,' said Sageworks analyst James Noe. Privately held office-supply, stationery and gift retailers operated with a net loss, on average, of 1.2% of sales in 2013, compared with a net profit margin of 3.7% in 2012, according to 'Sageworks' industry data."

Source: "Office-Supply Stores Seeing Profit Margins Erased," by Mary Ellen Biery, www.forbes.com April 13, 2014

Oil and Gas Related Businesses

Rules of Thumb

➢ 4 times EBITDA

Pricing Tips

- "Very few sales are based on a percent of sales, most are a multiplier of EBITDA. When EBIDTA is above $2.0 million, it is not unusual to see a sale in the 6 x; above $4.0 million, depending on customer concentration and other issues similar to any other industries, they could value in the 6–8 x. Drilling companies may be priced more on the value of their equipment as opposed to EBITDA."
- "Industry rule of thumb for:
  "Roustabout (SIC 1389)
    - ✓ 2x SDE plus FFE & inventory
    - ✓ 3–4x SDE
    - ✓ 75–90% of sales (100%+ when talking over $10+mil in sales)

  "Drilling (water well) (SIC 1781) [O&G companies need water wells and core samples]
    - ✓ 2xSDE plus FFE & inventory
    - ✓ 3x SDE
    - ✓ 3.5x EBITDA
    - ✓ 150% of sales

  "Excavation/Construction (NAICS 213112) [specifically for O&G industry with MSAs (other excavations site preps {SIC 1794} are vulnerable to the housing/real estate market and deem lower pricing)]
    - ✓ 1.5x SDE plus FFE & inventory
    - ✓ 3–4x SDE
    - ✓ 80–90% of sales"
- "Adjust for age/condition of equipment."
- "The typical discount for all cash versus terms applies."
- "The oil and gas industry is a very broad cross section of industry segments and varies widely in size. Value parameters will vary widely and are probably most associated with individual market segments such as manufacturing or services."

- "The typical measure of earnings used is EBITDA. The multiple will range between 3.2X and 4X for transactions up to $20 million. The variance is based upon qualitative factors such as customer concentrations, equipment age and condition, middle management depth and experience, safety records, and nature of services being performed. Equipment rental companies will be higher in the range while companies providing products or services with material intensive cost of sales will be somewhat lower, again depending upon qualitative factors.
"A key factor is the number of Master Service Agreements (MSA's) a company has in place. These are master agreements with an oil company. They do not guarantee any certain volume of work, but rather indicate the manner in which work will be performed, liabilities and hold harmless, rate sheets, insurance coverage required, etc."

Expert Comments

"It is no different than any other industry. Find the right buyer! To do that, the seller must take the time to clearly understand what kind of transaction he is most interested in. Will there be enough money after taxes and expenses for me and my family to live in style for the rest of my life? What will I do after I sell? For a buyer, ask himself, can I see myself working in this business? Does it fit my skill set? Exactly why is the seller wanting out? Are there key people in the business and will they remain after the sale. If I decide this business isn't for me, can I successfully sell it? and the most important of all; What is my exit plan?"

"All businesses geared to the O & G industry are potentially high profit with a high degree of risk due to the relationship of the price of a barrel of oil. However, many service and repair companies not only survive the downturns but also flourish. Because of the high cost of entry due to the equipment required, it is a difficult industry for new businesses."

"Industry trends are heavily influenced by commodity based pricing of the underlying oil and gas products. The industry may be subject to boom-bust cycles."

"High risk if a few top accounts take the majority of the sales. Lose one and lose 70–90% of the business."

"The oil and gas sector is very cyclical over 7- to 8-year cycles, normally. Natural gas and oil prices dictate the demand for services; hence, the profitability and revenues within the industry. Replication of products and/or services is difficult without sufficient industry knowledge."

Benchmark Data

- "All costs are dependent on the particular nature of the business. Is it service, manufacturing, repair, drilling, waste water hauling and disposal? All are unique in their own way."
- "Roustabout—(SIC 1389)
  - ✓ Payroll 40–45%
  - ✓ Profit 25%
"Drilling (water well)—(SIC 1781) [O&G companies need water wells and core samples]
  - ✓ Payroll 15%
  - ✓ Profit 50%

"Excavation/Construction—(NAICS 213112)
- ✓ Payroll 15%
- ✓ Profit 20–25%"

- "The cost of goods sold percentages vary widely. Companies providing materials in addition to their service or value added features tend to have much lower gross profit per dollar of revenues."

Industry Trend

- "Generally up, but with ups and downs. Rapid increases are unlikely, but rapid falls are possible as the world supply seeks equilibrium."
- "Because of the low price of oil, all businesses in this space are affected in a negative manner. However, we know oil will come back. It usually takes about one to two years for a rebound to come into play for these businesses, so the future looks very bright. No one knows if oil will get back to $100 per barrel but the good news is it doesn't have to for these businesses to flourish. We should see an upward trend beginning in 2017 and in 2018 we should see that trend continue."
- "Difficult profitability issues will likely remain over the short term. The long-term trend has been positive, but there are substantial periods of high volatility."
- "Currently in a strong downturn, but upturn is expected to follow price recovery over next 6 months to 3 years."
- "Steady to upward. The industry has historically seen boom-bust cycles. Today it is clearly booming."
- "Steadily increasing in revenues and earnings, depending upon the demand and pricing of oil and natural gas fluctuations."

Seller Financing

- "In today's market, buyers, including private equity, look to the owners for some financing and or investment back into the business, usually in the 25% range of owner carry or investment. Many owners are willing to do this due to the tremendous upside in the industry."
- "Normally a combination of owner and institutional financing"
- "Most have significant third-party financing, with some seller financing, frequently in the form of an earnout or clawback. The factors affecting that are usually the customer diversity or customer concentration."

Questions

- "Why is he selling? How can I grow the business? What specific relationships does the seller have with customers, suppliers, etc.?"
- "Equipment should be the number one question—age/condition. Ask for service maintenance logs. Find out the turnover rate. How often is the equipment replaced with better and newer equipment? Get a third-party equipment appraisal."

Resources

Websites
- American Petroleum Institute: www.api.org

Trade Publications

- The Oil & Gas Journal: www.ogj.com
- Hart Energy: www.hartenergy.com
- Shale Play Water Management: www.shaleplaywatermanagement.com

Associations

- American Association of Professional Landmen: www.landman.org
- PMAA— Petroleum Marketers Association of America: www.pmaa.org
- Pipe Line Contractors Association: www.plca.org
- Society of Petroleum Engineers: www.spe.org

	Franchise

Once Upon A Child

(See also Clothing Stores—Used, Consignment Shops, Franchises)

Approx. Total Investment	$244,800 to $376,600
SIC 5932-05	NAICS 453310	Number of Businesses/Units 320

Rules of Thumb

- ➤ 25 percent of annual sales plus inventory
- ➤ 30 percent of annual sales includes inventory

Optical Stores (See also Optometry Practices)

	NAICS 446130	Number of Businesses/Units 16,236

Rules of Thumb

- ➤ 50 to 60 percent of annual sales includes inventory (Sales do not include regular exam fees)
- ➤ 2 times SDE includes inventory (Sales do not include regular exam fees)

Pricing Tips

- "Another benchmark is 1 x SDE, plus tangible assets."
- "Adjust price up or down depending on how updated the equipment is."
- "How many days do they perform exams? For whom?"

Expert Comments

"Very limited buyer pool; must have OD degree and state license."

"The aging population will increase the demand for eyecare."

"National chains seem to be weaker. Mom and pops seem to be hanging in there, so they may be keeping optometrists busy."

"Surgery has made the industry shrink. However many chains have contracted, giving independents some breathing room. Walmart still looms."

Benchmark Data

Statistics (Eye Glasses & Contact Lens Stores)

Number of Establishments	16,236
Average Profit Margin	5.1%
Revenue per Employee	$133,300
Average Number of Employees	5.5
Average Wages per Employee	$27,056

Products and Services Segmentation

Prescription eyeglasses	64.9%
Nonprescription eyewear	14.4%
Contact lenses	10.8%
Other	6.5%
Eye examinations	3.4%

Industry Costs

Profit	5.1%
Wages	20.2%
Purchases	45.7%
Depreciation	4.6%
Marketing	3.3%
Rent & Utilities	7.0%
Other	14.1%

Market Share

Luxottica Group S.p.A.	48.7%
National Vision Inc.	8.2%
Highmark Inc.	8.1%

Source: IBISWorld, March 2016

- "$300 average revenue per exam"
- "$250 revenue/patient is low. $500 is very good."
- "Should give exams at least one full day a week. The more days they offer exams, the better."
- "The retail industry is highly fragmented but concentrated at the top: 90 percent of companies operate a single store, but about a dozen chains operate more than 100 and account for half of industry revenue."

Source: www.findarticles.com

Expenses as a percentage of annual sales

Cost of goods	35% to 45%
Payroll/labor Costs	10% to 15%
Occupancy	15% to 20%
Profit (estimated pretax)	25% to 30%

Industry Trend

- "Eyewear is big business. Market sources estimate that the global market, which includes frames, contact lenses and sunglasses, is worth $90 billion, and will reach $140 billion by 2020. In 2012, Exane BNP Paribas estimated that frames and sunglasses represented 40 percent of the eyewear market. Within that segment it estimates that premium frames and sunglasses, the sort produced by fashion labels, represent 35 percent. Applying those estimates to today's market values the premium fashion segment at just below $13 billion."

Source: https://www.businessoffashion.com/articles/intelligence/
a-closer-look-at-the-13-billion-premium-eyewear-market

- "More group practices and fewer single-doctor practices"
- "Perhaps stable. Surgery options will continue downslide."

Questions
- "Contact lens sales? Do they keep the profits from opticians?"
- "Probability of staff retention. Number of active patient records."
- "Days they have exams. If only one or two, could be tough to generate sales."
- "What kind of equipment? Leased? Referral sources? Insurances accepted?"
- "Does he have a lab? How many lanes (exam room)? What type of finishing does he do? How many days is a doctor available for exams?"

Resources

Trade Publications
- Eyecare Business: www.eyecarebusiness.com

Optometry Practices (See also Optical Stores)		
SIC 5999-04	NAICS 621320	Number of Businesses/Units 36,633

Rules of Thumb
➢ 55% to 65% percent of annual revenues includes inventory

➢ 3 to 4 times SDE includes inventory

➢ 2 to 2.5 times EBIT

➢ 2.5 to 3.5 times EBITDA

Pricing Tips
- "Location, brand name optical and sufficiently stocked inventory are all very important in this industry. They will significantly affect time on the market."
- "The purchase price will be somewhat lower in rural areas due to supply and demand."
- "Practices with EHR systems in place sell for a higher multiple."
- "Practices with SDE below $100,000 are basically worth the value of equipment and inventory. Reduce price for outdated equipment and/or below benchmark inventory level."
- "Optometry professional fees are generally 40% of total sales if the office includes dispensary, 60% sales from eyewear and contacts. Cost of goods averages about 25%. Premises expense about 8%–12%."
- "Pricing based on % of sales and cash flow are more applicable at sales exceeding $500,000."
- "The inventory that's included in the selling price should be an average inventory amount. The selling price should be adjusted up or down if the figure is above or below that amount. The selling price should be adjusted downward if the practice has not installed an EHR system."
- "Increased value with more sophisticated instrumentation and conversion to electronic health records"
- "Pricing varies based on % of medical services and product sales. Also, considerations in the percentage of private pay to insurance sourced revenue.

(i.e., low-volume Medicaid practice vs. high-end cash patients."

- "Reduce price for lack of lease transferability."
- "Values vary depending on the percent of professional fees to material sales. Offices with higher professional-only fees as a percent of gross collections will have a lower multiple."
- "Another benchmark is 1 x SDE, plus tangible assets."
- "Smaller offices are more asset based."
- "Offices without a dispensary typically have a lower multiple."
- "The intangible assets are difficult to value. Goodwill is 'the expectations of future profits under the ownership of someone other than the present owner.' According to the Internal Revenue Service, 'Goodwill is based upon earning capacity and its value, therefore it rests upon the excess of net earning over and above a fair return on net tangible assets...such factors as prestige and renown of successful operation over a prolonged period in a locality may be included in tangible value.' The American Medical Association simply defines goodwill as, 'the opportunity to take over the health care of a seller's patient base.'

Expert Comments

"Sellers—keep clean financial records with very little in the way of personal expenses. The valuation is heavily based on your practice's financial performance in the past two years. To get the most value for your practice, your tax returns should show a minimum of $140,000 in salary and net profit for a single practitioner. Larger ($750,000) and multi-office locations are in demand."

"Florida requires a licensed optometrist to own a practice. A non-licensed person could lease space to the optometrist and hire an optician, however that does affect seller's earnings."

"The seller should have accurate, up-to-date records. The buyer should insist on complete up-to-date records. The buyer should also make sure the equipment is in good shape and technologically up-to-date."

"Someone selling should develop an exit plan at least 3 to 5 years prior to the expected sale."

"A buyer should examine the practice momentum. Is the practice declining, stable, or growing—and what is the perceived reason."

"Replication is easy, however it requires a valid license for each respective state. Marketability is best in urban areas and can be poor in rural, less populated areas."

"Competition would be lower if not for increased pressure from the growth of chains and the impact of the Internet on retailing (eyewear sales)."

"While entry is rather easy (provided you are a doctor), it's customer service oriented and that takes years to build goodwill if you are starting from scratch. Other pressures include changes in healthcare reimbursements and retail online and store eyewear and contact lens sales."

"Offices that sell eyewear benefit from improved locations. Very customer driven service profession. Must be licensed OD in most states to own an optometry office"

"The aging population will increase the demand for eyecare."

Benchmark Data

Statistics (Optometrists)

Number of Establishments	36,633
Average Profit Margin	26.7%
Revenue per Employee	$114,500
Average Number of Employees	4.0
Average Wages per Employee	$37,290

Products and Services Segmentation

Prescription eyewear	43.0%
Eye exams	22.0%
Medical eye care	17.0%
Contact lenses	16.0%
Other	2.0%

Major Market Segmentation

Patients' out-of-pocket payments	42.4%
Private insurers	36.5%
Government payers	13.6%
Other patient care revenue	7.4%
Investment and property income	0.1%

Industry Costs

Profit	26.7%
Wages	32.7%
Purchases	22.2%
Depreciation	1.3%
Marketing	0.5%
Rent & Utilities	8.1%
Other	8.6%

Source: IBISWorld, May 2016

- "The 33% profit reflects SDE (income before a production wage for the owner/doctor. After all expenses, including a reasonable production wage for the owner, the net profit will average 10–15%"
- "Ideally each doctor should generate over $700,000 annual gross revenue."
- "New patient ratio should be at least 25%"
- "43 annual complete exams per 100 active patients. Eyewear sales as 43% of gross revenue. $550,000 annual revenue per full-time OD."
- "25% profit is SDE before paying doctor wages. Net profit to owner after all doctor wages is around 10%. Must be optometrist or ophthalmologist to own a practice. Many states and opticians cannot hire a doctor to do exams."
- "SDE percentage runs about 30% before debt service and before doctor production wages. Fixed costs play a large part because of the need for retail/visible setting. Therefore practice grossing under $500K might underperform."

Expenses as a percentage of annual sales

Cost of goods	25% to 35%
Payroll/labor Costs	10% to 20%
Occupancy	07% to 15%
Profit (estimated pretax)	20% to 30%

Industry Trend

- "Older optometrists are looking to get out as the complexity of insurance, billing and medical records increases. Many would prefer to sell rather than try to implement an EHR."
- "The number of Americans with visual impairment or blindness will climb to more than eight million by the year 2050—approximately twice the current number—and an additional 16.4 million Americans are expected to have vision impairment due to uncorrected refractive error, based on a National Institutes of Health analysis of six large studies."

  Source: Visual Loss, Blindness to Double by 2050, by Bill Kekevian, June 15, 2016, https://www.reviewofoptometry.com/article/visual-loss-blindness-to-double-by-2050
- "Competition continues to increase, consolidation has slowed the growth of business entities."
- "Other than a limited pool of buyers, the optometry industry is very secure and profitable. Aging baby boomers have created an increased demand and fewer millennial optometrists entering the field have decreased supply. Larger franchises are failing and consumers are returning to Mom and Pop' eye care centers for their needs. Most practices see around 8.1% in profit margins and predict 5% growth every year until 2019. This $6 billion dollar industry is great to be in, just challenging to leave."

  Source: http://www.vikingmergers.com/blog/2015/your-exit-strategy-selling-an-optometry-practice/
- "More use of the internet (online appointments, etc.) and social media. (marketing, patient relations, etc.). Movement towards multiple OD practices with larger patient bases. Expanding role of OD's in healthcare. OD alliances will be on the increase to keep independent OD's competitive."
- "Continued pressure from the internet sales and chains will put pressure on independent's revenues and profits."
- "The scope of optometry practice will continue to broaden as the supply of ophthalmologists fails to expand at the necessary pace."
- "Long term good, stable. Smaller offices shrinking in value. Larger offices stable (over $1MM)."
- "The independent optometrist is operating in a highly dynamic retail environment, as online sales growth rapidly outpaces physical retail across categories. For example, nearly 20% of contact lenses sales are now moving online."
- "A trend for solo practices to join alliances or merge with larger practices. Medical optometry will increase due to anticipated shortages of ophthalmologists and primary care physicians. Third-party reimbursements will account for a growing share of OD revenue."

Seller Financing

- "Outside financing"
- "It's almost all outside financing. Zero down is very common and financing is available for debt restructuring, relocation, remodeling, expansion and acquisition—good credit is the key."
- "Outside financing is typically used to fund the sale of optometry practices due to a number of organizations that specialize in financing medical (including optometry) practices. They also offer far more attractive terms than the typical commercial bank."
- "Buyers should have their financing lined up ahead of time. Seller should have their practice valued prior to selling."
- "The sale of well-run, profitable optometry practices are usually easy to bank finance. Many banks have separate practice acquisition financing departments

that allow a qualified OD to purchase a practice with little or no money down."
- "Either 100% financing from specialty lenders or seller financing. Buyers don't have the funds."

Questions
- "Insurance makeup (payors), review patient records."
- "Payor mix, market share, patient demographic data."
- "What would you do to expand the patient base?"
- "Carefully check out the risks associated with the seller continuing to practice in an area or in a manner that would siphon past patients to him/her. The details of the Non-Compete Agreement are very important."
- "Review revenue by source. Fee schedules? List of insurance panels they are currently with? Determine what services are done and what could be added."
- "What is your rate of new patient generation? What have been the obstacles to growing your practice? Have you converted to electronic health records?"
- "Obtain fee schedules, review exam charts, review insurance panels (payor mix) and top billing codes. Also review frames and contact lens inventory"
- "Days they have exams? If only one or two, could be tough to generate sales."
- "What kind of equipment? Leased? Referral sources? Insurances accepted?"

Resources

Websites
- OptiBoard: www.optiboard.com

Trade Publications
- Optometric Management: www.optometricmanagement.com
- Optometry Times: optometrytimes.modernmedicine.com
- Review of Optometry: www.revoptom.com
- Vision Monday: www.visionmonday.com

Associations
- American Academy of Optometry: www.aaopt.org
- American Optometric Association: www.aoa.org

		Franchise
Orange Julius (See also Franchises)		
Approx. Total Investment		$345,000 to $375,000
	NAICS 722515	Number of Businesses/Units 465

Rules of Thumb
- ➢ 32 percent of annual sales plus inventory

Resources

Websites
www.orangejulius.com

	Franchise

Original Italian Pie (See also Franchises, Pizza Shops)

Approx. Total Investment	$328,000 to $617,500

	NAICS 722513	Number of Businesses/Units 14

Rules of Thumb

➤ 35 to 40 percent of annual sales plus inventory

Resources

Websites
- www.italianpie.com

Outpatient Care Centers (Other)

Rules of Thumb

➤ 51 percent of annual sales plus inventory

➤ 1.6 times SDE plus inventory

➤ 5.1 times EBIT

➤ 5.0 times EBITDA

Benchmark Data

Expenses as a percentage of annual sales

Cost of goods..11%
Payroll/labor Costs.. 05%
Profit (estimated pretax) 14%

	Franchise

OXXO Care Cleaners (See also Dry Cleaners, Franchises)

Approx. Total Investment	$160,000 to $450,000

SIC 7212-01	NAICS 812320	Number of Businesses/Units 33

Rules of Thumb

➤ 60 percent of annual sales plus inventory

Resources

Websites
- OXXO Care Cleaners: www.oxxousa.com

Packaging (Industrial)		
	NAICS 561910	Number of Businesses/Units 10,344

Rules of Thumb

➤ 5 to 6 times EBIT

➤ 60 to 70 percent of annual sales plus inventory

Benchmark Data

Statistics (Packaging & Labeling Services)

Number of Establishments	10,344
Average Profit Margin	6.8%
Revenue per Employee	$149,400
Average Number of Employees	5.4
Average Wages per Employee	$36,970

Products and Services Segmentation

Packaging and labeling services	56.3%
Other services	20.2%
Assembly and fulfillment services	15.8%
Warehousing services	7.7%

Major Market Segmentation

Other consumer goods manufacturers	40.9%
Food and beverage manufacturers	38.0%
Pharmaceuticals and medical	8.6%
Chemical and petrochemical	6.2%
Automotive aftermarket manufacturers	5.1%
Other	1.2%

Industry Costs

Profit	6.8%
Wages	25.0%
Purchases	62.5%
Depreciation	2.2%
Marketing	0.5%
Rent & Utilities	2.5%
Other	0.5%

Source: IBISWorld, June 2016

Expenses as a percentage of annual sales

Cost of goods	60% to 65%
Payroll/labor Costs	08% to 10%
Occupancy	0
Profit (estimated pretax)	10% to 15%

Industry Trend

- "Global demand for flexible packaging is projected to reach $210 billion in 2015 according to a new market report by Smithers Pira.

   "The market is forecast to grow at an annual average rate of 3% reaching

$248 billion in 2020. Flexible packaging has been one of the fastest growing packaging sectors over the past 10 years, thanks to increased consumer focus on convenience and sustainability, and this rapid development will continue to accelerate, the report has found.

"The report shows that the global consumer flexible packaging market value is estimated at $91.7 billion for 2015 and is forecast to grow at an annual average rate of 4.4% during the period 2015–20 to reach $114 billion. The market tonnage of this segment is estimated at 26.2 million tons in 2015 and is forecast to grow on average by 3.8% during the period 2015–20 to reach 31.7 million tons."

Source: http://www.smitherspira.com/news/2015/july/global-flexible-packaging-market-sees-rapid-growth

- "Consolidation will rule the packaging industry. Cheaper to buy than to grow market share in a mundane, non-innovative business, lacking pricing power and vulnerable to relocation of key accounts to offshore facilities."

Questions

- "How stable is your customer base—what is your customer retention record? What % of total sales do your top 10 accounts represent? Is there really any real 'free cash flow' in the business?"

Paint & Decorating (Wallpaper) Retailers		
SIC 5231-07	NAICS 444120	Number of Businesses/Units 8,859

Rules of Thumb

➤ 20 percent of annual sales plus inventory

Pricing Tips

- "They should have a nationally known brand name plus 2 competitive paint lines. A wide variety of wallpaper from lesser priced to higher priced lines should be offered. National averages tell us these stores make from 16 to 17 percent plus reasonable wages for the owner/operators. The average markup is 40 percent. These stores are sold for fixtures, equipment plus inventory at cost."

Benchmark Data

Statistics (Paint Stores)

Number of Establishments	8,859
Average Profit Margin	12.2%
Revenue per Employee	$298,200
Average Number of Employees	4.2
Average Wages per Employee	$37,476

Products and Services Segmentation

Interior paint	44.0%
Stains, varnishes and other coatings	20.5%
Exterior paint	17.3%
Painting equipment and supplies	16.1%
Wallpaper and other flexible wall coverings	2.1%

Major Market Segmentation

Professional contractors	53.5%
Household consumers	29.3%
Other	17.2%

Industry Costs

Profit	12.2%
Wages	12.7%
Purchases	54.9%
Depreciation	1.1%
Marketing	2.7%
Rent & Utilities	6.9%
Other	9.5%

Market Share

The Sherwin-Williams Company	63.7%
PPG Industries Inc.	11.0%

Source: IBISWorld, March 2016

Industry Trend

- "The global market for paints and coatings is expected to reach $155 billion by 2020, which would represent a compound annual growth rate of 4%, according to BCC Research. Asia is expected to post significant gains, especially China and India.
  "The US paint and wallpaper store industry includes about 7,000 establishments (single-location companies and units of multi-location companies) with combined annual revenue of about $10 billion."
  Source: http://www.firstresearch.com/Industry-Research/Paint-and-Wallpaper-Stores.html

- "The Painting and Decorating Franchises industry is in the mature stage of its life cycle, indicated by its cyclicality with the construction sector and wholehearted acceptance of industry services by downstream markets. Industry value added (IVA), a measure of the industry's contribution to the overall economy, is expected to rise at an annualized rate of 3.8% over the 10 years to 2021. In comparison, US GDP is projected to grow at an annualized rate of 2.2% over the same period. Close growth with the overall economy shows that the industry is in the mature stage of its life cycle."
  Source: http://clients1.ibisworld.com/reports/us/industry/industryoutlook.aspx?entid=5575

Resources

Associations

- Paint and Decorating Retailers Association (PDRA): www.pdra.org

	Franchise
Pak Mail (See also Franchises, Mail and Parcel Centers)	
Approx. Total Investment	$138,020 to $180,215
NAICS 561431	Number of Businesses/Units 227

Rules of Thumb

➤ 50 percent of annual sales plus inventory

Resources

Websites
- www.pakmail.com

Franchise

Panera Bread (See also Franchises)	
Approx. Total Investment	Net Worth of $7.5 million
Estimated Annual Sales/Unit	$2.5 million
NAICS 722513	Number of Businesses/Units 1,926

Rules of Thumb
- ➢ 35 to 40 percent of sales plus inventory

Industry Trend
- "As of June 30, 2015, there are 1,926 bakery-cafes in 46 states, the District of Columbia, and in Ontario, Canada, operating under the Panera Bread®, Saint Louis Bread Co.® and Paradise Bakery & Café® names, delivering fresh, authentic artisan bread served in a warm environment by engaging associates."

Resources

Websites
- www.panerabread.com

Franchise

Papa John's Pizza (See also Franchises, Pizza Shops)		
Approx. Total Investment		$200,000 to $300,000
Estimated Annual Sales/Unit		$850,000
SIC 5812-22	NAICS 722513	Number of Businesses/Units 3,922

Rules of Thumb
- ➢ 38% to 40% of annual sales

Benchmark Data
- For Benchmark Data, see Pizza Shops

Resources

Websites
- wwwpapajohns.com

Franchise

Papa Murphy's Take 'N' Bake Pizza (See also Franchises, Pizza Shops)

Approx. Total Investment	$216,430 to $381,220
Estimated Annual Sales/Unit	$575,000

	NAICS 722513	Number of Businesses/Units 1,350

Rules of Thumb
➢ 35 to 40 percent of annual sales plus inventory

Benchmark Data
▪ For Benchmark Data, see Pizza Shops

Resources
Websites
▪ www.papamurphys.com

Franchise

Parcel Plus (See also Franchises, Mail and Parcel Centers)

Approx. Total Investment	$206,720 to $245,795

	NAICS 561431	Number of Businesses/Units 59

Rules of Thumb
➢ 25 percent of annual sales plus inventory

Resources
Websites
▪ Parcel Plus: www.parcelplus.com

Parking Lots and Garages

	NAICS 812930	Number of Businesses/Units 19,848

Rules of Thumb
➢ "[In some cities] they have been selling for 1.5 times their annual net before taxes, plus the value of fixtures, equipment and inventory at cost—plus real estate."

Benchmark Data

Statistics (Parking Lots and Garages)

Number of Establishments	19,848
Average Profit Margin	22.1%
Revenue per Employee	$62,100
Average Number of Employees	7.7
Average Wages per Employee	$20,303

Products and Services Segmentation

Off-street parking—hourly or daily	38.3%
Off-street parking in buildings—weekly or monthly	24.3%
Valet parking	12.7%
Off-street parking on lots—weekly or monthly	9.1%
Management fees for the operation of parking facilities	9.0%
Other	6.6%

Major Market Segmentation

Privately operated central business district	40.5%
College and university	14.2%
Off-premise airport	12.3%
On-premise airport	12.2%
Hotel	10.3%
Hospital	5.5%
Municipal central business district	5.0%

Industry Costs

Profit	22.1%
Wages	32.5%
Purchases	8.4%
Depreciation	1.1%
Marketing	0.8%
Rent & Utilities	28.2%
Other	6.9%

Market Share

SP Plus Corporation	16.4%
Vinci	10.3%
ABM Industries Inc.	7.0%

Source: IBISWorld, July 2016

- "Nearly four in 10 responding parking professionals are with organizations that currently contract with commercial operators for varying services. Contracted services include frontline attendants (39 percent), collections (36 percent), maintenance (36 percent), customer service (33 percent), transit/shuttle (31 percent), special events (30 percent), enforcement (29 percent), and security (29 percent). Of those surveyed, 18 percent outsource their entire operations to a commercial operator for turnkey services."

Source: 2015 Survey by the International Parking Institute

Industry Trend

- "However, while data suggests positive events on the horizon for the parking industry, there are a number of risk factors, such as increased taxes and increased government regulation"

Source: http://weareparking.org/?page=Parking_Demand.

- "In the five years to 2021, IBISWorld expects revenue for the Parking Lots and Garages industry to increase at an annualized rate of 1.0% to $11.3 billion. Employment, domestic trips and vehicle registrations will rise during this period, increasing the need for parking services at airports, entertainment venues and central business districts."

Source: http://clients1.ibisworld.com/reports/us/industry/industryoutlook.aspx?entid=1739

- "Most respondents' programs also include a variety of elements beyond parking, such as improving conditions for bicyclists and pedestrians (47 percent) and bike/transit integration (43 percent), special event management (43 percent), shuttle services (40 percent), carsharing (40 percent), park and ride (33 percent), and ridesharing (33 percent). About one quarter of all those surveyed are also involved with shared parking, commuter trip reduction programs, traffic calming, bikeshare programs, and a wide range of programs that promote alternative transportation modes.

  "Among the top 10 emerging trends in parking, half relate directly to a range of different technologies that have revolutionized the parking sector in the past few years. Topping the list are 'innovative technologies that improve access control and payment automation' (53 percent), the 'demand for electronic cashless payment' (44 percent), 'prevalence of mobile applications' (47 percent) and 'real-time communication of pricing and availability to mobile/smartphones' (41 percent), and 'wireless sensing devices for traffic management' (22 percent). Good news for parking professionals: A top trend remains greater 'collaboration between parking, transportation, and decision-makers,' which industry experts believe is a pathway to solving many problems."

  Source: 2015 Survey by the International Parking Institute

- "Factors Driving Parking Demand—Parking demand is a function of a number of factors, all working in tandem to affect demand and usage. When looking at macroeconomic, demographic, employment, and industry statistics, we see a picture of patterns that influence parking demand in North America.

  - ✓ Population: Fundamental population growth of 9.6% from the 2000 U.S. Census to the 2010 U.S. Census is expected to continue into the future.
  - ✓ Employment: In the U.S., 92% employment provides sustained parking demand, 6.2% unemployment as of August 2014.
  - ✓ Baby Boomers: The Baby Boomer population will increase to 63 million by 2025, an 80% increase over 2000 levels.
  - ✓ Colleges/Universities: College/University enrollment increased 30% from 2000–2009, from 15.3 million to 20.4 million.
  - ✓ Municipalities: Public sector parking is beset by financial pressures; this pressure will accelerate automation and rate increases that will drive revenue.
  - ✓ Pricing: Demand will be affected by demand pricing, mobile rate promotions, pre-paid parking and price increases both public/private, as well as price rates for peak parking periods.

  However, while data suggests positive events on the horizon for the parking industry, there are a number of risk factors, such as increased taxes and increased government regulation."

  Source: "National Parking Association 2013–2015 Parking Demand Report"

Resources

Associations
- National Parking Association: weareparking.org
- International Parking Institute: www.parking.org

Parking Lot Sweeping		
SIC 1611-04	NAICS 561790	

Rules of Thumb

➤ 60 to 65% percent of annual sales includes inventory

➤ 2 to 2.5 times SDE includes inventory

➤ 5 to 5.5 times EBIT

➤ 5 to 6 times EBITDA

Pricing Tips

- "Some value factors are types of accounts, large box stores, nat'l shopping centers, small strips, construction, colleges, corporations. The stronger the account base with good contracts, the higher the value. Condition of equipment, quality of labor force and quality of service to the accounts separate the top companies from the rest."

- "Most of the time, prospective buyers for a sweeping company will primarily look at two factors, your sweeping equipment and your accounts. For the former, that's when you'll want to have preventative and scheduled maintenance documents on each piece of equipment available. If you know you're putting your business onto the market, you may even want to go through your sweepers and improve their cosmetics, installing items like seat covers and floor mats. These are low-cost items that provide a better overall impression to prospective buyers. It's best if you have all safety and normal operational items working, as well.

  "When it comes to your contracts, savvy buyers will want to look at several areas of your accounts. Although quantity and margin are important, their perception of the quality of your accounts is perhaps even more so. This includes such factors as longevity on the books, ease of cancellation, whether or not escalation clauses are in the contract and more. For example, if all of your contracts allow for a 30-day, 'no reason required' cancellation by the customer, your business won't be worth as much as when you want to sell it.

  "In most buy/sell transactions, at least for sweeping businesses that have been operational for a number of years, 'goodwill' is also a factor. The seller typically wants money to compensate for having developed the business to its current state. As a buyer, your goal is to keep this amount to a minimum.

  "'Everyone wants lots of money for the business they've put however many years of blood, sweat and tears into,' said Presutti. The reality, however, is often different. That will often become apparent when, as a buyer, you sit down with the owner and go through the actual current valuations of both contracts and depreciated equipment. This is central to the negotiation process.

  "Since most business owners plan ahead to sell, the machinery has typically not been replaced recently. Contracts usually have a 30-day cancellation clause where the customer can cancel for no reason. You have to ask yourself what that type of contract is really worth to you. 'In my view, giving more than 60 days of revenue to such an account is really a crapshoot.'"

Source: "Operate Your Business With a Resale in Mind"
by Jay Presutti and Ranger Kidwell-Ross, October 2005, http://www.worldsweeper.com/
This is a very informative site and should be visited by anyone who has an interest in this business.
Don't let the date fool you, still excellent information.

Expert Comments

"This industry has been unable to support national or regional consolidation. Mostly local, statewide, or small regional players."

Benchmark Data

- "$125K/employee or $150–$200K/driver"
- "Very generally speaking, using 2005 prices, it is not uncommon for a contractor with a smaller parking area sweeper, such as a three-yard-capacity sweeper on a 1-ton chassis, to be able to charge between $55 and $65 per hour, for a gross earnings of between $9,000 and $11,000 per month.

  "For a larger sweeper, one which is suitable for performing a variety of duties other than parking lot cleanup, the same rule of thumb is a charge of between $65 and $75 per hour; this should net you a gross of between $11,000 and $14,000 per month. Street sweeping pricing should be about $90, since it is harder on your equipment, and the sweepers cost substantially more.

  "Again, these are simply generalizations, and actual earnings are quite dependent upon work performed, charges in your area, etc. They are definitely, however, numbers which have been attained by many in the industry who have worked hard at developing their businesses."

  Source: Schwarze Industries, Inc. Although this information is dated, it is still interesting.

Expenses as a percentage of annual sales

Cost of goods	20%
Payroll/labor Costs	15%
Occupancy	05%
Profit (estimated pretax)	10% to 12%

Questions

- "Must establish the quality of the accounts, condition of equipment, review contracts, examine labor force, etc. Is the owner tied to any special interests, people or other connections responsible for a significant portion of his company's business? If so how will this affect these accounts/sites? Future growth in a local area or region? Competition?"

Resources

Websites

- www.worldsweeper.com

Associations

- North American Power Sweeping Association (NAPSA): www.powersweeping.org

---

Pawn Shops (See also Used Goods)

SIC 5932-29	NAICS 522298	Number of Businesses/Units 9,849

Rules of Thumb

➢ 3 times SDE includes inventory

➢ 3 to 5 times EBIT

➢ 3.5 times EBITDA

> 40 to 70 percent of annual sales plus inventory. Since money is loaned using items of value belonging to the customer and said items serve as collateral for the loan, inventory against money loaned has to be taken into account.

Pricing Tips

- "Pricing pawnshops usually is far from the norm of a multiple of SDE, EBIT or EBITA. Typically the values that drive a pawnshop are the 'Money on the street' (value of the daily loans) and the inventory, with great interest in the MIX of all the items that have been taken and used as collateral and the type of inventory, i.e., if a certain shop has 80% Jewelry and 20% guns, tools, and electronics the inventory will be worth more than cost since gold and silver are extremely valuable. If the mix is 20% jewelry and 80% tools and electronics then it possibly could be worth less than cost due to depreciation. Not all shops handle guns but if they are a large percentage or even half of the inventory then it is a pretty safe bet it should be valued no less than cost. Today's buyers are typically corporate buyers and rely heavily on good records and computer systems. They will shy away from shops that are not computerized and the seller is telling them (wink wink) the shop makes more than it shows. Keep a close eye on the scrap gold sales and whether or not they are being recorded in the income for the shop. It is very common for those sales to not be recorded and will generally be $15,000–$25,000 per month for a shop doing $2 million in gross sales. This will drastically change the SDE for you."
- "Quality of inventory is very important. Stores with lots of unwanted 'junk' will not be of interest to educated pawn buyers. Need to understand pawn renewal rate, average loan, do they buy gold and at what rate."

Expert Comments

"Let me take these one by one. The amount of competition is directly affected by the part of town and possibly the state you are in. Some states have very difficult pawn laws and others do not, so the competition is stiff in Detroit but none at all in San Francisco.

"Amount of risk is very little if you are somewhat educated in the pawn business; even a poorly run shop can be profitable if they know how to make educated loans. If you make poor loans your retail side will not be enough to sustain you for a long time.

"Location and facilities are key to your survival. You must be in the right location and contrary to popular belief that does not mean you want to be in a poor neighborhood. Areas with blue collar incomes are much more desirable than welfare or extremely poor neighborhoods. Marketability is very high for both small and large shops alike. The shops with at least $150,000 on the street are desirable to small to medium size chain buyers and anything smaller will be sought after by mom and pops. Any store with $400,000 or more on the street will be sold quickly. Remember that money on the street is the number one thing that all educated buyers of pawnshops look for. A high loan balance on good loans will eventually bring high revenue.

"Industry trend: with the boom in pawnshop reality shows pawnshops are getting some much needed positive spotlight from Hollywood and the TV world. This is driving the industry forward with both patrons and individuals wanting to try their hand at being a pawnshop owner.

"Ease of replication: the industry is growing and cities/municipalities are seeing the need for more ordinances to govern the business and practices of some of the owners. Therefore opening new shops is getting very difficult in some areas.

"Risk is actually very low if you make educated loans on a daily basis. There are many factors that weigh in on this and typically 'education' in this field comes from 'learning the hard way,' but several large chains have been very successful in training personnel quickly to run shops successfully."

Benchmark Data

Statistics (Pawn Shops)

Number of Establishments	9,849
Average Profit Margin	10.1%
Revenue per Employee	$230,700
Average Number of Employees	2.4
Average Wages per Employee	$29,421

Products and Services Segmentation

Merchandise sales	58.1%
Secured loans for personal collateral	41.9%

Industry Costs

Profit	10.1%
Wages	12.9%
Purchases	39.8%
Depreciation	1.1%
Marketing	0.9%
Rent & Utilities	6.5%
Purchases	28.7%

Market Share

Cash America International Inc.	9.3%
EZCorp Inc.	10.9%

Source: IBISWorld, June 2016

- "The average pawn customer:
  - ✓ Age: 36
  - ✓ Household Income: $29,000
  - ✓ 80% are employed
  - ✓ 82% have high school diploma or GED
  - ✓ 33% are homeowners
  - ✓ All ethnicities
  - ✓ National Average Loan Amount: $150"

Source: http://pawnshopstoday.com/the-customer/

- "According to the National Pawnbrokers Association, 80 percent of all customers do end up reclaiming their items."

- "The National Pawnbrokers Association reports that there are over 30 million pawn store customers per year and they appreciate this unique form of credit and tend to borrow only what they need, as evidenced by the relatively low national average loan amount of $80. NPA President and pawn shop owner Dave Crume says, 'Pawn customers repay their loans and redeem their collateral at a correspondingly high average national redemption rate of 80 percent. These parameters appear to be holding constant, despite the current economy."

Expenses as a percentage of annual sales

Cost of goods	62%
Payroll/labor Costs	09%
Occupancy	04%
Profit (estimated pretax)	18%

Industry Trend

- "IBISWorld forecasts moderate growth for the Pawn Shops industry over the five years to 2019, with revenue projected to increase at an average annual rate of 1.5% to $7.1 billion. The industry will likely experience steady demand throughout the period, driven by cautious consumers who continue to seek out discounted goods at pawn shops to save money."

    Source: http://clients1.ibisworld.com/reports/us/industry/industryoutlook.aspx?entid=4741

- "The National Pawnbrokers Association (NPA) today announced the results of the NPA 2015 Trend Survey that assesses how changes in the U.S. economy have affected the pawn industry since the beginning of 2014. Findings of the survey demonstrate conservative growth within the industry over the past year, as well as a dip in the number gold-based loans and gold-buying transactions. This decrease in gold-based transactions, according to industry experts, is due to consumers having released disposable gold during peak gold price periods.

    "While gold-based transactions may have leveled off, the majority of pawnbrokers surveyed reported a three to five percent increase in overall business. Collateral loans, also known as pawn loans, remain the core of pawnbrokers' businesses, with over 80 percent of pawnbrokers reporting that pawn loans are the most common transactions. According to the survey, the national average pawn loan amount remained at $150.

    "'Americans continue to turn to pawn stores for non-recourse, collateral based loans,' said Ben Levinson, president of the National Pawnbrokers Association. 'While business has grown more conservatively in recent years, increased public awareness, a positive image, and consumer-friendly stores attract new customers to pawn stores every day.'"

    Source: http://pawnshopstoday.com/trends/

- "The new wave of pawnbrokers, or collateralized lenders, as they like to be known, isn't just betting that people will pledge cars, planes, or, in the case of one ultrapawn customer, an earth mover. They are betting that as long as traditional bank lending remains tight for individuals, there will be repeat customers."

    Source: "Rich, too, find need for a good pawnshop," Paul Sullivan, *Boston Globe*, January 13, 2014

    "Trend is more competition and a steady customer base."

    "The pawn business model is diverse, including retail, jewelry sales and pawn loans. While one element of the pawn business may thrive in a slow economy, such as pawn loans, other elements such as retail sales, will decrease. Dave

Crume notes, 'While many of our association members are making it through the dip in the economy, there are many pawn shops in the U.S. that are struggling and closing. Just like all sectors of the American economy, the pawn industry is challenged by the recent economy, the pawn industry is challenged by the recent economic trends."

Source: www.pawnshopstoday.com

Seller Financing
- "2–3 years max"

Questions
- "What type of software do you use to track pawn receivables and inventory? How do you value pawned items? What is the quality of your pawn receivable? How do you measure and track bad inventory? What are the state laws regarding pawn shops, gun sales, and interest rates on loans?"
- "Do you have a good POS program and do you use it correctly? How is your accounting done? What type of software and is all income recorded?"

Resources

Websites
- Pawn Shops Today: www.pawnshopstoday.com

Associations
- National Pawnbrokers Association: www.nationalpawnbrokers.org

Payday Loans (See also Check Cashing Services)		
	NAICS 522291	Number of Businesses/Units 20,092

Rules of Thumb
➢ 70 percent of annual sales

Benchmark Data

Statistics (Check Cashing & Payday Loan Services)
Number of Establishments 20,092
Average Profit Margin 13.7%
Revenue per Employee $127,200
Average Number of Employees 4.5
Average Wages per Employee $37,653

Products and Services Segmentation
Payday loans for recurring expenses 46.0%
Check cashing 33.3%
Payday loans for unexpected emergencies/expenses 10.7%
Payday loans for other reasons 10.0%

Industry Costs

Profit	13.7%
Wages	29.4%
Purchases	33.9%
Depreciation	1.6%
Marketing	2.2%
Rent & Utilities	2.8%
Other	16.4%

Market Share

AARC LLC	7.1%
Cash America International Inc.	5.6%

Source: IBISWorld, November 2015

- Miscellaneous Statistics:
    - ✓ "97 percent of borrowers agree that their payday lender clearly explained the terms of the loan to them, including nearly nine in 10 (88 percent) who strongly agree.
    - ✓ 68 percent prefer a payday loan over incurring a late fee of approximately $30 (4 percent) or an overdraft fee of $35 from their bank (3 percent) when faced with a short-term financial crisis and unable to pay a bill.
    - ✓ Fewer than one in 10 (8 percent) said that a payday loan was their only option and they had no other resources available.
    - ✓ 95 percent say payday loans can provide a safety net during unexpected financial difficulties.
    - ✓ 94 percent say they were able to repay their loan in the amount of time they had expected to.
    - ✓ 89 percent say they feel more in control of their financial situation because of this option when they need it.
    - ✓ 68 percent say they would be in worse financial condition than they are now without the option of taking out a payday loan."
        Source: "New Harris Poll: 9 in 10 Payday Loan Borrowers Felt Product Met Their Expectations," http://cfsaa.com/our-resources/communications/recent-news/article-detail/newsid/77.aspx
- "Consequently, revenue for the Check Cashing and Payday Loan Services industry is expected to increase at an annualized rate of 2.0% from 2009 to 2014 to reach $11.1 billion; this growth includes a 2.2% rise in revenue expected in 2014 alone.
    "According to The Pew Charitable Trusts, 5.5% of domestic adults have used a payday loan. In general, younger individuals that lack a college degree and generate less than $40,000 in annual income are the most likely to rely on payday loans. The average borrower takes out eight loans of $375 each and pays $520 in interest annually. Moreover, this average borrower is typically indebted for five months out of the year."
        Source: "Check Cashing & Payday Loans Services in the US Industry Market Research Report Now Available from IBISWorld," www.prweb.com, February 19, 2014
- "For the payday lending industry, and as previously discussed, smaller loans cost more to originate than larger ones on a cost-per-dollar basis. This is because lenders, regardless of their structure, incur fixed costs in originating a loan, whatever its size. In the case of payday lending, these costs include:
    - ✓ Defaults on extensions of unsecured credit to borrowers of moderate means;

✓ Operating costs, such as salaries, facilities, processing applications, and collection of payments;

✓ Taxes; and

✓ Return on investment capital."

- "Available data on defaults suggest that unpaid obligations to payday lenders amount to about 10 to 20 percent of the finance charges they levy over the course of a year.

"The operating costs, which represent the largest part by far, are fixed and are not affected by the loan amount. While the fixed costs of facilitating a $200 loan are not substantially different from those likely to be incurred to facilitate and place a $20,000 home equity loan or $5,000 cash advance on a credit card, actual labor costs associated with servicing payday loans are higher.

"Within the parameters of the marketing proposition—i.e., a quick, convenient loan, as an alternative to credit card borrowing—payday lenders can be expected to do as much as they can to ensure that the risk of default is low.

"For example, payday lenders require borrowers to produce proof of a checking account, identification and a pay-stub; some lenders screen for histories of bounced checks.

"For payday loans—as for other unsecured, subprime loans—the costs relating to collection of payments is significant. Our reading of Prof. Caskey's analysis suggests that payday lenders are exceptionally close to their borrowers. Payday loans are generally originated and serviced by local loan offices."

Source: www.CIFA.net, Community Financial Services Association of America. This is a very informative site.

Industry Trend

- "Sweeping new rules proposed Thursday by the Consumer Financial Protection Bureau (CFPB) could upend the payday loan industry, which consumer advocates say often traps cash-strapped workers into a vicious cycle of borrowing. If enacted, the rules generally will require lenders to verify that borrowers can afford the loans and cap the number of times people can take out successive loans. The rules also would go beyond payday loans to target other costly short-term loans, including some high-interest installment loans and car title loans.

"The CFPB says that because of the way the loans work now, borrowers who use them can often be overwhelmed by fees and trapped into a cycle of debt that forces them to skip important bills or make other difficult financial choices. For instance, the agency found that about 80 percent of payday loans are rolled over into a repeat loan, causing fees to pile up for borrowers. Roughly 45 percent of payday customers take out at least four loans in a row.

"And each loan comes with steep fees. The CFPB found that payday borrowers pay a median $15 in fees for every $100 they borrow, amounting to an annual percentage rate of 391 percent on a median loan of $350. The rates on installment loans and auto title loans can be similarly high."

Source: by Steve Helber, https://www.washingtonpost.com/news/get-there/wp/2016/06/02/
what-consumers-need-to-know-about-the-rules-proposed-for-payday-loans/

- "Despite an improving macroeconomic landscape, the Check Cashing and Payday Loan Services industry is forecast to continue expanding over the five years to 2020, albeit at a similar rate. While the unemployment rate is anticipated to fall gradually over the five-year period, this fails to reflect the number of individuals that have dropped out of the workforce entirely."

Source: http://clients1.ibisworld.com/reports/us/industry/industryoutlook.aspx?entid=5408

- "The agency (the Consumer Financial Protection Bureau) subsequently released a startling study of 12 million payday loans issued all across the country that thoroughly debunked the industry's claim that the loans were necessary to help people make it to the next payday—customarily two weeks away—at which point they could comfortably pay off what they owed. It turned out that only 15 percent of borrowers could find the money to repay the full debt without borrowing again within 14 days, which meant they were hit with more fees.

  "One in five borrowers eventually defaulted on the loan; nearly two-thirds ended up renewing a loan, some more than 10 times, turning what began as a short-term loan into a long-term debt trap. The debt typically grew as the borrowers moved from one loan to the next, instead of being paid down, as happens with a traditional bank loan. In three-fifths of the cases studied, the fees ended up exceeding the original amount of the loan."

  Source: "Progress on Payday Lending," *New York Times*, March 29, 2015

- "Each month, more than 200,000 needy US households take out what's advertised as a brief loan.

  The government is seeking to set standards for a multibillion-dollar industry that has historically been regulated only at the state level. The payday industry warns that if the rules are enacted, many impoverished Americans would lose access to any credit."

  Source: Associated Press as reported in *Boston Globe*, March 27, 2015

- "Notably, borrowers almost unanimously agree that it should be their choice whether or not to use payday lending, not the government's choice (95 percent)."

  Source: "New Harris Poll: 9 in 10 Payday Loan Borrowers Felt Product Met Their Expectations," http://cfsaa.com/our-resources/communications/recent-news/article-detail/newsid/77.aspx

Resources

Associations

- Community Financial Services of America: www.cfsaa.com

Pest Control		
SIC 7342-01	NAICS 561710	Number of Businesses/Units 26,931

Rules of Thumb

➢ 80 to 90 percent of annual sales plus inventory

➢ 2 to 3 times SDE plus inventory

➢ 3 to 4 times EBIT

➢ 3 to 4 times EBITDA

Pricing Tips

- "Price should equal 4 to 5 times real profit where provable."
- "Pest control companies tend to be less based on a multiple of cash flow than other industries. The multiple is taken into account along with whether the customers are under contract, the longivity of the customer base, as well as whether they are serviced monthly, bi-monthly or quarterly and the cost per service."

- "Most buyers are looking for repetitive income. The buyer can reap the benefits of the purchase for multiple years but only pay once for the customers. A pest control company with contracts or year to year consistent sales and profits would be valued at a higher multiple than one with less consistent sales."
  "Profit x 4 to 6 plus or minus time in business as a %—plus or minus size of business in a %—plus or minus price of service as a %."
- "Length of time in business, methods used in treating, % of profit on total sales (higher=more value), annual contracts add value, increased sales each year adds value, no tax liens or other liens, good reputation with competitors and customers add value."
- "It is all about transferring profit from one company to the other. Profit being 10% to 45%, how much is transferable to the new owner? The more transferable, the higher the price."
- "Range .60 to 1.15 times sales, as high as 1.5 annual sales for commercial pest control."
- "Pricing is based on recurring contractual revenue. Pest control companies generally sell for about 100% of recurring sales and between 20% and 50% of nonrecurring sales. SDE is generally not applicable to pest control companies, rather, use EBITDA. A company with a high degree of contractual recurring revenue will sell for the closer to 5 or 6 times EBITDA, whereas a company with a low proportion of contractual recurring revenue will sell for the low end of the range of 2 to 3 times EBITDA."

Expert Comments

"Takes 3 years to be a certified operator."

"Most states require licensing which makes it more difficult to get into the industry. It eliminates those wanting to get into the industry without proper training."

"Owner needs a pest control license; 4 categories—be sure you know the one you are working in. Possibly hire a certified operator. Use consultants as often as possible. Get a good marketing manager because things are changing as fast as technology."

"Location and facilities are not important in this industry as long as they meet the needs of the business. Customers rarely visit the business."

Benchmark Data

Statistics (Pest Control)

Number of Establishments	26,931
Average Profit Margin	9.5%
Revenue per Employee	$130,100
Average Number of Employees	4.1
Average Wages per Employee	$43,468

Products and Services Segmentation

Insect control, including bed bugs, cockroaches and ants	55.1%
Termite control	17.0%
Other services, including bird-proofing and mosquito control	16.4%
Rodent extermination and control	11.5%

Major Market Segmentation

Residential homes	68.3%
Commercial establishments	29.4%
Government institutions	2.3%

Industry Costs

Profit	9.5%
Wages	33.4%
Purchases	18.2%
Depreciation	1.4%
Marketing	5.4%
Rent & Utilities	4.8%
Other	27.3%

Market Share

The ServiceMaster Company	11.1%
Rollins Inc.	10.6%

Source: IBISWorld, March 2016

- "$125k to $150k production per technician. Profit 20% or better."
- "Cost per hour to provide service + a reasonable amount of profit"

Expenses as a percentage of annual sales

Cost of goods	08% to 15%
Payroll/labor Costs	25% to 30%
Occupancy	05%
Profit (estimated pretax)	20% to 30%

Industry Trend

- "Mergers and acquisitions, big fish eating little fish."
- "In this industry there are always more buyers than sellers. I believe this should continue in the future."

Seller Financing

- "Some owner financing and not more than 70% in cash up front."
- "Since this is not an inventory or equipment intensive business, the majority of buyers rely on seller financing or pay cash for the business. Lender financing is frequently based on the profits of the business."
- "Typical financing is seller financing. Banks don't loan money to service businesses."
- "Depends on the size of the business. Normally 3 to 5 years. A larger company would be eligible for an SBA loan or other lender financing and could be financed for up to 10 years."
- "Financing is directly related to the profits of the business. The buyer needs to feed his family and pay the debt service. When the seller is willing to finance a portion of the sale, it is normally between 3 and 7 years."

Questions

- "Why are you selling? What are you going to do after the sale? How long will you be available for consulting?"

- "Any recent significant changes in your business such as the loss of a major account? What portion of your business is your largest customer?"
- "Why are you getting out of the business? What is your employee turnover rate? Have you paid all of your federal and state taxes and can you prove it?"
- "Like most businesses, a quality company sells for more. New equipment, good books and records, and a high profit margin make a business worth more. Repeat commercial accounts also affect the bottom line positively when pricing a business."
- "Breakdown of services: commercial versus residential; general pest versus wood destroying."

Resources

Websites
- Al Woodward, pest control brokerage specialist: www.servicebusinessconsulting.com

Trade Publications
- Pest Management Professional—an excellent site with lots of informative articles: www.mypmp.net
- PestWeb: www.pestweb.com

Associations
- Arizona Pest Control Professional Organization: www.azppo.org
- National Pest Management Association: www.pestworld.org

Pet Grooming (See also Dog Kennels)		
SIC 0752-04	NAICS 812910	Number of Businesses/Units 113,279

Rules of Thumb

➢ 40 to 45 percent of annual sales plus inventory

➢ 1.5 times SDE plus inventory

Pricing Tips
- "Gross Income is not a reliable Rule of Thumb at all. SDE most accurate revenue stream against which multiplier is to be used, as most of these businesses are owner operated. Deduct any income owner/seller directly generates (grooming, training) as that revenue will most likely disappear with a sale. Owner involvement and client dependency on the owner needs to be carefully examined as the owner is a high risk factor in this loyalty based, customer service industry. If owner also owns property, a Fair Market Value of Rent needs to be adjusted in the recast. Some owners pay no rent, some pay too little or too high."

Expert Comments

"Low barriers to entry of competition, except due to zoning requirements. High growth, high profit industry that attracts a lot of 'dog lovers.' Competition includes pet sitters, friends & family. Industry expected to grow 3% to 5% annually for the next 5 years. Boarding revenue is more 'protected' from economic fluctuations than daycare, which relies heavily on discretionary income."

Benchmark Data

Statistics (Pet Grooming and Boarding)

Number of Establishments	113,279
Average Profit Margin	13.9%
Revenue per Employee	$34,400
Average Number of Employees	1.8
Average Wages per Employee	$15,022

Products and Services Segmentation

Pet boarding	38.4%
Pet grooming	29.5%
Other	24.7%
Pet training	7.4%

Industry Costs

Profit	13.9%
Wages	43.0%
Purchases	12.2%
Depreciation	2.7%
Marketing	2.5%
Rent & Utilities	11.6%
Other	14.1%

Source: IBISWorld, April 2016

- "Annual occupancy for boarding should be around 50% to 55%. Labor between 35% to 45%, excluding owners. SDE in the 25% range."

Industry Trend

- "Estimated 2016 Sales within the U.S. Market—For 2016, it estimated that $62.75 billion will be spent on our pets in the U.S. In 2015, $60.28 was actually spent.

Estimated Breakdown:

Food	$24.01 billion
Supplies/OTC Medicine	$14.98 billion
Vet Care	$15.92 billion
Live animal purchases	$2.11 billion
Other Services	$5.73 billion"

Source: http://www.americanpetproducts.org/press_industrytrends.asp

- "Nationwide the average grooming fee in 2015 increased by a modest $1.25 for non-mobile groomers, and by $1.75 for mobile groomers. As a result the average U.S. grooming fee broke the $50.00 barrier for the first time, coming in at $51.00. Likewise, mobile groomers broke the $70.00 barrier for the first time with an average U.S. grooming fee of $70.25.

"Housecall groomers (grooming inside pet owners' homes, no mobile conversion) recorded a similar modest increase of an average price increase of $1.50. The average housecall fee in 2015 rose to $57.00.

"The majority of groomers (63%) indicated they would increase prices modestly in 2016. The average predicted price increase was $2.25 for non-mobile groomers and $3.25 for mobile and housecall groomers."

Source: "2015 Grooming Prices Survey Results," PetGroomer.com, January/March 2016

- "Growth. More modern facilities will take over market share from older, chainlink type facilities. Luxury resorts will become more popular."
- "The pet industry in the United States and many other countries is booming. Americans, for example, own more pets than ever before. Growth in the sector is derived both from increasing pet ownership as well as from increased spending per pet. Pet pampering is becoming the norm, as pet owner spending has moved far beyond simple food and grooming expenses to include innovative and specialized premium products. The bottom line: people increasingly view their pets as part of the family and are willing to spend even during difficult economic times.

  "A Golden Age for Pets and Pet Businesses—An overall rise in the number of pets in the US and increased spending per pet are the main factors that will contribute to the pet industry's growth in the years ahead. Even with the overall economic recovery taking longer than expected, annual revenue growth in pet products and services is anticipated to clock in at some 4.4% through 2016 (one of the few industries that can say so). As the recovery takes hold, household disposable income will rise even faster, and spending on pets will pick up even more."

  Source: Pet Care Industry in 2015 at a Glance, https://www.franchisehelp.com/
  industry-reports/pet-care-industry-report/

Seller Financing
- "SBA financing for solid businesses, owner financing for others."

Resources

Websites
- PetGroomer—An amazing site, well worth visiting if you have any interest at all in the subject: www.petgroomer.com

Associations
- American Pet Products Association: www.americanpetproducts.org
- National Dog Groomers Association of America: www.nationaldoggroomers.com

		Franchise
Petland (See also Franchises, Pet Stores)		
Approx. Total Investment		$400,000 to $850,000
	NAICS 453910	Number of Businesses/Units 145

Rules of Thumb
➤ 50 percent of annual sales plus inventory

Resources

Websites
- www.petland.com

Pet Stores

SIC 5999-30	NAICS 453910	Number of Businesses/Units 17,926

Rules of Thumb

➢ 25 to 30 percent of annual sales plus inventory

➢ 2 times SDE plus inventory

Pricing Tips

- "Be sure to check inventory turnover rate to make sure inventory is saleable."
- "Dealing with reputable breeders increases value."
- "If they have an 'acceptable' system for acquiring pets for sale, increase the price by 5%."

Expert Comments

"This takes into consideration that the store would be privately owned and not a 'big box' store. Many of these privately owned businesses have been able to successfully compete on price against the big box stores. Stores in small towns tend to do well."

"Location is a key factor in pricing, as many people travel to pick out the 'right' dog. Location to major intersections is a definite plus. Although it is fairly easy to duplicate a pet or pet supply store, knowing the mechanics of the industry can be tricky. Risk is primarily associated with dealing with reputable breeders that stand by their product; diseases such as parvo and kennel cough can cost quite a bit."

Benchmark Data

Statistics (Pet Stores)

Number of Establishments	17,926
Average Profit Margin	4.6%
Revenue per Employee	$159,354
Average Number of Employees	6.9
Average Wages per Employee	$20,551

Products and Services Segmentation

Pet food	45.7%
Pet supplies	40.6%
Pet services	9.0%
Live animals	4.7%

Industry Costs

Profit	4.6%
Wages	12.9%
Purchases	57.2%
Depreciation	0.9%
Marketing	1.9%
Rent & Utilities	10.2%
Other	12.3%

Market Share

PetSmart Inc.	36.8%
PETCO Animal Supplies Inc.	23.0%

Source: IBISWorld, August 2016

Number of U.S. Households that Own a Pet (millions)

Bird	6.1
Cat	42.9
Dog	54.4
Horse	2.5
Freshwater Fish	12.3
Saltwater Fish	1.3
Reptile	4.9
Small Animal	5.4

- According to the 2015–2016 APPA National Pet Owners Survey, basic annual expenses for dog and cat owners in dog and cat owners in dollars include:

Item	Dogs	Cats
Surgical Vet Visits	$551	$398
Routine Vet	$235	$196
Food	$269	$246
Food Treats	$61	$51
Kennel Boarding	$333	$130
Vitamins	$62	$33
Groomer/Grooming Aids	$83	$43
Toys	$47	$28

Source: 2015–2016 APPA National Pet Owners Survey

- "The keys to success in this industry are low rent, knowledgeable and caring employees, spotlessly clean store, publicly accepted pet sales system, and competition in price against 'big box' stores."
- "Cost of goods should not exceed 75%."

Expenses as a percentage of annual sales

Cost of goods	50% to 60%
Payroll/labor Costs	08% to 10%
Occupancy	04% to 05%
Profit (estimated pretax)	20% to 25%

Industry Trend

- "But the really good news for the industry is that the even more massive Millenial generation—born between 1985 and 2010, and numbering 100 million strong—is just now entering its prime spending years. These folks are the future of the pet industry, and they are embracing pets as enthusiastically as the Boomers. Keep providing them with products and services they need to have a rewarding experience as pet parents, and you'll have a customer for the next 40 to 50 years."

Source: "2016 will be another good year for the pet industry," by Steve King, http://www.petbusiness.com/December-2015/Three-Pet-Industry-Predictions/

P - Rules of Thumb

- "For 2016, it estimated that $62.75 billion will be spent on our pets in the U.S.
  Estimated Breakdown:
  Food.. $24.01 billion
  Supplies/OTC Medicine .... $14.98 billion
  Vet Care .... $15.92 billion
  Live animal purchases ....$2.11 billion
  Other Services .... $5.73 billion"

  Source: "2015–2016 APPA National Pet Owners Survey Statistics"

- "To the industry's benefit, demand for pets, especially cats and dogs, is expected to rise over the five years to 2021, with single-person households and the aging population, two demographics that increasingly own pets, driving demand. IBISWorld projects that the number of pet cats and dogs will increase at an annualized rate of 1.8% during the five-year period, which will contribute to the industry's growing revenue."

  Source: http://clients1.ibisworld.com/reports/us/industry/industryoutlook.aspx?entid=1103

- "Thanks in part to the many calls from PAWS Chicago supporters, the Illinois state legislature unanimously passed a bill that strengthens disclosure requirements on all dogs or cats made available for adoption or sale by pet shop operators in Illinois pet stores, including adoptions or sales available over the Internet."

  Source: "Pet Store Disclosure Bill Passes" www.pawschicago.org/news

Questions

- "Where do you get your puppies from and what is their guarantee?"
- "Do they have a publicly accepted way of selling pets?"
- "Do your customers have a desire to know about the food products? (This will give you an idea of the service the seller is providing.) How do you go about recruiting employees?"

Resources

Websites
- Pet Industry Joint Advisory Council: www.pijac.org

Associations
- American Pet Products Association: www.americanpetproducts.org
- World Pet Association: www.worldpetassociation.org

Pharmacies and Drug Stores		
SIC 5912-05	NAICS 446110	Number of Businesses/Units 53,858

Rules of Thumb

➢ 18 to 42 percent of annual sales—depending on profits and includes inventory

➢ 70 times average daily sales (range 60 to 80 times) plus inventory

➢ 25 percent of annual sales (range 20% to 30%) plus inventory

➢ 6.5 times EBIT (range 5 to 8 times) plus inventory

Pricing Tips

- "Average total Rx filled daily, % new, % refills, & total Rx average price for year, % Rx third-party insurance & Medicaid & % cash sales, % charge sales. Inventory value in date & salable. Inventory turns per year; total cost of goods sold + inventory on hand (8 times); age analysis of all accounts receivable including welfare, Workers' Comp; hours open per day, per week, per month, # days per year open; lease."
- "Good front business, e.g., gifts and greeting cards that improve profits. Look for niche business & profits."
- "Number of prescriptions filled daily, monthly, annually; divide by number of days open to arrive at number of prescriptions filled per day. Retail & cost of ingredients. In medical professional building—number of physicians in building. Does pharmacy do its own prescription compounding, & what percentage of business is third party; i.e., Medicare (welfare) & insurance company paid?"
- "Try 22% of [annual] sales. Net income, i.e., return on investment. Future income of business at least 5 years down the line. Demographics and customer review."

Benchmark Data

Statistics (Pharmacies and Drug Stores)

Number of Establishments	53,858
Average Profit Margin	3.3%
Revenue per Employee	$431,000
Average Number of Employees	12.7
Average Wages per Employee	$36,634

Products and Services Segmentation

Branded prescription drugs	51.5%
Generic drugs	20.1%
Other	11.2%
Nonprescription medicines	5.1%
Personal health supplies	4.8%
Groceries and food items	4.0%
Cosmetics	1.8%
Vitamins, minerals and dietary supplements	1.5%

Industry Costs

Profit	3.3%
Wages	9.1%
Purchases	68.4%
Depreciation	0.5%
Marketing	0.6%
Rent & Utilities	5.1%
Other	13.0%

Market Share

Walgreen Co.	32.6%
CVS Caremark	21.7%
Rite Aid Corporation	10.7%

Source: IBISWorld, April 2016

P - Rules of Thumb

- "You might think of doctors, who have to go to medical school, as making six figures or more, but not pharmacists. In fact, the median salary for pharmacists in the U.S. is $113,000, according to Salary.com. It's not just filling out prescriptions, it's offering advice on dosage and side effects and interacting with doctors. Becoming a pharmacist requires a bachelor's degree and an advanced degree in pharmacy. The job prospects are expected to be good over the next decade—the number of pharmacist jobs is expected to jump 17 percent, according to the Labor Department."

    Source: http://www.salary.com

- "Among multi-store owners, the average number of pharmacies owned is 2.8. For the independent sector as a whole, the average is 1.2 pharmacies."

Expenses as a percentage of annual sales

Cost of goods	75%
Payroll/labor Costs	09%
Occupancy	02% to 03%
Profit (estimated pretax)	03% to 04%

Industry Trend

- "Most independent community pharmacists consistently encounter misleading and confusing fees imposed by prescription drug middlemen that negatively impact both pharmacies and patients and distort medication costs and reimbursement rates, according to a recent survey of 640 pharmacists conducted by the National Community Pharmacists Association (NCPA). "Sometimes weeks or months after medication is dispensed to a patient and a pharmacy is reimbursed, community pharmacies are assessed "DIR fees" that can turn a modest profit into a financial loss."

    Source: "Pharmacists Survey: Prescription Drug Costs Skewed by Fees on Pharmacies, Patients by NCPA," June 28, 2016, http://www.ncpanet.org/newsroom/news-releases/2016/06/28/pharmacists-survey-prescription-drug-costs-skewed-by-fees-on-pharmacies-patients

- "The Pharmacy Forecast 2016–2020 from the American Society of Health-System Pharmacists (ASHP) Foundation analyzed pharmacy trends and described strategies for health-system pharmacists to keep pace with the evolving scope of their practice. Here are 4 pharmaceutical market trends to watch in the year ahead:
    - ✓ Generic Drug Pricing
    - ✓ Enforced Product Tracing
    - ✓ Specialty Drug Spending
    - ✓ Limited Drug Distribution Channels"

    Source: "4 Pharma Market Trends to Watch in 2016," by Allison Gilchrist, January 25, 2016, http://www.pharmacytimes.com/news/4-pharma-market-trends-to-watch-in-2016

- "Over the five years to 2021, industry revenue is forecast to rise at an annualized rate of 6.1% to $374.2 billion due to the projected shortage of primary care physicians, according to the US Department of Health and Human Services."

    Source: http://clients1.ibisworld.com/reports/us/industry/industryoutlook.aspx?entid=1054

- "Over the years, pharmacy retailers have greatly accelerated their function in healthcare delivery. The pharmacy has evolved from a location where prescriptions are dispensed and a few necessities can be picked up, to a media channel powerhouse where a large and receptive audience can be reached. Here are some of the key trends for this booming platform:
    - ✓ Over 250 million people visit pharmacies each week; that's three-quarters of the U.S. population.
    - ✓ "47% of OTC purchases are made in chain drug stores. Only 1% of

consumers surveyed make an OTC purchase online.
- ✓ "85% of prescription drugs are dispensed in retail pharmacy channels: independent—18%; supermarket—12%; chain—55%. Only 6% are dispensed via pharmacy mail order.
- ✓ "70% of Americans are now taking at least one prescription drug; 50% of Americans take at least two prescription drugs; 20% of Americans are taking five or more prescription medications at the same time.
- ✓ "94% of Americans plan to continue filling their prescriptions at their primary pharmacy.
- ✓ "Pharmacists are increasingly providing services to patients beyond drug dispensing.
- ✓ "The number of retail clinics is estimated to grow by 25%–30% annually; 73% of adults who have visited a retail clinic would go again."

Source: http://www.pm360online.com/pharmacy-channel-trends-and-facts-2014/

Seller Financing
- "Mostly all cash sales. Owner finance 3 to 7 years with interest at prime +/- 1% or 2 %"
- 10 years

Questions
- "Number of years on lease? Do you own the building?"

Resources

Associations
- National Community Pharmacists Association: www.ncpanet.org

---

Photographers & Photographic Studios (See also Camera Stores)

	NAICS 541921	Number of Businesses/Units 195,510

Rules of Thumb

➤ 45 to 50 percent of SDE; add fixtures, equipment & inventory

➤ 2.5 to 3 times monthly sales; add inventory

Pricing Tips
- "They are usually sold for the new cost of fixtures and equipment, plus inventory, plus 30 percent of one year's net profit. National average states the gross profit usually runs about 62 percent, leaving a net profit of about 24 percent after expenses."

Benchmark Data

Statistics (Photography)

Number of Establishments	195,510
Average Profit Margin	6.6%
Revenue per Employee	$45,400
Average Number of Employees	1.2
Average Wages per Employee	$11,493

Products and Services Segmentation

Personal and group portrait photography	34.1%
Commercial and technical photography	23.8%
School portrait photography	15.9%
Weddings, holidays and other special occasions photography	14.7%
Other	11.5%

Industry Costs

Profit	6.6%
Wages	25.6%
Purchases	19.4%
Depreciation	2.9%
Marketing	2.4%
Rent & Utilities	7.3%
Other	35.8%

Market Share

Lifetouch Inc.	15.3%

Source: IBISWorld, February 2016

Industry Trend

- "As revenue streams recover, the number of industry operators is expected to increase at an average rate of 2.1% per year to 205,805 in the five years to 2021. Most of this growth will occur within the nonemployer segment, particularly in the less-saturated institutional and commercial photography areas."

Source: http://clients1.ibisworld.com/reports/us/industry/industryoutlook.aspx?entid=1443

Resources

Associations

- PhotoMarketing Association International - this contains valuable information on the photography business including the school market, the portrait business, etc.: www.pmai.org

---

Physical Therapy		
	NAICS 621340	Number of Businesses/Units 117,849

Rules of Thumb

➤ 60 to 75 percent of annual sales

➤ 1.8 to 2.5 times SDE

➤ 1.5 to 2 times EBIT

➤ 1.5 to 3 times EBITDA

Pricing Tips

- "The value of PT and medical practices dependent on insurance reimbursement is generally at an all-time low. Decisions regarding what, where, when and how to practice are influenced by numerous factors, including: personal preferences, market forces, state and federal policies and programs, and institutions that constitute the health care system and medical education infrastructure. Increasing retirement, plus the trend toward shorter working hours, increases the supply of practices for sale, and decreases the available FTE workforce available as buyers. The increasing rate of Boomer retirement and decreasing count of new physicians contributes to a reduction of value of practices for sale. A significant shortfall of physicians could develop over the next 15 or more years in the absence of increased output from U.S. medical schools, increased recruitment of foreign-trained physicians, or both. The American College of Physicians is concerned that the practice environment for those in medical practice has become so encumbered with regulation and practice hassles, at a time when reimbursement for care provided by physicians is declining, that physicians are finding it increasingly difficult to provide for their patients. Of particular concern when determining value of a medical practice is ensuring not only that the purchase price is Fair Market Value, but also that the valuation method does not take into account the volume or value of referrals that the selling physician has made or may make to the purchaser, such that the purchase price could be challenged as a kickback or inducement. The OIG has provided guidance on the question of how to value a physician practice or other healthcare provider. The ailing economy is leading many Americans to skip doctor visits, skimp on their medicine, and put off tests. Employment by hospitals is paying more, and insurance-reimbursement and gross income is often dropping, so the results of the Income Approach of valuation identifying 'dividends' [(SDE minus market rate compensation of one working owner) x 1.5 (ie 65% Cap rate)] is becoming more important for more specialties. 'Percentage of annual gross sales' or 'SDE multiplier' as valuation Rules of Thumb are obsolete, if ever valid. Growth Rates are available through the Congressional Budget Office reports; rarely above 2% historically. Medical practice is riskier—and demands higher Cap rates—than other professional practices like accounting, law, architecture and engineering which are not subject to clinical malpractice risks, or subject to Medicare or insurance company changing reimbursement limitations or denials. Many practices can't even sell at the value of the liquidated assets, since jobs pay more without asset purchase. The impact of specialty and location is profound, as is the FTE work-schedule and leverage of employed licensed providers. Medicare is continually reducing reimbursement, which impacts other insurances which often base their payment on a percent of Medicare (i.e., 80–120% of Medicare), so dependence on insurance reimbursement is an important consideration in value. In addition; specific diagnosis and procedure (ICD/CPT) billing-code reimbursement changes—like what has happened in dermatology, ophthalmology, allergy, cardiology, and other specialties—have further reduced reimbursement and profits during the past decade. The Goodwill Registry on sale data is helpful in some cases, but the often-quoted running average 10-year median goodwill value as a percentage of gross is irrelevant; as the average of many specialties reflects the midpoint of 10 years' steady decline. You need to acquire the full database and evaluate the underlying data to be useful; and look in particular at the Price:SDE data. The effect of the Medicare cuts which began in 2005 can distort the Registry summary statistics and need to be adjusted; and you need to remove results from court valuations, divorces and other non-transactional data."

- "In an ACO, the family physician may be penalized, or prohibited, from referring patients to PTs not employed by the ACO. Many ACOs are building fully vertically integrated delivery systems that employ the PCPs, orthopaedists, and PTs, increasing risk of loss of business for independent PTs. ACOs should focus management efforts on reducing leakage to hospitals and specialists that are not part of the ACO. This will increase volume to ACO providers and help offset revenue loss due to improved utilization management. Hospitals are on an ACO practice-acquisition, and mergers binge. This is reducing the number of physicians available or interested in buying practices, and therefore limiting referrers to PTs. Even though patients can self-refer, many will follow their physician's referral. From the private practice perspective, the ACO question mark boils down to this: Will physical therapists participate as employees or as independent clinicians? Physicians have voted en masse to participate as employees. Record numbers of mergers and acquisitions, especially by large, publicly owned hospitals, have decreased independently owned physician practices to single digits in many regions of the country. Will 'integration,' in the name of health safety and cost-consciousness, destroy private enterprise in outpatient physical therapy?"

- "There is a national shortage of PTs, compensation for employment is increasing, so dividends to equity is decreasing. A full educational video on healthcare practice valuation is available at MedicalPracticeAppraisal.com homepage."

- "Most appraisers favor the Income Approach in valuing small, privately held professional services businesses, as it best reflects the impact of profit or dividends rather than just gross collections. It is the income above what the buyer could earn in employment that creates value in medical practices."

- "It's very important that when pricing a practice that is expected to go to market, calculating EBITDA is important. The first $70,000 to $95,000 in SDE is not important to buyers as many of them already earn this as a practicing PT. The income above that amount is one of the most important components of value. Also, diversification of referral sources increases value. When a practice has more than 25% of its referral sources coming from only one physician group, the structure of a transaction must be in the form of an earn-out and/or reduced value.

  "Another important factor in value is location. Most buyers of physical therapy practices with less than $500,000 in SDE are physical therapists. Physical therapy practices located in livable areas sell for a higher multiple. The definition of livable means an attractive safe community, some physical beauty (mountains/oceans), good schools and additional employment opportunities for non-PT spouses. Practices in areas that are less desirable, even with very high SDEs, have a very limited market and are difficult to sell."

- "Industry is challenged with declining reimbursements. Pricing is dependent on whether practice is owner/operated or has DPT's on staff. Non-owner-operated will generate higher multiple. Lease is critical. Most practice sales need a minimum of 5 years with a 5-year option to maximize value. Outside billing service preferred for control and highest revenue possible."

Expert Comments

"Don't try to use boilerplate broker contracts to sell medical practices, as it is easy to violate state or federal regulations—have all the paperwork and terms done by a medical practice transaction specialist attorney."

"You have to be a licensed PT or physician in most states to be an owner. There is currently a national shortage of physical therapists. There are over 2,700 PT jobs posted on the American Physical Therapist Association website, up from 2,300 just last year. A PT shortage reduces the availability of prospective purchasers of practices and drives up wages, reducing future profits-above-wages (i.e., 'dividends') for owners."

"A PT can learn how to start and run a practice in a day's consult with an expert. As a field of medicine, it is subject to most of the same hassle factors, like insurance and laws. Obamacare is causing ACOs to take over PT and control referrals. On the other hand, larger chains of PT practices are selling for a premium to private equity groups at up to 4–5x EBITDA, but I think it can't last due to PPACA laws and ACOs. "

"Owners of practices need to have a managing physical therapist. Many PTs are now incurring very high education expenses and the debt load on many of them may prevent them from owning practices in the future."

"The reductions in insurance reimbursements have affected buyer's interest level in owning a practice."

"Investment should include a gym and treatment area."

Benchmark Data

Statistics (Physical Therapists)
Number of Establishments	117,849
Average Profit Margin	12.2%
Revenue per Employee	$68,562
Average Number of Employees	4.0
Average Wages per Employee	$39,574

Products and Services Segmentation
Diseases of the musculoskeletal system and connective tissue	59.3%
Other	17.6%
Symptoms, signs and ill-defined conditions	8.2%
Injury and poisoning	7.3%
Diseases of the nervous system and sense organs	4.4%
Mental disorders	3.2%

Industry Costs
Profit	12.2%
Wages	57.3%
Purchases	8.4%
Depreciation	1.1%
Marketing	1.6%
Rent & Utilities	8.2%
Other	11.2%

Source: IBISWorld, August 2016

P - Rules of Thumb

- "Employs at least 2–3 PTs and 2–3 PT Aides."
- "At least a 2-week waiting list for new patient visits. No PPACA ACOs locally."
- "The best benchmark is revenue per employee. Revenue per full-time PT and patient visits by month are also helpful."
- "Need to have 3–4 patients per hour for high utilization. Each physical therapist should account for approximately $250,000 of billing."

Expenses as a percentage of annual sales

Cost of goods	27%
Payroll/labor Costs	15% to 25%
Occupancy	06% to 10%
Profit (estimated pretax)	12% to 25%

Industry Trend

- "While the PT industry experienced modest growth from 2010 to 2015, it has entered a new era of growth and is expected to increase by 3.6% annually to become a $34.6 billion sector by 2020. U.S. Physical Therapy (the only public pure play ORF provider) anticipates the outsourced rehab market could grow at +5% over the same period. Growth within the ORF and IRF sectors are largely being fueled by the aging US population, healthcare reforms and the recognized benefits of rehabilitation services."

  Source: http://www.capstonellc.com/sites/default/files/Capstone%20Outpatient%20
  Physical%20Therapy%20Report_Q1%202016_0.pdf

- "The physical therapy and rehabilitation care industry market is large and growing. Merger and acquisition activity continues to be on the radar for many of our nation's largest rehab therapy providers with six of the ten largest players now owned by private equity firms. There are several reasons for this industry phenomenon, which has driven multiples to a 20-year high and has attracted both financial and strategic buyers from all walks of life."

  "We are seeing one to five clinics drive one to three multiple of EBITDA while larger groups of 20 or more exceed ten times EBITDA. These are general observations and may vary for a variety of reasons."

  Source: https://www.webpt.com/blog/post/mastering-metrics- exit

- "According to the US Department of Labor, 'Employment of physical therapists is expected to increase for all occupations. The impact of proposed Federal legislation imposing limits on reimbursement for therapy services may adversely affect the short-term job outlook for physical therapists. However, over the long run, the demand for physical therapists should continue to rise as growth in the number of individuals with disabilities or limited function spurs demand for therapy services. Job opportunities should be particularly good in acute hospital, rehabilitation, and orthopedic settings, because the elderly receive the most treatment in these settings. The growing elderly population is particularly vulnerable to chronic and debilitating conditions that require therapeutic services. Also, the baby-boom generation is entering the prime age for heart attacks and strokes, increasing the demand for cardiac and physical rehabilitation. Further, young people will need physical therapy as technological advances save the lives of a larger proportion of newborns with severe birth defects. Future medical developments also should permit a higher percentage of trauma victims to survive, creating additional demand for rehabilitative care. A growing number of employers are using physical therapists to evaluate worksites, develop exercise programs, and teach safe work habits to employees in the hope of reducing injuries in the workplace.'"

- "PT reimbursement is legislated to also decrease like physicians, but the PT shortage will keep salaries stable, so costs will be going up while reimbursement is going down, decreasing profits."
- "Under PPACA, many hospitals and other entities are forming vertically integrated systems, taking control of physician referrers to PTs, and likely following with integration of PT practices, keeping services in-house and reducing referrals to independent PTs."
- "Integration into ACOs."
- "Declining reimbursements will force owners to increase patient time with aides and assistants, and reduce time with highly paid physical therapists."
- "Rollups and combination due to insurance issues. However, with the aging of the population and more joint replacements, there will be a demand for services."

Seller Financing

- "100% bank financing"
- "75% SBA guaranteed financing is generally available."
- "Seller financing is low especially if referral sources is widely diversified. 10–20% of a deal is seller financing with the remaining amount in the form of an SBA loan."
- "Financing is available through SBA guaranteed loans for those with good financial statements. Otherwise, they are seller financed. Banks generally approve of financing doctor practices although this has not been extended to physical therapists (unlike dentists and other medical and doctor
- practices)."

Questions

- "How long have they been practicing physical therapy? Have they managed people before? Why are they looking for a practice? What location is important to them and why?"
- "Patient visits per hour, per day, per week are critical. Trends in the revenue. Orthopedic referral sources and relationships. Hospital contacts. Length of lease and terms."
- "Many about state, federal and Medicare compliance, insurance contracts, ACO trends in market."

Resources

Websites
- Physical Therapy Practice Valuation: medicalpracticeappraisal.com

Trade Publications
- ADVANCE for Physical Therapy & Rehab Medicine: physical-therapy. advanceweb.com

Associations
- American Physical Therapy Association: www.apta.org

Picture Framing

SIC 5999-27	NAICS 442299	Number of Businesses/Units 9,811

Rules of Thumb

> 45 percent of annual sales plus inventory

Pricing Tips

- "Not a lot of activity to report in the framing industry. While there have been some transactions, most involve private sales where numbers aren't reported. I have valued a few businesses in the past year and found the same formulae apply as in the past. Values were less, but that is as a result of lower sales, inventories and other assets."
- "Perhaps most critical is the impact of a change in ownership. If the shop is small, that is the owner is the face of the business, rarely is the business worth any more than 10% of sales."

Expert Comments

"Location and co-tenancy is extremely important to value as long as lease is secure."

Benchmark Data

Statistics (Picture Framing Stores)

Number of Establishments	9,811
Average Profit Margin	5.5%
Revenue per Employee	$116,100
Average Number of Employees	2.4
Average Wages per Employee	$23,621

Products and Services Segmentation

Custom framing	67.5%
Ready-made frames	15.6%
Photo frames	9.4%
Other	7.5%

Industry Costs

Profit	5.5%
Wages	20.4%
Purchases	53.3%
Depreciation	0.8%
Marketing	2.7%
Rent & Utilities	4.6%
Other	12.7%

Market Share

Aaron Brothers Inc. 17.9%

Source: IBISWorld, March 2016

Expenses as a percentage of annual sales

Cost of goods	25%
Payroll/labor Costs	12%
Occupancy	10%
Profit (estimated pretax)	14%

Industry Trend

- "Custom frame jobs will remain a discretionary purchase for most consumers in the next five years. Therefore, the ability and willingness of consumers to purchase the goods and services available at frame shops will hinge on their ability to spend on nonessential goods. To that end, per capita disposable income is forecast to rise at an annualized rate of 2.4% in the five years to 2021, with growth accelerating from the previous period. A greater number of Americans returning to work will make consumers more willing to spend on higher-value discretionary purchases, including custom and ready-made frames."
  Source: http://clients1.ibisworld.com/reports/us/industry/industryoutlook.aspx?entid=4270

Questions

- "In addition to the usual financial questions, you should conduct a market evaluation to determine the viability of the present pricing structure."

Resources

Associations

- Professional Picture Framers Association: www.ppfa.com

	Franchise
Pillar to Post— Home Inspection (See also Franchises, Home Inspection)	
Approx. Total Investment	$31,550 to $36,550
NAICS 541350	Number of Businesses/Units 455

Rules of Thumb

➢ 25 to 30 percent of annual sales plus inventory

Resources

Websites

- www.pillartopost.com

	Franchise
Pizza Factory (See also Franchises, Pizza Shops)	
Approx. Total Investment	$150,000 to $400,000
Estimated Annual Sales/Unit	$375,000
NAICS 722513	Number of Businesses/Units 110

Rules of Thumb

➢ 30% to 35% of annual sales plus inventory

		Franchise
Pizza Inn (See also Franchises, Pizza Shops)		
Approx. Total Investment		$80,000 to $764,000
Estimated Annual Sales/Unit		$450,000
	NAICS 722513	Number of Businesses/Units 181

Rules of Thumb

➤ 45 percent of annual sales plus inventory

Resources

Websites
- www.pizzainn.com

Pizza Shops		
SIC 5812-22	NAICS 722513	Number of Businesses/Units 88,059

Rules of Thumb

➤ 35 percent of annual sales plus inventory for independent shops

➤ 38 percent of annual sales plus inventory for franchised or chain pizza shops

➤ 1.5 to 2 times SDE; plus fixtures, equipment and inventory

➤ 1.5 to 1.6 times EBIT

➤ 1.5 times EBITDA

➤ 4 times monthly sales plus inventory

Pricing Tips

- "As a baseline, Edelstein says a restaurant valuation is typically anywhere from two to three times the adjusted cash flow, a number that rarely matches the cash flow number listed on the restaurant's P&L since so many operators place various expenses on the business—cars, cell phones, life insurance, and the like—to maximize deductions."

  Source: http://www.pizzatoday.com/departments/back-office/valuation- whats-pizzeria- worth/

- "Good books can help raise all of the pricing Rules of Thumb. If there is substantial 'goodwill' being included in the sell price, positive online reviews will play an important part of the marketing of the pizza shop for sale."
- "Expect some business owners to purchase a fair amount of food in cash. Good employees are the most important part of this business. Large cash flow in and large cash flow out."
- "Typical pricing is 20 to 24 times weekly gross sales. Industry insiders and purchasers use this barometer consistently."
- Pizza Franchise Rules of Thumb and Annual Sales—Quick Check

Blackjack's Pizza	40% of annual sales
Domino's Pizza	50% of annual sales—$800,000
Gatti's Pizza	30% of annual sales—$1,000,000
Godfather's Pizza	25% of annual sales—$380,000
Hungry Howie's Pizza	35% of annual sales—$550,000

Little Caesars Pizza	50% of annual sales—$830,000
Mountain Mike's Pizza	30% of annual sales—$525,000
Mr. Jim's Pizza	35% of annual sales—$440,000
Papa Murphy's Take 'N' Bake	35% of annual sales—$550,000
Pizza Factory	30% of annual sales—$375.000
Pizza Inn	45% of annual sales—$450,000

September 2016

Note: Several of the businesses had a percentage multiple of, for example, 35% to 40%. The lower figure was the one used in tabulating an average. This produced an average rule of thumb of 38% of annual sales = the "ballpark" price. The above represent an average rule of thumb for franchised pizza restaurants. As you can see from the information above, independent pizza shops have an average rule of thumb of 35%. This slight difference may be due to more information being available for franchised units than independents.

Expert Comments

"Location is important, as most shopping centers have an existing pizza shop. It is important to get in on the ground floor."

"High profile locations are not as important if there is emphasis being put on delivery service. If that is the case, more rooftops in the area of the shop becomes the important factor."

"You must make the process as simple as possible if you are going to expand to multiple locations."

Benchmark Data

Statistics (Pizza Restaurants)

Number of Establishments	88,059
Average Profit Margin	5.5%
Revenue per Employee	$43,000
Average Number of Employees	10.8
Average Wages per Employee	$13,245

Products and Services Segmentation

Takeout and delivery	53.0%
Sit-down service	33.0%
Catering	14.0%

Industry Costs

Profit	5.5%
Wages	30.5%
Purchases	37.2%
Depreciation	2.9%
Marketing	2.6%
Rent & Utilities	12.7%
Other	8.6%

Market Share

Pizza Hut Inc.	14.8%
Domino's Inc.	9.6%
Little Caesars	8.1%
Papa John's International Inc.	6.4%

Source: IBISWorld, November 2015

P - Rules of Thumb

- "Sales per employee should exceed $40,000. Food Costs can vary depending on what you are doing with the dough; scratch dough can bring the food cost to 30%, where buying a fully sheeted pie could bring food cost to 34%."
- "Top Ten U.S. chains according to number of units:
  - ✓ Pizza Hut
  - ✓ Domino's Pizza
  - ✓ Little Caesars
  - ✓ Papa John's
  - ✓ Papa Murphy's Pizza
  - ✓ CiCi's Pizza
  - ✓ Round Table Pizza
  - ✓ Chuck E. Cheese's
  - ✓ Hungry Howie's Pizza
  - ✓ Godfather's Pizza"

Source: "2015 Pizza Power Report," *PMQ*, December 2015

- "Imperative to watch food costs for this business. Cannot be run absentee. Theft by employees sometimes a problem. Trend was seven days per week, seems to be changing in some areas to six. Expect 11AM to 11PM hours. Delivery is a must."

Expenses as a percentage of annual sales

Cost of goods	30% to 32%
Payroll/labor Costs	25% to 30%
Occupancy	07% to 10%
Profit (estimated pretax)	08% to 12%

Industry Trend

- "Overall, pizza restaurant sales in the United States were flat for the year ending September 30, 2015, even while the total number of units increased. Pizza sales reached $38,504,164.116, a slight drop of .05% from the same time period in 2014. Average store sales also went down to $514,679, a decrease of 2.34%.

  "A closer look at the past year's sales figures from CHD Expert reveals some particularly discouraging news for independent operators (those with fewer than 10 stores). Their sales dropped by 5.01% to a total of $14,967,292,162, while chain operators (10 or more units) logged an increase of 3.38% to $23,536,871,954. Independents' average sales dropped by 3.21% to $384,524 per store, while the chains saw an increase in average sales of 3.82% to $655,846. The chains also added more units, with a 7.33% increase to a total of 35,888 stores, even as more independent stores closed their doors, dropping to 38,924, a decrease of 1.85% from the previous year.

  "All of this points to a shrinking market share for independent pizzerias—they now account for a little under 39% of all pizza sales, compared to slightly more than 61% for the chains. That's about a 2% drop compared to the same period in 2014."

Source: "2015 Pizza Power Report"

- "Consumer confidence in the economy's outlook is expected to increase over the next five years, boosting spending as a result. The U.S. economy is exhibiting consistent growth and Americans are increasingly becoming more confident that the worst is over; even the more price-conscious consumers are forecast to increase their spending in the next five years. In addition, the number of households earning more than $100,000 is expected to rise 0.8% per year on average over the five years to 2020. This growth of wealthy households will induce higher demand for more expensive pizza restaurants and gourmet pizzas, which will help boost industry growth. According to market research firm Mintel, pizza chains currently experiencing the greatest growth are those targeting consumers from higher income brackets. Chains catering to lower incomes are competing in a very saturated marketplace, thus limiting their opportunity for organic growth.

"Similar to the previous five-year period, the industry will continue to deal with rising input prices, especially fresh meats. Some restaurants will increase prices to help with the rise in expenses and others will change some of their menu offerings to better cope with the shift. However, these changes may not be significant enough for smaller operators to offset the costs, which could potentially harm their profit margins. Large chains that are able to buy in bulk will be in a better position to manage the rise in expenses, keeping their profit margins relatively stable as a result. With revenue expanding consistently, IBISWorld expects more restaurants to open up, albeit at a slow rate. Over the five years to 2020, the number of industry establishments is projected to increase at an average rate of 1.7% per year to 94,717 restaurants. Employment numbers are projected to follow suit. As more restaurants open, more employees will be needed to help run the establishments. In the five years to 2020, employment will increase at an annualized rate of 2.1% to 1.0 million workers."

Source: http://clients1.ibisworld.com/reports/us/industry/industryoutlook.aspx?entid=4320

- "Technology is killing off independent pizzerias in the United States at the rate of roughly 2,549 locations per year (in 2015 alone). The pizza category is being reshaped by both big new tech deployed by chains and fresh threats from sophisticated emerging brands that are taking slices of the pie from tens of thousands of ill-equipped and low-tech independent pizzerias.

"With an AUV of $657,000 (on par with the segment average), Domino's now sees over 50 percent of its sales generated by online platforms (though, in some regions like the U.K., that number is higher, with 75 percent of the company's 2015 pizza orders made through digital channels). Take away these sales, and you're left with an AUV of $328,500.

"If that number looks familiar, it absolutely should—it's only $56,000 less than the AUV of your typical independent pizza restaurant. The evidence is pretty plain that, in the case of the plummeting mom-and-pop pizza profits, the failure to get with the program and get online, once categorized by consultants and onlookers as a 'highly recommended' strategy, is now requisite, not just to compete but to stay in business."

Source: "How Tech is Killing Off Independent Pizzerias," by Aaron D. Allen, LinkedIn.com, March 3, 2016

- "A lot of the same as far as total numbers of establishments. Turnover of pizza shops is high because of competition. People are always interested in buying for the relatively low entry costs."

Seller Financing
- "Seller financing with 35–50% down with the balance being paid back in 3-5 years."
- "Five to seven years"

Questions
- "What is the reason for selling? Will you open another pizza shop and where? How long have you been in business and what were your sales trends?"

P - Rules of Thumb

- "Why is the business for sale? Net Income? Unreported Income? Employees off the books? Number of employees? Amount of hours he or she personally works?"

Resources

Trade Publications

- Guide to a Successful Pizza Business & Pizza Business Manual by Paul Shakarian: www.pizzabusiness.com
- National Restaurant News: www.nrn.com
- Pizza Magazine Quarterly: www.pmq.com
- Franchise Times: www.franchisetimes.com

		Franchise
Planet Beach (See also Franchises, Medical Spas, Tanning Salons)		
Approx. Total Investment		$177,000 to $351,000
	NAICS 812199	Number of Businesses/Units 205

Rules of Thumb

- 35 to 40 percent of annual sales
- Planet Beach has day spa franchises in the U.S., Canada and Australia.

Resources

Websites
- www.planetbeach.com

		Franchise
Play It Again Sports (See also Franchises)		
Approx. Total Investment		$242,200 to $392,500
	NAICS 453310	Number of Businesses/Units 295

Rules of Thumb

- 40 to 45% of annual sales plus paid-for inventory

Resources

Websites
- www.playitagainsports.com

Podiatrists

SIC 8043-01	NAICS 621391	Number of Businesses/Units 12,151

Rules of Thumb

➤ 35 to 40 percent of annual sales plus inventory

➤ 3 to 4 times SDE plus inventory

➤ 1.5 times EBITDA

Pricing Tips

- "Doctors of Podiatric Medicine (DPMs) are podiatric physicians and surgeons, also known as podiatrists, qualified by their education and training to diagnose and treat conditions affecting the foot, ankle and related structures of the leg. Podiatrists are defined as physicians by the federal government and in most states. DPMs receive medical education and training comparable to medical doctors, including four years of undergraduate education, four years of graduate education at accredited podiatric medical colleges and two or three years of hospital residency training. Within the field of podiatry, practitioners can focus on many different specialty areas, including surgery, sports medicine, biomechanics, geriatrics, pediatrics, orthopedics or primary care."

- "Most podiatric practices are small. Most of the practices have only one or two doctors. The average partnership has 2 doctors and the typical podiatric medical group had 3 podiatrists, according to an APMA study. The median podiatrist has about $750,000 In annual collections, with a $180,000-$200,000 income, including benefits. Prescription foot orthoses are a foundation of non-surgical treatments utilized by podiatrists. The vast majority of orthotics dispensed by podiatrists are custom functional orthoses. The custom orthotic industry is headed into a crisis based upon a number of issues: ethics & accountability, verification of outcomes, coding & reimbursement, increased operational costs, and reduced profitability. As insurance companies look to reduce their services or payments, they have looked to orthotics as a way to cut costs, according to an article in *Podiatry Today*."

- "Dividends are a better measure than EBITDA given the lack of need of capital assets."

- "Inventory varies widely. Some podiatrists sell products and some don't. Product sales can be profitable, but surgical podiatry is usually the most profitable."

Expert Comments

"Easy for a podiatrist to learn how to do a startup in a day. Podiatry is a field of medicine accepting all the same insurances and Medicare, and subject to the same laws."

"The value of podiatric practices is generally at an all-time low. Decisions regarding what, where, when and how to practice are influenced by numerous factors, including: personal preferences, market forces, state and federal policies and programs, and institutions that constitute the health care system and podiatric education infrastructure. Increasing retirement, plus the trend toward shorter working hours, increases the supply of practices for sale, and decreases the available FTE workforce available as buyers. The increasing rate of boomer retirement and decreasing count of new physicians contribute to a reduction of value of practices for sale. A significant shortfall of physicians could develop over the next 15 or more years in the absence of increased output from U.S. podiatric schools, increased recruitment of foreign-trained physicians, or both. The American College of Physicians is concerned that the practice environment for those in medical practice has become so encumbered with regulation and practice hassles, at a time when reimbursement for care provided by physicians is declining, that physicians are finding it increasingly difficult to provide for their patients. Of particular concern when determining value of a podiatric practice is ensuring not only that the purchase price is Fair Market Value, but also that the valuation method does not take into account the volume or value of referrals that the selling physician has made or may make to the purchaser, such that the purchase price could be challenged as a kickback or inducement. The OIG has provided guidance on the question of how to value a physician practice or other healthcare provider. The ailing economy is leading many Americans to skip doctor visits, skimp on their medicine, and put off tests. Employment by hospitals is paying more, and insurance-reimbursement and gross income is often dropping, so the results of the Income Approach of valuation identifying 'dividends' [(SDE minus market rate compensation of one working owner) x 1.5 (i.e., 65% Cap rate)] is becoming more important for more specialties. 'Percentage of annual gross sales' or 'SDE multiplier' as valuation Rules of Thumb are obsolete, if ever valid. Growth rates are available through the Congressional Budget Office reports, rarely above 2% historically. Podiatric practice is riskier—and demands higher Cap rates—than other professional practices like accounting, law, architecture and engineering which are not subject to clinical malpractice risks, or subject to Medicare or insurance company changing reimbursement limitations or denials. Many practices can't even sell at the value of the liquidated assets, since jobs pay more without asset purchase. The impact of specialty and location is profound, as is the FTE work-schedule and leverage of employed licensed providers. Medicare is continually reducing reimbursement, which impacts other insurances which often base their payment on a percent of Medicare (i.e., 80–120% of Medicare), so dependence on insurance reimbursement is an important consideration in value. In addition, specific diagnosis and procedure ('ICD/CPT') billing-code reimbursement changes—like what has happened in dermatology, ophthalmology, allergy, cardiology, and other specialties—have further reduced reimbursement and profits during the past decade. Cash and cosmetic practices are usually worth more since there is a higher profit for less work, and often provide a better lifestyle, but even those can be difficult to sell. Many specialties are having trouble attracting new doctors no matter the income, so guaranteed wages are increasing, sales are becoming more difficult, and values are dropping. Make sure to read the white papers on supply and demand available on many specialty professional association websites. The best overhead statistics are usually available at http://www.NSCHBC.org. The best market rate compensation stats are usually available at http://www.MGMA.com. The Goodwill Registry on sale-data is helpful in some cases, but the often-quoted running-average 10-year median goodwill-value as a percentage of gross is irrelevant, as the average of many specialties reflects the midpoint of 10 years' steady decline. You need to acquire the full database and evaluate the underlying data to be useful; and look in particular at the Price:SDE data. The effect of the Medicare cuts which began in 2005 can distort the Registry summary statistics and need to be adjusted; and you need to remove results from court-valuations, divorces and other non-transactional data.

"Podiatric record charts are not a true asset of the practice since they can't be put on the balance sheet as an asset using the Asset Approach valuation methodology. Podiatric record valuation is only used to specifically allocate intangibles, assuming they exist at the time of the valuation. The physician has the physical chart but usually cannot legally sell or dispose of it without the patient's consent (per state statutes), only transfer custodianship. So the physician is basically a custodian of the record rather than an owner of an asset with independent value. When paper charts are involved, I have come to the opinion that the value of the chart is zero because of the attendant custodianship liability costs. With EMR, a digital record may need to be converted from one digital platform to another either by custodianship transfer or technology succession, in which case a printout and re-entry may be required, probably exceeding in labor costs any physical value to the original digital chart.

"The library in a smaller pediatric practice—as opposed to a university or a 'super-group'—is presumed to not include historical or rare publications, be organized with bibliographic cataloging, nor represent a complete or unique collection for the specialty. Materials are presumed to be of mixed currency and technological validity. No value is therefore assigned to the practice library.

"The billing process in a podiatric practice is very complex, both in generating the charges using appropriate diagnosis and treatment codes, and in recording the payment and adjustments for uncollectable amounts. Accounts Receivable represent past gross charges for services rendered and as yet uncollected or adjusted-off. These receivables must be discounted to reflect both insurance company reimbursement disallowances, plus the decreasing value over time due to difficulty in collections of past due accounts. In other words, the historic collection ratio of the practice does not yet include the "standing wave" of uncollectable accounts at practice end, or at a particular point in time, as in a valuation at a particular date."

"Serious shortages expected, plenty of jobs available, reduces need to buy business."

"Medicare and insurance dominated revenues and profits"

"An aging population will result in increased foot related issues. There will be increased growth in outpatient surgery."

"Competition in the primary markets is high, but low in rural markets. Risk is high due to medical malpractice issues, just like other specialties of surgery."

Benchmark Data

Statistics (Podiatrists)

Number of Establishments	12,151
Average Profit Margin	17.7%
Revenue per Employee	$142,000
Average Number of Employees	3.4
Average Wages per Employee	$41,594

Products and Services Segmentation

Musculoskeletal system and connective tissue diseases	37.4%
Skin and subcutaneous tissue diseases	20.3%
Other	14.6%
Infectious and parasitic diseases	7.7%
Endocrine, nutritional and metabolic diseases	7.1%
Merchandise Sales	5.2%
Circulatory system diseases	5.1%
Nervous system and sense organ diseases	2.6%

Industry Costs

Profit	17.7%
Wages	30.5%
Purchases	25.3%
Depreciation	1.4%
Marketing	1.2%
Rent & Utilities	2.2%
Other	21.7%

Source: IBISWorld, December 2015

- "The value of podiatry practices is generally at an all-time low."
- "At least a 2-week waiting list for patient appointments"
- "Most podiatrists see approximately 100 visits per 40-hour workweek"
- "Variables include whether 'midlevels' like nurse practitioners or P.A.'s are employed; orthotic sales or referral; surgical components."

Expenses as a percentage of annual sales

Cost of goods	05% to 06%
Payroll/labor Costs	20% to 23%
Occupancy	06% to 07%
Profit (estimated pretax)	40% to 43%

Industry Trend

- "Competition is high and steady, growth is expected for the next 5 years, fragmentation should remain relatively constant."
- "Poor due to Obamacare, or whatever replaces it"
- "Increasing demand by baby boomers"
- "There will be a trend to fewer solo practices and more group practices. There will be a trend toward group practices involving other health care disciplines."

Seller Financing

- "100% bank financing is usually available from specialty banks."
- "SBA will finance 75%."
- "Financing term of 5 to 7 years"
- 2 to 5 years

Questions

- "Payor mix, market share, patient demographic data"
- "State and federal compliance"
- "Do you have nursing home contracts? Do you have Medicaid patients?"

Resources

Trade Publications
- Podiatry Today: www.podiatrytoday.com

Associations
- American Academy of Podiatric Practice Management: www.aappm.org
- American Podiatric Medical Association: www.apma.org

Pool Service (Swimming)		
SIC 7389-09	NAICS 561790	Number of Businesses/Units 53,821

Rules of Thumb

➤ 10 to 12 times the "Monthly Service Only Gross Income"—swimming pool routes throughout the country sell for this multiple.

➤ "Note: The monthly service gross income is just that. It does not include income from maintenance or repair. This is already considered in the multiple, because most pool service technicians agree that whatever your monthly service billing is, half of that again will translate into maintenance/repair income."

Pricing Tips

- "Pricing is typically 10–12 times monthly service income. This usually does not include repairs or other services, but does include inventory."
- "Average is 1 year gross service billing, not including repairs."
- "These figures will vary based upon a solo business owner and one that has employees. A great estimate of profit without employees will be 80%; if employees are a factor, you should anticipate 40% profit margins. Both of these issues will affect pricing of a business for sale, and will also affect sale price."
- "As stated, there are two main sources of income, monthly service billing and maintenance/repair income. Throughout the United States the purchase price of a pool service route is based on a multiple times the Monthly Service Billing Only income. The multiple will vary from state to state and even within some states. However, it is an industry standard to use a multiple times the Monthly Service Billing Only income. In other words, the maintenance/repair income should not be included to arrive at a fair purchase price. Any other method of appraising the value of a pool route would be contrary to the industry standards. The maintenance and repair income is already considered in the multiple, because most pool service technicians agree that whatever your monthly service billing is, half of that again will translate into maintenance/repair income.

  "We have been selling businesses for over 28 years. Pool routes are our specialty. We can tell that the most important step in purchasing a pool route is in verifying the monthly service billing. Financial statements, profit and loss statements, and balance sheets are usually not available, mainly because it is not necessary to keep an expensive bookkeeping system for one person operating out of their home. Therefore, there are not usually records available to satisfy a bank or financial institution to borrow the money to buy the route. Individual tax returns usually will not help either, because if you were buying 50 accounts of a route of 100, the tax returns would not be broken down that way. Also, if he is a pool builder or does a lot of business in major pool repairs or pool remodeling, again the tax returns would reflect all this income. What if he had 100 accounts and sold 50 accounts? His tax return would show an income for 100 accounts and you would have no way of knowing this.

"Pool routes are sold for cash and no terms are generally available. Therefore, you should have the funds available at the time of purchase, unless you are arranging for an equity loan, line of credit or other means to enable you to purchase a pool route.

"While most pool routes have the same expenses, they do not have the same income. Income is what you will be purchasing. One of the best ways to get a handle on the monthly service income, as well as what the owner is charging for repairs, is to look at his ledger cards. A ledger card is a monthly history for each account. A ledger card should show when an account was billed and when the account was paid. The payment history of the customer is one of the most important items to review during purchase. Who wants an account that does not pay his or her bill? The ledger card also shows what the account was billed for repairs. This part of the ledger card will show if the owner is charging for the proper extras. In addition, the ledger card will show how long the account has been on service. While this is very important to some, the length of time on service is not as important as the payment history. If the average age of the accounts is over a year and they have a good payment history that would be a good account.

"Another big question on the minds of most potential purchasers is the radius of the route and the quality of the neighborhoods. The overall radius of a pool route is not as important as the daily radius. Almost everyone has to drive to work or the office. Some people drive 30 minutes, some an hour, some much more. If you purchase a pool route that is within an overall radius of twenty miles but is under a five-mile daily radius, this would be considered a good route in the industry. Try to keep your pools clustered tight by service day. The neighborhood of your accounts is not as important as the way they pay their bills. There are several high-priced neighborhoods where collection is a problem. Most people in just average neighborhoods have a far better collection record than some so-called upper class neighborhoods."

Source: Contributed by Frank Passantino, Pool Route Brokers, Inc. Frank is a veteran business broker and the information provided has been taken from his Web site—www.poolroutebrokers. He is one of the country's leading pool route brokers. His firm is in California and the phone number is 800-772-6002

Expert Comments

"Sellers: Document all of your accounts and work so you can verify income. Minimize expenses where possible. Take great care of your customers so they trust you. Buyers: Buy a route that is closely run with minimal driving. You lose money any time you are sitting in the truck. Make sure you are making enough money per pool to justify the price."

"As a Seller: Provide the necessary training & support to the buyer and keep good books to verify income. As a Buyer: Provide your best customer service skills to keep your customers, learn the trade and attend trade shows and training classes"

"A business that has a strong long-term customer base should anticipate receiving a higher multiple of sales than someone who has a short-term history. If someone is willing to wait for the right buyer, expecting a 12-month multiple is realistic; however if someone is looking for a quick sale on a well-designed route, 10 times monthly income is realistic."

Benchmark Data

Statistics (Swimming Pool Cleaning Services)

Number of Establishments	53,821
Average Profit Margin	11.1%
Revenue per Employee	$50,500
Average Number of Employees	1.3
Average Wages per Employee	$16,424

Products and Services Segmentation

General cleaning services	41.1%
Equipment cleaning and maintenance	27.7%
Chemical adjustments	19.2%
Other	12.0%

Industry Costs

Profit	11.1%
Wages	32.4%
Purchases	25.2%
Depreciation	2.7%
Utilities	3.5%
Rent	4.5%
Other	20.6%

Source: IBISWorld, March 2015

- "Customer service is the backbone of a successful business."
- "On a well-designed route, each employee should generate $100k of gross sales based simply upon service; this figure should increase if repairs are included."
- "How many pools can I service in a day? A good question, but difficult to answer. The average pool service technician will service approximately 16 full-service pools a day, while some can service 25 to 30 in a day. It depends on the individual and what type of pools he or she is servicing. The average pool service technician will service two pools an hour including driving time. If the accounts are chemical only, he can do many more. If the accounts are commercial, he or she will do less.

"The average pool service technician, if running his route correctly, should be netting between $75,000.00 and $80,000.00 per year. If you have a monthly gross service billing income of $4,000.00 per month, that equates to $48,000.00 per year generated from weekly 'service only.' Your expenses should be approximately 2 months of your service income or in this example $8,000.00. This will cover your three major expenses, gas, insurance and chemical replacement. Therefore, your service income totaling $48,000.00 for the year, less estimated expense of $8,000.00, should produce a net profit of $40,000.00, assuming you are operating in a diligent manner. In addition to this profit, you will have a second income on the same accounts for maintenance (filter cleaning, algae, conditioner treatments and other preventive maintenance) charges that you will bill your account extra, plus repairs (motors, pumps, heaters, etc.). This second income should be fifty percent of your service net. If your net income from service is $40,000.00 then your net from maintenance and repairs should be $20,000.00. This is assuming that you are providing full service to your accounts."

Source: Contributed by Frank Passantino, Pool Route Brokers, Inc.

Expenses as a percentage of annual sales

Cost of goods	20%
Payroll/labor Costs	40%
Occupancy	0
Profit (estimated pretax)	40%

Industry Trend

- "I think profits should continue to increase with the new construction of more pools."
- "Steady"
- "On the franchising side, most of the attention has been given to the service-tech side of the industry. There's an important reason for that: It costs less. Return on investment is the major concern when starting a franchise, so prospects like the relatively low start-up costs of a service business. 'The ones that tend to grow fastest are the ones that have the lowest level of investment,' Siebert (Mark, CEO of iFranchise Group) says. 'So the service industry would probably be the one that would ultimately get the most franchisees.'

  "When Baron (Kevin, President of Probity Pools) wanted to expand his company, he chose the franchise model because he figured it best suited the kind of work done by service companies. To just grow a company organically removes the company owner farther and farther from the work itself as the organizational chart expands, he says, while franchising allows the owners to stay near those maintaining the pools.

  "While some professionals are quick to point out examples where these types of models did not work in the pool industry, others say the time for franchising and outside investment has come, and examples will only become more prevalent. But Porter (Paul, CEO of Premier Pools Management Corp.) doesn't see the transition going smoothly. 'It will happen … kicking and screaming because we have a lot of people who are very resistant to change in our industry,' he says. But Baron expects it will be long-term. 'I think when the dust settles in 10 years, every city's probably going to have a half dozen or so major pool-maintenance brands,' he says."

  Source: http://www.poolspanews.com/business/coming-together_o.aspx?dfpzone=general
- "This industry should expand."
- "Competition getter stronger and more government enforcement of licensing."

Seller Financing

- "Typically they are all cash deals, but if any financing is involved it is typically very short-term owner financing."
- "All cash, or 3rd party financing"

Questions

- "How long have you had the pools? Any previous problems with payments from customers. Where did your pools come from (did you buy route, build it, etc.?)"
- "How long have your clients been on service, do they all pay on time, do you have any challenging customers or difficult pools?"
- "Find out how long they have had the clients. Determine the driving time of the route. Clearly understand what services are being delivered for what price."

Resources

Websites
- Pool Pro: www.poolpro.com

Trade Publications
- SQUA Magazine: www.aquamagazine.com
- Pool and Spa News: www.poolspanews.com
- Service Industry News: www.serviceindustrynews.net

Associations
- Independent Pool and Spa Service Association: www.ipssa.com
- National Swimming Pool Foundation: www.nspf.org
- Florida Swimming Pool Association: www.floridapoolpro.com
- Association of Pool and Spa Professionals: www.apsp.org

Portable Toilet Companies		
SIC 7359-22	NAICS 562991	Number of Businesses/Units 9,126

Rules of Thumb
➢ $1,000 per unit
➢ 85 to 90 percent of annual revenues

Pricing Tips
- "An interesting statistic is that experienced purchasers anticipate the loss of customers when buying a company. The percentage, although not a scientific number, has been expressed as high as 25%. In terms of fast numbers, a business with gross sales of $500,000 along with a price conscious customer base could fall to $375,000 as fast as the ink dried on the check.
"In reality, it has been more common during the last three to five years for portable restroom businesses to sell for approximately 90.62% of annual sales.
"In revealing the percentage rate, it is important to note that the average percentage rate includes transactions where businesses sold for as little as 50% and as high as 150% of annual sales. Consideration for profitability is included with a highly profitable portable sanitation business demanding a higher price. Again, as an example, a business that does $500,000 in annual sales and is not a good fit or is not running profitably might fall into the lower percentage rate, while a company running the same numbers and showing an annual profit of $125,000 with good equipment and verifiable records might attract a buyer for 100% of annual sales."
Source: "What Is My Portable Restroom Business Worth?" *Sanitation Journal*, www.sanitationjournal.com

Benchmark Data

Statistics (Portable Toilet Rental & Septic Tank Cleaning)

Number of Establishments	9,126
Average Profit Margin	7.2%
Revenue per Employee	$139,600
Average Number of Employees	4.3
Average Wages per Employee	$42,001

Products and Services Segmentation

Portable toilet rentals	38.9%
Septic tank maintenance services	24.2%
Other services	20.9%
Drain and sewer services	16.0%

Major Market Segmentation

Businesses, farms and nonprofit organizations	54.0%
Individuals	31.2%
State and local governments	10.8%
Federal government	2.0%
Other	2.0%

Industry Costs

Profit	7.2%
Wages	30.2%
Purchases	22.3%
Depreciation	6.8%
Marketing	1.0%
Rent & Utilities	5.7%
Other	26.8%

Source: IBISWorld, October 2015

- "The portable sanitation industry has developed into a $4 billion-a-year business. There are an estimated 3 million portable restrooms in use, serviced by a fleet of over 10,000 trucks. The industry includes more than 3,600 businesses and 39,000 employees worldwide."

Source: Portable Sanitation Association International

Industry Trend
- "The toilet-rental business is up 25 percent in the past year or so."

Resources

Associations
- Portable Sanitation Association International: www.psai.org

Power/Pressure Washing		
	NAICS 561790	

Rules of Thumb

➤ 50 percent of annual revenues

		Franchise
Precision Tune Auto Care (See also Franchises)		
Approx. Total Investment		$123,000 to $208,075
	NAICS 811118	Number of Businesses/Units 384

Rules of Thumb

➤ 35 to 40 percent of annual sales plus inventory

Resources

Websites

▪ www.precisiontune.com

Printing/Flexographic		
	NAICS 323111	

Rules of Thumb

➤ 2 to 5 times EBITDA

➤ 3 times EBIT

➤ Note: "It is a different area—they print labels on Web presses using plates that are made of curved rubber. Web presses use rolls of material rather than sheets. Think newspaper printing. However, apparently the pricing multiples are similar."

Pricing Tips

▪ "Depending on size, EBITDA ranges from 2 to 4 unless special circumstances are present like exceptional profit or none"
▪ "Multiples range from 2 to 5 depending on size and sector."

Expert Comments

"It is probably the most stable section of the printing industry, but it is not growing."

"There is generally lots of competition but less than those of commercial printers. Profits have stabilized in recent years. Marketability is generally high. Replication is relatively easy, but can you get the business and can you keep going until you make a profit? This is a good sector of the printing industry."

Benchmark Data

▪ "Look for stable customer base with no heavy concentration with one or two clients."

Expenses as a percentage of annual sales

Cost of goods	43%
Payroll/labor Costs	43%
Occupancy	05%
Profit (estimated pretax)	05% to 09%

27th Edition

Industry Trend

- "Thanks to rising global demand for corrugated packaging and flexible packaging, the flexographic printing market is set to grow by 3% per annum in real terms over the period 2014-2019 to $194 billion (2013 prices)."

  Source: http://www.smitherspira.com/industry-market-reports/printing/flexography/
  flexographic-printing-future-in-a-digital-world

Questions

- "Does the owner handle major customers personally and can they be transitioned to a new owner? Do they have contracts? What sets this company apart from others? Do you have non-compete agreements with your salesmen?"

Resources

Websites

- Greeneville Plate Services: www.greenevilleplateservices.com

---

Printing/Silk Screen

SIC 7336-09	NAICS 323113	

Rules of Thumb

- ➢ 40 to 45 percent of annual sales plus inventory
- ➢ 2.5 to 3 times SDE includes inventory
- ➢ 3.5 to 4 times EBITDA
- ➢ 3.5 to 4 times EBIT

Pricing Tips

- "SDE 2.5–3.0 range. Sales growth, market potential, age/quality of equipment, staffing, lease will determine which end of range to use."
- "Value affected by equipment, customer base, skilled labor, location and sales growth."
- "Value of any long-term contracts that are in place. Are contracts assignable?"
- "National/corporate accounts as customers increases value vs. small local accounts."

Expert Comments

"Can be high capital investment to start up."

"Anyone can open a small screen printing shop or store. Most companies do screen printed and embroidered products. They also sell small signs, graphics, etc. This industry can be capital intensive. High-speed equipment is necessary to produce larger volume and some companies add a second and third shift."

Benchmark Data

- "$60,000 to $90,000 sales per employee, depending upon area of country located, type of printing and products manufactured."

- "$100,000/employee; $175–$200 sq. ft."
- "Sales $75–$100K/employee"

Expenses as a percentage of annual sales

Cost of goods	60%
Payroll/labor Costs	20% to 25%
Occupancy	05%
Profit (estimated pretax)	05% to 10%

Industry Trend

- "Digital technology, specifically inkjet printing, was forecast by many to be the death knell of screen printing when the first systems were first showcased at the SGIA Expo in the early 1990s. While inkjet has taken much of the large-format graphics market and DTG printers are extending their reach into textiles, inkjet has not forced screen printing into obsolescence. In fact, the two disciplines seem to complement each other, giving screen printers more choices and variety of services to sell."

  Source: "Stencilmaking in the Age of CTS," by Dave Dennings, May 3, 2016, http://www.screenweb.com/content/stencilmaking-age-cts#.V42Dn6KhmQ8

- "As such, the industry is still expanding. In the 10 years to 2020, the number of industry operators is expected to increase an average annual rate of 1.7%, reaching 6,234 companies."

  Source: http://clients1.ibisworld.com/reports/us/industry/industryoutlook.aspx?entid=4211

- "Consolidation as weaker competitors are either sold or shut the doors."
- "Increased competition & pressure on margins."
- "Growth due to U.S. society continuing to be more visually oriented"
- "Transition from traditional screen printing to digital printing output"

Questions

- "Sales & profit trend over past 3 years, and especially over most recent 12-month period."
- "Monthly revenue over past 3 years to gauge seasonality of business and to analyze competitive environment."
- "Provide concentration of customers. Any range, one-time orders in sales figures? Maintenance schedule for all equipment?"
- "How are sales generated? Competition? Breakdown of revenues? Condition of equipment? Maintenance records? Seasonality? Sales Structure? Website?"

Resources

Websites
- ScreenWeb: http://www.screenweb.com/

Trade Publications
- Screen Printing Magazine: http://stmediagroupintl.com/brands/screen-printing/

27th Edition

Print Shops/Commercial Printers (See also Print Shops (General))		
SIC 2752-02	NAICS 323111	

Rules of Thumb

➤ 50 to 55 percent of annual sales plus inventory

➤ 2 to 3 times SDE includes inventory

➤ 2.5 to 3 times recast EBITDA if sales under $2 million

➤ 2.5 to 3.5 times recast EBITDA if sales $2 to $5 million

➤ 3.5 times recast EBITDA if sales $5 to $25 million

➤ 4 times EBIT

➤ 1 to 1.5 SDE plus fair market value of assets (for smaller companies)

Pricing Tips

- "As with other small businesses, commercial printers can be valued using a number of income and asset-based business valuation methods. For owner-operator managed printers, the Multiple of Discretionary Earnings method is a frequent choice. This well-known method lets you determine the value of your business based on its earnings and a set of financial and operational performance factors. For a well-established commercial printing business, the Capitalized Excess Earnings method is a good choice. You can calculate the value of your business and its goodwill—an important part of what makes a successful business worth more."
  Source: https://www.valuadder.com/blog/2008/11/19/valuing-printing- businesses/
  (A bit dated, but still of interest)

- "Smart sellers are well positioned and organized relative to qualitative and quantitative monitoring systems. Buyers buy on potential of the seller's enterprise."

- "RMA Benchmarks/Industry Ratios—EBITDA calculations"

- "Print for Pay is declining as volume users have purchased equipment and produce in-house. Walk-in trade is inconsistent, commercial accounts provide stability. Newer equipment is important to allow a greater range of products delivered in an efficient manner."

- "Be careful of long-term contracts that might go away if the business ownership changes."

- "Having current technology in computer to plate is a big plus."

- "There are two primary ways of valuing printing companies. Fair value of assets plus a half multiple of EBITDA for goodwill and customer lists. The other is 2–4 times EBITDA depending on size, profitability, equipment, sector, etc."

- "The bigger the printer, the higher the multiple."

Expert Comments

"Because of the various types and sizes of printing companies [e.g., large vs. small format equipment, digital vs. analog, screen vs. digital signage, etc.] the speed of technological changes makes the above factors inconsistent throughout this industry. More than any other industry I've seen through my 12 years in M&A, there is no greater challenge than selling a printing company."

"Market share, customer base, equipment capabilities, niche markets"

"Person-to-person relationships are still very important."

"The current regional market shows excess capacity and possibly short-term declines in sales. There is brisk competition, but capitalization costs are high to replicate these businesses. Consolidations are needed."

"Trend is toward large online providers. Level of technical knowledge is critical."

"Customer base important. Hard to steal customers from competition."

"Printing is a mature industry that is growing at barely the growth in population."

"Price competition from on-line providers. Short-run color work is being done on in-house printers and copiers. 'Pleasing quality' has become acceptable for the small-business owner."

Benchmark Data
- For additional Benchmark Data see Print Shops (General)
- "COGS, net profits, annual sales trend over $4 million"
- "Sales per employee should exceed $200K."
- "Payroll less than 30% of sales"

Expenses as a percentage of annual sales

Cost of goods	40% to 50%
Payroll/labor Costs	35% to 45%
Occupancy	03% to 10%
Profit (estimated pretax)	05% to 15%

Industry Trend
- "Consolidation—baby boomers vast exits."
- "Because (1) new production equipment is becoming increasingly available and appropriate for the largest customers of printing companies; (2) traditional printing work is continuing to be replaced by digital media—for email and the Web; and (3) much of the printing equipment [digital & analog] remains in operation, long after they might be considered obsolete, there is an imbalance of supply (of services) and demand, so downward pressure on prices will continue for the foreseeable future."
- "Positive outlook—big players expanding with M&A strategies."
- "The industry is splitting into two distinct segments: specialty wholesale printers 'gang running' for the trade (other printers) and full-service B2B printers incorporating design, Web services, etc. as part of their offerings."
- "Greater competition from large online providers"

Seller Financing
- "New owner & outside financing"
- "More typical to be outside financing"
- 5 to 10 years

27th Edition

P - Rules of Thumb

Questions
- "Do you have skilled & experienced people in place?"
- "1. Real estate options 2. IP advantages 3. Lean or sustainability programs 4. Owner financing options 5. Proforma forecasts 6. Management skill set 6. Supplier discounts"
- "Why are you leaving and are there any contracts still honored."
- "Commercial account base? Outside salespeople? What role(s) does owner fill? Product mix? Specialty vs. commodity."
- "Look for any niche they serve; client concentration is a risk; client contracts are rare and would be a premium multiple."
- "Is production equipment leased or owned?"
- "How up-to-date is their equipment? Do they have a niche? Do they do digital printing? What is their salesperson(s) situation? Do they have non-compete agreements with salespeople?"
- "How tied to the customers is the owner, why do customers use this printer over others, does any customer account for more than 10% of revenue."
- "How has the business been trending over the past five years?"
- "Why would a customer do business with you, other than quality, price and turnaround time?"

Resources

Websites
- Printing Industries of America: www.printing.org
- Tag and Label Manufacturers Institute: www.tlmi.com

Trade Publications
- American Printer: www.americanprinter.com
- Printing Impressions, an online publication: www.piworld.com
- "Valuing Printing Businesses, Handbook of Business Valuation," West & Jones, 2nd Edition: www.wiley.com

Associations
- Idealliance + Epicomm: http://my.idealliance.org/
- Specialty Graphic Imaging Association: www.sgia.org

Print Shops (General)		
SIC 2752-02	NAICS 323111	Number of Businesses/Units 47,941

Rules of Thumb
- 30 to 45 percent of annual sales plus inventory
- 2 to 3.5 times SDE plus inventory
- 3.5 to 4 times EBITDA

Pricing Tips
- "Always consider the assets of any print shop business for sale, including mail order and website availability. The cost of an individual print shop business for sale will be dramatically reduced if the business does not have either in

their box of tricks. While it would be preferable if they have one of the two on board, this can be implemented for a price lower than the amount that would be added onto the overall asking price if they were in place already. You would also want to consider the contacts and customers on the books already, both of which should be included in any sale that was to go through. When you buy a print shop business, you will need those initial contacts in order to facilitate a smooth transition and a solid foundation for profitability."

Source: http://blog.globalbx.com/2009/02/11/how-to- buy-a- print-shop- for-sale/

- "Pricing is based on EBITDA—multiples are determined by the buyers—buyers are strategic and financial."
- "EBIT, EBITDA, 3–5 years of financial statements, outsourced industry specific appraisal, best to have audited statements every 5 yrs."
- "Market share in region, quality of accounts, no more than 20% of annual revenues per key account. Profit margin vs. industry benchmarks"
- "Owner benefit add-backs, IP protection, key account loyalty, key employees and non-compete agreements."
- "There are two primary methods of valuing printing companies. A multiple of EBITDA and fair market value of assets plus half times a multiple of EBITDA. If everything is equal, these two methods should come relatively close."
- "What is trend of business for the subject company?"

Expert Comments

"Focus on your niche; stay the course; be strategic and buy right; don't overpay on the short term."

"Leaders are in growing—M&A is a key strategy."

"Talent pool, key sales relationships, special capabilities, owner financing"

"Key accounts, brand awareness, strong sales force, experience of leadership, documented business plans and vision, funding and vendor relationships, diversity of markets, product mix."

"Some areas of printing are declining, which will cause support services to decline."

Benchmark Data

Statistics (Printing)

Number of Establishments	47,941
Average Profit Margin	4.8%
Revenue per Employee	$183,958
Average Number of Employees	9.0
Average Wages per Employee	$43,049

Products and Services Segmentation

Commercial lithographic printing	41.4%
Other printing	16.9%
Digital printing	11.5%
Commercial flexographic printing	10.5%
Commercial screen printing	9.6%
Book printing	6.0%
Commercial gravure printing	4.1%

Major Market Segmentation

Manufacturers	30.1%
Advertisers	20.7%
Publishing	17.6%
Other	17.1%
Financial and legal firms	9.1%
Exports	5.4%

Industry Costs

Profit	4.8%
Wages	23.3%
Purchases	42.3%
Depreciation	3.5%
Marketing	0.4%
Rent & Utilities	3.7%
Other	22.0%

Market Share

RR Donnelley & Sons Co.	7.4%
Quad/Graphics Inc.	4.3%

Source: IBISWorld, August 2016

- "The average sales revenue is almost $3 million, although the median was $877,500."
- "$180,000 per employee for a profitable business."
- "$200,000.00 per employee—great target."

Expenses as a percentage of annual sales

Cost of goods	35% to 45%
Payroll/labor Costs	25%
Occupancy	05%
Profit (estimated pretax)	20%

Industry Trend

- "Growth for print leaders; packaging, wide-format and labeling all growing. Baby boomers exiting; less family succession plans. Consolidation continues."
- "'Sales growth has been fairly constant over the past five years at somewhere between 3 and 5 percent,' said Sageworks analyst Jenna Weaver. 'In the year ended January 20, sales increased about 4 percent. That shows us this industry is still growing its revenue, even though the popular opinion is that this industry is dying or really struggling. Our data shows that's not the case, at least with these private companies.'

  "Weaver noted that net profit margin has increased to 5.2 percent from 1.4 percent four years ago. 'That's a real positive for the industry,' she said. Data on profit growth for the most recent period wasn't yet available, but Sageworks' preliminary results indicate another year of growth, which would follow four years in a row of double-digit percentage gains in pretax net profit. Weaver said the factors driving the sales increases and improved profitability are unclear, although outside reports have indicated some printing companies are diversifying, relying more on added services such as shipping, packing, signs, and graphic design."

Source: "Don't Print The Obituary For The Printing Industry Just Yet" by Mary Ellen Biery, January 25, 2015, Forbes.com

- "Higher capability and lower cost for in-house equipment to handle short-run requirements."

Seller Financing
- "Outside financing is the standard; sellers want out. Cash is king."
- "Two years maximum or don't do it."
- 3 to 5 years

Questions
- "Competitive advantages? Retained talent pool for transitions? Last year of 3rd party valuation of business? Reasons for selling? Best identified and suited buyers of your business?"
- "What is the business plan? Vision of business? Key employees secured by non-compete? IP status? What do the next 3 years look like in contacts, sales revenues?"
- "Systems, controls, leadership team, competitive advantages, ideal clients."
- "Who are your largest customers and what percentage of the total do they account for? Are these relationships personal and can they be transitioned to a new owner? What has been done to grow the business? "
- "What is customer mix? What is age and type of equipment?"

Resources
Associations
- Idealliance + Epicomm: http://my.idealliance.org/

Print Shops/Quick Print (See also Print Shops/Commercial Printers)

SIC 2752-02	NAICS 323111	Number of Businesses/Units 8,522

Rules of Thumb
- 45 to 55 percent of annual sales plus inventory
- 2.5 to 3.5 times SDE plus inventory
- 2 to 5 times SDE plus inventory—SDE (Owner's compensation) treats depreciation as an expense and thus it is not included in SDE.
- 4 times EBIT
- 3 to 4 times EBITDA

Pricing Tips
- "Fair market salary adjustment required prior to calculating SDE or excess earnings."
- "Excess earnings should exclude a fair-market salary for a new owner/ manager."
- "Quick printer valuations have been on the decline."
- "The terms of the leases on the digital equipment will affect the operating income and price."
- "The business should be a solutions provider to their clients."
- "Competitive equipment is very important, including lease terms and click

charges."

- "Review replacement cost of assets. Percentage of business with top ten clients. Receivable turn."

Expert Comments

"Printing customers today do not necessarily buy on price, but they are buying small quantities and cutting back . . . this favors smaller printers."

"Industry is equipment intensive and requires a high degree of marketing skills to succeed."

"Quick printers that don't adapt have been declining. The ease of publishing and printing with computers and various printing devices has taken business from the quick printers."

"These are marketable companies suitable for corporate dropouts or general business people."

Benchmark Data

Statistics (Quick Printing)

Number of Establishments	8,522
Average Profit Margin	4.5%
Revenue per Employee	$159,400
Average Number of Employees	3.0
Average Wages per Employee	$29,244

Products and Services Segmentation

Printing	63.9%
Other services	14.8%
Bindery and finishing services	8.2%
Prepress services	7.1%
Mailing services	6.0%

Major Market Segmentation

In-store customers	47.0%
Small businesses	23.5%
Non-employing businesses	18.5%
Online customers	11.0%

Industry Costs

Profit	4.5%
Wages	18.6%
Purchases	39.9%
Depreciation	4.1%
Marketing	0.9%
Rent & Utilities	5.9%
Other	26.1%

Market Share

FedEx Corporation	13.5%

Source: IBISWorld, January 2016

- "One that goes out and gets business instead of waiting for it to walk in the door; one that is more creative."
- "Sales per employee are more a measure of automation and type of work than a meaningful value. Net profit after allowance for equipment is the main factor."

Expenses as a percentage of annual sales

Cost of goods	30% to 40%
Payroll/labor Costs	25% to 30%
Occupancy	05% to 10%
Profit (estimated pretax)	10% to 20%

Industry Trend

- "Growth for the industry will remain elusive, as quick printing companies will continue to face competition from the use of household and business printers, photocopiers and computers. In the five years to 2020, the price of computers and peripheral equipment is expected to decrease at an annualized rate of 4.8%, increasing the affordability of DIY printing and raising external competition for the Quick Printing industry. . . .the Quick Printing industry is expected to experience slow, yet steady, decline in the five years to 2020."
  Source: http://clients1.ibisworld.com/reports/us/industry/industryoutlook.aspx?entid=437
- "Moderation of profits and growth"
- "Slight decline for companies unprepared to take necessary steps to modernize."
- "Very good for someone who is technically literate regarding computers and networks and has specific skills found in the printing industry."
- "Digital equipment is taking over this segment of the printing industry. Quick turns and high quality are important."
- "Sales and marketing skills important"
- "Continued decline as people do more with computers and advanced printers."

Questions

- "Percent of sales represented by top 3–5 customers?"
- "How did the seller arrive at his initial asking price? What was the basis for this price, and what references did he refer to?"
- "Describe competition, percentage of sales by category (products & customers)."
- "What percentage of customers makes up 80% of the business?"
- "Type of equipment, lease terms, click charges. What related services do they offer? How do they get and maintain sales?"
- "Sales per employee, how old is the equipment—and number of impressions. How long have the employees been with the business? How up-to date is the pre-press department?"

Resources

Trade Publications
- Quick Printing Magazine: http://magazine-directory.com/Quick-Printing.htm

Associations
- Idealliance + Epicomm: http://my.idealliance.org/

Process Serving

	NAICS 541199	

Rules of Thumb

➢ 35% to 40% sales includes inventory

Benchmark Data

Statistics (Conveyancing Services)

Number of Establishments	36,695
Average Profit Margin	12.8%
Revenue per Employee	$135,800
Average Number of Employees	3.6
Average Wages per Employee	$45,026

Products and Services Segmentation

Conveyancing and title abstract services	41.4%
Settlement and closing services	22.9%
Other legal services	18.2%
Title search and other document filing services	8.5%
Process services	4.8%
Arbitration and Mediation Services	2.2%
Patent copyright and other intellectual property document services	2.0%

Major Market Segmentation

Businesses	55.3%
Individuals	42.6%
Government and nonprofit organizations	2.1%

Industry Costs

Profit	12.8%
Wages	32.8%
Purchases	2.4%
Depreciation	1.1%
Marketing	2.2%
Rent & Utilities	8.7%
Other	40.0%

Market Share

Fidelity National Financial, Inc.	18.2%
First American Financial Corporation	9.2%
Stewart Information Services Corporation	4.1%

Source: IBISWorld, December 2015

Industry Trend

- "The trends show that as technology grows more pervasive into everyday life, it also has made its way into the civil process service industry. The bulk of the new rules implemented in 2016 are focused on modernizing processes, making them more efficient and compatible with today's technology. This should continue throughout 2016 and in the years to come.

"Just as the U.S. Post Office was revolutionized by the advent of email, we may see electronic service options increase for those who seek out civil process service. But, just as the US Post Office continues to be a communications staple in the U.S., so shall the traditional means of hand-delivered service.

"Be on the lookout for bills in the U.S. Congress that aim to streamline processes (e.g., decreasing time limits to get things done), as well as requiring and/or creating more options for civil process service. Hopefully, these changes will make processes easier—not more difficult —for process servers."

Source: https://www.serve-now.com/articles/2175/2016-new-rules-in-process-serving

Property Management Companies

SIC 6531-08	NAICS Residential Property 531311; Nonresidential 532312
	Number of Businesses/Units 251,774

Rules of Thumb

- ➢ 100 percent of annual revenues
- ➢ 6 to 7 months' revenues for firms selling under $500K
- ➢ 10 to 12 months' revenues for firms above $500K
- ➢ 2.5 to 5 times SDE based on a cash sale
- ➢ 3.5 to 6 times SDE with sales involving notes and/or contingencies
- ➢ 2.4 to 2.5 times EBIT
- ➢ 2.5 to 3 times EBITDA

Pricing Tips

- "When pricing for property management, particularly short-term rental homes, we take into consideration the number of properties managed by the business owner and the amount they charge as a management fee. Also whether or not the properties are good rentable homes which generate a decent nightly rental income."
- "Buyers should study and learn about the various sources of income from booking revenue, the relationship of homeowner mortgage position on cash flow."
- "These businesses have a tendency to sell between 2 and 2.6 times the owner benefit. In some cases individual contracts are sold, i.e., a seller may have 50 management contracts and sell off say 20, in which case they are sold on a contract basis according to the quality of the contract."
- "There are critical elements to valuation of these businesses that do not show in the financials. Booking sources for tenants, mortgage position of the property owners. In addition, the escrow monies must be measured and transferred at closing."
- "Length of time business owned, amount of work carried out by the seller, i.e., specifically in short-term rental homes owners can carry out lawn and pool care, as opposed to administration."
- "Occupancy is critical as is markup on services. Discovery of proximity of properties to attractions."
- "Key item is the longevity of accounts (i.e., any property managed for more

than 3 years is good). Also, the transition period should have the owner (seller) remain visible for 2 to 3 months."

Expert Comments

"Make sure you carry out your due diligence, check the books and records, do not just believe what someone tells you, get the facts."

"This is a very popular business in Central Florida. It lends itself to people from all walks of life, as there are numerous income streams and you can earn from rentals, management fees, lawn care, pool care, cleaning, maintenance. I find that it is very popular with people who are willing to work in a business doing any of the manual work; those who only wish to do administrative work can employ sub-contractors to carry out the cleaning, maintenance etc."

"We always make sure that the buyer has an independent accountant review the bookings and records of the business, preferably for three years. Should the buyer only be taking on contracts, as opposed to a full business, then have the accountant check the contracts thoroughly and if possible have a clause in the contract which allows for a replacement contract should one be lost during the first three months due to no fault of the buyer. For example a house is sold, then it should be replaced."

"After going through the recession, this industry has bounced back and it has been found that the demand for this type of business is still high but the supply has been lower."

"Home based generally, scalable, annuity revenue nature of some of the revenue streams"

Benchmark Data

Statistics (Property Management)

Number of Establishments	251,774
Average Profit Margin	23.2%
Revenue per Employee	$96,200
Average Number of Employees	3.1
Average Wages per Employee	$42,176

Products and Services Segmentation

Residential property management	55.4%
Non-residential property management	24.7%
Other	14.2%
Real estate brokerage	2.8%
Land management	1.9%
Construction	1.0%

Major Market Segmentation

Residential properties	67.5%
Other nonresidential properties	20.0%
Commercial	4.5%
Industrial buildings	4.0%
Office buildings	4.0%

Industry Costs

Profit	23.2%
Wages	43.5%
Purchases	9.5%
Deprecation	1.6%
Marketing	1.2%
Rent & Utilities	7.0%
Other	14.0%

Source: IBISWorld, May 2016

- "This business can be grown very well by the owners if they are willing to put effort into the business. I have seen this kind of business grow from 20 contracts at time of purchase to almost 100 within 4 to 5 years. This kind of business sells very fast."
- "Usually home based. $7,000 per house in vacation rental"
- "It is difficult to give an average for occupancy, labor and cost of goods sold, due to the fact these businesses are so diverse and you have to determine according to the business being sold. Some businesses have a higher owner involvement, i.e., the owner may do some of the maintenance work, lawn and pool care as well as the administration; whereas in other businesses the owner simply handles the administration, including placing rentals into the properties, which creates a much higher income for the business."
- "2x owner benefit. Some value on a per house basis....not valid if property is not apple to apple comparison with other units."
- "This type of business allows an owner to do a variety of work within the business, which makes it attractive to a buyer. It is not too difficult to expand this type of business providing the owner is an organized person. Over the last 10 years or so I have seen contracts per house for short-term rental homes sell from $5,000 to $8,000 per unit, subject to the type of property and age."

Expenses as a percentage of annual sales

Cost of goods	20% to 35%
Payroll/labor Costs	40% to 50%
Occupancy	05% to 10%
Profit (estimated pretax)	15% to 25%

Industry Trend

- "Upward trend"
- "I believe this business will continue to thrive. It is extremely popular and one should note that no real estate license is required for the short-term rental property management, as it is governed in the state of Florida by the hotel and motel licensing and not the Florida Real Estate Commission."

Seller Financing

- "I have been successful in obtaining SBA Loans for this kind of business."
- "I have been able to achieve all manner of financing. Many people have paid cash. I have also had success in SBA lending for a good solid business. Not much seller financing, the reason being, this is a very personal type of business and the sellers understand this. If a buyer does not have a good attitude, it could prevent the business expanding, and this is a fear for sellers, so they do not like to carry a large note."
- "Seller financing is less common for property management companies larger than $500,000 gross income, but for smaller companies it would be 3 to 5 years."
- "30% owner financing"

Questions

- "Are any of your owners in debt to you (seller) and if so how much and for how long have they owed that money."
- "Escrow account/operating account terms and transfer/"
- "Homeowner mortgage? How do you generate occupancy? What is the occupancy rate?"
- "What exactly do you do in the business? Do you hold escrow for the owners? Do you pay their bills without holding escrow? Can you show a contract for each of the owners you manage properties for?"
- "Insure that deposits and owner operating account funds transfer at closing."
- "How many homes? How many with pools? What are your service charges and corresponding costs for each? Your management fee? What is the homeowner's mortgage position? Occupancy rate seasonality?"
- "Why are you selling? Have there been any lawsuits or complaints?"

Resources

Websites
- Institute of Real Estate Management: www.irem.org

Associations
- Property Management Association: www.pma-dc.org
- National Property Management Association: www.npma.org
- Florida Vacation Rental Managers Association: https://fvrma.wildapricot.org/
- Vacation Rental Managers Association: www.vrma.com

Publishers—Books (See also Publishers—In General)		
SIC 2731-01	NAICS 511130	Number of Businesses/Units 28,987

Rules of Thumb

➢ 70 percent of annual sales plus inventory

➢ 4 to 6 times EBIT

➢ 4 to 6 times EBITDA

Pricing Tips

- "Professional publishing is valued higher than educational publishing, and both are valued higher than consumer publishing. Proprietary and niche-specific publishing is most attractive."

Benchmark Data

Statistics (Book Publishing)

Number of Establishments	28,987
Average Profit Margin	7.9%
Revenue per Employee	$333,600
Average Number of Employees	17.2
Average Wages per Employee	$57,218

Products and Services Segmentation

Textbooks	31.6%
Professional, technical and scholarly books	27.5%
Adult trade books	24.0%
Other books and services	10.3%
Children's books	6.6%

Industry Costs

Profit	7.9%
Wages	17.3%
Purchases	60.0%
Depreciation	1.4%
Marketing	3.2%
Rent & Utilities	1.5%
Other	8.7%

Market Share

Pearson PLC	11.7%
Bertelsmann SE & Co. KGaA	11.2%

Source: IBISWorld, February 2016

Industry Trend

- "2015 Overview: Net Revenue and Unit Growth

	2014	2015
Total net revenue	$27,957,086,149	$27,784,851,263
Total net units	2,702,337,737	2,714,877,707

"The area of largest growth for the trade category was Adult Books, which grew by 6.0% from $9.87 billion in 2014 to $10.47 billion in revenue in 2015. For the second consecutive year, Adult non-fiction books, which includes adult coloring books, was the category that sold the most units and provided the most revenue in the trade category. Within the Adult Books category, the fastest growing formats in terms of units sold were downloaded audio (up 45.9%), hardback (up 15.1%) and paperback (up 9.1%).

"Number of units sold by format

- ✓ Paperback & Mass Market: 1.18 billion
- ✓ Hardback: 577 million
- ✓ eBook: 424 million
- ✓ Children's Board Books: 89 million
- ✓ Physical Audio & Downloaded Audio: 81 million
- ✓ Other: 107 million"

Source: "U.S. Publishing Industry's Annual Survey Reveals Nearly $28 Billion in Revenue in 2015," July 11, 2016, http://newsroom.publishers.org/us-publishing-industrys-annual-survey-reveals-nearly-28-billion-in-revenue-in-2015/

- "As a result of fewer expenses and increased productivity, profit margins are projected to grow during the five years to 2021 to 8.1%. Profit margins largely depend on the actions of major e-book retailers, mainly Amazon. As e-books become more prominent in the market, major players like Amazon may demand higher margins from publishers as it has in its other operating segments. The growing dependency on e-books leaves publishers exposed to changes in downstream markets."

Source: http://clients1.ibisworld.com/reports/us/industry/industryoutlook.aspx?entid=1233

P - Rules of Thumb

- "Students are shouldering huge costs when it comes to the textbooks in their backpack, but companies are stepping in to lighten the load. Textbook prices increased 1,041% from January 1977 to June 2015, more than three times the rate of inflation, according to an NBC News analysis of Bureau of Labor Statistics data. As student loan debt continues to rise above the $1 trillion mark, the cost of a college education and all of its trappings is becoming increasingly unaffordable.

  "He (Mark Perry, professor at the University of Michigan-Flint) added that the consolidation of the market into a few major publishers, such as Cengage, McGraw Hill and Pearson, allows for further price gouging."
  Source: "How financial aid is driving up college textbook prices" by Kathleen Burke, August 6, 2015, marketwatch.com

Resources

Associations
- Association of American Publishers: www.publishers.org
- American Booksellers Association: www.bookweb.org
- Independent Book Publishers Association: www.ibpa-online.org

Publishers—In General

| | NAICS 511130 | |

Rules of Thumb

➢ 75 to 100 percent of annual sales includes inventory

➢ 3.5 to 7 times SDE includes inventory

➢ 4 to 6 times EBIT

➢ 4 to 7 times EBITDA

Pricing Tips

- "The size of the business is critical to valuation—larger higher multiples.. Also, publishing is a diverse business. The niche of a publishing company is critical. Also, the competitive situation. A business to business magazine which is #1 in its niche is worth far more than the #4 publication as an example. I try to sell a publishing property to synergistic publishers. They will pay far more for the publication due to cost savings and the advantages of integration into a current portfolio."
- "Pricing varies significantly by segment or niche, from a high of 1.5 times revenue and 8 to 10 times EBITDA for scientific technical publishing to 3 times EBITDA for trade book publishing."
- "Publishing is a diverse business. Electronic publications have higher multiples. Specialties such as scientific and technical publications have higher multiples. Books would have the lowest multiple. Magazines would be somewhere in the middle, with good trade magazines worth more than consumer magazines. City and local magazines are worth the least of the magazines with competition intense. Most print publications will have an electronic or digital component, and if they do not, the value is negatively impacted. The publications of

sufficient size and strategic interest to the major publishers such as Elsevier, Wiley or Wolters Kluwer are worth considerably more."
- "Businesses are essentially goodwill, with little consideration of fixed assets. Strategic and financial buyers (PEGs) figure predominantly in valuation with considerably higher valuations, some as high as 8 to 10 times EBITDA, possible for a publisher of strategic interest. Size is also a critical factor in valuation, as most strategic buyers will not be attracted to a publishing business with gross revenue less than $3 to $4 million annually."

Expert Comments

"Get a valuation. Price the business properly. Work with a broker who specializes in publishing. It is a unique and difficult business."

"Print publishing is on a downward trend. More publishers of value will have a digital component or a secondary marketing component such as trade shows. Print is not dead; there is a market for print publications, however, the publishers should be moving towards digital delivery if not already there."

"Publishing is a risky, competitive but profitable business for those who are successful. There are some declining segments which you should be aware of, such as general book publishing."

Benchmark Data

- "Gross Margin % and Operating Income %."
- "For magazines we use profit per page, cost per page and various other metrics of profitability and productivity."
- "A general benchmark has been one-times sales, but this is more difficult to measure now because of declining sales."

Expenses as a percentage of annual sales

Cost of goods	25%
Payroll/labor Costs	10% to 25%
Occupancy	05% to 08%
Profit (estimated pretax)	15% to 20%

Industry Trend

- "Downward trend for print publications, upward for digital and ancillary marketing services."
- "Continued downward due to online competition and, for books, loss of bookstores."
- "The trend is clearly to digital and electronic products. Also, the valuable properties have a very highly defined niche and a leadership position in that niche."
- "Internet will continue to negatively impact many segments of the publishing business."

Seller Financing

- "Both. Large businesses are outside financing generally."

Questions

- "Buyer has many questions to ask. For example, is there a database of customers and how up to date is it. This may be the number 1 question."
- "The position of the publication in its niche is critical. Where would competition come from? How protected is the competitive position of the business?"
- "For magazines, what is the definition of your market segment and what is your rank in the segment? Number 1 can be worth considerably more than number 2 for a business-to-business magazine. Where do you print, who are your suppliers? Questions about subscribership are critical for consumer magazines. Newsstand distribution is difficult for consumer magazines—how do you do it? Is the magazine paid or free, and so on."

Resources

Websites
- Editor and Publisher: www.editorandpublisher.com

Trade Publications
- Booklist: www.booklistonline.com
- Publishers Weekly: www.publishersweekly.com

Associations
- MPA: The Association of Magazine Media: www.magazine.org
- The Association of American Publishers: www.publishers.org
- International Association of Scientific, Technical & Medical Publishers: www.stm-assoc.org

Publishers—Internet (and Broadcasting)		
	NAICS 519130	

Rules of Thumb

- ➢ 100 percent of annual revenue includes inventory
- ➢ 6 times SDE includes inventory
- ➢ 6 times EBIT
- ➢ 5 times EBITDA

Pricing Tips

- "Size matters. Multiples for larger companies >$5 million will be in the 10X range. Same goes for companies with a subscription base that represents recurring revenues."
- "Faster growing companies will provide higher multiples. Higher multiples will also be paid for companies that can document recurring revenue streams, such as subscriptions or annual advertiser contracts. Publishers who provide original content or who own assets such as proprietary databases also can expect greater buyer interest."

Expert Comments

"Ease of replication; it really depends on the content provided. The best businesses have proprietary content and/or a market niche in which they operate."

"Online publishing is a popular business. The barriers to entry are low and the financial reward can be great. The key is developing something original that keeps users coming back to a site. Competition is growing, a factor that will make good sites more valuable while leading to the demise of weaker ones."

"The Web is the world's largest printing press. Everyone wants to be a publisher and competition for eyeballs, ad dollars, subscribers and market share is intense. Barriers to entry are low. On the flip side, publisher and broadcaster audiences tend to be loyal. If they like your site they will stay with you. This leads to lots of repeat business and higher profit margins."

Benchmark Data

- "A successful Internet business will generate revenues at the rate of 2x employee costs."

Expenses as a percentage of annual sales

Cost of goods	10%
Payroll/labor Costs	65%
Occupancy	05% to 10%
Profit (estimated pretax)	20%

Industry Trend

- "Businesses will continue to grow as 'old' media ad dollars continue to migrate to Web-based 'new' media."
- "There will be significant consolidation as smaller operations are rolled into larger ones."

Questions

- "I would ask about stability of earnings, renewal rates, staff turnover, number of advertising contracts, and if there is any revenue/customer concentration."
- "1. How much of your revenue base is recurring? 2. What is your renewal rate? 3. How much do you spend on customer acquisition?"
- "I'd want to know about revenue growth, subscriber/advertiser diversification and renewal rates. Professional publications/broadcasts should be in the 80% range; consumer oriented services should be at 50%. These are rough metrics, but demonstrate 'stickiness.'"

Publishers—Magazines/Periodicals

(See also Publishers—In General)

SIC 2721-02	NAICS 511120	Number of Businesses/Units 22,632

Rules of Thumb

- ➤ 7 times SDE includes inventory
- ➤ 2 to 5 times EBIT
- ➤ 2 to 5 times EBITDA

Pricing Tips

- "Publishers are generally selling for 2 to 5 times EBITDA, down from where they once were."
- "Publications generally sell for a multiple of EBITDA and have very little inventory. Depending on size, industry, if it is a consumer publication or business to business, profitability, etc., smaller ones will sell in the 2 to 5 times range, while the large companies will sell for as much as 12 times EBITDA."
- "Circulation questions are key, including various details of subscriptions and newsstand. Advertisers—number, new advertisers. Share of market in the specific specialty area such as log-home magazines, fishing—# of pages and revenue dollars."
- "Prices have been hurt due to low advertising and magazines not embracing an Internet strategy."

Expert Comments

"Publishing, especially trade publishing, is declining rapidly. People are looking to the Internet for trade information because it can be delivered daily and weekly and be received long before a magazine can even be produced."

Benchmark Data

Statistics (Magazine & Periodical Publishing)

Number of Establishments	22,632
Average Profit Margin	7.4%
Revenue per Employee	$271,100
Average Number of Employees	4.8
Average Wages per Employee	$69,549

Products and Services Segmentation

Entertainment magazines	30.6%
Academic and professional	28.8%
Home and living magazines	18.0%
General interest magazines	16.5%
Other periodicals	6.1%

Industry Costs

Profit	7.4%
Wages	25.8%
Purchases	34.8%
Depreciation	1.8%
Marketing	2.8%
Rent & Utilities	4.0%
Other	23.4%

Market Share

Advance Publications Inc.	11.5%
Hearst Corporation Inc.	8.9%
Time Inc.	6.5%

Source: IBISWorld, March 2016

Expenses as a percentage of annual sales

Cost of goods	50%
Payroll/labor Costs	35%
Occupancy	05%
Profit (estimated pretax)	10%

Industry Trend

- "The volume of magazines mailed annually has dropped for 15 years in a row, according to data released yesterday by the U.S. Postal Service. During those 15 years, 'Outside-County' Periodicals Class volume—by far the best proxy for total magazine volume—has dropped 44%. That means 4 billion fewer copies were mailed in 2015 than in 2000. (Outside-County periodicals are almost exclusively magazines and represent the vast majority of U.S. magazine distribution.) During that time, entire categories have disappeared or shrunk to the point of insignificance. For the past three years, the Outside-County declines have been 6%, then 5%, and then 4% in Fiscal Year 2015."

  Source: "A Magazine Resurgence? The Numbers Say No," July 13, 2016,
  http://deadtreeedition.blogspot.com/2016/07/a-magazine-resurgence-numbers-say-no.html

- "The Association of Magazine Media released The Magazine Media 360° Brand Audience Report for March and the Social Media Report for first quarter 2016 today, showing that magazine media brands continue to deliver meaningful growth across platforms, engaging consumers in all formats, including social media."

  Source: "Magazine Media Continues to Grow Audiences," April 28, 2016, http://www.magazine.org/industry-news/press-releases/mpa-press-releases/mpa/magazine-media-continues-grow-audiences

- "Publishing will continue to decline with the exception of the publishers that can embrace the Internet. Consumer magazines will fare better."

Questions

- "What are advertisers telling you? Look at circulation trends and costs."
- "What have you done to grow the company and how would you grow it in the future?"

Resources

Websites
- www.editorandpublisher.com

Associations
- MPA: The Association of Magazine Media: www.magazine.org

Publishers—Monthly Community Magazines		
	NAICS 511120	

Rules of Thumb

➤ 65–85 percent of annual sales includes inventory

➤ 3 times SDE includes inventory

➤ 3.5 EBIT

➤ 3.5 times EBITDA

Pricing Tips

- "The page count of the magazine and the size of the distribution is a key to attaining the higher number and the greater multiple suggested above. Most publications in this segment will be focused on an area or group within a geographical area, i.e., 'Lake Norman Woman,' 'Carolina Living,' or 'Iredell County Life' and will require that targeted readers identify themselves with the title implication and market. The attraction to a segment of the market creates a loyalty that should translate into long-time advertisers. Make sure the renewal rate is over 75% to confirm this loyalty is real & present."

- "If gross revenues exceed $500,000 then 1X sales is common. That usually equates to 3X SDE. A monthly that has the owner doing all of the sales is worth less than one with a good sales staff. Publications under $500,000 will sell closer to 2X SDE or 50% to 75% of sales."

Expert Comments

"The advertising industry as a whole is very competitive, which will show in the last 3 years' sales, but there is a strong opportunity for a great salesperson to make good money. Hiring great salespeople is very hard and a new owner should not count on a salesperson making a material difference in sales. This is the owner's primary responsibility."

"Monthlies are easy to start up and competition is great. Look for the thickest book (largest number of pages). Advertising should be around 70% of total pages. The thinner books will have the hardest time staying alive. Advertisers tend to stick with the publication they are in, so it's hard to be the new kid on the block."

Benchmark Data

- "The average cost is about $700 a page to print and distribute. The average sales commission should not exceed 25% of the sale. Most vanity magazines will operate out of a home or key-man office space with the occasional use of conference rooms for sales meetings. In any case, occupancy cost should not exceed 5% of sales."

- "Look for sales per salesperson of around $20,000 a month. That should pay a commission of $4,000 which is the minimum you need to keep good salespeople."

Expenses as a percentage of annual sales

Cost of goods	25%
Payroll/labor Costs	25% to 30%
Occupancy	05%
Profit (estimated pretax)	20% to 30%

Industry Trend

- "The boutique magazine industry trend is positive as a larger number of people see this industry as attractive because it affords them the opportunity for a specific lifestyle in a targeted community setting without a significant liability and risk"

Questions

- "What are the top five advertisers? How long have they been with you? Could you grow the circulation? How long have you been with your current printer? Describe your 'layout' process."
- "How long have you been publishing and what are your historical trends? How many salespeople and how long have they worked for you? Who do you consider your competition?"

Publishers—Newsletters		
	NAICS 511120	

Rules of Thumb
➢ 1 times revenues

Pricing Tips
- "High renewal rate (70 percent plus) increases value"

Publishers—Newspapers—Dailies		
(See also Publishers—Newspapers—Weeklies/Community Papers)		
SIC 2711-98	NAICS 511110	Number of Businesses/Units 6,511

Rules of Thumb

➢ 50% of annual sales includes inventory (only very large will get higher)

➢ 4 times EBITDA

➢ 4 times EBIT

➢ 5 times SDE includes inventory

Pricing Tips

- "EBITDA valuation multiples for mid and small market papers range from 3x to 6x. Publishing company values are currently in the 3x to 6x trailing EBITDA range with most transactions at 4x to 5x. Prices over 5x tend to be strategic acquisitions. Buyers typically look at the most recent performance, and the multiples indicated here are based on stable or improving performance. Companies with declining revenues and EBITDA tend to be valued at the lower end of the multiple scale."
  > Source: www.cribb.com—An excellent site, full of valuable information on the publishing business, especially newspapers.
- "In today's market, most valuation methods for newspapers are out the window."
- "Multiples for newspapers can range from four to ten times EBITDA depending on size and type. Dailies can easily sell at 10 times while smaller weekly publications will be at the lower range."
- "5x EBITDA is a current average for newspaper properties with a history of stable earnings. Number may be considerably higher if publication is

positioned for sale to a strategic buyer."

- "Key factors include: size of market, years in business. Is the newspaper geographically desirable by contiguous publishers or buyers looking to roll-up smaller publications into larger groups and take advantage of economies of scale? How active and dominant is the publication in its market and how dominant are its online activities?"

Expert Comments

"While the industry is certainly on a decline, there are still many strategic consolidation opportunities."

"Competition generally comes from other media such as TV and cable rather than other newspapers. As newspapers face new challenges, the risk will increase. Profits have historically been very high, reaching 30% EBITDA. Marketability is still strong but will probably decrease. Industry trend is down as circulation and advertising decline. You can replicate but you must sustain the losses for some time."

"Established newspapers with 10+ year track record tend to be extremely stable and low risk. Competition from Internet has not had a material impact on revenues or valuations . . . at least not yet."

"Subscriber acquisition and gaining solid market position takes many, many years for paid circulation newspapers, therefore time is the greatest barrier to entry."

Benchmark Data

Statistics (Newspaper Publishing)

Number of Establishments	6,511
Average Profit Margin	7.3%
Revenue per Employee	$130,600
Average Number of Employees	30.7
Average Wages per Employee	$40,718

Products and Services Segmentation

Print Advertising	49.8%
Sales and subscriptions	28.3%
Digital Advertising	11.0%
Other	7.3%
Printing services	3.6%

Industry Costs

Profit	7.3%
Wages	31.6%
Purchases	30.6%
Depreciation	3.7%
Marketing	1.7%
Rent & Utilities	3.1%
Other	22.0%

Market Share

Gannett Co. Inc.	10.1%
News Corp.	7.5%
Tribune Company	5.9%
The New York Times Company	5.8%

Source: IBISWorld, February 2016

- "Benchmarks vary greatly by type of publication. For instance, sellers of daily paid circulation newspapers may find that valuations based on subscriber base may be most advantageous. Publishers of free distribution publications are often tied to multiple of discretionary cash flow."
- "Generally multiple of EBITDA. Another is $50 to $400 per paid subscriber."
- "Sales per subscriber, number of subscribers, revenue per household reached (if free distribution publication)."

Expenses as a percentage of annual sales

Cost of goods	50% to 55%
Payroll/labor Costs	30%
Occupancy	05%
Profit (estimated pretax)	15%

Seller Financing
- 5 years

Questions
- "How effectively are you competing with online media? How are your renewal rates compared to your competitors'?"
- "How he would increase the circulation and advertising revenue and why he has not been successful if that is the case. Is the circulation audited?"

Resources

Websites
- Cribb, Greene and Associates—a newspaper appraisal and brokerage firm: www.cribb.com

Trade Publications
- Editor & Publisher: www.editorandpublisher.com

Associations
- National Newspaper Association: www.nnaweb.org
- Newspaper Association of America: www.naa.org

Publishers—Newspapers (In General)

SIC 2711-98	NAICS 511110	

Rules of Thumb
- ➤ 25 percent of annual sales includes inventory
- ➤ 3 times SDE plus inventory
- ➤ 3 to 5 times EBIT
- ➤ 3 to 5 times EBITDA

Pricing Tips

- "Depends on size and segment; for example, it would be very hard to sell a daily newspaper in today's environment."
- "Price can vary greatly depending on the size and frequency of publication, i.e., weekly, daily publication; if the company has its own printing plant; the value of printing equipment; and approximately 50% of gross revenue for recurring outside print work."
- "A stable weekly will sell for 5 to 7 times EBITDA. A strong weekly in a growth area can sell for as much as 9 to 11 times EBITDA. Variation in price is based upon age of property, market potential, competition, stability, growth history, community acceptance, reputation and market penetration. If printing equipment is owned, add value of equipment. If income is generated from outside printing, the profits for the printing portion of the business need to be separated and valued at 3 to 5 times EBITDA."
- "Each newspaper is unique and its strengths and weaknesses must be analyzed in order to arrive at a Fair Market Value. There are industry rules-of-thumb that apply to Gross Revenues and EBITDA, which change according to the dictates of the market."

Expert Comments

"The growth of online advertising has significantly reduced profitability and gross revenues of newspapers."

"Amount of competition from all media in the market is important because there is a limited amount of advertising dollars to go around. Historic performance and competition will be large factors in determining the amount of risk. Location is of minor importance because the customer rarely goes to the business. Most publications with reasonable profits are marketable as there are sufficient buyers in the market for local community operations. While the trend in large metro dailies is declining revenue and profits, smaller community publications continue to do well. It is easy to start a new publication, but a lot more difficult to build a reader and advertising base."

"Competition generally comes from other media such as TV and cable rather than other newspapers. Profits have historically been very high, reaching 30% EBITDA, but have been falling recently. Marketability is decreasing."

"The industry is in a state of turmoil and transition. Large metro dailies are being hardest hit, while smaller community newspapers have been able to weather the perfect storm of Internet competition and a changing economic environment."

Benchmark Data

- For additional Benchmark Data see Publishers—Newspapers—Dailies
- "At one time $200 per daily newspaper subscriber, but not anymore. It is a matter of profitability. Some smaller newspapers in rural areas have a better chance because there are not as many advertising options."
- "The ratio of advertising space to editorial space has a lot to do with profitability. Ideally one should have two-thirds advertising, one-third profit."

Expenses as a percentage of annual sales

Cost of goods	35% to 45%
Payroll/labor Costs	25% to 35%
Occupancy	05% to 10%
Profit (estimated pretax)	15% to 25%

Industry Trend

- "As more news moves online and demand for news grows in emerging markets, global newspaper circulation will continue to increase while revenues decline. These countervailing trends will see 2015's total global newspaper revenue of US$130.5bn fall to US$121.1bn in 2020, a compound annual decline of 1.5%."

  Source: http://www.pwc.com/gx/en/industries/entertainment-media/outlook/segment-insights/newspaper-publishing.html

- "Perhaps the biggest shift in the newspaper world is the revenue driven from circulation is now greater than revenue from advertising. But one area that everyone is worried about is adblocking!
  - ✓ 47% of Internet users use some form of ad blocking (Reuters Institute—June 2015)
  - ✓ 55% in the 18–24 year old demo.
  - ✓ 16% of all US traffic adblocked at start of 2015—20% now (Adobe)
  - ✓ Global loss of ad revenue to adblocking—$21.8 billion (Adobe)
  - ✓ AdBlock Plus averaging 2.3M global downloads a week for 2 years.
  - ✓ Higher income users more likely to adblock (their time is more important to them)
  - ✓ Adblocking effecting your analytics tags
  - ✓ CBS Interactive—05%–40% of pageviews adblocked across 20 properties

  "So what does this all mean? Newspapers are hungry for new revenue streams. While this should not come as a surprise, one area that newspapers are successfully recouping losses is online recruitment advertising. As the job advertisement becomes more similar to a hybrid of native advertising and an SEM result, job ads are the prime content for a newspapers audience. Whether in New York, Philadelphia, Eastern Tennessee, or numerous places across America, newspapers are using their local influence to help employers and job candidates find each other."

  Source: "State of the Newspaper Publishing Industry," by Yoav Guttman, May 25, 2016, http://blog.realmatch.com/publishers/state-of-the-newspaper-publishing-industry/

- "After a year of slight gains, newspaper circulation fell again in 2014 (though tracking these data is becoming more complicated each year due to measurement changes). Revenue from circulation rose, but ad revenue continued to fall, with gains in digital ad revenue failing to make up for falls in print ad revenue. Despite widespread talk of a shift to digital, most newspaper readership continues to be in print. Online, more traffic to the top newspaper websites and associated apps comes from mobile than from desktop users, and the average visitor only stays on the site for three minutes per visit. And several larger media conglomerates spun off their newspaper divisions as separate companies in an attempt to prevent the newspaper industry's woes from affecting the health of their broadcast divisions."

- "Readership—Although the public conversation about newspapers focuses on the shift to digital, most newspaper reading still happens in print. According to readership data from Nielsen Scarborough's 2014 Newspaper Penetration Report, 56% of those who consume a newspaper read it exclusively in print, while 11% also read it on desktop or laptop computers; 5% also read it on mobile; and another 11% read it in print, on desktop and on mobile. In total, more than eight-in-ten of those who read a newspaper do so in print, at least sometimes. Only 5% read newspapers exclusively on mobile devices.

"For the past five years, newspaper ad revenue has maintained a consistent trajectory: Print ads have produced less revenue (down 5%), while digital ads have produced more revenue (up 3%) – but not enough to make up for the fall in print revenue. Overall ad revenue fell 4%, to just $19.9 billion."

Source: Newspapers: Fact Sheet by Michael Barthel, April 29, 2015, journalism.org

- "Fully 69% of Americans—or more than 164 million adults in the United States—access newspaper media content in print or online during a typical week or on mobile devices during a typical month, according to the survey of some 206,000 U.S. adults collected by Scarborough Research."

Source: Executive Summary, Newspaper Association of America, www.naa.org

Seller Financing

- "About 50% of sales are financed. Larger papers generally sell for cash. Smaller papers will sell for as little as 30% down with terms averaging seven years."
- "Seller financing is typical with terms of five years or longer."

Questions

- "What is your online market position and share of market in each market that you serve?"
- "What are the reasons why you feel your media will continue to be relevant in the years to come?"
- "How would you increase the circulation and advertising? Why haven't you been successful in doing so?"
- "Revenue by category, cash flow, paid circulation and free circulation, average advertising percentage, competition, owner's duties, who sells the ads, number of ad contracts in place and dollar value?"
- "What contracts do you have; how are you handling the changes in the newspaper environment? Is it an all-cash sale or is the owner willing to carry some of the sale price?"
- "Subscription base, number of subscribers, subscriber retention, revenue trends, strength of online initiatives, years established"
- "Why they are selling; what their daily involvement is; what investment has been made to adapt to new technologies; how do they reach the individual reader and advertiser. Many more."
- "How are you positioned in your market relative to competition in the online market? How are you protecting your employment and classified advertising base from online competition?"

Resources

Websites
- Cribb, Greene and Associates: www.cribb.com

Trade Publications
Editor and Publisher Magazine: www.editorandpublisher.com

Associations
Newspaper Association of America: www.naa.org

Publishers—Newspapers—Weeklies/Community Papers
(See also Publishers/Newspapers—Dailies)

	NAICS 511110	

Rules of Thumb

➤ "100 percent of annual sales"

➤ "Some smaller weekly papers will have lower multiples in the 3 to 5 EBITDA area."

➤ "Community monthlies will sell for 3 x SDE if they produce at least $150,000 in SDE. Otherwise, multiple comes down to the 2 x SDE area."

➤ 3 times SDE

➤ 3 times EBIT

➤ 3 times EBITDA

➤ 1 times annual income for mid-sized weekly newspaper

Expert Comments

"Barriers to entry are low. This is a selling business. Getting good salespeople is very difficult. The buyers of this type of business should expect to spend half of their time selling."

Benchmark Data

- "The majority of community papers that answered the survey, however, still receive most of their ad income from grocery ads, 43.8 percent. The next two top earners are medical based (hospitals and urgent care clinics) 40.8 percent, and tied for third are new auto sales and banks or other financial institutions at 30.8 percent each."

    Source: "Survey: ad revenue showing improvement at community papers" by Stanley Schwartz, www.nnaweb.org July 3, 2013

- "Advertising to editorial should run 2/3rd to 1/3rd for maximum profitability."
- "Look for businesses where the owner does very little selling. You have to make a negative adjustment to SDE to account for sales commissions to replace an overactive seller."

Expenses as a percentage of annual sales

Cost of goods... 25%
Payroll/labor Costs... 25%
Occupancy.. 05%
Profit (estimated pretax) 20%

Industry Trend

- "Up. Local merchants are looking for a cost-effective way to reach their local customers. Major dailies are too expensive and provide too much reach for the local markets."
- "Community papers are following the rise in the housing market. New communities are receptive to local papers that educate them as to local restaurants, salons, etc. This trend will continue."

Questions
- "How many salespeople do you have?"

Resources

Websites
- Cribb, Greene & Associates—a newspaper appraisal and brokerage firm: www.cribb.com

Associations
- Association of Free Community Newspapers: www.afcp.org
- National Newspaper Publishers Association (NNPA): www.nnpa.org

Publishers—Software	
NAICS 511210	Number of Businesses/Units 12,029

Rules of Thumb
> "Varies widely, particularly on multiple (revenue, earnings) of historical performance. Many acquisitions are strategic in nature."

Expert Comments

"Market momentum of software products can change quickly, both up and down. With specialized niche firms, buyers can be international companies. This is a trans-national market."

Benchmark Data

Statistics (Software Publishing)

Number of Establishments	12,029
Average Profit Margin	20.8%
Revenue per Employee	$451,100
Average Number of Employees	38.8
Average Wages per Employee	$152,720

Products and Services Segmentation

Application software publishing	36.3%
System software publishing	33.0%
All others	19.2%
Re-sale of computer hardware and software	3.8%
Information technology technical consulting services	3.4%
Custom application design and development	3.2%
Information Technology related training services	1.1%

Major Market Segmentation

Business	62.2%
Household consumers and individual users	30.3%
Government	7.5%

Industry Costs

Profit	20.8%
Wages	33.6%
Purchases	11.0%
Depreciation	1.8%
Marketing	3.5%
Rent & Utilities	5.5%
Other	23.8%

Market Share

Microsoft Corporation	16.8%
Oracle Corporation	6.3%
International Business Machines Corporation	4.5%

Source: IBISWorld, July 2016

Industry Trend
- "Increasingly competitive"

	Franchise

Pump It Up (See also Franchises)

Approx. Total Investment	$366,250 to $790,000
NAICS 713990	Number of Businesses/Units 130

Rules of Thumb
➤ 30 percent of annual sales plus inventory

➤ (Provides children's parties with inflated/bouncy toys)

Resources
Websites
- www.pumpitupparty.com

	Franchise

Purrfect Auto (See also Franchises)

NAICS 811118	Number of Businesses/Units 100

Rules of Thumb
➤ 45 percent of annual sales plus inventory

➤ Note: This franchise is on the West Coast—primarily California, Nevada and Arizona.

Resources
Websites
- http://purrfectauto.com/

Franchise

Quaker Steak & Lube (See also Franchises)	
Approx. Total Investment	$1.2 million to $4.4 million
Estimated Annual Sales/Unit	$2,500,000
NAICS 722513	Number of Businesses/Units 44

Rules of Thumb
➤ 45 percent of annual sales

Resources
Websites
- www.thelube.com

Franchise

Quiznos Classic Subs (See also Franchises, Sandwich Shops)		
Approx. Total Investment		$182,912 to $231,246
Estimated Annual Sales/Unit		$325,000
SIC 5812-19	NAICS 722513	Number of Businesses/Units 1,935

Rules of Thumb
➤ 20 to 25 percent of annual sales plus inventory

Benchmark Data
- For Benchmark Data see Sandwich Shops

Resources
Websites
- www.quiznos.com

Radio Communications, Equipment and Systems		
	NAICS 443142	

Rules of Thumb
➤ 2 to 4 times SDE plus inventory

Pricing Tips
- "It is important to consider the revenue per customer and industry figures. A well-diversified company can weather downturns in business cycles that this industry may be subject to."

Expert Comments
"Not location dependent, but a well-trained staff and diversified product lines are important."

Benchmark Data

- "GP of 40%, payroll 20%, advertising 4%"

Expenses as a percentage of annual sales

Cost of goods	60%
Payroll/labor Costs	20%
Occupancy	07%
Profit (estimated pretax)	10% to 12%

Industry Trend

- "FCC rule changes mandate replacement of older 2-way radio equipment being used."

Questions

- "Product line diversification? Service and installation capabilities? Employee tenure?"

Radio Stations (See also Television Stations)		
SIC 4832-01	NAICS 515112	Number of Businesses/Units 6,703

Rules of Thumb

- ➤ 8 to 10 times EBITDA
- ➤ 10 to 12 times cash flow in medium markets
- ➤ 15 times cash flow—large markets
- ➤ 1.5 to 6 times annual sales

Pricing Tips

- "Many sellers continue to value their property based on multiples that were in place in the mid to late 1990's. Sadly, these valuations have dropped quite drastically in the past several years. Reality of today's true economic picture must enter into the mindset of those who are in a divestiture mode."

  Source: http://www.radiotvdeals.com/Seller%20Tools

- "Broadcast station 'stick' valuation or the conundrum of how to value a station that has never made any money…ever. Broadcast station valuation is usually done by using a multiple of the station's broadcast cash flow (BCF). Of course this assumes the station is producing a cash flow. Where there is no cash flow, it is the perceived value of what the license is worth plus any hard assets the station may have … commonly referred to as the 'stick' or base value. There are several scholarly tomes on broadcast or radio station valuation (Search: broadcast station valuation). The problem here is that many stations have gone through a succession of owners and have never shown any positive cash flow or just enough to keep the power on until the next sale/transfer. What is a station like this worth? Many new construction permits (CP) are coming on the market as a result of the recent FM allocation auctions. What are these worth?

  "In the case of a station that has never shown a positive cash flow you need to determine the reason. Is it an unfortunate combination of circumstances that has led to a succession of owners who had no clue as to what to do with the station? Poor market conditions? Improper format? Poor signal? Also, some stations can be artistic successes and commercial failures. Such a station might have a format that appeals to a significant audience but the station is unable to sell enough advertising to capitalize on the station's own success. This is frequently because the station has not developed a proper sales force. As any broadcast owner knows, the hardest positions to fill at a station are good sales representatives. I talk to would-be broadcasters all the time that have no clue as to what it takes to put together a sales staff.

"Back to how to evaluate a non-cash-flowing station or a dark station ready to go back on the air. A common industry approach has been to factor the amount of revenue a particular facility may generate by looking at the amount of advertising revenue the station may be able to secure out of the total revenue available for radio in the market if it reaches a particular audience level … whew … got that? The problem here is there are many pieces of the puzzle that have to be put together to get an idea of what the numbers should be. What is the financial condition of the market? Power of the station? Is it AM or FM? Is the ownership/management talented? In today's market we have to contend with how much advertising revenue is going to other competitors on the Internet. This is where the question is asked… 'Is the Internet going to be a foe of the station or a tool to be used by it?' To stream or not to stream? Interactive Web site or not? Maybe even podcasts?

"Another major factor to look at in evaluating a start-up property is the technical condition of the station. Failure to conduct an engineering inspection can be a costly mistake. What looks like a cheap price for an AM property could be a pig in a poke with some nasty surprises. Questions that need to be answered: What is the condition of the AM ground system and tower? Do either need to be painted (tower), repaired or even replaced? Are the copper radials in the ground damaged or corroded away? If the AM station is a directional system, is the pattern still in compliance? Has there been lightning damage to the phasor system and other transmitter/audio processing components? What is the age of the transmitter? Will it need to be replaced? To get the answers, hire a competent broadcast engineering firm to do an evaluation. You will need to pay for this but it can save you big money and headaches later."

Source: David Garland, Media Brokerage, www.radiobroker.com.
Garland is one of the most successful radio brokers in the country.

- "Normally depends on historical (and projected) Broadcast Cash Flow, or EBITDA plus certain non-recurring charges and management-unique expenses. Value of the intangible rights to the license can vary widely with supply and demand.

  "A multiple of broadcast cash flow (revenues minus operating expenses before interest, depreciation, taxes). Multiple varies by service (AM/FM/TV) & market size. All broadcasters need to own tower site. Consolidation opportunities within a market add value."

- "With rapid consolidation taking place in the radio industry sellers and buyers are happy with the multipliers they are achieving—buyers of multiple properties can reduce expenses. Ask about buyer's investment horizon. What expenses are in the business of the owner/operator that an investor may not have?"

Benchmark Data

Statistics (Radio Broadcasting)

Number of Establishments	6,703
Average Profit Margin	13.6%
Revenue per Employee	$197,300
Average Number of Employees	15.4
Average Wages per Employee	$58,804

Products and Services Segmentation

Other	37.5%
Country	14.8%
News/Talk	11.3%
Classics	10.7%
Urban	10.4%
Top 40	8.0%
Adult Contemporary	7.3%

Industry Costs

Profit	13.6%
Wages	30.0%
Purchases	40.1%
Depreciation	4.6%
Marketing	4.5%
Rent & Utilities	6.7%
Other	0.5%

Market Share

Sirius XM Radio Inc.	21.8%
iHeartMedia Inc.	16.3%
Cumulus Media Inc.	6.8%
CBS Corporation	6.1%

Source: IBISWorld, November 2015

- "Profit (estimated)—25 percent for well-run stations"

Industry Trend

- "Radio is the leading reach platform:
    - ✓ 93% of us listen to AM/FM radio over the airwaves, which is higher than TV viewership (85%), PC use (50%), smartphone use (74%), and tablet use (29%)
    - ✓ 265 million Americans 6+ listen to the radio each week;
    - ✓ 66 million Millennials use radio each week;
    - ✓ Audio consumers are listening for more than 12 hours each week; and
    - ✓ The majority of radio usage comes from employed listeners; nearly three-quarters of Generation X listeners work full-time."

Source: "Radio Facts and Figures,"
http://www.newsgeneration.com/broadcast-resources/radio-facts-and-figures/

Seller Financing

- "Rarely is there seller financing except for smallest of deals."

Questions

- "Can your signal be upgraded or moved to cover a larger market? How are you spending your revenue? How much do you do in trade? Can any barter be converted to cash? Do you really need to buy that new gadget, just because you have a few extra bucks this month? Spend the money to find out what can be done to expand or move that signal to more ears. Are you being a partner in your advertisers' business? The more you expand your advertisers' businesses, the more you expand yours and are therefore able to ask for more dollars on the selling market."

Source: www.buysellradio.com

R - Rules of Thumb

Resources

Websites
- David Garland, Media Brokerage, also, a brokerage site, but well worth a visit.: www.radiobroker.com

---

Real Estate Agencies		
SIC Real Estate: 6531-18; Business Brokerage: 7382-22		
	NAICS 531210	Number of Businesses/Units 834,730

Rules of Thumb

> 2 times SDE; may require earnout

> 33 percent of annual sales (real estate offices) includes inventory

Pricing Tips
- "Price will depend on agent splits."
- "Time in the market and number of listings"
- "This industry has taken a huge hit. The multiples must be on SDE that is sustainable."

Expert Comments

"There are a wide variety of real estate firm types, from residential to commercial and from tenant-rep leasing to agency leasing for landlords. However, barriers to entry remain low and access to capital is increasing through both community banks and private lenders."

Benchmark Data

Statistics (Real Estate Agency Franchises)
Number of Establishments	15,919
Average Profit Margin	15.5%
Revenue per Employee	$101,500
Average Number of Employees	13.5
Average Wages per Employee	$47,263

Products and Services Segmentation
Residential real estate agency franchises	68.5%
Commercial real estate agency franchises	31.5%

Major Market Segmentation
Sellers	45.0%
Lessors	30.0%
Buyers	25.0%

Industry Costs

Profit	15.5%
Wages	35.4%
Purchases	12.8%
Depreciation	0.7%
Marketing	5.4%
Rent and Utilities	7.1%
Other	23.1%

Source: IBISWorld, April 2016

Statistics (Real Estate Sales and Brokerage)

Number of Establishments	818,811
Average Profit Margin	15.5%
Revenue per Employee	$123,800
Average Number of Employees	1.3
Average Wages per Employee	$43,621

Products and Services Segmentation

Residential sales	64.5%
Commercial rentals	11.4%
Other services	11.1%
Commercial sales	8.4%
Residential rentals	4.6%

Major Market Segmentation

Married or partnered residential homeowners and renters	46.3%
Single residential homeowners and renters	22.8%
Office and professional space	12.7%
Retail space	11.1%
Warehousing and other commercial space	4.4%
Manufacturing space	2.7%

Industry Costs

Profit	15.5%
Wages	35.4%
Purchases	9.0%
Depreciation	0.7%
Marketing	5.4%
Rent & Utilities	3.9%
Other	30.1%

Source: IBISWorld, March 2016

Expenses as a percentage of annual sales

Cost of goods	65% (commission payout)
Payroll/labor Costs	10%
Occupancy	05% to 10%
Profit (estimated pretax)	15%

Industry Trend

- "According to the 2016 Emerging Trends in Real Estate, which was just released by the Urban Land Institute, the outlook for the next 12 months is rosy, with one analyst going so far as to call it 'doggone good.' Here's a breakdown of . . . some factors that the authors of the report, Urban Land Institute and PriceWaterhouseCoopers, and the hundreds of industry analysts they interviewed and surveyed, believe will shape the landscape for the year to come.

- ✓ Second Tier Cities Take Center Stage—It's no shocker that cities such as Austin are taking off. These 18-hour cities (as compared to high-profile, 24-hour cities such as New York and San Francisco), are expected to perform incredibly well this year.
- ✓ Millennial Parents Move to the 'Burbs—Millennials have traditionally been painted as a generation obsessed with urban living, but just like their parents and grandparents, they wants homes and good schools for their kids.
- ✓ Investment in the Changing Office Landscape—The maturing recovery has led to job growth, which in turn has strengthened the commercial sector. With the dominant trend towards open office plans—the average square foot per worker, which was 253 in 2000, is predicted to shrink to 138 by 2020.
- ✓ New Housing Options and Ideas—The concept of homeownership may be experiencing a significant, and serious, shift. Rates of homeownership has dropped from roughly 70 percent before the Great Recession, to 63.5 percent in the second quarter of 2015.
- ✓ Pulling Up Parking Lots?—As many younger American opt out of car ownership, and tech trends such as ride-sharing and autonomous cars begin to change transportation patterns, many urban planners, government officials, and real estate owners are questioning if parking lots are the best use of downtown real estate. Trends suggest that "existing parking represents a suboptimal use of land," and as cities change zoning regulations to reflect these shifts, developers are asking how they can take advantage. Are surface lots and parking structures potential development opportunities?

Source: by Patrick Sisson, January 27, 2016,
http://www.curbed.com/2016/1/27/10842856/top-10-real-estate-trends-of-2016

Seller Financing

- "Banks are generally friendly to borrowers with collateral. So on the investment or development side, inexpensive capital is often easy to come by. However, the increase in private lending has been a boon to quick-moving developers who don't mind a higher, short-term rate."

Questions

- "Are you in production? What contract do you have for advertising and services? Where do you get your leads? Have you recently lost top-producing agents?"
- "Do you produce? What are your splits? Do you have non-competes?"
- "Will the owner be available?"

Records Management		
	NAICS 541611	

Rules of Thumb

➢ 8 times SDE
➢ 200 percent of annual sales

Pricing Tips
- "Pricing [above] specifically for Records Management businesses"

Benchmark Data
- "Internal account growth of 5% to 7%. Sixty percent storage revenues with 40% service revenues."

Expenses as a percentage of annual sales

Cost of goods...0%
Payroll/labor Costs...35%
Occupancy...25%
Profit (estimated pretax) 30%

Industry Trend
- "Continued industry growth with emphasis on document-destruction services"

Recruiting Agencies		
SIC 7361-03	NAICS 56131	Number of Businesses/Units 25,923

Rules of Thumb
➤ 50 percent of annual revenues; may require earnout

➤ 1 to 1.5 times SDE; add fixtures equipment & inventory; may require earnout

Benchmark Data

Statistics (Employment and Recruiting Agencies)

Number of Establishments... 25,923
Average Profit Margin 5.3%
Revenue per Employee $91,493
Average Number of Employees...11.7
Average Wages per Employee $37,081

Products and Services Segmentation

Permanent placement services 49.9%
Executive search services 32.1%
Temporary staffing services 8.4%
Independent contractor placement services 5.9%
Other.. 3.7%

Major Market Segmentation

Executive and managerial 33.0%
Industrial 32.3%
Administrative and clerical 15.5%
Technical..11.4%
Healthcare 7.8%

Industry Costs

Profit	5.3%
Wages	40.9%
Purchases	20.2%
Depreciation	0.3%
Marketing	1.4%
Rent & Utilities	2.9%
Other	29.0%

Market Share

LinkedIn Corp.	5.1%
Randstad Holding NV	4.8%

Source: IBISWorld, August 2016

Industry Trend

- "When LinkedIn and online job applications first began to gain traction, they were seen as supplements to the traditional paper résumé and in-person interview. Today, the world of recruiting has gone nearly 100-percent digital.

  "'From the résumé to the search to the interview, we're moving toward a digital hiring model,' said Bob Myhal, director of digital marketing at CBC Advertising and former CEO of NextHire. 'Résumés will be displaced by constantly evolving representations of individual experiences, skills and aptitudes that exist purely in the digital realm. Innovative tools that use social media, big data and other technologies to give tremendous insight into individual job seekers will [be] the primary screening method.

  "Jon Bischke, CEO of Entelo, noted that digital profiles can provide far more insight into a candidate than a traditional résumé can, and many recruiters have realized that."

  Source: "Hiring in the Digital Age: What's Next for Recruiting?" by Nicole Fallon Taylor, January 11, 2016, http://www.businessnewsdaily.com/6975-future-of-recruiting.html

Recruiting Agencies (Online) (See also Recruiting Agencies)

	NAICS 56131	

Rules of Thumb

➢ 50% of Annual Gross Sales including inventory

➢ 6 times SDE plus inventory

➢ 5 times EBITDA

Benchmark Data

Expenses as a percentage of annual sales

Cost of goods	50%
Payroll/labor Costs	20%
Occupancy	05%
Profit (estimated pretax)	0

Industry Trend

- "The online recruitment business is challenging. There are many new and free and very inexpensive competitors."

Seller Financing
- "Typically uses outside financing"

Questions
- "Where is the majority of traffic coming from: SEO, natural search, PPC, other?"

Recycling		
	NAICS 562920	Number of Businesses/Units 1,611

Rules of Thumb
➤ 3 to 5 times SDE includes inventory

➤ 3 to 6 times EBIT

➤ 3 to 6 times EBITDA

Pricing Tips
- "Value is based on land and improvements, inventory (aged), earnings, and goodwill"
- "Once the EBITDA exceeds $1,000,000 most buyers will assume that normal levels of inventory, A/R, and FFE will be included in the transaction as working capital. The key is to understand how the buyer is structuring their offer and how they are accounting for these values."
- "Must consider if this is a commodity product that is sold. If so, consider the consistency of the source of the product as an important risk factor."

Benchmark Data

Statistics (Recycling Facilities)
Number of Establishments	1,611
Average Profit Margin	3.9%
Revenue per Employee	$214,000
Average Number of Employees	15.4
Average Wages per Employee	$37,899

Products and Services Segmentation
Recyclable material recovery and processing	47.4%
Sale of recycled materials	39.3%
Other	8.2%
Recyclables collection services	5.2%

Major Market Segmentation
Private businesses, including recycling commodity wholesalers and manufacturers	75.8%
Municipal governments	22.5%
State governments, nonprofit organizations and individuals	1.7%

R - Rules of Thumb

Industry Costs

Profit	3.9%
Wages	17.7%
Purchases	49.3%
Depreciation	5.5%
Marketing	0.6%
Rent & Utilities	4.0%
Other	19.0%

Market Share

Waste Management Inc.	20.9%
Republic Services Inc.	7.0%

Source: IBISWorld, April 2016

Expenses as a percentage of annual sales

Cost of goods	50%
Payroll/labor Costs	12%
Occupancy	10%
Profit (estimated pretax)	08%

Industry Trend

- "As we prepare to move into 2016, the solid waste management industry faces ongoing and new challenges that shape how companies do business. From the push to landfill less and reuse more, to the resulting economic toll of plummeting values of surplus recyclables, haulers, recyclers and landfill operators are finding new ways to thrive.

  "Here are six likely trends for the upcoming year, as projected by industry leaders.

  1. Best practices and new technologies will aim to improve safety.

  2. Automated collections to expand.

  3. Commodity prices will continue to decline while diversion costs climb.

  4. Municipal recycling programs to refuse glass, while some companies will invest in this material.

  5. Composting programs will expand in some regions6. CNG technology will continue to grow."

      Source: "6 waste and recycling trends to watch in 2016, as predicted by experts," by Arlene Karidis, December 14, 2015, http://www.wastedive.com/news/6-waste-and-recycling-trends-to-watch-in-2016-as-predicted-by-experts/410771/

- "With prices tumbling for scrap metal, used paper and old plastic bottles, recycling firms around Indiana are watching revenue drop. Most are working harder to find buyers that will pay a decent price for their truckloads of materials. Some are idling operations. The downturn is putting pressure on operators to cut costs and could take a bite out of government budgets that used to rake in money from the sale of paper, scrap and other recyclables.

  "But for all their work, a truckload of sorted scrap metal that would have fetched $120,000 two years ago from a mill or foundry now is likely to get only $65,000. Solotken's revenue has fallen 25 percent in the past two years, President Joseph M. Alpert said. 'There's too much supply and not enough demand,' he said. 'We're not losing money, but we're not making what we did two or three years ago.'

  "With the collapse in prices and tough times for operators, it would seem households and businesses would have a tough time finding anyone to haul away their recyclables."

Source: "Recycling industry buffeted by falling prices," by John Russell, February 27, 2016, http://www.ibj.com/articles/57397-recycling-industry-buffeted-by-falling-prices

- "And Waste Management, the biggest recycler in the country, has reduced the number of recycling facilities it operates to about 100, from 130, over the last two years, resulting in the loss of 900 jobs. Over the last three quarters, revenues from recycling operations are down 16 percent from the same time a year earlier, to $878 million from just over $1 billion.

  "'The recycling industry is being hit dramatically by falling commodity and oil prices,' said Michael Taylor, vice president of international trade at the Society of the Plastics Industry. 'A real fear now is that recycling rates might go down. That would be a horrible situation.'

  "Last year the city government in Washington, D.C., paid Waste Management $1.37 million to accept the recyclables it collected from residents. That represented a stark reversal from 2011, when the district earned $550,000 for sending the company roughly the same amount of material.

  "Orange County, N.C., which includes Chapel Hill, was making about $500,000 a year by selling its recyclables to a company called Sonoco. But as commodity prices have fallen, so, too, have the prices that Sonoco can offer local governments. Starting this month, Sonoco will not pay Orange County anything for the mixed paper, plastics and metals it collects."

Source: "Skid in Oil Prices Pulls the Recycling Industry Down With It" by David Gelles, *The New York Times*, February 13, 2016

- "Companies associated with the waste management industry will continue to be attractive as they provide a 'green' business opportunity to both individual and strategic buyers."
- "Trend is overall growth in the recycling industry with a consolidation with middle to large sized companies seeking to purchase smaller competitors."

Questions
- "What kind of contracts do you have with your paper suppliers? Are you contracted to sell your paper to certain mills or brokers? Who is your competition within 100 miles?"

		Franchise
Red Robin Gourmet Burgers (See also Franchises)		
Approx. Total Investment		$1,800,000 to $3,000,000
Estimated Annual Sales/Unit		$2,900,000
	NAICS 722513	Number of Businesses/Units 500

Rules of Thumb
➤ 30 to 35 percent of annual sales

Resources

Websites
- www.redrobin.com

Registered Investment Advisors

	NAICS 523930	Number of Businesses/Units 116,628

Rules of Thumb

➢ 150 percent of annual sales

➢ 3 to 5 SDE

Pricing Tips

- "The structure of your deal will depend on the willingness of the seller to hold an earnout vs. a note and cash down payment at closing."

Expert Comments

"There will be continued major consolidation in the industry."

Benchmark Data

Statistics (Financial Planning and Advice)

Number of Establishments	116,628
Average Profit Margin	22.5%
Revenue per Employee	$248,800
Average Number of Employees	1.7
Average Wages per Employee	$79,049

Products and Services Segmentation

Personal financial planning and advice	33.3%
Personal investment management	29.7%
Business and government financial planning and management	20.8%
Other services	16.2%

Major Market Segmentation

Individuals and households	42.9%
Businesses	27.7%
Other clients	15.8%
Governments	13.6%

Industry Costs

Profit	22.5%
Wages	32.1%
Purchases	4.8%
Depreciation	1.2%
Marketing	1.7%
Rent & Utilities	2.8%
Other	34.9%

Market Share

Morgan Stanley Wealth Management	17.9%
Wells Fargo & Company	13.7%
Bank of America Corporation	13.4%
Ameriprise Financial Inc.	4.9%

Source: IBISWorld, June 2016

- "Average account per client"

Expenses as a percentage of annual sales

Cost of goods	05% to 10%
Payroll/labor Costs	10% to 20%
Occupancy	05% to 15%
Profit (estimated pretax)	20% to 45%

Industry Trend

- "According to a survey conducted by TD Ameritrade Institutional, advisors said their business grew last year in terms of both assets under management and revenue, and they expect more of the same in 2016.

  "TD's survey of 302 independent registered investment advisors—both those who custody with TD and those who custody elsewhere— identified the biggest industry trends. It's anyone's guess how the markets will shake out this year. But financial advisors are feeling good about their own prospects for the year ahead.

  "Eighty percent of the advisors in the survey believe that their assets under management will increase; the average rate of growth is expected to be 17 percent.

  "'My guess is that we'll begin to see some migration out of robo-advisors,' said Norman Boone, president and founder of Mosaic Financial Partners. 'People realize they need more of a human touch.'"

  Source: "Higher tech spending, asset growth top RIA trends: Survey," Ilana Polyak, Monday, February 1, 2016, http://www.cnbc.com/2016/01/27/higher-tech-spending-asset-growth-top-ria-trends-survey.html

- "Continued major consolidation. Large players absorbing smaller operators for their higher margins. However, smaller players will have a disadvantage due to size."

Questions

- "Gross commissions? Net? Broker-dealer? Overhead? Fee-based or commission-based? Average fees? Average client investment, net worth?"

Remediation Services		
	NAICS 562910	Number of Businesses/Units 8,575

Rules of Thumb

- 4 to 5 times EBITDA
- 40 percent of annual sales includes inventory
- 2 to 3 times SDE includes inventory

Pricing Tips

- "Union vs non-union work force. Private vs. public projects."
- "Contract and client direct relationships will be worth more than those performed as a subcontractor for a general contractor. Size makes a big difference in price—larger businesses with $1 million + EBITDA sell for higher multiples."
- "Value of future jobs under contract is a major factor in value and salability."

Expert Comments

"Industry has become increasingly competitive as more players are chasing fewer projects."

"Demand for remediation services is tied to the construction remodeling and improvement market. As demand for building modifications has decreased with the economic crisis, so too have remediation services."

"Competition varies based on union vs. non-union, and public vs. private market. Revenue varies with commercial real estate renovation and development."

Benchmark Data

Statistics (Remediation & Environmental Cleanup Services)

Number of Establishments	8,575
Average Profit Margin	6.5%
Revenue per Employee	$216,700
Average Number of Employees	9.9
Average Wages per Employee	$57,539

Products and Services Segmentation

Site remediation services	47.4%
Building remediation services	26.8%
Environmental emergency response services	13.1%
Other services	12.7%

Major Market Segmentation

Businesses	55.0%
Federal government	23.5%
State and local government	11.5%
Individuals	5.0%
Nonprofit organizations	5.0%

Industry Costs

Profit	6.5%
Wages	26.5%
Purchases	25.8%
Depreciation	7.9%
Marketing	0.8%
Rent & Utilities	4.5%
Other	28.0%

Market Share

CH2M Hill Inc.	8.2%
CB&I	5.5%

Source: IBISWorld, January 2016

- "Owner compensation 3% of sales"
- "Flat management structure with an engaged owner will be much more profitable. Sales, estimating and production responsibility for each project should be with the same manager."
- "Gross margin should be 25%–30% and SDE 20% of revenue."

Expenses as a percentage of annual sales

Cost of goods.. 70%
Payroll/labor Costs... 07%
Occupancy... 04%
Profit (estimated pretax) .... 03% to 05%

Industry Trend

- "Project opportunities are a function of the overall commercial construction industry. Business will pick up when commercial renovation work picks up."

Questions

- "Have there been any DEP violations? Worker's comp claims?"
- "Check for hidden liabilities. Union vs. non-union is important difference. Reputation is also important—how many jobs have they abandoned or not completed on time?"

	Franchise

Renaissance Executive Forums (See also Franchises)

Approx. Total Investment	$61,500 to $150,000
NAICS 611430	Number of Businesses/Units 54

Rules of Thumb

➢ 70 percent of annual sales includes inventory

Resources

Websites
- www.executiveforums.com

Rental Centers (See also Rent-To-Own Stores)

SIC 7359-59	NAICS 532310	Number of Businesses/Units 20,114

Rules of Thumb

➢ 95 to 100 percent of annual sales includes inventory

➢ 3 times SDE includes inventory

➢ 4 times EBITDA

➢ Depending on type of business (general, tool, construction, industrial, party) values will range from 3.0 to 5.5 EBITDA, $1.00 to $2.00 per annual revenues.

➢ 5 times SDE (party and tent rental)

Pricing Tips

- "Age of equipment, depreciation expense. If equipment is old and depreciation expense getting lower each year, then examine equipment carefully. Equipment may be old and worn out requiring replacement with new."

- "A. Type of rental business: tool versus construction equipment versus party/ event rental —earnings have a different set of criteria. B. Key ratios: rental equipment inventory; rental revenues; EBITDA percent of net revenues."
- "Percentage of rent to sales; capitalization versus expense policy for equipment purchases; age of rental fleet (inventory for rent); rental inventory is a fixed asset, not a current asset such as inventory for sale."
- "ROI—Return on Investment (annual rental revenues divided by original cost of equipment). Varies from $0.70:$1.00 to $2.00:$1.00, 1:1 depending on whether equipment is construction, general tool, or party. Values primarily based on multiple of EBITDA, net revenues, value of assets plus goodwill factor, customer base, organizational structure/employees & staff, physical plant facilities, including location and expansion area availability."

Expert Comments

"Business location is very important relative to competition and accessibility for customers."

Benchmark Data

Statistics (Tool and Equipment Rental)

Number of Establishments	8,882
Average Profit Margin	17.0%
Revenue per Employee	$116,400
Average Number of Employees	3.2
Average Wages per Employee	$40,244

Products and Services Segmentation

Contractor equipment	46.9%
Home tools and DIY equipment rental	27.3%
Rental of other goods	11.6%
Consumer goods rental	8.7%
Delivery, repair and other services	5.5%

Major Market Segmentation

Construction firms	24.8%
Industrial firms	21.2%
Independent builders and contractors	19.6%
Private households	18.1%
Other	8.9%
Government	7.4%

Industry Costs

Profit	17.0%
Wages	35.0%
Purchases	25.5%
Depreciation	5.1%
Marketing	1.5%
Rent & Utilities	7.7%
Other	8.2%

Market Share

United Rentals Inc. 52.1%
Sunbelt Rentals 15.4%
Hertz Global Holdings Inc. 6.4%

Source: IBISWorld, June 2016

Statistics (Party Supply Rental)

Number of Establishments	11,232
Average Profit Margin	11.2%
Revenue per Employee	$92,600
Average Number of Employees	4.6
Average Wages per Employee	$32,659

Products and Services Segmentation

Wedding rentals	34.8%
Corporate event rentals	31.3%
Other event rentals	18.7%
Birthday rentals	15.2%

Industry Costs

Profit	11.2%
Wages	35.2%
Purchases	21.6%
Depreciation	6.8%
Marketing	2.1%
Rent & Utilities	10.4%
Other	12.7%

Market Share

Classic Party Rentals	5.1%

Source: IBISWorld, November 2015

Expenses as a percentage of annual sales

Cost of goods	<10%
Payroll/labor Costs	<30%
Occupancy	<10%
Profit (estimated pretax)	05% to 15%

Industry Trend

- "The American Rental Association (ARA) latest forecast calls for equipment rental industry revenue growth in the United States of 6.7 percent in 2016 and 2017, 6.2 percent in 2018, and 5.8 percent in 2019 to reach $48.7 billion."

  Source:http://www.ararental.org/Portals/0/Documents/Press%20Releases/11.15.2015
  ForecastCallsForEvenGrowth.pdf

- "Growing industry with growth areas. Dependent on construction cycle."

Seller Financing

- "Limited to 20 percent of the sales price"
- "7-year amortization"

Questions

- "Get a depreciation schedule and verify equipment age and condition. Do a thorough due diligence. If a stock sale, find out about lawsuits and environmental issues."
- "How does business account for equipment maintenance—expense or capitalize?"

Resources

Trade Publications
- Rental Management: www.rentalmanagementmag.com

Associations
- American Rental Association: www.ararental.org

Rent-To-Own Stores (See also Rental Centers)		
SIC 7359-30	NAICS 532310	Number of Businesses/Units 6,693

Rules of Thumb

➢ 55 percent of annual sales includes inventory

Pricing Tips

- "Eight (8) times monthly gross receipts (tops), includes lock, stock (inventory) and barrel. All underlying debts would be paid off by seller at this price. I think the multiple is now less because the industry has sustained a shakeout."

Benchmark Data

Statistics (Consumer Electronics & Appliances Rental)

Number of Establishments	6,693
Average Profit Margin	10.6%
Revenue per Employee	$342,100
Average Number of Employees	3.4
Average Wages per Employee	$51,574

Products and Services Segmentation

Electronics	45.3%
Appliances	39.1%
Computers	14.5%
Other	1.1%

Industry Costs

Profit	10.6%
Wages	15.1%
Purchases	23.9%
Depreciation	11.8%
Marketing	2.1%
Rent & Utilities	7.0%
Other	29.5%

Market Share

Rent-A-Center Inc.	26.8%
Aaron's Inc.	21.9%

Source: IBISWorld, September 2016

- "The average store has annual revenue of $736,000 and serves 360 customers each year."
- "Operating costs for rent-to-own businesses are higher than traditional retail because of the ultimate return of merchandise, merchandise repair and replacement expenses, and the need to continually market the industry's services to a rotating customer base."

Product Breakdown

Furniture	36.7%
Appliances	18.6%
Electronics	24.9%
Computers	10.7%
Jewelry	.06%
Other	7.6%

Source: Association of Progressive Rental Organizations (APRO), www.rtohq.org, 2015

- The following data is a bit dated, but still of interest

"Rental Revenue per Employee—Rent-A-Center 2007 Rental Revenue per employee rose to its highest level ever—$153,930.54, up from $121,209.57 in 2006.

"Rental Revenue per Home Office Employee—After declining for four consecutive years, Rent-A-Center's Rental Revenue per Home Office Employee increased to $5,402,090.57 up from $4,843,475.71 in 2006.

"Monthly Revenue per Location—Rent-A-Center's 2007 average monthly rental revenue per location reached its highest level ever at $77,439.90, up from $58,540.74 in 2006. Note: Based on store count at the end of 2007. If based on weighted average store count, average revenue per location for 2007 would have been $70,673.08. Rent-A-Center's lowest average monthly rental revenue per location ($29,797.00) was reported in 1998, the year Renters Choice acquired Rent-A-Center. For the entire 12-year period—1996 through 2007—Rent-A-Center's average monthly revenue per location is $58,701.53.

"Rental Revenue per Square Ft.—Rent-A-Center's 2007 Rental Revenue per Square Ft., increased sharply to $202.02 up from $152.71 in 2006.

"Average Store Size—Rent-A-Center's average store size remained at 4,600 square ft. in 2007. The company's average store size has grown from a low of 3,800 square ft. in 1998."

Source: Rent-to-Own Industry Statistics, www.rtoonline.com.

Resources

Associations
- Association of Progressive Rental Organizations (APRO)—a very good site : www.rtohq.org

Repair Services

Rules of Thumb

➤ "General type—When establishing a price for a repair business which caters to the general public, the selling price should be fixtures and equipment; inventory, which is usually rather small; plus two-thirds of one year's profit."

Repossession Services

	NAICS 561491	

Rules of Thumb

➤ 85 to 95 percent of annual sales includes inventory

➤ 4 times SDE

➤ 2.5 to 3.5 times EBITDA

Pricing Tips

- "Some industry consolidation is happening by various large conglomerates."
- "Be careful of the depreciation associated with trucks. Towing is also a supplement of this industry."

Expert Comments

"There are barriers to entry in certain states which require licensing. The insurance costs are very high."

Benchmark Data

- "A successful company tracks on average how much fuel is consumed per recovery and also makes an allocation for insurance cost."
- "The average repo fee is $300.00 +."

Expenses as a percentage of annual sales

Cost of goods	10% to 15%
Payroll/labor Costs	35% to 45%
Occupancy	10% to 15%
Profit (estimated pretax)	35% to 45%

Industry Trend

- "The business will grow as the economy continues to improve."

Resale Shops

(See also Clothing Stores—Used, Consignment Shops, Used Goods)

	NAICS 453310	

Rules of Thumb

➤ 40 to 45 percent of annual sales plus paid-for inventory

Benchmark Data

- For additional Benchmark Data see Used Goods
- "According to America's Research Group, a consumer research firm, about 16–18% of Americans will shop at a thrift store during a given year. For consignment/resale shops, it's about 12–15%. To keep these figures in perspective, consider that during the same time frame, 11.4% of Americans shop in factory outlet malls, 19.6% in apparel stores and 21.3% in major department stores.

  "Resale is a multi-billion dollar a year industry. First Research estimates the resale industry in the U.S. to have annual revenues of approximately $16 billion including revenue from antique stores, which are 13% of their statistics."

  Source: "Industry Statistics & Trends," NARTS, The Association of Resale Professionals

Industry Trend

- "For the fifth year in a row, Plato's Closet and Once Upon A Child, both resale stores, made Entrepreneur Magazine's Franchise 500 List. In the 36th annual rankings, these two retailers nabbed the No. 108 and No. 140 spots overall, proving that the trend in growth of the resale industry is only growing."

  Source: "Two resale stores make top 150 franchise list" by Jacqueline Renfrow, February 3, 2015, http://www.fierceretail.com/story/two-resale-stores-make-top-150-franchise-list/2015-02-03

- "While many businesses close their doors every day, resale remains healthy and continues to be one of the fastest growing segments of retail. With new stores entering the industry and current establishments opening additional locations, the industry has experienced a growth—in number of stores—of approximately 7% a year for the past two years. This percentage reflects the estimated number of new stores opening each year, minus the businesses that close."

  Source: Industry Statistics & Trends, http://www.narts.org/

- "Name Brand Exchange, another resale company based in Phoenix, also is doing well. 'Every hanger in the store is being used,' said Tamra Thomas, sales manager for the Mesa store. 'But we never turn it away, even though we have no room in the stores.' Thomas said the resale turnover and customer traffic at Name Brand are very high. 'It is crazy busy right at this time,' she said. 'People are selling clothes to get money for vacation, save up for college or for gas.' As a result, sales have increased at the two Name Brand locations. 'We make at least $10,000 to $15,000 more a month in sales than we did five years ago.' Traci Nelson, another manager at the Mesa location, said business depends on the economy. 'Everyone is trying to get something any way they can to get extra gas money,' she said."

  Source: "Business is booming at used clothing, consignment shops during economic downturn" by Ashley Macha, www.bizjournals.com/phoenix/stories

- "The resale industry is one of the few recession-proof segments of retailing. Not only does it survive during economic slowdowns, but it grows and thrives. The appeal is twofold… consumers are attracted to buying quality merchandise at a fraction of the original cost, and there is a financial incentive to sell, consign, or donate their unused or unwanted items."

  Source: www.narts.org

Residential Care—Other Facilities

Rules of Thumb

➤ 51% percent of annual revenues includes inventory

➤ 1.8 times SDE includes inventory

➤ 3 times EBIT

➤ 2.9 times EBITDA

Benchmark Data

Expenses as a percentage of annual sales

Cost of goods	08%
Payroll/labor Costs	03%
Occupancy	0
Profit (estimated pretax)	07%

Industry Trend

- "Revenue, profit, and demand projected to decline, industry expected to contract."

Seller Financing

- "Outside financing"

Questions

- "Payor mix, market share, patient demographic dat."

Restaurants—An Introduction

Restaurants—QUICK CHECK—2016

Bagels	30% of annual sales (not as much interest today)
Bars	50% of annual sales (very much in demand)
Bar & Grill (40% liquor)	40% of annual sales (very popular)
Barbecue	30% of annual sales (limited pool of buyers)
Bistros	30% of annual sales (typically chef owned)
Brew Pubs	40% of annual sales (a lot of interest in craft beer)
Billiard Parlors	40% of annual sales (limited pool of buyers)
Cajun	30% of annual sales (not big in New England)
Catering Businesses	30% to 40% of annual sales (seller may have to stay for an earnout)
Caribbean	30% of annual sales
Chicken	30% of annual sales
Chinese	30% of annual sales (of reported sales)
Coffee Houses	30% of annual sales
Continental	30% of annual sales (heavy/rich menus, not in vogue today)
Delis	30% to 40% of annual sales (higher value if only5/6 days)
Diners	30% of annual sales (competing with coffee shops)
Fine Dining	30% of annual sales (goodwill lost when chef/owner leaves)
Gourmet Shops	20% of annual sales (+ cost of inventory which can be expensive)
Hamburgers	30% to 40% of annual sales (very popular today)
Ice Cream	30% to 40% of annual sales (higher price in warmer climate)

Irish ....40% of annual sales (if higher liquor sales)
Italian .... 30% of annual sales (popular because of low food costs)
Mexican .... 30% of annual sales (popular concept today)
Night Clubs .... 30% of annual sales (high risk rate lowers value)
Pancake Houses... 30% of annual sales
Pizza (if delivery) .... 30% of annual sales
Pizza (if no delivery) .... 40% of annual sales
Sandwiches .... 40% of annual sales (not expensive to open)
Seafood ....30% of annual sales (very high food costs)
Sports Bars .... 40% of annual sales (beverage sales over 40%)
Steakhouses .... 30% of annual sales (higher food costs)

Source: Business Brokerage Press and the Boston Restaurant Group, 2016

VALUING A RESTAURANT

- FAIR MARKET VALUE
  "The asking price is what the seller wants. The selling price is what the seller receives. Fair Market Value is the highest price the buyer is willing to pay and the lowest price the seller is willing to accept."

  There is no formula for valuing a restaurant. Each business needs to be considered on an individual basis. There are, however, certain benchmarks and valuation approaches and methods that enable an experienced appraiser to determine the most probable price for which the business could be sold on the open market

- INCOME STATEMENT ANALYSIS
  The restaurant's operating expenses will be consolidated into four categories to more accurately reflect industry format and to allow for more meaningful comparisons with the industry averages:

SALES	$	%	COMMENTS
Cost of Goods			
Payroll/Benefits			
Other Expenses			
Occupancy Costs			
Income			

- CASH FLOW ANALYSIS
  When valuing a company it is customary to analyze the financial statements and make adjustments, where necessary, to better indicate the true earnings capacity of the business:

ADJUSTMENTS
1.
2.
3. etc.
Total Adjustments

- VALUATION ANALYSIS

  The following approaches and methods should be considered in the valuation of any restaurant:

Approaches/Methods	Sales/Cash Flow		Multiple	Indicated Value
Multiple of Sale		X		
Multiple of Cash Flow		X		
Sales to Investment Ratio		%		
Appraisal Databases		X		
Industry Rules of Thumb		X		

Source: Charles Perkins, The Boston Restaurant Group

- WHY RESTAURANTS FAIL

  A Cornell University study noted that the first year failure rate for restaurants is between 20 percent and 25 percent. Major contributors to a restaurant's failure in today's market: 1.The concept is not well defined – you know what you are going to get at Five Guys Burgers. 2. Poor management and lack of leadership skills. 3. Inconsistent customer service and product preparation. 4. The business being undercapitalized. 5. Ownership being unable or unwilling to react.

  Source: Charles Perkins, The Boston Restaurant Group

Benchmark Data

- "Summary of Industry standards
  Prime Cost
  - ✓ Full-service—65% or less of total sales
  - ✓ Table-service—60% or less of total sales

  Food Cost
  - ✓ Generally—28% to 32% of total food sales

  Alcoholic Beverage Costs
  - ✓ Liquor—18% to 20% of liquor sales
  - ✓ Bar consumables—04% to 05% of liquor sales
  - ✓ Bottled beer—24% to 28% of bottled beer sales
  - ✓ Draft beer—15% to 18% of draft beer sales
  - ✓ Wine—35% to 45% of wine sales

  Nonalcoholic Beverage Costs
  - ✓ Soft drinks (post-mix) 10% to 15% of soft drink sales
  - ✓ Regular coffee—15% to 20% of regular coffee sales
  - ✓ Specialty coffee—12% to 18% of specialty coffee sales
  - ✓ Iced tea—05% to 10% of iced tea sales

  Paper Cost
  - ✓ Full-service—01% to 02% of total sales
  - ✓ Limited-service—03% to 04% of total sales

  Payroll Cost
  - ✓ Full-service—30% to 35% of total sales
  - ✓ Limited-service—25% to 30% of total sales

Management Salaries
- ✓ 10% or less of total sales

Hourly Employee Gross Payroll
- ✓ Full-service—18% to 20% of total sales
- ✓ Limited-service—15% to 18% of total sales

Employee Benefits
- ✓ 05% to 06% of total sales
- ✓ 20% to 23% of gross payroll

Sales per Square Foot
- ✓ Losing Money: Full-service—$150 or less; Limited-service—$200 or less
- ✓ Break-even: Full-service—$150 to $250; Limited-service—$200 to $300
- ✓ Moderate Profit: Full-service—$250 to $350; Limited-service—$300 to $400
- ✓ High Profit: Full-service—More than $350; Limited-service—More than $400

Rent and Occupancy
- ✓ Rent—06% or less of total sales
- ✓ Occupancy—10% or less of total sales"

Source: Information provided by Jim Laube, founder of www.RestaurantOwner.com

- "Profitability Standards

Full-service
- ✓ Under $150/square foot = little chance of generating a profit
- ✓ At $150 to $250/square foot = break even up to 05% of sales
- ✓ At $250 to $325/square foot = 05% to 10% of sales

Limited-service
- ✓ Under $200/square foot = little chance of averting an operating loss
- ✓ At $200 to $300/square foot = break even up to 05% of sales
- ✓ At $300 to $400/square foot = 05% to 10% of sales (before income taxes)"

Source: www.bakertilly.com

- "Facts at a Glance 2016
  - ✓ $782.7 billion: Restaurant industry sales.
  - ✓ 1 million+: Restaurant locations in the United States.
  - ✓ 14.4 million: Restaurant industry employees.
  - ✓ 1.7 million: New restaurant jobs created by the year 2026.
  - ✓ 10%: Restaurant workforce as part of the overall U.S. workforce.
  - ✓ Nine in 10: Restaurant managers who started at entry level.
  - ✓ Eight in 10: Restaurant owners who started their industry careers in entry-level positions.
  - ✓ Nine in 10: Restaurants with fewer than 50 employees.
  - ✓ Seven in 10: Restaurants that are single-unit operations."

Source: www.restaurant.org/News-Research/Research/Facts-at-a-Glance

- "Top challenges facing restaurant owners:

Finding and keeping quality employees	48%
Minimum wage increases or pressures	27%
Health care costs	10%
Changing consumer menu expectations	06%
Securing prime real estate	04%
Other	04%"

Source: NRN 2016 Operator Survey

Industry Trend

- "Restaurant industry sales are expected to reach $783 billion in 2016. Although this will represent the seventh consecutive year of real growth in restaurant sales, the rate of growth remains moderate. The restaurant industry will remain the nation's second-largest private sector employer with a workforce of 14.4 million."

  Source: http://www.restaurant.org/News-Research/Research/Forecast-2016

- "If you haven't yet partnered with a delivery service, it's time to do so, according to a recent report from market researcher company The NPD Group. If the group's Delivery—A Growth Opportunity on the Horizon forecast is correct, off-premise foodservice will continue to outpace overall restaurant industry traffic growth over the next decade.

  "While restaurant delivery is nothing new, it was until recently the purview of pizza places and, in urban markets, small, independent Asian restaurants. Now, of course, foodservice delivery outfits like DoorDash are making it easier for restaurants to meet customers on their own turf.

  "Delivery services such as Eat24, Grub Hub and Seamless continue to roll out in some smaller markets, while UberEATS and Amazon Prime Now restaurant delivery are making significant headway nationally. As these operations expand, delivery will continue to see significant growth and even outpace regular restaurant traffic growth.

  "How much has the demand for delivery risen? Delivery traffic, outside of pizza, has increased 33 percent since 2012. Much of this gain seems to be at the expense of traditional quick-service pizza delivery, which decreased three percent over the same period, according to NPD."

  Source: "Report: Delivery shows double-digit growth," February 16, 2016, http://restaurant-hospitality.com/consumer-trends/report-delivery-shows-double-digit-growth

- "Studies vary, but a report published by a Cornell University journal found that about 60 percent of restaurants fail in their first three years. . . . 'There are two main reasons restaurants fail,' the chef said. The first one was insufficient startup capital. 'The second,' he said, holding the creamer cup at eye level for inspection, 'is waste.'"

  Source: *Boston Globe Magazine*, May 29, 2016

- "The restaurant industry remains the nation's second-largest private-sector employer, with 13.5 million people working in the business. Restaurants are projected to add jobs at a national rate of 2.8% this year. Over the next 10 years, the fastest restaurant job growth is projected to occur in Arizona with a rate of 15.6%, followed by Texas with 15.3%, and Florida with 15%. Nevada (14.7%) and Georgia (14.4%) round out the top five states with the fastest restaurant job growth."

  Source: "2015 Pizza Power Report," *PMQ Pizza Magazine*

- "According to Technomic, Americans now dine outside the home an average of 4.2 times per week. That practically makes it America's kitchen."

  Source: "Top 10 trends in food service industry" by Jim Sullivan, for Post-Crescent Media, May 16, 2015

- "Sixty-one percent of the 1,000 people surveyed by the NRA said they eat Italian food at least once a month, and 26 percent said they eat it a few times a year. By comparison, the other two of the 'big three' ethnic cuisines in the United States, Mexican and Chinese, were eaten at least once a month by 50 percent and 36 percent of those surveyed, respectively, and a few times a year by 31 percent and 42 percent of respondents, respectively.

  "The NRA defines 'ethnic' cuisine broadly as any cuisine originating in a different country or within a specific region of the United States. The recently released study was the first the NRA has conducted in 16 years."

  Source: "Survey: Italian remains most popular ethnic cuisine" by Bret Thorn, August 28, 2015, nrn.com

- "A three percent drop in independent restaurant unit counts compared to a year ago brought the total U.S. restaurant count down by one percent to 630,511 units, according to a census of U.S. commercial restaurant locations compiled in the spring and fall each year by industry tracker NPD Group. Full-service independent operators took the biggest hit, with a unit loss of three percent. Quick-service independent units held their ground, NPD says."

  Source: www.restaurant-hospitality.com August 3, 2015

- "For the first time on record in December, monthly sales at restaurants exceeded grocery stores sales, according to data from the U.S Census Bureau. This development was hinted at through preliminary data releases in recent months, but was officially confirmed by today's annual benchmark of Census data.

  "The gap between monthly grocery store sales and restaurant sales started gradually shrinking in 2010—a trend that was partially due to the increase in consumers buying their groceries at big box stores. However, the most striking part of the chart is the dramatic shift toward restaurants that occurred in the last 10 months. In June 2014, grocery store sales exceeded restaurant sales by $1.6 billion. By April 2015, the gap had essentially reversed, with restaurant sales moving out in front by $1.5 billion. In fact, the $3.1 billion sales shift registered during the last 10 months is nearly as much as occurred during the previous 4.5 years."

  Source: http://www.restaurant.org/News-Research/News/Restaurant-sales-surpass-grocery-store-sales-for-t

---

Restaurants—Asian (See also Restaurants, Restaurants—Chinese)

	NAICS Full Service—722511; Limited Service—722513

Rules of Thumb

➤ 30 to 32 percent of annual sales plus inventory

Benchmark Data

Statistics (Sushi Restaurants)

Number of Establishments	3,450
Average Profit Margin	7.2%
Revenue per Employee	$77,300
Average Number of Employees	8.9
Average Wages per Employee	$27,044

Products and Services Segmentation

Full-service dining sushi sales	62.0%
Beverage sales	26.0%
Take-out sushi sales	12.0%

Industry Costs

Profit	7.2%
Wages	35.0%
Purchases	24.8%
Depreciation	2.4%
Marketing	4.6%
Rent/Utilities	5.5%
Other	20.5%

Source: IBISWorld, June 2016

Industry Trend

- "And Asian in general is one of the fastest growing categories in the U.S., though it's very fragmented.

Resources

Trade Publications

- Asian Restaurant News: www.a-r-n.net/

Restaurants—Barbecue (See also Restaurants)

	NAICS 722513	

Rules of Thumb

➤ 30 percent of annual sales plus inventory

Benchmark Data

- Estimated Annual Sales: Sonny's Real Pit Bar-B-Q: $1.9 million; Smokey Bones Bar & Fire Grill: $2.6 million

---

Restaurants—Chinese (See also Restaurants, Restaurants—Asian)

	NAICS full service—722511; limited service—722513	

Rules of Thumb

➤ 30 percent of annual sales plus inventory

Restaurants—Full Service

(See also Restaurants—An Introduction, Limited Service)

SIC 5812-08	NAICS 722511	

Rules of Thumb

➤ 20 to 35 percent of annual sales includes inventory

➤ 1 to 3 times SDE includes inventory

➤ 2.5 to 3.5 times EBIT

➤ 3 to 4 times EBITDA

➤ Note: California restaurants seem to be receiving higher multiples than the rest of the country with the possible exception of New York City. For example: 35 to 40 percent of annual sales and 2 to 5 times SDE.

Pricing Tips

- "Profitable restaurants are being sold between 2 to 3 times SDE. However, distressed or closed restaurants sell as an 'Asset Sale' and sometimes are a great buy. Even some landlords are asking for key money for a closed or second-generation restaurant. Removing an unprofitable seller from the lease liability may be a good deal for the seller... even if the seller does not make money."

- "Depends on following:
  1. Years in business (should be at least three)
  2. Terms and conditions of current or negotiated lease.
  3. Location of business
  4. Type or nature of business; small or large cafe, ethnic or standard food service, large or small restaurant, etc."

- "Restaurants must be valued on a case by case basis. Many factors affect value: location, equipment, discretionary earnings and the valuation of long-term leases. Because restaurants in Florida and other tourism locales tend to be seasonal, often adjustments can be made for other services or potential profit streams in other areas: catering, etc. Because financing is often offered, a value to the financial package can be given. We evaluate restaurants with regard to the leasehold improvements and value of the negotiated long- term lease. Recasting can often be challenging because of the cash unaccounted for in these types of businesses, so sellers will often augment the deal with financing or earned-out options. With rising housing costs in Florida it is challenging in many markets to find good restaurant space. 'Key money' or 'opportunity cost' is not unheard of."

- "Asset sale for restaurant/bar that is not profitable is common. There is no rule of thumb for an asset sale valuation. Prices vary according to desirability of the location, the type of permits/licenses (i.e., entertainment permit, dance permit, alcohol license) that come with the premises and the condition of the FFE."

- "Gross sales are no longer a valid indicator in my market. There is a wide range of values because it is a large category and encompasses everything from a deli franchise to a fine dining restaurant, or bar and club. The lease terms are always important, as a percentage of sales and for the length of time. Perceived risk of transferability based on skill level required and role of owner, hours of operation, and age and condition of equipment are other factors."

- "Location and the value of the lease (is it undermarket? Length of time left on the lease)"

- "Occupancy cost should be in the 7% area...payroll in the area of 25%. Obviously there are a number of facets of operation that affect any rule of thumb."

- "The value of a license to sell alcohol varies from town to town. It is critical to find out what the market value of a license is in a subject's particular town or city. For example an all-alcohol license in Boston can cost $375,000–$400,000 in today's marketplace.

  "Another pricing tip is to make sure the rent is competitive within the market place. If the rent is high on a dollar-per-square-foot basis or the annual escalations are unsustainable it will have an adverse impact on the selling price of the business."

- "Unlike in other industries, many buyers in this sphere care more about top line revenues and significant fixed costs like rents than they do cash flow. This is the case because most experienced operators know the expense ratios a given operation should be able to achieve."

- "Generally there are four different valuation methods used to place a value to a restaurant or bar.

  "A. PERCENTAGE OF REVENUE: One method is the percentage of revenue method. To derive a value, one merely selects a percentage, say 30%, and multiplies it by the revenue or sales of the business not including sales taxes. For example, if the business had revenues of $1,000,000 and the percentage factor of 30% was used, then the business value is $300,000. This method is used when the financials are not readily available or are not accurate.

"To determine the percentage to use, one takes into account five factors. (1) the strength of the revenue, (2) the condition of the facility, (3) the lease and location (4) the strength of the management and cost management of the business and finally (5) the type of restaurant business. I generally look at each item and assign a number between 1 and 4, 4 being it's awesome and 1 being it's awful. The closer the average is to 4, the closer the percentage factor is to 40%–45%. The closer to 1, then the percentage will be closer to 20%. This method, in my opinion, has some serious flaws and leads to bad valuations. I don't suggest using it.

"B. SELLER'S DISCRETIONARY INCOME (SDI): This method takes some education and skills to accurately apply the concepts, but it is the standard the banks use to give loans to buyers. Simply put, SDI attempts to identify all the seller's perks including salary, payroll taxes, personal auto expenses, medical insurance and any other personal items included in the profit and loss statement that's truly not a business expense. To arrive at a value, one uses the SDI and multiples it by a market multiple. Every region and country has differing multiples and only a well-trained and educated broker can help you determine what you should use. For example, the average multiple across the U.S. is about 2.2 times. That means one takes the SDI and multiples it by 2.2 to determine the value. However, every region has differing multiples. In New Jersey for example, the multiple tends to be significantly higher than say Delaware. Why? I think it is in the variability of the earnings. The higher the variability, the lower the certainty; therefore the lower the multiple. I use the same logic to determine the multiple as I do in the example of Percentage of Revenue method described above, and adjust for regions. A 4 will receive a multiple in the 2.8–3.0 range, while a 1 will receive a 1–1.5 range.

"C. CAPITALIZATION OF INCOME: This technique is widely used to value income producing assets such as commercial real estate. The premise is based on what the market expected return on investment is at the time the transaction takes place. The SDI must be calculated first as described above. Then that income is divided by the capitalization rate (Cap rate) to derive the value. For example, if the business' SDI is $100,000 and the determined Cap Rate is 30%, then the math is $100,000/.3 or $333,333.

"To determine the cap rate is the challenge and a simple drop of a few percentage points can make a huge difference in price. For example, in the above example, if the Cap Rate were 35% the value would be $285,000. There are several considerations to think about when trying to determine the proper Cap Rate. First, the higher the risk of the investment, the higher the percentage used. In other words, when the income is risky, the expected return the market demands is higher. Restaurants are very risky. So I like to start out at the 35–40% range and go from there. Then again I apply the method described above and assign a number to the business. The closer the number is to 4, the closer my cap rate will be to 25–30%. The closer the number is to 1 the closer my cap rate will be to 50%.

"D. REPLACEMENT COST METHOD: Finally, the replacement cost method assumes a buyer pays the seller a large premium over the income value and annual gross revenue techniques in order to benefit from the existing investment in the restaurant facility, the lease and the location of the restaurant. In other words, a buyer will pay for the right to avoid spending hundreds of thousands and even possibly a million+ dollars to avoid all the city regulations, delays and headaches of building a new restaurant. How much a buyer pays depends on the buyer's need. Some buyers will pay more for the same space because they may see the value in a lease or location while others may see that they have too much improvements to make to convert to their existing concept."

- "Be careful with add backs. Some pricing varies heavily by market and saturation levels by segments."
- "A national franchise restaurant will typically sell for higher multiples than a mom & pop; key factors to consider include rent as a percentage of revenue, payroll cost and food cost."
- "Rent and lease terms are an important part of the equation. Lease costs need to stay under 9% annually. Longevity can boost value. Sales numbers need to be verified against bank deposits along with credit card statements. Cash that cannot be verified will not justify an add back for valuation purposes. A lot of times small Mom & Pop type restaurants have family members working there. If that is the case a negative add back needs to be done to show cost of replacing that person or persons. Seller financing will help increase the value of the restaurant."
- "Occupancy costs must be in line with revenues and usually not exceed 7–10%."
- "Equipment age and maintenance important. Lease with market rent and good terms very important."
- "Don't put a lot of weight for rule of thumb on annual sales, since the occupancy cost has increased significantly in the last 3 years. It's the same for the labor cost, therefore, it is very critical to multiply with SDE. The multiple of SDE goes up for the restaurants with $100,000 + SDE, and if the restaurant has a full liquor license type 47, B&W type 41 license, catering license type 58, entertainment license, etc."
- "Most restaurants with liquor sell for 70% multiple. Without liquor the ratio drops to 35-40% of sales. Light menu a big plus. Home cooking hard to duplicate for a buyer."
- "Price can vary with cash flow and, with leased properties, the quality and length of the lease."
- "Does the owner just manage the business or is he the chef or cook? Business is more valuable if owner just manages the business."
- "Ease of operation—five-day operation worth more than a seven-day. Always look at food to bar sales as to what percent."
- "Lease should be no more than six to eight percent of sales. Food cost and payroll costs are the key items to control after lease costs."
- "Much depends on the size of the revenues and earnings; the multiples increase above $500k in sales. Gross profit should be 70% or better."
- "We never use gross sales to determine a price. Only a multiple of SDE is used. For businesses that rent their space, the average is 2X SDE with 1.7–1.8X selling faster than 2X. For businesses that own their real estate, the formula becomes 1.4X SDE plus real estate--either appraised value or agreed. "The main factor that drives pricing from a sales perspective is if the restaurant has liquor or is just food. From an EBITDA or SDE provable figures drive the

multiple as well as the condition of the equipment and decor in addition to the lease terms. The type of food served also will be a factor; the more ethnic, the more difficult to sell."

- "The more technical the business, the lower the percentage of gross sales. Another way to say that is the more difficult to operate the business and the more intense the management involvement, the lower the multiple. Fast food sells at higher multiples than a white tablecloth restaurant."

- "Lease terms and rent are a key factor. There is a great range of complexity within the industry that also contributes to determination within the range of 2.0–2.75."

- "Pricing based on cash flow can range from 2.0 to approx. 2.5 depending on several factors: lease terms, condition of FF&E, stability and years established, hours of operation, complexity of operations. Location is always a factor but is generally already reflected in the financials. Unprofitable restaurants are marketable based on location, infrastructure in place, ABC Licensing, quality of FF&E, and lease terms."

- "In suburban markets occupancy costs should not exceed 10%. Restaurants with revenue under $1 MM are less desirable and likely treated as startups from a lending standpoint unless significant cash flow can be shown."

- "Including real estate, the price can be up to gross sales and up to 35–40% in leased space, but debt service should always be calculated to see if it makes sense for a buyer. This is going down as restaurants have become less desirable in recent years. The higher end restaurants are the toughest to sell, as the down payment needed is greater."

- "Each deal has a different set of circumstance depending on four factors I use: (1) strength of revenue—is it growing, flat, declining? (2) profitability—is it growing, flat decreasing? (3) lease and location—is it a high traffic location or a destination location? Are there plenty of years left on the lease? How's the rent compared to market and compared to the sales volume? And are there restrictions in the lease that could hurt a sale? (4) Finally, the condition of the restaurant and its equipment. Is the place in great shape or a bit worn? Is it clean or filthy? I score each of these factors to generate an average score and relate that to an estimated value."

- "Since 95% of all restaurant sales are seller-financed, the determined price is a direct function of 4 components: goodwill (sales), lease (7% of sales is ideal), equipment, seller financing...how is it structured."

- "Occupancy costs should be in line with industry averages of 6–8%."

- "90% of the restaurants in this market are sold as asset sales and have no verifiable cash flow or books and records. These are priced according to the market which is typically between $50K and $250K, depending on type of restaurant, and if the restaurant has a hood, grease trap, etc... Rent is a major factor in determining price. Restaurants with above market leases stay on the market a long time and are difficult to sell. The value of a full 4COP liquor license in Miami Dade is in the $175K range and this must be added to the price of the FF&E and Leasehold Improvements. Neighborhood is a huge factor in this market with restaurants in the top neighborhoods selling at higher levels. Restaurants for sale with good books and records and verifiable payroll records that are cash flowing are scarce in this market, and when they are available they typically sell at a premium.(3X SDE all day) There are many buyers in this market looking to obtain their visas. The most common type of visa buyer that we are seeing is for the E2 Investor visa program where the purchase requirement seems to be in the $100K range. The story of the guy that needs to obtain his visa and is willing to substantially overpay for a restaurant is a myth. Gross sales and rent are the best value indicators to me."

- "Proper use of the SDE formula is the most accurate way of valuing an independent restaurant with sales under $3 million per year."
- "Seasonal restaurants, 'takeout,' and 'to-go' style restaurants with strong cash flow are desirable and trade at a higher SDE multiple and gross sales multiple (40%). Year-round full-service restaurants with sales under $500k are less desirable and trade at (20–30% of sales) depending on profit."
- "The multiples increase as revenue and earnings increase due to economies of scale. Cost of goods should be at or below 30%. Must look for cash that is unaccounted for and non-operating assets and expenses."
- "Multiples are the highest possible. Need to look at prime costs to make sure they are within industry averages, must normalize owner's salary, and rent needs to be less than 8% as a ratio of sales (6% is ideal but not achievable in some markets)."
- "Twice the probable yearly seller's profit"
- "Key factors are the food cost, payroll cost and rent expense as a percentage of total revenue. Rent should be about 6% to 8% of total revenue. Food costs and payroll costs vary depending on the type of restaurant. Franchised units typically sell for more than mom and pop units."
- "You need to take into consideration the location, rent, any way to bring expenses down within reason and the concept."
- "Age of equipment and F&F very important and lease. Numerous leases are priced over market rents; it is important on a feasible rent structure ideal 6%-8% of sales volume. Equipment ages quickly in this industry key in that it is maintained on a regular basis."
- "We use Owner's Discretionary Benefit exclusively because a new owner wants to know what will be available for them. The cash component of a restaurant owner's owner benefit must be clearly proved; otherwise we refuse the listing."
- "100% of gross sales if the real estate is included and 30% if in leased space."
- "Rent ratio over 10% lowers the SDE, EBIT, EBITDA and the percent of annual sales. The percent of annual sales is reduced point for point on every point rent ratio above 10%."
- "% of annual gross needs to be supported by SDE so higher prices get higher % of sales and lower %'s may have no SDE and may be just the sale of the tangible and intangible assets. Lots of other factors to consider including comps for like businesses."
- "Obtain bank statements showing deposits to help verify income. Obtain check register to verify expenses. POS numbers will usually be higher as most of the cash will show on the POS (but maybe not the deposits). Taking a really good prospect to lunch or dinner almost always pays off! For businesses conveying real estate, our 13-year average of multiples for scores of restaurant sales shows a multiple of owner's discretionary income of 3.1X which includes real estate. These same sales show a multiple of 1.6X owner's discretionary income plus negotiated real estate value. I have averaged 98% of the asking price for 13 years using these formulas."
- "Make sure to adjust the pay for family members working in the restaurant to current market rates for equal skill level."

- "Compare COG to industry standards. Rent factor vs. sales. Extraneous cost to generate sales, e.g., music, price deals, advertising, hours of operation."
- "Adjust for exceptionally low operating hours vs. extremely long hours."
- "Restaurants with small profits are worth more as an asset sale than based on sales or net cash flow. The cost of opening a new restaurant makes over 50% of the restaurants for sale only worth what the buyer feels he would have to spend to open a new one. The cost of permits and fees has driven the cost of new restaurants through the roof, and buyers should always consider taking over an existing one even if not profitable."
- "May require reverse gross margin proofing. EBITDA formulas typically larger restaurants."
- "Minimum length of lease: 10 years; consistent sales history over three years. Assumes no major renovations required. Pricing for going concern only with market rent."

Expert Comments

"Buying a restaurant may take a couple of months, so it is very important to prepare the buyer or the seller for this event. It is not an easy task.

"The buyer should have experience and reserves before even thinking of owning a restaurant . It is a real job that requires long hours and lots of energy. The most important items on the list are the lease and the landlord's approval. If the buyer does not have extensive restaurant experience, a sandwich/sub shop or a smoothie or juice bar will be recommended. A long lease with options is highly desirable. The ideal lease will be a percentage over the gross (08% to 12%).

"Experienced restaurant owners are looking for 2nd generation restaurants either closed or in distress. The value, even if it is closed, is immense. Most likely there is a hood and grease trap fire suppression system, and all the impact fees have been paid. It may take up to a year or more to open a restaurant from zero. Buying a second generation one will save you time and money."

"Restaurants are a very risky business, and lots of competition is always present. 70 to 80 % of restaurants close the doors within 5 years or less."

"Buy when you have plenty of money to carry you for 6 months. Sell when you're making money! Never wait until you must sell!"

"SDE is and should be a key factor in any analysis of this business."

"BUYING: Use a seasoned consultant and broker in the restaurant industry who knows how to interpret the seller's financials and look for hidden problems.

SELLING: Again, use a seasoned consultant and business broker who can properly vet your potential buyers for a match that will succeed. Closing a sale is not enough—you want to see a buyer candidate who has the skills and resources to continue to be successful in this very challenging business."

"For a small- to moderate-sized operation, ease of replication is very high. Location is often key."

"With all of the TV shows and glamorization around restaurants, we see more people diving in from other backgrounds."

"Restaurants have high turnover rates."

"If the person has a family, it is important to have their support due to the long hours involved. I try to give sellers advice on how to categorize their expenses and make sure they can validate any addbacks. Buyers don't accept the creative adjustments to cost of goods these days. Sales must be documented, including catering which is often outside of the POS system. Sellers should continue with maintenance of both the front of the house and kitchen. Make sure to always ask for another option on the lease whenever exercising an option to extend. It is not a good idea to be on a month-to-month basis when trying to sell."

"In my market area, consumers continue to dine out so the customer base is strong, but expenses continue to increase so the margins are thin. There is a trend toward more limited service versus full-service, due to the cost of labor."

"Be willing to share the risk with owner financing."

"Restaurants have become a bit of a commodity. The plus side of this is there is a large and fluid market. The negative is that barriers to entry are low and competition high."

"Be smart and keep the owner involved if you are the buyer and seller finances the sale."

"The industry is experiencing shrinking profitability and shrinking disposable income per household—all making the risk greater for startup restaurants. Startups are needed to find the best locations and fair rent. Today, because the leasing market is recovering, the search for the ideal location and rent is becoming increasingly difficult but more important. 'Better to buy a printing press already printing money rather than building a new one and hoping it works.' This is my philosophy when speaking with a client who wants to open a new restaurant business."

"The restaurant/food service industry can be volatile and needs hard work. If a restaurant has systems and procedures in place, it can be very valuable and worth a lot."

"Food industry is highly competitive and easily duplicated in some cases. Real estate has become more critical in recent years."

"The industry can change quickly depending on many factors. Consumer spending is the key economic factor to consider---when the economy slumps, restaurants have a tougher time. Facilities need periodic remodeling and upgrades in order to remain competitive. The minimum wage battle is of great concern to restaurants."

"Do not buy a restaurant if you've never worked in one before, unless it's large enough that you can hire a knowledgeable GM and you as owner would have only that one employee to supervise."

"Verify the figures and inspect the equipment and insure the lease term is good."

"Buyer should consider the minimum wage increase for the next 5 years and factor that into the labor expenses. Sales should be in the financial statement; today's buyers are very careful, and don't want to pay for just guessing. If the seller wants top dollar, then the seller has to show the top books. Gone are those days of buying a restaurant with observation only, with no books and records. If the restaurant doesn't have good books, then I value it based on sale of assets in place."

"With liquor, hard to duplicate. Without liquor, much easier to open a restaurant."

"It's all about leasing and location in pricing and marketing."

"With the overreach of government regulation and the shrinking profit margins, success becomes a daunting task that is only attained with hard work, a competent staff, a good location, and hands-on management."

"A significant portion of the restaurant/bar business is from cash sales. A buyer should verify that sales reported by the owner are accurate."

"The restaurant business is a grueling one, and most sales are motivated by burnout of the owner after some period of years. Restaurants serving three meals, 7 days a week are most difficult to sell as they are burnout-prone operations. Primary traits of successful operators are drive, ability to multitask, human relations skills, ability to analyze a business and stay on top of costs. Everyone wants a restaurant because they think it is a dinner party every evening and don't realize the commitment a restaurant takes."

"Costs of food and labor result in small profit margin. Very competitive, but industry overall has demand from consumers. Cost of entry can be very high relative to return on investment if doing a new build-out. Recommend second generation facility for this reason. Usually cost effective to buy an existing restaurant even if paying some goodwill and then changing the concept."

"Sellers need to understand that if they are the ones who made the initial capital investment, they may not recoup their investment. I try to make them understand that when they opened it was based on returning the investment in the form of operating profits over the course of ownership (years). Market value based on cash flow may not justify a price that would equal the high cost of investment. Normally the reason for sale is something other than, or in addition to, simply making money from the sale. Buyers should ask the typical questions about reason for sale and what the seller would do if he or she were to stay longer. The landlord relationship should be discussed. Competitive changes in the area should be researched."

"There is typically a very large capital investment to open a restaurant in compliance with building and health codes. Restaurants can usually be sold, whether profitable or not, mainly because of the high cost of build-out. Asset sales for conversion are common unless the restaurant is not viable, usually due to lease or location. Industry trend—there will always be a need for restaurants as people dine out for convenience or pleasure, but cost of goods, cost of labor, and regulatory environment continue to squeeze the profit margin which makes the business challenging and risky. Ease of replication—in relation to some other businesses I would say it is easy to create and open with the exception of the high cost of initial build-out and remodeling. It is not too difficult to open especially if the infrastructure is already in place, but it can be difficult to make a profit. Operational experience is important although many enter the business without the recommended experience, which then justifies the opinion that this is a high risk category."

"Experience is not required but preferred. Successful owners can run all aspects of their operation (including the kitchen); for restaurants performing $1MM or under this is a must, whereas larger operations (>$1MM) can allocate more payroll for specialists."

"Make sure you have a busy location with a lease no more than 10% of the gross sales."

"The buyer should first sit down with an expert and let the expert explain to them the pluses and minuses of buying a restaurant. Too many buyers function strictly on an emotional level. With the help of someone who knows that type of business, ask for actual food and beverage purchases. Get a list of the suppliers and call them to verify."

"This is a lifestyle, not a business, in most cases. Be prepared to put in long hours until systems, policies, procedures and a reliable staff (including managers) are in place. Restaurant experience is nearly always required to obtain financing due to the high risk and historical failure rate."

"Location, location, location. Also critically important, cleanliness, customer service and food quality."

"Normalize owner and/or manager salaries. Question how many hours the owner is working. Be very careful with lease options that are at market rent. If it is a triple net lease, check and see if the building is for sale. As an example; the current owner paid $800K 10 years ago. He wants to sell as an investment property. New landlord pays $1,600,000. Taxes that the tenant must pay just went from $15,000 annual to $30,000 or more. Nothing the buyer of the business can do but he should be prepared that it may happen in strong markets."

"I will advise the buyer to make sure that he watches the activity during the busy times, to be ready to spend enough time in the business in order to manage it correctly, that this type of business needs a full time owner operator to be successful and grow the business, and to make sure that he hires a due diligence expert that is familiar with restaurants. I will advise the seller to price the business in a realistic way since most of the businesses on the market for sale are restaurants. I will show the seller sold comps in his area, and also tell him to keep all his records in order to prove the numbers during due diligence."

"If the restaurant is leased, make sure that the lease is assumable and that renewal options exist so that similar rent going forward can be obtained."

"Understand the industry plan, budget, P&L weekly. Work hard to have the best service and food; understand the numbers and what they tell you."

"Develop a good business plan and make your changes slowly. Don't spend all your money on leasehold improvements! Buy the real estate if you can."

"Experience is very important in this field. Majority of restaurants close the door or sell within the first 5 years."

"The rental rate per the lease agreement is very important. Watch out for percentage rent clauses as well. A below-market lease with years to go is a big benefit. A short lease or above-market rent is a problem."

"Barrier to entry can be restricted by number of pouring licenses in town or municipality."

R - Rules of Thumb

"Competition in the surrounding area is not much of a factor because more restaurants together become a reason to visit a location (provided they are different concepts)."

"1. Competition is daunting. Big chains can & do kill independents. 2. Very risky business due in large part to competition but also changing customer attitudes and the media. 3. Profit trends are down due to increasing labor costs and competition. 4. Location, location, location! 5. Tough to sell due to all other factors. 6. The field is growing but is being diluted by grocery and big discount stores selling pre-packaged meals. 7. Most any concept can be fairly easily replicated in menu and design. The key is in quality, quantity and service."

"You never know why one concept works or doesn't, but location is key and you're only as good as your servers!"

Benchmark Data

Statistics (Chain Restaurants)

Number of Establishments	32,319
Average Profit Margin	4.5%
Revenue per Employee	$58,200
Average Number of Employees	58.1
Average Wages per Employee	$18,805

Products and Services Segmentation

American food	56.6%
Breakfast foods	17.0%
Italian-American food	9.3%
Seafood	5.8%
Other food	5.7%
Specialty burgers	3.8%
Asian cuisine	1.8%

Industry Costs

Profit	4.5%
Wages	32.3%
Purchases	32.1%
Depreciation	2.3%
Marketing	2.2%
Rent & Utilities	12.9%
Other	13.7%

Market Share

DineEquity Inc.	7.7%
Darden Restaurants Inc.	5.9%

Source: IBISWorld, July 2016

Statistics (Single Location Full-Service Restaurants)

Number of Establishments	264,256
Average Profit Margin	4.5%
Revenue per Employee	$52,500
Average Number of Employees	13.3
Average Wages per Employee	$17,964

Products and Services Segmentation

Asian restaurants	25.5%
American restaurants	20.2%
European restaurants	14.5%
Other	13.7%
Mexican restaurants	12.9%
Pizza restaurants	6.4%
Seafood restaurants	4.0%
Steakhouses	2.8%

Industry Costs

Profit	4.5%
Wages	34.3%
Purchases	38.9%
Depreciation	2.3%
Marketing	2.2%
Rent & Utilities	11.9%
Other	5.9%

Source: IBISWorld, June 2016

Statistics (Premium Steak Restaurants)

Number of Establishments	2,432
Average Profit Margin	6.2%
Revenue per Employee	$66,100
Average Number of Employees	45.5
Average Wages per Employee	$20,128

Products and Services Segmentation

Classic steak restaurants	35.0%
Steak and seafood restaurants	32.6%
Other premium steak restaurants	22.0%
Premium Brazilian steak restaurants	10.4%

Industry Costs

Profit	6.2%
Wages	30.1%
Purchases	33.5%
Depreciation	1.9%
Marketing	3.0%
Rent & Utilities	6.2%
Other	19.1%

Market Share

Ruth's Hospitality Group, Inc.	9.2%
Darden Restaurants Inc.	6.4%

Source: IBISWorld, April 2015

- "Cost of food should be between 20% and 30%. The initial cost of a brand new restaurant may go up to $300K and higher."
- "$250–$300 would be a benchmark for a good profit. We look for food costs of 29–30 percent, but they need to be evaluated by the owner operator on a weekly basis. We look for good accounting systems (POS) and book systems

such as Quickbooks backup. You cannot use what you cannot see, so a well-implemented accounting system is very important and adds value to a business."

- "Keep Gross Profit at 40%."
- "Need to be under 65% for combined food and payroll."
- "As a percentage of sales rent should not exceed 6% net or 8% of gross sales annually. Pizzerias and fast casual concepts typically sell around 40% of gross annual sales. Businesses where alcohol sales make up 50% or more of the annual gross sales typically sell in the 40–45% range."
- "Cost of goods varies by type of food (seafood & prime meats vs. pastas and burgers) and category (casual vs. white tablecloth fine dining) and amount of alcohol being sold."
- "Food cost range between 28% and 35% depending on the concepts."
- "Successful units will control food costs, payroll costs and rent as a percentage of total revenue. These benchmarks vary depending on the type of restaurant."
- "Food costs will vary depending on the concept. Typically will run between 27% & 36%. Because of the high cost and availability of labor in some markets, restaurants are purchasing more prepared food that in the past. As a result of that, their food costs are increasing; however their labor costs are going down. Because of this, sometime you have to combine the labor and food costs to determine if there is an issue. Combined they should run under 60%. Restaurants with high check averages, typically your fine steak houses & fresh seafood restaurants, will run a 40%–44% food cost."
- "Food cost should be 28-33%, Labor should be 25-27% including taxes, Occupancy cost should be 06%–08%."
- "Today prime cost cannot be over 60%."
- "Benchmark sales per square foot for a steakhouse are $400+, Food costs at a steakhouse typically average 40% +/-."
- "Must be able to keep food costs down. Spoilage kills lots of good restaurants."
- "Ideal prime cost is 50%."
- "$10,000 to $12,000 per seat per year."
- "Need to keep rent below 8% of gross sales to have a good chance of success."
- "Food costs vary according to the type of restaurant. Many fast food enterprises can be in the 28% to 33% range; full-service restaurants typically have a higher cost of sales in the 35% to 38% area. Controlling payroll costs while still covering shifts well requires good management."
- "The more alcohol in the sales mix, the greater the profitability should be; requires inventory controls."
- "The major controllable expenses are FLP >> food goal 33–34%; labor goal, including employer payroll taxes, 25–27%; paper goal 1.5–2%. Occupancy cost should be between 6–8%; above 8% you have another partner, that being the landlord."
- "We look at margins as a common benchmark. Also income per hour opened per week."
- "Too often the RE has gotten too valuable for the sales level, thus the occupancy cost to the next buyer could go higher than industry averages, thus the seller is going to have to carry back more of the deal to make it work."
- "$300–$500 PSF sales yield, $50,000–$75,000 per employee per year. Casual category specific can go up to $75,000–$100,000. Food cost should average 32–40 % depending on type food (steaks & seafood) high vs. burgers and fries and southwestern (Mexican) low and competition in the market. Owner operators are more successful than absentee owners."

- "Occupancy cost (including all NNN/CAM charges) should not exceed 10% of annual revenue. This is a very difficult benchmark in high urban areas or sought-after vacation destinations, i.e., Nantucket; however, for one to be successful, reasonable occupancy cost is crucial."
- "COGS is a blend. With high protein costs I am finding food COGS are climbing to 34–36%;, liquor costs have been constant with a target of 19–21%. Payroll target is 30–35%. In theory if the prime costs are within industry averages, rent is 6–8%; a decent operator will drive 10% in EBITDA or more."
- "Prime cost needs to be 60%"
- "It's all over the board but a 6% lease in a hot location with a good assignment clause is like gold!"

Expenses as a percentage of annual sales

Cost of goods	25% to 35%
Payroll/labor Costs	25% to 35%
Occupancy	06% to 10%
Profit (estimated pretax)	08% to 20%

Industry Trend

- "Lots of new restaurants are appearing with a different kind of concept. QSR, quick service restaurants, are becoming more popular since there is no waiter service, and there is no tip, which is 15% to 20% in some restaurants."
- "Good, particularly in more affluent areas like SF Bay area. The more money people make, they are less inclined to eat at home. This is true for people under 50 working in our Silicon Valley."
- "Farm-to-table demands from consumers are high, but tourists, travelers and budget-conscious consumers like the convenience and familiarity of chain restaurants, so both will be contenders. Greatest challenge will be employee costs and retention. The large focus should be on millennials who eat out often and are a growing population."
- "Strong, more conservation efforts"
- "Though a high-risk opportunity, restaurant business will continue to be a desirable form of investment."
- "Due to increased costs, labor in particular, I think the true mom & pops may continue to thrive if they don't require paid staff for key positions. The large multi-unit chains and franchisees may continue to grow but will operate on very thin margins. I am concerned that those who own 2–5 restaurants, especially in the full-service category. These may find it challenging, as minimum wage in our area is increasing to $15 per hour and waitstaff are paid minimum wage with no offset for tips. This also creates disparity between what the servers earn as compared to kitchen staff. I think there will always be an active market for restaurants though, because people will continue to eat out."
- "More upscale quick service restaurants, less full-service restaurants."
- "Slow growth"
- "Pressure on profitability. Severe staffing problems. Strong companies will survive, the weaker ones will fail."
- "The trend in our market is increased competition with many new concepts flooding into the market."
- "I see flat sales and lesser profits for the industry."
- "Marginal annual growth. The energy situation was only a brief reprieve. We

will see higher energy costs and that will impact costs across the board in all business categories."

- "Increased move to automation, lower human labor, smarter equipment including iPad style ordering at the table. This can help improve business efficiency and standard daily costs."
- "Strong growth, higher rent and stiff competition for prime real estate."
- "The industry is on an upswing currently. Competition is always fierce. Restaurants like to congregate in the same areas as customers like variety."
- "Sales have stabilized; however wages and occupancy cost continue to be major challenges."
- "Authentic restaurant in right location will do great, since people are looking for original and unique types of restaurants. People are tired of seeing the same franchise restaurant and will want something different. Of course the taste and the service is very critical, therefore, hiring a great chef is a must."
- "High-end steakhouses will continue to feel the pressure as more restaurants enter the market and the restaurant industry continues to become more promotionally driven."
- "Flat business growth. Economy a big factor."
- "A growing brand awareness among consumers = more chain and franchise units."
- "I see minimal growth with an increase in expenses creating a smaller profit for restaurants."
- "Business is getting better slowly after the recession."
- "Hopefully with a new president, repealing of a plethora of executive regulations, and a recovering economy, the well-funded, professionally managed operations will continue to thrive...those businesses that have been struggling will fall by the wayside and get picked up by the growing class of entrepreneurs that have a solid vision."
- "Expect things to remain very competitive—tough to compete against national chains, but it can be done if management is exceptional."
- "With the amount of new products emerging from the market with flavored wines, vodka, whisky...one has to stay up on what is in."
- "Restaurants and bars will continue to be a sought-after type of business. Turnovers will remain high. As rent will continue to rise, restaurant owners will be more creative in finding less popular locations and turn to social media for marketing and to promote their locations."
- "As the economy turns, if gas prices stay down thus putting more disposable income in consumers' hands, business should continue to improve for the restaurants with low to mid menu price points. The higher end restaurants will continue to have economic pressures."
- "Much the same as we have seen over the last 3–5 years. Costs will rise. Limited disposable income will cause customers to be more selective. Owners will need to become more focused on limited menus and higher sales revenues on higher margins."
- "The demand for restaurants in general seems stable and strong, but it may become more difficult for the independently owned single operators to maintain market share when dealing with costs and regulatory environment including minimum wage increases. California is more burdensome than many other states in this regard and some franchises and chain restaurants have avoided expansion to the area. People are more health conscious and particular with

their food in general and there is an opportunity to cater to this market if the restaurant can provide a good value for the product. Bars and clubs including microbreweries and craft cocktail houses are doing well."

- "There will continue to be strong demand for restaurants in general, but it is challenging for the independent restaurants to compete with the franchises and chains. The independent owner must have a way of differentiating from the many choices available, in terms of the menu, or personal service. Ethnic and specialty restaurants (vegetarian for example) are increasing in popularity. However, in my experience, people say they are interested in healthy alternatives, but they are not willing to sacrifice taste or variety when dining out, so expectations are high."
- "These have been tougher to sell in recent years, less buyers interested."
- "Pricing trends up due to inflation and national pressure on minimum wage. A shift away from casual dining and fast food to fast casual dining growing rapidly. National chains grabbing more market share from mom and pop operations. Continued sluggish growth."
- "Very good in terms of people going out to eat. Poor for independents opening new businesses due to gov't regulations and shrinking profit margins. Successful chains can sustain increased operating costs."
- "Pretty steady with more working spouses and our busy lifestyle(s). Take-out or pick-up should continue to grow."
- "Good service and good food priced fairly will always be popular."
- "Increased diversity of competition and the increase in independent restaurants."
- "I continue to see a very moderate sales increase in the independent restaurant business. Sales stagnant and expenses increasing lead to lower profits. That coupled with pressure on the salary and wage front leads me to think that sales will continue to be slow and financing very difficult."
- "Lots of downsizing and specialty food operations. Menu food types specific."
- "I see the trend in the restaurant business over the next few years as a large turnover of existing restaurants as people move in and out of the industry. A major push for the large chains will continue to move into city locations and squeeze the margins and business of the independent main street businesses."
- "As global economy improves, the U.S. will continue to flourish and families/ individuals will have more disposable income which should help the industry. Massachusetts is a growing area and melting pot for restaurant entrepreneurs. Many multi-unit operators (with 5 or under locations) are now entering into high occupancy cost destinations such as new outdoor shopping center developments to compete with area chains. This trend is helping grow the restaurateur's concept organically without franchising their concept. These decisions are high risk/high reward for the multi-unit operator."
- "Depends on the area—baby boomers will likely eat out more as long as they can. Tourist and sunbelt areas are expected to be hot markets."
- "It has great potential for growth when an owner has industry experience and pays attention to the competition in his area. Giving great service and serving a quality product. Treating every customer like royalty and not letting a single patron leave his business unhappy. Satisfied customers are great advertising."
- "The industry is improving—highly competitive."
- "Will be turnover as it always has been; education and hard work will pay off"

R - Rules of Thumb

- "Less independent sales, more franchised sales, more tenant reps for lease of both 2nd generation spaces and new startups! Landlords are paying big bucks to get credit worthy, experienced tenants!"
- "There should be a small increase."

Seller Financing

- "Banking financing is rare, almost impossible, due to the risk involved. Seller financing is an option, 20% to 30% may be possible if seller wants to hold note."
- "1. All cash
  2. Cash down of 30% to 50% and owner carries rest as a loan
  3. SBA financing with less than 10% of transactions
  4. Don't waste your time with the big banks!"
- "Seller financing is often the key to closing these types of businesses. The more financing offered, generally the greater yield in sales price. Although SBA loans are possible, without good real estate, restaurants generally have low valued hard assets so books and records must be impeccable."
- "SBA loans are the minority. Cash or seller financing are the norm. We try to have at least 60+% for buyer down payment, and the norm would be about 70% cash down. Sales for under $100,000 are primarily all cash."
- "Seller financing 40–50% down."
- "90–95% are sold with seller financing."
- "There typically is very little outside financing in a sale unless it includes real estate."
- "Seller financing is the norm. Few banks, national, regional or community, have an appetite for restaurant transactions. That said, we frequently see five-year terms with sub-10% rates from sellers. Additionally, most buyers come to the table with private investors."
- "Today, there is little or no outside financing for the food service industry without pledging personal assets and experience in the industry and a solid successful financial background in the industry. Sellers are learning the advantages and importance of owner financing transactions. They are able to get higher prices for the business and sell faster. The proceeds include interest and are higher, and taxes are lower."
- "A mix of outside and seller financing is typical. Terms can be all over, but typically 5 years around 5%–7%."
- "For franchises bank financing, independents primarily cash or owner financing."
- "Mom and pop units are difficult to finance; sellers will likely have to carry financing. National franchise affiliates can be financed if the seller reported all of the revenue and has good records."
- "There is very little opportunity for traditional financing of restaurants. Usually for a restaurant to qualify for traditional financing, they would need to have been in business for 10–15 years and have some real estate that is included in the sale. Seller financing is usually the only alternative with 60–70% of the sale being required as a down payment. Terms usually are under 6% for periods of 3–5 years."
- "Old-line restaurants that are paid for tend to have sellers willing to finance. 3rd party lenders are very conservative in their lending practices."

- "I have seen both. However banks and SBA have a tendency to not finance restaurants. SBA 10 year Prime plus 1 or 2%. Most of the time seller financing with 50% down balance financed over 5 years at fixed % 6–8%."
- "Owner finance ten years with a balloon after three years."
- "Seller financing is typical, since SBA not excited to loan on restaurants, but the down payment should be large enough for restaurants with ABC liquor license; the liquor license has lot of value in case the restaurant fails."
- "Seeing many cash transactions on entry level businesses."
- "Smaller restaurants use seller financing. Bigger facilities can get institutional lending."
- "If the numbers can be substantiated on tax returns, bank financing is possible; if not, more seller financing will be needed."
- "Business with real estate outside financing is more common. Restaurant business with revenue under $1 MM seller financing."
- "In today's market it is mostly owner financing for small food service businesses because the financials are not typically good. This would apply for single owner businesses; in partnerships the businesses typically have better financials. Food service operations with over $1.5 million–$2.0 million sales are generally better managed and have better financial controls and frequent financial reporting. In those cases some outside financing is possible if the numbers are good and meet standard and theoretical costs."

Questions

- "What is the reason for selling? What is the relationship with the landlord, length of the lease? What is the competition around? Cost of goods, percentage of revenue? Selling financing? Any family members in the restaurant? Does the lease transfer? What Is the cash flow of the restaurant? What Is the condition of the equipment? Is there a transferable beer and wine or liquor license? Willing to sign a non-compete? What is restaurant's reputation in the community? Are there existing liabilities? Any suggestions to improve the business? "
- "1. Tell me about your typical bad day.
  2. How much money do you set aside for your worst month?
  3. Why are none of the employees here interested in buying this business?
  4. What is your highest cost menu item and why do you keep it on the menu?
  5. Who is your toughest competition?
  6. How many customers are on your mailing list?
  7. How do you determine who your vendors should be?
  8. How do you determine where to spend marketing dollars?"
- "Do your financials reflect cash and credit card sales? Is the business free and clear of any liens or encumbrances? Have you had employee relations issues?"
- "Make sure to understand the labor picture in detail, including how people are being paid. Ask about any discounting programs that have been used (Groupon for example). These can distort both sales and expenses and have liabilities that must be considered. Gift cards and Inventory can also be sticky issues with a sale. Knowing the reason for selling and whether it makes sense is a good idea for any business. Ask if recipes and menus are documented and included."

R - Rules of Thumb

- "Why are you selling? If you were keeping the restaurant what changes would you make?"
- "What has the sales trend been for past 3 years?"
- "Can you prove sales and profitability figures?"
- "Why are you selling? What is there a demand for locally? What would you do differently?"
- "Provide all purchase receipts. Sales trends."
- "What do you do every day? How do you justify your pricing?"
- "How much time a week has the seller spent in the business—the buyer will need to know what adjustments need to be made for management if the seller has been very hands on and the buyer does not plan to be hands on."
- "Why are you selling? Why did you pick this type of food and why this location? Is your equipment—including hoods, grease traps, septic system—in sound working condition and in compliance with all city/county codes and regulations? Can the new owner get a certificate of occupancy and or a liquor permit for this type of business in this exact location?"
- "How many employees; do you perform maintenance on equipment."
- "Verify funds or credit, secure loan with buyers outside interest."
- "How many hours owner works, if it's more than 40 to 45; I do adjust for employees."
- "What are the sales trends and respective profits. A buyer needs to dig into the financials and get a thorough understanding of all expenses. If they don't understand, they should ask an accountant for help. What are the terms of the lease. How is the landlord to deal with. Does he take care of his property and respond to your needs as a tenant. Is the seller current with payments to the landlord & vendors."
- "Staff loyal? Menu same for how long? Personal receipt? Age of kitchen equipment? Delivery?"
- "How much time is left on the lease; are renewal options fixed or at 'market.' How many hours a week does the owner spend in the restaurant."
- "The business is not for the faint of heart but can be very fun to operate. Must ask the seller to prove the figures. Are all recipes written down? Is the kitchen staff trained, or is the owner required to do all the cooking?"
- "Buyer should review all sales tax payments and actual food and liquor receipts, not just the P&L, especially if there is a lot of unreported income."
- "Tell the seller that no one is going to buy their business unless they can answer three questions: 1. What does the business take in? 2. What are the necessary expenses to operate the business? 3. What is left over for the owner as profit (SDE)? We cover our document, *What Every Seller Should Know*, to school sellers on working with a business broker. In part it states that 'selling a business is nothing like selling a house where the seller doesn't even have to play a role in the sales process.' That cooperation is mandatory when questions are asked or documents are requested and an immediate response is required 'even to the occasional inconvenience' of the seller."
- "Are you willing to finance the sale? Buy what is on the financials."
- "Learn about the landlord. Understand the cost of goods. Know whether there are promos and discounts being used to generate revenue and what may be outstanding. Know who the key employees are in the kitchen and whether any are being paid outside of normal channels. Look into past health department reports and ABC conditions."
- "1.) Is the seller in good standing with the state Department of Revenue (DOR) and Department of Unemployment Assistance (DUA)? Failure to comply can result in delay of transfer and delay in transfer of liquor license.

Business Reference Guide **2017**

2.) How old/how many tons are the heating/cooling units. I advise purchasers to inspect these, as this can be a large unforeseen cost."

- "How many hours have you been working? Are all sales recorded? Are there any employees being paid in cash? Do you know of any new competition coming to the area?"
- "How old is the air conditioning unit(s)? Inspect the A/C thoroughly. This is commonly overlooked by inexperienced buyers and can be a large unforeseen expense. Read your lease thoroughly and hire an attorney to review/negotiate it. Make sure to look at the gross sales to rent ratio"
- "What areas do you think you could grow your business? The seller should know where he sees room for instant growth and where they should 'trim.' What are the day to day roles of each employee? Many times employees can work additional jobs to save on labor. High labor cost can eat up your profit fast!"
- "Why did you buy or start this business and what do you think of it now?"
- "How many hours the owner works, food and beverage costs and payroll costs. How long is the lease—is there percentage rent, what are the escalations in the lease?"
- "Reason for selling, history of the business, what makes it special compared to competitors, any lawsuits pending, three years' P&Ls and tax returns, list of FF&E, personnel info (duties, tenure, pay, hrs. worked weekly, any benefits), hours worked by owner, competitors' names and estimated market shares, areas for growth of the business, catering done, monthly sales for past 3 years, published newspaper or magazine articles, names of professional advisers, zoning-license or EPA issues, inventory value, business hours, etc."
- "What are the food costs. Do you have trouble getting help. What type of marketing do you do."
- "How much are liabilities?"
- "What does the future look like for the location? Zoning, competition, lease rate, etc."
- "Percentage of cash vs. credit. Is there reliance on a key chef?"
- "Is the price/sq. ft. of the lease within market?"
- "Which equipment is leased and which is paid, and the condition of the equipment. Is there a grease trap? What kind and what size? Any key employee, especially the cook, and whether he or she wants to stay."
- "Will the owner offer financing, training, non-compete (for how many miles); is the lease assignable; is all equipment approved by the NSF (many states do not allow domestic appliances in a commercial location); are trade name, Website, recipes and training manuals included in the deal?"
- "It is useful to know if the owner has experimented with different hours (breakfast, lunch, dinner, weekend brunch, late night entertainment). Of course the reason for sale is good to know. Any expected modifications from health dept. or franchisor? Any liquor license violations or restrictions?"
- "Ask about cash payroll. Many sellers pay all or part of their payroll in cash. Check if the POS computer is connected to the corporate headquarters or franchise. How long the seller has owned the business might be a good indication that after they bought it they decided that they made a mistake and want out."
- "Work histories of staff? Staffing resources? What vendors should I not deal with and why? Suggestions for growth or expansion?"
- "Do they have good and current tax returns; are the federal, state and payroll taxes current; and does the family have non-essential employees on the payroll? Are sales taxes and gratuities being included in the sales? Some

accountants will permit the operator to do that, then remove them as an expense."

- "Which equipment do you own that is leased? Do you have any gift-card programs?"
- "Does a refurbishment need to occur? Why are you selling now?"
- "What is your strongest area in your business? What part of your business needs the most improvement?"

Resources

Websites
- Today's Restaurant News: www.trnusa.com
- Muradian Business Opportunities: http://muradianbusiness.com
- ServSafe: www.servsafe.com

Trade Publications
- Restaurant Hospitality: www.restaurant-hospitality.com
- Restaurant Start-up and Growth: www.rsgmag.com
- Restaurant Business Magazine: http://www.restaurantbusinessonline.com/
- "Appetite for Acquisition": www.wesellrestaurants.com
- Restaurant Finance Monitor: www.restfinance.com
- Nation's Restaurant News: www.nrn.com

Associations
- National Restaurant Association: www.restaurant.org
- Massachusetts Restaurant Association (MRA): http://www.themassrest.org/
- Ohio Restaurant Association: www.ohiorestaurant.org

Restaurants—Limited Service

(See also Franchises, Restaurants—Full Service, Restaurants—An Introduction)

SIC 5812-08	NAICS 722513	Number of Businesses/Units 302,418

Rules of Thumb

➤ 30 to 40 percent of annual sales for independents; 45 to 60 percent for many franchises—plus inventory

➤ 1.5 to 2.5 times SDE plus inventory

➤ 2 to 3 times EBIT

➤ 2.5 to 3.5 times EBITDA

➤ For a rule of thumb for many limited-service franchises see Franchised Food Businesses, Franchises, and the specific franchise listing, if available.

Pricing Tips
- "Location and lease will affect the sale price directly"
- "Add liquor license cost & value of FF&E"
- "Food and labor costs are value drivers."
- "Not all restaurants are valued the same—each segment has their own value."

- "Analyze food costs—ideally, they should be less than 30%. Industry average ranges from 30–40%. Look for non-operating assets and unreported cash."
- "Location and history are important. Independents are less attractive but often more profitable than franchises. The key is low overhead, and most franchises have high overhead. Considering owner financing is a must."
- "Limited-service may be lower volume than a full-service restaurant allowing for some higher rent as a % of sales. Make sure that true profitability is over 20% (near 25%)."
- "Independent restaurants priced to sell should be around 1.5 to 2.0 times EBITDA (real estate not included) and owner must be willing to consider some sort of owner financing. Franchised limited-service restaurants may go for as high as 3 times EBITDA but be prepared to go through the franchise-transfer process. You will need patience."
- "Price: twice the yearly net income"
- "You arrive at two sets of figures, based on profit and sales. Price tends to move towards higher figure when a new store, has length of lease, volume increasing, and favorable market placement. Price tends to go lower if short lease, declining volume, no franchise term, equipment old, store tired, dropping profitability."
- "Gross revenue is the key, but if the SDE doesn't support the debt service requirements and a reasonable salary, then the % of gross will have to come down."
- "Sales are a much better indicator of value than bottom-line numbers. Different operators can have a huge impact on food and labor costs running the same business."
- "Limited menu a bonus; delivery and length of lease major considerations."
- "Location, lease, concept, operating manuals, recipes"
- "Normal situation—I would take last year's net plus any adjustments such as cars, insurance for owner, depreciation and interest, and make it a multiple of .72 to 2 times that number depending upon location, growth or decline of sales, age of fixtures and condition of building, then add value of FF&E, liquor license and other assets for a good value number."
- "Increase in upcoming rental amount; ease of menu; delivery and competition in the market"

Expert Comments

"Fast casual with concentrating on one item is the hottest trend; it provides a full-service meal at almost a fast-food price, and if the owner or manager ran it efficiently, will be more profitable than full service; examples: Chipotle, Schnitzel and Things, etc. This kind of operation has lower food and labor cost."

"Operations closing, which will help the ones left as long as consumers keep spending. Expensive to equip and furnish without knowing if the concept will go. Takes a lot of money to find out. Controlling overhead is key."

"Established independents often are better deals than the franchises as far as net cash flow."

"Tough to compete against national chains and big franchises"

"Most models project labor as a percentage of total sales, but I find this method highly inaccurate. I view the majority of labor as a fixed expense. A restaurant needs the majority of its staff whether or not any customers are served. As a result, unpredictable sales generate high labor cost as a percentage of sales. Sending an hourly employee home can reduce labor only slightly. Therefore I recommend treating labor as a fixed expense."

Source: "The New Restaurant Entrepreneur" by Kep Sweeney

"Highly competitive; tied to economic outlook"

"Large capital investment in equipment required. Makes resales a bargain!"

"Increasing food costs squeezing profits"

"Restaurants are tough work. They are usually profitable but owners tend to burn out very quickly. Too many owners have a good thing, try to expand, and then spread themselves too thin and end up failing at both locations. One good location does not assure you the 2nd one will be as profitable. Keep your overhead under control."

"Easy to open, hard to master. Very difficult to run absentee; owner must be present."

"Lots of competition. Risk factor: must give consistent product, with good quality. Catering a plus for today's business environment. Many sandwich shops add catering. Some catering-only locations with delivery, in low-rent areas with little highway exposure."

Benchmark Data

Statistics (Fast Food Restaurants)

Number of Establishments	302,418
Average Profit Margin	5.2%
Revenue per Employee	$53,000
Average Number of Employees	14.4
Average Wages per Employee	$13,663

Products and Services Segmentation

Burgers	42.0%
Sandwiches	14.0%
Asian	10.0%
Chicken	10.0%
Pizza and Pasta	9.0%
Mexican	8.0%
Other	7.0%

Industry costs

Profit	5.2%
Wages	25.8%
Purchases	36.4%
Depreciation	2.9%
Marketing	2.8%
Rent & Utilities	13.1%
Other	13.8%

Market Share

McDonald's Corp.	16.1%
Yum! Brands Inc.	9.0%
Subway	5.0%

Source: IBISWorld, August 2016

Statistics (Coffee & Snack Shops)

Number of Establishments	76,801
Average Profit Margin	6.7%
Revenue per Employee	$57,900
Average Number of Employees	9.1
Average Wages per Employee	$14,912

Products and Services Segmentation

Coffee beverages	51.0%
Food	36.0%
Other beverages	9.0%
Other	4.0%

Industry Costs

Profit	6.7%
Wages	25.8%
Purchases	38.5%
Depreciation	3.7%
Marketing	3.5%
Rent & Utilities	11.1%
Other	10.7%

Market Share

Starbucks Corporation	39.8%
Dunkin' Brands Inc.	21.9%

Source: IBISWorld, May 2016

- "Prime cost (cost of goods plus payroll costs divided by sales) must remain below 60%."
- "Food costs—sub shops < 30%, fine dining 35% +, breakfast/lunch < 30%, pizza & pasta 29%–32%."
- "Food costs under 33% are critical, and labor costs under 30% are important."
- "2 times EBITDA plus real estate is most often used."
- "Food costs should be in 28% to 30% range."
- "Again sales must be at a point that there is enough margin to cover fixed costs and then some."
- "Lower quartile per seat is $5,115, median is $7,510, and $14,293 is upper. $10,000 per seat is a benchmark for a successful quick-service restaurant."
- "Food usually maximum of 35%. Sandwich shops very popular today. Catering a plus, hard to prove without good reliable records."
- "I look for a 20% plus EBIT and 'Prime Costs' (Cost of Sales & Labor) combined below 50%."
- "Good menu can add to success. Location, visibility, and parking key ingredients for profitable business."
- "Ownership of real estate very desirable. Franchise stores more marketable than independents. Franchise presence in marketplace very important."

R - Rules of Thumb

Expenses as a percentage of annual sales

Cost of goods	28% to 32%
Payroll/labor Costs	25% to 35%
Occupancy	08% to 12%
Profit (estimated pretax)	15% to 20%

Industry Trend

- "Fast-casual restaurants and new quick-service chains are entering the market with narrower, more specialized menus. 'Fast casual and new QSRs have very focused menus,' said Jana Mann, senior director of menu trends at Datassential. 'They might be smaller in size. They focus on one item. If you want the best taco, or you want the best burger, do you go to someone that specializes in them, or one that has a general menu?'

  "Existing quick-service restaurants are responding by cutting menus or limiting menu additions to focus more on quality, speed and service. 'QSRs' game is being upped,' Mann said. 'They now know there is competition with these places and the whole industry is being elevated.'

  "Chick-fil-a, the Atlanta-based chicken sandwich chain, has all three day parts, a menu that is half the size of McDonald's, and unit volumes over $3 million per location. Plus, it's not open on Sundays. In-N-Out, headquartered in Irvine, Calif., likewise has high unit volumes and a narrow menu. Raising Cane's Chicken Fingers' systemwide sales have grown 52 percent over the past two years, according to Nation's Restaurant News Top 100 data. The chain, based in Baton Rouge, LA, sells chicken fingers—and that's about it."
  Source: "Quick-service restaurants take a bite out of menus" by Jonathan Maze, August 7, 2015, nrn.com
- "Slow sales, higher expenses"
- "Lots of turnover"
- "Many units with expensive leases are likely to close."
- "Less upscale dining, more family-oriented businesses"

Seller Financing

- "Five years—8 percent"
- 3 to 4 years
- "7 to 10 years with a 3 to 5 year stop"
- "Average of 5 years and prime plus 2 percent"
- "Depends on size and cash flow; 8 years is an average of our last 20 restaurant transactions."

Questions

- "This kind of operation that requires low supervision, why are you selling?"
- "What can be done to improve the business that you are not doing?"
- "Sales, purchase invoices, detail of expenses"
- "Food costs & payroll costs"
- "Who are your key people? How many hours per week do you work? How long have you been in business?"
- "Tax issues. Relationship with franchisor if applicable. Any mandatory remodeling in near future. Lease terms and length. CAM charges."
- "When was the last time you had a menu change or price change?"
-

Restaurants—Mexican

	NAICS full service—722511; limited service—722513
	Number of Businesses/Units 46,691

Rules of Thumb

➢ 30 per cent of annual sales

Expert Comments

"Chains that specialize in Mexican food do well, but not at the expense of independent competitors that serve authentic fare and outnumber them by a wide margin."

Source: "Mom-and-pop model endures in the Mexican segment," by Brad Bloom
restaurant-hospitality.com, June 23, 2015

Benchmark Data

Statistics (Mexican Restaurants)

Number of Establishments	46,691
Average Profit Margin	5.6%
Revenue per Employee	$43,300
Average Number of Employees	19.4
Average Wages per Employee	$13,473

Products and Services Segmentation

On-premises limited-service restaurants	32.0%
Drive-thru limited-service restaurants	27.0%
Full-service restaurants	22.0%
Off-premises (take out) limited-service restaurants	15.0%
Cafeterias and buffets	4.0%

Industry Costs

Profit	5.6%
Wages	31.2%
Purchases	31.5%
Depreciation	3.6%
Marketing	2.6%
Rent & Utilities	6.9%
Other	18.6%

Market Share

Taco Bell Corp.	23.0%
Chipotle Mexican Grill	12.2%

Source: IBISWorld, April 2015

- "According to CHD FIND there are approximately 57,000 Mexican restaurants in the U.S., of which approximately 15,000 are classified as chain restaurants. As the third most popular menu type, Mexican accounts for eight percent of all restaurants in the U.S. Texas tops the list for states with the largest share of Mexican restaurants at 17 percent. California and New Mexico follow with 14 percent each. Arizona and Colorado come in with 13 percent and 12 percent, respectively. "The average Mexican restaurant, whether chain or independent, grosses $735,000 per year. According to CHD FIND, 58 percent of independent Mexican restaurants gross between $500,000 and $1,000,000. Surprisingly, just 33 independent Mexican restaurants make up the top tier of this menu type by grossing more than $5 million in annual sales."

Source: "Mom-and-pop model endures in the Mexican segment," by Brad Bloom, restaurant-hospitality.com, June 23, 2015

Industry Trend

- "While prominent chains like Chipotle, Qdoba, and Taco Bell maintain their place in the media with hip add-ons like tofu, innovative breakfast meals and efforts to use fresh local ingredients, it's the smaller independent Mexican restaurants that are using this market to their advantage.

  "In order to accurately evaluate the current Mexican restaurant landscape in the U.S., we pulled Mexican Menu Type data from CHD Expert's Foodservice Industry National Database (FIND). CHD collects, manages and analyzes data for the away-from-home global foodservice market, with information on more than five million foodservice operators around the world."

Source: "Mom-and-pop model endures in the Mexican segment," by Brad Bloom, restaurant-hospitality.com, June 23, 2015

Retail Businesses (In General)

Rules of Thumb

➢ 30 to 35 percent of annual sales plus inventory

➢ 1.5 to 3 times SDE plus inventory

➢ 10 times EBIT

➢ 12 times EBITDA

Pricing Tips

- "Location, remodel, condition of the business/equipment, lease, stability of revenue and general market conditions are some of the factors which will have an effect on valuation."
- "Excess Inventory or slow moving inventory may have to be included in normal level of inventory."

Expert Comments

"Sell more through the Web. Increase social media."

"Different industries within retail segment are valued differently at different times in the economic cycle. Generally retail industry is stable and is generally well balanced."

Benchmark Data

- "Sales per square foot $500."
- "Location is a critical factor in retail, and business needs to be attractive."
- "Most independent retails average around $240 per square foot but this can vary dramatically based on product lines carried and store concept, i.e., big box, boutique, etc."

- "No business lends itself more to benchmarking than retailing. Two important benchmarks for retail operations that may measure profitability, or just how a particular business may stack up against its peers, are sales per square foot and sales per employee."
- "Pat O'Rourke, the creator of BizStats, has written a very interesting—and informative—article titled "Why Sales per Foot Is the Critical Benchmark for Retailers." Here are a few excerpts—a bit dated, but still of interest.

"Think of sales per foot in terms of sun protection factor—SPF—a healthy SPF will help prevent you from getting burned in a retail business. SPF is one of many retail benchmarks, but I believe it's the best gauge of a retailer's efficiency, and, ultimately, its profitability. It's also easy to compute—just divide sales by the store's gross square feet. Some retailers calculate SPF based on selling feet (excluding in-store administrative, storage and other space), but this can be subjective and impair meaningful comparisons.

"SPF differs among industries. For example, a big box discounter with high inventory turnover (such as Costco) is going to have a much higher SPF than a clothing chain or sports equipment outlet. Another key element is location, SPF is typically much higher for merchants in a destination mall, than for similar stores in a local shopping center—of course you pay much higher rent in the big mall.

"An upward trend in SPF is almost always a positive sign of a retailer's health, whereas a downward trend in SPF is often a warning sign that business performance is suffering—even if the company's total sales are increasing.

"There can be many reasons for a low SPF. The first reason is obvious—the retailer simply has too much space. By having excessive space, a retailer will be adversely impacted by high fixed costs:

- ✓ Rent costs are excessive
- ✓ Labor costs are excessive, since additional floor space requires additional personnel
- ✓ Flooring costs are excessive, since additional space requires additional merchandise
- ✓ Insurance utilities and theft costs all increase with additional floor space
- ✓ "Assuming the store size is reasonable, there are many reasons for a poor SPF relative to competitors. Here are 10 primary reasons for a low SPF—these are considerations for retailers of all sizes:
- ✓ Poor product/merchandising mix
- ✓ Insufficient floor inventory (e.g., empty shelves, missing sizes)
- ✓ Un-competitive pricing
- ✓ Poor location
- ✓ Poor sales and customer service personnel
- ✓ Non-optimal store hours
- ✓ Poor store layout and design
- ✓ Cannibalization of nearby owned stores
- ✓ Insufficient/poor marketing
- ✓ Fixed consumer perception"

Expenses as a percentage of annual sales

Cost of goods	25%
Payroll/labor Costs	20% to 25%
Occupancy	15% to 18%
Profit (estimated pretax)	28% to 30%

R - Rules of Thumb

Industry Trend
- "3% annual growth."
- "There has been tremendous growth in this industry in the past few years. I believe the industry is going to settle down in the next few years and the market conditions may even force some 'cleanup' of businesses that overexpanded."
- "Always competing with 'big retailers'"
- "According to GE Capital, the key trends in retail include the following:
  - ✓ Channel shift to continue: Consumers' focus on value and convenience will continue to shift discretionary spending away from traditional retail channels in favor of e-commerce and discount venues.
  - ✓ Margin pressure from accelerated growth in e-commerce: The accelerated growth and shift to e-commerce/m-commerce has diminished the pricing power of most retailers. This trend has increased margin pressure, given increased competition on free shipping and negative leverage of in-store fixed costs due to declining traffic.
  - ✓ Retail square footage rationalizing: Mall traffic will remain difficult, exacerbated by accelerated growth of the online channel on top of the encroachment by the discounters for many years.
  - ✓ Contrarily, the secularly pressured sectors, such as office products, consumer electronics, teen apparel retailers and department stores will continue to rationalize their retail locations."

  Source: "GE Capital: 2015 retail industry trends" by Marianne Wilson, February 5, 2015, http://www.chainstoreage.com/article/ge-capital-2015-retail-industry-trends
- "Retail will continue to shift to the Internet and any retail concept must contain a fully functional retail shopping site that must be managed like it is a completely separate facility. The value and business the Internet will bring is very dependent on the product line, with commodity type goods being very vulnerable."

Seller Financing
- "Seller financing. 30 percent down, 70 percent financed over 5 years."
- "Seller financing unless the property is also being sold."
- "Typically there is a large amount of seller financing. This doesn't mean you can get a partial loan for the purchase price but collateralization is a big issue in buying a retail operation. Most retail transactions also involve some nature of outside collateral to make a lender comfortable enough to deal with the large amount of goodwill involved with retail companies."

Questions
- "Cash sales, stale inventory, inventory turnover compared to prior years, justification for a 3% annual growth when the business only grew 2% last year, employee turnover."
- "How long in business; trend of sales; expected new competition; why selling, product mix and industry changes, industry trade shows. Will the seller help the new owner in buying?"
- "A buyer needs to look at more than just the P&L and balance sheet. Look hard at the inventory. Do they have excessive amounts of merchandise that haven't moved? Are the racks empty? Are the payables up to date? A retail company can be showing a profit and still go out of business because of poor

cash management. Does the P&L have any shrinkage? All retail companies are subject to significant amount of theft. If they don't show any losses on the P&L, then they aren't properly inventorying the store and the inventory on the balance sheet can be way off. Don't buy inventory without going in and doing a physical count at cost. If the inventory is out of line with the balance sheet, be sure the selling price is adjusted at close to reflect the proper amount."

Resources

Trade Publications
- Stores Magazine: https://nrf.com/connect-us/stores-magazine

Associations
- National Retail Federation: https://nrf.com/

Retail Stores (Small Specialty)		
		Number of Businesses/Units 139,674

Rules of Thumb

- ➢ 15 to 20 percent of annual sales plus inventory
- ➢ 1.8 to 2.2 times SDE plus inventory
- ➢ Misc. Small Retail Stores:
    - ✓ Tobacco Stores—15 percent of annual sales plus inventory
    - ✓ Bridal Shops—10 to 15 percent of annual sales plus inventory (see also Bridal Shops entry)
    - ✓ Souvenir Shops—15 to 20 percent of annual sales plus inventory
    - ✓ Collectible Stores—15 to 20 percent of annual sales plus inventory (see also Collectibles entry)
    - ✓ Coin/Stamp Shops—5 to 10 percent of annual sales plus inventory
    - ✓ Religious Goods (not books)—5 to 10 percent of annual sales plus inventory
    - ✓ Process Serving—35–40 percent of annual sales

Pricing Tips

- IBISWorld includes such businesses in this category as tobacco stores, artists' materials, souvenirs & collectibles, coin & stamp shops, religious goods (not books), occupational supplies and other similar type businesses. Approximately 85 percent of them are single-owner/small family businesses. Eighty-eight percent of these businesses have 9 or fewer employees.

Benchmark Data

Statistics (Small Specialty Retail Stores)

Number of Establishments	139,674
Average Profit Margin	4.1%
Revenue per Employee	$132,200
Average Number of Employees	1.7
Average Wages per Employee	$16,320

Products and Services Segmentation

Tobacco product and smokers' accessories	31.2%
Collectibles and monuments	20.9%
Other	20.5%
Pools, pool chemicals, pool supplies and accessories	15.8%
Home goods	7.9%
Groceries and alcoholic beverages	3.7%

Industry Costs

Profit	4.1%
Wages	12.4%
Purchases	48.8%
Depreciation	0.9%
Marketing	1.7%
Rent & utilities	5.6%
Other	26.5%

Source: IBISWorld, August 2016

Industry Trend

- "IBISWorld expects market conditions for the Small Specialty Retail Stores industry to improve over the next five years. Although revenue growth will remain constrained as external competition intensifies, overall industry performance is expected to be significantly more robust. As the economic recovery continues to gain traction, consumers will allocate more disposable income to the purchase of quality products, driving up industry demand. However, recovery will be tempered by residually low prices and increasing competition, both of which will likely keep revenue and profit low."

Source: http://clients1.ibisworld.com/reports/us/industry/industryoutlook.aspx?entid=1106

Retirement Communities—Continuing Care

Rules of Thumb

- ➢ 51 percent of annual sales plus inventory
- ➢ 2.5 times SDE plus inventory
- ➢ 2.8 times EBIT
- ➢ 2.6 times EBITDA

Benchmark Data

Expenses as a percentage of annual sales

Cost of goods	11%
Payroll/labor Costs	05%
Occupancy	0
Profit (estimated pretax)	06%

Industry Trend

- "Revenue projected to grow, demand projected to grow, profit expected to grow, consolidation has slowed."

Seller Financing

- "Outside financing"

Questions
- "Payor mix, market share, patient demographic data"

Resources

Websites
- The National Center for Assisted Living: www.ahcancal.org

Associations
- The American Seniors Housing Association: www.seniorshousing.org

Retirement Homes (See also Assisted Living, Nursing Homes)	
	NAICS homes with nursing care—623110;
	NAICS homes without nursing care—623312

Rules of Thumb

> "Selling price is quite varied, from $2,000 to $3,000 + per bed, depending upon the number of beds. There is no hard and fast rule of thumb which will apply because of the condition of the real estate, whether or not there are quarters for the owner/operator, and the size of the home."

	Franchise
Rita's Italian Ice (See also Franchises, Ice Cream/Yogurt Shops)	
Approx. Total Investment	$140,500 to $414,200
Estimated Annual Sales/Unit	$230,000
NAICS 722515	Number of Businesses/Units 600

Rules of Thumb

> 80 to 100 times annual sales plus inventory

Resources

Websites
- www.ritasice.com

	Franchise
Rocky Mountain Chocolate Factory (See also Candy Stores, Food Stores—Specialty)	
Approx. Total Investment	$126,300 to $421,400
Estimated Annual Sales/Unit	$350,000
NAICS 311352	Number of Businesses/Units 235

Rules of Thumb

> 50 to 55 percent of annual sales plus inventory

Resources

Websites
- www.sweetfranchise.com

		Franchise
Roly Poly Sandwiches (See also Franchises, Sandwich Shops)		
Approx. Total Investment		$101,050 to $220,200
	NAICS 722211	Number of Businesses/Units 125

Rules of Thumb

> 35 percent of annual sales plus inventory

Benchmark Data
- For Benchmark Data see Sandwich Shops

Resources

Websites
- www.rolypoly.com

Route Distribution Businesses

Rules of Thumb

> 35 to 40% percent of annual sales plus inventory

> 1 to 4 times SDE plus inventory

> 3 times SDE plus inventory—3 to 4 times for name brands; 1 to 2 times for no-name brands

> 1 to 4 times EBIT

> 10 to 20 times weekly gross plus inventory

Pricing Tips
- "Actual SDE & EBIT ranges from 1–4 according to the type of distribution business."
- "Ascertain where geographically the route accounts are located; are the accounts spread out or cohesive; what time is the route operated; age of the truck used on route; how well established is the route; how close is the product pick-up point to where the accounts are located."
- "The larger transactions involve a multiple of sales. The multiple range is 1–2 x sales. 1x sales—sometimes even less, depending on a number of factors—is common for the smaller transactions. The larger ones are clearly in the M &

A field, as these can be $5 million to $50 million also involving land, bottling plants, spring sources and truck fleets.

"The sales that are in our ranges of $50,000 to about $2 million are in the multiple range of .75 to 1.5 x sales and usually include assets that are needed to run the business (office, warehouse, inventory, and trucks). The .75 range or even less is for the smallest of these under $200,000 with owners that are very anxious to sell. The higher multiple is generated when buyers are very anxious to buy for strategic regions and the sellers are not forced to sell.

"Profitability, EBITDA, etc. are not factors, because the buyer rolls the accounts into his own operation inheriting none of the overhead. Often there is not even an increase in the cost of delivery. This depends on how large an operation the buyer has and the size of the business he is buying. Therefore the sales less COGS drops to the bottom line and is extremely profitable for the buyer. COGS in the water industry is only 10%–20% of sales. In coffee, it would be 33%–50%."

- "Major factors involved in pricing a route include: (1) Where the route is located; (2) What is the year & condition of the vehicle included? (3) Is the truck owned or leased? (4) How many years the route is established; (5) Is the route protected stops territory or is it an unprotected route? (6) What is the brand of the product that the route is distributing? (7) How close to the depot is the route?"
- "Franchised Routes: Approximately 2 times SDE. Note that franchised routes, which usually exist on the more consumer-recognized products, have 'Distribution Agreements' in force between wholesales and distributor.

"Non-Franchised Routes: Approximately 1 times SDE. Non-franchised routes have no such contracts [Distribution Agreements] and they usually distribute staple items and/or non-consumer recognized products."

Expert Comments

"Test ride the route you are looking at for several days before making up your mind to purchase. Remember the word route comes from the word routine. So if you don't enjoy the work during your short test ride, it ain't for you!"

"Easy to check out business, learn business, operate business and grow business."

Benchmark Data

- "Bread, chip & provisions routes sometimes try to use a multiple of weekly sales. Beverage & juice routes usually use a price/case. Majority of routes, even those mentioned above, are priced at a multiple of annual net profit."
- "Each category (bread, coffee, chips, candy & nut, cookie, dairy, juice, paper, pie & pastry, provisions, soda & beverage, vending, package delivery (FedEx, etc.) of route businesses is priced differently. Even within categories, such as soda & beverage, a Snapple route will go for a higher multiple then an independent beverage route."
- "Routes usually are priced at a multiple of net earnings. That multiple is commonly in the 1 to 2 times range. Overall, this price range can be less than 1 times a year's income to as much as four times. The most important variable that determines where in the range the price falls is connected with the name

of the product sold (is it a consumer recognized brand?) & whether or not the route business is franchised or non-franchised (independent). Commonly most name brand products that are offered for sale in the marketplace are distributed by franchised routes...with perhaps the most common exception being Tropicana juice products!"

- "The route must net a minimum of $175 per day after all expenses. What are categorized as 'A' routes are the most common in the market. They are one-man routes that operate out of a truck that does not require a CDL license; operate 4–5 days per week & net an income between $700–$1400 per week. The next larger category of routes is classified as 'B' routes. They may require a helper; may operate out of a CDL truck & net a weekly income of $1400–$2500 per week. The largest routes are classified as 'C' routes. They require the use of helper(s), operate out of CDL trucks & net a weekly income of more than $2500 per week."

- "Most routes sell at a multiple of 'weekly sales' from 12 to as high as 50:1 on each dollar of sales."

- "Cost of goods should never be more than 35 percent."

Expenses as a percentage of annual sales

Cost of goods	35%
Payroll/labor Costs	08% to 15%
Occupancy	10%
Profit (estimated pretax)	10% to 20%

Industry Trend

- "Distribution is still on an upward trend despite the floundering economy. However, one should be most cautious in getting involved with a franchised route that is handling a weak or 'for sale' product line. A perfect example of this was the recent sale of Bachman Pretzels to Utz Snacks. Bachman had at one time been the most popular pretzel product in the northeast part of this country...but as its customer based was undermined by Snyder's...the product's sales weakened. The result of the sale of Bachman to Utz resulted in many Bachman route investors having their investments diminish (or disappear) in value as the metro market was revamped by Utz!"

- "Questions are on the minds of industry professionals about whether to switch from a DSD (Direct Store Delivery) to centralized distribution model, or a combination of both. The steady growth of online purchases (led by Amazon with almost $70b of sales in 2013alone) is showing no signs of slowing down. Aside from worrying brick-and-mortar retailers and emptying malls, it's also creating more awareness of the expansive array of products available to consumers. It's not just the long-haul sector that is having difficulty replacing a workforce that is beginning to age out—distribution in general is suffering from a lack of visibility for new job-seekers.

"The DOT seems to modify the HOS (Hours of Service) rules for commercial drivers on a fairly consistent basis, creating both confusion and uncertainty for some carriers and their drivers. These HOS mandates are even more onerous for short-haul delivery drivers, besieged by a frenetic workday (with an average of 14 stops a day) they generally have little time for keeping HOS logbooks up-to-date. Add to this the new ELD rules coming into effect during 2015 and the high probability of more compliance changes to come, and it's not surprising that 2015 will be the year that a lot of fleets will be eager to adopt automated solutions to make sure drivers (and route planners) stay HOS compliant."

Source: http://www.telogis.com/blog/3-big-trends-distribution-2015-telogis-industry-forecast

- "Over the years there has been much consolidation within the industry, with larger regional firms buying smaller regionals, the smaller regionals buying larger local firms, and the larger locals buying smaller (under $500,000) companies. Today super-large national companies such as Nestle (which controls 50% of the U.S. market and is worldwide) bought most of the regional brands, and DS Waters, another national water company, bought the rest. So virtually all of the mega-consolidation has already taken place. However there is still plenty of consolidation being done on a smaller basis, with transactions ranging from $50,000 to $5,000,000. There are still a number of smaller regional bottlers and distributors buying companies in this range."
- "One difficult issue facing vending is the shrinking customer base at locations. During the past 10 years there has been a lot of consolidation in the business sector. This has left vendors with a high percentage of B&I accounts in a delicate position. They have been forced to reevaluate the machines at locations. Sometimes the drop in sales is the only notice vendors get that now there are fewer employees at a location. Despite the recovering economy there are areas where employee levels haven't returned to normal. This makes the issue of evaluating if you have the right number of machines and types of products at a location even more important to profitability."

Source: "Location Intel—How do you know who is really there?" by Emily Refermat,
VendingMarketWatch.com, March 19, 2015

Seller Financing

- "Typically, when financing is available, it is through the seller with 5-year terms and interest rates currently averaging around 5–7%."
- "Most routes are sold with owner financing. There are several big franchised routes (like Pepperidge Farm) which offer outside financing to buyers."
- "90% may be seller financed, with the exception of some companies (like Bimbo & Pepperidge Farm) that provide financing to buyers looking to come into their company with a route purchase."
- "Sellers often tend to be more apprehensive in offering financing in these businesses for 2 reasons: it is a low asset business with little to attach & it is very dependent upon the seller's relationship with his customer base. Thus many sellers (most of the time incorrectly) believe that the buyer coming in cannot be as successful in taking care of his customer base as he has been."

Questions

- "Documentation of purchases, sales and expenses."
- "Ask for the past full year's worth of purchase and/or sales records; copy of contract (if franchised) for review; permission to take truck in for inspection; list of active (& inactive) accounts."
- "Look for verification of his last year's purchase history, a representation of % profit worked on, & then do a random sampling of customer invoices to confirm the % profit margin."
- "Where is route operated? Is it franchised? Hours of operation? Type/year truck included?"

Resources

Websites
- www.routebrokers.com

RV Dealerships

SIC 5561-03	NAICS 441210	Number of Businesses/Units 6,581

Rules of Thumb

> ➤ 15 percent of annual sales plus RV inventory & parts, etc.

Pricing Tips

- "A good formula: ease of entry, big secular swings, keep the price in the 4x range for smaller, privately owned companies. Also, balance sheets generally are not critical."

Expert Comments

"Learn the business from the first company you buy—and a year or so later look for an add-on."

"Elkhart has had 19% unemployment to 2% above full employment, back and forth. The last ten years have seen big consolidation moves and only a handful of companies dominate now, but new companies come along regularly. Basically an assembly business, not much capital required to start."

Benchmark Data

Statistics (Recreational Vehicle Dealers)

Number of Establishments	6,581
Average Profit Margin	3.7%
Revenue per Employee	$444,100
Average Number of Employees	6.3
Average Wages per Employee	$45,001

Products and Services Segmentation

Travel trailers	63.3%
Fifth-wheel trailers	18.2%
Class A	5.8%
Class C	5.8%
Parts and services	2.5%
Folding trailers	2.3%
Truck campers	1.2%
Class B	0.9%

Industry Costs

Profit	3.7%
Wages	10.2%
Purchases	81.9%
Depreciation	0.4%
Marketing	1.2%
Rent & Utilities	1.9%
Other	0.7%

Source: IBISWorld, August 2016

- "High direct costs, low period costs, so when you go by break-even, about 15% of sales drops to the bottom line. C.O.D. business, which also helps ease of entry and rapid growth."

"By the Numbers
- ✓ 8.9 million US households own an RV
- ✓ There are 460 RV rental outlets across the country
- ✓ The RV rental business is $350 million annual industry"

Source: Cruise America, Recreation Vehicle Industry Association, www.gorving.com

Industry Trend

- "Very strong right now. Gas is cheap, credit is cheap; millions of families already own a vehicle."
- "The RV market continued to race ahead through the first half of 2016 with total RV wholesale shipments reaching 226,286 units, an 11.7% increase over this same period last year, according to RVIA's June survey of RV manufacturers. The monthly total for June was 40,072 units, rising 18.7% above June one year ago and marking the third monthly total in excess of 40,000 units this year."
- "Shipments through June were at a seasonally adjusted annualized rate of nearly 415,000 units and the six-month total this year was the best since 1977. Towable RV shipments led the way in volume total with shipments reaching 197,515 units through June, an 11% gain over the 177,939 units shipped during the same six-month time frame in 2015. Meanwhile, motorhome shipments showed the largest percentage gain with the market segment up 16.4% to 28,771 units compared to 24,714 units last year at the same point."

Source: http://rvia.org/?ESID=preleases&PRID=1769&SR=1 August 4, 2016

- "General Electric one of the RV industry's largest lenders, expects the trend to continue. 'What we have seen since 2015 has begun is very strong attendance at retail shows,' said Tim Hyland, president of the RV group at Commercial Distribution Finance for GE. The growth in attendance has been consistent nationwide, and it speaks to current consumer interest.

"In a survey conducted by GE at the annual RVIA trade show in Louisville, Kentucky, in December, 41 percent of survey respondents—the majority of which were RV dealers—said they expected sales to rise 5 percent to 10 percent next year, and 26 percent expected a 10 to 15 percent growth."

Source: "The RV industry, thriving, is getting younger," by Rebecca Ungarino, cnbc.com 3/28/15

Seller Financing

- "Outside financing and maybe some seller paper to keep the transaction kosher"

Questions

- "Gross margin—it's really important to have that straight."

Resources

Websites
- RV Pro: https://rv-pro.com

Associations
- Recreational Vehicle Industry Association, (RVIA)—A very informative site: www.rvia.org

RV Parks (See also Campgrounds)

SIC 7033-02	NAICS 721211	

Rules of Thumb

➢ 3.3 percent of annual sales plus inventory

➢ 8.5 times SDE plus inventory

Pricing Tips

- "Cap rates range from 7% to 12%."
- "RV parks are a very high-yielding investment, with returns from 10% to 20%+ on your money. RV parks are among the highest yielding of all real estate asset classes. So if your goal is to maximize the return on your money, RV parks are not a bad starting spot."
  Source: http://www.rvparkuniversity.com/articles/is-buying- an-rv- park-worth- the-investment.php
- "The industry is getting more sophisticated at marketing and pricing. Many hotel/motel pricing strategies are starting to work for campgrounds."
- "Too variable for Rules of Thumb. Cap rates of 9 to 15 percent. Urban parks at low end of cap rate spectrums. Destination parks are at higher end. Number of ancillary revenue sources will affect cap rates on destination parks—more revenue sources, lower cap rates. Parks with fewer than 100 sites are very inefficient, and value tends to be exclusively in the real estate, with little or no intrinsic value."

Expert Comments

"Have a business plan that is achievable based on improving all areas of opportunities that the current owner is not maximizing."

"The RV and campground industry did very well during the recession in Florida."

"It is difficult to build new facilities due to permitting."

Benchmark Data

Expenses as a percentage of sales:

Marketing	10%
Utilities	14%
Payroll	25%
G&A	05%

- "Below 5,000 camper nights per year is difficult to operate the business and make a profit."
- "Expenses should run between 40 and 60% of gross profit"
- Note: See Campgrounds for additional Benchmark Data

Industry Trend

- "Increased revenues based on limited supply and high demand."
- "Gradually better"
- "Affordable travel that should grow. Retired baby boomers should keep the business strong for several years."

Seller Financing
- "Outside financing based on low interest rates."
- 20 years
- 50% of all sales

Questions
- "What would you do to maximize the income?"

Resources

Trade Publications
- Guide to Appraising Recreational Vehicle Parks published by the Appraisal Institute: www.appraisalinstitute.org
- RV Life—an industry publication: www.rvlife.com

Associations
- Florida Association of RV Parks and Campgrounds: www.FARVC.org
- National Association of RV Parks and Campgrounds: www.arvc.org

		Franchise
Safe Ship (See also Franchises)		
Approx. Total Investment		$39,900 to $94,800
	NAICS 488991	Number of Businesses/Units 40

Rules of Thumb
➤ 40 percent of annual sales

Resources

Websites
- www.safeship.com

Sales Businesses (In General)
Rules of Thumb
➤ 1 to 2 times SDE plus inventory

Pricing Tips
- "In this industry, there is an abundance of owner benefits such as: high-end automobiles that are not necessary to conduct business, but are definitely a benefit, extensive travel throughout the world, dining out at five-star restaurants, etc."

Benchmark Data
- "40% of your gross commission should equate to your owner's benefit"

S - Rules of Thumb

Seller Financing
- 36 months

Questions
- "Are all of your lines paying 5 % or more? How long have you had each line? How many of your lines are industry leaders?"

Sales Consulting		
SIC 8748-08	NAICS 541613	

Rules of Thumb
➢ 33 percent of annual sales includes inventory

Pricing Tips
- "Price paid should be affected by current accounts surviving the exit of the owner."

Franchise

Samurai Sam's Teriyaki Grill		
(See also Franchises, Restaurants—Asian)		
Approx. Total Investment		$115,600 to $427,050
	NAICS 722513	Number of Businesses/Units 29

Rules of Thumb
➢ 45 percent of annual sales

➢ 1.5 times SDE

Resources

Websites
- www.samuraisams.net

Sand and Gravel Mining		
SIC 5032-11	NAICS 212321	Number of Businesses/Units 2,131

Rules of Thumb
➢ 100 percent of annual sales plus inventory

➢ 5 times EBITDA

Benchmark Data

Statistics (Sand and Gravel Mining)

Number of Establishments	2,131
Average Profit Margin	14.0%
Revenue per Employee	$581,600
Average Number of Employees	13.0
Average Wages per Employee	$62,669

Products and Services Segmentation

Industrial (silica) sand	48.8%
Construction sand and gravel	42.5%
Kaolin	5.2%
Other clays and ceramic minerals	2.8%
Common clay	0.7%

Industry Costs

Profit	14.0%
Wages	10.8%
Purchases	12.9%
Depreciation	7.6%
Marketing	0.1%
Rent & Utilities	11.2%
Other	43.4%

Market Share

CRH PLC	8.0%
HeidelbergCement AG	5.7%

Source: IBISWorld, August 2016

- "At least 150,000 tons/year is the minimum usually necessary for a profitable site."

Industry Trend

- "The outlook of the Sand and Gravel Mining industry will remain heavily dependent on demand from downstream markets, particularly infrastructure construction. Over the five years to 2021, industry revenue is expected to rise at an average annual rate of 2.4% to $15.4 billion, including an anticipated 2.6% bump in 2017. Despite the end of federal stimulus programs, a stronger economy will spur greater demand in downstream construction markets, including residential, nonresidential and infrastructure. Demand for clay and refractory materials is projected to continue to deteriorate in several downstream manufacturing industries, but this decline will be offset by stronger demand from the housing market and buoyant demand from the highway and bridge construction market."

Source: http://clients1.ibisworld.com/reports/us/industry/industryoutlook.aspx?entid=129

Sandwich Shops (See also Individual Franchised Sandwich Shops)		
SIC 5812-19	NAICS 722513	Number of Businesses/Units 38,124

Rules of Thumb

➢ 40 to 50 percent of annual sales plus inventory

➢ 2 times SDE plus inventory

➢ 3 times EBIT

➢ Franchised Sandwich Shops:
  - ✓ Blimpie—45% to 50% of annual sales
  - ✓ Lil' Dino's—50% of annual sales
  - ✓ Quiznos—25% to 30% of annual sales
  - ✓ Roly Poly—35% of annual sales
  - ✓ Jimmy John's—60% to 65% of annual sales
  - ✓ Jersey Mike's—50% of annual sales
  - ✓ Subway—60% to 65% of annual sales

➢ All above Rules of Thumb are plus inventory

➢ Average Rule of Thumb for above franchises is 46% of annual sales plus inventory

➢ Note: In averaging the Rules of Thumb for some of the larger franchised sandwich shops, it turns out that it is just about the same as sandwich shops in general—independent or franchised. However, they seem to be more saleable than independents.

Benchmark Data

Statistics (Sandwich & Sub Store Franchises)

Number of Establishments	38,124
Average Profit Margin	4.6%
Revenue per Employee	$42,000
Average Number of Employees	14.0
Average Wages per Employee	$10,198

Products and Services Segmentation

Limited-service restaurants	46.8%
Cafeteria restaurants	33.5%
Takeout restaurants	19.7%

Industry Costs

Profit	4.6%
Wages	24.3%
Purchases	36.9%
Depreciation	3.1%
Marketing	2.9%
Rent & Utilities	11.9%
Other	16.3%

Market Share

Subway	57.1%
Jimmy John's	9.7%

Source: IBISWorld, October 2015

Expenses as a percentage of annual sales

Cost of goods	28%
Payroll/labor Costs	22%
Occupancy	10%
Profit (estimated pretax)	20%

Industry Trend

- "Although most sandwiches are made at home, restaurant sandwiches rank a very strong second place, such that the sandwich strides proudly on menus across restaurant sectors. On the high side, MenuTrends tracking shows that 74% of quick-service restaurants feature sandwiches on the menu. Even on the (relatively) low side, in the fine dining sector, 62% serve sandwiches on their white tablecloths or polished wood. Across the board, sandwiches are more prevalently featured than portable, sandwich-like competition such as burgers, hot dogs, and pizza (which arguably is an open-faced hot sandwich)."

Source: "Let Them Eat Brioche! Sandwich Trends Impacting the Food Industry," Posted by David Sprinkle, marketresearch.com June 18, 2015

		Franchise
Sarpino's Pizzeria (See also Franchises, Pizza Shops, etc.)		
Approx. Total Investment		$246,995 to $333,795
SIC 5812-22	NAICS 722513	Number of Businesses/Units 46
Rules of Thumb		

- ➢ 50 percent of annual sales plus inventory

Resources

Websites
- www.sarpinosfranchise.com

Schools—Educational & Non-Vocational		
	NAICS 61	
Rules of Thumb		

- ➢ 40% to 50% of Annual Gross Sales
- ➢ 2 to 3 times SDE
- ➢ 4 times EBITDA

Pricing Tips

- "40–50% staffing, 15–20% facility, 20–25% other."

S - Rules of Thumb

- "Simple rule for schools: preschools 20% rent or bank loan, 20% other expenses, 40 to 45% staff, balance is yours. As for private schools up to 12th grade, staff is 50 to 55%."
- "Sales can be based on the number of students in the school. Today's range is from $5,000 to $12,000 per student."
- "For small schools (revenues < $5M 3 to 4 X Adjusted EBITDA.
  For medium schools (revenues between $5M and $20M) 4 to 5 X Adjusted EBITDA.
  For large schools (revenues > $20M) 5 to 6 X Adjusted EBITDA.
  Accreditation adds to value. Good regulatory metrics add to value."
- "Use cash flow to determine price and what the lenders will do with that figure."

Expert Comments

"Have good strong financials that show what the business is doing."

"The current US Executive Branch and the Department of Education, in particular, have been toughening regulations for private sector schools. The regulatory environment in the current administration appears to favor only public sector schools, with an intent of pushing private sector schools out of business. This trend is being challenged in the courts and is likely to become more fair with any new administration."

"Look at books, enrollment numbers, staff expense. You do not have to go back far; look at more current data. You're buying today, not 3 years ago."

"High school and college type schools are in big demand and there is a limited number of schools on the market. Trade school is a new area that is in demand."

"Both school buyers and sellers should work with M&A intermediaries who are extremely knowledgeable in the industry. Because of the challenging regulatory environment, logic alone cannot be relied upon. Buyers and sellers need to know the right questions to ask and what information to request. Most importantly, they need to clearly understand the answers that are provided. Additionally, every transaction requires an industry-experienced attorney. There are many nuances in today's regulatory environment that require the knowledge that only experience can provide."

"Overall there are more childcare centers in the country than private schools, adult ed schools, and other types of schools. There is a market for schools."

"There are no physical barriers to entry, but creating a quality school or day care takes more than a facility. It takes quality teachers and leaders. Finding these is the real barrier to entry."

Benchmark Data

Statistics (Business Certification & IT Schools)

Number of Establishments	1,531
Average Profit Margin	8.4%
Revenue per Employee	$165,800
Average Number of Employees	9.8
Average Wages per Employee	$54,643

Products and Services Segmentation

Professional development and management training..39.5%
Computer and information sciences 26.9%
Basic education and improvement courses..15.9%
Business, management and public administration 13.2%
Other occupational, technical and trade skill training 4.5%

Industry Costs

Profit 8.4%
Wages...33.3%
Purchases..10.1%
Depreciation..2.4%
Marketing 4.8%
Rent & Utilities 9.0%
Other..32.0%

Source: IBISWorld, May 2016

- "Student roster and valuation per student enrolled"
- "Cash flow of the school will determine price. It's hard to use per employee, per student or per foot."

Expenses as a percentage of annual sales

Cost of goods..10% to 20%
Payroll/labor Costs...40% to 50%
Occupancy...15% to 20%
Profit (estimated pretax) ....10% to 20%

Industry Trend
- "Not many opening, but a lot will sell."
- "As the population grows so does the business. Parents need care in preschool, and education leads to better jobs."
- "The sale of schools is coming back. Buyers are looking for good investments that have a good track record."
- "There are many trends that affect transactions:
    - ✓ Currently baby-boomer school owners are ready for retirement. They have built great schools and want to divest to help support their retirement.
    - ✓ Increased regulations are forcing some good as well as bad schools to sell. This creates opportunities for qualified and knowledgeable buyers.
    - ✓ The international market is growing. International schools and investors are seeking U.S. acquisitions in international-friendly cities."
- "There is plenty of growth as the population increases. Franchises and corporate-owned schools are increasingly popular."
- "Always students who need help, fall behind, need passing grades to pass"

Seller Financing
- "Smaller schools—seller financing; larger Schools—outside financing"
- 5 years

Questions

- "Financials and reason for selling."
- "Look at the books, look at staff cost, look at student income and make sure your debt if you get a loan can service the loan and give you a profit."
- "Do you have programs for kids? How is the establishment record with community care licensing? Do you provide snacks, lunch? What curriculum is being utilized and what is the average experience of the teachers? Do you have a director? What are his or her responsibilities?"
- "A buyer of a career school should ask all the questions that would be asked during any business transaction. In addition, of great importance for a career school acquisition, are:
    - ✓ Names and contact information of all regulatory bodies
    - ✓ Updates on past and current regulatory issues
    - ✓ Status of all approvals and dates of upcoming renewals
    - ✓ Enrollment trends
    - ✓ Job saturation for programs and community served
    - ✓ How long the owners will stay on."
- "What is your market area?"

Resources

Websites
- U.S. Department of Education: www.ed.gov

Associations
- New England Association of Schools and Colleges (NEASC): www.neasc.org
- Northwest Commission on Colleges and Universities (NWCCU): www.nwccu.org
- The Southern Association of Colleges and Schools Commission on Colleges: www.sacscoc.org
- Accrediting Bureau of Health Education Schools (ABHES): www.abhes.org
- Accrediting Commission of Career Schools and Colleges (ACCSC): www.accsc.org
- Accrediting Council for Continuing Education and Training (ACCET): www.accet.org
- Accrediting Council for Independent Colleges and Schools (ACICS): www.acics.org
- The Higher Learning Commission: https://www.hlcommission.org
- Distance Education Accrediting Commission: http://www.deac.org
- Career Education Colleges and Universities: http://www.career.org

Schools—Tutoring & Driving Schools	
(See also Schools/Educational, Vocational)	
	NAICS tutoring—611691; driving schools—611692
	Number of Businesses/Units 142,836

Rules of Thumb

➤ Driving Schools/Instruction

➤ 1 times SDE + fair market value of fixed assets

➤ 40 to 45 percent of annual sales + fair market value of fixed assets

Pricing Tips

- Driving Schools/Instruction
- "High barrier to entry due to increasingly higher and stricter state regulations and standards."
- The rule of thumb above applies to "learn-to-drive schools" that primarily teach teenagers to drive and pass a state driving test. It is mandatory in many states. However, there are many other types of driving schools such as: winter driving, commercial driving (trucks, etc.), race driving, etc.

Benchmark Data

Statistics (Tutoring & Driving Schools)

Number of Establishments	161,661
Average Profit Margin	6.4%
Revenue per Employee	$31,300
Average Number of Employees	1.9
Average Wages per Employee	$12,832

Products and Services Segmentation

Test preparation	44.4%
Tutoring	26.2%
Other schools	10.6%
Driving schools	10.6%

Industry Costs

Profit	6.4%
Wages	40.7%
Purchases	10.1%
Depreciation	3.1%
Marketing	2.8%
Rent & Utilities	6.3%
Other	30.6%

Source: IBISWorld, January 2016

Schools—Vocational & Training

(See also Schools—Educational/Non-Vocational)

	NAICS 611210	

Rules of Thumb

➤ 75 to 100 percent of annual sales plus inventory

➤ 2 to 4 times SDE plus inventory

➤ 1.5 times EBIT

➤ 3 to 5 times EBITDA

Pricing Tips

- "Home-based franchise sells for much higher multiple of 4 or above, if it's generating $300K+ in revenue. Educational franchise that allows office location contributes to higher SDE. Customer base of 4–14 years is highly preferred due to high demand."
- "Accreditation and Title IV funding provides for higher pricing."
- "Pricing is all over the board because of the size of a facility. The larger the school, the more the owners profit."
- "Value is driven by type of program (longer, more expensive programs are more valuable), enrollment, and enrollment growth."

Expert Comments

"Great industry with room to grow. The childcare, private school and adult education industry is on the move."

Benchmark Data

Statistics (Trade and Technical Schools)

Number of Establishments	8,886
Average Profit Margin	9.7%
Revenue per Employee	$103,600
Average Number of Employees	14.7
Average Wages per Employee	$38,832

Products and Services Segmentation

Other professional development programs	57.6%
Flight training programs	18.5%
Cosmetology and barber schools	14.5%
Apprenticeship training programs	9.4%

Industry Costs

Profit	9.7%
Wages	37.2%
Purchases	19.4%
Depreciation	3.4%
Marketing	7.8%
Rent & Utilities	6.4%
Other	16.1%

Source: IBISWorld, February 2016

- "Sales per license cap can range from $6,000 to $ 14,000. An example: a 100-student licensed school could sell for as much as $1.4 million. Most schools sell based on Cash Flow."

Expenses as a percentage of annual sales

Cost of goods	10% to 20%
Payroll/labor Costs	35% to 40%
Occupancy	05%
Profit (estimated pretax)	20% to 30%

Industry Trend

- "Trend is going up in terms of new type of businesses. Trend is going down if the franchise does not innovate and provide new services."
- "Generally increasing revenues"

Seller Financing

- "Most of the time seller finance due to lack of tangible assets"
- 10 years

Questions

- "Customer retention rate; method of new customer acquisition; employee qualifications, turnaround and hiring process."
- "Is the school accredited and what is the status?"

Resources

Websites

- RWM provides a database of private post-secondary vocational schools in all 50 states: www.schoolsforsale.com

---

		Franchise
Sears Carpet and Upholstery Care & Home Services		
(See also Carpet Cleaning, Franchises)		
Approx. Total Investment		$26,00 to $192,000
	NAICS 561740	Number of Businesses/Units 138

Rules of Thumb

➤ 35 percent of annual sales plus inventory

➤ Note: Sears offers three home service franchises to choose from: Carpet & Upholstery Cleaning; Air Duct Cleaning & Indoor Air Quality; Garage Solutions (Doors, Repairs, Repairs, etc.). We believe that the rule of thumb above would apply to any of the three franchises.

Resources

Websites

- www.searsclean.com
- www.ownasearsfranchise.com

Secretarial Services		
	NAICS 561410	

Rules of Thumb

➤ 50 percent of annual revenues includes inventory

Security Services/Systems (See also Guard Services)

SIC 7382-02	NAICS 561621	Number of Businesses/Units 78,869

Rules of Thumb

➢ 50 percent of annual sales includes inventory

➢ 2 to 3 times SDE includes inventory

➢ 3 times EBIT

➢ 4 times EBITDA

➢ 24 to 28 times monthly revenue based on an average $25 mo. per account plus inventory

Pricing Tips

- "Security Alarm companies generally sell on a multiple of their Recurring Monthly Revenue. Currently, the multiple is 33 times, excluding assets. Monitoring contracts is key to the deal."
- "Typically, an alarm company sells for a multiple of Recurring Monthly Revenue (RMR), plus any additional assets the company may own. In addition, the multiple of RMR may vary for contract vs non-contracted customers. Typically, contracted customers generate between 33x–36x RMR and non-contracted will get between 10x–25x RMR."
- "Weighted monthly billing times 4"

Expert Comments

"There are many barriers to entry, specifically having the licenses in place to run the business. A buyer with no experience would need 4 years just to obtain the licensing."

"An alarm company can be run from any location because all work is completed at a customer's home or business. They are very marketable and are not easy to replicate. The hurdle is that a new owner needs to hold a Class C & D license for low-voltage wiring, which is a 3–5 year process to obtain."

Benchmark Data

Statistics (Security Alarm Services)

Number of Establishments	59,311
Average Profit Margin	3.5%
Revenue per Employee	$121,600
Average Number of Employees	3.2
Average Wages per Employee	$34,901

Products and Services Segmentation

Residential security alarm system services with monitoring	48.0%
Nonresidential security alarm system services with monitoring	26.6%
Nonresidential security system and lock installation without monitoring	16.2%
Residential security system and lock installation without monitoring	9.2%

Major Market Segmentation

Residential clients.. 51.0%
Business and commercial clients.. 37.0%
Government clients.. 12.0%

Industry Costs

Profit 3.5%
Wages.. 28.6%
Purchases.. 34.6%
Depreciation.. 0.7%
Marketing... 2.2%
Rent & Utilities 4.4%
Other.. 26.0%

Market Share

ADT Security Services Inc. 15.1%

Enterprises by Employment Size

Number of Employees	Share
1–4	63.8%
10–19	9.4%
20–99	7.1%
100–499	1.1%

Source: IBISWorld, April 2016

Statistics (Security Services)

Number of Establishments.. 16,801
Average Profit Margin 4.2%
Revenue per Employee $39,800
Average Number of Employees 48.6
Average Wages per Employee $25,862

Products and Services Segmentation

Security guard services for buildings and grounds 70.6%
Investigation services 15.9%
Armored vehicle services... 6.7%
Security guard services for special events 4.4%
Other services... 2.4%

Major Market Segmentation

Corporations 29.7%
Financial institutions 19.0%
Government clients... 18.5%
Residential and other... 17.8%
Retail and leisure 15.0%

Industry Costs

Profit 4.2%
Wages.. 65.2%
Purchases.. 9.5%
Depreciation... 0.4%
Marketing 1.0%
Rent & Utilities 2.6%
Other.. 17.1%

Market Share

Securitas AB	14.3%
G4S PLC	7.8%
Allied Universal	6.0%

Source: IBISWorld, February 2016

- "Generally, there should be 500 paying monthly monitoring accounts for every 1 technician."

Dealers' Revenue Segmented by Business Services

Monitoring	49%
Sales/Installation	30%
Service contracts	09%
Non-contracted service	05%
Test & inspection	03%
Other	02%
Hosted & managed services	01%

Source: "Performance Remains Solid" by Laura Stepanek, sdmmag.com, May 8, 2015

Expenses as a percentage of annual sales

Cost of goods	40%
Payroll/labor Costs	40%
Occupancy	05% to 10%
Profit (estimated pretax)	10%

Industry Trend

- "Despite growing concerns over a potential global economic slowdown, the outlook for the Private Security Services industry in the U.S. and abroad continues to be upbeat. As security concerns continue to escalate, government and private entities are expected to increase spending to improve all aspects of their security programs. The following statistics and trends suggest that the Private Security Services Industry is poised for continued growth in 2016:
    - ✓ Worldwide annual spending on private contract security services is predicted to climb to $244 billion this year, according to a report from the Freedonia Group.
    - ✓ The Freedonia Group report also notes that security guard services will attract the largest share of overall U.S. security spending through 2019, highlighting the continued importance of having skilled, qualified personnel to conduct security system monitoring and incident response.
    - ✓ IBISWorld's Security Services market research report predicts an annual growth rate of 2.4% for the security services sector over the next 10 to 15 years.
    - ✓ Fiscally strapped municipalities are increasingly turning to contract security services providers as an alternative to expanding their more expensive police forces, notes a research report from Robert H. Perry & Associates."

  Source: www.summitsecurity.com/looking-forward-security-industry-trends-and-outlook-for-2016-and-beyond/

- "This industry is very stable and a strong housing market with support the industry."

Seller Financing

- "Easily financed through SBA. In any deal, there will be a hold back of 10%-25% of the deal for a period of 13 months for any customer loss."
- "There are industry specific financing companies that will hold contracted accounts as collateral. Also the SBA has gone 10 years because of the RMR."
- "3 to 5 years and an average of 20 to 50 percent of transaction value financed by seller"

Questions

- "A buyer wants to see a seller contracts and the terms of the contract."
- "1. Do they own the central station? 2. If not, do they own the phone lines that connect to central station? 3. What % of their customers are contracted?"
- "What are the contract terms? How long have you had this account? Buyers do not like government contracts."
- "Type of guard services and customer list. Most guard companies have one major client."

Resources

Websites

- The American Society for Industrial Security (ASIS): www.asisonline.org

Trade Publications

- www.sdmmag.com

Associations

- National Burglar & Fire Alarm Association: www.alarm.org
- Security Industry Association (SIA): www.siaonline.org

Self Storage (Mini Storage)		
	NAICS 531130	Number of Businesses/Units 57,632

Rules of Thumb

➤ 1 times EBITDA

Pricing Tips

- "Very few buyers or appraisers will count revenues in excess of 90% of potential rents, except in very unusual circumstances."
- "What are We Selling—Dirt, Bricks or Income? The reality is that while the dirt and bricks will be transferred by the deed, it is the income stream that creates the value in self-storage properties.

   "Operating Expenses: It is considered a rule of thumb that operating expenses generally run between 35%–45% with many in the range of 40%. However, this is just a rule of thumb, and if your project falls out of this range further analysis may be required.

   "Typical Operating Expense Categories:
   - ✓ Real estate taxes
   - ✓ On-site salaries & benefits
   - ✓ Property insurance

S - Rules of Thumb

 ✓ Utilities
 ✓ Repairs and maintenance
 ✓ Off-site management fees
 ✓ Marketing & advertising
 ✓ Office expenses
 ✓ Capital reserves"

Source: "Market Monitor," June 2015 by Ben Vestal, President of the Argus Self Storage Sales Network

- "These are difficult because they are often a means of holding land until it reaches the point where it is more profitable to redevelop it for another use. Most buyers look for a cash on cash return of about 20% on the amount they must invest to purchase the property compared to the purchase price/financing that can be obtained."
- "Key factors are vacancy and turnover of units. Buyers want to get at least a 20% cash-on-cash return."
- "Most involve the real estate"
- "Pricing is driven by capitalization rates and expense ratios."

Cap Rate Adjustments

The little chart that follows outlines specific business issues and assigns them an adjustment to the cap rate. What is good about this chart is the specific areas it covers and that it essentially assigns a rating to each one that impacts the valuation or pricing of each business.

Item	9.50–10.00	10.00–11.00	11.00–11.50
Occupancy (last 2 years)	95%–100%	90%–95%	<90%
Rates (last 2 years)	Continuous Rise	Steady	Falling
Size	>45,000	30,000–45,000	<30,000
Competition (3 mile radius)	None	One	More than One
Competition's Vacancy	95%–100%	90%–95%	<90%
Surrounding Area	Growing Metro	Large City	Rural
Density (5 mile radius)	>200,000	100,000–200,000	<100,000
Median Household Income	Above Average	Average	Below Average
Manager	Full-time	Full-time	Other
Records (last 3 years)	Computerized & Professionally Audited	Computerized	Other
Computer System	Computers & SS Accounting Software	Computers	None
Construction	Concrete or Brick	Combination Brick & Metal	Metal
Maintenance	Pristine	Little Deferred Maintenance	Modest Deferred Maintenance
Security	Full Gate & Card Access	Full Gate	Other
Access	Very Direct	Clear, but Not Direct	Difficult
Visibility	Can see Sign & Facility	Can see Sign & Entrance	Can see Sign only
Drives	Concrete	Paved	Gravel

Source: Argus Real Estate, Inc., Denver, CO

Note: This is from an excellent article by Michael L. McCune, Cap Rates and Sales Prices. For more information visit www.selfstorage.com—an excellent site. The above is a bit dated but still of interest.

- "You can look at it a couple of different ways. It depends on your location; but here in southern Indiana, mini-storage facilities are being appraised based upon the number of units. Age, condition and income are also looked at. Our appraiser just today told us that they are ranging from $3,000 to $3,500 per unit. So your 131-unit facility would appraise for around $393,000 if it were located here.

  "Another way to figure out what your potential income will be: if you are totally full, then multiply that number by 60 to 75 percent, because of the reality of occupancy. Use those numbers to figure out what your income/expense ratio will be. Your income should be at least 1.25 over your debt service (if it's not, then you're paying too much for the property). That extra 25 percent will help cover vacancies, utilities, labor, etc."

  Source: www.autocareforum.com

Expert Comments

"Storage units are a great way to warehouse land until the highest and best use changes."

"This is a real-estate purchase with a business element attached to it. The value of the underlying real estate controls a large part of the value of the property. Management is more important than most people realize."

Benchmark Data

Statistics (Storage and Warehouse Leasing)

Number of Establishments	57,632
Average Profit Margin	40.0%
Revenue per Employee	$238,700
Average Number of Employees	2.5
Average Wages per Employee	$30,673

Products and services Segmentation

10-by-10-foot storage spaces	23.1%
10-by-20-foot storage spaces	20.6%
Other	15.6%
10-by-15-foot storage spaces	14.4%
Five-by-10-foot storage spaces	11.3%
10-by-30-foot storage spaces	6.2%
10-by-25-foot storage spaces	5.3%
Five-by-5-foot storage spaces	3.5%

Major Market Segmentation

Long-term residential customers	48.9%
Short-term residential customers	21.0%
Commercial firms	18.4%
Military	5.9%
Students	5.8%

Industry Costs

Profit	40.0%
Wages	13.0%
Purchases	6.6%
Depreciation	14.5%
Marketing	2.2%
Rent & Utilities	11.9%
Other	11.8%

Market Share

Public Storage Inc.. 7.2%

Source: IBISWorld, June 2016

- Here is some data from the Self Storage Industry Fact Sheet:
  - ✓ "The self storage industry has been one of the fastest-growing sectors of the United States commercial real estate industry over the period of the last 40 years.
  - ✓ There are now over 48,500 'primary' self storage facilities in the United States as of year-end 2014; another 4,000 are 'secondary' facilities ('primary' means that self storage is the 'primary' source of business revenue—U.S. Census Bureau).
  - ✓ Total self storage rentable space in the US is roughly 2.5 billion square feet [more than 210 million square meters]. That figure represents more than 78 square miles of rentable self storage space, under roof—or an area well more than 3 times the size of Manhattan Island (NY).
  - ✓ The distribution of U.S. self storage facilities (Q2-2015) is as follows: 32% urban, 52% suburban and 16% rural.
  - ✓ The average revenue per square foot varies from facility to facility; however, here are the data for Q2 2015: $1.25 PSF for a non-climate controlled 10 x 10 unit and $1.60 PSF for a climate controlled 10 x 10 unit.
  - ✓ U.S. self storage facilities employed more than 170,000 persons, or an average of 3.5 employees per facility.
  - ✓ The average (mean) size of a 'primary' self storage facility in the US is approximately 56,900 square feet.
  - ✓ Occupancy rates for self storage facilities as of Q2 2015 were 90% (percentage of units rented per facility) up from 86.8% at year-end 2013.
  - ✓ Of over 10,000 facilities surveyed, the mean facility size is 546 units and the median facility size is 517 units.
  - ✓ About 13% of all self storage renters say they will rent for less than 3 months; 18% for 3-6 months; 18% for 7–12 months; 22% for 1–2 years; and 30% for more than 2 years.
  - ✓ Some 47% of all self storage renters have an annual household income of less than $50,000 per year; 63% have an annual household income of less than $75,000 per year.
  - ✓ The top-5 self storage companies, including 4 real estate investment trusts (Public Storage, Extra Space, Sovran and CubeSmart) plus U-Haul (a public company/non-REIT), own, operate and/or manage some 5,600 self storage facilities, or about 11.5% of all U.S. facilities. Several public companies are now offering third-party management of facilities owned by other investors. Hundreds of facilities are now being managed by the three public companies that have moved into this service area.
  - ✓ In addition to the public companies in the industry (above), there are more than 150 privately held firms that own and operate 10 or more self storage facilities. In addition, there are some 4,000 firms that own and operate from 2–9 self storage facilities. Lastly, there are more than 26,000 firms that own and operate just one facility."

Source: 2015–2016 Self Storage Industry Fact Sheet, July 1, 2015

Business Reference Guide **2017**

"Sample facility

Size	40,000 SF
Average Rent	$71/month
Rent/SF	$8.52/yr.
Current Occupancy	88%
Market Occupancy	70%
Potential Rent	$341,000
Rents Collected @ 88%	$300,000/yr.
Expenses	$100,000
Net Operating Income	$200,000/yr.
Value @ 9.5	$2,100,000
Loan Amount @ 75%	$1,575,000
Debt Service @ 6.5%	$128,000/yr."

Source: "The State of Self Storage Real Estate" by Michael L. McCune, Argus Self-Storage Sales Network

Expenses as a percentage of annual sales

Cost of goods	0
Payroll/labor Costs	0
Occupancy	0
Profit (estimated pretax)	05%

Industry Trend

- "IRR (Integra Realty Resources) forecasts $32.7 billion in self-storage transactions in 2016. Population gains, especially in the South and Southwest, have led to an increase in demand for apartment units, which has propelled an increase in multifamily construction. This, in turn, has driven renter demand in storage space.

  "The intense pace of multifamily development and demand are key leading indicators for long-term self-storage demand. On the investment side, the inventory of self-storage properties available remains low, due to a pullback in construction during the Great Recession and its aftermath. Though new construction is increasing, especially in metro areas, it's not nearly enough to meet the current demand. As a result the sector has been boasting strong occupancy and revenue gains, and attracting first-time buyers. Sellers are experiencing record-level prices, while those acquiring are keeping an eye out for value-add opportunities.

  "REITs are actively expanding their portfolios, while industry consolidation is a trend that will likely continue. It does need to be mentioned, however, that self-storage is a highly fragmented industry, with low barriers to entry. Still, investors are becoming comfortable with owning self-storage properties. As such, aggressive asset pricing has continued into 2016. IRR forecasts that, given continued demand, lack of supply and plenty of investors from within the industry as well as from other property types, the self-storage sector will remain a very strong investment type for the remainder of the year and into 2017."

  Source:http://www.irr.com/_FileLibrary/Office/P885/IRR_2016%20SelfStorage%20 Report_April%2018%202016%20by%20Steve%20Johnson.pdf

Seller Financing

- 10 to 15 years

Questions

- "Who manages the site and are they willing to stay on? Can existing financing be assumed?"
- "Occupancy and waiting list"
- "Management turnover"

Resources

Websites
- Argus Self-Storage Sales Network: www.argusselfstorage.com

Trade Publications
- Mini Storage Messenger—excellent resources: www.selfstoragenow.com

Associations
- Self Storage Association—An excellent site with lots of information: www.selfstorage.org

			Franchise
Senior Helpers (See also Franchises, Home Health Care—Care Giving)			
Approx. Total Investment			$81,300 to $117,300
	NAICS 621610	Number of Businesses/Units	265

Rules of Thumb

➢ 40 to 45 percent

Resources

Websites
- www.seniorhelpers.com

Service Businesses (In General)

Rules of Thumb

➢ 35 percent to 50 percent of annual revenues [sales] plus inventory; however it is not unusual for service businesses to sell for a much higher figure

➢ 72 percent of annual sales plus inventory

➢ 2 times SDE

Pricing Tips

- "One of the most important factors is determining how replaceable the owner is, and how much of the revenue the owner generates him/herself."
- "Consider the last 3 to 5 years—is it an up or down trend? Is the business expandable or is it at its peak?"
- Valuation Issues for Service Companies

  "On the plus side, almost all service companies have recurring revenue. Some, like funeral homes, have very little, while others, like Paychex (payroll service), Cintas (uniform rental) and Dun & Bradstreet (credit reports) have a lot of recurring revenue with each customer. Another plus is that service companies usually have modest capital equipment requirements resulting in a high return on assets. Expansion and geographic roll-outs like retail and restaurant chains can be readily expedited. Additionally, service companies are less impacted by foreign competition. From a macro-economic view, the U.S. had a $65 billion service trade surplus in 2002 while the U.S. had a large manufactured goods deficit in 2002. And, from a competitive point of view, large service companies can source services off-shore just as manufacturing companies have done in order to reduce costs. For example, the annual cost for a computer-related employee in the U.S. is $61,600 compared to India at $5,800.

"On the minus side, service companies are largely dependent on their management team and employees. They are, by and large, the assets of the company... so imagine what would happen to the value of an architectural firm or a law firm if the people walked off their job. Since labor is the major expense of service companies, they are more difficult to substantially increase sales (or scale-up) compared to manufacturing companies where labor might only represent 20% of sales.

"From a service owner's perspective, rarely can they fully cash-out at closing or rarely can they walk away from the business at closing, as service companies are highly relationship driven... not only with the customers but with the employees. Further, unlike some small niche manufacturers, many service companies need to reach a higher revenue threshold of $10+ million to prove the company's viability of not being dependent on just a few key people or a few key customers.

"The valuation multiples vary widely across the various sectors and equally divergent are the various structures of the transactions. Of course, the critical issues in the valuation of service companies include the extent of their profitability, relative size, proprietary nature of the service firm's capabilities and the potential growth. Conventional wisdom dictates that service firms are valued between .5 x to 1.0 x revenues, but a closer look at the following sectors shows a wide differential of valuation metrics based on Last Twelve Months (LTM) of revenues and EBITDA." (A bit dated, but still of interest)

Expert Comments

"Competition and the industry trends (growing or constant) are important for calculating the ROI on the intangible part."

Benchmark Data

Expenses as a percentage of annual sales

Cost of goods	30%
Payroll/labor Costs	30%
Occupancy	05%
Profit (estimated pretax)	20%

Industry Trend
- "Growth."

	Franchise

ServiceMaster Clean	
(See also Franchises, Janitorial Services, Maid Services, etc.)	
Approx. Total Investment	$51,000 to $260,000
NAICS 561720	Number of Businesses/Units 3,077

Rules of Thumb
➤ 55 to 60 percent of annual sales plus inventory

Resources

Websites
- www.ownafranchise.com

		Franchise
Servpro (See also Franchises, Janitorial Services, Maid Services, etc.)		
	NAICS 561720	Number of Businesses/Units 1,000

Rules of Thumb

➢ 90 to 95 percent of annual sales plus inventory

Resources

Websites
- www.servpro.com

Shoe Stores		
SIC 5661-01	NAICS 451110	Number of Businesses/Units 31,000

Rules of Thumb

➢ 15 to 20 percent of annual sales plus inventory

Benchmark Data

Statistics (Shoe Stores)

Number of Establishments	31,000
Average Profit Margin	3.6%
Revenue per Employee	$166,500
Average Number of Employees	7.3
Average Wages per Employee	$18,561

Products and Services Segmentation

Women's shoes (not including athletic)	32.3%
Men's athletic shoes	22.5%
Children's shoes	15.0%
Men's shoes (not including athletic)	14.8%
Women's athletic shoes	11.1%
Slippers and other shoes	4.3%

Industry Costs

Profit	3.6%
Wages	11.1%
Purchases	58.1%
Depreciation	0.9%
Marketing	4.3%
Rent & Utilities	9.5%
Other	12.5%

Market Share

Foot Locker Inc.	12.0%
Payless ShoeSource	7.3%
Designer Shoe Warehouse Inc.	6.4%
Brown Shoe Company Inc.	6.0%

Source: IBISWorld, December 2015

Industry Trend

- "IBISWorld expects the Shoe Stores industry to experience solid growth as consumers continue to regain confidence and purchasing power in the five years to 2020. During the five-year period, the Consumer Confidence Index is forecast to grow at an annualized rate of 0.9%, while disposable income is expected to increase at an annualized rate of 2.5%. Instead of simply purchasing necessities, shoppers will increasingly return to shopping for discretionary items. Recovering purchasing habits are expected to help boost industry revenue; IBISWorld projects revenue to grow at an annualized rate of 2.7% to $42.5 billion over the five years to 2020.

  "Athletic shoes are a significant source of revenue for this industry; they currently account for more than a third of the total. As sporting activity increases, so will demand for appropriate shoes. This trend will help support industry revenue growth over the next five years."

  Source: http://clients1.ibisworld.com/reports/us/industry/industryoutlook.aspx?entid=1073

- "The U.S. market for athletic shoes is one of the strongest of the global markets. However, U.S.-based companies and their competitors have long been multi-national firms operating in diverse overseas markets selling footwear and also athletic apparel in increasingly competitive markets. The athletic footwear is highly dependent on fashion trends, customer preferences and other fashion-related factors. Many of the industry's highest-margin products are sold to young males between the ages of 12 and 25 and are subject to frequent shifts in fashion trends."

  Source: "Athletic Shoe Industry Analysis" by Robert Shaftoe, Demand Media
  http://smallbusiness.chron.com/athletic-shoe-industry-analysis-74098.html

Resources

Trade Publications
- Footwear News: footwearnews.com

Associations
- National Shoe Retailers Association: www.nsra.org

Short Line Railroads		
	NAICS 482112	

Pricing Tips

- "These are highly regulated businesses that, as businesses, tend to be basically real estate businesses. Many buyers tend to be hobby buyers. Historically, buyers have grossly overpaid to purchase these businesses, then not exploited the potential of the real estate business. Buyers are almost always industry related in some way. Sellers are mainly large operating corporations who cannot operate these units economically."

- "Buyers are quoting 1.6 to 1.85 times gross revenues and in most cases it is a seller's market."

- "If it's for sale, that pretty much guarantees that someone with expertise has determined that they cannot operate it profitably and/or make the capital investments required. Sellers have usually deferred capital investment and maintenance to an extreme degree prior to sale."

Industry Trend

- "The U.S. economy continues to grow, and strong demand for rail service demonstrates that the freight rail industry is integral to this growth. By providing cost-effective transportation of goods, from lumber to oil to auto parts, freight rail is playing a central role in positive economic trends—including rising gross domestic product, improving employment statistics and low gasoline prices.

   "Freight rail is ready for this and more. In 2015, the nation's major freight railroads plan to spend an estimated $29 billion—which would set an annual record—to build, maintain and grow the rail network. This private spending will go to expenditures like new equipment and locomotives, installation of new track and bridges, the raising of tunnels and new technology used to keep America's rail network the best in the world.

   "With the right federal policies in place, measures that support market pricing and do not stifle railroad investment, the world's best rail network is on track to be even better."

   Source: "For 2015, Freight Rail Will Carry the Economy," https://www.aar.org/policy/2015-outlook

- "America's short line railroads provide fuel savings and environmentally friendly shipping for small businesses and communities around the country. One freight rail car can carry a ton of cargo 436 miles on just one gallon of fuel. Short line railroads take the equivalent of nearly 33 million truck loads off the highways, saving the country over $1.4 billion annually in highway repair costs and improving highway safety and congestion."

   Source: American Short Line and Regional Railroad System (ASLRRA)

Shuttle Services & Special Needs Transportation	
	NAICS shuttle services—485999;
	NAICS special needs transportation—485991

Rules of Thumb

➤ 3 times EBITDA plus the value of the vehicles

Benchmark Data

Statistics (Airport Shuttle Operators)

Number of Establishments	619
Average Profit Margin	8.5%
Revenue per Employee	$64,900
Average Number of Employees	20.8
Average Wages per Employee	$26,389

Products and Services Segmentation

Local shuttle services for leisure.. 67.0%
Local shuttle services for business 30.5%
Other.. 1.9%
Long-distance shuttle services 0.6%

Industry Costs

Profit 8.5%
Wages... 40.5%
Purchases.. 13.1%
Depreciation.. 6.1%
Marketing 0.5%
Rent & Utilities 3.2%
Other.. 28.1%

Source: IBISWorld, August 2016

		Franchise
Signarama (See also Franchises, Manufacturing—Signs, Sign Companies)		
Approx. Total Investment		$168,000 to $172,000
	NAICS 339950	Number of Businesses/Units 875

Rules of Thumb

➢ 55 to 60 percent of annual sales plus inventory

Resources

Websites

- www.signarama.com

Sign Companies (See also Manufacturing—Signs)		
	NAICS 339950	

Rules of Thumb

➢ 48 percent to 50 percent of annual sales includes inventory

➢ 2.5 times SDE includes inventory

➢ 3.5 to 5 times EBITDA

Pricing Tips

- "Relative to annual revenue—critical to have a 3rd party certified valuation of the business & commercial real estate when optional."

- "Businesses with gross sales of over $1M typically will get slightly higher #'s than the rule of thumb. Technology can have an impact on the sales price. Large format printers and flatbed printers have become more commonplace and are expected to be in-house by many buyers."

- "Margins do vary significantly in this industry. The product is custom made, and there are a variety of products that can be produced, with margins varying within the product ranges. So, one company that is producing one product 'niche' within the category may be more profitable than another company focusing on a different product 'niche.'"

- "Most sign companies are small independents—SDE is a better calculation than EBIT or EBITDA. Inventory is not usually an excessive number, and usually included as part of a 2.5–3 x multiple of SDE."

Expert Comments

"Difficulty in selling operations—real estate is usually more valuable than the business."

"There are many segments/areas of specialization within the industry that can affect margins and equipment needed. Additionally, some buyers will view the location as a critical element and others do not. The industry is a B2B service, so there are varying points of view on the issue of 'location.'"

"Make sure that customer base is diverse—both in terms of types of industries served as well that one or two key customers aren't a huge percentage of the total revenue."

Benchmark Data

Statistics (Sign & Banner Manufacturing Franchises)

Number of Establishments	37
Average Profit Margin	4.8%
Revenue per Employee	$150,400
Average Number of Employees	7.2
Average Wages per Employee	$40,602

Products and Services Segmentation

Banners and flags	24.6%
Building signs	23.2%
Trade show exhibits	20.6%
Point-of-sale displays	13.6%
Electric signs	13.2%
Other	4.8%

Major Market Segmentation

Accommodation and food services	48.6%
Other retailers	21.1%
Car dealers and gas stations	16.5%
Professional services	8.8%
Other	5.0%

Industry Costs

Profit	4.8%
Wages	28.0%
Purchases	40.4%
Depreciation	1.6%
Marketing	1.5%
Rent & Utilities	0.8%
Other	21.2%

Market Share

Signarama	51.5%
Fastsigns International Inc.	33.9%
Image360	14.5%

Source: IBISWorld, July 2016

- "Sales per employee—$150,000 to $180,000"

Expenses as a percentage of annual sales

Cost of goods	25% to 28%
Payroll/labor Costs	20% to 25%
Occupancy	15% to 20%
Profit (estimated pretax)	20% to 25%

Industry Trend

- "Digital signage is today used in numerous market verticals such as retail, healthcare, transportation, office and enterprise, education, foodservice and outdoor signage. At the end of 2014, there were approximately 25.4 million connected digital screens in use worldwide. Berg Insight forecasts that this number will grow at a CAGR of 20.2 percent to reach 63.8 million units by 2019."

  Source: "Shipments Of Connected Digital Signs Will Reach 17.2 Million In 2019," http://www.signs.org/Newsroom/IndustryNews/IndustryNewsItem.aspx?NewsID=3358

- "IBISWorld estimates that total advertising expenditure will increase at an average annual rate of 4.4% over the five years to 2021. Furthermore, traditional mass-market print media is anticipated to continue declining, strengthening the appeal of billboards as one of the few remaining options for advertisers seeking to reach a general audience. As companies increase their marketing budgets, businesses in the related Billboard and Outdoor Advertising industry will likely purchase more billboards and displays from manufacturers."

  Source: http://clients1.ibisworld.com/reports/us/industry/industryoutlook.aspx?entid=902

- "Big transitions: outdoor signage going to digital wide-format printing, installation, even car wraps. Promotional, fragmented, small players, local. Very few regional, national players interested in operations; focus is on project management."

- "The ascendency of large format digital printing has changed the picture of the sign industry considerably. Franchise companies like Fast Signs with the ability to invest and manage large scale printing equipment have grown tremendously and are now penetrating wayfinding and rebrand markets.

  "Specialty printing companies in non-sign markets like exhibition and retail have also begun to move into sign markets. On the other hand, traditional sign companies have been using large format printing to move into wider areas including exhibition and placemaking.

  "Wendy's alone is spending up to $750,000 per restaurant, or over a half billion dollars, to renovate its company-owned restaurants with a large part of that going to signs and graphics. Competitive pressures have made rebranding a necessity, and constant corporate mergers have forced airlines and banks to change frequently.

  "Lately, though, there has been a bit of a backlash identified by sign fabricators. Mark Andreasson of DCL states, 'Customers want to see products that are durable and work long term, and not just be a momentary fad. This includes durable paint and materials.'

S - Rules of Thumb

"This skepticism on the benefits of sustainable products and services could benefit companies that take a more holistic view. Sustainability, though, will remain an important feature of sign companies with approaches like lifecycle management where sustainability is part of the entire fabrication process and becomes part of the maturing of the field."

Source: Mike Santos, October 1, 2014
http://www.novapolymers.com/5-leading-trends-impacting-sign-companies-in-2015/

Seller Financing
- "Cash; very few sellers have options to offer financing. Buyers are offering bargain prices."
- "Outside financing is usually available, although we have seen some seller finance deals over the last few years."
- "Typically use outside financing"
- 3 to 5 years

Questions
- "Ensure that the customer database is diverse and that no one customer dominates the sales."
- "How do they secure customers? What kind of repeat customer base do they have? How much of the business/sales depends on their personal relationship with customers?"

Resources

Trade Publications
- Signs of the Times Magazine: www.stmediagroupintl.com
- Sign & Digital Graphics Magazine: www.sdgmag.com

Associations
- International Sign Association: www.signs.org
- Specialty Graphic Imaging Association: www.sgia.org

		Franchise
Sir Speedy Printing (See also Franchises, Print Shops)		
Approx. Total Investment		$275,000 to $350,000
	NAICS 323111	Number of Businesses/Units 480

Rules of Thumb
> 55 to 60 percent of annual sales plus inventory

Resources

Websites
- www.sirspeedy.com

Business Reference Guide **2017**

Ski Shops

SIC 7011-10	NAICS 532292	Number of Businesses/Units 395

Rules of Thumb

➢ 1.8 to 2.5 times EBIT; very rare 3.0 times (plus inventory), unless store is very exclusive with no competition in area.

➢ 40 percent of gross annual sales plus inventory

➢ 2.5 to 3.5 times SDE plus inventory

Pricing Tips

- "It depends if the business is retail, service, rental, or some combination of all of these offerings. We find we are able to get good multiples because of the desirability of the businesses."

- "Key is long-term lease, since location is so important in resort retail sales. If lease is less than 3 years, a heavy discount in percentage of gross sales is appropriate. The price goes down the higher the inventory—which is always in addition to price [calculated on Rules of Thumb]. Every store is different. Be careful—the trend is for ski companies to get into the retail business and compete with independent shops."

- "In resort businesses, location is key. Businesses must be in the tourist foot traffic areas. A strong lease securing such a location is the key in determining the multiple of cash flow. Since most areas have limited real estate, competition plays a large factor in determining price; e.g., how many ski shops are in your immediate area?"

Expert Comments

"Our market tends to be competitive and the bar is set high. The businesses are expected to be very knowledgeable and have a lot of inventory in stock. We have seen a trend in retailers having difficulty in maintaining margins in order to keep or increase market share. In certain industries, having the right brands or product lines is very important."

Benchmark Data

Statistics (Ski & Snow Board Resorts)

Number of Establishments	395
Average Profit Margin	8.2%
Revenue per Employee	$38,200
Average Number of Employees	213.2
Average Wages per Employee	$10,390

Products and Services Segmentation

Skiing facilities	53.7%
Equipment Rental	12.6%
Ski schools	12.5%
Food and beverages	8.3%
Merchandise	7.2%
Other	5.7%

Major Market Segmentation

Destination visitors	58.7%
Local visitors	41.3%

Industry Costs

Profit	8.2%
Wages	27.2%
Purchases	24.3%
Depreciation	9.6%
Utilities	5.2%
Rent	6.6%
Other	19.0%

Market Share

Vail Resorts Inc.	37.9%
Intrawest Corporation	8.1%
Boyne Resorts	7.3%
POWDR Corporation	4.8%

Source: IBISWorld, January 2016

- "Gross profit is the single biggest benchmark for success. After that it's sales per square foot and inventory turns that matter."

Expenses as a percentage of annual sales

Cost of goods	45% to 50%
Payroll/labor Costs	22% to 28% (rising due to labor shortages)
Occupancy	08% to 12% (seeing some 18% to 20%)
Profit (estimated pretax)	0

Industry Trend

"Total Number of Snow Sports Participants

Season	Alpine	Snowboarding	Freeski	Cross Country
2014/2015	9,378,000	7,676,000	4,464,000	4,146,000
2013/2014	9,004,000	7,339,000	4,361,000	4,291,000

Products Purchased At Snow Sports Specialty Stores

Season	Equipment	Outerwear	Apparel Accessories	Equipment Accessories	Total*
2015/16	$677,463,583	$742,545,624	$371,153,610	$298,897,871	$2,550,075,533
2014/15	$667,372,814	$742,544,826	$379,814,173	$314,785,564	$2,554,760,709
2013/14	$658,714,284	$686,020,022	$356,072,986	$279,573,525	$2,447,718,251

Products Purchased Online

Season	Equipment	Outerwear	Apparel Accessories	Equipment Accessories	Total*
2014/15	$175,808,290	$532,290,165	$105,761,414	$120,720,000	$997,062,248"

*Includes casualwear, rentals and services

Source: 2015 SIA Snow Sports Fact Sheet,
http://www.snowsports.org/research-surveys/snow-sports-fact-sheet/

- "Positive, based upon an improving economy and increased discretionary income. Recreation is a perceived need rather than perceived want. "

Seller Financing
- 3 years maximum

Resources

Websites
- Snowsports Industries America: www.snowsports.org

	Franchise
Smartbox Portable Storage & Moving (See also Franchises, Self Storage)	
Approx. Total Investment	$365,900 to $849,300
NAICS 484210	Number of Businesses/Units 25
Rules of Thumb	
➢ 45 to 50 percent of annual sales includes inventory	

Resources

Websites
- http://smartboxmovingandstorage.com/

	Franchise
Smoothie King (See also Franchises)	
Approx. Total Investment	$176,300 to $403,550
NAICS 722515	Number of Businesses/Units 711
Rules of Thumb	
➢ 40 to 45 percent of annual sales	

Resources

Websites
- www.smoothieking.com

	Franchise
Snap Fitness (See also Fitness Centers, Franchises)	
Approx. Total Investment	$109,525 to $285,620
NAICS 713940	Number of Businesses/Units 1,290
Rules of Thumb	
➢ 40 percent of annual sales plus inventory	

Resources

Websites
- www.snapfitness.com

Soft Drink Bottlers		
	NAICS 312111	Number of Businesses/Units 480

Rules of Thumb

➤ $10/case sold annually

Benchmark Data

Statistics (Soda Production)

Number of Establishments	480
Average Profit Margin	8.6%
Revenue per Employee	$845,800
Average Number of Employees	105.5
Average Wages per Employee	$57,673

Products and Services Segmentation

Regular carbonated soft drinks	50.5%
Energy and sports drinks	26.1%
Diet carbonated soft drinks and sparkling water	23.4%

Major Market Segmentation

Grocery Stores	42.0%
Gas stations and convenience stores	19.8%
Warehouse clubs and supercenters	15.4%
Vending machines	13.2%
Other	9.6%

Industry Costs

Profit	8.6%
Wages	6.2%
Purchases	64.9%
Depreciation	2.2%
Marketing	5.0%
Rent & Utilities	1.5%
Other	11.6%

Market Share

The Coca-Cola Company	32.5%
PepsiCo Inc.	25.7%
Dr. Pepper Snapple Group Inc.	9.7%
Monster Beverage Corp.	6.4%

Source: IBISWorld, May 2016

Industry Trend

- "The beverage industry is experiencing some major changes heading into the new year. Sugary sodas are under fire. Juice sales are slipping. Many of the brightest points are new brands and beverages that no one had heard of a few years ago.

  "Here are four key trends to watch out for in the industry in 2016, according to some of the biggest executives and experts in the business:

✓ The growth of energy, water, and sports drinks brands
✓ Reworking recipes
✓ Smaller cans and bottles
✓ Attempts at authenticity"

Source: "The 4 biggest ways American beverage consumption will change in 2016," by Kate Taylor, January 2, 2016, http://www.businessinsider.com/4-big-beverage-industry-trends-in-2016-2015-12

Software Companies		
	NAICS 511210	

Rules of Thumb

➤ 1to 3 times revenue (trailing 12 months) plus inventory
➤ 5.5 to 7.5 times SDE
➤ 5 to 7 times EBITDA
➤ 6 to 7 times EBIT

Pricing Tips

▪ "Enterprise value is a factor of:
  1. Recurring maintenance revenue (stable and adds more value)
  2. Recurring subscription revenue (increasing and adds more value)
  3. Legacy system license revenue (lessening and adds less value)
  4. Percentage of products engineered/re-engineered for SaaS
  5. Industry (stable)
  6. Client type (B2B, B2C, combo—value higher for B2B due to stickiness of base)
  7. Foundation (i.e., size of base and ability to influence demand of product type)
  8. Competitive inhibitors (can influence value dramatically, mostly to the negative)
  9. Organization (particularly engineering base—higher value for core engineering component and reasonable access to professionals, offshore use)
  10 . Architecture (engineering platform—more generally accepted/current technology gets better value)"

▪ "SDE, EBIT, & EBITDA ratios are meaningless in this industry because of the great differences in product, market, and development stage from company to company. Businesses even without profits or negative net worth can command multiples of gross revenue. Values are more focused on revenues trending upward, consistency and sustainability of the existing customer base, and potential for growth."

▪ "Software companies are guided by two major factors: new/existing product sales and most important, continuing maintenance dollars. A look under the covers to truly understand the sales pattern, not just the GL account sales are posted to, will greatly influence the value attached to any organization. Less sophisticated and entrepreneurial software companies tend to forget that the delineation of how they earn their income can drive their value, and in many cases will not breakdown or record their income correctly, thereby limiting potential value and possibly buyers and investors. If revenue is broken down correctly, you will place a larger multiple on maintenance (particularly maintenance for mission critical and higher cost software), than you would new sales. Additionally, companies that lack a SAAS (Software As A Service) model, tend to have lower multiples unless they service industries that have heavy data security requirements that diminish that need."

- "Pricing is determined by the type of software and customers a tech company seeks. Two major areas are Web-based/consumer centric vs. mission-critical/commercial based. Web-based has pre-determined value based upon subscriber base, whereas mission-critical based gain value from growing maintenance (recurring) revenue that organically grows over time."

Expert Comments

"Tech companies rely on skilled professionals, primarily at the technical ranks. These are high-paid individuals whose creation of intellectual property is difficult to reproduce in a short period of time. This can limit competition, but also encourages others to try and make a better 'mouse trap' because of the typically high gross margins. In order to encourage a limited qualified personnel pool, many companies have a higher benefit cost to employee ratio and offer better than average benefits including bonuses, time off, health, dental, 401K, and for certain companies, options. Location is important in the overall scope of attracting qualified employees."

"Software development and sales requires different cultures than typical brick, manufacturing, or other service-based companies. They tend to be younger, have complex requirements that cannot be easily learned, and have changing requirements that outpace many other industries.

"Because the products are people-centric in use, the ability to generate demand is based upon functionality, usability, and fitness for a particular purpose. Cost issues place demands on companies such that without traction, it's not cost effective to create competitive offerings against well-established companies. Personnel costs for qualified engineers, business analysts, designers, and QA/QC professionals is, per capita, expensive. As the Internet of Things (IoT) becomes more prevalent, the need for technology solutions that incorporate more complex solutions is growing geometrically."

"Software development is very difficult. The programming must be completed in view of superior user interface design, process modeling, and speed (response times). Because of the low cost as a barrier to entry, many individuals who gain education and skills don't fully understand that programming is not, in and of itself, a business. Getting product to market (i.e., in this case, deploying the software) is complex and costly, such as it is in many other industries.

"Many companies with 'great software products' never succeed because they lack first mover status, or the marketing prowess to gain mass customer adoption. Those are key to an enterprise value since the likelihood of continuous revenue when a customer has been acquired is high. The change from one software platform/program/application is difficult and costly. Cost-of-ownership models have been around for a long time, but the key metrics still exist and many companies will not make changes in their software very often accordingly."

"Software companies must attract highly qualified individuals who work both in teams and on their own. Their experience is difficult to replicate, as software can be developed in many different platforms and require knowledge in a wide array of languages and development methodologies. Accordingly, companies that are valuable tend to have very liberal benefits and workplace accommodations to keep their staff. Employee acquisition costs are high."

"Success in this business requires both technical talent and business acumen. One without the other is a recipe for disaster."

"Software, by its unique nature and protections through patents (algorithms), copyright, trade secret, and 'stealth' processes, is very difficult to replicate without extensive reverse engineering and creative paths around the legal boundaries."

"Software is unique. A company that has a product that is used in commerce, in a reasonably large deployment, has a lot of value since the cost to replace and deploy new systems is prohibitive. No two software systems are the same, although they may work to achieve a similar objective. Keep in mind, valuation is different in a B2B vs. B2C type software company. B2C will require a market plan that provides continuous R&D and product justification since loyalty, as well as replacement costs, are low. The better the history of product development and strength of the developers, the higher the multiple. In B2B it is different, and the higher multiple will come with large scale adoption, difficulty in system transition, and continuous development cycles that lock in long-term association with the product."

Benchmark Data

- "Typical models for rev/employee is difficult unless you split pre-revenue/ emerging companies from established ones. Also, in the software space, different types of software garner different KPI's. So ERP software development is different than consumer versus HR versus vertical software platforms."
- "Gross profit is very high on software. Typically companies will sell software and related services. Software typically 70% of revenues, services 30% for B2B companies. For B2C, Support contracts help to define continued customer contracts assist in customer relations, marketing, social media comments, etc."
- "Actual and replication costs per source code line is a significant measurement used by potential acquirers."
- "For B2B look at average length of maintenance agreement—not the length of the contract, but the length of time the average client stays with the vendor. For B2C software companies, its more sales focused, so gauge their development life cycle, and their ability to keep innovating, and remain ahead of the marketplace. Remaining ahead of the marketplace also includes ability to provide products that consumers need and want. In a larger scale B2B, with mission-critical type systems, look for average length of contracts in excess of 5 years to achieve a higher multiple. In a B2C, look for scheduled and periodic releases, their contribution to revenue, and their future development lifecycle. B2C companies have had pressure to drop prices over the years, as the model for less expensive 'throw away' software becomes more mainstream. Brand effectiveness is key. SaaS offerings are required in most cases to be considered 'current', but legacy systems will be around for a long time."

Expenses as a percentage of annual sales

Cost of goods	05% to 11%
Payroll/labor Costs	60% to 65%
Occupancy	10% to 15%
Profit (estimated pretax)	25%

Industry Trend

- "The Software Publishing industry is expected to continue growing over the five years to 2020. As private investment in computers and software continues to increase, and the proportion of households with at least one computer surges to more than 90.0%, software license purchases will follow suit. Increases in government spending and growth in mobile internet connections and smartphone ownership rates will also support industry growth, especially with security software.

  "In addition, higher corporate profit among downstream industries, such as healthcare and finance, and booming demand for security products and video games are expected to strongly contribute to revenue growth. Consequently, industry revenue is forecast to increase an annualized 3.0% to $222.9 billion by 2020.

  "Constantly improving technology and falling hardware prices will make computers, cell phones, video games and, ultimately, software more accessible to more people. Businesses will continue to use information technology to increase efficiency and security. For example, a major feature of the Obama administration's 2010 healthcare reform plan involves supplying tax incentives for health insurers and medical professionals to switch from paper-based record systems to digital records. Finance, insurance and healthcare companies also increasingly use security software, such as fraud detection, to protect the vast amounts of data they store. Competence in software programs is expected to become a prerequisite to employment in a wide range of industries."

  Source: http://clients1.ibisworld.com/reports/us/industry/industryoutlook.aspx?entid=1239

- "Software companies will continue to grow for the foreseeable future. As more and more aspects of everyday life become digital, more sophisticated software will become required to control it.

  "Further development in consumer based trends will transcend to other areas. For example, development in VR systems has multiple revenue channels including consumer, defense, and commercial (like driverless cars). Software companies are developing key AI components to provide to major software aggregators, whether through licensing or via acquisition.

  "Companies that develop process and control systems, especially those that enhance regulatory concerns in key industries like Pharma, have a smaller market, but can produce better than average return when they are introduced in a critical number of industry players. Software companies will be continually looking to new extensions of areas that in the past would never have been considering digitally connected."

- "The Internet of Things (IoT) promises to enhance the need for sophisticated technology in all aspects of life. From wearable tech like the Apple Watch, Fitbit, refrigerators, automotive, to clothing like Ralph Lauren shirts that measure various health factors through integrated threads that transmit wireless data, the confluence of everyday life and software systems to control them will give rise to many new companies. The key is to see who can generate an accepted marketplace and monetize it. Software companies will be continually looking to new extensions of areas that in the past would never have been considered digitally connected."

- "Accordingly, and in an attempt to gain traction, more companies specialize in segments they believe will become more commonplace in the future. Some companies develop software that are integral to future plans and offerings of larger entities and become competitive targets for acquisitions. That is where the true value is at."

- "As the industry continues its rise from the recession ashes, sales and profits will trend upward"

- "Growth Drivers (percent answering 'important' or 'most important'):
  Developing New Upgraded Products & Services 87.4%
  New Distribution Channels/Key Partnerships 76.4%
  Acquisition of Companies .... 35.4%"

Source: Spencer Stuart/Software & Information Association

Seller Financing

- "It varies. There is no average, as many software companies are sold with equity participation vs. seller notes in order to value the upside of the future software adoption."

- "Given the competitive landscape for this type of business, sales typically have significant cash or stock components. Sellers are requested to hold notes that vary in scale based upon the maturity of the product and customer base. When there is a large base of existing customers with a high probability of continuous maintenance or upgrade revenue to continue, the valuation will likely exceed normal/median valuation for an average company and have limited seller financing. If acquired by a public company, leverage using the company's public stock offering is used to sweeten the deal and lessen the need for outside or seller financing."

Questions

- "Some key questions: a) Define the marketplace served by your software products. b) What is the life cycle for product development (SDLC)? c) What percentage of your clients is on maintenance? (B2B). d) What percentage of your clients on maintenance has been on contracts for over 5 years? (B2B). e) What percentage of your total product income comes from maintenance? Over the last three years? (B2B). f) What do you sell your products for (MSRP)? (B2C). g) What is your policy for product updates (time and cost to consumer)? (B2C). h) Who is your competition? i) Explain your distribution model (B2B and B2C). j) Critique your development personnel, average longevity, and income patterns. k) Do you deploy a high percentage of your development or support offshore? l) Do you have an SaaS model? If not why not? If planned, when will it be released and what competition do you see in that marketplace? m) What is your revenue per employee over the last three years, and what has been your average tenure for engineers in your company? n) What is your average employee longevity? o) Explain in-house technical skill set. p) Explain benefit package and cost (remember, it will be different than average, and that is to be expected). q) What is unique about your business plan? r) Do you have a customer retention plan? s) How do you formulate your product/service pricing plan? t) Are you subject to any regulatory issues, especially if paving new ground with product introduction?"

- "Ask for a pro-forma income statement to maintain business. Industry trends. Competition and how the business/software compares. Similar questions as you would ask any business owner."
- "Calculations of net cash flow, consistently applied, are good for historical analysis. Discounted cash flow models vary widely, but commonly use higher rates because of risk and uncertainty. Premiums for control, discounts for illiquidity are usually magnified from more 'stable' industries. The broker/ intermediary should inquire about capitalization policies of the software 'asset.' Many companies will not capitalize their product; others will be based on cost accumulation. 'Niche' software with an established client base will attract buyers because of the ongoing service revenues."

Resources

Websites
- Industry/Company Analysis and Trends (fee based): www.factset.com

Trade Publications
- How to evaluate a Software Company:
  http://www.essensys.ro/whitepapers/How-to-Evaluate-a-Software-Company.pdf

Associations
Software & Information Industry Association: www.siia.net
Association for Computing Machinery: www.acm.org
Association of Information Technology Professionals: www.aitp.org
Association of Software Professionals: www.asp-software.org

Sound Contractors		
SIC 5065-07	NAICS 238210	

Rules of Thumb

➤ 75 percent of annual sales includes inventory

➤ 2 to 3 times SDE and/or 30 to 60 times monthly contract billing for music services includes inventory

➤ 5 times EBIT

➤ 3 times EBITDA

Pricing Tips
- "Most contractors in this industry supply some type of music service; if it is a recurring base and the contractors are on their paperwork, then this company will have more value to a buyer."
- "Any inventory over 24 months is dead inventory and should not be part of sale."

Expert Comments

"If company is a commercial contractor, the economy does not have much effect on industry. If they give good service and have experience in technical support, business will be stable."

"There are few good sound contractors with a great customer list."

Benchmark Data

- "Recurring services are a key in value to this industry."
- "One tech per $400K in revenue"

Expenses as a percentage of annual sales

Cost of goods	35%
Payroll/labor Costs	35%
Occupancy	10%
Profit (estimated pretax)	20%

Industry Trend

- "5% to 10% growth each year"
- "Business is stable."

Seller Financing

- 5 to 8 years

Questions

- "Inventory, how much is dead and on the books?"
- "Relationship to customers"

Sporting Goods Stores

SIC 5941-13	NAICS 451110	Number of Businesses/Units 45,468

Rules of Thumb

- ➢ 25 percent of annual sales plus inventory
- ➢ 4 times EBIT

Pricing Tips

- "Add or subtract based on nearby competition"
- "Inventory should be excluded due to rapid obsolescence."

Expert Comments

"Increasing competition from on-line retailers"

"Declining profitability due to ability of customers to comparison shop online"

Benchmark Data

Statistics (Sporting Goods Stores)

Number of Establishments	45,468
Average Profit Margin	3.4%
Revenue per Employee	$163,000
Average Number of Employees	6.4
Average Wages per Employee	$20,095

Products and Services Segmentation

Sporting equipment	61.5%
Athletic apparel	17.0%
Athletic footwear	10.8%
Other	10.7%

Industry Costs

Profit	3.4%
Wages	12.2%
Purchases	63.6%
Depreciation	0.9%
Marketing	2.2%
Rent & Utilities	6.1%
Other	11.6%

Market Share

Dick's Sporting Goods Inc.	16.6%
Academy Sports & Outdoor	10.2%
Cabela's Inc.	7.7%
REI	5.4%

Source: IBISWorld, July 2016

- "Cost of goods sold should be no more than 55%."

Expenses as a percentage of annual sales

Cost of goods	45% to 55%
Payroll/labor Costs	17%
Occupancy	15% to 20%
Profit (estimated pretax)	08%

Industry Trend

- "During the first two months of 2016, retail sales at U.S. sporting goods stores rose 9 percent over the same period in the previous year. Sporting goods stores' revenue is anticipated to grow at a rate of 2.9 percent in 2016.
"The popularity of various sports has changed in the last decade; running, gym workouts and target shooting have increased in popularity, while golf, in-line skating, skateboarding, and cross-country skiing have decreased according to a recent survey conducted by the National Sporting Goods Association (NSGA)."

  Source: http://www.gordonbrothers.com/expertise/industry-insights/R/Retail-Sporting-Goods

- "Over the next five years, the Sporting Goods Stores industry will grow as an increase in the sports participation rate spurs demand for industry goods. The sports participation rate is anticipated to grow 1.8% in the five years to 2021, causing more individuals to require athletic apparel and footwear for their sporting activities. Furthermore, rising consumer per capita disposable income, coupled with more health-conscious individuals, will stimulate industry revenue growth, as more consumers require sporting goods for their health and fitness regimens."

  Source: http://clients1.ibisworld.com/reports/us/industry/industryoutlook.aspx?entid=1079

- "Dick's Sporting Goods has put its thumb to the wind and judged that shoppers want less golf and more athletic apparel."

  Source: "Dick's Sporting Goods Follows the Trends to Earnings Beat"
  by Samantha Sharf, forbes.com, August 19, 2014

Questions

- "Are the sales personnel knowledgeable in their specific areas?"

Resources

Associations

- National Sporting Goods Association: www.nsga.org

Staffing Services (Health Care)

(See also Employment Agencies, Office Staffing & Temporary Agencies)

Rules of Thumb

➤ "Barry Asin, chief analyst at Staffing Industry Analysts, in Los Altos, California, says that most health care staffing firms sell for four to five times EBITDA."

Source: "Businesses For Sale" by Elaine Appleton Grant, *Inc. Magazine*, January 2008
(Dated but still of interest)

Industry Trend

- "Thirty-four staffing firms each generated at least $50 million in healthcare temporary staffing revenue in 2014; combined, they generated $6.5 billion and comprised 61% of the market. AMN and CHG each garnered 9% market share.
  "The report also provides four rankings of the largest firms in each healthcare sub-segment: travel nurse, per diem nurse, locum tenens and allied healthcare. This year's report ranks 21 travel nurse firms that generated in total $2.1 billion, 12 per diem nurse staffing firms that generated $1.0 billion, 10 locum tenens firms that generated $1.9 billion, and 21 allied healthcare staffing firms that generated $1.5 billion."

Source: "Healthcare Staffing Report: Sept. 3, 2015" staffingindustry.com

Resources

Websites

- Staffing Industry Analysts: www.staffingindustry.com

	Franchise
Subway (See also Franchises, Sandwich Shops)	
Approx. Total Investment	$116,000 to $300,000
Estimated Annual Sales/Unit	$400,000

SIC 5812-06	NAICS 722513	Number of Businesses/Units 36,000

Rules of Thumb

➤ 50 percent to 60 percent of annual sales includes inventory
➤ 3.3 to 3.8 times SDE includes inventory
➤ 3.5 times EBIT
➤ 3.5 times EBITDA
➤ 35 to 40 times weekly sales

Pricing Tips

- "Discount value for sales less than national average of $8,500 a week but compare with local average. Discount for remodeling required. Discount for short lease. Discount for rent over 10% of sales. Discount if SDE less than $50,000."
- "Factor in costs of high rent(>12%), remodel costs, short lease, new store coming nearby"
- "70% of asking price minus remodel cost if any."
- "Deduct for remodel expense; deduct for high rent; deduct for less than 7 yrs on lease. C-Store and Walmart locations need an adjustment too."
- "If sales less than $400,000, price is less than 50% of sales. If sales over $400,000 and closer to $500,000 and above, can get 60%. Subject to lease term over 7 yrs. and remodel done, rent 10–12% of sales."

Expert Comments

"60 hours a week to start, then 40. Must be hands-on owner operator for efficiencies. Buy a store with $350k plus price tag if you can find one, and sales about $550k plus. Always keep rent below 10%, mall stores not recommended."

"Subway has matured as a brand and I am starting to see cracks in their marketwide growth. Many owners leaving system now, and marginal stores closing rather than relocating. Cannibalization of sales by overexpansion is now showing its ugly face. We told them so several years ago.... taking a haircut from previous values, but overall they did OK."

"Quiznos is a non-entity for the most part, some new names are appearing in the market as people experiment or get tired of Subway, but Subway is still the segment leader and the juggernaut."

"Very high demand, low number of opportunities."

"Good franchise, happy owners"

Benchmark Data

- For additional Benchmark Data see Sandwich Shops
- "29% food, 18% labor with owner working 40 hours and rents below 8%. That is a winner."
- "True cost of goods is 30% in a well-run, owner-operated store. Rent should be less than 10% for real profitability. Valuation/pricing does range from 25% to 85% of sales, depending on the numbers and region."
- "Most stores are 1,000 s/f, have approximately 20 seats and are owner operated. Food cost is controllable."
- "Food costs—30% or below, rent 10% or below, average sales per store per week over $10,000 makes a good store. Subway average nationwide is about $7,300 per week in store sales."

Expenses as a percentage of annual sales

Cost of goods	30% to 31%
Payroll/labor Costs	20% to 21%
Occupancy	10%
Profit (estimated pretax)	15% to 25%

Industry Trend

- "Maturing, losing out market share gradually to new sandwich concepts, but that is not catastrophic as they command such presence and are market leaders. New generation are opting for more exotic fare and fancy chains to be hip."
- "More competition from other Subway stores opening near existing ones, cannibalization of sales but that is nothing new. New menu items and flavors."
- "Steady sales increase"

Seller Financing

- "Seller financing best option, but financing not very difficult as the brand is favoured."
- "Rarely seller financed"
- 5 years

Questions

- "Are they going to open a new store nearby? Does it need a remodel?"
- "Is the DA support good?"
- "Lease length and terms, trend of gross sales, years established"
- "Remodel due? Rent and CAM? Combo report?"

Resources

Websites

- Subway: http://www.subway.com/en-us

Sun Room and Awning Installation		
SIC 1521-22	NAICS 326199	

Rules of Thumb

➤ 35 percent of annual sales plus inventory

Pricing Tips

- "Strong, knowledgeable managers who have been with this specialty business for a long time can add a lot of value to the company. This would also increase the buyer pool greatly. A buyer with no knowledge or experience in this business could purchase it and be successful."

Expert Comments

"Competition—this is a specialty business; risk—there is an abundance of work in this field; profit trend—sales have shown steady increases; location—a shop and a central location is all you need; marketability—there is a high demand for this type of work; industry trend—new housing boom and damages from hurricane have this business booked for years; replication—this being a specialty business, most construction workers don't have the necessary knowledge to do these jobs."

S - Rules of Thumb

Benchmark Data

- "30%+ net income based on gross sales"

Expenses as a percentage of annual sales

Cost of goods	15%
Payroll/labor Costs	25% to 30%
Occupancy	15%
Profit (estimated pretax)	30%

Industry Trend

- "Growing due to housing boom in area"

Questions

- "What contracts do you have with whom?"

Resources

Websites

- National Sunroom: www.nationalsunroom.org

Supermarkets/Grocery Stores		
SIC 5411-05	NAICS 445110	Number of Businesses/Units 66,665

Rules of Thumb

➢ 10 to 22 percent of annual sales plus inventory

➢ 2 to 3 times SDE; add fixtures, equipment plus inventory

➢ 3 times EBIT

➢ 3 to 3.5 times EBITDA

Pricing Tips

- "There are different departments within a supermarket, with some departments having a gross profit of 30% or more and others having lower than 10% and even negative gross profit on sale items; so depending on the store customers' buying habits and how these departments are managed, the selling price will be adjusted."
- "3 times yearly net income"
- "When we benchmarked the typical hard-discounter P&L versus traditional grocers, we found that the discounters turn a 12 percentage-point disadvantage in gross margin into a 3.5 percentage-point advantage in EBITDA. They do this with carefully designed operations that leverage deep sourcing expertise, massive sales intensity per SKU on a small number of 'bull's eye' lines, low-labor merchandising and very small-footprint stores. The result is a store that can be profitable with prices up to 20 percent below Walmart's, and in locations that are too densely populated to support a Walmart Supercenter."
- "Since traditional grocers today run with 2 percent earnings before interest and tax (EBIT) and a 20 percent volume variable margin, a 10 percent market share to online would erase their aggregate profitability at current footprint."

- "Gas & lottery sales should not be included in gross sales."
- "EBITDA is most reliable. Gross sales are fairly irrelevant for smaller stores (sales under $5M)."
- "Location, demographics, and competition are the 3 biggest factors in pricing."
- "Rent above 3% of sales, or a short-term lease will reduce value of business."

Expert Comments

"Check out the current competitive environment and ask about any anticipated new competition."

"Competition is the most influential effect on a grocery store. There are many independent stores that thrive in areas that are too small or remote for a larger chain. However, the arrival of a new chain store, even if it is out of town, can drastically disrupt the business. Industry sales and profits are fairly steady. There is good buyer demand for well-located stores."

"A good location is difficult to secure, but once you have established a strong business it can be very lucrative. The food business is a low margin business with nice cash flow but there is always new competition coming aboard. Walmart, drug stores, dollar stores, and convenience stores require store operators to constantly run a tight ship."

"We see a high demand for established retail food stores. New or threatened competition can decrease value greatly and diminish buyer interest. Stores in smaller, rural areas have a reduced threat of larger operators and are in good demand."

Benchmark Data

Statistics (Supermarkets and Grocery Stores)

Number of Establishments	66,655
Average Profit Margin	1.5%
Revenue per Employee	$230,600
Average Number of Employees	39.8
Average Wages per Employee	$22,793

Products and Services Segmentation

Other food items	31.7%
Beverages (Including alcohol)	16.1%
Dairy Products	14.2%
Other non-food items	10.5%
Fresh and frozen meat	10.1%
Frozen foods	8.4%
Drugs and health products	6.1%
Fruit and vegetables	2.9%

Industry Costs

Profit	1.5%
Wages	9.9%
Purchases	73.3%
Depreciation	0.9%
Marketing	1.0%
Rent & Utilities	3.8%
Other	9.6%

Market Share

The Kroger Co.	16.1%
Albertsons LLC	9.7%
Publix Super Markets Inc.	5.6%

Source: IBISWorld, May 2016

- "As consumers adopt more healthy eating habits, organic and locally sourced products grow in importance. The study found that 48 percent prefer to buy organic products, when given a choice. Produce is by far the most popular organic item – 90 percent said they had purchased it in the previous 30 days. Meat wasn't far behind with 55 percent, dairy was a close third with 54 percent, and packaged canned (soups, sauces, etc.) and dry products (cereal, pasta, etc.) were each cited by 29 percent to tie for fourth. On the flip side, only 6 percent of shoppers reported purchasing organic baby products."

Source: http://www.progressivegrocer.com/industry-news-trends/
trader-joes-leads-market-force-ranking-favorite-grocers

Supermarket Facts:

Number of employees.. 3.4 million
Source: Bureau of Labor Statistics
Total supermarket sales—2015 .... $649.087 billion
Source: Progressive Grocer Magazine
Number of supermarkets—2015 ($2 million or more in annual sales)............... 38,015
Source: Progressive Grocer Magazine
Net profit after taxes—2014.. 1.5%
Source: Food Marketing Institute
Median Total Store Size in Square Feet—2014............................... 46,000
Source: Food Marketing Institute
Median weekly sales per supermarket—2014 .... $516,727
Source: Food Marketing Institute
Percentage of disposable income spent on food—USDA figure for 2013
    food-at-home 5.6%
    food away-from-home.. 4.3%
Weekly sales per square foot of selling area—2014........................$11.98
Source: Food Marketing Institute
Sales per customer transaction—2014................................... $29.90
Source: Food Marketing Institute
Sales per labor hour (median, unweighted)—2014 .... $148.00
Source: Food Marketing Institute
Average number of trips per week consumers
    make to the supermarket—2015 .... 1.5
Source: Food Marketing Institute
Average number items carried in a supermarket in 2014 42,214
Source: Food Marketing Institute

Source: http://www.fmi.org/research-resources/supermarket-facts

Expenses as a percentage of annual sales

Cost of goods	70% to 75%
Payroll/labor Costs	05% to 15%
Occupancy	05% to 05%
Profit (estimated pretax)	02% to 15%

Industry Trend

- "The Supermarkets and Grocery Stores industry is in the mature stage of its life cycle. However, in the 10 years to 2021, the industry's contribution to the overall economy is expected to increase at a slow annualized rate of 1.7%. Comparatively, US GDP is forecast to rise at an average annual rate of 2.2%. Typically, an industry is considered to be declining when industry growth falls below GDP. However, supermarket and grocery stores have historically suffered from low profit margins, which lowers this industry's contribution to the economy. Additionally, intense competition in the food retailing sector has also contributed to the industry's slow growth."

Source: http://clients1.ibisworld.com/reports/us/industry/industryoutlook.aspx?entid=1040

- "Sales will only increase at the rate of inflation. Competition will increase, putting a strain on already thin margins."

- "Independent grocery store owners are worried about their livelihoods as big supermarket chains such as Wegmans and BJ's Wholesale Club open more locations in Greater Boston neighborhoods. The arrival of new competition is particularly troubling for small grocers already struggling to gain market share in an industry dominated by large companies."

Source: "Fiercely Independent—Neighborhood grocery stores brace themselves for intense competition as big supermarket chains move onto their turf" by Taryn Luna, *Boston Globe*, April 18, 2014

- "Trader Joe's took the No. 1 spot out of the 14 grocery chains studied, with a score of 78 percent, and was closely followed by Publix with 74 percent. Aldi, Hy-Vee and H-E-B rounded out the top five. Brands such as WinCo Foods, Albertsons and Sam's Club made this year's list, after failing to garner enough mentions in 2014."

Source: http://www.progressivegrocer.com/industry-news-trends/trader-joes-leads-market-force-ranking-favorite-grocers

- "Grocers need to provide more targeted shopping experiences tailored to specific consumer needs and changing demographics, a new report from PricewaterhouseCoopers (PwC) suggests. The report, 'Front of the Line: How Grocers Can Get Ahead for the Future,' is based on a survey of more than 1,000 shoppers.

"'Grocers can no longer rely on providing a one-size-fits-all customer experience. The next wave of millennial consumers is likely to demand individualized attention and a shopping experience that meets their specific wants and needs,' said Steven Barr, PwC's U.S. retail and consumer practice leader. According to the London-based global professional services firm, 83 percent of survey respondents prefer to shop at traditional grocery stores.

"More than half of the shoppers surveyed complained of long lines and crowded stores. Grocers that provide a smoother in-store experience by taming congestion are likely to earn repeated shopper visits. Furthermore, shoppers will increasingly look to store employees as shopping advisers, whether for additional product information, new recipe tips or purchase recommendations, as consumers will want increased service and assistance with decision-making.

"Although online shopping is seeing exponential growth in the retail industry, the grocery segment has not shown the same levels of engagement. Only 1 percent of survey respondents consider online shopping their primary way of purchasing groceries, though 92 percent reported having the option to shop for groceries online.

"'While online channels may not become a common way to buy groceries in the near future, technology will still play a major role in the evolving grocery experience,' said Sabina Saksena, managing director in PwC's U.S. retail and consumer practice. 'Shoppers expect information at their fingertips, and, according to our survey, more than half of respondents want to integrate their mobile devices into their future grocery experience. Grocers that innovate and build on their digital channels to meet this demand will be most successful.'

"PwC's report provides five tips for grocery retailers to prepare for the future and stay ahead of the curve as demographics shift and consumer needs evolve:

- ✓ Tailor your brick-and-mortar stores
- ✓ Personalize your marketing strategies
- ✓ Empower your staff
- ✓ Transform your technology
- ✓ Reinvent your loyalty programs"

Source: "Consumers Want More Personalized Shopping Experiences: PwC Report," www.progressivegrocer.com, June 10, 2014 (A bit dated, but still of interest.)

Seller Financing

- "In more rural areas, grocery stores own their real estate. This makes bank financing easier. For stores without real estate, subordinate seller financing is often necessary in addition to bank financing."
- 5 years
- "Most larger stores are sold with outside financing. Smaller stores that do not include real estate usually require seller financing."
- "Generally, we are seeing sellers financing a small portion, along with a primary lender."

Questions

- "What are the prospects of new competition? How is pricing managed?"
- "Why are you selling? Check the store order history to determine what kind of clients are shopping the store. A store with high add ordering and low everyday items ordering is not a good store, and you have to examine the P&L very carefully."
- "What additional incentives do your suppliers provide that may not show on the financial statements?"
- "Consider the possibility of a new competitor coming into the market and what effect it will have on the store location. It is also important to have effective security measures in place to minimize employee theft. Look at the ability to expand the square footage of the store in order to offer more variety and departments within the business."

Resources

Websites
- Food Marketing Institute (FMI): www.fmi.org

Trade Publications
- Supermarket News: www.supermarketnews.com
- Progressive Grocer: www.progressivegrocer.com

Associations
- National Grocers Association (NGA): www.nationalgrocers.org
- Grocery Manufacturers of America (GMA): www.gmaonline.org
- New Hampshire Grocers Association (NHGA): www.grocers.org

Surgical and Emergency Centers—Ambulatory (Free-Standing)

Rules of Thumb

➤ 51 percent of annual sales plus inventory

➤ 2.9 times SDE plus inventory

➤ 6.3 times EBIT

➤ 5.6 times EBITDA

Benchmark Data

Expenses as a percentage of annual sales

Cost of goods	11%
Payroll/labor Costs	05%
Occupancy	0
Profit (estimated pretax)	27%

	Franchise

Swisher (Restroom Hygiene Service) (See also Franchises)

Approx. Total Investment		$100,000 to $150,000
	NAICS 561720	Number of Businesses/Units 110

Rules of Thumb

➤ 50% of annual sales plus inventory

	Franchise

Sylvan Learning Center (See also Children's Educational Franchises)

Approx. Total Investment		$92,614 to $191,343
	NAICS 611691	Number of Businesses/Units 565

Rules of Thumb

➤ 1.7 times SDE plus inventory

Pricing Tips

- "The multiples of SDE vary depending on the owner benefit. Higher owner benefits drive higher multiples."

Expert Comments

"With the advent of SylvanSync, Sylvan has brought technology to the forefront and no other competitor has such a product to offer."

Seller Financing

- 2 years

Questions

- "How much in prepaid revenues as of today?"

Resources

Websites
- http://franchise.sylvanlearning.com/brand-strength

Franchise

Synergy HomeCare (See also Franchises, Home Health Care—Care-Giving)	
Approx. Total Investment	$59,175 to $108,900
NAICS 621610	Number of Businesses/Units 300

Rules of Thumb
➤ 30 to 35 percent of annual sales includes inventory

Resources

Websites
- www.synergyhomecare.com

Franchise

Taco John's (See also Franchises)	
Approx. Total Investment	$336,000 to $1,094,000
Estimated Annual Sales/Unit	$850,000
NAICS 722513	Number of Businesses/Units 430

Rules of Thumb
➤ 30 percent of annual sales plus inventory

Resources

Websites
- www.tacojohns.com

Tanning Salons		
SIC 7299-44	NAICS 812199	Number of Businesses/Units 13,673

Rules of Thumb
➤ 2 to 2.5 times SDE includes inventory
➤ 50 to 60 percent of annual sales plus inventory
➤ 2 times EBIT
➤ 2 times EBITDA

Pricing Tips

- "Age of the equipment. Age of the tanning lamps. High pressure tanning beds & tanning booths vs low pressure ones. High pressure equipment has more value and brings in more revenue, but the lamp replacements cost more. They tend to be newer equipment. Variety & diversity of the equipment adds value, for example, having equipment that provides red light therapy for skin rejuvenation, equipment that senses skin sensitivity to prevent burning, having equipment with mostly UVA rays for very light skin or sensitive skin, having stand up booths & lay down beds, providing body wrap services, tooth whitening services."
- "Salons with standup beds and spray tanning have higher gross margins and levels of profitability. This type of salon can command a multiple of 3.0"
- "The recently imposed federal 10% surtax on tanning will most likely reduce the demand for services and thus impact cash flow."
- "If equipment is very new, calculate FMV less debt outstanding."
- "Pricing may vary based on the time of year the salon is sold, due to seasonality. Higher multiples will be achieved in the December to February time frames, as peak season is March until June. Buyers will seek to get in and implement changes prior to the busy season. Salon values are then depressed from June until November, as the salons are far less lucrative (or even operating in the red) during these months."

Expert Comments

"Good equipment is very expensive, thus it is not easy to replicate. It will cost a minimum of $100,000.00 in equipment alone to set up a new & modern salon. All new equipment can go up much higher."

"According to the American Academy of Dermatology and the World Health Organization, indoor tanning heightens the risk of developing melanoma by 59 percent, and the risk goes up with each use. Despite these risks, according to the American Cancer Society (ACS), thousands of Americans will opt for an indoor tan. The ACS estimates that nearly 13,000 people die each year from skin cancers—approximately 9,700 of which are from melanoma. The ACS predicts that in 2014, melanoma will account for 76,100 cases of skin cancer."

Source: www.fda.gov May 29, 2014

"Concern with skin cancer has dampened public interest. Also parents are controlling their teenage daughters from going to salons."

"Gyms, nail salons and beauty shops continue to add single tanning beds, so perceived competition or threat of new entrants is high due to the low cost in doing so. Such novice entrants are rarely successful in tanning, however, the perception may differ."

"While the industry is growing overall, competition has created saturation in many markets, especially high-growth areas that experienced a recent housing boom. New commercial development has enticed many new operators to enter the market. The older 'mom and pop' site locations are being overtaken by more upscale, higher end facilities."

"Locations are often difficult to replicate, but they are one of the most important factors in valuation. Adjacent anchor tenants, nearby gyms, or complementary neighbors such as hair and nail salons or day spas also influence value and provide a business a sustainable competitive advantage."

T - Rules of Thumb

"Tanning salons can vary greatly. People prefer the most modern beds and/ or stand-up booths. Also spray-on is very popular. An ideal location would be next to or near a health club like LA Fitness and/or a massage facility like Massage Envy."

"In a highly competitive industry like tanning, the ability to market to your target market is your business's life blood. The client base can be very fickle, so customer service is of the utmost importance."

"Competition varies greatly by location. California, Nevada, Arizona, Texas, and Florida are highly competitive in most areas. Some college towns (i.e., Ann Arbor, Michigan) also see a great deal of competition."

Benchmark Data

Statistics (Tanning Salons)

Number of Establishments	13,673
Average Profit Margin	8.7%
Revenue Per Employee	$65,500
Average Number of Employees	2.6
Average Wages per Employee	$23,776

Products and Services Segmentation

UV tanning	50.9%
Sunless tanning	30.6%
Merchandise sales	18.5%

Industry Costs

Profit	8.7%
Wages	36.3%
Purchases	22.8%
Depreciation	4.7%
Marketing	4.6%
Rent & Utilities	12.3%
Other	10.6%

Source: IBISWorld, June 2016

- "Average sales per tanner/client should be around $15 in addition to the membership fees."
- "Rent, payroll, COGS, and utilities should account for approximately 90% of total expenses."
- "One general manager and two (rotated) employees per store. If multi-unit, also include a regional manager."
- "It will be worthwhile to determine bed utilization, electrical power capacity utilization, sales per square foot, and percentage of sale percentages from monthly electronic fund transfers, recurring memberships or single sessions."
- "There are few industry benchmarks, as the industry has a broad spectrum of competitors."

Expenses as a percentage of annual sales

Cost of goods	10%
Payroll/labor Costs	20% to 25%
Occupancy	25%
Profit (estimated pretax)	30%

Industry Trend

- "The industry is shifting to more modern high-end salons versus the traditional mom and pop style locations. Gyms nail salons and beauty shops continue to add single tanning beds. This is perceived as a threat but novice entrants are rarely successful in tanning."
  Source: http://www.bizben.com/blog/posts/tanning-salons- should-you- consider-buying- one-6775.php

- "The Tanning Salons industry is in the mature stage of its economic life cycle. The industry is characterized by growth in line with the overall economy, a growing number of businesses with consolidation from larger players and moderate technological change. Demand for tanning services continues to rise with an estimated 30.0 million Americans using indoor tanning services each year according to the American Academy of Dermatology. The industry has grown over the past five years due to rising disposable income and consumer confidence, which translates into greater demand for personal care services and luxury merchandise items. However, mounting concerns over the potential health risks associated with tanning have caused industry growth to hold steady and regulators to become more stringent."
  Source: http://clients1.ibisworld.com/reports/us/industry/industryoutlook.aspx?entid=1721

- "More consolidation & better profit margin."

- "For decades, researchers saw indoor tanning as little more than a curiosity. But a review of the scientific evidence published last year estimated that tanning beds account for as many as 400,000 cases of skin cancer in the United States each year, including 6,000 cases of melanoma, the deadliest form.

  "There were about 14,000 salons across the country as of early 2014, according to John Overstreet, executive director of the Indoor Tanning Association. That does not count tanning beds in gyms and beauty parlors. The number is down by about a fifth in recent years, he said, as the recession eroded young women's disposable income and the tax imposed under the new health care law squeezed salons' profits."
  Source: "Warning: That Tan Could Be Hazardous" by Sabrina Tavernise, *New York Times,* January 11, 2015

- "Using sunlamp products such as tanning beds or tanning booths increases the risk of skin damage, skin cancer and eye injury, according to the Food and Drug Administration (FDA) and numerous other health organizations. A particularly dangerous result is melanoma, the deadliest type of skin cancer.

  "To help protect consumers and inform them about the risks of indoor tanning, FDA is changing its regulation of sunlamp products and UV lamps intended for use in sunlamp products. The changes strengthen the oversight of these devices, and require that sunlamp products carry a visible, black-box warning stating that they should not be used on people under the age of 18.

  "FDA is also requiring that certain user instructions and promotional materials for sunlamp products and UV lamps intended for use in sunlamp products include the following warnings and contraindications (a contraindication means that the risk outweighs the benefit):

  ✓ the product must not be used if skin lesions or open wounds are present;
  ✓ the product should not be used on people who have had skin cancer or a family history of skin cancer; and
  ✓ people repeatedly exposed to UV radiation should be regularly evaluated for skin cancer."
  Source: "Indoor Tanning Raises Risk of Melanoma: FDA Strengthens Warnings for Sunlamp Products," FDA Consumer Updates, May 29, 2014

T - Rules of Thumb

Questions

- "Seller to keep good books and records where the computer sales reports match the tax returns. Buyer should ask & verify the age of the equipment and age of the bulbs in each equipment. The good thing for a buyer is that a lot of information can be analysed, verified through the salon computer in terms of sales breakdown by demographics, age & gender of the clients, amount spent by each client, busy time of the day or busy time of the year and much more."
- "Have any of your competitors gone out of business within the last 12 months? Who has opened up within the last 12 months? How old are each of the beds? How old are the bulbs in each bed?"
- "How many hours are truly worked by owner? Are there any new competitors?"
- "Revenue trends"
- "How many members have you lost in the last 12 months? What is your retention percentage? How old is each piece of equipment? Do you have every bed metered? How do you check on your employees to make sure they are not giving away free time?"
- "How old is the equipment? How often is maintenance performed? Is there an EFT system in place?"

Resources

Trade Publications
- Smart Tan Magazine: www.smarttan.com
- ist Magazine: www.istmagazine.com

Associations
- The National Tanning Training Institute (NTTI): www.tanningtraining.com

Tattoo Parlors		
SIC 7299-43	NAICS 812199	Number of Businesses/Units 38,333

Rules of Thumb

➤ 50 percent of annual sales includes inventory

Benchmark Data

Tattoo Statistics (Tattoo Artists)
Number of Establishments	38,333
Average Profit Margin	14.5%
Revenue per Employee	$13,600
Average Number of Employees	1.5
Average Wages per Employee	$9,646

Products and Services Segmentation
Custom tattoos	69.0%
Body piercing	15.0%
Predesigned tattoos	12.0%
Aftercare tattoo services	4.0%

Industry Costs

Profit	14.5%
Wages	70.9%
Purchases	5.3%
Depreciation	2.8%
Marketing	1.5%
Rent & Utilities	4.0%
Other	1.0%

Source: IBISWorld, March 2015

Industry Trend

- "The Tattoo Artists industry is currently in the growth stage of its life cycle. In the 10 years to 2020, industry value added (IVA), which measures the industry's contribution to the overall economy, is expected to grow at an annualized rate of 9.5%. Comparatively, GDP is anticipated to grow at an average annual rate of 2.5% over the 10-year period. Over the period, tattoos have become less culturally taboo thanks to tattoo reality TV programs and more celebrities receiving tattoos. As a result, tattoo artists have benefited from the expansion of their demographic, with women exceeding men in their number of tattoos."

Source: http://clients1.ibisworld.com/reports/us/industry/industryoutlook.aspx?entid=4404

Taxicab Businesses (See also Ground Transportation, Limousine Services)		
SIC 4121-01	NAICS 485310	Number of Businesses/Units 357,359

Rules of Thumb

➢ 4 times EBITDA plus value of vehicles

Pricing Tips

- "Selling price should be between 1 year and 2 years' net profit, depending upon the number of cabs and their respective ages."

Benchmark Data

Statistics (Taxi & Limousine Services)

Number of Establishments	357,359
Average Profit Margin	8.9%
Revenue per Employee	$48,000
Average Number of Employees	1.2
Average Wages per Employee	$31,409

Products and Services Segmentation

Taxi services, taxi leasing and other car services	66.3%
Luxury and corporate sedan services	13.9%
Stretch limousines and buses	13.0%
SUVs and large cans	4.9%
Other	1.9%

T - Rules of Thumb

Industry Costs

Profit	8.9%
Wages	66.0%
Purchases	6.0%
Depreciation	6.6%
Marketing	1.6%
Rent & Utilities	9.6%
Other	1.3%

Source: IBISWorld, July 2016

Industry Trend

- "The Taxi and Limousine Services industry is in the mature stage of its life cycle. Industry value added (IVA), which measures the industry's contribution to GDP, is expected to grow at an average annual rate of 5.3% in the 10 years to 2021. During that same period, GDP is estimated to increase 2.1% per year on average. Industry demand is typically influenced by disposable income levels corporate profit and domestic trips by US residents. All of these factors have improved since 2011, enabling the industry's IVA's growth to remain in the positive. The industry's high IVA growth rate in part reflects the rapid expansion of e-hailing and ride-sharing services over the period."
  Source: http://clients1.ibisworld.com/reports/us/industry/industryoutlook.aspx?entid=1951#IO

- "As Transportation Network Companies (TNCs) continue to disrupt the transportation industry, there are a growing number of taxi drivers who are banding together in a unique way to compete with the likes of Uber and Lyft. Drivers in Denver, Portland, San Jose, New Jersey, and other areas are now teaming up to create cooperatives, a type of business in which each employee owns a share of the company and is able to participate in decision making. While cooperatives exist in many industries, including banking, retail, and manufacturing, there is a particular appeal for workers in the transportation industry who are often subject to long working hours and steep operating fees. Better working conditions and ownership of the business are two of the primary benefits of working for a cooperative business."
  Source: "Cooperatives a Growing Trend in the Taxi Industry" researchunderwriters.com, March 19, 2015

- "Taxis are losing business travelers to ride-hailing services like Uber, a survey shows. In the three months ended in June, Uber overtook taxis as the most expensive form of ground transportation, according to Certify, a provider of expense management systems. Uber accounted for 55 percent of ground transportation receipts, versus taxis at 43 percent. That's a big jump from just the beginning of the year. In the first quarter, Uber Technologies had 46 percent of receipts tracked by Certify, compared with 53 percent for taxis. Certify based its finding on the 28 million trip receipts its North American clients submit each year. Business travelers whose companies use other services to track expenses are not included in the results."
  Source: Associated Press as reported in *Boston Globe*, July 17, 2015

- "To drive a cab in Boston, drivers need access to one of the city's 1,825 taxi permits, generally known as medallions. Fatefully, the city long ago let medallions trade on the open market, and only a minority of Boston cab drivers have scraped together enough money to buy their own.
  "Instead, most Boston cabbies are independent contractors driving taxis owned by someone else. Just to work, they have to pay a medallion owner a fee that can top $100 for a single 12-hour period, and on slow nights only the driver suffers. For the medallion owner, meanwhile, the arrangement has been rather

cushy: Shift after shift, week after week, drivers' fees far exceed the cost of buying and maintaining cabs.

"Inevitably, the going rate for a medallion shot up over time, reaching $700,000 last spring. Because drivers need to cover the fees they pay to medallion owners, the inequity in this system filters down to street level in the form of some of the country's highest cab rates.

"The system was sustainable as long as passengers had no alternative. But with passengers—and even some drivers—defecting to the likes of Uber, Lyft, and Sidecar, the value of taxi medallions is in free fall. In October, a medallion changed hands for $561,000. In the last month, a medallion sold for $350,000 in a foreclosure auction. Lenders are abandoning the market, and sales have slowed to a trickle."

Source: "The $700,000 taxi medallion is doomed," *Boston Sunday Globe*, March 15, 2015

			Franchise
TCBY and Mrs. Fields (See also Franchises, Ice Cream/Yogurt Shops)			
Approx. Total Investment		$100,000 to $450,000	
	NAICS 722515	Number of Businesses/Units 880	

Rules of Thumb

➢ 40 to 45 percent of annual sales plus inventory

Resources

Websites
▪ www.tcby.com

Technology Companies—Information

Rules of Thumb

➢ 100 percent of annual sales plus inventory

➢ 3 times SDE plus inventory

➢ 3 times EBIT

➢ 3 times EBITDA

Pricing Tips

▪ "In fact, the best time to sell a technology company is when you are growing. Our rule of thumb is that while the company's revenues are growing greater than 20%, it is best to keep growing the company. When it starts teetering around 20% or dropping below 20%, it is best to sell the company. The reason is that selling a company exhibiting growing forecasts is much easier than selling a company exhibiting flat or nominally increasing forecasts. Buyers are typically looking at the forecasts of your company to determine its value, so it is much better being in a position to offer strong, growing forecasts that a buyer can believe."

Source: Orion Capital Group

- "Renewal rates are paramount, whether the business is advertiser supported or subscription supported."

Benchmark Data
- "The sales ratio to employee expense should exceed 1.5 to 1."

Expenses as a percentage of annual sales

Cost of goods..40%
Payroll/labor Costs...25%
Occupancy...05%
Profit (estimated pretax) 20%

Industry Trend
- "I see continued consolidation as smaller providers are rolled into larger companies. It is easier for larger companies to buy than to build."

Seller Financing
- 5 years

Technology Companies—Manufacturing		
	NAICS 334111	

Rules of Thumb
➤ Niche market—4.25 to 4.75 adjusted net plus inventory

➤ PCB—4.65 to 5.0 plus inventory

➤ Software—4.50 to 6.0 plus inventory

➤ Non-niche—4.35 to 5.5 plus inventory

Pricing Tips
- "Adjusted net times [EBIT] 4 to 5.5 (depending on prior growth curves)"
- "Additions: location, 1st impression on walk-through, how competitive is marketplace, how clear P&L is. High tech or low tech? How much is straightforward in P&L & how much has to be recast?"

Technology Companies—Service		
	NAICS 541	

Rules of Thumb
➤ Temporary Agencies—1.25 to 3.5 EBITDA

➤ Test Services—2.75 to 3.35 EBITDA

➤ Design Services—2.5 to 3.5 EBITDA

➤ 3 to 7 times EBITDA

➤ (Adjusted net for large companies is EBITDA, for smaller ones SDE is used as adjusted net)

Pricing Tips

- "The multiples are not consistent since every company has its own gross profit percentage and cost of goods sold. In most manufacturing and distribution companies, the net income margins are very thin, thus the overall percentage of net profit to revenue is also small."
- "Very specialized. Normal price or sales multiples are not normal at all. Sales multiples can go from 0.5 to 8, all depending on the scalability and profitability of the model. EBITDA multiples typically tend to be above par. 5 to 8x is normal for good deals."
- "Growth is very important; stagnating companies tend to be closer to 3xSDE or 4–5x EBITDA. Growth companies can get 4–5x SDE and 5–8x EBITDA"
- "There is usually no rule of thumb. Right combination of technology and customers can push deal prices up significantly. Typically financed by cash, stock and earnouts."
- "Usually goes for multiple of revenues—especially when the company is not highly profitable but has valuable technology."

Expert Comments

"Understanding the upcoming changes in the industry and understanding competition is critical to success."

"Competition for a lot of companies can come from anywhere in the world. Service companies tend to be more local. At the same time customers tend to be sticky. The more value added, the more sticky."

"Most companies in the industry have been around a while and have their own niche; lots of long-term customers; usually good downside protection."

Benchmark Data

- "For small service business, there should be at least $150K per year per employees; for high value added situations the number can be closer to $300K per year; net margins of high teens are common for successful companies."
- "Good businesses tend to have above $100K per employee in revenue; margins should almost always be more than 50%."

Expenses as a percentage of annual sales

Cost of goods	40% to 50%
Payroll/labor Costs	20% to 22%
Occupancy	04% to 05%
Profit (estimated pretax)	15% to 20%

Industry Trend

- "With shrinking margins, combinations are inevitable and occurring on a regular basis. The legacy owners of companies with less than $25M in volume are subject to takeover and acquisition due to the economies of scale. Larger companies can reduce the Cost of Goods Sold by 4–5%, savings which go to the bottom line."
- "Technology is an increasing part of everyone's life. The growth trend is likely to continue."

- "Stable segment; most of the high growth was in the past; still growing faster than overall economy."

Seller Financing

- "Smaller companies (less than $10M) are seller financed while others may qualify for bank or outside financing depending on inventory levels, receivable levels and past banking relationships."
- "SBA is difficult because most of the value is likely to be in goodwill. High cash component, seller carry and performance payouts are common."
- "Combination of cash and seller financing; buyer may tap into existing lines of credit; typically no new SBA financing."
- "Typically sellers get a good parity of value on earnouts, non-competes, etc."

Questions

- "1. What are the staffing issues;
  2. How consistent have the margins been for specific products;
  3. What is your biggest challenge in operating the business;
  4. What would you do to grow the business in the next 12–18 months."
- "Typically margins tell the story. If the margins are not in high teens, then there may not be too many barriers to the business. Probe about competition. That is the key."
- "Focus should be on strategic value of the business because most of the time the value has very little to do with current financials."

Tee Shirt Shops		
SIC 5699-17	NAICS 448190	

Rules of Thumb

> 30 percent of annual sales plus inventory

Telecommunication Carriers (Wired)		
	NAICS 517110	

Rules of Thumb

> 2.5 times SDE includes inventory

Pricing Tips

- "Need to understand how the carrier commission structure will impact the current client base and future sales. Trained, knowledgeable and professional sales staff is critical—this is not an order-taking environment."

Expert Comments

"Very robust, competitive landscape, but a savvy operator can carve out a healthy market share."

Benchmark Data
- "Sales per employee"

Expenses as a percentage of annual sales

Cost of goods	40%
Payroll/labor Costs	24%
Occupancy	12%
Profit (estimated pretax)	17%

Industry Trend
- "The Wired Telecommunications Carriers industry is anticipated to experience declining revenue over the next five years. The move away from copper infrastructure will underpin the gradual transition from traditional telephony to VoIP. Telecommunications providers are increasingly competing to be a one-stop shop for consumers, offering an array of services over the same infrastructure. Consequently, it is unlikely that carriers will continue to use copper infrastructure to provide voice services in areas where fiber-optic networks are available. By offering voice, data and video services through the same infrastructure, telecommunications carriers are able to spread their fixed costs not only across their subscriber base, but also across three different markets. Operators will likely choose to offer VoIP technology over this infrastructure because of its price attractiveness to consumers and the lower maintenance associated with sending voice transmission the same way data is already transmitted."

  Source: http://clients1.ibisworld.com/reports/us/industry/industryoutlook.aspx?entid=1268
- "Continued growth, especially in smart phones and data services"

Questions
- "Trends for client counts. Cancellation rates and velocity."

Telecommunications		
	NAICS 517110	

Rules of Thumb
- $700 to $1,400 per line
- 3 times SDE includes inventory
- 5 times EBITDA

Pricing Tips
- "Depends on the amount of equipment involved as well as the quality. Differentiate from fiber optic splicers and diggers."
- "Three variables—$1,000 to $2,000 per installed port; 20 to 40 percent of annual revenues, depending upon sales mix & earnings; earnings impact selling price, but on a case by case basis relating to the first two variables plus cash flow analysis. This industry is far from exact, as market share, client base revenues, product line exclusivity, market potential (saturation) & earnings all impact market value. The old adage 'beauty is in the eye of the beholder'

definitely applies to the telecom industry. Client (installed) base revenue mix & profit margin? New system sales product mix? Competition? Service reputation? Customer retention rate? Inventory obsolescence factor? Overall pretax profit?"

Industry Trend

- "A report from Ovum details the situation's stakes: telecom firms are projected to grow to over $297 billion just by 2020, with new information and communications technology (ICT) revenues kicking in the largest share of that growth, around $173 billion total. That represents a compound annual growth rate (CAGR) of 9.9 percent between 2015 and 2020, and that means a huge number of competitors eager to claim a slice of that rapidly-growing market."

  Source: "With Managed Services on the Rise, How Can Telcos Stay Ahead?" by Steve Anderson, August 2, 2016, http://www.msptoday.com/topics/msp-today/articles/ 423765-with-managed-services-the-rise-how-telcos-stay.htm

- "Major telecommunications companies include AT&T, Verizon and ComCast, but the bright future painted by our economy is not limited to these industry conglomerates. Small businesses in the telecommunications sector can expect a year of growth and advancement, making it an excellent time to start planning for their future."

  Source: http://www.vikingmergers.com/blog/2016/determining-the- value-of- a-telecom- company/

Seller Financing

- 3 to 5 years

Questions

- "Where do your customers come from?"
- "Are there any Competitive Local Exchange Carriers (CLECs) operational in market area? Do they have their own facilities or are they reselling?"

Resources

Trade Publications
- Telephony Magazine: www.tmcnet.com

Telephone Companies/Independent		
	NAICS 517110	

Rules of Thumb

➤ "Sales price throughout the nation has been established at between $800 and $1,200 per subscriber."

Television Sales & Service (See also Appliance Stores)		
	NAICS 443142	

Rules of Thumb

➤ 2 times monthly sales plus inventory

Television Stations (See also Radio Stations)

SIC 4833-01	NAICS 515120	

Rules of Thumb
➢ 9 to 12 times EBITDA

Industry Trend
- "Here are five biggest trends in the television industry investors should follow this year:
    - ✓ Netflix is stepping up its competition with traditional networks
    - ✓ Customers get more over-the-top options
    - ✓ Skinny bundles are everywhere
    - ✓ Cable is growing subscribers
    - ✓ Set set-top boxes free"

    Source: "5 TV Trends to Watch in 2016, by Adam Levy, February 8, 2016
- "Many of the 290 TV station purchases in 2013 occurred as group acquisitions by some of the largest owners, building their portfolios of stations even more. The Tribune Co. emerged from bankruptcy to make the richest single deal, spending $2.73 billion to acquire 19 stations from Local TV Holdings. Gannett completed a $2.2 billion transaction to buy 17 stations from Belo Corp., almost doubling Gannett's TV holdings and giving it national reach. Twelve stations changed hands when Media General merged with New Young Broadcasting."

    Source: "A Surge in Local TV Acquisitions Puts More Stations in the Hands of a Few," by Deborah Potter and Katerina Eva Matsa, www.journalism.org March 26, 2014

		Franchise

The Maids (See also Franchises, Janitorial Services, Maid Brigade, Molly Maid)

Approx. Total Investment		$93,000 to $125,000
	NAICS 561720	Number of Businesses/Units 1,092

Rules of Thumb
➢ 40 to 45 percent of annual sales plus inventory

Resources
Websites
- www.maids.com

Therapists—Offices of Occupational, Physical, Speech and Audiologists
Rules of Thumb
➢ 50 percent of annual sales plus inventory

➢ 2.3 times SDE plus inventory

➢ 4.5 times EBIT

➢ 4.8 times EBITDA

Expenses as a percentage of annual sales

Cost of goods	22%
Payroll/labor Costs	04%
Occupancy	0
Profit (estimated pretax)	10%

Industry Trend
- "Competition is steady, growth is expected for the next 5 years, fragmentation should remain constant."

Seller Financing
- "Outside financing"

Questions
- "Payor mix, market share, patient demographic data"

Ticket Services

SIC 7999-73	NAICS 561599	

Rules of Thumb

➤ 2 times SDE

➤ 4 times EBITDA for small to midsize operations; 5 times EBITDA for larger companies

Pricing Tips
- "Due to StubHub, RazorGator and private equity shops, multiple has increased."

Questions
- "Number of corporate clients?"
- "Length of time in business? Stability of earnings? How do they get tickets? Average markup? Repeat business?"

Resources

Associations
- National Association of Ticket Brokers: www.natb.org

Tire Stores

SIC 5531-23	NAICS 441320	Number of Businesses/Units 39,960

Rules of Thumb

➤ 25% of Annual Gross Sales

➤ 1 to 3 times SDE plus inventory

➤ 3 to 4 times EBIT

➤ 2.5 to 3 times EBITDA

Pricing Tips

- "Tire Centers with some aftermarket services (minimum 5 bays, the average tire store has 6 to 8 bays), non-franchise multiples shown below. For franchises like Big O Tire, Goodyear, Firestone, etc. you would add an additional .20 to the multiple.

  Index Owner's Cash Flow (SDE)

  1.5 x to $50K + inv.

  2.0 x to $75K + inv.

  2.5 x to $100K + (sales normally exceed $800K)

  3.0 x from $125k to $250k (sales exceed $1MM+)"

- "Tire stores grossing over $1 million are very desirable, despite low margins, and are fetching a 3–3.5 multiple."

- "The buyer needs to know what percentage of the revenues are tires vs. auto repair. A good mix is 50/50, tires to auto repair."

- "This business has shown some growth but has been affected by the price of oil per barrel. Tire prices have gone up as well as the other normal business expenses, i.e., rent, utilities, parts and labor costs have increased and these are four main variables. As such the owner needs to increase his hourly labor rate and product costs to offset these increases."

- "A product name identity on the business as shown above does generate a greater multiple as shown. If the business does not have a name identity or management in place, you will need to reduce the multiple by 10%. The above multiples do not include inventory, at cost; the multiples do include equipment, FF&E."

Expert Comments

"For a buyer—you want to do your books and records check along with the staff in place, who are their suppliers and their proximity to the store. Are there any commercial accounts that attribute more than 20% of the revenues and the number of customers in their database.

"For a seller—you need to have your books and tax returns in order, an operations manual, mgt. in place, all employees on a W-2, good monthly records showing average ticket and number of vehicles for the same period. Keep your shop very clean and upgrade the customer area annually."

"This business has shown some growth but has been affected by the competition from the big box stores and major discount stores. Tire prices have gone up as well as the other normal business expenses, i.e., rent, utilities, parts and labor costs have increased and these are four main variables. As such the owner needs to increase his car count their hourly labor rate and product costs to offset growing expenses, like labor and rent factors."

"The tire industry has seen a higher number of new tire lines coming into the marketplace, mostly from Japan, China, and Korea. The gross profit on tire sales is not as high compared to auto service repair, so you prefer at least a 70/30 mix, tires to auto repair services."

Benchmark Data

Statistics (Tire Dealers)

Number of Establishments	39,960
Average Profit Margin	3.7%
Revenue per Employee	$199,800
Average Number of Employees	5.5
Average Wages per Employee	$34,187

Products and Services Segmentation

Automotive services	49.8%
Passenger car and light-truck tires	38.9%
Medium- and heavy-duty truck tires	8.5%
Off-road tires	2.1%
Farm tires	0.7%

Industry Costs

Profit	3.7%
Wages	17.1%
Purchases	70.0%
Depreciation	1.1%
Marketing	1.4%
Rent & Utilities	3.7%
Other	3.0%

Market Share

Discount Tire Co.	10.1%
Sumitomo Corporation	8.2%

Source: IBISWorld, March 2016

- "Most common trend to look for in this industry is number of service bays as each service bay should produce at least $25k per month in sales if the shop is a top producer. Tires are a high price commodity and the average vehicle that purchases four tires with mounting and balancing will cost over $550; with some higher priced vehicles the cost will be over $1000.

  "Some trends to look for when you are analyzing a tire store value or their success are the revenues; if they exceed $900,000 annually you can feel good about the fact it's making a six figure adjusted net."

U.S. Consumer Tire Retail Market Share (based on retail sales)

Distribution channel	2014
Independent tire dealers	60.5%
Mass merchandisers	13.0%
Warehouse clubs	9.0%
Auto dealerships	8.0%
Tire company-owned stores	7.5%
Miscellaneous outlets	2.0%

Source: Modern Tire Dealer, January 2015

- "Benchmark in this industry is determined by daily car count vs. the average price per invoice per vehicle. This is an integral factor for each customer who walks through the door."

Business Reference Guide **2017**

Expenses as a percentage of annual sales

Cost of goods	36% to 43%
Payroll/labor Costs	20% to 28%
Occupancy	09% to 15%
Profit (estimated pretax)	13% to 20%

Industry Trend

- "Tire dealers can expect greater business activity as the economy strengthens and consumers and commercial customers increase purchasing activity. Demand for replacement tires is projected to grow in the five years to 2021, as unemployment rates fall and per capita disposable income rises. Additionally, consumer trends in tire purchases that favor niche products such as fuel-efficient (low-rolling resistance tires) and high-performance tires will continue to strengthen. Since these tire types require more frequent replacement than conventional tires, the potential for revenue growth increases. As a result, revenue is forecast to rise at an average annual rate of 2.9% to $46.2 billion over the five years to 2021."

  Source: http://clients1.ibisworld.com/reports/us/industry/industryoutlook.aspx?entid=1013#IO

- "However, as a company, Bridgestone Americas Inc. accounts for the greatest share of not only the replacement passenger tire market, but also the consumer (passenger and light truck) tire market. Its three main brands represent 38.1 million tires, ahead of Michelin North America Inc. (37.9 million) and Goodyear Tire & Rubber Co. (36.2 million). The three companies combined account for 48% of the replacement consumer tire market."

  Source: http://www.moderntiredealer.com/uploads/stats/facts-section16.pdf

- "Highly competitive with many smaller lower grossing tire centers leaving for lack of earnings."

- "Although it is 6,000 miles away, the People's Republic of China is the center of the universe to the U.S. tire industry. In 2014, China exported a record 60.5 million passenger and light truck tires to the United States, representing one-quarter of all domestic replacement consumer tire shipments.

  "U.S. Consumer Tire Imports by country (units, in parentheses, are in millions)

2014 rank/country	% change vs. 2013
1. China (60.5)	+17.9%
2. Canada (19.6)	-4.8%
3. South Korea (18.0)	-9.0%
4. Thailand (12.2)	+10.9%
5. Indonesia (11.1)	-0.9%
6. Mexico (10.8)	-0.9%
7. Japan (10.1)	-2.9%
8. Taiwan (7.3)	+1.4%
9. Chile (6.8)	+13.3%
10. Germany (3.7)	+5.7%"

  Source: Modern Tire Dealer, January 2015

- "The trend on tire centers is stability, and the industry should hold its own for the next five years. The competition is stronger than, let's say, 10 years ago, with discount tire companies and major big box companies selling tire brands."

- "Half of dealers expect tire sales to improve in the next six months, according to industry analyst Nick Mitchell, senior vice president research for Northcoast Research in Cleveland, Ohio, and author of Modern Tire Dealer's Your Marketplace column. The other half expects sales to remain level.

"Truck tire dealers likewise are evenly split, with 50% seeing business improving and 50% believing it will stay level. None of the respondents to Modern Tire Dealer's exclusive 'Your Marketplace' survey feel business levels will drop."

Source: http://www.moderntiredealer.com/news/story/2015/03/
half-of-dealers-expect-to-sell-more-tires.aspx 3/24/15

Seller Financing

- "When the revenues exceed $1MM you will generally see outside financing, for the smaller producing stores you will generally see seller financing."
- "Normally five years, note of 30 to 35% of the total price, at 6% interest."
- "5 to 7 years, on average"

Questions

- "Ask the owner what is their percentage of revenues on tires vs. aftermarket services. The split for a good store would be 50% tires to 50% services; however, the average normally comes in at 70% tires to 30% services. You may also ask what is their vehicle count and average ticket on a monthly basis. Do they have a manager and key techs, the tenure of each one, are all employees W-2, and what are their benefits."
- "Where do they obtain their tires from (suppliers) and what is their delivery process timewise."
- "Reason for selling. What he/she does on a daily basis. Worker's comp mode rate. Upside potential."
- "Key employees, their duties and positions. Will mgr. stay, will key techs stay? Term of the lease? Any major changes in the industry?"

Resources

Trade Publications

- Tire Review: www.tirereview.com
- Tire Business: www.tirebusiness.com
- Modern Tire Dealer—a great Website, one of the best: www.moderntiredealer.com

Title Abstract and Settlement Offices		
SIC 6541-02	NAICS 541191	

Rules of Thumb

➢ 60 percent of annual sales

➢ 3 times SDE

➢ 5 times EBIT

➢ 4.5 times EBITDA

Pricing Tips

- "'Affiliated Business Arrangements' (ABAs) are in vogue. Make sure the ABA is transferable upon sale. Title agencies will command higher prices in states with higher filed premiums."

- "Criteria include the sales history and trends. Title companies' revenues are affected by interest rates, but the stronger ones will maintain profits through the ups and downs by adjustments of variable expenses."

Expert Comments

"Although there is significant competition, this is a highly profitable industry with relatively low barriers to entry."

"Buyers for title agencies have increased due to legislative changes."

Benchmark Data

Statistics (Conveyancing Services)

Number of Establishments	36,695
Average Profit Margin	12.8%
Revenue per Employee	$135,800
Average Number of Employees	3.6
Average Wages per Employee	$45,026

Products and Services Segmentation

Conveyancing and title abstract services	41.4%
Settlement and closing services	22.9%
Other legal services	18.2%
Title search and other document filing services	8.5%
Process services	3.3%
Arbitration and Mediation Services	2.2%
Patent copyright and other intellectual property document services	2.0%

Major Market Segmentations

Businesses	55.3%
Individuals	42.6%
Government and nonprofit organizations	2.1%

Industry Costs

Profit	12.8%
Wages	32.8%
Purchases	2.4%
Depreciation	1.1%
Marketing	2.2%
Rent & Utilities	8.7%
Other	40.0%

Market Share

Fidelity National Financial, Inc.	18.2%
First American Financial Corporation	9.2%
Stewart Information Services Corporation	4.1%

Source: IBISWorld, December 2015

- "Title companies typically retain 70% of the premium on title insurance policies issued, with remaining 30% going to the underwriter."
- "Labor/Gross Revenues = <35% for metropolitan markets
Labor/Gross Revenues = <30% for rural markets"

T - Rules of Thumb

Expenses as a percentage of annual sales

Cost of goods	30%
Payroll/labor Costs	20%
Occupancy	07%
Profit (estimated pretax)	35%

Questions

"How many referral sources does the company have solid relationships with?"

Tobacco Stores (See also Retail Stores—Small Specialty)		
SIC 5993-01	NAICS 453991	

Rules of Thumb

➤ 15 to 20 percent of annual sales plus inventory

Industry Trend

- "The Cigarette and Tobacco Products Wholesaling industry will continue to face major challenges over the next five years, including gradual drops in smoking rates, higher excise taxes and greater levels of illicit trade across state lines. Unlike the current five-year period, however, the industry is unlikely to continue growing during the following five-year period, especially as demand for all product segments begins to slow down in response to broader regulatory pressure by the Food and Drug Administration (FDA), Federal Trade Commission, Alcohol and Tobacco Tax and Trade Bureau and other public or private institutions.

  "Operators also face the threat of wholesale bypass from retailers and manufacturers. Several major tobacco product manufacturers have their own wholesaling operations, making merchant wholesalers, particularly at the regional level, increasingly obsolete. As a result, total industry revenue is expected to contract at an average annual rate of 0.5% to $119.2 billion in the five years to 2019, although industry revenue is expected to grow 0.7% in 2015 to reach $122.8 billion. Over this five-year period, the trajectory of establishment and enterprise growth will reverse course. In particular, the number of establishments is expected to decline an annualized 2.4% to reach 2,537 locations, while the number of enterprises will decline at a faster 2.5% per year on average to reach 2,318 operators over the five years to 2019. Likewise, total employment is expected to continue falling at an annualized 2.4% to reach 40,321 workers over the same period."

  Source: http://clients1.ibisworld.com/reports/us/industry/industryoutlook.aspx?entid=997

Resources

Associations

- Tobacco Merchants Association (TMA): www.tma.org

		Franchise

Togo's Eatery (See also Franchises, Sandwich Shops)	
Approx. Total Investment	$257,813 to $419,796
Estimated Annual Sales/Unit	$650,000

	NAICS 722513	Number of Businesses/Units 245

Rules of Thumb
➤ 60 percent plus inventory

Resources

Websites
▪ www.togos.com

Tour Operators		
SIC 4725-01	NAICS 561520	Number of Businesses/Units 8,139

Rules of Thumb

➤ 2 to 4 times SDE

➤ 2 times SDE for small companies

➤ 3 to 5 times EBITDA—multiple expands as profits go up

Pricing Tips
▪ "Upscale or mid-grade?"
▪ "Average mark up? Wholesale or direct?"
▪ "Length of time in business? Single destination operators warrant a bit higher; type of travel (golf, ski, scuba, etc.)—specialist vs. generalist. Wholesale via agents or direct business? Inbound or outbound?"

Expert Comments

"Travel & tourism is universal. World is shrinking. Huge inheritance in USA to fuel 20-year boom."

Benchmark Data

Statistics (Tour Operators)
Number of Establishments	8,139
Average Profit Margin	5.1%
Revenue per Employee	$229,400
Average Number of Employees	3.9
Average Wages per Employee	$41,237

Products and Services Segmentation

International packaged tours	33.5%
Domestic packaged tours	28.8%
International customized tours	12.2%
Domestic customized tours	11.0%
Reservation services	7.9%
Reselling tours	4.2%
Other	2.4%

Major Market Segmentation

Individuals	52.4%
Travel agencies	32.6%
Businesses	9.0%
Other	6.0%

Industry Costs

Profit	5.1%
Wages	18.0%
Purchases	60.8%
Depreciation	2.0%
Utilities	2.5%
Rent	3.7%
Other	7.9%

Market Share

The Travel Corporation	8.6%
The Mark Travel Corporation	6.4%
Flight Centre Ltd.	4.7%

Source: IBISWorld, December 2015

Expenses as a percentage of annual sales

Cost of goods	80%
Payroll/labor Costs	55% (after COG)
Occupancy	15% (after COG)
Profit (estimated pretax)	20%

Industry Trend

- "Six trends for 2016:
  - ✓ Continued strength of the Chinese market
  - ✓ Travellers wanting to unplug
  - ✓ Discovering untouched and unique places
  - ✓ Fewer barriers to travel
  - ✓ Millennials are looking for adventure
  - ✓ Staycations, or travelling closer to home"

  Source: "6 Travel Trends for 2016 that will drive the global tourism industry," by Lucy Fuggle, December 11, 2015, https://www.trekksoft.com/en/blog/travel-industry-trends-2016

- "As the industry begins to stabilize, operators are expected to experience higher competition. Due to the intensifying competition among tour operators, merger and acquisition activity is expected to accelerate as companies seek cost savings from economies of scale and grow market share. The markets that this industry sells to are clearly defined. Downstream travel agents, businesses and private citizens have long been the largest downstream markets for operators. Older individuals have tended to travel more, as a result of increased income and leisure time, and, even as younger individuals have sought out travel opportunities, the age segmentation of individuals that buy from this industry has largely stayed the same. Many smaller operators opened in an effort to appeal to those with specialized interests, such as food, beverage and historical tours. Larger companies will likely acquire these smaller businesses to expand their client portfolios and increase market share. As a result, concentration is anticipated to increase over the five years to 2020, which is common among mature industries."

Source: http://clients1.ibisworld.com/reports/us/industry/industryoutlook.aspx?entid=1482

Questions
- "Which key employees stay post-sale? Are wholesale contracts transferable?"

Resources

Associations
- National Tour Association: www.ntaonline.com

Towing Companies		
SIC 7549-01	NAICS 488410	Number of Businesses/Units 36,936

Rules of Thumb
- ➢ 70 percent of annual revenues plus inventory
- ➢ 2.75 times EBITDA

Pricing Tips
- "Extreme care with adding back depreciation, and/or allowance to replace trucks. Define which segment of industry, and check to see if the insurance premium is fair market value. Small companies and those in non-consent business are hard to sell."
- "The last of the consolidators has liquidated its acquisitions at a loss. The implication is that there are negative economies of scale at both ends of the scale, large and small, i.e., above some size these businesses based on revenue, etc. have a declining value, and that optimal values are found within the span of control of one person. Ease of entry has been increasing, so going-concern values have been declining."

Expert Comments
"These businesses vary widely. Hands-on management is almost always a critical element. Control of operating real estate is usually a major element in profitability."

Benchmark Data

Statistics (Automobile Towing)
Number of Establishments	36,936
Average Profit Margin	7.9%
Revenue per Employee	$73,500
Average Number of Employees	2.3
Average Wages per Employee	$23,774

T - Rules of Thumb

Products and Services Segmentation

Passenger car towing services 43.5%
Light duty truck towing services 34.7%
Roadside assistance services 21.8%

Major Market Segmentation

Individuals 43.0%
Local and state governments 35.0%
Commercial customers 22.0%

Industry Costs

Profit 7.9%
Wages 32.2%
Purchases 32.5%
Depreciation 7.2%
Marketing 2.3%
Rent & Utilities 4.9%
Other 13.0%

Source: IBISWorld, May 2016

Expenses as a percentage of annual sales

Cost of goods 30%
Payroll/labor Costs 30%
Occupancy 08%
Profit (estimated pretax) 20%

Industry Trend

- "Trend is positive, but competition is fierce. Many companies come and go."
- "More than 85 percent of all tows in the U.S. involve passenger cars and light trucks. The majority of these tows are provided by small, family-owned towing businesses."

Source: Towing and Recovery Association of America (TRAA)

Seller Financing

- 5 years

Resources

Trade Publications
- Tow Times Magazine: www.towtimes.com

Toy Stores (See also Hobby Shops)		
SIC 5945-17	NAICS 451120	

Rules of Thumb

> 20 to 25 percent of annual sales plus inventory

Benchmark Data

- For more Benchmark Data see Hobby Shops
- "Year-end sales data for 2015 shows a 7% increase in domestic toy sales from 2014. All dollars shown in billions.

Total Traditional Toy Categories	Annual 2015	Change 2014 vs. 2015
Grand Total	$19.48	07%
Action Figures & Accessories	$1.44	09%
Arts & Crafts	$1.00	-04%
Building Sets	$2.04	09%
Dolls	$2.59	09%
Games/Puzzles	$1.62	11%
Infant/Toddler/Preschool Toys	$3.07	06%
Youth Electronics	$0.60	-05%
Outdoor & Sports Toys	$3.59	09%
Plush	$1.00	02%
Vehicles	$1.42	10%
All Other Toys	$1.12	05%

Source: http://www.toyassociation.org/TIA/Industry_Facts/salesdata/IndustryFacts/Sales_Data/Sales_Data.aspx?hkey=6381a73a-ce46-4caf-8bc1-72b99567df1e#.V6vToKKhmQ8

Industry Trend

- "By providing comparable products at low prices, large external retailers have attracted price-sensitive customers away from this industry. In response to decreased demand, small players have left the industry and the total number of enterprises has declined at an annualized rate of 0.5% over the past five years. As competition from discount retailers sustains, IBISWorld expects the number of operators to continue to fall, at an annualized rate of 1.0% in the five years to 2021. The Hobby and Toy stores industry exhibits a relatively stable market, although electronic toys have emerged as a growing industry product line for younger children, due to the age compression phenomenon. However, large online and brick-and-mortar retailers, including Amazon, Walmart and Best Buy, limit the potential growth impact of these products on the Hobby and Toy Stores industry, dominating sales of electronic and video games."
  Source: http://clients1.ibisworld.com/reports/us/industry/industryoutlook.aspx?entid=1080

- "Robotics, drones, creative playthings and family-inclusive toys and games will be among the top toy trends of 2016, according to experts at the U.S. Toy Industry Association (TIA). The trade group announced this year's hottest trends in toys and play during a packed seminar held this afternoon for media and buyers at TIA's 113th North American International Toy Fair.
  "'This year, the toy box will be filled with products from both ends of the spectrum. From high-tech toys to classic and outdoor-based products, there's something for each child's interests. The best toys hitting the market are ones that challenge kids and foster their development, all while maintaining an element of fun,' said Adrienne Appell, TIA trend expert. 'While the focus is on kids, what's noteworthy is that many elements of these toys and games encourage parents to join the activities.'"

- "A summary of the five top trends follows:
  - ✓ Tech: Drones, Robots and Toys-to-Life
  - ✓ Family Matters
  - ✓ Ultimate Creator
  - ✓ Brain Boosters/STEAM
  - ✓ Coveted Collectibles"

Source: "Top Toy Trends of 2016 Announced by Toy Industry Association (TIA), the Official Voice of Toy Fair," February 14, 2016, http://www.toyassociation.org/PressRoom2/News/2016_News/Top_Toy_Trends_of_2016_AnnouAnno_by_Toy_Industry_Association__TIA____the_Official_Voice_of_Toy_Fair.aspx#.V6vUN6KhmQ8

- "Since the launch of Skylanders in 2011, toys-to-life have been one of the fastest-growing product categories in toys and games. With the launch of LEGO Dimensions in late 2015 the market is poised for dynamic growth in 2015 and 2016. However, the product's limited appeal in emerging markets and competition from emerging technologies such as smart toys and virtual reality gaming mean that the market will saturate very quickly and growth will slow significantly in 2017.

  "LEGO Dimensions is expected to be a major growth driver over the second half of 2015 and 2016. The product brings together a large array of popular licensed characters and settings with significant cross-generational appeal and real world playability that is not matched by rival offers."

  Source: "The Future of Toys-to-Life: Prospects and Forecasts" euromonitor.com, September 2015

- "With limited appeal in emerging markets and growing competition from emerging gaming and entertainment technologies such as virtual and augmented reality gaming demand for toys-to-life will start to stagnate by 2018."

  Source: "Key Global and Regional Trends Shaping Toys Licensing" euromonitor.com, September 2015

- "The holiday season is a crucial time for many specialty toy-store owners. The period from Black Friday to Christmas can account for as much as 50% of a small toy shop's yearly sales, and the season can make up for losses during the rest of the year.

  "The number of small toy stores plummeted 40%, to 1,500 from 2,500, over the past 10 to 15 years, estimates Kathleen McHugh, the president of the American Specialty Toy Retailing Association. 'Toys are being sold now in a lot of different places, like bookstores, gift shops and educational supply stores,' she adds."

  Source: "Peruse the Puzzles, Have Some Wine" by Adam Janofsky, *Wall Street Journal*, December 4, 2014

Resources

Associations

- Toy Industry Association—good site: www.toyassociation.org

Translation and Interpretation Services		
SIC 7389-20	NAICS 541930	Number of Businesses/Units 58,269

Rules of Thumb

> 40 to 45 percent of annual sales plus inventory

Benchmark Data

Statistics (Translation Services)

Number of Establishments	58,269
Average Profit Margin	26.2%
Revenue per Employee	$70,700
Average Number of Employees	1.4
Average Wages per Employee	$15,063

Products and Services Segmentation

Interpretation services	59.5%
Written translation services	37.8%
Other	2.7%

Major Market Segmentation

Technology, finance, and retail	46.4%
State and local governments	30.4%
Marketing and advertising	10.8%
Medicine, engineering and natural sciences	7.0%
Other	5.4%

Industry Costs

Profit	26.2%
Wages	21.2%
Purchases	12.4%
Depreciation	1.6%
Marketing	5.6%
Rent & Utilities	4.0%
Other	29.0%

Market Share

LanguageLine Solutions	8.2%
Lionbridge Technologies Inc.	5.7%

Source: IBISWorld, April 2016

- "It's all about supply and demand and since the U.S. became involved in Afghanistan after the Sept. 11 attacks, there has been demand for linguists or interpreters of the two main Afghan languages, Dari and Pashto. The average salary for a linguist or interpreter who speaks Dari is $187,000 and it's $193,000 for those who speak Pashto, according to Indeed.com. The jobs range from an interpreter for military personnel to a media desk officer who would translate Afghan news stories and communicate with Afghan media."

Source: http://www.salary.com

Industry Trend

- "It is a fact that the translation market is not heavily affected by recessions. However, it is a very fragmented market, with spot number 1 claimed by military contractors and the Top 100 firms ranging from $427M down to $4M according to studies by Common Sense Advisory, a translation industry think tank which estimated the size of the industry to be $33.5 billion in 2012. According to a report by IBISWorld, translation services are expected keep on growing and reach $37 billion in 2018. The United States represents the largest single market for translation services. Europe is a close second and Asia is the largest growth area. Currently, business is generated from the government and private industries alike. According to the U.S. Bureau of Statistics, the translation industry is expected to grow by 42% between 2010–2020."

Source: http://www.pangeanic.com/knowledge_center/size-of-the-translation-industry/

- "The Translation Services industry is in the growth phase of its life cycle. Over the 10 years to 2021, IBISWorld expects that the industry's value added (IVA), which measures its overall contribution to the economy, will increase at an average annual rate of 5.3%. This represents significantly faster growth than US GDP, which is forecast to grow at an annualized rate of 2.3% during the same period."

Source: http://clients1.ibisworld.com/reports/us/industry/industryoutlook.aspx?entid=1446

Travel Agencies		
SIC 4724-02	NAICS 561510	Number of Businesses/Units 26,064

Rules of Thumb

➢ 45 percent of annual gross profit

➢ 1.8 to 3 times SDE plus inventory

➢ 2 to 3 times EBIT for small to mid-size agencies

➢ 3 to 5 times EBITDA for larger agencies

➢ "Small operations, $1 to $3 million—35 percent of annual commissions and fees; $4 to $8 million—40 percent; $9 to $20 million—45 percent; 3.5 times EBITDA above $20 million in volume; 5 times EBITDA for shops earning over $1 million net profit."

➢ "For agencies with $1 to $4 million in sales, 1.5 to 2.0 SDE is customary. If $5 to $10 million, then 2.0 to 2.5 SDE"

Pricing Tips

- "1. Goodwill is the most important; inside vs. independent employees is another factor.
  2. Quality & diversity of the client base
  3. ARC & IATAN appointments
  4. How long in business
  5. Seller's Covenant not to Compete"

- "There is no inventory in this business as it is service; the travel agent is only an agent of the airlines, hotels, cruise companies and the tour company."
  "There are no hard and fast rules on pricing, he explained, but the more profitable an agency, the higher the multiple. For instance:
  • An agency that generates up to $150,000 in free cash flow each year will likely sell for 2.5 to three time earnings.
  • An agency that generates between $150,000 and $500,000 in free cash flow each year will likely sell for 4.5 times earnings.
  • An agency that generates between $500,000 and $1 million in free cash flow each year will likely sell for about 5.5 times earnings.
  "The typical purchase price is around five times EBITDA, according to Adams. There is always room for adjustments based on specific situations such as less productive family members on the payroll or particularly valuable accounts tied to specific agents."

Source: http://www.travelmarketreport.com/articles/How-Much- Is-Your- Agency-Worth

- "It is important to have good clean financials, e.g., a P & L that has a breakdown of the expenses that would go away after the sale. Having 2–3 years' worth of financials to start is important; don't buy new office equipment, sign a new building lease, or other long-term contracts prior to listing your business. Net profit and excess owner's compensation, potential replacement cost of an owner to stay on all contribute to the valuation. Multiple of EBITDA typically average 2–4 times, and 2–3 for SDE."

- "Multiples expand as profit level rises...anywhere between 2 to 5x is the range of earnings paid."
- "Top importance is: 1. The gross income not gross sales 2. In-house income not independent agent income. Income verification is easy in this business as there is a paper trail for all transactions."
- "Profitability? Agency more than 3 years old? Agency does not depend on more than one account for more than 10 percent of gross? Agency does not rebate? Manager stays on?"
- "Would need last 18 months' financials to spot any trends"
- "Buyers simply need to receive what they pay for. With zero tangible assets, all transactions now include performance-laden contracts."
- "Always include service charges, fees and markups to the gross sales. These are becoming a more and more important part of agencies' income."
- "Several factors. Most important staff, goodwill. Airline contracts for net rates, specialty clients, etc."
- "Look at commission and fee income; both are important."
- "Most important are long-term good employees, long-term goodwill, owner's covenant not to compete, high volume and special contracts net or override with the vendors. It's important to count all service fees as well as commissions from suppliers when calculating SDE. Also overrides and CRS money."

Expert Comments

"These are general factors, airline bookings have been impacted by the Internet for last 6-8 years."

"However most corporate & high end clients pay travel agent service fees. Still new Domestic & International buyers are interested to buy, as well as existing travel Agents looking to acquire for the client base & good employees to increase their profitability"

"For outside the industry, do your homework; it is a tough business to slide into and think you will now own a sexy travel company. For inside the industry already, by acquiring the assets of another travel company you can greatly enhance your bottom line, increase destinations, gain new agents, increase profits with suppliers and expand your client database."

"Obviously you want to list your business while sales are trending up; location can be important, but with technology, this may not be an issue. Companies that would grow with new marketing is great, especially if there hasn't really been any marketing due to the seller holding off, little or no passion left or fire in the belly. The travel industry is filled with risk."

"Supply and demand has made it a seller's market."

"Good financials are important and a good spread of business, i.e., not one big client"

"With the aging of the baby boomers more and more demand will be put on agents for leisure travel and tours."

"Must have continued growth with various client bases, groups, incentives, meeting & conventions, constant marketing, stable staff, industry trend is upwards."

"The small travel agency's income has declined due to commission cuts & Internet, however the industry is growing due to more people traveling and many people willing to pay service fees for good travel agents. It is good to have corporate & leisure mix to weather all possibilities. The bigger the volume, the bigger the ratio of income."

"Service is most important, ARC & IATAN appointments transfer require a 2 years' experienced manager. Better to purchase an agency with goodwill."

Benchmark Data

Statistics (Travel Agencies)

Number of Establishments	26,064
Average Profit Margin	2.5%
Revenue per Employee	$166,300
Average Number of Employees	8.1
Average Wages per Employee	$57,743

Products and Services Segmentation

Tours and packaged travel bookings	32.0%
Cruise bookings	26.0%
International and domestic airline bookings	23.0%
Accommodation bookings	11.0%
Other services	5.0%
Car rental	3.0%

Major Market Segmentation

Leisure—international travel	52.0%
Leisure—domestic travel	25.0%
Corporate—unmanaged	11.0%
Corporate—managed	8.0%
Other	4.0%

Industry Costs

Profit	2.5%
Wages	35.1%
Purchases	20.0%
Depreciation	0.4%
Marketing	4.3%
Rent & Utilities	6.1%
Other	31.6%

Market Share

Expedia Inc.	12.6%
Priceline.com LLC	5.5%

Source: IBISWorld, September 2016

- "Please note travel agents do not buy any tickets &/or goods; they provide service and get a commission. The average commission income is 10% for the gross sales. Major expense is the employees. Rental space can be small or average; the appointments, insurance & utilities are low."

- "Good leisure agent should book $59k in commission fee income...good corporate agent over $1 million"
- "Each agent should produce 2.5x their salary."
- "Sales per employee should be high. Most important factor: the ratio between inside (salary) or outside (independent contractor) employees. On sale of the business independent employees can leave & goodwill will be lost."
- "Higher net commissions due to special contracts. Service fee income. Overall control on expenses."
- "Look for preferred supplier and override agreements, written contractual agreements with corporate customers, relationships with wholesalers on airline tickets. GDS (airline computer system) contract situation is a key factor."

Expenses as a percentage of annual sales

Cost of goods	10% to 20%
Payroll/labor Costs	50% to 60%
Occupancy	15% to 20%
Profit (estimated pretax)	05% to 15%

Industry Trend

- "People are traveling more than ever. The travel industry is overall healthy. It is the second biggest industry in the world next to food."
- "The two main segments of the Travel Agencies industry are in distinctively different stages of their life cycles. Travel websites are in the growth stage of their life cycle, as consumers flock to the internet to make travel bookings directly. Meanwhile, traditional brick-and-mortar travel agents have reached maturity and face increasing threats from travel websites and vendors that take online bookings directly. Overall, the industry is mature. Industry value added, which measures the industry's contribution to the overall economy, is expected to remain flat, exhibiting growth of 0.8% per year on average over the ten years to 2021. This compares with a GDP growth rate of 2.3% per year on average over the same period. While the industry is contributing less to the overall economy, the industry is not yet in decline, as the travel agencies that remain in the industry following the past decade of turmoil have found profitable niches and travel websites are still growing."
Source: http://clients1.ibisworld.com/reports/us/industry/industryoutlook.aspx?entid=1481
- "More and more travel related businesses will be selling as the age of the owners, on average, is high amongst a large percentage of travel companies."
- "Losing great baby boomer agents daily."
- "Meanwhile, from 2003 to 2014, the number of independent agents working primarily from their homes rose 434%, and as of 2013, they now eclipse the number of U.S. retail location agents. However, even though 40,000 independent agents have entered the marketplace in the 21st century, their combined sales are relatively small compared to storefront and corporate agencies.
  "'Consumers are increasingly using travel advisors and I think the data bears that out,' says Kerby (Zane Kerby, president/CEO of ASTA). 'Average sales are on the rise, and agencies are thriving with 84% of our members in the first three quarters of 2014 reporting that their revenues were better than the year before. I think the reason behind that is there is so much information available now to people on the Internet that you need a professional guide to make sense of it all.'"
Source: "Travel Agent Industry Executives Argue That Agents Are Coming Back" by Greg Oates, skift.com, February 3, 2015
- "Good and getting better with baby boomers retiring"

T - Rules of Thumb

- "Good if geopolitical factors stay in calm state"
- "Expedia said Thursday that it will buy online booking rival Orbitz Worldwide for roughly $1.6 billion, cementing its place as the No. 1 digital travel provider while potentially disrupting the hotel and airline industries. With the acquisition, the largest online travel agency in the U.S., will be incorporating the sector's third-largest player. Together, Expedia and Orbitz had 29.4 million unique visitors in the U.S. in December, according to comScore.

  "Airlines get 10% to 15% of their bookings through online travel agencies, but they don't have to haggle with those portals as much since they generally don't pay them commissions. Hotels may be the travel sector with the most concern. Online travel agencies are responsible for roughly 19% of their sales, Harteveldt (Henry Harteveldt, a travel industry analyst) says. And hotels pay fees, on average of 15%, to online sites for bookings that are steered their way, Cole (Robert Cole, a travel industry analyst and consultant) says."

  Source: "Traveling together: Expedia to buy rival Orbitz" by Charisse Jones, http://www.usatoday.com/story/money/business/2015/02/12/expedia-is-buying-orbitz-worldwide-for-12-per-share/23283797/ 2/13/15

- "Supply is dwindling, demand is there."

Seller Financing

- "Usually all cash, seller financing or sometimes based on an earnout."
- "Most travel related business buyers are in the industry."
- 2 to 5 years

Questions

- "How secure is the client base & employees as the income & expenses are easy to check in their business?"
- "It's all about accurate financials, sales trend, current vendor/supplier list, and if any employee issues—just to name a few."
- "Tell me about ghosts...look at monthly year-over-year comps."
- "Buyer should check ARC reports right up to closing. Any big accounts up for bid?"
- "What is the client base stability? What is the mix of in-house vs. outside independent agent business? What is the promotion budget? Reason for sale?"
- "The breakdown of revenue for salary & independent employees. Covenant not to compete clause."
- "Who stays on post-sale? Any client over 10% of biz? How long have your key accounts and employees been on board? Are you 100% credit card? Willing to do earnout on performance basis?"
- "Ask about who controls the business, is it under contract? Length of GDS contract, location, lease expiration date? Any net pricing? Do customers have written contracts to use the agency? Is there a database of past leisure customers? How often is this database contacted? The net commissions earned, service price charged, special override commission contracts from the vendors. Employees' goodwill, inside or independent contractors, all licenses, covenant not to compete."

Resources

Trade Publications

- Travel Agent Magazine: www.travelagentcentral.com
- Travel Weekly: www.travelweekly.com
- TravelAge West: www.travelagewest.com

Associations
- U.S. Travel Association: www.ustravel.org
- American Society of Travel Agents (ASTA): www.asta.org
- National Tour Association: www.ntaonline.com

Travel Wholesalers/Consolidators		
	NAICS 561520	

Rules of Thumb

➢ 3 to 5 times EBITDA

➢ "3 times EBITDA for small to midsize companies; 4 times EBITDA when profits exceed $350,000"

Pricing Tips
- "Airlines not giving out as many contracts as they have in the past due to 90 percent of all airline seats being filled as number of aircraft has decreased. Airlines pushing more direct channels to their own Websites. Value of wholesaler is under some pressure."

Questions
- "Are the contracts owned or are they subcontracted?"
- "Length of time in business? Salary vs. commission? Who controls the business? How long are contracts valid?"

Trophy Studios		
	NAICS 453998	

Rules of Thumb

➢ 40 to 45 percent of annual sales plus inventory

Industry Trend
- "Should be about the same as it has been, but technology is changing the business."

	Franchise
Tropical Smoothie Café (See also Franchises)	
Approx. Total Investment	$195,550 to $427,130
Estimated Annual Sales/Unit	Approximately $490,000
NAICS 722515	Number of Businesses/Units 465

Rules of Thumb

➢ 50 to 55 percent of annual sales plus inventory

Trucking Companies		
	NAICS 484230	Number of Businesses/Units 593,922

Rules of Thumb

➢ 50 percent of annual sales
➢ 5 times EBIT
➢ 2 to 3 times EBITDA
➢ 1 to 2 times SDE + market value of assets
➢ $4,000 to $6,000 per driver

Pricing Tips

- "Focus should be on strategic value of the business because most of the time the value has very little to do with current financials"
- "Gross Sales important of course; understand all costs involved from licensing, broker (trucking brokers) fees, fuel surcharges, trailer and truck parking and driver salaries; all are important to understand. Understand the length of contracts; some contracts are not for actual work, but allow for bids to do the work/deliveries."

Expert Comments

"This is difficult because of the variations in different types of motor carriers."

Benchmark Data

Statistics (Long-Distance Freight Trucking)

Number of Establishments	378,057
Average Profit Margin	7.5%
Revenue per Employee	$170,500
Average Number of Employees	2.9
Average Wages per Employee	$44,852

Products and Services Segmentation

Other transportation services	38.1%
Truckload carriers	37.4%
Less-than-truckload carriers	24.5%

Major Market Segmentation

Manufacturing sector	62.1%
Retail and wholesale sector	32.9%
Other	5.0%

Industry Costs

Profit	7.5%
Wages	26.3%
Purchases	41.3%
Depreciation	1.9%
Marketing	3.7%
Rent & Utilities	11.0%
Other	8.3%

Source: IBISWorld, September 2016

Statistics (Local Freight Trucking)

Number of Establishments 215,865
Average Profit Margin 6.4%
Revenue per Employee $112,600
Average Number of Employees 1.7
Average Wages per Employee $35,883

Products and Services Segmentation

Truckload transportation 44.4%
Less-than-truckload transportation 23.1%
Other Services 15.4%
Intermodal transportation 10.3%
Dry bulk transportation 6.8%

Major Market Segmentation

Retail and wholesale sectors 53.7%
Manufacturing sector 46.3%

Industry Costs

Profit 6.4%
Wages 32.0%
Purchases 29.7%
Depreciation 3.9%
Marketing 0.8%
Rent & Utilities 7.2%
Other 20.0%

Source: IBISWorld, July 2016

Expenses as a percentage of annual sales

Cost of goods 0
Payroll/labor Costs .... 40% to 60%
Occupancy 0
Profit (estimated pretax) .... 08% to 15%

Industry Trend

- "The 10 most critical issues facing trucking companies:

  1. Hours of Service
  2. CSA
  3. Driver Shortage
  4. Driver Retention
  5. Truck Parking
  6. ELD Mandate
  7. Driver Health/Wellness
  8. Economy
  9. Infrastructure/Congestion/Funding
  10. Driver Distraction"

Source: American Transportation Research Institute survey

- "The Long-Distance Freight Trucking industry is in the mature stage of its life cycle. Volatile industry performance in the five years to 2016 was primarily the result of volatile oil prices and their dampening effect on demand for freight.

The industry generally moves in line with the overall economy and is a good measure of economic health. As the economy improves and demand for freight traffic increases, industry revenue and profit are expected to rise, though profit will be somewhat limited by competition from the Rail Transportation industry (IBISWorld Report 48211) and increased diesel prices. In the 10 years to 2021, the industry's contribution to the overall economy, measured by industry value added (IVA), is expected to grow at an average annual rate of 3.7%. Over the same period of time, US GDP will grow at an annualized rate of 2.2%. Labeling this industry as mature seems counterintuitive as the industry's IVA is growing faster than US GDP; however, this growth is skewed by the massive levels of growth in 2011, which were largely due to the end of the recession."

Source: http://clients1.ibisworld.com/reports/us/industry/industryoutlook.aspx?entid=1150

- "Trucking is becoming even more important as Internet sales and the need for packages to be moved from place to place increase."

Seller Financing
- "2 years, up to 50%. Earnouts can work in this industry."

Questions
- "How old are the trucks? Who owns the trailers? Where do you park and do you offer warehousing?"

Resources

Associations
- America's Independent Truckers Association: www.aitaonline.com

Truck Stops (See also Gas Stations)		
SIC 5541-03	NAICS 447190	

Rules of Thumb
➢ 75 percent of annual sales

➢ 5 times SDE plus inventory, may deduct cost of cosmetic update.

➢ 5 times EBITDA

Pricing Tips
- "The rule of thumb for truck stops is going to be 5–6 times EBITDA with the factors coming into play like the quality of the assets, and are there any environmental issues that will need to be deducted from the value of the truck stop. However, to arrive at an EBITDA one must add up all of the different profit centers that comprise the truck stop such as: income from the scales, truck wash, video games, gift shop, restaurant income or restaurant lease income if the unit is leased out, and sometimes there are other ancillary forms of income that will all need to be added together to get to the EBITDA of the truck stop."
- "A lot of people will try to pump up the value of a truck stop by stating how much property is comprised by the truck stop, because it takes several acres to make a truck stop, but anything beyond the basic amount of property needed that is being used to support the business should not be included as additional value. For example there may be a truck stop that sits on a 10-acre tract of

ground and the seller has another 5 acres that he thinks add additional value to the truck stop, but it doesn't. Only the property that is being used at the present time."

- "Be sure to check to see if they have any additional profit centers such as scales and if the scales are leased or owned. Other profit centers such as gambling machines (video poker, etc.) sometimes are not included in the P & L's due to skimming."
- "Due to the multiple streams at one location the goodwill can go for a premium."
- "Limited buyers who buy this kind of business, due to the large number of employees and size of operation."
- "I only do cash deals. Environmental risk can turn into a nightmare on contract sales."

Expert Comments

"The truck stop industry has taken a severe beating lately due to the increased diesel fuel prices. Plus added to that the fact that the major truck stop operators such as Love's, Petro, Flying J, and Pilot are ruthless on their competition and have decreased the fuel margins considerably. Plus the majors that I just mentioned have made it a point to have fueling agreements with most of the major truck carriers across the country leaving only the independent truckers who will stop at the independent truck stops."

"Very expensive to replicate and build, few buyers, due to the heavy labor involvement and the 24X365 days business, yet very profitable."

"Even though the travel plazas are profitable, the size of operation and management acumen required can be daunting. Also the upfront monies required are pretty hefty as compared to most small businesses."

"The average return on investment for a truck stop is 6 to 8 percent. The high profit return on investment for a truck stop is 16 to 17 percent. In order for a buyer to determine a good deal—12 to 15 percent ROI for a truck stop should provide a good rule of thumb."

"Replication is difficult because 5 to 25 acres of prime real estate is required, and the cost can be between $5 million and $10 million to build one. Truck stops/travel plazas have been steady, but also the older or small mom/pops are being eliminated due to competition."

Benchmark Data

- "To be a profitable truck stop it seems inevitable that there is a restaurant connected to the facility. Many of the truck stops are now partnering with Hardee's, Wendy's, McDonald's, Arby's etc., while the others have a sit-down restaurant."
- "Convenience/Retail combined is approx. $500 per sq. ft."
- "Per employee sales annually: $135,000
  Gross Profit Margins: 24%
  Net Profit Margins: 1.8%"
- "Typical Full-Service Travel Plaza Statistics
  At a typical full-service travel plaza you will find:
    ✓ Convenience or retail stores (97%)
    ✓ Check cashing (98%)
    ✓ Private showers (89%)

- ✓ Free parking (93%)
- ✓ Buses welcome (82%)
- ✓ Public fax machines (81%)
- ✓ Restaurants or delis (77%)
- ✓ Platform scales (59%)
- ✓ Laundry facilities (58%)
- ✓ Truck repair (50%)
- ✓ Emergency road service (63%)
- ✓ ATM machines (91%)
- ✓ Security/local police patrol (54%)
- ✓ Load boards (75%)
- ✓ Postal service (53%)
- ✓ Truck washes (28%)
- ✓ Hotels or motels (28%)
- ✓ Driver lounges (48%)
- ✓ Recreational vehicle facilities (23%)
- ✓ On-site fast food (51%)
- ✓ Church services (38%)
- ✓ Food court (15%)
- ✓ Internet services (39%)"

Expenses as a percentage of annual sales

Cost of goods	63%
Payroll/labor Costs	08%
Occupancy	02% to 03%
Profit (estimated pretax)	04%

Industry Trend

- "There are not many independent truck stops left in the country with Pilot acquiring Flying J and making deals with other operators like Road Ranger to sell their Pilot fuel. It has been said that Pilot alone controls almost 60% of the diesel fuel sales in the United States."
- "Large chains will survive and mom and pops will have to specialize or get out."
- "Very slow growth due to the nature of the business. Large lots of 10+ acres required, and investments upwards of $10+ million per site make the field of players very limited."

Seller Financing

- "Property and land included: 10 to 15 years (8% to 11%); business only: 3 to 8 years (8% to 10%)"

Questions

- "Do they own the restaurant or lease it out? What is the environmental situation?"
- "Does it have any fuel agreements with any trucking lines? Does he have Fuel Man or similar fuel agreements that would be in place to draw regional or national trucking companies to him? Any hidden income, i.e., video machines, laundry, showers etc.?"
- "As much paperwork as possible including tax returns."

"When valuing the business be sure to question the Seller about all of the sources of income. Most units have income from video games which is very lucrative, but that doesn't make it to the P & L; scale income and do they own the scales or lease them, any contracts with carriers, do they have Mr. Fuel or other recognized fuel discount programs, shower income etc.? The money is still made on the inside so the higher the fuel volume, the more people that visit the facility, the more money they will spend inside. Is the unit branded with Shell, BO, TA etc.? If so how much time is left on the contract with them and what are their costs to them? Who do they buy their fuel from? To purchase fuel you must have a fuel purchase agreement with your supplier and what is the length of the term and the charge for the fuel? Most agreements are for 7–10 years and if it is a branded unit you will be required to pay them back if you do not fulfill the length of the agreement, and this can be very costly. Are there any rebates coming back from the fuel supplier? How much over rack are they charging you? Very important that you know what the cost to buy fuel is. If you are doing 400,000 gallons of fuel per month and you are paying 1 cent over the posted rack price, that is $4,000 per month plus freight to bring it to your facility. The seller will know this and the buyer should know it too."

Resources

Websites
- www.npnweb.com
- America's Independent Truckers' Association, Inc.: www.aitaonline.com

Associations
- National Ass. of Truck Stop Operators—an excellent site: www.natso.com

	Franchise
Two Men and a Truck (See also Franchises, Trucking Companies)	
Approx. Total Investment	$178,000 to $555,500
NAICS long distance—48412; local—48411	
	Number of Businesses/Units 255

Rules of Thumb
➢ 40 to 45 percent of annual sales plus inventory

Benchmark Data
- "The first year, the franchise generated $835,000 in gross revenue. This year, he expects that figure to reach $1.8 million. Crain started with two trucks, added a third that November and two more in March 2008. He currently owns nine trucks and leases a 10th during the busy summer season. Three more are on order."

Source: "Young entrepreneur moves up with franchise" by Susan Jacobson, *Orlando Sentinel*, August 31, 2014

Resources

Websites
www.twomenandatruck.com

Uniform Rental (See also Hospital Laundry)	
NAICS 812331	Number of Businesses/Units 4,568

Rules of Thumb

➢ 40 to 45 times weekly sales plus inventory

Pricing Tips

- An industry expert says that if there are contracts with the accounts serviced, the rule of thumb will be 70 percent of gross annual sales.

Benchmark Data

Statistics (Industrial Laundry & Linen Supply)

Number of Establishments	4,568
Average Profit Margin	8.5%
Revenue per Employee	$125,200
Average Number of Employees	25.5
Average Wages per Employee	$39,528

Products and Services Segmentation

Work uniform rental and cleaning	30.6%
Flat linens rental and cleaning	20.3%
Other	17.6%
Linen garments rental and cleaning	15.2%
Industrial mats rental and cleaning	11.5%
Industrial wiping cloths rental and cleaning	4.8%

Major Market Segmentation

Healthcare	24.8%
Food service	19.3%
Retail and service	18.8%
Hospitality and lodging	16.0%
Manufacturing and distribution	12.4%
Other	8.7%

Industry Costs

Profit	8.5%
Wages	30.8%
Purchases	32.7%
Depreciation	4.6%
Marketing	0.9%
Rent & Utilities	4.4%
Other	18.1%

Market Share

Cintas Corporation	26.9%
Aramark Corporation	11.0%
UniFirst Corporation	9.4%
G&K Services Inc.	5.8%

Source: IBISWorld, May 2016

	Franchise

UPS Store (See also Franchises, Mail & Parcel Centers)

Approx. Total Investment	$139,673 to $353,580
NAICS 561431	Number of Businesses/Units 4,700

Rules of Thumb

➤ 35 to 40 percent of annual sales plus inventory

➤ 2 to 3 times SDE plus inventory

➤ "Franchises will sell for higher % of Annual Gross Sales. High volume UPS stores sell for over 1 times annual sales (STR Subject to Royalty)."

Resources

Websites
▪ www.theupsstore.com

	Franchise

U-Save Car and Truck Rental (See also Auto Rental, Franchises)

Approx. Total Investment	$60,000 to $681,300
NAICS 532111	Number of Businesses/Units 170

Rules of Thumb

➤ "10 percent of annual sales (price does not include cost of vehicles, and revenues do not include auto & truck sales)"

Resources

Websites
▪ www.usave.net

Used Goods

(See also Clothing Stores—Used, Consignment Shops, Resale Shops)

NAICS 45331	Number of Businesses/Units 82,836

Rules of Thumb

➤ 20 to 25 percent of annual sales plus inventory unless it is on consignment

Benchmark Data

Statistics (Used Goods Stores)

Number of Establishments	82,836
Average Profit Margin	5.4%
Revenue per Employee	$75,400
Average Number of Employees	3.2
Average Wages per Employee	$15,762

Products and Services Segmentation

Clothing, footwear and accessories	47.7%
Furniture, appliances and home furnishings	17.8%
Antiques and collectibles	13.8%
Other	12.3%
Entertainment, recreation and culture product	8.4%

Industry Costs

Profit	5.4%
Wages	20.9%
Purchases	49.9%
Depreciation	1.0%
Marketing	3.6%
Rent & Utilities	5.6%
Other	13.6%

Market Share

Goodwill Industries International Inc.	21.6%
Savers Inc.	5.2%
Winmark Corporation	5.1%

Source: IBISWorld, May 2015

Industry Trend

- "With per capita disposable income expected to rise an annualized 2.4% over the five years to 2021, industry revenue growth is expected to slow. Although revenue increased during the previous period despite the strengthening economy, such growth was unexpected and was largely a result of an influx of young consumers. Although demand from young consumers is expected to bolster industry revenue over the next five years, rising income levels will entice many consumers to shop at big-box stores for new items. Additionally, sales from niche establishments, such as antique and collectable items shops, are expected to struggle, as consumers demand less of these items than in previous years."
- "Over the five years to 2021, the number of establishments is expected to rise an annualized 1.0% to reach 86,400. These for-profit companies are anticipated to buoy profit margins to a certain extent despite falling sales volumes; the average industry profit margin is anticipated to fall slightly to 5.3% of revenue in 2021."

Source: http://clients1.ibisworld.com/reports/us/industry/industryoutlook.aspx?entid=1101

	Franchise
Valpak Direct Marketing Systems	
(See also Coupon Books, Franchises, SuperCoups)	
Approx. Total Investment	$32,500 to $2,000,000
NAICS 541870	Number of Businesses/Units 165

Rules of Thumb

➢ 40 to 45 percent of annual sales plus inventory

> 2 times SDE plus inventory

> "If a cooperative direct mail business, such as Money Mailer or SuperCoups is making $100,000, it could be sold for $150,000 to $225,000, and $250,000 if it was a perfect situation. Now, on the other hand if it is a Valpak, I believe you could get up to 3 times what it is making because Valpak is the undisputed leader."

Resources

Websites
- www.valpak.com

	Franchise
Valvoline Instant Oil Change (See also Auto Lube/Oil Change, Franchises)	

Approx. Total Investment		$200,000 to $2,000,000
	NAICS 811191	Number of Businesses/Units 900

Rules of Thumb

> 50 percent of annual sales

Resources

Websites
- www.viocfranchise.com

Vending Machine Industry (See also Route Distribution Businesses)		
SIC 2599-02	NAICS 454210	Number of Businesses/Units 22,487

Rules of Thumb

> SDE is from 2–3 times depending on gross sales. Under $500k in sales usually 2 times SDE; over $500k gross 2.5–3 times SDE.

> 65 to 75 percent of annual sales plus inventory

> 2 to 3 times SDE plus inventory

> 3 to 4 times EBIT

> 2 to 4 times EBITDA

> "Smaller, one-man operations sell for less than one year's gross sales. Larger vending businesses are based on cash flow and asset value. A common rule of thumb would be 1 to 2 times SDE plus assets. Again, companies with new assets would be closer to 2 times SDE plus hard assets."

Pricing Tips

- "One must know if machines are owned outright, if there are E-ports on machines, how to access the accounts to be serviced, age of equipment, commissions paid, vend prices attained at each location, and age of accounts."

- "Prices for coffee service will typically be on the higher end of the spectrum. Values for vending businesses very dependent on the age and quality of equipment."
- "Inventory in machines on location & coins in coin machines are included in the price—estimate at $100 per machine. Inventory in trucks and warehouse is not included. Most machines should be MDB capable—this allows machines to be fitted for credit cards and inventory control software."
- "Major factors involved in pricing a route include: (1) Where the route is located; (2) What is the year & condition of the vehicle included? (3) Is the truck owned or leased? (4) How many years the route is established; (5) Is the route protected stops, territory or is it an unprotected route? (6) What is the brand of the product that the route is distributing? (7) How close to the depot is the route? (8) Value of equipment included (vending machines, validators, step-climbing hand trucks, coin & bill counters)?"
- "How much does a route cost? The net profit of the route is the main factor in determining its value. Other significant factors include the type of route, the gross, the area, days and hours, and the vehicle. A general rule to keep in mind for the purchase of a route is 'double net.' The amount that you net in one year will be the approximate down payment amount, and double that figure will be the total purchase price. (Example: route netting $1,000/wk would cost approximately $100,000 with $50,000 down.) As a rule of thumb, the bigger the name a brand route is, the more the route will cost. Independent routes and service routes, on the other hand, cost usually 1 to 1 ½ year's net as opposed to 2 years' net (double net)."

  Source: Mr. Route, www.mrrouteinc.com—a very informative Web site

- "These factors will also influence price determination: ownership status of the machines coming with the sale; are they leased, owned, financed; the type of machines that the route consists of and the service schedule that they would need to have the machines produce income (sandwiches need daily servicing … soda/snacks many need weekly servicing); the locale of the machines … inside, outside, 24-hour access, limited access; is the commission paid to accounts above the normal 10% to 15%?"
- "Ratios of investment dollars (borrowed or asset) and estimated length of return"

Expert Comments

"It seems to be a very easy business to enter, which is the reason it is highly plagued by scam artists who promise one 'the stars,' but usually deliver nothing!! The problem of securing good producing accounts—ones that make the cost of the equipment needed to properly serve that account worthwhile—is the problem that most of the time can only be circumvented by buying established routes with a track record!"

"Buyer: Recognize the maintenance capital requirement to replace worn/ obsolete equipment and trucks. Seller: Begin preparing to sell three years ahead of the target date. Get financials up-to-date and in good order. Pay down debt. Obtain customer contracts whenever possible."

"'The vending industry and atmosphere is not the same as it was ten, or even five years ago,' said Rosset (Marc Rosset, CEO of Professional Vending Consultants). 'It is a different industry in many ways, and that includes buying and selling.' According to Rosset, there are four things every operator should consider when thinking about selling.

"One: The region your company serves—'Within the last few years there has been so much consolidation in the industry that there are only a handful of vending operations in each state that are looking to buy,' said Rosset.

"Two: Technology investment history—When it comes to investing to make a vending company look more desirable, many operators look towards technology. Rosset says this is a good idea for some, but not all. 'Sometimes it is not appropriate to invest in technology,' he said.

"Three: Life outside of the industry—Rosset recommends that operators think about life outside of vending. 'For many, the vending company has been their life. It's an emotional process and once it's sold, you don't get it back. It's life changing, so really be sure that you're ready to let go.'

"Four: Obtain professional help—Obtaining professional help, such as that of an acquisitions consultant, may also ease the process."

Source: "4 Things to Consider When Selling Your Vending Business," Marc Rosset, contributor
www.vendingmarketwatch.com

- "The industry is experiencing consolidation as baby boomer owners are retiring. Further, the implementation of technology is narrowing the ranks as less sophisticated owners are leaving the industry."

Benchmark Data

Statistics (Vending Machine Operators)

Number of Establishments	22,487
Average Profit Margin	3.4%
Revenue per Employee	$144,100
Average Number of Employees	2.2
Average Wages per Employee	$22,992

Products and Services Segmentation

Beverages	29.9%
Movies and games	29.8%
Food	29.6%
Other products	10.7%

Major Market Segmentation

Retail sites	34.7%
Manufacturing sites and offices	30.9%
Other	24.4%
Schools and colleges	10.0%

Industry Costs

Profit	3.4%
Wages	16.3%
Purchases	50.6%
Depreciation	4.4%
Marketing	0.6%
Rent & Utilities	3.9%
Other	20.8%

V - Rules of Thumb

Market Share

Outerwall Inc.	21.2%
Compass Group PLC	12.5%
Aramark Corporation	9.0%

Source: IBISWorld, June 2016

- "Food cost on product sold should not be higher than 55%. Accounts should have an in-house head count of a minimum of 75 ...with hopefully transient/walk-by traffic as well."
- "Labor costs less than 20%; cost of goods sold at less than 50%; sales per route of $500,000 per year or greater."

"Operator Sales

Size	Revenue Range	% of 2015 operators	Projected 2015 sales	% of 2015 sales
Small	under $1M	50.5%	$1.77B	08%
Medium	$1M–$4.9M	26.6%	$5.81B	28%
Large	$5M–$9.9M	9.1%	$5.27B	25%
Extra large	$10M+	13.8%	$8.06B	39%

Machines by Location

Manufacturing	18.4%
Offices	13.1%
Hotels/motels	6.6%
Restaurants, bars, clubs	7.3%
Retail sites	9.6%
Hospitals, nursing homes	10%
Universities, colleges	6.8%
Elementary, middle, high schools	9.7%
Military bases	8.7%
Correctional facilities	5.6%
Other	4.7%

Share of Sales by Category

Candy/snacks/confections	40.4%
Ice cream	1.9%
Vended food	7.1%
Cold beverages	38%
Hot beverages	3.8%
Milk	1%
Cigarettes	0.2%
Sundries	0.4%
Other	7.1%

Source: 2016 State of the Vending Industry Report from Automatic Merchandiser

- "The higher the 'head count' in that particular location (minimum of 20), the more potential that account should have in generating income. For a small independent vending operator, the rule of thumb in account volume is usually a modest $75–$100 per week in sales...as the vending company gets bigger this desired sale goes up as it costs that vendor more (payroll, etc.) to service each account."
- "Profit depends on volume and percentage paid to customer providing space & power."

Expenses as a percentage of annual sales

Cost of goods	35% to 50%
Payroll/labor Costs	25% to 30%
Occupancy	02% to 10%
Profit (estimated pretax)	15% to 20%

Industry Trend

- "The global installed base of Intelligent Vending Machines is projected to reach 2.7 million units by 2020, driven by benefits such as ease of use, higher energy and operating efficiency, and ability to offer a more engaging retail experience. Rapid urbanization and the resulting increase in traffic at public places is further strengthening the business case for Intelligent Vending Machines. The United States represents the largest market worldwide, supported by factors such as robust demand for healthy vended foods, and development of cashless and credit card systems for vending machines. Asia-Pacific is forecast to emerge as the fastest growing market with a projected CAGR of 15% over the analysis period. The growth in the region is led by urban lifestyles, rising disposable income of the middle class population, and changing food consumption habits in favor of convenience food."

  Source: June 10, 2015, http://www.strategyr.com/MarketResearch/
  Intelligent_Vending_Machines_Market_Trends.asp

- "One difficult issue facing vending is the shrinking customer base at locations. During the past 10 years there has been a lot of consolidation in the business sector. This has left vendors with a high percentage of B&I accounts in a delicate position. They have been forced to reevaluate the machines at locations. Sometimes the drop in sales is the only notice vendors get that now there are fewer employees at a location. Despite the recovering economy there are areas where employee levels haven't returned to normal. This makes the issue of evaluating if you have the right number of machines and types of products at a location even more important to profitability."

  Source: "Location Intel—How do you know who is really there?" by Emily Refermat, March 19, 2015

- "The Vending Machine Operators industry is in the mature phase of its life cycle. Over the ten years to 2021, industry value added (IVA), which measures an industry's contribution to the overall economy, is expected to decrease at an annualized rate of 1.9%. In contrast, US GDP (Gross Domestic Product) is projected to grow at an annualized rate of 2.2% during the same period. Typically, an industry is considered to be in the decline phase of its life cycle when IVA growth is below GDP growth over a 10-year period. There are other signs that the industry is in the decline phase of its life cycle. One key indicator that an industry is in decline is a shrinking market, as shown by declining revenue. Since 2005, the industry has experienced constantly declining revenue, except for a small growth in 2012. Over the 10-years to 2021, IBISWorld estimates total revenue to continue to decline."

  Source: http://clients1.ibisworld.com/reports/us/industry/industryoutlook.aspx?entid=1113

- "With a history that dates back to ancient times, vending machines are likely to remain a part (and perhaps a growing part) of the world's diet in the future. But several current trends have left the vending machine industry at a crossroads.
  "Current Trend 1: The obesity epidemic. In case you've been hiding in a vending machine for the past decade, there's an ongoing obesity epidemic, including an obesity epidemic among children, which has motivated a closer look at where people, especially children, get their food and drink. More and more states and municipalities have been considering policies that more

strongly regulate what is available in vending machines that fall under their jurisdiction.

"Current Trend 2: Busy schedules and laziness. . . . the demand for ready-to eat- food seems to be growing.

"Current Trend 3: Online ordering and mobile applications. As turnaround and delivery times get faster, the convenience of online ordering could eventually begin to rival the convenience of vending machines.

"So what does this mean for the future of vending machines? Well, these are likely to lead to several future trends in vending machines:

"Future Trend 1: Vending machines that provide healthy food.

"Future Trend 2: Vending machines that provide nutritional and health education. The Food and Drug Administration (FDA) already requires operators who own or operate 20 or more vending machines to disclose calorie information for food sold from vending machines, subject to certain exemptions.

"Future Trend 3: Vending machines that can customize, cook, and prepare food.

"Future Trend 4: Vending machines that provide other products related to food.

"Future Trend 5: Online vending machines. This doesn't mean purchasing vending machines over the Internet, which you can already do. This means vending machines that are connected to the Internet to allow ordering or purchasing over the web or a smartphone app.

"Future Trend 6: Vending machines in new locations.

"Future Trend 7: More interactive vending machines.

Source: "Current and Future Trends in Vending Machines," by Bruce Y. Lee, Forbes, April 22, 2016

- "Lot less small players . . . with the big guys getting bigger!"

- "The industry is becoming much more technology driven as operators implement remote monitoring of the machines at customer locations. A higher degree of owner sophistication will be required in order to successfully deploy the technology to drive efficiencies."

- "A majority, 82.7 percent, of operators report having locations request healthier products be placed in the machines. This is a trend that is not receding.

    "In 2014, 16.1 percent of operators report making an acquisition, compared to 17.7 percent the year before. However, there was a small increase, 1.4 percent, to the number of vendors who sold off parts of their businesses.

    "There are five factors really pulling at today's vending operation. Those factors are rising product costs from manufacturers; technology adoption in operators management and at the vending machine; regulations that changed the face of school vending; changing consumer preferences; and, most importantly, taking advantage of new product and service opportunities."

Source: Automatic Merchandiser 2015 State of the Vending Industry Report

- "Both margins and operating results should steadily improve as technology makes the operators more efficient and able to better manage their businesses."

- "Growing in popularity as more people look for secondary sources of income."

- "Disappearing 'middle class'; gross sales more than $300k and less than $2MM; big operators getting bigger and going into smaller locations; there will always be the mom & pops. Micro markets for larger locations. Credit card reader technology coming down in price—will see more machines taking credit cards."

- "Profits are up due to price increases by operators. Replication difficult as purchase price is usually near asset value which does not take into account the marketing and effort to locate the machines."

Seller Financing

- "Seller financing for 35–50% of price is usually obtainable . . . and many times the equipment can be used as a source of collateral for purchasing the route."
- "Seller financing is typical in the vending industry. Normally in the 30–40% of purchase price range. Bank financing can be difficult to obtain as the hard collateral (vending machines) are scattered at customer locations."
- "We see both outside and seller financing. The recent trend has been for an increased willingness of the banking/lending sector to loan into the industry reducing the need for seller financing."

Questions

- "Do you have contracts in place with your major customer? What cash controls do you have in the business? When did you last raise selling prices? Is any of your business controlled by third parties?"
- "Seller: 1) Get your books and records in order, 2) Make sure you have clean financial statements, 3) Have a professional valuation completed. Buyer: 1) Fully grasp the capital requirements for both new business and the maintenance of existing business, 2) Be prepared to invest in technology."
- "Are machines owned or leased? How old is equipment? Is any equipment supplied with E-Ports? Commissions paid? How geographically far apart are the accounts located? Access to machines? 24/7?"
- "Are your machines DEX capable? What controls do you have on the cash in the machines? Is all the money going into the bank? If no, they have to hold paper."
- "Head count at the particular location & permissible servicing time for each account."
- "Do you have contracts?"
- "How many people work at a location? How close are accounts? Are commissions paid to all or some customers? Do you pay commissions to accounts; do machines carry perishable food stuffs?"
- "Will seller finance the deal? Lenders do not want to own a lot of vending machines in case the loan would go bad."

Resources

Websites
- www.vendingmarketwatch.com

Trade Publications
- Vending Times: www.vendingtimes.com
- Automatic Merchandiser: www.vendingmarketwatch.com/magazine/

Associations
- National Automatic Merchandising Association (NAMA)—good site: https://namanow.org/
- Amusement & Music Operators Association (AMOA): www.amoa.com

V - Rules of Thumb

Veterinary Hospitals

	NAICS 541940	

Rules of Thumb

➤ 65 to 70 percent of annual revenues plus inventory

Industry Trend

- "Veterinary hospital growth—Average annual revenue growth for veterinary hospitals was 5.1%, slightly behind average annual growth in 2012–2013. "Despite the slight decline in industry growth and improving economy, roughly one-quarter of hospitals exhibited annual growth of more than 10% ('Outgrowers'). This is approximately the same percent as we saw last year, demonstrating practices cannot solely depend on economic or industry factors to drive growth.
  - ✓ Active patients grew 0.9% in 2014 relative to 2013.
  - ✓ Patient visits grew 1.4% in 2014 (canine, 1.9%; feline, -0.4%).
  - ✓ Average annual veterinary hospital revenue grew 5.1% in 2014 relative to 2013, slightly below average growth for 2012–2013.
  - ✓ 24% of hospitals exhibited annual revenue growth of more than 10% ('Outgrowers'). By contrast, 51% of hospitals had growth of 0%–10% ('Growers') and 25% of hospitals had negative growth ('Decliners').
  - ✓ 49% of the Outgrowers exhibited annual revenue growth of more than 10% two years in a row ('Consistent Outgrowers').
  - ✓ 58% of the Consistent Outgrowers exhibited annual revenue growth of more than 10% three years in a row ('Power Outgrowers').
  - ✓ AAHA-accredited hospitals exhibited more active clients, more new clients in a year, higher average transaction value and higher income per veterinarian."
    Source: "2015 AAHA State of the Industry Fact Sheet," https://www.aaha.org/graphics/original/professional/resources/library/aaha_state_of_the_industry_2015_fact_sheet.pdf

Veterinary Practices

SIC 0742-01	NAICS 541940	Number of Businesses/Units 51,914

Rules of Thumb

➤ 70 to 75 percent of annual sales includes inventory

➤ 2 to 3 times SDE for small-animal practices includes inventory

➤ 2 to 5.2 times EBIT

➤ 3 to 5 times EBITDA

➤ "Usually 70 to 80 percent of past 12 months' gross revenues [sales] (includes tangible and intangible assets)"

Pricing Tips

- "On average veterinary practices sell for about 70% of annual gross income. However the range is quite wide. It is not uncommon for the price range to be between 40% to 100% on annual gross income. Many factors come into play:

type of practice (e.g., small-animal vs. equine vs. ER vs. specialty referral), number of veterinarians, number of hours worked by the veterinarians, amount and type of furniture and equipment, drug inventory, etc. These and other factors can skew price above or below the average price by significant amounts."

- "Small-animal practices (dogs/cats) are most common type. Most veterinarian buyers are looking for this type of practice. Goodwill tends to transfer well with small-animal practices. Still a very fragmented market with many independent practices. There are a number of corporate nationals with large numbers of practices nationwide who buy practices. However, they usually want larger, multidoctor practices, with gross income of over $1 million."

- "Good financing for doctor/veterinarian buyers...up to 100% financing provided there is sufficient cash flow."

- "Typically a practice needs 1400–1500 active clients to support each full time veterinarian."

- "Demographic trend for veterinarians is strongly skewed to female doctors. Most new graduates are female."

- "For highly profitable practices (profit greather than 20%) most traditional lenders don't want to lend more than 100% of the annual revenues, so seller financing would usually be required for such transactions involving high-value practices."

- "Mixed-animal, large-animal and rural practices typically sell for lower multiples."

- "There is a wide variation in sales price for veterinary practice sales. The most common range for percent of gross sales is 65% to 80%, however, very profitable practices will sell for 90% or more. Almost all sales are asset sales, not stock. For companies with revenues greater than $2,000,000, there are several national corporate purchasers, who will pay 5 times or greater than 5 times EBITDA. Using SDE is very accurate for single-owner practices, but it becomes less helpful in multi-doctor practices."

- "Pricing is strongly associated with a multiple of EBITDA, after adjustments for non-operating, non-recurring and discretionary expenses. The largest factors affecting the size of the selected multiple are location, local demographics, local competition, curb appeal and growth or decline in earnings. Multiples of gross sales have declined over the past 20 years because of increased costs of labor and supplies. The major factors affecting profitability are COGS, staff wages and rent expense. Poor management of these expenses leads to poor profitability and decreased value."

- "In regard to financial analysis, the gross multiple has declined over the past 30 years because of increased cost for labor, outside services and products. It should not be relied upon for a sales valuation, but can be used as a test for reasonableness of pricing. The most reliable multiples are for SDE (solo doctor practice, only) and EBITDA (solo and multi-doctor practice), both based on a normalized income statement or tax return. Fundamental factors, such as location, curb appeal, practice growth, quality of equipment, average transaction fee and competition are all very important to buyers. Large animal practices will have lower multiples. Rural and remote small animal practices are difficult sales."

- "Inventory included in the sale is usually a working level or 30-day supply. Most sales are asset sales and include equipment, furniture, removable fixtures, working levels of consumable inventory, and intangibles (goodwill)."

Expert Comments

"The culture and relationships within a veterinary practice may have a significant impact on the success of a veterinary hospital, according to survey data revealed during the American Animal Hospital Association 2016 State of the Industry presentation. The AAHA 2016 State of the Industry, which was presented during the AAHA Austin 2016 Yearly Conference, examined data from a fall 2015 survey AAHA conducted with the Daniels College of Business at the University of Denver that studied organizational culture in veterinary practices.

"The culture study surveyed over 1,000 veterinary hospitals to study the qualities of organizational culture in veterinary practices, evaluate the overall and specific subcultures in veterinary hospitals, and determine how culture affects veterinary practice metrics.

"On the economic front, data from the 2016 State of the Industry indicated that more practices have moved into the 'Outgrower' category of practices that demonstrate growth of more than 10 percent year-over-year. Thirty-five percent of practices are now considered Outgrowers, compared to 24 percent from the 2015 State of the Industry.

"Other key points from the economic data revealed:
- ✓ Active patients in 2015 grew 2.6% relative to 2014
- ✓ Patient visits in 2015 grew 3.2% relative to 2014
- ✓ Overall practice revenue in 2015 grew by 6.4% relative to 2014
- ✓ Outgrowers exhibit 8.7% growth in active patients
- ✓ Growers exhibit .9% growth in active patients
- ✓ Decliners exhibit a 7.1% decrease in active patients

"'We know that successful veterinary practices such as Outgrowers focus on strengthening bonds and building relationships,' Cavanaugh said. 'We'll see that category continue to grow as more and more practices focus on strengthening the bonds and improving culture within their own practices.'"

Source: AAHA 2016 State of the Industry, http://www.aaha.org/blog/NewStat/post/2016/04/04/102724/
Culture-can-impact-veterinary-practice-success-AAHA-2016-State-of-the-Industry-reveals.aspx

"The market is mostly vets selling to other vets. Very few non-veterinarian buyers/sellers outside of large corporate nationals."

"Competition varies city by city. Some locations can be saturated. Risk is typically very low. This is reflected by excellent financing terms. Strong industry. Very good projected growth nationwide. Most facilities are good. Most practices in suburban locations. Can be in leased space/strip malls or standalone buildings. Marketability is good for practices with good cash flow. Replication is fairly easy in that startup financing is plentiful for veterinarians."

"- A buyer should study each aspect about the available practices, from location to financial performance, and determine whether a specific practice will meet his/her needs.

- Have a building inspection done, if acquiring the real estate.

- A seller needs to be prepared to provide a smooth transition. Typically the seller should be prepared to work in the practice for at least a couple months after the sale, and normally the seller is compensated."

"The veterinary world is changing. Single-doctor practices are becoming a thing of the past. There are a lot of corporate buyers like VCA Antech Inc. who are acquiring practices."

"For buyers, be sure to have experts on your side—consultants, accountants and attorneys. Then perform your due diligence. For sellers, keep working hard and do not let the revenues decline. Practices that are declining are red flags to both buyers and lenders."

"Since the great recession, most practices have been steadily growing. The amount of risk with new ownership is low because the goodwill transferability remains high. The clients and the support staff are basically the buyer's to lose. Most transitions are successful. The larger risks are related to practices that have very high average transaction fees. It takes are very confident buyer to purchase a high-end practice. Marketability tends to be good. Practices in more rural locations take much longer to sell because of the limited amount of buyers for rural practices. Curb appeal of the facility and modern equipment add to marketability. Practices with low revenues or low profitability are more difficult sales. It requires a confident buyer, who knows that he or she can grow the practice."

"Competition can be quite variable, tending to moderate to heavy in desirable places to live. The risk is low, as evidenced by the ease of lender financing up to 100% of the acquisition price. Trends in historical profit have been variable through the economic downturn. High fee practices have suffered declines in revenues, while moderate fee practices have actually grown during the past few years. Location and facilities are variable. Most practices are located in accessible sites within a community, but some communities, mainly rural locations, have a limited number of potential buyers making sales difficult. Marketability is good because there is currently strong demand for practices by potential buyers. Trends are good because pet-owning clients will take care of their animals, even in difficult economic times. Replication is hard because of the extensive education, training and licensing requirements."

"The practice transition process is so complex that both seller and buyer should utilize consultants who are knowledgeable in veterinary practice sales transactions."

"Competition has been growing because of many new veterinary colleges that have opened in the past 20 years, producing more graduates. Risk is low because lenders have a very low default rate with licensed veterinarians, indicating most acquisitions are successful. Profitability has been difficult to maintain because of the economic downturn, competition from human and online pharmacies, animal shelters providing vaccinations and spays and neuters. Small-animal practices are giving up lower cost margin income sources because many procedures and treatments are referred to specialty centers. Facilities are generally good because practice clients expect a clean and presentable clinic/hospital. Urban/suburban locations are the best. Marketability has been good because there are many buyers and few sellers. Many Boomers, who should retire, are holding on to their practices because their revenues have declined, and their real estate holdings and retirement accounts took a big hit during the recession. Industry trends are positive because animal owners will still spend money on their pets and sacrifice discretionary income for other types spending. Ease of replication is very dependent on the buyer's ability to replace the seller's skill level and communication abilities (bedside manner). Most buyers are quite competent in the practice of veterinary medicine, but the change in the practice's culture and perceived quality of care, whether better or worse, can be a challenge to a new owner. Typically, it is best for a new buyer to change the acquired practice's culture and the fees gradually."

"Competition varies by region. The typical small-animal vet needs about 1,500 active clients to make a decent living. Small-animal fixed base practices sell best. Mobile practices usually have little value other than asset value."

"Fewer young veterinarians desire their own business. The costs of veterinary practice are increasing."

"Stable pet care market but more competition for the discretionary dollars used to underwrite the cost of care. Costs to provide services are increasing."

"Risk is low. Loan default rates very low. Can get up to 100% financing. Cost of entry for vet practice is higher than for human medical practice."

Benchmark Data

Statistics (Veterinary Services)

Number of Establishments	51,914
Average Profit Margin	11.4%
Revenue per Employee	$101,700
Average Number of Employees	7.2
Average Wages per Employee	$35,343

Products and Services Segmentation

Nonsurgical treatments	26.6%
Routine examinations	23.2%
Laboratory services	16.4%
Surgical treatments	14.9%
Merchandise sales	11.0%
Other	3.6%
Boarding services	2.9%
Pet grooming services	1.4%

Major Market Segmentation

Companion animal exclusive practices	65.7%
Companion animal predominate practices	9.1%
Food animal exclusive practices/predominate practices	6.8%
Mixed animal practices	6.3%
Other	6.3%
Equine	5.8%

Industry Costs

Profit	11.4%
Wages	34.7%
Purchases	37.7%
Depreciation	2.7%
Marketing	1.1%
Rent & Utilities	7.8%
Other	4.6%

Market Share

VCA Antech Inc.	5.9%

Source: IBISWorld, May 2016

- "- Per the AAHA's most recent 'Financial & Productivity Pulsepoints', the Average Client Transaction (ACT) was $137.
  - Per AAHA, the average annual revenue/veterinarian is $516,000."
- "Sales per support staff of $150,000 to $180,000 indicate average to above average productivity. Cost of supplies, including drugs and diet foods of 20% of revenues or less is positive. However, many practices have COGS much greater, but it the practice sells a lot of product, then the impact on profitability can be lessened because many product sales contribute to ancillary income. The three major expenses that cut into profitability are staff wages (not including doctors) greater than 20% of revenues, COGS greater than 20% of revenues and facility rents greater than 8% of revenues. Shopping center practices often have high rents that can affect the practice earnings."
- "The expenses above are the most common benchmarks used for expenses. Revenues per full-time veterinarian= $525,000 to $600,000. Revenues per full-time employee (non-veterinarian)=$130,000 to $170,000 (median about $150,000). Ancillary income (grooming, boarding, diet food and retail sales) of 14% to 16% of revenues is desirable because higher ancillary income tends to increase the productivity of the doctors."
- "Average annual gross income per DVM is about $500K, of which about $450K is professional services (as opposed to retail, prescription refills, grooming, etc.). Average transaction charge is $114. Income per square foot is $338. Should have about 4 support staff for every full-time veterinarian."

Expenses as a percentage of annual sales

Cost of goods	15% to 20%
Payroll/labor Costs	20% to 30%
Occupancy	05% to 11%
Profit (estimated pretax)	20% to 30%

Industry Trend

- "Plenty of buyers for good practices. Good growth for pet industry and veterinary medicine services."
- "More and more Baby Boomer owner-operator veterinarians will be selling their practices."
- "Larger practices (>$2,000,000) are increasingly selling to consolidators (larger corporate companies). Smaller practices still hold their own because clients feel that they are receiving more personalized services. There is a concern in the industry that there may an over-supply of veterinarians leading to increased competition in the future. The current market is still favorable to sellers because of the large number of buyers."
- "For practice acquisitions, there may be a change in supply and demand. Boomers, who have been holding on to their practices, may be forced to sell because of age and health reasons. As the economy rebounds, the aging Boomers may feel more comfortable retiring because their real estate holdings and investment accounts have returned to pre-recession levels. Many veterinary practice analysts expect far more practices to become available in

the coming years."
- "Will continue to grow."
- "The trend will continue toward larger practices with more upscale facilities."
- "Good stable revenue. Smaller offices exhibit downward pressure on values."
- "An increase in consumer demand for better access, convenience, technology, diagnosis, and feedback will continue to shape veterinary practices."

Seller Financing

- "Outside financing very common. 10 years, 5%–6%. Both commercial and SBA loans."
- "Veterinarians are a preferred business type for SBA lenders. It is possible to obtain 100% loan to value financing with a 25-year amortization when purchasing an existing, profitable practice and building. Sometimes this requires the vet selling the practice/building to take back a second mortgage of 10–25%."
- "A financially sound buyer (good credit score and personal liquidity) can typically borrow most of the sale price. Weaker buyers will require some form of seller participation. The typical seller may not have to finance greater than 10% of the sale price. There are both conventional lenders and SBA lenders. Interest rates for both are quite low now. Many conventional loans have fixed interest rates between 4.0% to 4.5%. SBA loans are around 5%, but they are variable quarterly."
- "Many lenders, both conventional and SBA, are ready to lend 100% of the acquisition price. Seller financing tends to be minimal."
- "For qualified buyers, greater than 90% of practices sold are completed with outside financing. Sellers typically receive all cash or contribute minimally (<20%) to buyer financing."
- "Financing can be 100% (no down payment) with 7- to 10-year notes if credit is good."

Questions

- "Type of practice; hours worked per week; number of client transactions per day; ancillary services; % of revenue (grooming, boarding, retail); types of procedures performed; types of species treated; drug inventory levels; in-house lab and equipment capabilities"
- "What is the value of the procedures currently being referred out of the office? Do you have agreements with suppliers of practice services, such as laboratory services and are those agreements transferable to a buyer? What are the demographics in the area and what are the demographics of the clients in this practice?"
- "Learn their practice philosophy and see if it is compatible with yours. Next, ask for three years of tax returns, supporting documents, practice performance reports, equipment list and information on the staff."
- "Gross hours worked, type of patients seen, and percentage mix; ancillary profit centers support staff info; number active clients in last 2 years"
- "What is the turnover rate, large vs. small animal, surgery vs. treatment, retail sales, inventory size, payroll costs?"
- "Ask what medical services they do not provide that could be added."
- "Review cash flow. Check conditional use permits. Fees schedule and list of

procedures."

- "What percentages of revenues are from: vaccines, surgery, boarding, retail sales and grooming?"
- "Are they willing to sign a covenant not to compete? Can they work in the practice after the sale? How was price arrived at and justified? What is the value of the real estate and how was the price arrived at? What is being sold for the asked price? How many hours per week are worked by the owner/doctor? How are emergencies calls covered?"
- "At least 5 years of financial statements and tax returns, current detailed depreciation schedule, practice management and production reports, and payroll and staffing information to begin analysis. Then follow up information and details. Site visit is extremely informative!"
- "Standard recasting info for sellers. Types of surgery performed? 1 or 3 vaccination schedule? Relationship with local shelters/humane societies? How are emergencies handled?"

Resources

Websites
- Vet Quest Classifieds: www.vetquest.com
- Veterinary Information Network: www.vin.com
- VetPartners: www.vetpartners.org

Trade Publications
- Veterinary Economics: http://veterinarybusiness.dvm360.com/
- Veterinary Practice News: www.veterinarypracticenews.com/

Associations
- American Veterinary Medical Association: www.avma.org
- American Animal Hospital Association: www.aahanet.org

Video Stores		
SIC 7841-02	NAICS 532230	Number of Businesses/Units 3,353

Rules of Thumb
- "Most buyers want to recover their investment within 24 months, so 2 times SDE is a safe bet, including inventory."
- "It used to be one year's SDE plus the fair market value of the tapes and games, but inventory drops in value too dramatically after the 'new release' prime period (90 days) has passed."
- "1 to 2 times SDE to a working owner plus fair market value for videos, games & DVDs"
- .65 to 1.0 annual revenues plus inventory

Pricing Tips
- "The inventory price of the videos and games drops drastically from its original retail. Unit prices can be as low as $5.00 or less."

V - Rules of Thumb

- "If the current owner can computer-generate a video rental report that shows you how many times each video in inventory has been rented and the income associated with it, you will see how much 'dead inventory' could be replaced to increase revenues. Special- interest videos and games like Nintendo and PlayStation 2, etc. would be good profit generators."

Expert Comments

"The industry has changed with the switch to games."

Benchmark Data

Statistics (DVD, Game & Video Rental)

Number of Establishments	3,353
Average Profit Margin	2.8%
Revenue per Employee	$278,300
Average Number of Employees	3.5
Average Wages per Employee	$23,087

Products and Services Segmentation

Nonsubscription rental	62.3%
Subscription rental	32.0%
Other	5.7%

Industry Costs

Profit	2.8%
Wages	8.6%
Purchases	40.1%
Depreciation	6.5%
Marketing	1.9%
Rent & Utilities	10.9%
Other	29.2%

Source: IBISWorld, August 2016

Expenses as a percentage of annual sales

Cost of goods	33%
Payroll/labor Costs	27%
Occupancy	15%
Profit (estimated pretax)	25%

Industry Trend

- "The Entertainment Merchants Association's recently released 2016 D2: Disc to Digital annual report on the home entertainment industry demonstrates that the DVD and Blu-ray Disc market is not dead or dying; rather it remains a significant and important segment of our evolving industry.

  "While the physical goods market has slowly declined since its heyday in 2004, it remains strong. Citing figures released by DEG, the report notes that spending on rental and purchases accounted for half of the overall home video market in 2015, and is expected to still represent 30% of the market in 2019. Both disc rental and disc retail spending currently far exceed their digital equivalents.

"Discs contribute significantly to the bottom lines of the studios, as disc sales and rentals are almost equal to theatrical box office. They continue to be an integral part of the economics of the motion picture industry."

Source: "The Disc is not Dead," by Mark Fisher, President and CEO of EMA (Entertainment Merchants Association), May 2016, http://entmerch.org/press-room/marks-remarks/the-disc-is-not-dead.html

- "The DVD, Game and Video Rental industry has contracted considerably over the 10 years to 2020 and is in the declining life stage cycle. Alongside the continuing trends of industry consolidation and store closures, industry value added (IVA), which measures the industry's contribution to the economy, is expected to decline at an annualized rate of 18.2% through 2020, which pales in comparison to the 2.2% annualized growth GDP is expected to experience over the same period."

Source: http://clients1.ibisworld.com/reports/us/industry/industryoutlook.aspx?entid=1370

- "Over 70% of video consumption takes place on the television.
Younger viewers are selecting other screens as their primary entertainment platforms. The laptop is ranked ahead of the television for those ages 18–34.
Household penetration of set-top and portable streaming devices reached 25% at the end of 2014.
51% of U.S. households own a dedicated game console.
53% of video gamers say they prefer to buy the physical game over the digital version."

Source: "EMA's 2015 D2 Report: Discs and Digita—The Business of Home Entertainment Retailing"

- "Almost half of all U.S. households subscribe to Amazon Prime, Hulu Plus, Netflix or a combination of these services. UltraViolet has over 21 million users with 110 million movies and TV shows in their libraries."

Source: http://entmerch.org/industry/facts-home-video-mkt.html

Seller Financing
- 12 to 24 months
- 3 years

Resources

Associations
- Entertainment Merchants Association: www.entmerch.org/

Visa/Passport Companies

Rules of Thumb
➢ 3 to 5 times EBITDA

➢ 3 times EBITDA for small to midsized operations, 4.5 times EBITDA for larger ones.

Pricing Tips
- "Immigration is rising."
- "Total number of applications processed year over year (up or down?)"
- "Due to new U.S. Government requirements, this industry multiple has increased."

Expert Comments

"This industry deals as expeditors of government travel documents."

Questions
- "How do they execute quick turnaround? How long does it take them to fulfill applications?"

Waste Collection		
	NAICS 56211	Number of Businesses/Units 11,193

Rules of Thumb

➤ 95 percent of annual sales

➤ 3 times SDE

➤ 5 times EBIT

➤ 4 times EBITDA

Pricing Tips
- "For a company with predictable repeat earnings with service contracts, eleven times the last twelve months' revenue. For a company involved in the construction industry, there may be a holdback of an amount multiple to adjust for homebuilder risk. The most valued are ongoing commercial accounts, which might have an adjustment or an earnout up or down. The best buyers are the 'big boys' in waste management."

Expert Comments

"This has been a very difficult business dominated by a few large companies."

Benchmark Data

Statistics (Waste Collection Services)
Number of Establishments	11,193
Average Profit Margin	7.3%
Revenue per Employee	$221,900
Average Number of Employees	18.0
Average Wages per Employee	$52,327

Products and Services Segmentation
Residential waste collection services	37.2%
Nonresidential waste collection services	35.2%
Transfer and storage facility services	8.8%
Recyclable material collection services	7.3%
Hazardous waste collection services	5.5%
Construction and demolition site waste collection services	3.8%
Other	2.2%

Major Market Segmentation

Individuals and households	40.9%
Retail and office businesses	30.1%
Industrial companies	14.7%
Government and not-for-profit organizations	7.6%
Construction and demolition companies	6.7%

Industry Costs

Profit	7.3%
Wages	23.7%
Purchases	21.9%
Depreciation	8.1%
Marketing	2.8%
Rent & Utilities	7.2%
Other	29.0%

Market Share

Waste Management Inc.	21.5%
Republic Services Inc.	18.2%

Source: IBISWorld, May 2016

Expenses as a percentage of annual sales

Cost of goods	20%
Payroll/labor Costs	50%
Occupancy	05%
Profit (estimated pretax)	25%

Industry Trend

- "Here are 10 trends that are driving the industry toward relevant and important changes:

  1. CNG trucks are being widely used to cut costs and increase efficiencies

  2. Cities from coast to coast are implementing programs and legislation to reach zero waste goals

  3. More landfills are seeking expansions, causing controversy between owners and residents

  4. Mergers and acquisitions — especially between small companies — continue to drive businesses forward

  5. Municipalities are taking action to cut food and organic waste

  6. Bans and fees are being placed on common products — such as Styrofoam and plastic bags — to prevent them from reaching landfills

  7. The concept of waste-to-energy is growing as more companies find ways to turn refuse into reusable products

  8. Interstate waste transportation is becoming a burden for some states

  9. Low levels of commodity recycling are leading to changes in municipal recycling programs

  10. Companies are creating more innovative and advanced trash and recycling containers"

Source: "10 trends defining the waste industry — and why they matter," by Kristin Musulin, August 31, 2015, http://www.wastedive.com/news/10-trends-defining-the-waste-industry-and-why-they-matter/404810/

- "The US waste management industry includes about 24,000 establishments (single-location companies and units of multi-location companies) with combined annual revenue of about $60 billion."

Source: www.firstresearch.com

- "The top two companies, Waste Management and Republic Services accounted for 39 percent of total industry revenue. All of the publicly traded companies together comprised 61 percent of total revenues. All told, the private sector represents 78 percent of the industry while the municipal sector controls the remaining 22 percent. This is a sharp contrast to 1992 when municipalities controlled 35 percent of industry revenue.

  "Recent mergers, including that of Veolia's U.S. waste business by Advanced Disposal, promise a reshaped industry much further along its path of privatization. The companies understand that one way to deal with turbulent economic times amidst rising fuel, labor and equipment costs is to streamline operations and vertically integrate their markets.

  "Rising costs have focused company managers on disciplined price increases especially now that the industry is more consolidated, more attentive to return on invested capital, more rational about valuing existing landfill capacity and mindful of lessons in the past when pricing was sacrificed."

  Source: "New Report Details the $55 Billion U.S. Waste Industry,"
  http://www.wastebusinessjournal.com/overview.htm

- "Growing by leaps with no bounds"

Resources

Websites
- Waste 360: www.waste360.com

Water Companies		
	NAICS 22131	

Rules of Thumb

➢ "The market price varies greatly, between $75 and $150 per metered customer. The normal meter hookup charge is approximately $100. These are not saleable unless they have a minimum of 250 customers with growth potential."

Industry Trend

- "The Water Supply and Irrigation Systems industry is in the mature stage of its life cycle. Industry value added (IVA), a measure of an industry's contribution to the overall economy, is forecast to grow at an annualized rate of 1.8% over the 10 years to 2021."

  Source: http://clients1.ibisworld.com/reports/us/industry/industryoutlook.aspx?entid=161

Web Hosting		
	NAICS 518210	

Rules of Thumb

➢ 3 to 4 times EBITDA

Pricing Tips

- "Prices are down from 2 years ago."

Expert Comments

"Industry was growing by 50% per year prior to the economic downturn. Still growth in the industry."

Benchmark Data

- "Most are netting between 33% and 44% of gross income."

Expenses as a percentage of annual sales

Cost of goods	n/a
Payroll/labor Costs	n/a
Occupancy	n/a
Profit (estimated pretax)	33%

Industry Trend

- "The Internet Hosting Services industry is expected to experience strong growth over the next five years as maintaining an attractive web presence becomes increasingly important for businesses. The desire to improve the customer experience online, coupled with the continued shift to online services, will drive demand for industry services. Growing corporate profit will incentivize businesses to invest in their digital property. As a result, IBISWorld expects industry revenue to grow at an annualize rate of 5.5% to $20.7 billion over the five years to 2020."

  Source: http://clients1.ibisworld.com/reports/us/industry/industryoutlook.aspx?entid=608

- "Massive growth"

Weight Loss Services/Centers

SIC 7299-34	NAICS 812191	Number of Businesses/Units 40,768

Rules of Thumb

➢ 50 to 55 percent of annual sales

Benchmark Data

Statistics (Weight Loss Services)

Number of Establishments	40,768
Average Profit Margin	7.8%
Revenue per Employee	$56,100
Average Number of Employees	1.4
Average Wages per Employee	$16,832

Products and Services Segmentation

Meeting fees	48.5%
Internet fees	32.4%
In meeting product sales	13.2%
Other	5.9%

Industry Costs

Profit	7.8%
Wages	34.1%
Purchases	30.2%
Depreciation	4.4%
Marketing	6.2%
Rent & Utilities	10.5%
Other	6.8%

Market Share

Weight Watchers International Inc.	21.7%
Nutrisystem Inc.	17.2%
MediFast International Ltd.	8.5%

Source: IBISWorld, August 2016

Industry Trend

- "A new study by Transparency Market Research (TMR), titled 'Weight Loss Services Market—Global Industry Analysis, Size, Share, Growth, Trends and Forecast 2016–2023,' states that the global weight loss services market is poised to grow in the coming years, thanks to increasing awareness among people about their health and well-being. The huge consumer base is a key market driver for the growth of global weight loss services market and will continue to remain due to increasing global population, particularly in the Asia Pacific and rest of the world."

  Source: July 11, 2016, https://globenewswire.com/news-release/2016/07/11/854979/0/
  en/Weight-Loss-Services-Market-set-to-Grow-in-Coming-Years-Driven-by-Huge-
  Consumer-Base-Transparency-Market-Research.html

- "During the next five years, the Weight Loss Services industry is expected to rebound from the previous five-year period. As more health-conscious individuals become aware of how weight loss plays an integral role in health and overall wellness, industry revenue will grow.

  "Over the five years to 2021, industry revenue is forecast to grow at an annualized rate of 2.6% to $2.6 billion. As more individuals become time strapped over the period, many obese or overweight individuals will purchase weight loss services to achieve their fitness, weight and nutritional goals in short time increments. Profit is expected to rise from 7.8% of industry revenue in 2016 to 9.1% in 2021, as many weight loss companies raise their membership rates, rather than offer discount and promotional pricing like the previous period."

  Source: http://clients1.ibisworld.com/reports/us/industry/default.aspx?entid=1719

- "To grasp the plight of the diet industry these days, consider these two statistics: 77% of Americans are actively trying to eat healthier, according to a poll conducted this month for Fortune by SurveyMonkey—but only 19% say they're on a diet.

  "It's not that Americans have slimmed down; more than a third of U.S. adults are still considered obese. It's the fact that more and more people are focused on health first—and calories second. The percentage of women reporting they are on a diet has dropped 13 points over the past two decades, according to research firm NPD Group.

  "The result: crimped revenues for companies in the business of helping people lose weight. Market leader Weight Watchers has reported sales declines for two consecutive years and is projecting a weak 2015. Revenues have also shriveled at Jenny Craig and meal provider Medifast. Another meal provider, Nutrisystem, whose revenues were soaring a few years ago, has seen sales tumble 21% compared to four years ago."

  Source: "Lean times for the diet industry" by John Kell, fortune.com, 5/22/15

Franchise

Wienerschnitzel (See also Franchises)

Approx. Total Investment	$350,000 to $1,000,000
Estimated Annual Sales/Unit	$1,000,000
	NAICS 722513	Number of Businesses/Units 325

Rules of Thumb
➢ 30 to 35 percent of annual sales plus inventory

Franchise

Wild Birds Unlimited (See also Franchises)

Approx. Total Investment	$123,331 to $192,099
	NAICS 453910	Number of Businesses/Units 292

Rules of Thumb
➢ 30 percent of annual sales plus inventory

Resources

Websites
- www.wbu.com

Wind Farms (Energy)

	NAICS 333611	

Rules of Thumb
➢ 10 times EBITDA

Pricing Tips
- "Use a cap rate, similar to pricing commercial real estate."

Expert Comments
"This industry is, for a number of reasons, going to grow dramatically over the next decade. The economic model is very similar to that of commercial real estate—high upfront capital costs followed by extremely consistent cash flows, with upside appreciation potential. The smart money will get in early and ride the wave."

Benchmark Data
- "Revenue per kilowatt hour, capacity factor, PPA rate"

Industry Trend
- "The leading 25 owners of wind assets have seen their share of global installed

W - Rules of Thumb

capacity fall from 47% to 41% over the past three years, according to a report by Make Consulting."

Source: August 10, 2016,
http://www.windpowermonthly.com/article/1405306/top-asset-owners-losing-market-share

- "U.S. Wind Energy Capacity Statistics

  Total U.S. installed wind capacity, through end of 2015: 73,992 MW

  Equivalent number of average American homes powered in a year by current installed wind capacity: 20 million

  Wind energy's percentage share of power capacity additions in 2015: 41%

  Total number of operating utility-scale wind turbines: >48,800

  Number of U.S. states with operating utility-scale wind energy projects: 40 plus Puerto Rico"

  Source: "Wind Energy Facts at a Glance,"
  http://www.awea.org/Resources/Content.aspx?ItemNumber=5059&navItemNumber=742

- "The Wind Turbine industry is in the decline stage of its life cycle. Industry value added, which measures its contribution to the overall economy, is projected to decline at an annualized rate of 5.6% over the 10 years to 2021. US GDP, by contrast, is forecast to grow an annualized 2.2% over the same period. This indicates that the industry is rapidly falling as a share of the overall economy, largely due to the scheduled expiration of government renewable energy incentives, which have been the primary driver of demand for wind turbines over the past decade."

  Source: http://clients1.ibisworld.com/reports/us/industry/industryoutlook.aspx?entid=715

- "Low-cost, zero-emission wind energy will become even more valuable as states and utilities develop plans to cost-effectively reduce carbon pollution to comply with EPA's Clean Power Plan, according to new economic analysis from the Energy Information Administration (EIA), a nonpartisan branch of the Department of Energy (DOE). EIA's analysis modeled a range of options for complying with EPA's proposed rule across a variety of scenarios, and wind energy consistently emerged as the lowest cost option for reducing emissions.

  "EIA's analysis saw a large role for wind across more than a dozen different scenarios. As shown below, EIA saw a large amount of wind deployment in all scenarios it examined, even with low gas prices, more use of energy efficiency, and greater use of nuclear energy. As a result, states and utilities should look to wind energy as a 'no-regrets' option that will be valuable under any scenario for unexpected market changes, creating further impetus for states and grid operators to begin planning now for infrastructure to connect cost-effective wind."

  Source: "EIA finds wind energy will have largest role in cost-effectively meeting Clean Power Plan"
  by Michael Goggin, http://www.aweablog.org/eia-finds-wind-energy-will-have-
  largest-role-in-cost-effectively-meeting-clean-power-plan/ May 27, 2015

Resources

Trade Publications
- Windpower Monthly: www.windpowermonthly.com

Associations
- American Wind Energy Association: www.awea.org/

Window Cleaning

	NAICS 561720	

Rules of Thumb

➤ 60 percent of annual sales

Resources

Associations

- International Window Cleaning Association—a site with a lot of valuable information: www.iwca.org

Window Treatment/Draperies

	NAICS 442291	

Rules of Thumb

➤ 35 to 40 percent of annual sales plus inventory

Industry Trend

- "One of the most significant factors that will drive sales of window treatments in the years ahead is the rising homeownership rate. Although the millennials' future home-buying behavior is in question, the homeownership rate over the next five years is anticipated to increase as a result of purchases made by Generation X (those born between the early 1960s and the early 1980s)."

  Source: http://clients1.ibisworld.com/reports/us/industry/industryoutlook.aspx?entid=4971

		Franchise
Wine Kitz (Canada) (See also Franchises)		
Approx. Total Investment	$106,000 to $135,000 (See Rule of Thumb)	
	NAICS 312130	Number of Businesses/Units 95

Rules of Thumb

➤ 55 percent of annual sales plus inventory

➤ Note: The investment above is for a retail store with an in-store winery. The investment for a retail only is approximately $73,000 to $100,000.

Wineries

SIC 2084-01	NAICS 312130	Number of Businesses/Units 7,124

Rules of Thumb

➤ 25 percent of annual sales (does include real estate)

➤ 10 times SDE

➤ 60 times EBIT (does include real estate)

➤ 89 times EBITDA (does include real estate)

W - Rules of Thumb

Expert Comments

"Wineries take 1–2 years to sell if they are priced well."

Benchmark Data

Statistics (Wineries)

Number of Establishments	7,124
Average Profit Margin	11.0%
Revenue per Employee	$421,100
Average Number of Employees	6.1
Average Wages per Employee	$51,693

Products and Services Segmentation

Chardonnay	26.4%
Zinfandel, Riesling and other blends	19.8%
Cabernet Sauvignon	19.4%
Merlot	10.8%
Pinot Grigio	10.3%
Pinot Noir	7.6%
Sauvignon Blanc	5.7%

Industry Costs

Profit	11.0%
Wages	12.0%
Purchases	42.6%
Depreciation	5.4%
Marketing	4.1%
Rent & Utilities	2.0%
Other	22.9%

Market Share

E. & J. Gallo Winery	23.5%
Constellation Brands Inc.	12.7%
The Wine Group, Inc.	8.7%

Source: IBISWorld, April 2016

- "California Wine Profile 2015
  - ✓ America's top wine producer—California makes 85% of all U.S. wine and is the world's 4th leading wine producer after France, Italy and Spain.
  - ✓ 4,600 bonded wineries—Up 102% from 2,275 wineries in 2005; nearly all are family owned businesses.
  - ✓ 229 million cases—California wine sales volume into the U.S. market, with shipments growing 23% since 2005's 185.5 million cases.
  - ✓ $31.9 billion retail value—Estimated retail value of California wine sales in the U.S.
  - ✓ 60% share of U.S. market by volume—Three of every five bottles sold in the U.S. is a California wine.
  - ✓ $1.6 billion in export revenue—U. S. wine exports, 90% from California, reached an all-time record, up 7.6% from 2014 by value. California exports 51.2 million cases to 135 countries.
  - ✓ 5,900 winegrape growers—Our partners in sustainable winegrowing.
  - ✓ 608,000 acres/246,000 hectares of winegrapes—Winegrapes are grown

in 49 of 58 counties in California; 138 federally approved American Viticultural Areas.
- ✓ 3.7 million tons/3.4 million tonnes harvested of winegrapes—More than 110 winegrape varieties.
- ✓ $2.5 billion in farmgate value to growers—Farmgate value of California winegrapes; one of California's top five agricultural commodities by value.

Source: http://www.discovercaliforniawines.com/media-trade/statistics/

Expenses as a percentage of annual sales

Cost of goods	59%
Payroll/labor Costs	20%
Occupancy	20%
Profit (estimated pretax)	10%

Industry Trend

- "Impact of California wine and winegrapes on the U.S. economy in 2015:
  - ✓ Employment—786,000 full-time equivalent jobs: 325,000 jobs in California, 461,000 jobs in other states
  - ✓ Annual Economic Activity—$114.1 billion
  - ✓ Wages—$34.9 billion annually
  - ✓ Taxes—$15.2 billion total: $8.9 billion in federal taxes, $6.3 billion in state and local taxes
  - ✓ Charitable Contributions—$249 million annually"

Source: "California Wine Shows Strength in Challenging Economy," August 4, 2016, http://www.wineinstitute.org/resources/pressroom/08042016

- "The Wineries industry is expected to grow at a slower pace over the next five years. IBISWorld forecasts revenue will increase at an annualized 0.1% to $18.4 billion, including projected growth of 0.3% in 2017. Exports are expected to grow an average 4.0% per year to $2.2 billion, while imports are expected to grow an average of 4.4% per year to $9.2 billion. Operating profit will likely decline slightly as consolidation continues throughout the supply chain and Californian wineries struggle with uncharacteristically low levels of rainfall."

Source: http://clients1.ibisworld.com/reports/us/industry/industryoutlook.aspx?entid=289

- "It is expected an increase in properties will go up for sale, especially if adult children do not share mom & dad's dream. But selling even a marginally profitable business is a challenge. Typically, it takes three years or more to find a qualified buyer."

Source: http://www.hagarty-on-wine.com/OnWineBlog/?p=7130

Questions
- "Will you [the seller] stay on as a consultant?"

Resources

Websites
- California Wineland: www.winesandvines.com

Trade Publications
- Wine Business Monthly: www.winebusiness.com

Associations
- Family Winemakers of California: www.familywinemakers.org
- American Society for Enology and Viticulture: www.asev.org

Franchise

Wingstop Restaurants (See also Franchises, Restaurants—Limited Service)	
Approx. Total Investment	$242,787 to $569,528
Estimated Annual Sales/Unit	$950,000
NAICS 722513	Number of Businesses/Units 537

Rules of Thumb

➤ 30 to 35 percent of annual sales plus inventory

Resources

Websites
- www.wingstop.com

Wireless Communications
(Carriers, dealers & resellers of cellular, PCs, & paging)

SIC 5999-02	NAICS 517210	

Rules of Thumb

➤ 30 percent of annual gross sales

➤ 2 to 3 times SDE plus inventory

➤ 2.5 to 5 times EBITDA includes inventory

➤ $50 to $130 per pop for operational market—less if naked license

Pricing Tips

- "It is important to consider revenue per customer."
- "Strong employee technical base/tenure desirable along with non-competes for key personnel"
- "Trend upward in volume and downward in service income is not abnormal"
- "Subscribers, physical plant capacity, client retention and gross margins"
- "Calculating furniture, fixtures and equipment value along with any real estate involved"

Expert Comments

"Multi-store operators with strong sales and net earnings are in demand."

"Difficult to replicate due to technical nature of business as well as myriad supplier relationships required"

"Expanding into synergistic product lines is becoming the norm."

"This is a fairly mature market, however, the advent of the Internet and Voice over Internet Protocol are changing the landscape of the wired telecommunications market. While core services (long distance and data) have become a commodity, there is plenty of opportunity to differentiate with platform applications and custom architecture."

Benchmark Data

- "3 x SDE is a good place to begin. Inventory/chargebacks and deactivations can be an issue if not clearly discussed."
- "35%–40% percent gross profit"
- "COGS 25%, payroll 20%, profit 28%, occupancy cost 18%"
- "Sales per employee"
- "Number of years owner has operated the business, along with how long they will stay and train. Are the employees staying or leaving? Location of the business and any customer lists they may have are all similar factors."

Expenses as a percentage of annual sales

Cost of goods	60%
Payroll/labor Costs	20%
Occupancy	05% to 10%
Profit (estimated pretax)	10%

Industry Trend

- "The Wireless Telecommunications Carriers industry is well positioned for future growth. Expanding demand for wireless data services is anticipated to offset declining demand for voice-only services, particularly as more broadband-enabled mobile devices, such as tablet computers and e-readers, achieve wider penetration. Over the five years to 2021, the number of wireless subscribers is expected to continue increasing. As a result, revenue is projected to grow at an annualized rate of 3.2% over the next five years, reaching $300.1 billion in 2021."

  Source: http://clients1.ibisworld.com/reports/us/industry/default.aspx?entid=1267
- "Trend toward commodity-based marketing and addition of synergistic product lines in an effort to offset eroding equipment profits"

Seller Financing

- "1–2 years"
- "Depends on size and complexity of transaction."

Questions

- "Seller Financing? Lease issues? Any problems with the carrier transferring the business to a buyer and what are those exact requirements? Timing."
- "Ask if market is built out (to what percentage of population and geography) and if it is operational (how long)."
- "Number of activations per month currently doing? How many deactivations per month? What is advertising budget? How long at this location? Are employees on commission or salary or both? Number of locations?"
- "Pricing strategy and debt owed"
- "How will inventory be paid for and when? Period of time post-close that seller will be responsible for chargebacks and de-activations for pre-sale customers."

Resources

Trade Publications

- Wireless Dealer Magazine: www.wirelessdealermag.com
- Wireless Week: www.wirelessweek.com
- RCR Wireless News: www.rcrwireless.com

	Franchise
Wireless Toyz (See also Cellular Telephone Stores, Franchises)	
Approx. Total Investment	$219,000 to $648,000
Estimated Annual Sales/Unit	$650,000
NAICS 443142	Number of Businesses/Units 187

Rules of Thumb

➢ 45 to 50 percent of annual sales plus inventory

Resources

Websites

- www.wirelesstoyz.com

Women's Clothing

SIC 5621-01	NAICS 448120	Number of Businesses/Units 57,117

Rules of Thumb

➢ 20 percent of annual sales plus inventory

➢ 2 times monthly sales plus inventory

Benchmark Data

Statistics (Women's Clothing Stores)

Number of Establishments	57,117
Average Profit Margin	3.3%
Revenue per Employee	$112,500
Average Number of Employees	6.5
Average Wages per Employee	$15,666

Products and Services Segmentation

Tops	30.0%
Bottoms	20.3%
Dresses	15.5%
Other apparel and accessories	15.3%
Outerwear	10.5%
Underwear	8.4%

Industry Costs

Profit	3.3%
Wages	13.9%
Purchases	54.5%
Depreciation	1.1%
Marketing	3.7%
Rent & Utilities	12.7%
Other	10.8%

Market Share

Ascena Retail Group Inc. 11.9%

Source: IBISWorld, June 2016

Industry Trend

- "Industry value added (IVA), or the industry's contribution to the overall economy, is expected to decline an annualized 0.5% over the 10 years to 2021, while GDP is estimated grow 2.2% per year on average over the same period. IVA growth below GDP usually indicates a declining industry, however, the Women's Clothing Stores industry exhibits characteristics typical of a mature industry. Women's clothing stores have a wholehearted market acceptance, as proven by their recovery from the short lapse in sales, but many of the major players are merging in the wake of weak mall sales. External competition has also plagued industry operators, and continues to hamper sales.

  "Moreover, the number of industry establishments is growing at a slow yet steady pace and is expected to continue in this fashion over the next five years. Between 2011 and 2021, the number of brick-and-mortar women's clothing stores is forecast to grow at an annualized rate of 0.9% to 58,327. This steady growth is indicative of the stable demand for women's apparel."

Source: http://clients1.ibisworld.com/reports/us/industry/industryoutlook.aspx?entid=1067

		Franchise
World Wide Express (See also Delivery Services, Franchises)		
Approx. Total Investment		$25,000 to $150,000
	NAICS 561431	Number of Businesses/Units 138

Rules of Thumb

➤ 50 to 55 percent of annual sales plus inventory

Resources

Websites

- www.wwex.com

		Franchise
Your Office USA (See also Franchises)		
Approx. Total Investment		$200,000 to $500,000+
	NAICS 531120	Number of Businesses/Units 7

Rules of Thumb

➤ 60 percent of annual sales plus inventory

Resources

Websites

- www.youroffice.com

27th Edition

Franchise

You've Got Maids (See also Franchises, Janitorial Services, Molly Maid, etc.)

Approx. Total Investment		$45,000 to $123,000
SIC 7349-23	NAICS 561720	Number of Businesses/Units 40

Rules of Thumb

➢ 60 percent of annual sales plus inventory

Resources

Websites
- You 've Got Maids: www.youvegotmaids.com

Franchise

Ziebart International (Auto Services) (See also Franchises)

Approx. Total Investment		$167,000 to $326,000
	NAICS 8111	Number of Businesses/Units 400

Rules of Thumb

➢ 42 percent of annual sales plus inventory

Resources

Websites
- www.ziebart.com

Franchise

Zoo Health Club (See also Fitness Centers, Franchises)

Approx. Total Investment		$73,899 to $278,499 (equipment purchased),
		$48,399 to $189,249 (equipment leased)
	NAICS 713940	Number of Businesses/Units 25

Rules of Thumb

➢ 20 percent of annual sales

Resources

Websites
- www.zoogym.com